SOLARIS™ INTERNALS

Core Kernel Components

SOLARIS INTERNALS

Core Kernel Components

Jim Mauro and Richard McDougall

Sun Microsystems Press
A Prentice Hall Title

The publisher offers discounts on this book when ordered in bulk quantities.
For more information, contact: Corporate Sales Department, Phone: 800-382-3419; Fax: 201-236-7141; E-mail: corpsales@prenhall.com; or write: Prentice Hall PTR, Corp. Sales Dept., One Lake Street, Upper Saddle River, NJ 07458.

Editorial/production supervision: *Mary Sudul*
Cover design director: *Jerry Votta*
Cover design: *Anthony Gemmellaro*
Manufacturing manager: *Alexis R. Heydt*
Marketing manager: *Debby Van Dijk*
Acquisitions editor: *Gregory G. Doench*
Sun Microsystems Press:
Marketing manager: *Michael Llwyd Alread*
Publisher: *Rachel Borden*

10 9 8 7 6 5 4 3 2

ISBN 0-13-022496-0

Sun Microsystems Press
A Prentice Hall Title

For Traci.

For your love and encouragement . . .

Richard

For Donna, Frankie and Dominick.

All my love, always . . .

Jim

CONTENTS

INTRODUCTION TO SOLARIS INTERNALS

PART TWO 123

THE SOLARIS MEMORY SYSTEM

PART THREE 255

THREADS, PROCESSES, AND IPC

8. The Solaris Multithreaded Process Architecture 257

PART FOUR 469

FILES AND FILE SYSTEMS

LIST OF FIGURES

LIST OF TABLES

LIST OF HEADER FILES

PREFACE

The internals of the UNIX kernel are fairly well-documented, most notably by Goodheart and Cox [10], Bach [1], McKusick et al. [19], and Vahalia [39]. These texts have become a common source of reference information for those who want to better understand the internals of UNIX. However little has been written about the specifics of the Solaris kernel.

The paucity of Solaris specific information led us to create our own reference material. As we published information through white papers, magazine columns, and tutorials, the number of folks expressing interest motivated us to produce a complete work that discussed Solaris exclusively.

About This Book

This book is about the internals of Sun's Solaris Operating Environment. The rapid growth of Solaris has created a large number of users, software developers, systems administrators, performance analysts, and other members of the technical community, all of whom require in-depth knowledge about the environment in which they work.

Since the focus of this book is the internals of the Solaris kernel, the book provides a great deal of information on the architecture of the kernel and the major data structures and algorithms implemented in the operating system. However, rather than approach the subject matter from a purely academic point of view, we wrote the book with an eye on the practical application of the information contained herein. Thus, we have emphasized the methods and tools that can be used on a Solaris system to extract information that otherwise is not easily accessible with the standard bundled commands and utilities. We want to illustrate how you can apply this knowledge in a meaningful way, as your job or interest dictates.

To maximize the usefulness of the text, we included specific information on Solaris versions 2.5.1, 2.6, and Solaris 7. We cover the major Solaris subsystems, including memory management, process management, threads, files, and file systems. We do not cover details of low-level I/O, device drivers, STREAMS, and networking. For reference material on these topics, see "Writing Device Drivers" [28], the "STREAMS Programming Guide" [29], and "UNIX Network Programming" [32].

The material included in this book is not necessarily presented at an introductory level, although whenever possible we begin discussing a topic with some conceptual background information. We assume that you have some familiarity with operating systems concepts and have used a UNIX-based operating system. Some knowledge of the C programming language is useful but not required.

Because of the variety of hardware platforms on which Solaris runs, it is not practical to discuss the low-level details of all the different processors and architectures, so our hardware focus, when detail is required, is admittedly Ultra-SPARC-centric. This approach makes the most sense since it represents the current technology and addresses the largest installed base. In general, the concepts put forth when detail is required apply to other processors and platforms supported. The differences are in the specific implementation details, such as per-processor hardware registers.

Throughout the book we refer to specific kernel functions by name as we describe the flow of various code segments. These routines are internal to the operating system and should not be construed as, or confused with, the public interfaces that ship as part of the Solaris product line—the systems calls and library interfaces. The functions referenced throughout the text, unless explicitly noted, are private to the kernel and not callable or in any way usable by application programs.

Intended Audience

We hope that this book will serve as a useful reference for a variety of technical staff members working with the Solaris Operating Environment.

- **Application developers** can find information in this book about how Solaris implements functions behind the application programming interfaces. This information helps developers understand performance, scalability, and implementation specifics of each interface when they develop Solaris applications. The system overview section and sections on scheduling, interprocess communication, and file system behavior should be the most useful sections.

- **Device driver and kernel module developers** of drivers, STREAMS modules, loadable system calls, etc., can find herein the general architecture and implementation theory of the Solaris Operating Environment. The Solaris kernel framework and facilities portions of the book (especially the locking and synchronization primitives chapters) are particularly relevant.

- **Systems administrators, systems analysts, database administrators, and ERP managers** responsible for performance tuning and capacity planning can learn about the behavioral characteristics of the major Solaris subsystems. The file system caching and memory management chapters provide a great deal of information about how Solaris behaves in real-world environments. The algorithms behind Solaris tunable parameters (which are detailed in Appendix A) are covered in depth throughout the book.

- **Technical support staff** responsible for the diagnosis, debugging, and support of Solaris will find a wealth of information about implementation details of Solaris. Major data structures and data flow diagrams are provided in each chapter to aid debugging and navigation of Solaris Systems.

- **System users who just want to know more** about how the Solaris kernel works will find high-level overviews at the start of each chapter.

In addition to the various technical staff members listed above, we also believe that members of the academic community will find the book of value in studying how a volume, production kernel implements major subsystems and solves the problems inherent in operating systems development.

How This Book Is Organized

We organized *Solaris Internals* into several logical parts, each part grouping several chapters containing related information. Our goal was to provide a building block approach to the material, where later sections build on information provided in earlier chapters. However, for readers familiar with particular aspects of operating systems design and implementation, the individual parts and chapters can stand on their own in terms of the subject matter they cover.

- *Part One:* Introduction to Solaris Internals
  - *Chapter 1* — An Introduction to Solaris
  - *Chapter 2* — Kernel Services
  - *Chapter 3* — Kernel Synchronization Primitives

Solaris Source Code

In February 2000, Sun announced the availability of Solaris source. This book provides the essential companion to the Solaris source and can be used as a guide to the Solaris kernel framework and architecture.

It should also be noted that the source available from Sun is the Solaris 8 source. Although this book covers Solaris versions up to and including Solaris 7, almost all of the material is relevant to Solaris 8.

Updates and Related Material

To complement this book, we created a Web site where we will place updated material, tools we refer to, and links to related material on the topics covered. The Web site is available at

http://www.solarisinternals.com

We will regularly update the Web site with information about this text and future work on *Solaris Internals*. We will place information about the differences between Solaris 7 and 8 at this URL, post any errors that may surface in the current edition, and share reader feedback and comments and other bits of related information.

Notational Conventions

Table P-1 describes the typographic conventions used throughout the book, and Table P-2 shows the default system prompt for the utilities we describe.

Table P-1 Typographic Conventions

Typeface or Symbol	Meaning	Example
AaBbCc123	Command names, file names, and data structures.	The vmstat command. The `<sys/proc.h>` header file. The proc structure.
AaBbCc123()	Function names.	page_create_va()
AaBbCc123(2)	Manual pages.	Please see vmstat(1M).
AaBbCc123	Commands you type within an example.	$ **vmstat** r b w swap free re mf 0 0 0 464440 18920 1 13
AaBbCc123	New terms as they are introduced.	A *major page fault* occurs when...

Table P-2 Command Prompts

Shell	Prompt
C shell prompt	machine_name%
C shell superuser prompt	machine_name#
Bourne shell and Korn shell prompt	$
Bourne shell and Korn shell superuser prompt	#
The crash utility prompt	crash >

A Note from the Authors

We certainly hope that you get as much out of reading *Solaris Internals* as we did from writing it. We welcome comments, suggestions, and questions from readers.

ACKNOWLEDGMENTS

It's hard to thank all people who helped us with this book. As a minimum, we owe:

- Thanks to Brian Wong, Adrian Cockcroft, Paul Strong, Lisa Musgrave, and Fraser Gardiner for all your help and advice for the structure and content of this book.

- Thanks to Tony Shoumack, Phil Harman, Jim Moore, Robert Miller, Martin Braid, Robert Lane, Bert Beals, Calum Mackay, Allan Packer, Magnus Bergman, Chris Larson, Bill Walker, Keith Bierman, Dan Mick, and Raghunath Shenbagam for helping to review the material.

- A very special thanks to David Collier-Brown, Norm Shulman, Dominic Kay, Jarod Jenson, Bob Sneed, and Evert Hoogendoorn for painstaking page-by-page reviews of the whole book.

- Our thanks to the engineers in the Solaris business unit—Jim Litchfield, Michael Shapiro, Jeff Bonwick, Wolfgang Thaler, Bryan Cantrill, Roger Faulker, Andy Tucker, Casper Dik, Tim Marsland, Andy Rudoff, Greg Onufer, Rob Gingell, Devang Shah, Deepankar Das, Dan Price, and Kit Chow for their advice and guidance. We're quite sure there are others, and we apologize up front to those whose names we have missed.

- Thank you to the systems engineers and technical support staff at Sun for the corrections and suggestions along the way.

- Thanks to Lou Marchant—for the endless search for engine pictures, and Dwayne Schumate at Lotus Cars USA for coordinating permission to use the images of the Lotus V8 engine.

- Thanks to the folks at Prentice Hall—Greg Doench for his patience (we did slip this thing a few times) and support.

- Thanks to our enduring copy editor, Mary Lou Nohr, for her top-notch editorial work and style suggestions.

Without your help, this book wouldn't be what it is today.

From Jim:

I wish to personally acknowledge Jeff Bonwick and Andy Tucker of Solaris kernel engineering. They demonstrated great patience in clarifying things that were complex to me but second nature to them. They answered innumerous emails, which contributed significantly to the accuracy of the text, as well as ensuring all the key points were made. They also provided some wonderful explanations in various areas of the source code, which definitely helped.

Roger Faulkner and Jim Litchfield, also of Solaris kernel engineering, deserve an additional note of thanks for their efforts and time.

Thanks to Nobel Shelby and Casey Palowitch for reviewing sections of the manuscript and providing insightful feedback and suggestions.

I owe a debt of gratitude to Hal Stern that goes way beyond his support for this work. His mentoring, guidance, and friendship over the years have had a profound impact on my development at Sun.

Last, but certainly not least, comes the family acknowledgment. This may appear cliché, as every technical book I've ever seen recognizes the writer's family in the acknowledgments section. Well, there's a very good reason for that. There are only 24 hours in a day and 7 days in a week. That doesn't change just because you decide to write a book, nor do the other things that demand your time, like your job, your house, your lawn, etc., all of a sudden become less demanding. So the people who end up getting the short end of the stick are invariably your family members. Thus, my deepest gratitude goes to my wife Donna, and my sons, Frankie and Dominick. Without their love, sacrifice, and support, I would not have been able to complete this work. Thanks guys—I'm back now (of course, there is that pesky little matter of the updated version for Solaris 8...).

Jim Mauro

`jim.mauro@eng.sun.com`

Green Brook, New Jersey

June 2000

From Richard:

I would like to thank Adrian Cockcroft and Brian Wong for first giving me the opportunity to join their engineering group in 1995, working from my remote outpost in Australia. Their leadership and guidance has meant a lot to me during my career at Sun.

Thank you to our friends, visitors, and family who seemingly understood for two years when I abstained from many invites to dinners, day trips, and fun events citing, "When the book's done . . ." Yes—it *is* done now!

And yes, a special thank you to my wife Traci, who provided a seemingly endless amount of encouragement and personal sacrifice along the way. This project would have been forever unfinished without her unquestionable cooperation and support.

Richard McDougall

rmc@eng.sun.com

Cupertino, California

June 2000

Part One

INTRODUCTION TO SOLARIS INTERNALS

- An Introduction to Solaris
- Kernel Services
- Kernel Synchronization Primitives
- Kernel Bootstrap and Initialization

1

AN INTRODUCTION TO SOLARIS

The UNIX system is very successful. At the time of writing there are over 3000 UNIX systems in active use throughout the world.

—S.R. Bourne, *The UNIX System*, 1983

Sun systems have shipped with a UNIX-based operating system since the first Sun-1 workstation was introduced in 1982. Steve Bourne's quote indicates how relatively small the UNIX market was at that time. Today, millions of UNIX systems are deployed, running a variety of applications ranging from single-user systems, to real-time control systems, to mission- and business-critical environments—and Solaris represents a large percentage of these systems.

The Solaris installed base has rapidly increased in size since its inception. It is available on SPARC processor architectures from Sun and OEMs and on standard Intel-based systems. Solaris scales from single-processor systems to the 64-processor Sun Enterprise 10000 system.

1.1   A Brief History

Sun's UNIX operating environment began life as a port of BSD UNIX to the Sun-1 workstation. The early versions of Sun's UNIX were known as SunOS, which is the name used for the core operating system component of Solaris.

SunOS 1.0 was based on a port of BSD 4.1 from Berkeley labs in 1982. At that time, SunOS was implemented on Sun's Motorola 68000-based uniprocessor workstations. SunOS was small and compact, and the workstations had only a few MIPS of processor speed and around one megabyte of memory.

In the early to mid-1980s, networked UNIX systems were growing in popularity; networking was becoming ubiquitous and was a major part of Sun's computing strategy. Sun invested significant resources in developing technology that enabled distributed, network-based computing. These technologies included interfaces for building distributed applications (remote procedure calls, or RPC), and operating system facilities for the sharing of data over networks (Network Information System, or NIS) and a distributed computing file system: NFS. The incorporation of remote file sharing into SunOS required extensive operating system changes. In 1984, SunOS 2.0 offered the virtual file system framework to implement multiple file system types, which allowed support for the NFS file system. The network file system source was made openly licensable and has subsequently been ported to almost every modern operating system platform in existence today.

The volume of applications running on the Sun platform increased steadily, with each new application placing greater demand on the system, providing the catalyst for the next phase of innovation. Applications needed better facilities for the sharing of data and executable objects. The combination of the need for shared program libraries, memory mapped files, and shared memory led to a major re-architecting of the SunOS virtual memory system. The new virtual memory system, introduced as SunOS version 4, abstracted various devices and objects as virtual memory, facilitating the mapping of files, sharing of memory, and mapping of hardware devices into a process.

During the 1980s, the demand for processing capacity outpaced the industry's incremental improvements in processor speed. To satisfy the demand, systems were developed with multiple processors sharing the same system memory and Input/Output (I/O) infrastructure, an advance that required further operating system changes. An asymmetric multiprocessor implementation first appeared in SunOS 4.1—the kernel could run on only one processor at a time, while user processors could be scheduled on any of the available processors. Workloads with multiple processes could often obtain greater throughput on systems with more than one processor. The asymmetric multiprocessor implementation was a great step forward; however, scalability declined rapidly as additional processors were added. The need for a better multiprocessor implementation was obvious.

At this time, Sun was participating in a joint development with AT&T, and the SunOS virtual file system framework and virtual memory system became the core of UNIX System V Release 4 (SVR4). SVR4 UNIX incorporated the features from SunOS, SVR3, BSD UNIX, and Xenix, as shown below. International Computers Limited (ICL) ported the new SVR4 UNIX to the SPARC processor architecture and delivered the reference source for SVR4 on SPARC.

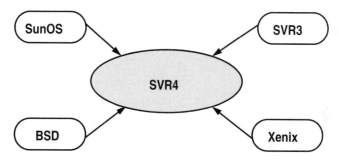

With the predicted growth in multiprocessor systems, Sun invested heavily in the development of a new operating system kernel with a primary focus on multiprocessor scalability. The new kernel allowed multiple threads of execution and provided facilities for threading at the process (application) level. Together with fine-grained locking, the new kernel provided the foundation for the scalability found in Solaris today. The new kernel and the SVR4 operating environment became the basis for Solaris 2.0.

This change in the base operating system was accompanied by a new naming convention; the Solaris name was introduced to describe the operating environment, of which SunOS, the base operating system, is a subset. Thus, the older SunOS retained the SunOS 4.X versioning and adopted Solaris 1.X as the operating environment version. The SVR4-based environment adopted a SunOS 5.X versioning (SunOS 5.0 being the first release) with the Solaris 2.X operating environment. The naming convention has resulted in most people referring to the pre-SVR4 releases as SunOS, and the SVR4-based releases as Solaris. Table 1-1 traces the development of Solaris from its roots to Solaris 7.

The new Solaris 2.0 operating environment was built in a modular fashion, which made possible its implementation on multiple platforms with different instruction set architectures. In 1993, Solaris was made available for Intel PC-based architectures, greatly expanding the platforms on which Solaris is available. In October 1999, Sun announced support for Solaris on the Intel Itanium processor.

The next major milestone was the introduction of a 64-bit implementation, in Solaris 7. Full 64-bit support allows the kernel and processes to access large address spaces and to use extended 64-bit data types. Solaris 7 also provides full compatibility for existing 32-bit applications, supporting concurrent execution of 32-bit and 64-bit applications.

Table 1-1 Solaris Release History

Date	Release	Notes
1982	Sun UNIX 0.7	• First version of Sun's UNIX, based on 4.BSD from UniSoft. • Bundled with the Sun-1, Sun's first workstation based on the Motorola 68000 processor; SunWindows GUI.
1983	SunOS 1.0	• Sun-2 workstation, 68010 based.
1985	SunOS 2.0	• Virtual file system (VFS) and vnode framework allows multiple concurrent file system types. • NFS implemented with the VFS/vnode framework.
1988	SunOS 4.0	• New virtual memory system integrates the file system cache with the memory system. • Dynamic linking added. • The first SPARC-based Sun workstation, the Sun-4. Support for the Intel-based Sun 386i.
1990	SunOS 4.1	• Supports the SPARCstation1+, IPC, SLC. • OpenWindows graphics environment
1992	SunOS 4.1.3	• Asymmetric multiprocessing (ASMP) for sun4m systems (SPARCstation-10 and -600 series MP (multiprocessor) servers).
1992	Solaris 2.0	• Solaris 2.x is born, based on a port of System V Release 4.0. • VFS/vnode, VM system, intimate shared memory brought forward from SunOS. • Uniprocessor only. • First release of Solaris 2, version 2.0, is a desktop-only developers release.
1992	Solaris 2.1	• Four-way symmetric multiprocessing (SMP).
1993	Solaris 2.2	• Large (> 2 Gbyte) file system support. • SPARCserver 1000 and SPARCcenter 2000 (sun4d architecture).
1993	Solaris 2.1-x86	• Solaris ported to the Intel i386 architecture.
1993	Solaris 2.3	• 8-way SMP. • Device power management and system suspend/resume functionality added. • New directory name lookup cache.

Table 1-1 Solaris Release History (Continued)

Date	Release	Notes
1994	Solaris 2.4	• 20-way SMP. • New kernel memory allocator (slab allocator) replaces SVR4 buddy allocator. • Caching file system (cachefs). • CDE windowing system.
1995	Solaris 2.5	• Large-page support for kernel and System V shared memory. • Fast local interprocess communication (Doors) added. • NFS Version 3. • Supports sun4u (UltraSPARC) architecture. UltraSPARC-I-based products introduced—the Ultra-1 workstation.
1996	Solaris 2.5.1	• First release supporting multiprocessor Ultra-SPARC-based systems. • 64-way SMP. • Ultra-Enterprise 3000–6000 servers introduced.
1996	Solaris 2.6	• Added support for large (> 2 Gbyte files). • Dynamic processor sets. • Kernel-based TCP sockets. • Locking statistics. • UFS direct I/O. • Dynamic reconfiguration.
1998	Solaris 7	• 64-bit kernel and process address space. • Logging UFS integrated. • Priority Paging memory algorithm.

The information in Table 1-1 shows the significant features incorporated in each major release of Solaris. Details of *all* of the features can be found in the Solaris release *What's New* document, which is part of the documentation supplied with Solaris.

1.2   Key Differentiators

Solaris development continued aggressively throughout the 1990s. Several key features distinguish Solaris from earlier UNIX implementations.

- **Symmetric multiprocessing** — Solaris is implemented on systems ranging from single-processor systems to 64-processor symmetric multiprocessor servers. Solaris provides linear scalability up to the currently supported maximum of 64 processors.

- **64-bit kernel and process address space** — A 64-bit kernel for 64-bit platforms provides an LP64 execution environment. (LP64 refers to the data model: long and pointer data types are 64 bits wide.) A 32-bit application environment is also provided so that 32-bit binaries execute on a 64-bit Solaris kernel alongside 64-bit applications.

- **Multiple platform support** — Solaris supports a wide range of SPARC and Intel x86 microprocessor-based architectures. A layered architecture means that over 90 percent of the Solaris source is platform independent.

- **Modular binary kernel** — The Solaris kernel uses dynamic linking and dynamic modules to divide the kernel into modular binaries. A core kernel binary contains central facilities; device drivers, file systems, schedulers, and some system calls are implemented as dynamically loadable modules. Consequently, the Solaris kernel is delivered as a binary rather than source and object, and kernel compiles are not required upon a change of parameters or addition of new functionality.

- **Multithreaded process execution** — A process can have more than one thread of execution, and these threads can run concurrently on one or more processors. Thus, a single process can use multiple processors for concurrent thread execution, thereby using multiprocessor platforms more efficiently.

- **Multithreaded kernel** — The Solaris kernel uses threads as the entity for scheduling and execution: The kernel schedules interrupts and kernel services as regular kernel threads. This key feature provides interrupt scalability and low-latency interrupt response.

  Previous UNIX implementations manipulated processor priority levels to ensure exclusive access to critical interrupt data structures. As a result, the inability of interrupt code to block led to poor scalability. Solaris provides greater parallelism by scheduling interrupts as threads, which can then use regular kernel locks to ensure exclusive access to data structures.

- **Fully preemptable kernel** — The Solaris kernel is fully preemptable and does not require manipulation of hardware interrupt levels to protect critical data—locks synchronize access to kernel data. This means threads that need to run can interrupt another, lower-priority thread; hence, low latency scheduling and low latency interrupt dispatch become possible. For example, a process waking up after sleeping for a disk I/O can be scheduled immediately, rather than waiting until the scheduler runs. Additionally, by not raising priority levels and blocking interrupts, the system need not periodically suspend activity during interrupt handling, so system resources are used more efficiently.

- **Support for multiple schedulers** — Solaris provides a configurable scheduler environment. Multiple schedulers can operate concurrently, each with its own scheduling algorithms and priority levels. Schedulers are supplied as kernel modules and are dynamically loaded into the operating system. Solaris offers a table-driven, usage-decayed, timesharing user scheduler (TS); a window system optimized timeshare scheduler (IA); and a real-time fixed priority scheduler (RT). An optional fair-share scheduler class can be loaded with the Solaris Resource Manager package.

- **Support for multiple file systems** — Solaris provides a virtual file system (VFS) framework that allows multiple file systems to be configured into the system. The framework implements several disk-based file systems (UNIX File System, MS-DOS file system, CD-ROM file system, etc.) and the network file system (NFS V2 and V3). The virtual file system framework also implements pseudo file systems, including the process file system, procfs, a file system that abstracts processes as files. The virtual file system framework is integrated with the virtual memory system to provide dynamic file system caching that uses available free memory as a file system cache.

- **Processor partitioning and binding** — Special facilities allow fine-grained processor control, including binding processes to processors. Processors can be configured into scheduling groups to partition system resources.

- **Demand-paged virtual memory system** — This feature allows systems to load applications on demand, rather than loading whole executables or library images into memory. Demand-paging speeds up application startup and potentially reduces memory footprint.

- **Modular virtual memory system** — The virtual memory system separates virtual memory functions into distinct layers; the address space layer, segment drivers, and hardware-specific components are consolidated into a hardware address translation (HAT) layer. Segment drivers can abstract memory as files, and files can be memory-mapped into an address space. Segment drivers enable different abstractions, including physical memory and devices, to appear in an address space.

- **Modular device I/O system** — Dynamically loadable device and bus drivers allow a hierarchy of buses and devices to be installed and configured. A device driver interface (DDI) shields device drivers from platform-specific infrastructure, thus maximizing portability of device drivers.

- **Integrated networking** — With the data link provider interface (DLPI), multiple concurrent network interfaces can be configured, and a variety of different protocols—including Ethernet, X.25, SDLC, ISDN, FDDI, token bus, bi-sync, and other datalink-level protocols—can be configured upon them.

- **Integrated Internet protocol** — Solaris implements TCP/IP by use of the DLPI interfaces.

- **Real-time architecture** — The Solaris kernel was designed and implemented to provide real-time capabilities. The combination of the preemptive kernel, kernel interrupts as threads, fixed priority scheduling, high-resolution timers, and fine-grained processor control makes Solaris an ideal environment for real-time applications.

The differentiators listed above represent many innovative features integrated in the Solaris kernel. In the remaining chapters, we closely examine the core modules and major subsystems of the kernel.

1.3 Kernel Overview

The Solaris kernel is the core of Solaris. It manages the system hardware resources and provides an execution environment for user programs. The Solaris kernel supports an environment in which multiple programs can execute simultaneously. The primary functions of the kernel can be divided into two major categories: managing the hardware by allocating its resources among the programs running on it; and supplying a set of system services for those programs to use.

The Solaris kernel, like that of other operating systems implementations, provides a virtual machine environment that shields programs from the underlying hardware and allows multiple programs to execute concurrently on the hardware platform. Each program has its own virtual machine environment, with an execution context and state.

The basic unit that provides a program's environment is known as a *process*; it contains a virtual memory environment that is insulated from other processes on the system. Each Solaris process can have one or more *threads of execution* that share the virtual memory environment of the process, and each thread in effect executes concurrently within the process's environment. The Solaris kernel scheduler manages the execution of these threads (as opposed to management by scheduling processes) by transparently time-slicing them onto one or more *processors*. The threads of execution start and stop executing as they are moved on and off the processors, but the user program is unaware of this. Each time a thread is moved off a processor, its complete execution environment (program counter, stack pointers, registers, etc.) is saved, so when it is later rescheduled onto a processor, its environment can be restored and execution can resume. Processes and scheduling are covered in detail in Part 3 of this book.

The kernel provides mechanisms to access operating system services, such as file I/O, networking, process and thread creation and termination, process control and signaling, process memory management, and interprocess communication. A process accesses these kernel services through the use of *system calls*. System calls are programming interfaces through which the operating system is entered so that the kernel can perform work on behalf of the calling thread.

1.3.1 Solaris Kernel Architecture

The Solaris kernel is grouped into several key components and is implemented in a modular fashion. The key components of the Solaris kernel are described in the following list and illustrated in Figure 1.1.

- **System Call Interface** — The system call interface allows user processes to access kernel facilities. The system call layer consists of a common system call handler, which vectors system calls into the appropriate kernel modules.

- **Process Execution and Scheduling** — Process management provides facilities for process creation, execution, management, and termination. The scheduler implements the functions that divide the machine's processor resources among threads on the system. The scheduler allows different scheduling classes to be loaded for different behavior and scheduling requirements.

- **Memory Management** — The virtual memory system manages mapping of physical memory to user processes and the kernel. The Solaris memory management layer is divided into two layers: the common memory management functions and the hardware-specific components. The hardware-specific components are located in the hardware address translation (HAT) layer.

- **File Systems** — Solaris implements a virtual file system framework, by which multiple types of file system can be configured into the Solaris kernel at the same time. Regular disk-based file systems, network file systems, and pseudo file systems are implemented in the file system layer.

- **I/O Bus and Device Management** — The Solaris I/O framework implements bus nexus node drivers (bus-specific architectural dependencies, e.g., a PCI bus) and device drivers (a specific device on a bus, e.g., an Ethernet card) as a hierarchy of modules, reflecting the physical layout of the bus/device interconnect.

- **Kernel Facilities (Clocks, timers, etc.)** — Central kernel facilities, including regular clock interrupts, system timers, synchronization primitives, and loadable module support.

- **Networking** — TCP/IP protocol support and related facilities. The Solaris networking subsystem is implemented as streams-based device drivers and streams modules.

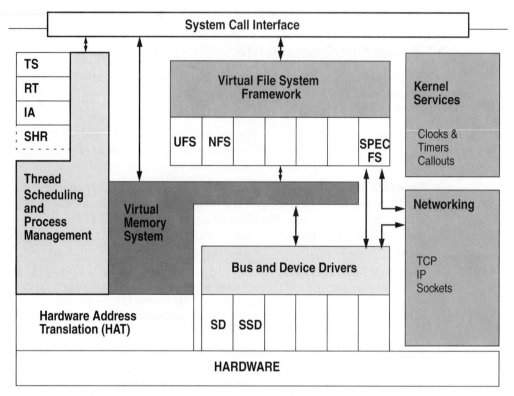

Figure 1.1 Solaris Kernel Components

1.3.2 Modular Implementation

The Solaris kernel is implemented as a core set of operating system functions, with additional kernel subsystems and services linked in as dynamically loadable modules. This implementation is facilitated by a module loading and kernel runtime linker infrastructure, which allows kernel modules to be added to the operating system either during boot or on demand while the system is running.

The Solaris 7 module framework supports seven types of loadable kernel modules: scheduler classes, file systems, loadable system calls, loaders for executable file formats, streams modules, bus or device drivers, and miscellaneous modules. Figure 1.2 shows the facilities contained in the core kernel and the various types of kernel modules that implement the remainder of the Solaris kernel.

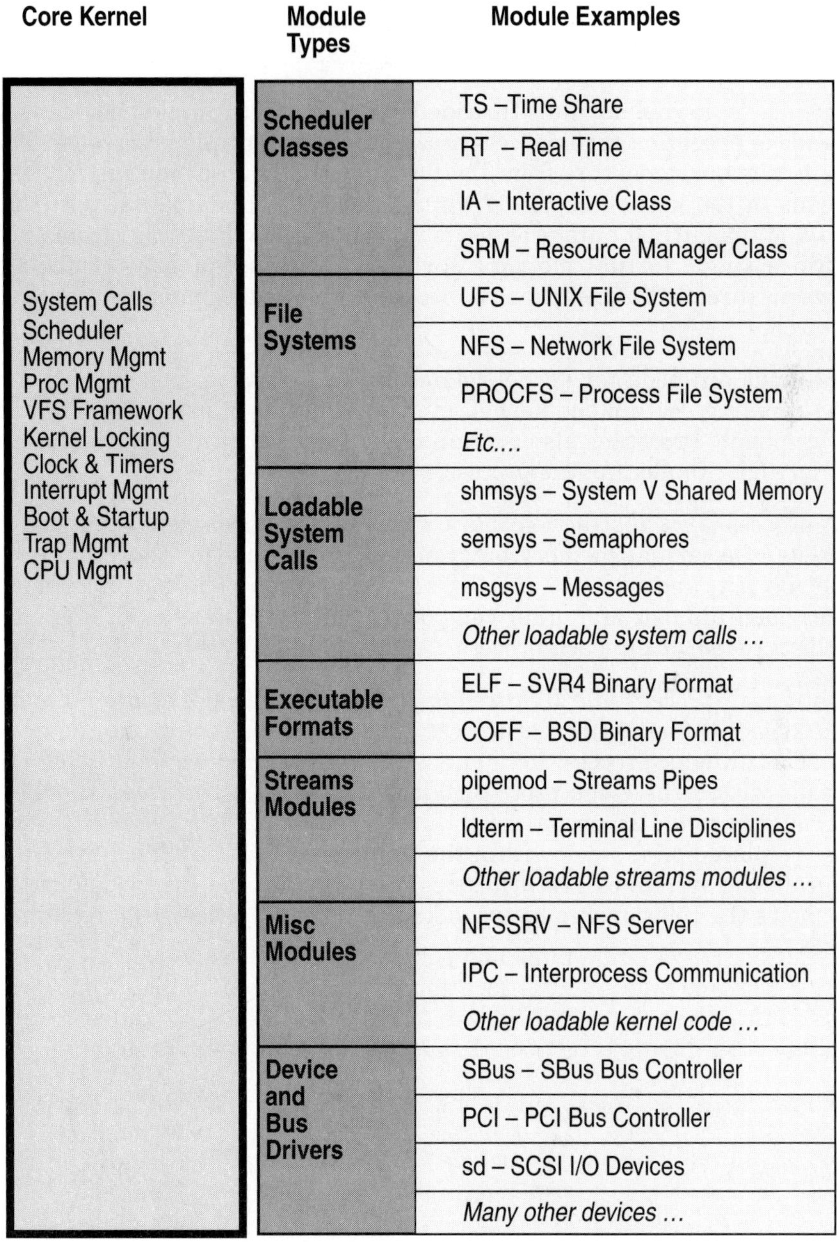

Core Kernel	Module Types	Module Examples

Core Kernel	Module Types	Module Examples
System Calls Scheduler Memory Mgmt Proc Mgmt VFS Framework Kernel Locking Clock & Timers Interrupt Mgmt Boot & Startup Trap Mgmt CPU Mgmt	**Scheduler Classes**	TS –Time Share
		RT – Real Time
		IA – Interactive Class
		SRM – Resource Manager Class
	File Systems	UFS – UNIX File System
		NFS – Network File System
		PROCFS – Process File System
		Etc....
	Loadable System Calls	shmsys – System V Shared Memory
		semsys – Semaphores
		msgsys – Messages
		Other loadable system calls ...
	Executable Formats	ELF – SVR4 Binary Format
		COFF – BSD Binary Format
	Streams Modules	pipemod – Streams Pipes
		ldterm – Terminal Line Disciplines
		Other loadable streams modules ...
	Misc Modules	NFSSRV – NFS Server
		IPC – Interprocess Communication
		Other loadable kernel code ...
	Device and Bus Drivers	SBus – SBus Bus Controller
		PCI – PCI Bus Controller
		sd – SCSI I/O Devices
		Many other devices ...

Figure 1.2 Core Kernel and Loadable Modules

1.4   Processes, Threads, and Scheduling

The Solaris kernel is multithreaded; that is, it is implemented with multiple threads of execution to allow concurrency across multiple processors. This architecture is a major departure from the traditional UNIX scheduling model. In Solaris, threads in the kernel, or *kernel threads*, are the fundamental unit that is scheduled and dispatched onto processors. Threads allow multiple streams of execution within a single virtual memory environment; consequently, switching execution between threads is inexpensive because no virtual memory context switch is required.

Threads are used for kernel-related tasks, for process execution, and for interrupt handling. Within the kernel, multiple threads of execution share the kernel's environment. Processes also contain one or more threads, which share the virtual memory environment of the process.

A process is an abstraction that contains the environment for a user program. It consists of a virtual memory environment, resources for the program such as an open file list, and at least one thread of execution. The virtual memory environment, open file list, and other components of the process environment are shared by the threads within each process.

Within each process is a *lightweight process*, a virtual execution environment for each kernel thread within a process. The lightweight process allows each kernel thread within a process to make system calls independently of other kernel threads within the same process. Without a lightweight process, only one system call could be made at a time. Each time a system call is made by a thread, its registers are placed on a stack within the lightweight process. Upon return from a system call, the system call return codes are placed in the lightweight process. Figure 1.3 shows the relationship between kernel threads, processes, and lightweight processes.

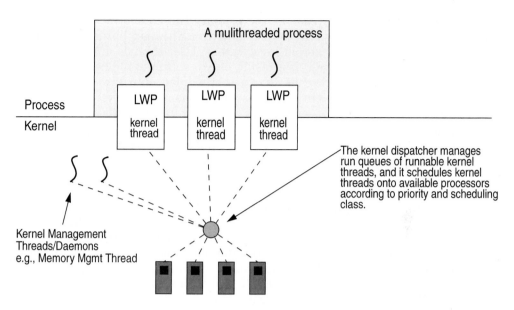

Figure 1.3 Kernel Threads, Processes, and Lightweight Processes

1.4.1 Two-Level Thread Model

Although it is relatively inexpensive to switch between multiple threads within a process, it is still relatively expensive to create and destroy threads. In addition, each kernel thread within a process requires a lightweight process containing a stack that consumes kernel resources. For these reasons, an additional level of thread management is implemented within each process to manage *user threads*, as shown in Figure 1.4.

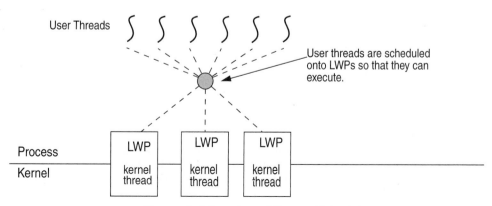

Figure 1.4 Two-Level Thread Model

Solaris exposes user threads as the primary thread abstraction for multithreaded programs. User threads are implemented in a thread library and can be created and destroyed without kernel involvement. User threads are scheduled on and off the lightweight processes. As a result, only a subset of the user threads is active at any one time—those threads that are scheduled onto the lightweight processes. The number of lightweight processes within the process affects the degree of parallelism available to the user threads and is adjusted on-the-fly by the user thread library

1.4.2 Global Process Priorities and Scheduling

The Solaris kernel implements a global thread priority model for kernel threads. The kernel scheduler, or *dispatcher*, uses the model to select which kernel thread of potentially many runnable kernel threads executes next. The kernel supports the notion of *preemption*, allowing a better-priority thread to cause the preemption of a running thread, such that the better- (higher) priority thread can execute. The kernel itself is preemptable, an innovation providing for time-critical scheduling of high-priority threads. There are 170 global priorities; numerically larger priority values correspond to better thread priorities. The priority name space is partitioned by different *scheduling classes*, as illustrated in Figure 1.5.

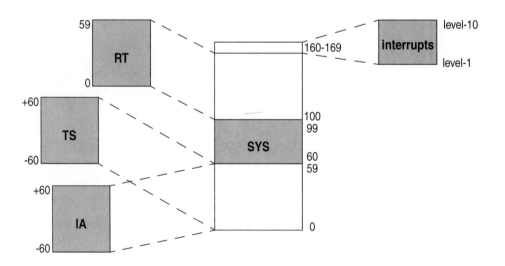

Figure 1.5 Global Thread Priorities

The Solaris dispatcher implements multiple scheduling classes, which allow different scheduling policies to be applied to threads. The three primary scheduling classes—TS (IA is an enhanced TS), SYS, and RT—shown in Figure 1.5 are described below.

- **TS** — The timeshare scheduling class is the default class for processes and all the kernel threads within the process. It changes process priorities dynamically according to recent processor usage in an attempt to evenly allocate processor resources among the kernel threads in the system. Process priorities and time quantums are calculated according to a timeshare scheduling table at each clock tick, or during wakeup after sleeping for an I/O. The TS class uses priority ranges 0 to 59.
- **IA** — The interactive class is an enhanced TS class used by the desktop windowing system to boost priority of threads within the window under focus. IA shares the priority numeric range with the TS class.
- **SYS** — The system class is used by the kernel for kernel threads. Threads in the system class are bound threads; that is, there is no time quantum—they run until they block. The system class uses priorities 60 to 99.
- **RT** — The realtime class implements fixed priority, fixed time quantum scheduling. The realtime class uses priorities 100 to 159. Note that threads in the RT class have a higher priority over kernel threads in the SYS class.

The interrupt priority levels shown in Figure 1.5 are not available for use by anything other than interrupt threads. The intent of their positioning in the priority scheme is to guarantee that interrupt threads have priority over all other threads in the system.

1.5   Interprocess Communication

Processes can communicate with each other by using one of several types of interprocess communication (IPC). IPC allows information transfer or synchronization to occur between processes. Solaris supports four different groups of interprocess communication: basic IPC, System V IPC, POSIX IPC, and advanced Solaris IPC.

1.5.1 Traditional UNIX IPC

Solaris implements traditional IPC facilities such as local sockets and pipes. A local socket is a network-like connection using the socket(2) system call to directly connect two processes.

A pipe directly channels data flow from one process to another through an object that operates like a file. Data is inserted at one end of the pipe and travels to the receiving processes in a first-in, first-out order. Data is read and written on a pipe with the standard file I/O system calls. Pipes are created with the pipe(2) system call or by a special pipe device created in the file system with mknod(1) and the standard file open(2) system call.

1.5.2 System V IPC

Three types of IPC originally developed for System V UNIX have become standard across all UNIX implementations: shared memory, message passing, and semaphores. These facilities provide the common IPC mechanism used by the majority of applications today.

- **System V Shared Memory** — Processes can create a segment of shared memory. Changes within the area of shared memory are immediately available to other processes that attach to the same shared memory segment.

- **System V Message Queues** — A message queue is a list of messages with a head and a tail. Messages are placed on the tail of the queue and are received on the head. Each messages contains a 32-bit type value, followed by a data payload.

- **System V Semaphores** — Semaphores are integer-valued objects that support two atomic operations: increment or decrement the value of the integer. Processes can sleep on semaphores that are greater than zero, then can be awakened when the value reaches zero.

1.5.3 POSIX IPC

The POSIX IPC facilities are similar in functionality to System V IPC but are abstracted on top of memory mapped files. The POSIX library routines are called by a program to create a new semaphore, shared memory segment, or message queue using the Solaris file I/O system calls (open(2), read(2), mmap(2), etc.). Internally in the POSIX library, the IPC objects exist as files. The object type exported to the program through the POSIX interfaces is handled within the library routines.

1.5.4 Advanced Solaris IPC

A new, fast, lightweight mechanism for calling procedures between processes is available in Solaris: doors. Doors are a low-latency method of invoking a procedure in local process. A door server contains a thread that sleeps, waiting for an invocation from the door client. A client makes a call to the server through the door, along with a small (16 Kbyte) payload. When the call is made from a door client to a door server, scheduling control is passed directly to the thread in the door server. Once a door server has finished handling the request, it passes control and response back to the calling thread. The scheduling control allows ultra-low-latency turnaround because the client does not need to wait for the server thread to be scheduled to complete the request.

1.6   Signals

UNIX systems have provided a process signaling mechanism from the earliest implementations. The signal facility provides a means to interrupt a process or thread within a process as a result of a specific event. The events that trigger signals can be directly related to the current instruction stream. Such signals, referred to as synchronous signals, originate as hardware trap conditions arising from illegal address references (segmentation violation), illegal math operations (floating point exceptions), and the like.

The system also implements asynchronous signals, which result from an external event not necessarily related to the current instruction stream. Examples of asynchronous signals include job control signals and the sending of a signal from one process or thread to another, for example, sending a kill signal to terminate a process.

For each possible signal, a process can establish one of three possible signal dispositions, which define what action, if any, will be taken when the signal is received. Most signals can be *ignored*, a signal can be *caught* and a process-specific signal handler invoked, or a process can permit the *default* action to be taken. Every signal has a predefined default action, for example, terminate the process. Solaris provides a set of programming interfaces that allow signals to be masked or a specific signal handler to be installed.

The traditional signal model was built on the concept of a process having a single execution stream at any time. The Solaris kernel's multithreaded process architecture allows for multiple threads of execution within a process, meaning that a signal can be directed to specific thread. The disposition and handlers for signals are process-wide; every thread in a multithreaded process has the same signal disposition and handlers. However, the Solaris model allows for signals to be masked at the thread level, so different threads within the process can have different signals masked. (Masking is a means of blocking a signal from being delivered.)

1.7   Memory Management

The Solaris virtual memory (VM) system can be considered to be the core of the operating system—it manages the system's memory on behalf of the kernel and processes. The main task of the VM system is to manage efficient allocation of the system's physical memory to the processes and kernel subsystems running within the operating system. The VM system uses slower storage media (usually disk) to store data that does not fit within the physical memory of the system, thus accommodating programs larger than the size of physical memory. The VM system is what keeps the most frequently used portions within physical memory and the lesser-used portions on the slower secondary storage.

For processes, the VM system presents a simple linear range of memory, known as an *address space*. Each address space is broken into several *segments* that represent mappings of the executable, heap space (general-purpose, process-allocated memory), shared libraries, and a program stack. Each segment is divided into equal-sized pieces of virtual memory, known as *pages*, and a hardware memory management unit (MMU) manages the mapping of page-sized pieces of virtual memory to physical memory. Figure 1.6 shows the relationship between an address space, segments, the memory management unit, and physical memory.

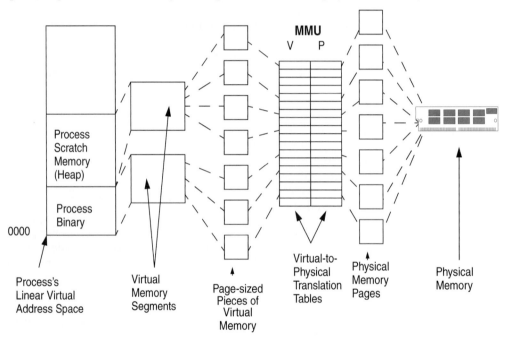

Figure 1.6 Address Spaces, Segments, and Pages

The virtual memory system is implemented in a modular fashion. The components that deal with physical memory management are mostly hardware platform specific. The platform-dependent portions are implemented in the hardware address translation (HAT) layer.

1.7.1 Global Memory Allocation

The VM system implements demand paging. Pages of memory are allocated on demand, as they are referenced, and hence portions of an executable or shared library are allocated on demand. Loading pages of memory on demand dramatically lowers the memory footprint and startup time of a process. When an area of virtual memory is accessed, the hardware MMU raises an event to tell the kernel that an access has occurred to an area of memory that does not have physical memory mapped to it. This event is a *page fault*. The heap of a process is also allocated in a similar way: initially, only virtual memory space is allocated to the process. When memory is first referenced, a page fault occurs and memory is allocated one page at a time.

The virtual memory system uses a global paging model that implements a single global policy to manage the allocation of memory between processes. A scanning algorithm calculates the least-used portion of the physical memory. A kernel thread (the page scanner) scans memory in physical page order when the amount of free memory falls below a preconfigured threshold. Pages that have not been used recently are stolen and placed onto a free list for use by other processes.

1.7.2 Kernel Memory Management

The Solaris kernel requires memory for kernel instructions, data structures, and caches. Most of the kernel's memory is not pageable; that is, it is allocated from physical memory which cannot be stolen by the page scanner. This characteristic avoids deadlocks that could occur within the kernel if a kernel memory management function caused a page fault while holding a lock for another critical resource. The kernel cannot rely on the global paging used by processes, so it implements its own memory allocation systems.

A core kernel memory allocator—the *slab allocator*—allocates memory for kernel data structures. As the name suggests, the allocator subdivides large contiguous areas of memory (slabs) into smaller chunks for data structures. Allocation pools are organized so that like-sized objects are allocated from the same continuous segments, thereby dramatically reducing fragmentation that could result from continuous allocation and deallocation.

1.8   Files and File Systems

Solaris provides facilities for storage and management of data, as illustrated in Figure 1.7. A *file* provides a container for data, a *directory* contains a number of files, and a *file system* implements files and directories upon a device, typically a storage medium of some type.

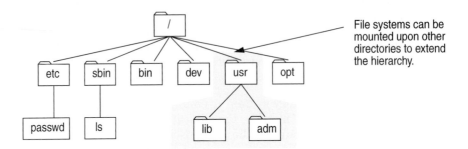

File systems can be mounted upon other directories to extend the hierarchy.

Figure 1.7 Files Organized in a Hierarchy of Directories

A file system can be mounted on a branch of an existing file system to extend the hierarchy. The hierarchy hides the mount so that it is transparent to users or applications that traverse the tree.

Solaris implements several different types of files:

- **Regular files** store data within the file system.
- **Special files** represent a device driver. Reads and writes to special files are handled by a device driver and translated into I/O of some type.
- **Pipes** are a special type of file that do not hold data but can be opened by two different processes so that data can be passed between them.
- **Hard links** link to the data of other files within the same file system. With hard links, the same data can have two different file names in the file system.
- **Symbolic links** point to other path names on any file system.
- **Sockets** in the file system enable local communication between two processes.

1.8.1 File Descriptors and File System Calls

Processes interface with files through file-related system calls. The file-related system calls identify files by two means: their path name in the file system and a *file descriptor*. A file descriptor is an integer number identifying an open file within a process. Each process has a table of open files, starting at file descriptor 0 and progressing upward as more files are opened. A file descriptor can be obtained with the `open()` system call, which opens a file named by a path name and returns a file descriptor identifying the open file.

```
fd = open("/etc/passwd",flag, mode);
```

Once a file has been opened, a file descriptor can be used for operations on the file. The `read(2)` and `write(2)` operations provide basic file I/O, along with several other advanced mechanisms for performing more complex operations. A file descriptor is eventually closed by the close(2) system call or by the process's exit. By default, file descriptors 0, 1, and 2 are opened automatically by the C runtime library and represent the standard input, standard output, and standard error streams for a process.

1.8.2 The Virtual File System Framework

Solaris provides a framework under which multiple file system types are implemented: the *virtual file system framework*. Earlier implementations of UNIX used a single file system type for all of the mounted file systems; typically, the UFS file system from BSD UNIX. The virtual file system framework, developed to enable the network file system (NFS) to coexist with the UFS file system in SunOS 2.0, became a standard part of System V in SVR4 and Solaris.

Each file system provides file abstractions in the standard hierarchical manner, providing standard file access interfaces even if the underlying file system implementation varies. The file system framework allows almost any objects to be abstracted as files and file systems. Some file systems store file data on storage-based media, whereas other implementations abstract objects other than storage as files. For example, the procfs file system abstracts the process tree, where each file in the file system represents a process in the process tree. We can categorize Solaris file systems into the following groups:

- **Storage Based** — Regular file systems that provide facilities for persistent storage and management of data. The Solaris UFS and PC/DOS file systems are examples.
- **Network File Systems** — File systems that provide files which appear to be in a local directory structure but are stored on a remote network server; for example, Sun's network file system (NFS).
- **Pseudo File Systems** — File systems that present various abstractions as files in a file system. The /proc pseudo file system represents the address space of a process as a series of files.

The framework provides a single set of well-defined interfaces that are file system independent; the implementation details of each file system are hidden behind these interfaces. Two key objects represent these interfaces: the virtual file, or *vnode*, and the virtual file system, or *vfs* objects. The vnode interfaces implement file-related functions, and the vfs interfaces implement file system management functions. The vnode and vfs interfaces call appropriate file system functions depending on the type of file system being operated on. Figure 1.8 shows the file system layers. File-related functions are initiated through a system call or from another kernel subsystem and are directed to the appropriate file system via the vnode/vfs layer.

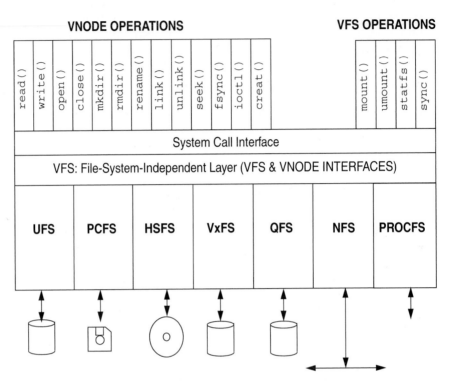

Figure 1.8 VFS/Vnode Architecture

Table 1-2 summarizes the major file system types that are implemented in Solaris.

Table 1-2 File Systems Available in Solaris File System Framework

File System	Type	Device	Description
ufs	Regular	Disk	UNIX Fast File system, default in Solaris
pcfs	Regular	Disk	MS-DOS file system
hsfs	Regular	Disk	High Sierra file system (CD-ROM)
tmpfs	Regular	Memory	Uses memory and swap
nfs	Pseudo	Network	Network file system
cachefs	Pseudo	File system	Uses a local disk as cache for another NFS file system
autofs	Pseudo	File system	Uses a dynamic layout to mount other file systems
specfs	Pseudo	Device Drivers	File system for the /dev devices
procfs	Pseudo	Kernel	/proc file system representing processes

Table 1-2 File Systems Available in Solaris File System Framework (Continued)

File System	Type	Device	Description
sockfs	Pseudo	Network	File system of socket connections
fdfs	Pseudo	File Descriptors	Allows a process to see its open files in /dev/fd
fifofs	Pseudo	Files	FIFO file system

1.9 I/O Architecture

Traditional UNIX implements kernel-resident device drivers to interface with hardware devices. The device driver manages data transfer and registers I/O and handles device hardware interrupts. A device driver typically has to know intimate details about the hardware device and the layout of buses to which the device is connected. Solaris extends traditional device driver management functions by using separate drivers for devices and buses: a *device driver* controls a device's hardware, and a *bus nexus driver* controls and translates data between two different types of buses.

Solaris organizes I/O devices in a hierarchy of bus nexus and instances of devices, according to the physical connection hierarchy of the devices. The hierarchy shown in Figure 1.9 represents a typical Solaris *device tree*.

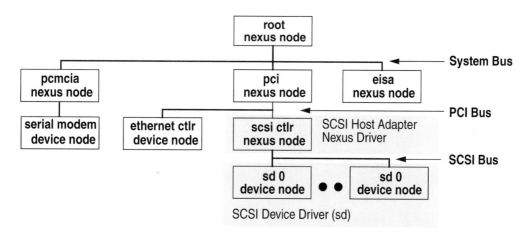

Figure 1.9 The Solaris Device Tree

Each bus connects to another bus through a bus nexus. In our example, nexus drivers are represented by the PCI, EISA, PCMCIA, and SCSI nodes. The SCSI host adapter is a bus nexus bridging the PCI and SCSI bus it controls, underneath which the SCSI disk (sd) device driver implements device nodes for each disk on the SCSI chain.

The Solaris device driver interface (DDI) hides the implementation specifics of the platform and bus hierarchy from the device drivers. The DDI provides interfaces for registering interrupts, mapping registers, and accessing DMA memory. In that way, the kernel can interface with the device.

Device drivers are implemented as loadable modules, that is, as separate binaries containing driver code. Device drivers are loaded automatically the first time their device is accessed.

2

KERNEL SERVICES

T he Solaris kernel manages operating system resources and provides facilities to user processes. In this chapter we explore how the kernel implements these services. We begin by discussing the boundary between user programs and kernel mode, then discuss the mechanisms used to switch between user and kernel mode, including system calls, traps, and interrupts.

2.1 Access to Kernel Services

The Solaris kernel insulates processes from kernel data structures and hardware by using two distinct processor execution modes: nonprivileged mode and privileged mode. Privileged mode is often referred to as *kernel mode;* nonprivileged mode is referred to as *user mode*.

In nonprivileged mode, a process can access only its own memory, whereas in privileged mode, access is available to all of the kernel's data structures and the underlying hardware. The kernel executes processes in nonprivileged mode to prevent user processes from accessing data structures or hardware registers that may affect other processes or the operating environment. Because only Solaris kernel instructions can execute in privileged mode, the kernel can mediate access to kernel data structures and hardware devices.

If a user process needs to access kernel system services, a thread within the process transitions from user mode to kernel mode through a set of interfaces known as *system calls*. A system call allows a thread in a user process to switch into kernel mode to perform an OS-defined system service. Figure 2.1 shows an example of a user process issuing a `read()` system call. The `read()` system call executes special machine code instructions to change the processor into privileged mode, in order to begin executing the `read()` system call's kernel instructions. While in privileged mode, the kernel `read()` code performs the I/O on behalf of the calling thread, then returns to nonprivileged user mode, after which the user thread continues normal execution.

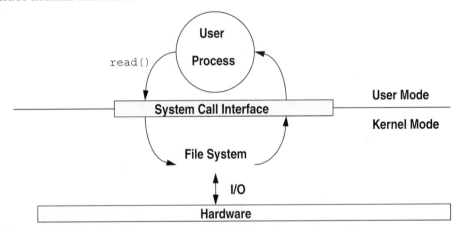

Figure 2.1 Switching into Kernel Mode via System Calls

2.2   Entering Kernel Mode

In addition to entering through system calls, the system can enter kernel mode for other reasons, such as in response to a device interrupt, or to take care of a situation that could not be handled in user mode. A transfer of control to the kernel is achieved in one of three ways:

- Through a system call
- As the result of an interrupt
- As the result of a processor trap

We defined a *system call* as the mechanism by which a user process requests a kernel service, for example, to read from a file. System calls are typically initiated from user mode by either a trap instruction or a software interrupt, depending on the microprocessor and platform. On SPARC-based platforms, system calls are initiated by issuing a specific trap instruction in a C library stub.

An *interrupt* is a vectored transfer of control into the kernel, typically initiated by a hardware device, for example, a disk controller signalling the completion of an I/O. Interrupts can also be initiated from software. Hardware interrupts typically occur asynchronously to the currently executing thread, and they occur in interrupt context.

A *trap* is also a vectored transfer of control into the kernel, initiated by the processor. The primary distinction between traps and interrupts is this: Traps typically occur as a result of the current executing thread, for example, a divide-by-zero error or a memory page fault; interrupts are asynchronous events, that is, the source of the interrupt is something unrelated to the currently executing thread. On SPARC processors, the distinction is somewhat blurred, since a trap is also the mechanism used to initiate interrupt handlers.

2.2.1 Context

A context describes the environment for a thread of execution. We often refer to two distinct types of context: an execution context (thread stacks, open file lists, resource accounting, etc.) and a virtual memory context (the virtual-to-physical address mappings).

2.2.1.1 Execution Context

Threads in the kernel can execute in process, interrupt, or kernel context.

- **Process Context** — In the process context, the kernel thread acts on behalf of the user process and has access to the process's user area (*uarea*), and process structures for resource accounting. The uarea (struct u) is a special area within the process that contains process information of interest to the kernel: typically, the process's open file list, process identification information, etc. For example, when a process executes a system call, a thread within the process transitions into kernel mode and then has access to the uarea of the process's data structures, so that it can pass arguments, update system time usage, etc.

- **Interrupt Context** — Interrupt threads execute in an interrupt context. They do not have access to the data structures of the process or thread they interrupted. Interrupts have their own stack and can access only kernel data structures.

- **Kernel Context** — Kernel management threads run in the kernel context. In kernel context, system management threads share the kernel's environment with each other. Kernel management threads typically cannot access process-related data. Examples of kernel management threads are the page scanner and the NFS server.

2.2.1.2 Virtual Memory Context

A virtual memory context is the set of virtual-to-physical address translations that construct a memory environment. Each process has its own virtual memory context. When execution is switched from one process to another during a scheduling switch, the virtual memory context is switched to provide the new process's virtual memory environment.

On Intel and older SPARC architectures, each process context has a portion of the kernel's virtual memory mapped within it, so that a virtual memory context switch to the kernel's virtual memory context is not required when transitioning from user to kernel mode during a system call. On UltraSPARC, features of the processor and memory management unit allow fast switching between virtual memory contexts; in that way, the process and kernel can have separate virtual memory contexts. See "Virtual Address Spaces" on page 130 and "Kernel Virtual Memory Layout" on page 205 for a detailed discussion of process and kernel address spaces.

2.2.2 Threads in Kernel and Interrupt Context

In addition to providing kernel services through system calls, the kernel must also perform system-related functions, such as responding to device I/O interrupts, performing some routine memory management, or initiating scheduler functions to switch execution from one kernel thread to another.

- **Interrupt Handlers** — Interrupts are directed to specific processors, and on reception, a processor stops executing the current thread, context-switches the thread out, and begins executing an interrupt handling routine. Kernel threads handle all but high-priority interrupts. Consequently, the kernel can minimize the amount of time spent holding critical resources, thus providing better scalability of interrupt code and lower overall interrupt response time. We discuss on kernel interrupts in more detail in "Interrupts" on page 38.

- **Kernel Management Threads** — The Solaris kernel, just like a process, has several of its own threads of execution to carry out system management tasks (the memory page scanner and NFS server are examples). Solaris kernel management threads do not execute in a process's execution context. Rather, they execute in the *kernel's* execution context, sharing the kernel execution environment with each other. Solaris kernel management threads are scheduled in the system (SYS) scheduling class at a higher priority than most other threads on the system.

Figure 2.2 shows the entry paths into the kernel for processes, interrupts, and threads.

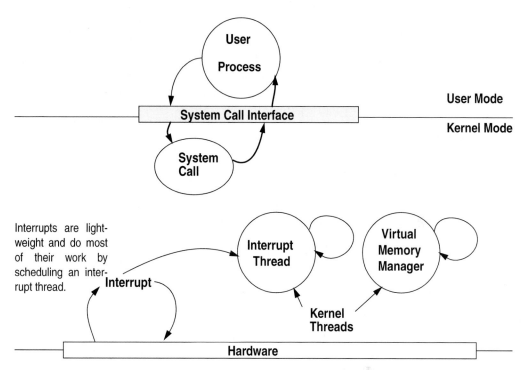

Figure 2.2 Process, Interrupt, and Kernel Threads

2.2.3 UltraSPARC I & II Traps

The SPARC processor architecture uses traps as a unified mechanism to handle system calls, processor exceptions, and interrupts. A SPARC trap is a procedure call initiated by the microprocessor as a result of a synchronous processor exception, an asynchronous processor exception, a software-initiated trap instruction, or a device interrupt.

Upon receipt of a trap, the UltraSPARC I & II processor enters privileged mode and transfers control to the instructions, starting at a predetermined location in a *trap table*. The trap handler for the type of trap received is executed, and once the interrupt handler has finished, control is returned to the interrupted thread. A trap causes the hardware to do the following:

- Save certain processor state (program counters, condition code registers, trap type, etc.)
- Enter privileged execution mode
- Begin executing code in the corresponding trap table slot

When an UltraSPARC trap handler processing is complete, it issues a SPARC DONE or RETRY instruction to return to the interrupted thread.

The UltraSPARC I & II trap table is an in-memory table that contains the first eight instructions for each type of trap. The trap table is located in memory at the address stored in the trap table base address register (TBA), which is initialized during boot. Solaris places the trap table at the base of the kernel (known as kernelbase) in a locked-down (non-pageable) 4-Mbyte page so that no memory-related traps (page faults or TLB misses) will occur during execution of instructions in the trap table. (For a detailed kernel memory map, see Appendix B, "Kernel Virtual Address Maps".)

2.2.3.1 UltraSPARC I & II Trap Types

The trap table contains one entry for each type of trap and provides a specific handler for each trap type. The UltraSPARC I & II traps can be categorized into the following broad types:

- **Processor resets** — Power-on reset, machine resets, software-initiated resets
- **Memory management exceptions** — MMU page faults, page protection violations, memory errors, misaligned accesses, etc.
- **Instruction exceptions** — Attempts to execute privileged instructions from nonprivileged mode, illegal instructions, etc.
- **Floating-point exceptions** — Floating-point exceptions, floating-point mode instruction attempted when floating point unit disabled, etc.
- **SPARC register management** — Traps for SPARC register window spilling, filling, or cleaning.
- **Software-initiated traps** — Traps initiated by the SPARC trap instruction (Tcc); primarily used for system call entry in Solaris.

Table 2-1 shows the UltraSPARC I & II trap types, as implemented in Solaris.

Table 2-1 Solaris UltraSPARC I & II Traps

Trap Definition	Trap Type	Priority
Power-on reset	001	0
Watchdog reset	002	1
Externally initiated reset	003	1
Software-initiated reset	004	1
RED state exception	005	1
Reserved	006...007	n/a
Instruction access exception	008	5
Instruction access MMU miss	009	2
Instruction access error	00A	3
Reserved	00B...00F	n/a
Illegal instruction	010	7

Table 2-1 Solaris UltraSPARC I & II Traps (Continued)

Trap Definition	Trap Type	Priority
Attempt to execute privileged instruction	011	6
Unimplemented load instruction	012	6
Unimplemented store instruction	013	6
Reserved	014...01F	n/a
Floating-point unit disabled	020	8
Floating-point exception ieee754	021	11
Floating-point exception – other	022	11
Tag overflow	023	14
SPARC register window clean	024...027	10
Division by zero	028	15
Internal processor error	029	4
Data access exception	030	12
Data access MMU miss	031	12
Data access error	032	12
Data access protection	033	12
Memory address not aligned	034	10
Load double memory address not aligned	035	10
Store double memory address not aligned	036	10
Privileged action	037	11
Load quad memory address not aligned	038	10
Store quad memory address not aligned	039	10
Reserved	03A...03F	n/a
Asynchronous data error	040	2
Interrupt level n, where $n=1...15$	041...04F	32-n
Reserved	050...05F	n/a
Vectored interrupts	060...07F	Int. Specific
SPARC register window overflows	080...0BF	9
SPARC register window underflows	0C0...0FF	9
Trap instructions Tcc	100...17F	16
Reserved	180...1FF	n/a

2.2.3.2 UltraSPARC I & II Trap Priority Levels

Each UltraSPARC I & II trap has an associated priority level. The processor's trap hardware uses the level to decide which trap takes precedence when more than one trap occurs on a processor at a given time. When two or more traps are pending, the highest-priority trap is taken first (0 is the highest priority).

Interrupt traps are subject to trap priority precedence. In addition, interrupt traps are compared against the *processor interrupt level* (PIL). The UltraSPARC I & II processor will only take an interrupt trap that has an *interrupt request level* greater than that stored in the processor's PIL register. We discuss this behavior in more detail in "Interrupts" on page 38.

2.2.3.3 UltraSPARC I & II Trap Levels

The UltraSPARC I & II processor introduced nested traps; that is, a trap can be received while another trap is being handled. Prior SPARC implementations could not handle nested traps (a "watchdog reset" occurs on pre-UltraSPARC processors if a trap occurs while the processor is executing a trap handler). Also introduced was the notion of *trap levels* to describe the level of trap nesting. The nested traps have five levels, starting at trap level 0 (normal execution, no trap) through trap level 4 (trap level 4 is actually an error handling state and should not be reached during normal processing).

When an UltraSPARC I & II trap occurs, the CPU increments the trap level (TL). The most recent processor state is saved on the trap stack, and the trap handler is entered. On exit from the handler, the trap level is decremented.

UltraSPARC I & II also implements an alternate set of global registers for each trap level. Those registers remove most of the overhead associated with saving state, making it very efficient to move between trap levels.

2.2.3.4 UltraSPARC I & II Trap Table Layout

The UltraSPARC I & II trap table is halved: the lower half contains trap handlers for traps taken at trap level 0, and the upper half contains handlers for traps taken when the trap level is 1 or greater. We implement separate trap handlers for traps taken at trap levels greater than zero (i.e., we are already handling a trap) because not all facilities are available when a trap is taken within a trap.

For example, if a trap handler at trap level 0 takes a memory-related trap (such as a translation miss), the trap handler can assume a higher-level trap handler will take care of the trap; but a higher-level trap handler cannot always make the same assumption. Each half of the trap table contains 512 trap handler slots, one for each trap type shown in Table 2-1.

Each half of the trap table is further divided into two sections, each of which contains 256 hardware traps in the lower section, followed by 256 software traps in the upper section (for the SPARC `Tcc` software trap instructions). Upon receipt of a trap, the UltraSPARC I & II processor jumps to the instructions located in the trap table at the trap table base address (set in the TBA register) plus the offset of the trap level and trap type. There are 8 instructions (32 bytes) at each slot in the table; hence, the trap handler address is calculated as follows:

TL = 0: trap handler address = TBA + (trap type x 32)

TL > 0: trap handler address = TBA + 512 + (trap type x 32)

As a side note, space is reserved in the trap table so that trap handlers for SPARC that register clean, spill, and fill (register window operations) can actually be longer than 8 instructions. This allows branchless inline handlers to be implemented such that the entire handler fits within the trap table slot.

Figure 2.3 shows the UltraSPARC I & II trap table layout.

	Trap Table Contents	Trap Types
	Hardware Traps	000...07F
Trap Level = 0	**Spill/Fill Traps**	080...0FF
	Software Traps	100...17F
	Reserved	180...1FF
	Hardware Traps	000...07F
Trap Level > 0	**Spill/Fill Traps**	080...0FF
	Software Traps	100...17F
	Reserved	180...1FF

Figure 2.3 UltraSPARC I & II Trap Table Layout

2.2.3.5 Software Traps

Software traps are initiated by the SPARC trap instruction, Tcc. The opcode for the trap instruction includes a 6-bit software trap number, which indexes into the software portion of the trap table. Software traps are used primarily for system calls in the Solaris kernel.

There are three software traps for system calls: one for native system calls, one for 32-bit system calls (when 32-bit applications are run on a 64-bit kernel), and one for SunOS 4.x binary compatibility system calls. System calls vector through a common trap by setting the system call number in a global register and then issuing a trap instruction. We discuss regular systems calls in more detail in "System Calls" on page 44.

There are also several ultra-fast system calls implemented as their own trap. These system calls pass their simple arguments back and forth via registers. Because the system calls don't pass arguments on the stack, much less of the process state needs to be saved during transition into kernel mode, resulting in a much faster system call implementation. The fast system calls (e.g., get_hrestime) are time-related calls.

Table 2-2 lists UltraSPARC software traps, including ultra-fast system calls.

Table 2-2 UltraSPARC Software Traps

Trap Definition	Trap Type Value	Priority
Trap instruction (SunOS 4.x syscalls)	100	16
Trap instruction (user breakpoints)	101	16
Trap instruction (divide by zero)	102	16
Trap instruction (flush windows)	103	16
Trap instruction (clean windows)	104	16
Trap instruction (do unaligned references)	106	16
Trap instruction (32-bit system call)	108	16
Trap instruction (set trap0)	109	16
Trap instructions (user traps)	110 – 123	16
Trap instructions (`get_hrtime`)	124	16
Trap instructions (`get_hrvtime`)	125	16
Trap instructions (`self_xcall`)	126	16
Trap instructions (`get_hrestime`)	127	16
Trap instructions (trace)	130-137	16
Trap instructions (64-bit system call)	140	16

2.2.3.6 A Utility for Trap Analysis

An unbundled tool, `trapstat`, dynamically monitors trap activity. The tool monitors counts of each type of trap for each processor in the system during an interval specified as the argument. It is currently implemented on UltraSPARC and Intel x86 processor architectures, on Solaris 7 and later releases.

You can download `trapstat` from the website for this book: `http://www.solarisinternals.com`. Simply untar the archive and install the driver with the `add_drv` command.

Note: `trapstat` *is not supported by Sun. Do not use it on production machines because it dynamically loads code into the kernel.*

```
# tar xvf trapstat28.tar
-r-xr-xr-x   0/2     5268 Jan 31 03:57 2000 /usr/bin/trapstat
-rwxrwxr-x   0/1    33452 Feb 10 23:17 2000 /usr/bin/sparcv7/trapstat
-rwxrwxr-x   0/1    40432 Feb 10 23:16 2000 /usr/bin/sparcv9/trapstat
-rw-rw-r--   0/1    21224 Sep  8 17:28 1999 /usr/kernel/drv/trapstat
-rw-r--r--   0/1      188 Aug 31 10:06 1999 /usr/kernel/drv/trapstat.conf
-rw-rw-r--   0/1    37328 Sep  8 17:28 1999 /usr/kernel/drv/sparcv9/trapstat
# add_drv trapstat
```

Once `trapstat` is installed, use it to analyze the traps taken on each processor installed in the system.

```
# trapstat 3
vct  name                   | cpu0   cpu1
----------------------------+--------------
 24  cleanwin               |  3636    4285
 41  level-1                |    99       1
 45  level-5                |     1       0
 46  level-6                |    60       0
 47  level-7                |    23       0
 4a  level-10               |   100       0
 4d  level-13               |    31      67
 4e  level-14               |   100       0
 60  int-vec                |   161      90
 64  itlb-miss              |  5329   11128
 68  dtlb-miss              | 39130   82077
 6c  dtlb-prot              |     3       2
 84  spill-1-normal         |  1210     992
 8c  spill-3-normal         |   136     286
 98  spill-6-normal         |  5752   20286
 a4  spill-1-other          |   476    1116
 ac  spill-3-other          |  4782    9010
 c4  fill-1-normal          |  1218     752
 cc  fill-3-normal          |  3725    7972
 d8  fill-6-normal          |  5576   20273
103  flush-wins             |    31       0
108  syscall-32             |  2809    3813
124  getts                  |  1009    2523
127  gethrtime              |  1004     477
----------------------------+--------------
ttl                         | 76401 165150
```

The example above shows the traps taken on a two-processor Ultra-SPARC-II-based system. The first column shows the trap type, followed by an ASCII description of the trap type. The remaining columns are the trap counts for each processor.

We can see that most trap activities in the SPARC are register clean, spill, and fill traps—they perform SPARC register window management. The level-1 through level 14 and int-vec rows are the interrupt traps. The itlb-miss, dtlb-miss, and dtlb-prot rows are the UltraSPARC memory management traps, which occur each time a TLB miss or protection fault occurs. (More on UltraSPARC memory management in "The UltraSPARC-I and -II HAT" on page 193.) At the bottom of the output we can see the system call trap for 32-bit systems calls and two special ultra-fast system calls (`getts` and `gethrtime`), which each use their own trap.

The SPARC V9 Architecture Manual [30] provides a full reference for the implementation of UltraSPARC traps. We highly recommend this text for specific implementation details on the SPARC V9 processor architecture.

2.3   Interrupts

An interrupt is the mechanism that a device uses to signal the kernel that it needs attention and some immediate processing is required on behalf of that device. Solaris services interrupts by context-switching out the current thread running on a processor and executing an *interrupt handler* for the interrupting device. For example, when a packet is received on a network interface, the network controller initiates an interrupt to begin processing the packet.

2.3.1 Interrupt Priorities

Solaris assigns priorities to interrupts to allow overlapping interrupts to be handled with the correct precedence; for example, a network interrupt can be configured to have a higher priority than a disk interrupt.

The kernel implements 15 interrupt priority levels: level 1 through level 15, where level 15 is the highest priority level. On each processor, the kernel can mask interrupts below a given priority level by setting the processor's interrupt level. Setting the interrupt level blocks all interrupts at the specified level and lower. That way, when the processor is executing a level 9 interrupt handler, it does not receive interrupts at level 9 or below; it handles only higher-priority interrupts.

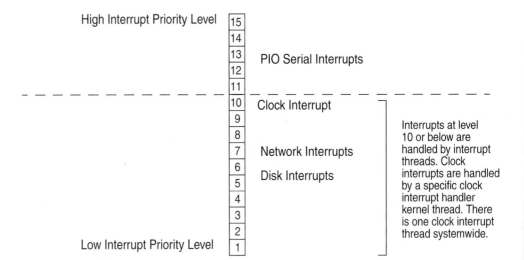

Figure 2.4 Solaris Interrupt Priority Levels

Interrupts that occur with a priority level at or lower than the processor's interrupt level are temporarily ignored. An interrupt will not be acknowledged by a processor until the processor's interrupt level is less than the level of the pending interrupt. More important interrupts have a higher-priority level to give them a better chance to be serviced than lower-priority interrupts.

Figure 2.4 illustrates interrupt priority levels.

2.3.1.1 Interrupts as Threads

Interrupt priority levels can be used to synchronize access to critical sections used by interrupt handlers. By raising the interrupt level, a handler can ensure exclusive access to data structures for the specific processor that has elevated its priority level. This is in fact what early, uniprocessor implementations of UNIX systems did for synchronization purposes.

But masking out interrupts to ensure exclusive access is expensive; it blocks other interrupt handlers from running for a potentially long time, which could lead to data loss if interrupts are lost because of overrun. (An overrun condition is one in which the volume of interrupts awaiting service exceeds the system's ability to queue the interrupts.) In addition, interrupt handlers using priority levels alone cannot block, since a deadlock could occur if they are waiting on a resource held by a lower-priority interrupt.

For these reasons, the Solaris kernel implements most interrupts as asynchronously created and dispatched high-priority threads. This implementation allows the kernel to overcome the scaling limitations imposed by interrupt blocking for synchronizing data access and thus provides low-latency interrupt response times.

Interrupts at priority 10 and below are handled by Solaris threads. These interrupt handlers can then block if necessary, using regular synchronization primitives such as mutex locks. Interrupts, however, must be efficient, and it is too expensive to create a new thread each time an interrupt is received. For this reason, each processor maintains a pool of partially initialized interrupt threads, one for each of the lower 9 priority levels plus a systemwide thread for the clock interrupt. When an interrupt is taken, the interrupt uses the interrupt thread's stack, and only if it blocks on a synchronization object is the thread completely initialized. This approach, exemplified in Figure 2.5, allows simple, fast allocation of threads at the time of interrupt dispatch.

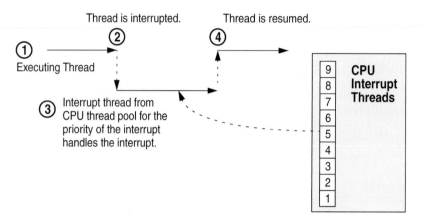

Figure 2.5 Handling Interrupts with Threads

Figure 2.5 depicts a typical scenario when an interrupt with priority 9 or less occurs (level 10 clock interrupts are handled slightly differently). When an interrupt occurs, the interrupt level is raised to the level of the interrupt to block subsequent interrupts at this level (and lower levels). The currently executing thread is interrupted and *pinned* to the processor. A thread for the priority level of the interrupt is taken from the pool of interrupt threads for the processor and is context-switched in to handle the interrupt.

The term *pinned* refers to a mechanism employed by the kernel that avoids context switching out the interrupted thread. The executing thread is pinned under the interrupt thread. The interrupt thread "borrows" the LWP from the executing thread. While the interrupt handler is running, the interrupted thread is pinned to avoid the overhead of having to completely save its context; it cannot run on any processor until the interrupt handler completes or blocks on a synchronization object. Once the handler is complete, the original thread is unpinned and rescheduled.

If the interrupt handler thread blocks on a synchronization object (e.g., a mutex or condition variable) while handling the interrupt, it is converted into a complete kernel thread capable of being scheduled. Control is passed back to the interrupted thread, and the interrupt thread remains blocked on the synchronization object. When the synchronization object is unblocked, the thread becomes runnable and may preempt lower-priority threads to be rescheduled.

The processor interrupt level remains at the level of the interrupt, blocking lower-priority interrupts, even while the interrupt handler thread is blocked. This prevents lower-priority interrupt threads from interrupting the processing of higher-level interrupts. While interrupt threads are blocked, they are pinned to the processor they initiated on, guaranteeing that each processor will always have an interrupt thread available for incoming interrupts.

Level 10 clock interrupts are handled in a similar way, but since there is only one source of clock interrupt, there is a single, systemwide clock thread. Clock interrupts are discussed further in "The System Clock" on page 54.

2.3.1.2 Interrupt Thread Priorities

Interrupts that are scheduled as threads share global dispatcher priorities with other threads. See Chapter 9, "The Solaris Kernel Dispatcher" for a full description of the Solaris dispatcher. Interrupt threads use the top ten global dispatcher priorities, 160 to 169. Figure 2.6 shows the relationship of the interrupt dispatcher priorities with the real-time, system (kernel) threads and the timeshare and interactive class threads.

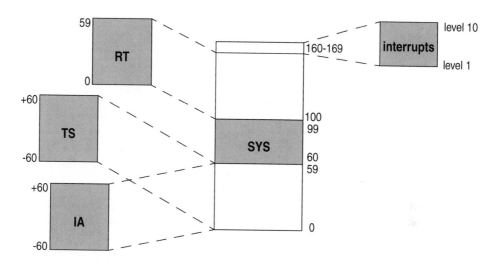

Figure 2.6 Interrupt Thread Global Priorities

2.3.1.3 High-Priority Interrupts

Interrupts above priority 10 block out all lower-priority interrupts until they complete. For this reason, high-priority interrupts need to have an extremely short code path to prevent them from affecting the latency of other interrupt handlers and the performance and scalability of the system. High-priority interrupt threads also cannot block; they can use only the spin variety of synchronization objects. This is due to the priority level the dispatcher uses for synchronization. The dispatcher runs at level 10, thus code running at higher interrupt levels cannot enter the dispatcher. High-priority threads typically service the minimal requirements of the hardware device (the source of the interrupt), then post down a lower-priority software interrupt to complete the required processing.

2.3.1.4 UltraSPARC Interrupts

On UltraSPARC systems (sun4u), the `intr_vector[]` array is a single, system-wide interrupt table for all hardware and software interrupts, as shown in Figure 2.7.

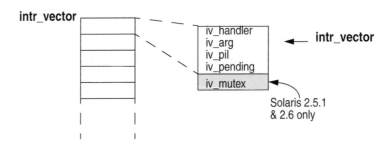

Figure 2.7 Interrupt Table on sun4u Architectures

Interrupts are added to the array through an `add_ivintr()` function. (Other platforms have a similar function for registering interrupts.) Each interrupt registered with the kernel has a unique interrupt number that locates the handler information in the interrupt table when the interrupt is delivered. The interrupt number is passed as an argument to `add_ivintr()`, along with a function pointer (the interrupt handler, `iv_handler`), an argument list for the handler (`iv_arg`), and the priority level of the interrupt (`iv_pil`).

Solaris 2.5.1 and Solaris 2.6 allow for unsafe device drivers—drivers that have not been made multiprocessor safe through the use of locking primitives. For unsafe drivers, a mutex lock locks the interrupt entry to prevent multiple threads from entering the driver's interrupt handler.

Solaris 7 requires that all drivers be minimally MP safe, dropping the requirement for a lock on the interrupt table entry. The `iv_pending` field is used as part of the queueing process; generated interrupts are placed on a per-processor list of interrupts waiting to be processed. The `pending` field is set until a processor prepares to field the interrupt, at which point the `pending` field is cleared.

A kernel `add_softintr()` function adds software-generated interrupts to the table. The process is the same for both functions: use the interrupt number passed as an argument as an index to the `intr_vector[]` array, and add the entry. The size of the array is large enough that running out of array slots is unlikely.

2.3.2 Interrupt Monitoring

You can use the `mpstat(1M)` and `vmstat(1M)` commands to monitor interrupt activity on a Solaris system. `mpstat(1M)` provides interrupts-per-second for each

CPU in the intr column, and interrupts handled on an interrupt thread (low-level interrupts) in the ithr column.

```
# mpstat 3
CPU minf mjf xcal  intr ithr  csw icsw migr smtx  srw syscl  usr sys  wt idl
  0    5   0    7    39   12  250   17    9   18    0   725    4   2   0  94
  1    4   0   10   278   83  275   40    9   40    0   941    4   2   0  93
```

2.3.3 Interprocessor Interrupts and Cross-Calls

The kernel can send an interrupt or trap to another processor when it requires another processor to do some immediate work on its behalf. Interprocessor interrupts are delivered through the poke_cpu() function; they are used for the following purposes:

- **Preempting the dispatcher** — A thread may need to signal a thread running on another processor to enter kernel mode when a preemption is required (initiated by a clock or timer event) or when a synchronization object is released. Chapter 9, "The Dispatcher," further discusses preemption.

- **Delivering a signal** — The delivery of a signal may require interrupting a thread on another processor.

- **Starting/stopping /proc threads** — The /proc infrastructure uses interprocessor interrupts to start and stop threads on different processors.

Using a similar mechanism, the kernel can also instruct a processor to execute a specific low-level function by issuing a processor-to-processor *cross-call*. Cross-calls are typically part of the processor-dependent implementation. UltraSPARC kernels use cross-calls for two purposes:

- **Implementing interprocessor interrupts** — As discussed above.

- **Maintaining virtual memory translation consistency** — Implementing cache consistency on SMP platforms requires the translation entries to be removed from the MMU of each CPU that a thread has run on when a virtual address is unmapped. On UltraSPARC, user processes issuing an unmap operation make a cross-call to each CPU on which the thread has run, to remove the TLB entries from each processor's MMU. Address space unmap operations within the kernel address space make a cross-call to *all* processors for each unmap operation.

Both cross-calls and interprocessor interrupts are reported by mpstat(1M) in the xcal column as cross-calls per second.

```
# mpstat 3
CPU minf mjf xcal intr ithr  csw icsw migr smtx  srw syscl  usr sys  wt idl
  0    0   0    6  607  246 1100  174   82   84    0  2907   28   5   0  66
  1    0   0    2  218    0 1037  212   83   80    0  3438   33   4   0  62
```

High numbers of reported cross-calls can result from either of the activities mentioned in the preceding section—most commonly, from kernel address space unmap activity caused by file system activity.

2.4   System Calls

Recall from "Access to Kernel Services" on page 27, system calls are interfaces callable by user programs in order to have the kernel perform a specific function (e.g., opening a file) on behalf of the calling thread. System calls are part of the application programming interfaces (APIs) that ship with the operating system; they are documented in Section 2 of the manual pages. The invocation of a system call causes the processor to change from user mode to kernel mode. This change is accomplished on SPARC systems by means of the trap mechanism previously discussed.

2.4.1   Regular System Calls

System calls are referenced in the system through the kernel sysent table, which contains an entry for every system call supported on the system. The sysent table is an array populated with sysent structures, each structure representing one system call, as illustrated in Figure 2.8.

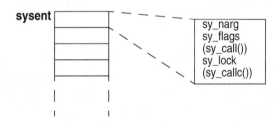

Figure 2.8 The Kernel System Call Entry (sysent) Table

The array is indexed by the system call number, which is established in the /etc/name_to_sysnum file. Using an editable system file provides for adding system calls to Solaris without requiring kernel source and a complete kernel build. Many system calls are implemented as dynamically loadable modules that are loaded into the system when the system call is invoked for the first time. Loadable system calls are stored in the /kernel/sys and /usr/kernel/sys directories.

The system call entry in the table provides the number of arguments the system call takes (sy_narg), a flag field (sy_flag), and a reader/writer lock

(sy_lock) for loadable system calls. The system call itself is referenced through a
function pointer: sy_call or sy_callc.

Historical Aside: The fact that there are two entries for the system call functions is the result of a rewriting of the system call argument-passing implementation, an effort that first appeared in Solaris 2.4. Earlier Solaris versions
passed system call arguments in the traditional UNIX way: bundling the arguments into a structure and passing the structure pointer (*uap* is the historical
name in UNIX implementations and texts; it refers to a *user argument pointer*).
Most of the system calls in Solaris have been rewritten to use the C language
argument-passing convention implemented for function calls. Using that convention provided better overall system call performance because the code can
take advantage of the argument-passing features inherent in the register window implementation of SPARC processors (using the *in* registers for argument
passing—refer to [31] for a description of SPARC register windows).

---

sy_call represents an entry for system calls and uses the older uap pointer convention, maintained here for binary compatibility with older versions of Solaris.
sy_callc is the function pointer for the more recent argument-passing implementation. The newer C style argument passing has shown significant overall performance improvements in system call execution—on the order of 30 percent in some
cases.

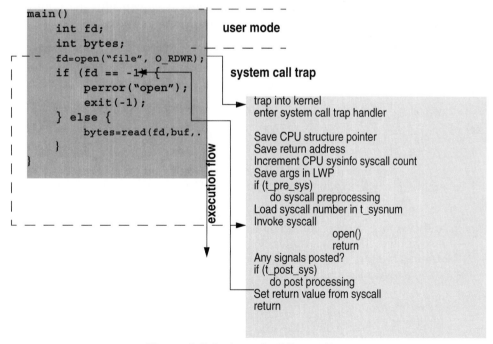

Figure 2.9 System Call Execution

The execution of a system call results in the software issuing a trap instruction, which is how the kernel is entered to process the system call. The trap handler for the system call is entered, any necessary preprocessing is done, and the system call is executed on behalf of the calling thread. The flow is illustrated in Figure 2.9.

When the trap handler is entered, the trap code saves a pointer to the CPU structure of the CPU on which the system call will execute, saves the return address, and increments a system call counter maintained on a per-CPU basis. The number of system calls per second is reported by mpstat(1M) (*syscl* column) for per-CPU data; systemwide, the number is reported by vmstat(1M) (*sy* column).

Two flags in the kernel thread structure indicate that pre-system call or post-system call processing is required. The t_pre_sys flag (preprocessing) is set for things like truss(1) command support (system call execution is being traced) or microstate accounting being enabled. Post-system-call work (t_post_sys) may be the result of /proc process tracing, profiling enabled for the process, a pending signal, or an exigent preemption. In the interim between pre- and postprocessing, the system call itself is executed.

2.4.2 Fast Trap System Calls

The overhead of the system call framework is nontrivial; that is, there is some inherent latency with all system calls because of the system call setup process we just discussed. In some cases, we want to be able to have fast, low-latency access to information, such as high-resolution time, that can only be obtained in kernel mode. The Solaris kernel provides a fast system call framework so that user processes can jump into protected kernel mode to do minimal processing and then return, without the overhead of the full system call framework. This framework can only be used when the processing required in the kernel does not significantly interfere with registers and stacks. Hence, the fast system call does not need to save all the state that a regular system call does before it executes the required functions.

Only a few fast system calls are implemented in Solaris versions up to Solaris 7: gethrtime(), gethrvtime(), and gettimeofday(). These functions return time of day and processor CPU time. They simply trap into the kernel to read a single hardware register or memory location and then return to user mode.

Table 2-3 compares the average latency for the getpid()/time() system calls and two fast system calls. For reference, the latency of a standard function call is also shown. Times were measured on a 300 MHz Ultra2. Note that the latency of the fast system calls is about five times lower than that of an equivalent regular system call.

Table 2-3 System Call Latency

System Call	Latency (ns)
getpid()	2138
time()	2134
gethrtime()	320
gethrvtime()	413
Standard C function call	93

2.5 The Kernel Callout Table

The Solaris kernel provides a callout facility for general-purpose, time-based event scheduling. A system callout table is initialized at boot time, and kernel routines can place functions on the callout table through the timeout(9F) interface. A callout table entry includes a function pointer, optional argument, and clock-tick value. With each clock interrupt, the tick value is tested and the function is executed when the time interval expires. The kernel interface, timeout(9F), is part of the device driver interface (DDI) specification and is commonly used by device drivers. Other kernel facilities, such as the page fsflush daemon, which sleeps at regular intervals, make use of callouts as well.

2.5.1 Solaris 2.6 and 7 Callout Tables

The kernel callout table in Solaris 2.6 and Solaris 7 is laid out as shown in Figure 2.10.

At boot time, the callout_table array is initialized with pointers to callout_table structures; the structures are also created at boot time. There are 16 callout tables—8 for each of the two callout types, *normal* and *real-time*. Normal callouts are those callout entries created with a timeout(9F) call. The kernel also supports real-time callouts, created with the internal realtime_timeout() function. Real-time callouts are handled more expediently than are normal callouts through a soft interrupt mechanism, whereas normal callouts are subject to scheduling latency. Once the callout mechanism has executed the function placed on the callout queue, the callout entry is removed.

Each callout entry has a unique callout ID, c_xid, the extended callout ID. The callout ID contains the table ID, indicating which callout table the callout belongs to, a bit indicating whether this is a short-term or long-term callout, and a running counter.

The callout ID name space is partitioned into two pieces for short-term and long-term callouts. (A long-term callout is defined as a callout with a tick counter greater than 16,384, a value derived through testing and monitoring of real pro-

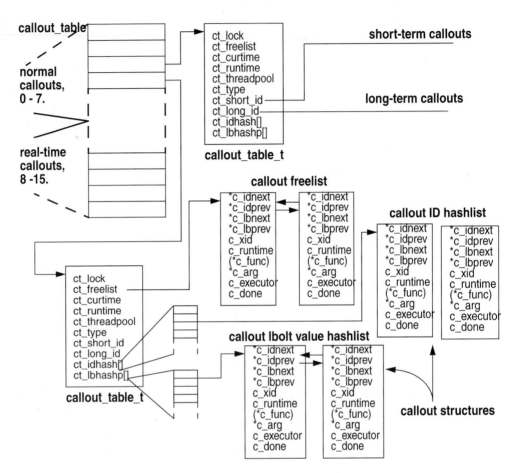

Figure 2.10 Solaris 2.6 and Solaris 7 Callout Tables

duction systems.) This partitioning prevents collisions on the callout ID, which can result from the high volume of timeout(9f) calls typically generated by a running system. It's possible to run out of unique callout IDs, so IDs can be recycled. For short-term callouts, ID recycling is not a problem; a particular callout will likely have been removed from the callout table before its ID gets reused. A long-term callout could collide with a new callout entry reusing its ID.

High-volume, short-term callout traffic is handled on a callout table with short-term callouts, and the relatively few long-term callouts are maintained on their own callout table. The callout table maintains a ct_short_id and ct_long_id, to determine if a callout table is supporting long-term or short-term callout entries.

The short and long IDs are set to an initial value at boot time in each callout table structure, with short IDs ranging from 0x10000000 to 0x1000000f and long IDs ranging from 0x30000000 to 0x3000000f. The other callout table structure fields set at boot time are the `ct_type` field (eight each of normal or real-time) and the `ct_runtime` and `ct_curtime`, both set to the current `lbolt` value when the initialization occurs.

The callout entries, each represented by a callout structure, are linked to a callout table through the `ct_idhash[]` and `ct_lbhash[]` arrays, where each array element is either null or a pointer to a callout structure. The callout entries are stored on each array; one hash is on the callout ID, the other hashes on the `lbolt` value. At initialization, the kernel also creates two callout threads with each callout table. The callout threads are signalled through a condition variable when the `callout_schedule()` function executes (called from the clock handler) if there are functions with expired timers that need to execute.

As we alluded to, the insertion and removal of callout table entries by the `timeout(9F)` function is a regular and frequent occurrence on a running Solaris system. The algorithm for placing an entry on the callout queue goes as follows (the `timeout(9F)` flow):

- `timeout(function_pointer, argument_pointer, time value (delta))` enters `timeout_common()`, with all the arguments passed to `timeout(9F)`, along with an index into the `callout_table` array. The index derivation is based on the CPU `cpu_seqid` (sequential ID) field and on the callout type, where normal callouts are placed on tables indexed between array locations 8 through 15 (real-time callouts, 0 through 7).

  Basically, the algorithm causes callout entries to cycle through indexes 8 through 15 as CPU IDs increment; the same CPU will reference the same index location every time.

- `timeout_common()` grabs a callout structure from the `ct_freelist` if one is available, or the kernel memory allocator allocates a new one.

- The `c_func` and `c_arg` fields are set in the callout structure, and the `c_runtime` field is set to the sum of the current `lbolt` value and the passed timer value.

- `timeout_common()` establishes the ID in the callout table structure, setting either the `ct_short_id` or `ct_long_id` (if the timer is larger than 16,384, it's a long ID).

  We saw earlier that the ID fields are initialized at boot time. As callout entries are added, the algorithm essentially counts up until it wraps around and starts over again. This process leads to the reuse problem we just discussed, which is why we have short-term and long-term IDs.

- The `c_xid` in the callout structure is set to the same ID value as the callout table ID.

- The algorithm inserts a callout entry (callout structure) into the callout table by adding the entry to both the `ct_idhash[]` and `ct_lbhash[]` arrays in the callout table. It derives the array index by hashing on the ID for `ct_idhash[]` placement and hashing on the `c_runtime` value set in the callout structure for the entry for `ct_lbhash[]`. If the array index already has a pointer, the algorithm links the callout structure by means of the `next` and `prev` pointers.

The callout entry is now established on the callout table, and `timeout(9F)` returns the ID to the calling function. The sequence of events for `realtime_timeout()` is the same.

The work done when `callout_schedule()` is called from the clock interrupt handler essentially happens through multiple loops. The outer loop hits all the callout *tables*, and the inner loop hits the callout *entries* in the table.

- A local function variable set to the current `lbolt` value is used for entry to the inner loop, and the callout entries' `c_runtime` values determine whether the callouts are due for execution.

- If the callout is not due or is already running, the code moves on to the next entry. Otherwise, it's time for the function in the callout entry to run.

- For normal callout types, a condition variable signal function is set to wake up one of the callout threads to execute the function. For real-time callouts, the kernel `softcall()` function is invoked to generate a soft interrupt, which will interrupt a processor, resulting in the function executing without going through the dispatcher.

- Once the callout table is processed in the inner loop, the outer loop moves the code on to the next callout table. A mutex lock (`ct_lock`) is acquired in the inner loop to prevent another processor from processing the same callout table at the same time. The mutex is released when the inner loop through the callout table is completed.

- The callout threads created at initialization (two per callout table) then loop, waiting for the `ct_threadpool` condition variable. They're signaled through the condition variable when a normal callout entry is due to execute (as above), at which point they call the `callout_execute()` function. `callout_execute()` is also invoked through the `softcall()` interrupt function to run a function placed on a callout table by `realtime_timeout()`.

  To reiterate, a normal callout can be exposed to some additional latency for the callout threads to be scheduled once they are signaled by the condition variable. The `softcall()` method will force a processor into the `callout_execute()` function sooner through the interrupt facility.

- `callout_execute()` will loop again through the callout table, testing the conditions for function execution. It's possible that another processor took care of things in the interim between function calls and lock releases, so the kernel tests the time values and running flag for the entries in the table before actually executing the function.

- Assuming that it is time to run, `callout_execute()` sets the `CALLOUT_EXECUTING` flag in the callout entry's `c_xid` field, and the function is invoked.

- The callout entry is then removed from the callout table, the callout structure is placed on the freelist (`ct_freelist`), and a condition variable is broadcasted if any threads are sleeping on the `c_done` condition variable. This condition variable is part of the callout entry and provides a method of generating a notification that a function placed on the callout table has executed.

The kernel also provides an `untimeout(9F)` interface, which will remove a callout. `untimeout(9F)` is passed the ID (which was returned from `timeout(9F)` when the function was placed on the callout table). The entry is located by means of the `ct_idhash[]` array and removed, with the callout structure being added to the freelist. Callout entries added by `realtime_timeout(9F)` can also be removed with `untimeout(9F)`. There is no separate function for the removal of real-time callouts.

2.5.2 Solaris 2.5.1 Callout Tables

Callout tables in Solaris 2.5.1 are functionally identical to those we described for Solaris 2.6 and Solaris 7; the implementation is different. Solaris 2.5.1 maintains two callout tables—one for normal callouts and one for real-time callouts—which are initialized at boot time. The overall structure of callout tables in Solaris 2.5.1 is illustrated in Figure 2.11.

As you can see, many of the structure fields are identical in name (and function) to those described previously. The link to each callout table is made with a `callout_state` pointer (normal callout table) and an `rt_callout_state` pointer (real-time callout table, not shown in the figure, but identical). The tables implement an array of 256 buckets; each bucket links to a callout structure and maintains the ID for the entry.

The initialization process happens at boot time, with two distinct setup phases: one for the normal callout table and one for the real-time callout table. The `cs_bucket[]` array of the `callout_state` structure (the callout table, really) is implemented as a circular, singly linked list. At initialization, the `b_first` pointer is set to point back to itself, and as callouts are added to the bucket, the last callout's `c_next` will reference the first entry on the bucket. The ID fields represent a long and a short ID name space, as in the Solaris 2.6 and 7 implementations. These fields are set to initial values in each bucket head during the init phase.

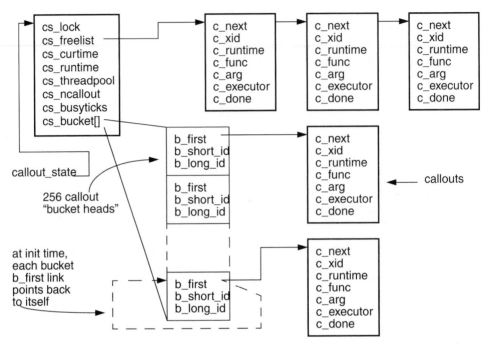

Figure 2.11 Solaris 2.5.1 Callout Tables

The c_xid (extended ID) field in each callout entry has multiple roles: It identifies the callout entry, the callout table (normal or real-time), the bucket ID, and a flag indicating a long-term callout if that is the case.

The process of placing a function on the callout list by timeout(9F) or realtime_timeout() is effectively the same as that described for Solaris 2.6 and Solaris 7. The primary difference is in identifying which bucket, among the 256 possibilities, the callout entry goes in. The bucket selection is relatively random, where the low-order bits of the sum of the current lbolt value and the tick count passed with the timeout(9F) call determine the bucket array index. The sum of lbolt and the tick count is set in the callout entry's c_runtime field, used later to determine when it's time to execute the callout. The callout ID maintained in the bucket (short or long ID) is set, based on the same criteria used in Solaris 2.6 and Solaris 7—a callout tick count greater than 16,384 (16K) is a long-term callout, which of course results in b_long_id getting set. Otherwise, b_short_id is used.

The remaining functions are algorithmically the same in Solaris 2.5.1 as they are in Solaris 2.6 and Solaris 7. One salient difference is that the clock interrupt handler in Solaris 2.5.1 makes two explicit calls to callout_schedule(): the first for real-time callouts, the second for normal callouts. That aside, normal callouts are processed through callout threads, signaled by a condition variable sent from the callout schedule loop; real-time callouts are handled through the interrupt facility by the `softint()` interface.

You can examine the callout table on a running system (all releases) with the callout function in the `crash(1M)` utility.

```
# /etc/crash
dumpfile = /dev/mem, namelist = /dev/ksyms, outfile = stdout
> callout
FUNCTION               ARGUMENT              TIME                 ID
polltime               00000300008df260      00000000006a4971     7fffffffffff761f0
realitexpire           000003000090ed80      00000000006adf39     7fffffffffff79890
setrun                 000002a10034fd60      000000000069bd97     3fffffffff925a31
schedpaging            0000000000000000      000000000069bd0f     3fffffffffb7c618
mi_timer_fire          0000030000a36820      000000000069bd20     3fffffffffb7c628
sigalarm2proc          0000030000974ac0      000000000069be19     3fffffffffb7c648
ts_update              0000000000000000      000000000069bd4c     3fffffffffb7c658
seg_pupdate            0000000000000000      000000000069c139     3fffffffffb7cb88
kmem_update            0000000000000000      000000000069c139     3fffffffffcb3069
.
.
```

Note that the example output from the callout function in `crash(1M)` is not a complete listing. Note, too, that the output is from a 64-bit Solaris 7 system, which is why the ARGUMENT, TIME, and ID columns are 8-byte (64-bit) data types. On a 32-bit kernel, they are 32-bit data types.

Some of the kernel functions that you will consistently find on the callout table of a running Solaris system include the following:

- **polltime** — A real-time callout. Set from the `poll(2)` system call and based on the poll interval. `polltime()` wakes up a thread waiting on a poll event.

- **realitexpire** — A real-time callout. Used in the real-time interval timer support when a timer is set. Callout ticks are derived from timer value. `realitexpire()` generates the `SIGALRM` to the process.

- **setrun** — A real-time callout. Placed on the callout queue by sleep/wakeup code (condition variables) to force a thread wakeup when the sleep event has a timeout value; for example, an `aiowait(2)` call can specify a maximum tick count to wait for the I/O to complete. `aiowait(2)` with a timeout specificity uses a timed condition variable, which in turn places a `setrun()` event on the callout queue to force a thread wakeup if the time expires before the I/O has completed.

- **schedpaging** — A normal callout. Part of the pageout subsystem in the VM system, used to manage the pageout rate.

- **mi_timer_fire** — A normal callout. Part of the STREAMS-based TCP/IP protocol support. `mi_timer_fire()` generates regular message block processing through a STREAMS queue.

- **sigalarm2proc** — A normal callout. The alarm(2) system call places sigalarm2proc on the callout queue to generate a SIGALRM when the timer expires.

- **ts_update** — A normal callout. Checks a list of timeshare and interactive class threads and updates their priority as needed.

- **seg_pupdate** — A normal callout. Used by the address space segment reclaim thread to find pagelocked pages that have not been used in a while and reclaim them.

- **kmem_update** — A normal callout. Performs low-level kernel memory allocator management.

This is by no means a complete list of all the kernel functions placed on the callout queue, and of course you will typically see several of the same functions on the callout queue at the same time, with different IDs and timeout values.

2.6   The System Clock

The Solaris kernel relies on hardware timer interrupts for general housekeeping chores that need to be done at regular intervals. For example, the system clock triggers the dispatcher to recalculate process priorities at regular intervals and also initiates callout queue processing.

The kernel (software) sets up the programmable interrupt generator (hardware) to generate a clock interrupt at regular intervals, by default 100 times per second. The clock interrupts at interrupt level 10 (SPARC); nothing else on the system generates interrupts at this level. With each clock interrupt, a handler is entered. It performs the following functions:

- Sets available kernel anon space (anon_free) value, for tracking and reporting.

- Sets free memory (freemem) value, for tracking and reporting.

- Adjusts the time of day clock for possible jitter.

- Calculates CPU usage (user, system, idle, and wait I/O) and system dispatch (run queue) queue size.

- Does clock-tick processing for the thread running on the CPU (except the CPU running the clock interrupt thread) and threads that are exiting. Note that kernel threads that do not have an associated LWP—kernel service threads that are an integral part of the operating system—are not subject to tick processing.

- Updates the `lbolt` counter. `lbolt` counts the number of clock ticks since boot.

- Processes the kernel callout table (described in the next section).

- If on a one-second interval, calculates kernel swap parameters (free, reserved, and allocated swap) and adjusts systemwide run queue size and swap queue size.

Once the clock interrupt handling is completed, the clock interrupt thread is context-switched off the processor, and the thread that was executing when the interrupt occurred resumes.

2.6.1 Process Execution Time Statistics

The CPU usage work and thread tick processing is done on a per-CPU basis; the code loops through the list of online processors and does the work for each CPU. Usage information is maintained in the `cpu[]` array in each CPU's `sysinfo` structure. The four-member `cpu[]` array stores an integer value, one for each of USER, SYSTEM, IDLE, and WAIT—the four possible states that the CPU will be in. A CPU in the QUIESCED state is charged with idle time. A CPU running an interrupt thread is charged with system time. A CPU running its idle thread is charged with idle time unless the `cpu_syswait.iowait` value is set; in that case, the CPU is charged wait I/O time.

`cpu_syswait.iowait` is set in the `biowait()` routine, which is called from the file system support code when a buffered I/O is issued (see Part Four, Files and File Systems, for specifics on buffered I/O). `biowait()` is also called from the disk drivers in the kernel; thus, wait I/O time reflects I/O through the file system as well as raw disk I/O; wait I/O reflects disk I/O only, and network I/O is not reflected. The algorithm for calculating wait I/O was flawed in releases prior to Solaris 7, and CPUs that were idle may be charged incorrectly with wait I/O time. Finally, if a thread that is not the idle thread or an interrupt thread is running on a CPU, the state of the thread is checked to determine if the CPU should be charged with user time (the thread is executing in user mode) or system time.

The last bullet item in the previous section indicates that some of the clock interrupt processing is not done in every clock interrupt (100 times a second), but rather at one-second intervals. For the services indicated, one-second granularity is sufficient.

Tick processing is done for each kernel thread (if that thread is not an interrupt handler or an operating system kernel thread) running on a CPU. Each kernel thread maintains a `t_pctcpu` (percent of CPU time) and `t_lbolt` value, where `t_pctcpu` is used for per-thread usage information (e.g., accounting) and `t_lbolt` provides a point of reference for tick processing. The kernel determines whether it is necessary to do tick processing for the thread by comparing t_lbolt against lbolt.

```
if (lbolt - t_lbolt) = 0
        no need to do tick processing
else

        set t_pctcpu
        t_lbolt = lbolt
        call clock_tick(current thread)
```

The clock_tick() code is passed the kernel thread ID and invokes the scheduling-class-specific clock-tick function, that is, ts_tick() for timeshare and interactive class threads and rt_tick() for real-time class threads. These functions are discussed in Chapter 4, "Kernel Bootstrap and Initialization." Briefly, the functions determine if the thread has used up its time quantum, and they take the thread off the processor if it has. Back in the clock_tick() function, the following actions are performed:

- The user or system time values in the process and the LWP are incremented, based on the mode the thread is in (system or user). Note that if a thread is executing in short bursts between clock samples, not all CPU time will be accounted for.

- The per-thread interval timers are tested (profiling and virtual timer, enabled with the setitimer(2) system call), and the appropriate signal—SIGPROF or SIGVTALRM—is sent if either timer has expired.

- The per-process CPU resource limit is checked (maximum CPU seconds the process can consume), and if that threshold has been reached, a SIGXCPU is sent.

- The process memory usage is updated in the uarea u_mem, which reflects the total address space size of the process.

The update completes the clock-tick processing for the thread.

2.6.2 High-Resolution Clock Interrupts

By default, a system clock interval of 10 milliseconds (100 interrupts per second) is used. You can set a kernel parameter, hires_tick, in the /etc/system file to increase the clock interrupt frequency to 1000 interrupts per second (set hires_tick = 1 in /etc/system). Increasing the clock frequency results in the system entering the dispatcher (among other things) more frequently. Exercise great care if you are considering setting high-resolution ticks—they can reduce system performance dramatically. As with any system tunable, this setting should never, ever be made on a production system without extensive testing first.

2.6.3 High-Resolution Timer

The kernel also maintains a high-resolution timer for nanosecond-level timing functions. On UltraSPARC-based systems, the hardware TICK register is used; it is incremented with every processor clock tick, that is, every 2.5 nanoseconds on a 400 MHz processor. An internal gethrestime() (get high-resolution time) function is used in a few areas of the kernel where fine-grained time is needed, such as the support for real-time interval timers (the setitimer(2) system call with the ITIMER_REAL flag). A gethrtime(3C) interface provides programs with nanosecond-level granularity for timing. The gethrtime(3C) function has an optimized code path to read the TICK register and return a normalized (converted to nanoseconds) value to the calling program.

2.6.4 Time-of-Day Clock

All computer systems—from desktop PCs to high-end multiprocessor systems—have a clock circuit of some sort. SPARC-based systems include clock circuitry in the EEPROM area of the hardware (e.g., the Mostek 48T59 clock chip is used on UltraSPARC-based systems). This Time-of-Day (TOD) clock chip is addressable by the kernel as part of the firmware address space and has a hardware register specification; a kernel interface to the TOD hardware is implemented as a TOD device driver.

The chip itself implements several registers, readable and writable by the kernel through the device driver, that provide multiple counters for the numeric components that make up the date and time (e.g., minute-of-the-hour, hour-of-the-day, day-of-the-week, month-of-the-year, etc.).

Figure 2.12 illustrates the hardware and software hierarchy for the TOD.

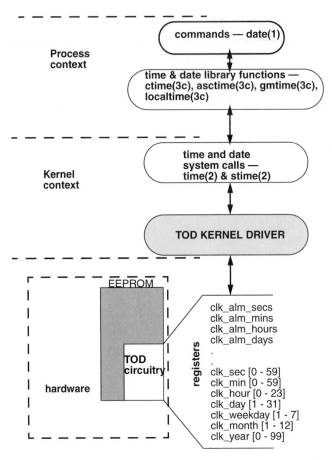

Figure 2.12 Time-of-Day Clock on SPARC Systems

Each component of a day and time value is stored as a separate counter value in the clock chip, and each counter increments the next logical value when it reaches its top value; for example, seconds count values 0–59, then increment minutes and restart at 0. Executing the date(1) command to set the date calls the stime(2) system call, which in turn calls the tod_set() device driver interface that sets the values in the TOD clock hardware.

To comply with industry-standard interfaces (system calls and library routines), the kernel provides functions for converting the date values read from the clock hardware to the UNIX convention of the number of seconds since the epoch, and vice versa.

3

KERNEL
SYNCHRONIZATION
PRIMITIVES

In this chapter, we continue our discussion of core kernel facilities, with an examination of the synchronization objects implemented in the Solaris kernel.

3.1 Synchronization

Solaris runs on a variety of different hardware platforms, including multiprocessor systems based on both the SPARC and Intel processors. Several multiprocessor architectures in existence today offer various trade-offs in performance and engineering complexity in both hardware and software. The current multiprocessor architecture that Solaris supports is the symmetric multiprocessor (SMP) and shared memory architecture, which implements a single kernel shared by all the processors and a single, uniform memory address space. To support such an architecture, the kernel must synchronize access to critical data to maintain data integrity, coherency, and state. The kernel synchronizes access by defining a lock for a particular kernel data structure or variable and requiring that code reading or writing the data must first acquire the appropriate lock. The holder of the lock is required to release the lock once the data operation has been completed.

The synchronization primitives and associated interfaces are used by virtually all kernel subsystems: device drivers, the dispatcher, process and thread support code, file systems, etc. Insight into what the synchronization objects are and how they are implemented is key to understanding one of the core strengths of the Solaris kernel—scalable performance on multiprocessor systems. An equally important component to the scalability equation is the avoidance of locks altogether whenever possible. The use of synchronization locks in the kernel is constantly being scrutinized as part of the development process in kernel engineering, with an eye to minimizing the number of locks required without compromising data integrity.

Several alternative methods of building parallel multiprocessor systems have emerged in the industry over the years. So, in the interest of conveying the issues surrounding the implementation, we need to put things in context. First, we take a brief look at the different parallel systems architectures that are commercially available today, and then we turn to the specifics of support for multiprocessor architectures by the Solaris kernel.

3.2   Parallel Systems Architectures

Multiprocessor (MP) systems from Sun (SPARC-processor-based), as well as several Intel-based MP platforms, are implemented as symmetric multiprocessor (SMP) systems. Symmetric multiprocessor describes a system in which a peer-to-peer relationship exists among all the processors (CPUs) on the system. A master processor, defined as the only CPU on the system that can execute operating system code and field interrupts, does *not* exist. All processors are equal. The SMP acronym can also be extended to mean Shared Memory Multiprocessor, which defines an architecture in which all the processors in the system share a uniform view of the system's physical address space and the operating system's virtual address space. That is, all processors share a single image of the operating system kernel. Sun's multiprocessor systems meet the criteria for both definitions.

Alternative MP architectures alter the kernel's view of addressable memory in different ways. Massively parallel processor (MPP) systems are built on nodes that contain a relatively small number of processors, some local memory, and I/O. Each node contains its own copy of the operating system; thus, each node addresses its own physical and virtual address space. The address space of one node is not visible to the other nodes on the system. The nodes are connected by a high-speed, low-latency interconnect, and node-to-node communication is done through an optimized message passing interface. MPP architectures require a new programming model to achieve parallelism across nodes.

The shared memory model does not work since the system's total address space is not visible across nodes, so memory pages cannot be shared by threads running on different nodes. Thus, an API that provides an interface into the message-passing path in the kernel must be used by code that needs to scale across the various nodes in the system.

Other issues arise from the nonuniform nature of the architecture with respect to I/O processing, since the I/O controllers on each node are not easily made visible to all the nodes on the system. Some MPP platforms attempt to provide the illusion of a uniform I/O space across all the nodes by using kernel software, but the nonuniformity of the access times to nonlocal I/O devices still exists.

NUMA and ccNUMA (nonuniform memory access and cache coherent NUMA) architectures attempt to address the programming model issue inherent in MPP systems. From a hardware architecture point of view, NUMA systems resemble MPPs—small nodes with few processors, a node-to-node interconnect, local memory, and I/O on each node. Note it is not required that NUMA/ccNUMA or MPP systems implement small nodes (nodes with four or fewer processors). Many implementations are built that way, but there is no architectural restriction on the node size.

On NUMA/ccNUMA systems, the operating system software provides a single system image, where each node has a view of the entire system's memory address space. In this way, the shared memory model is preserved. However, the nonuniform nature of speed of memory access (latency) is a factor in the performance and potential scalability of the platform. When a thread executing on a processor node on a NUMA or ccNUMA system incurs a page fault (references an unmapped memory address), the latency involved in resolving the page fault varies according to whether the physical memory page is on the same node of the executing thread or on a node somewhere across the interconnect. The latency variance can be substantial. As the level of memory page sharing increases across threads executing on different nodes, a potentially higher volume of page faults needs to be resolved from a nonlocal memory segment. This problem adversely affects performance and scalability.

The three different parallel architectures can be summarized as follows.

- **SMP** — Symmetric multiprocessor with a shared memory model; single kernel image.

- **MPP** — Message-based model; multiple kernel images.

- **NUMA/ccNUMA** — Shared memory model; single kernel image.

Figure 3.1 illustrates the different architectures.

The challenge in building an operating system that provides scalable performance when multiple processors are sharing a single image of the kernel and when every processor can run kernel code, handle interrupts, etc., is to synchronize access to critical data and state information. Scalable performance, or scalability, generally refers to accomplishing an increasing amount of work as more hardware resources are added to the system. If more processors are added to a multiprocessor system, an incremental increase in work is expected, assuming sufficient resources in other areas of the system (memory, I/O, network).

To achieve scalable performance, the system must be able to support multiple processors executing operating system code concurrently. Whether that execution is in device drivers, interrupt handlers, the threads dispatcher, file system code, virtual memory code, etc., is, to a degree, load dependent. Concurrency is key to scalability.

The preceding discussion on parallel architectures only scratched the surface of a very complex topic. Entire texts discuss parallel architectures exclusively; you should refer to them for additional information. See, for example, [11], [21] and [23].

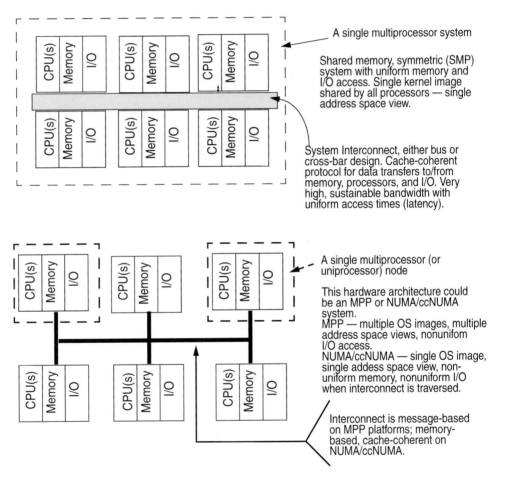

Figure 3.1 Parallel Systems Architectures

The difficulty is maintaining data integrity of data structures, kernel variables, data links (pointers), and state information in the kernel. We cannot, for example, allow threads running on multiple processors to manipulate pointers to the same data structure on the same linked list all at the same time. We should prevent one processor from reading a bit of critical state information (e.g., is a processor online?) while a thread executing on another processor is changing the same state data (e.g., in the process of bringing online a processor that is still in a state transition).

To solve the problem of data integrity on such systems, the kernel implements locking mechanisms. It requires that all operating system code be aware of the number and type of locks that exist in the kernel and comply with the locking hierarchy and rules for acquiring locks before writing or reading kernel data. It is worth noting that the architectural issues of building a scalable kernel are not very different from those of developing a multithreaded application to run on a shared memory system. Multithreaded applications must also synchronize access to shared data, using the same basic locking primitives and techniques that are used in the kernel. Other synchronization problems, such as dealing with interrupts and trap events, exist in kernel code and make the problem significantly more complex for operating systems development, but the fundamental problems are the same.

3.3 Hardware Considerations for Locks and Synchronization

Hardware-specific considerations must enter into the implementation of lock primitives on a system. The first consideration has to do with the processor's instruction set and the availability of machine instructions suitable for locking code. The second deals with the visibility of a lock's state when it is examined by executing kernel threads.

To understand how these considerations apply to lock primitives, keep in mind that a lock is a piece of data at a specific location in the system's memory. In its simplest form, a lock is a single byte location in RAM. A lock that is *set*, or *held* (has been acquired), is represented by all the bits in the lock byte being 1's (lock value 0xFF). A lock that is available (not being held) is the same byte with all 0's (lock value 0x00). This explanation may seem quite rudimentary, but is crucial to understanding the text that follows.

Most modern processors shipping today provide some form of byte-level *test-and-set* instruction that is guaranteed to be *atomic* in nature. The instruction sequence is often described as read-modify-write; that is, the referenced memory location (the memory address of the lock) is read, modified, and written back in one atomic operation. In RISC processors (such as Sun SPARC), reads are *load* operations and writes are *store* operations. An atomic operation is required for consistency. An instruction that has atomic properties means that no other store operation is allowed between the load and store of the executing instruction. Mutex and RW lock operations must be atomic, such that when the instruction execution to get the lock is complete, we either have the lock or have the information we need to determine that the lock is already being held. Consider what could happen without an instruction that has atomic properties. A thread executing on one processor could issue a load (read) of the lock, and while it is doing a test operation to determine if the lock is held or not, another thread executing on another processor issues a lock call to get the same lock at the same time. If the lock is not held, both threads would assume the lock is available and would issue a store to hold the lock. Obviously, more than one thread cannot own the same lock at the same time, but that would be the result of such a sequence of events. Atomic instructions prevent such things from happening.

SPARC processors implement memory access instructions that provide atomic test-and-set semantics for mutual exclusion primitives, as well as instructions that can force a particular ordering of memory operations (more on the latter feature in a moment). UltraSPARC processors (the SPARC V9 instruction set) provide three memory access instructions that guarantee atomic behavior: ldstub (load and store unsigned byte), cas (compare and swap), and swap (swap byte locations). These instructions differ slightly in their behavior and the size of the datum they operate on.

Figure 3.2 illustrates the ldstub and cas instructions. The swap instruction (not shown) simply swaps a 32-bit value between a hardware register and a memory location, similar to what cas does if the compare phase of the instruction sequence is equal.

The implementation of locking code with the assembly language test-and-set style of instructions requires a subsequent test instruction on the lock value, which is retrieved with either a cas or ldstub instruction.

For example, the ldstub instruction retrieves the byte value (the lock) from memory and stores it in the specified hardware register. Locking code must test the value of the register to determine if the lock was held or available when the ldstub executed. If the register value is all 1's, the lock was held, so the code must branch off and deal with that condition. If the register value is all 0's, the lock was not held and the code can progress as being the current lock holder. Note that in both cases, the lock value in memory is set to all 1's, by virtue of the behavior of the ldstub instruction (store 0xFF at designated address). If the lock was already held, the value simply didn't change. If the lock was 0 (available), it will now reflect that the lock is held (all 1's). The code that releases a lock sets the lock value to all 0's, indicating the lock is no longer being held.

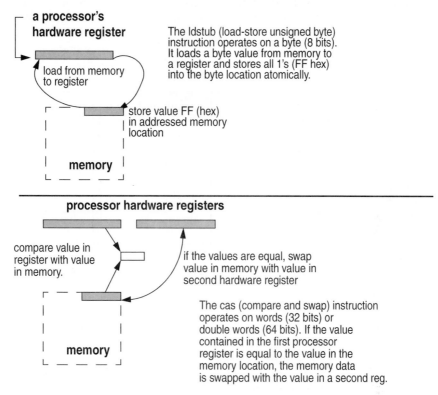

a processor's hardware register

load from memory to register

The ldstub (load-store unsigned byte) instruction operates on a byte (8 bits). It loads a byte value from memory to a register and stores all 1's (FF hex) into the byte location atomically.

store value FF (hex) in addressed memory location

memory

processor hardware registers

compare value in register with value in memory.

if the values are equal, swap value in memory with value in second hardware register

The cas (compare and swap) instruction operates on words (32 bits) or double words (64 bits). If the value contained in the first processor register is equal to the value in the memory location, the memory data is swapped with the value in a second reg.

memory

Figure 3.2 Atomic Instructions for Locks on SPARC

The Solaris lock code uses assembly language instructions when the lock code is entered. The basic design is such that the entry point to acquire a lock enters an assembly language routine, which uses either ldstub or cas to grab the lock. The assembly code is designed to deal with the simple case, meaning that the desired lock is available. If the lock is being held, a C language code path is entered to deal with this situation. We describe what happens in detail in the next few sections that discuss specific lock types.

The second hardware consideration referred to earlier has to do with the visibility of the lock state to the running processors when the lock value is changed. It is critically important on multiprocessor systems that all processors have a consistent view of data in memory, especially in the implementation of synchronization primitives—mutex locks and reader/writer (RW) locks. In other words, if a thread acquires a lock, any processor that executes a load instruction (read) of that memory location must retrieve the data following the last store (write) that was issued. The most recent state of the lock must be globally visible to all processors on the system.

Modern processors implement hardware buffering to provide optimal performance. In addition to the hardware caches, processors also use load and store buffers to hold data being read from (load) or written to (store) memory, in order to keep the instruction pipeline running and not have the processor stall waiting for data or a data write-to-memory cycle. The data hierarchy is illustrated in Figure 3.3.

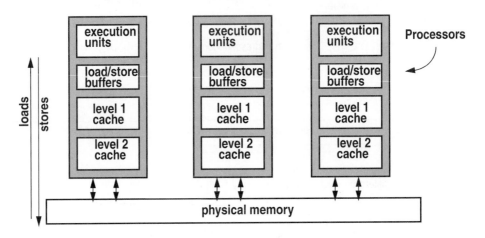

Figure 3.3 Hardware Data Hierarchy

The illustration in Figure 3.3 does not depict a specific processor; it is a generic representation of the various levels of data flow in a typical modern high-end microprocessor. It is intended to show the flow of data to and from physical memory from a processor's main execution units (integer units, floating point units, etc.).

The sizes of the load/store buffers vary across processor implementations, but they are typically several words in size. The load and store buffers on each processor are visible only to the processor they reside on, so a load issued by a processor that issued the store fetches the data from the store buffer if it is still there. However, it is theoretically possible for other processors that issue a load for that data to read their hardware cache or main memory before the store buffer in the store-issuing processor was flushed. Note that the store buffer we are referring to here is *not* the same thing as a level 1 or level 2 hardware instruction and data cache. Caches are beyond the store buffer; the store buffer is closer to the execution units of the processor. Physical memory and hardware caches are kept consistent on SMP platforms by a hardware bus protocol. Also, many caches are implemented as *write-through* caches (as is the case with the level 1 cache in Sun UltraSPARC), so data written to cache causes memory to be updated.

The implementation of a store buffer is part of the *memory model* implemented by the hardware. The memory model defines the constraints that can be imposed on the order of memory operations (loads and stores) by the system. Many processors implement a *sequential consistency* model, where loads and stores to memory are executed in the same order in which they were issued by the processor. This model has advantages in terms of memory consistency, but there are performance trade-offs with such a model because the hardware cannot optimize cache and memory operations for speed. The SPARC architecture specification [41] provides for building SPARC-based processors that support multiple memory models, the choice being left up to the implementors as to which memory models they wish to support. All current SPARC processors implement a Total Store Ordering (TSO) model, which requires compliance with the following rules for loads and stores:

- Loads (reads from memory) are blocking and are ordered with respect to other loads.

- Stores (writes to memory) are ordered with respect to other stores. Stores cannot bypass earlier loads.

- Atomic load-stores (ldstub and cas instructions) are ordered with respect to loads.

The TSO model is not quite as strict as the sequential consistency model but not as relaxed as two additional memory models defined by the SPARC architecture. SPARC-based processors also support Relaxed Memory Order (RMO) and Partial Store Order (PSO), but these are not currently supported by the kernel and not implemented by any Sun systems shipping today.

A final consideration in data visibility applies also to the memory model and concerns instruction ordering. The execution unit in modern processors can reorder the incoming instruction stream for processing through the execution units. The goals again are performance and creation of a sequence of instructions that will keep the processor pipeline full.

The hardware considerations described in this section are summarized in Table 3-1, along with the solution or implementation detail that applies to the particular issue.

Table 3-1 Hardware Considerations and Solutions for Locks

Consideration	Solution
Need for an atomic test-and-set instruction for locking primitives.	Use of native machine instructions. ldstub and cas on SPARC, cmpxchgl (compare/exchange long) on x86.
Data global visibility issue because of the use of hardware load and store buffers and instruction reordering, as defined by the memory model.	Use of memory barrier instructions.

The issues of consistent memory views in the face of a processor's load and store buffers, relaxed memory models, and atomic test-and-set capability for locks are addressed at the processor instruction-set level. The mutex lock and RW lock primitives implemented in the Solaris kernel use the `ldstub` and `cas` instructions for lock testing and acquisition on UltraSPARC-based systems and use the `cmpxchgl` (compare/exchange long) instruction on Intel x86. The lock primitive routines are part of the architecture-dependent segment of the kernel code.

SPARC processors provide various forms of *memory barrier (membar)* instructions, which, depending on options that are set in the instruction, impose specific constraints on the ordering of memory access operations (loads and stores) relative to the sequence with which they were issued. To ensure a consistent memory view when a mutex or RW lock operation has been issued, the Solaris kernel issues the appropriate `membar` instruction after the lock bits have changed.

As we move from the strongest consistency model (sequential consistency) to the weakest model (RMO), we can build a system with potentially better performance. We can optimize memory operations by playing with the ordering of memory access instructions that enable designers to minimize access latency and to maximize interconnect bandwidth. The trade-off is consistency, since the more relaxed models provide fewer and fewer constraints on the system to issue memory access operations in the same order in which the instruction stream issued them. So, processor architectures provide memory barrier controls that kernel developers can use to address the consistency issues where necessary, with some level of control on which consistency level is required to meet the system requirements. The types of `membar` instructions available, the options they support, and how they fit into the different memory models described would make for a highly technical and lengthy chapter on its own. Readers interested in this topic should read [4] and [23].

3.4   Introduction to Synchronization Objects

The Solaris kernel implements several types of synchronization objects. Locks provide mutual exclusion semantics for synchronized access to shared data. Locks come in several forms and are the primary focus of this chapter. The most commonly used lock in the Solaris kernel is the mutual exclusion, or *mutex* lock, which provides exclusive read and write access to data. Also implemented are *reader/writer* (RW) locks, for situations where multiple readers are allowable but only one writer is allowed at a time. Kernel *semaphores* are also employed in some areas of the kernel, where access to a finite number of resources must be managed. A special type of mutex lock, called a *dispatcher lock*, is used by the kernel dispatcher where synchronization requires access protection through a locking mechanism, as well as protection from interrupts.

Condition variables, which are not a type of lock, are used for thread synchronization and are an integral part of the kernel sleep/wakeup facility. Condition variables are introduced here and covered in detail in Chapter 5, "Solaris Memory Architecture."

The actual number of locks that exist in a running system at any time is dynamic and scales with the size of the system. Several hundred locks are defined in the kernel source code, but a lock count based on static source code is not accurate because locks are created dynamically during normal system activity—when kernel threads and processes are created, file systems are mounted, files are created and opened, network connections are made, etc. Many of the locks are embedded in the kernel data structures that provide the abstractions (processes, files) provided by the kernel, and thus the number of kernel locks will scale up linearly as resources are created dynamically.

This design speaks to one of the core strengths of the Solaris kernel: scalability and scaling synchronization primitives dynamically with the size of the kernel. Dynamic lock creation has several advantages over static allocations. First, the kernel is not wasting time and space managing a large pool of unused locks when running on a smaller system, such as a desktop or workgroup server. On a large system, a sufficient number of locks is available to sustain concurrency for scalable performance. It is possible to have literally thousands of locks in existence on a large, busy system.

3.4.1 Synchronization Process

When an executing kernel thread attempts to acquire a lock, it will encounter one of two possible lock states: free (available) or not free (owned, held). A requesting thread gets ownership of an available lock when the lock-specific get lock function is invoked. If the lock is not available, the thread most likely needs to block and wait for it to come available, although, as we will see shortly, the code does not always block (sleep), waiting for a lock. For those situations in which a thread will sleep while waiting for a lock, the kernel implements a sleep queue facility, known as *turnstiles*, for managing threads blocking on locks.

When a kernel thread has completed the operation on the shared data protected by the lock, it must release the lock. When a thread releases a lock, the code must deal with one of two possible conditions: threads are waiting for the lock (such threads are termed *waiters*), or there are no waiters. With no waiters, the lock can simply be released. With waiters, the code has several options. It can release the lock and wake up the blocking threads. In that case, the first thread to execute acquires the lock. Alternatively, the code could select a thread from the turnstile (sleep queue), based on priority or sleep time, and wake up only that thread. Finally, the code could select which thread should get the lock next, and the lock owner could hand the lock off to the selected thread. As we will see in the following sections, no one solution is suitable for all situations, and the Solaris kernel uses all three methods, depending on the lock type. Figure 3.4 provides the big picture.

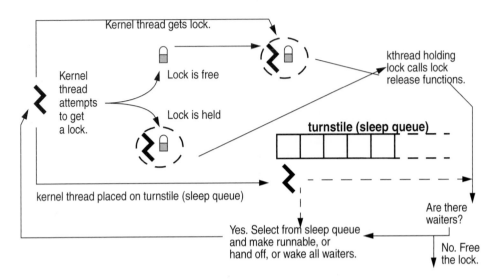

Figure 3.4 Solaris Locks — The Big Picture

Figure 3.4 provides a generic representation of the execution flow. Later we will see the results of a considerable amount of engineering effort that has gone into the lock code: improved efficiency and speed with short code paths, optimizations for the hot path (frequently hit code path) with well-tuned assembly code, and the best algorithms for lock release as determined by extensive analysis.

3.4.2 Synchronization Object Operations Vector

Each of the synchronization objects discussed in this section—mutex locks, reader/writer locks, and semaphores—defines an operations vector that is linked to kernel threads that are blocking on the object. Specifically, the object's operations vector is a data structure that exports a subset of object functions required for kthreads sleeping on the lock. The generic structure is defined in /usr/include/sys/sobject.h.

```
/*
 * The following data structure is used to map
 * synchronization object type numbers to the
 * synchronization object's sleep queue number
 * or the synch. object's owner function.
 */
typedef struct _sobj_ops {
        syncobj_t        sobj_type;
        kthread_t        *(*sobj_owner)();
        void             (*sobj_unsleep)(kthread_t *);
        void             (*sobj_change_pri)(kthread_t *, pri_t, pri_t *);
} sobj_ops_t;
```

Header File <sys/sobject.h>

The structure shown above provides for the object type declaration. For each synchronization object type, a type-specific structure is defined: `mutex_sobj_ops` for mutex locks, `rw_sobj_ops` for reader/writer locks, and `sema_sobj_ops` for semaphores.

The structure also provides three functions that may be called on behalf of a kthread sleeping on a synchronization object:

- An *owner* function, which returns the ID of the kernel thread that owns the object.
- An *unsleep* function, which transitions a kernel thread from a sleep state .
- A *change_pri* function, which changes the priority of a kernel thread, used for priority inheritance. (See "Turnstiles and Priority Inheritance" on page 88.)

We will see how references to the lock's operations structure is implemented as we move through specifics on lock implementations in the following sections.

It is useful to note at this point that our examination of Solaris kernel locks offers a good example of some of the design trade-offs involved in kernel software engineering. Building the various software components that make up the Solaris kernel is a series of design decisions, when performance needs are measured against complexity. In areas of the kernel where optimal performance is a top priority, simplicity might be sacrificed in favor of performance. The locking facilities in the Solaris kernel are an area where such trade-offs are made—much of the lock code is written in assembly language, for speed, rather than in the C language; the latter is easier to code with and maintain but is potentially slower. In some cases, when the code path is not performance critical, a simpler design will be favored over cryptic assembly code or complexity in the algorithms. The behavior of a particular design is examined through exhaustive testing, to ensure that the best possible design decisions were made.

3.5 Mutex Locks

Mutual exclusion, or *mutex* locks, are the most common type of synchronization primitive used in the kernel. Mutex locks serialize access to critical data, when a kernel thread must acquire the mutex specific to the data region being protected before it can read or write the data. The thread is the lock *owner* while it is holding the lock, and the thread must release the lock when it has finished working in the protected region so other threads can acquire the lock for access to the protected data.

3.5.1 Overview

If a thread attempts to acquire a mutex lock that is being held, it can basically do one of two things: it can *spin* or it can *block*. Spinning means the thread enters a tight loop, attempting to acquire the lock in each pass through the loop. The term *spin lock* is often used to describe this type of mutex. Blocking means the thread is placed on a sleep queue while the lock is being held and the kernel sends a wakeup to the thread when the lock is released. There are pros and cons to both approaches.

The spin approach has the benefit of not incurring the overhead of context switching, required when a thread is put to sleep, and also has the advantage of a relatively fast acquisition when the lock is released, since there is no context-switch operation. It has the downside of consuming CPU cycles while the thread is in the spin loop—the CPU is executing a kernel thread (the thread in the spin loop) but not really doing any useful work.

The blocking approach has the advantage of freeing the processor to execute other threads while the lock is being held; it has the disadvantage of requiring context switching to get the waiting thread off the processor and a new runnable thread onto the processor. There's also a little more lock acquisition latency, since a wakeup and context switch are required before the blocking thread can become the owner of the lock it was waiting for.

In addition to the issue of what to do if a requested lock is being held, the question of lock granularity needs to be resolved. Let's take a simple example. The kernel maintains a process table, which is a linked list of process structures, one for each of the processes running on the system. A simple table-level mutex could be implemented, such that if a thread needs to manipulate a process structure, it must first acquire the process table mutex. This level of locking is very coarse. It has the advantages of simplicity and minimal lock overhead. It has the obvious disadvantage of potentially poor scalability, since only one thread at a time can manipulate objects on the process table. Such a lock is likely to have a great deal of contention (become a *hot* lock).

The alternative is to implement a finer level of granularity: a lock-per-process table entry versus one table-level lock. With a lock on each process table entry, multiple threads can be manipulating different process structures at the same time, providing concurrency. The disadvantages are that such an implementation is more complex, increases the chances of deadlock situations, and necessitates more overhead because there are more locks to manage.

In general, the Solaris kernel implements relatively fine-grained locking whenever possible, largely due to the dynamic nature of scaling locks with kernel structures as needed.

The kernel implements two types of mutex locks: *spin locks* and *adaptive locks*. Spin locks, as we discussed, spin in a tight loop if a desired lock is being held when a thread attempts to acquire the lock. Adaptive locks are the most common type of lock used and are designed to dynamically either spin or block when a lock is being held, depending on the state of the holder. We already discussed the trade-offs of spinning versus blocking. Implementing a locking scheme that only does one or the other can severely impact scalability and performance. It is much better to use an adaptive locking scheme, which is precisely what we do.

The mechanics of adaptive locks are straightforward. When a thread attempts to acquire a lock and the lock is being held, the kernel examines the state of the thread that is holding the lock. If the lock holder (owner) is running on a processor, the thread attempting to get the lock will spin. If the thread holding the lock is not running, the thread attempting to get the lock will block. This policy works quite well because the code is such that mutex hold times are very short (by design, the goal is to minimize the amount of code to be executed while a lock is held). So, if a thread is holding a lock and running, the lock will likely be released very soon, probably in less time than it takes to context-switch off and on again, so it's worth spinning.

On the other hand, if a lock holder is not running, then we know that minimally one context switch is involved before the holder will release the lock (getting the holder back on a processor to run), and it makes sense to simply block and free up the processor to do something else. The kernel will place the blocking thread on a turnstile (sleep queue) designed specifically for synchronization primitives and will wake the thread when the lock is released by the holder. (See "Turnstiles and Priority Inheritance" on page 88.)

The other distinction between adaptive locks and spin locks has to do with interrupts, the dispatcher, and context switching. The kernel dispatcher is the code that selects threads for scheduling and does context switches. It runs at an elevated Priority Interrupt Level (PIL) to block interrupts (the dispatcher runs at priority level 10 on SPARC systems). High-level interrupts (interrupt levels 11–15 on SPARC systems) can interrupt the dispatcher. High-level interrupt handlers are not allowed to do anything that could require a context switch or to enter the dispatcher (we discuss this further in "Dispatcher Locks" on page 96). Adaptive locks can block, and blocking means context switching, so only spin locks can be used in high-level interrupt handlers. Also, spin locks can raise the interrupt level of the processor when the lock is acquired.

```
struct kernel_data {
        kmutex_t klock;
        char *forw_ptr;
        char *back_ptr;
        long data1;
        int data2;
} kdata;

void function()
        .
        mutex_init(&kdata.klock);
        .
        mutex_enter(&kdata.klock);
        klock.data1 = 1;
        mutex_exit(&kdata.klock);
```

The preceding block of pseudocode illustrates the general mechanics of mutex locks. A lock is declared in the code; in this case, it is embedded in the data structure it is designed to protect. Once declared, the lock is initialized with the kernel mutex_init() function. Any subsequent reference to the kdata structure requires that the klock mutex be acquired with mutex_enter(). Once the work is done, the lock is released with mutex_exit(). The lock type, spin or adaptive, is determined in the mutex_init() code by the kernel. Assuming an adaptive mutex in this example, any kernel threads that make a mutex_enter() call on klock will either block or spin, depending on the state of the kernel thread that owns klock when the mutex_enter() is called.

3.5.2 Solaris 7 Mutex Lock Implementation

The implementation description in this section is based on Solaris 7. Algorithmically, Solaris 2.5.1 and Solaris 2.6 are very similar but have some implementation differences, which we cover in the sections that follow.

The kernel defines different data structures for the two types of mutex locks, adaptive and spin, as shown in Figure 3.5.

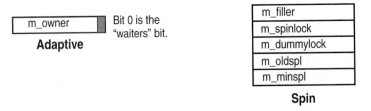

Figure 3.5 Solaris 7 Adaptive and Spin Mutex

In Figure 3.5, the m_owner field in the adaptive lock, which holds the address of the kernel thread that owns the lock (the kthread pointer), plays a double role, in that it also serves as the actual lock; successful lock acquisition for a thread means it has its kthread pointer set in the m_owner field of the target lock. If threads attempt to get the lock while it is held (waiters) the low-order bit (bit 0) of m_owner is set to reflect that case. We ensure that kthread pointer values do not require bit 0 to make this work.

The spin mutex, as we pointed out earlier, is used at high interrupt levels, where context switching is not allowed. Spin locks block interrupts while in the spin loop, so the kernel needs to maintain the priority level the processor was running at prior to entering the spin loop, which raises the processor's priority level. (Elevating the priority level is how interrupts are blocked.) The m_minspl field stores the priority level of the interrupt handler when the lock is initialized, and m_oldspl gets set to the priority level the processor was running at when the lock code is called. The m_spinlock fields are the actual mutex lock bits.

Each kernel module and subsystem implementing one or more mutex locks calls into a common set of mutex functions. All locks must first be initialized by the `mutex_init()` function, where the lock type is determined on the basis of an argument passed in the `mutex_init()` call. The most common type passed into `mutex_init()` is MUTEX_DEFAULT, which results in the init code determining what type of lock, adaptive or spin, should be used. It is possible for a caller of `mutex_init()` to be specific about a lock type (e.g., MUTEX_SPIN), but that is rarely done.

If the init code is called from a device driver or any kernel module that registers and generates interrupts, then an *interrupt block cookie* is added to the argument list. An interrupt block cookie is an abstraction used by device drivers when they set their interrupt vector and parameters. The `mutex_init()` code checks the argument list for an interrupt block cookie. If `mutex_init()` is being called from a device driver to initialize a mutex to be used in a high-level interrupt handler, the lock type is set to spin. Otherwise, an adaptive lock is initialized. The test is the interrupt level in the passed interrupt block; levels above 10 (on SPARC systems) are considered high-level interrupts and thus require spin locks. The init code clears most of the fields in the mutex lock structure as appropriate for the lock type. The `m_dummylock` field in spin locks is set to all 1's (0xFF). We'll see why in a minute.

The primary mutex functions called, aside from `mutex_init()` (which is only called once for each lock at initialization time), are `mutex_enter()` to get a lock and `mutex_exit()` to release it. `mutex_enter()` assumes an available, adaptive lock. If the lock is held or is a spin lock, `mutex_vector_enter()` is entered to reconcile what should happen. This is a performance optimization. `mutex_enter()` is implemented in assembly code, and because the entry point is designed for the simple case (adaptive lock, not held), the amount of code that gets executed to acquire a lock when those conditions are true is minimal. Also, there are significantly more adaptive mutex locks than spin locks in the kernel, making the quick test case effective most of the time. The test for a lock held or spin lock is very fast. Here is where the `m_dummylock` field comes into play: `mutex_enter()` executes a compare-and-swap instruction on the first byte of the mutex, testing for a zero value. On a spin lock, the `m_dummylock` field is tested because of its positioning in the data structure and the endianness of SPARC processors. Since `m_dummylock` is always set (it is set to all 1's in `mutex_init()`), the test will fail for spin locks. The test will also fail for a held adaptive lock since such a lock will have a nonzero value in the byte field being tested. That is, the `m_owner` field will have a kthread pointer value for a held, adaptive lock.

If the lock is an adaptive mutex and is not being held, the caller of `mutex_enter()` gets ownership of the lock. If the two conditions are not true, that is, either the lock is held or the lock is a spin lock, the code enters the `mutex_vector_enter()` function to sort things out. The `mutex_vector_enter()` code first tests the lock type. For spin locks, the `m_oldspl` field is set, based on the current Priority Interrupt Level (PIL) of the processor, and the lock is tested. If it's not being held, the lock is set (`m_spinlock`) and the code returns to the caller. A held lock forces the caller into a spin loop, where a loop counter is incremented (for statistical purposes; the lockstat(1M) data), and the code checks whether the lock is still held in each pass through the loop. Once the lock is released, the code breaks out of the loop, grabs the lock, and returns to the caller.

Adaptive locks require a little more work. When the code enters the adaptive code path (in mutex_vector_enter()), it increments the cpu_sysinfo.mutex_adenters (adaptive lock enters) field, as is reflected in the smtx column in mpstat(1M). mutex_vector_enter() then tests again to determine if the lock is owned (held), since the lock may have been released in the time interval between the call to mutex_enter() and the current point in the mutex_vector_enter() code. If the adaptive lock is not being held, mutex_vector_enter() attempts to acquire the lock. If successful, the code returns.

If the lock is held, mutex_vector_enter() determines whether or not the lock owner is running by looping through the CPU structures and testing the lock m_owner against the cpu_thread field of the CPU structure. (cpu_thread contains the kernel thread address of the thread currently executing on the CPU.) A match indicates the holder is running, which means the adaptive lock will spin. No match means the owner is not running, in which case the caller must block. In the blocking case, the kernel turnstile code is entered to locate or acquire a turnstile, in preparation for placement of the kernel thread on a sleep queue associated with the turnstile.

The turnstile placement happens in two phases. After mutex_vector_enter() determines that the lock holder is not running, it makes a turnstile call to look up the turnstile sets the waiters bit in the lock, and retests to see if the owner is running. If yes, the code releases the turnstile and enters the adaptive lock spin loop, which attempts to acquire the lock. Otherwise, the code places the kernel thread on a turnstile (sleep queue) and changes the thread's state to sleep. That effectively concludes the sequence of events in mutex_vector_enter().

Dropping out of mutex_vector_enter(), either the caller ended up with the lock it was attempting to acquire, or the calling thread is on a turnstile sleep queue associated with the lock. In either case, the lockstat(1M) data is updated, reflecting the lock type, spin time, or sleep time as the last bit of work done in mutex_vector_enter().

lockstat(1M) is a kernel lock statistics command that was introduced in Solaris 2.6. It provides detailed information on kernel mutex and reader/writer locks.

The algorithm described in the previous paragraphs is summarized in pseudocode below.

```
mutex_vector_enter()
        if (lock is a spin lock)
                lock_set_spl() /* enter spin-lock specific code path */
        increment cpu_sysinfo.ademters.
spin_loop:
        if (lock is not owned)
                mutex_trylock() /* try to acquire the lock */
                if (lock acquired)
                        goto bottom
                else
                        continue /* lock being held */
        if (lock owner is running on a processor)
                goto spin_loop
        else
                lookup turnstile for the lock
                set waiters bit
                if (lock owner is running on a processor)
                        drop turnstile
                        goto spin_loop
                else
                        block /* the sleep queue associated with the turnstile */

bottom:
        update lockstat statistics
```

When a thread has finished working in a lock-protected data area, it calls the `mutex_exit()` code to release the lock. The entry point is implemented in assembly language and handles the simple case of freeing an adaptive lock with no waiters. With no threads waiting for the lock, it's a simple matter of clearing the lock fields (`m_owner`) and returning. The C language function `mutex_vector_exit()` is entered from `mutex_exit()` for anything but the simple case.

In the case of a spin lock, the lock field is cleared and the processor is returned to the PIL level it was running at prior to entering the lock code. For adaptive locks, a waiter must be selected from the turnstile (if there is more than one waiter), have its state changed from sleeping to runnable, and be placed on a dispatch queue so it can execute and get the lock. If the thread releasing the lock was the beneficiary of priority inheritance, meaning that it had its priority improved when a calling thread with a better priority was not able to get the lock, then the thread releasing the lock will have its priority reset to what it was prior to the inheritance. Priority inheritance is discussed in "Turnstiles and Priority Inheritance" on page 88.

When an adaptive lock is released, the code clears the `waiters` bit in `m_owner` and calls the turnstile function to wake up *all* the waiters. Readers familiar with sleep/wakeup mechanisms of operating systems have likely heard of a particular behavior known as the *"thundering herd problem,"* a situation where many threads that have been blocking for the same resource are all woken up at the same time and make a mad dash for the resource (a mutex in this case)—like a herd of large, four-legged beasts running toward the same object. System behavior tends to go from a relatively small run queue to a large run queue (all the threads have been woken up and made runnable) and high CPU utilization until a thread gets the resource, at which point a bunch of threads are sleeping again, the run queue normalizes, and CPU utilization flattens out. This is a generic behavior that can occur on any operating system.

The wakeup mechanism used when `mutex_vector_exit()` is called in Solaris 7 may seem like an open invitation to thundering herds, but in practice it turns out not to be a problem. The main reason is that the blocking case for threads waiting for a mutex is rare; most of the time the threads will spin. If a blocking situation does arise, it typically does not reach a point where very many threads are blocked on the mutex—one of the characteristics of the thundering herd problem is resource contention resulting in a lot of sleeping threads. The kernel code segments that implement mutex locks are, by design, short and fast, so locks are not held for long. Code that requires longer lock-hold times uses a reader/writer write lock, which provides mutual exclusion semantics with a selective wakeup algorithm. There are, of course, other reasons for choosing reader/writer locks over mutex locks, the most obvious being to allow multiple readers to see the protected data.

In the following sections, we differentiate the implementation of mutexes in Solaris 2.5.1 and 2.6. As we said, Solaris 2.5.1 and 2.6 are similar to the previously described Solaris 7 behavior, especially in the area of lock acquisition (`mutex_enter()`). The more salient differences exist in the lock release algorithm, and associated wakeup behavior.

3.5.2.1 Solaris 2.6 Mutex Implementation Differences

First, an examination of the lock structures, as illustrated in Figure 3.6.

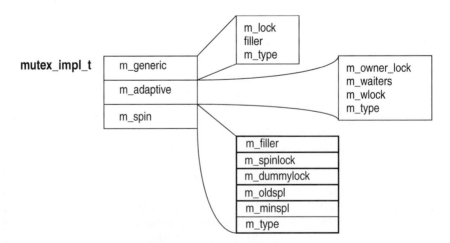

Figure 3.6 Solaris 2.6 Mutex

Solaris 2.6 defines all possible mutex lock types within the same structure. The spin lock is the same as for Solaris 7, with the addition of a type field. The adaptive mutex has more fields, which are fairly self-descriptive. m_owner_lock is the same as m_owner in Solaris 7; it is the lock itself, and the value represents the kthread ID of the holder when the lock is held. m_waiters stores the turnstile ID of a waiting kernel thread, and m_wlock is a dispatcher lock (see "Dispatcher Locks" on page 96) that synchronizes access to the m_waiters field in the mutex. m_type describes the lock type (adaptive or spin).

The structure differences aside, the basic algorithm and implementation of assembly and C code are essentially the same in Solaris 2.6 for lock acquisition (mutex_enter()). The differences exist in the sleep mechanism—the turnstile implementation has been improved in Solaris 7. These differences are in the interfaces and subroutines called to facilitate turnstile allocation and priority inheritance. (See "Turnstiles and Priority Inheritance" on page 88.)

On the lock release side, Solaris 2.6 implements separate routines for releasing spin locks and adaptive locks: mutex_vector_exit() and mutex_adaptive_release(), respectively. When an adaptive lock with waiting threads is released, the 2.6 code wakes only the thread with the highest priority. If multiple threads of the same (highest) priority are waiting for the same lock, the thread waiting longest is selected.

3.5.2.2 Solaris 2.5.1 Mutex Implementation Differences

The data structure of Solaris 2.5.1 looks very much like that of Solaris 2.6. It has another possible instantiation of an adaptive lock, m_adaptive2, which combines the lock owner and lock bits in the same field of the adaptive mutex data structure, as illustrated in Figure 3.7.

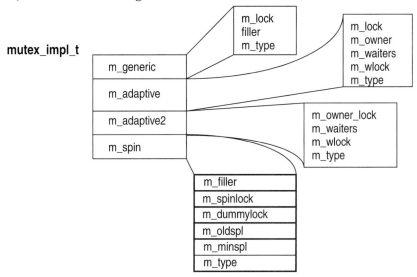

Figure 3.7 Solaris 2.5.1 Adaptive Mutex

The implementation of the mutex code in Solaris 2.5.1 is quite different from the other releases, although algorithmically the behavior is essentially the same. Solaris 2.5.1 defines a mutex operations vector array. Each element in the array is a `mutex_ops` structure, one structure for each type of mutex defined in Solaris 2.5.1. The array is indexed according to the lock type and the function call. The design is such that specific functions handle lock operations for each of the different types of mutex locks. Common entry points into the mutex code pass control to the lock-specific functions by switching through the operations array, as determined by the lock type and function offset. This is illustrated in Figure 3.8.

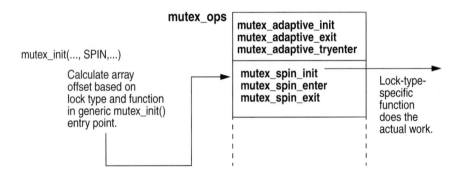

Figure 3.8 Solaris 2.5.1 Mutex Operations Vectoring

Solaris 2.5.1 implements a wakeup method similar to that of Solaris 2.6 when an adaptive mutex is released with waiting threads; the highest priority waiter is selected for wakeup and should get ownership of the lock. It is, of course, possible for another thread to come along and acquire the lock before the wakeup is completed, so the newly awakened thread is not guaranteed to get the lock.

Finally, note that the `lockstat` utility was first implemented in Solaris 2.6 and thus is not part of the 2.5.1 release.

3.5.2.3 Why the Mutex Changes in Solaris 7

We wanted to avoid getting mired in subtle differences that would not add real value to the text, but at the same time we want to point out relevant differences in implementations. The subsections describing the implementation differences across releases serve two purposes. The first and most obvious is completeness, to meet our goal of covering multiple Solaris releases. Second, and even more compelling, we show the evolution and refinements that have gone into the lock code from release to release. What we see is something that is functionally similar but significantly scaled down in size. The actual lock manipulation and turnstiles code follow the same trend shown in the data structures—scaled down, leaner, and more efficient.

The rationale for changing the wakeup behavior in Solaris 7 stems from exhaustive testing and examination of all possible options; then, the designers selected what works best most of the time.

To summarize, when a mutex lock is being released with waiters, there are essentially three options:

- Choose a waiting thread from the turnstile and give it lock ownership *before* waking it. This approach is known as *direct handoff* of ownership.

  This approach has a downside when there is even moderate lock contention, in that it defeats the logic of adaptive locks. If direct handoff is used, there is a window between the time the thread was given ownership and the time the new owner is running on a processor (it must go through a state change and get context-switched on). If, during that window, other threads come along trying to get the lock, they will enter the blocking code path, since the "is the lock owner running" test will fail. A lock with some contention will result in most threads taking the blocking path instead of the spin path.

- Free the lock and wake one waiter, as Solaris 2.5.1 and Solaris 2.6 do.

  This option has a much more subtle complication because of the potential for a lock to have no owner, but multiple waiters. Consider a lock having multiple waiters. If the lock is released and the code issues a wakeup on one waiter, the lock will have no owner (it was just released). On a busy system, it could take several seconds for the selected thread to be context-switched and take ownership of the lock. If another thread comes along and grabs the lock, the mutex_enter() code must examine the blocking chain (all the threads sitting on a turnstile waiting for the lock) to determine if it should inherit a higher priority from a sleeping thread. This complicates the mutex_enter() code, putting an unnecessary burden on a hot code path.

- Wake all the waiters, which is what we do in Solaris 7.

  This option has the benefit of not having to preserve the waiters bit—since we're waking all the waiters, the action can simply be cleared in one operation. The approach simplifies the code and is more efficient. Extensive testing has shown that the blocking case is relatively rare, so this algorithm works quite well.

Statistical information on mutex locks is readily available, but not in Solaris 2.5.1. Releases 2.6 and 7 include a lockstat(1M) utility, which collects and displays information on mutex and reader/writer lock activity. lockstat(1M) is implemented with a pseudodevice, /dev/lockstat, and associated pseudo device driver. The interfaces are not public, meaning there are no open, read, write, etc., calls into the lockstat driver. The lockstat(1M) manual page provides information on how to use lockstat(1M) and how to interpret the displayed data. Several options enable you to select particular events to watch, data collection methods (statistics, stack tracing, etc.), and the method by which to display data, so go through the manual page carefully.

3.6   Reader/Writer Locks

Reader/writer (RW) locks provide mutual exclusion semantics on write locks. Only one thread at a time is allowed to own the write lock, but there is concurrent access for readers. These locks are designed for scenarios where it is acceptable to have multiple threads reading the data at the same time, but only one writer. While a writer is holding the lock, no readers are allowed. Also, because of the wakeup mechanism, a writer lock is a better solution for kernel code segments that require relatively long hold times, as we will see shortly.

The basic mechanics of RW locks are similar to mutexes, in that RW locks have an initialization function (rw_init()), an entry function to acquire the lock (rw_enter()), and an exit function to release the lock (rw_exit()). The entry and exit points are optimized in assembly code to deal with the simple cases, and they call into C language functions if anything beyond the simplest case must be dealt with. As with mutex locks, the simple case is that the requested lock is available on an entry (acquire) call and no threads are waiting for the lock on the exit (release) call.

The implementation of RW locks is almost identical in Solaris 7 and Solaris 2.6. The Solaris 2.5.1 code is somewhat different. As we did with mutex locks, we'll discuss the Solaris 7 implementation first and point out differences in the other releases later.

3.6.1 Solaris 7 Reader/Writer Locks

In Solaris 7, RW locks are implemented as a single-word data structure in the kernel, either 32 bits or 64 bits wide, depending on the data model of the running kernel, as depicted in Figure 3.9.

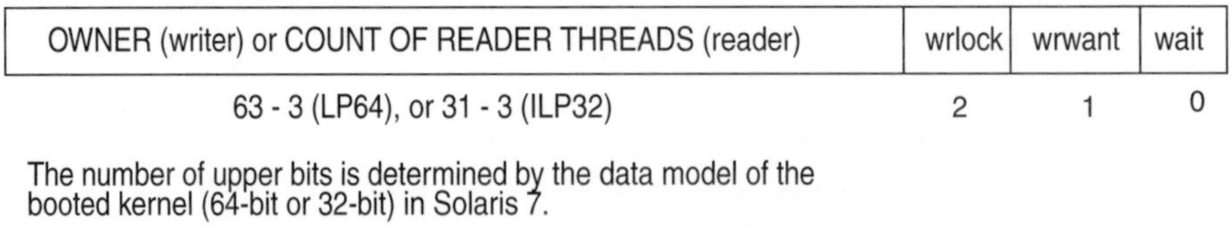

OWNER (writer) or COUNT OF READER THREADS (reader)	wrlock	wrwant	wait
63 - 3 (LP64), or 31 - 3 (ILP32)	2	1	0

The number of upper bits is determined by the data model of the
booted kernel (64-bit or 32-bit) in Solaris 7.

Figure 3.9 Solaris 7 Reader/Writer Lock

The Solaris 7 RW lock defines bit 0, the wait bit, set to signify that threads are waiting for the lock. The wrwant bit (write wanted, bit 1) indicates that at least one thread is waiting for a write lock. Bit 2, wrlock, is the actual write lock, and it determines the meaning of the high-order bits. If the write lock is held (bit 2 set), then the upper bits contain a pointer to the kernel thread holding the write lock. If bit 2 is clear, then the upper bits contain a count of the number of threads holding the lock as a read lock.

The simple cases for lock acquisition through `rw_enter()` are the circumstances listed below:

- The write lock is wanted and is available.

- The read lock is wanted, the write lock is not held, and no threads are waiting for the write lock (`wrwant` is clear).

The acquisition of the write lock results in bit 2 getting set and the kernel thread pointer getting loaded in the upper bits. For a reader, the hold count (upper bits) is incremented. Conditions where the write lock is being held, causing a lock request to fail, or where a thread is waiting for a write lock, causing a read lock request to fail, result in a call to the `rw_enter_sleep()` function.

Important to note is that the `rw_enter()` code sets a flag in the kernel thread used by the dispatcher code when establishing a kernel thread's priority prior to preemption or changing state to sleep. We cover this in more detail in Chapter 6, "Kernel Memory." Briefly, the kernel thread structure contains a `t_kpri_req` (kernel priority request) field that is checked in the dispatcher code when a thread is about to be preempted (forced off the processor on which it is executing because a higher priority thread becomes runnable) or when the thread is about to have its state changed to sleep. If the `t_kpri_req` flag is set, the dispatcher assigns a kernel priority to the thread, such that when the thread resumes execution, it will run before threads in scheduling classes of lower priority (timeshare and interactive class threads). More succinctly, the priority of a thread holding a write lock is set to a better priority to minimize the hold time of the lock.

Getting back to the `rw_enter()` flow: If the code falls through the simple case, we need to set up the kernel thread requesting the RW lock to block.

- `rw_enter_sleep()` establishes whether the calling thread is requesting a read or write lock and does another test to see if the lock is available. If it is, the caller gets the lock, the `lockstat(1M)` statistics are updated, and the code returns. If the lock is not available, then the turnstile code is called to look up a turnstile in preparation for putting the calling thread to sleep.

- With a turnstile now available, another test is made on the lock availability. (On today's fast processors, and especially multiprocessor systems, it's quite possible that the thread holding the lock finished what it was doing and the lock became available.) Assuming the lock is still held, the thread is set to a sleep state and placed on a turnstile.

- The RW lock structure will have the `wait` bit set for a reader waiting (forced to block because a writer has the lock) or the `wrwant` bit set to signify that a thread wanting the write lock is blocking.

- The `cpu_sysinfo` structure for the processor maintains two counters for failures to get a read lock or write lock on the first pass: `rw_rdfails` and `rw_wrfails`. The appropriate counter is incremented just prior to the turnstile call; this action places the thread on a turnstile sleep queue.

mpstat(1M) sums the counters and displays the fails-per-second in the *srw* column of its output.

The acquisition of a RW lock and subsequent behavior if the lock is held are straightforward and similar in many ways to what happens in the mutex case. Things get interesting when a thread calls rw_exit() to release a lock it is holding—there are several potential solutions to the problem of determining which thread gets the lock next. We saw with mutex locks that a change was made from Solaris 2.6 (and previous releases) to Solaris 7 in the wakeup mechanism. A wakeup is issued on all threads that are sleeping, waiting for the mutex in Solaris 7, and we know from empirical data that this solution works well for reasons previously discussed. With RW locks, we're dealing with potentially longer hold times, which could result in more sleepers, a desire to give writers priority over readers (why let a reader in when a thread is apparently waiting to change the data?), and the potential for the priority inversion problem described in "Turnstiles and Priority Inheritance" on page 88.

For rw_exit(), which is called by the lock holder when it is ready to release the lock, the simple case is that there are no waiters. In this case, the wrlock bit is cleared if the holder was a writer, or the hold count field is decremented to reflect one less reader. The more complex case of the system having waiters when the lock is released is dealt with in the following manner:

- The kernel does a direct transfer of ownership of the lock to one or more of the threads waiting for the lock when the lock is released, either to the next writer or to a group of readers if more than one reader is blocking and no writers are blocking.

  This situation is very different from the case of the mutex implementation, where the wakeup is issued and a thread must obtain lock ownership in the usual fashion. Here, a thread or threads wake up owning the lock they were blocking on.

  The algorithm used to figure out who gets the lock next addresses several requirements that provide for generally balanced system performance. The kernel needs to minimize the possibility of starvation (a thread never getting the resource it needs to continue executing) while allowing writers to take precedence whenever possible.

- rw_exit_wakeup() retests for the simple case and drops the lock if there are no waiters (clear wrlock or decrement the hold count).

- When waiters are present, the code grabs the turnstile (sleep queue) associated with the lock and saves the pointer to the kernel thread of the next write waiter that was on the turnstile's sleep queue (if one exists).

  The turnstile sleep queues are organized as a FIFO (first in, first out) queue, so the queue management (turnstile code) makes sure that the thread that was waiting the longest (the first in) is the thread that is selected as the next writer (first out). Thus, part of the fairness policy we want to enforce is covered.

The remaining bits of the algorithm go as follows:

- If a writer is releasing the write lock and there are waiting readers and writers, readers of the same or higher priority than the highest-priority blocked writer are granted the read lock.

- The readers are handed ownership, and then woken up by the `turnstile_wakeup()` kernel function in Solaris 7.

  These readers also inherit the priority of the writer that released the lock if the reader thread is of a lower priority (inheritance is done on a per-reader thread basis when more than one thread is being woken up). Lock ownership handoff is a relatively simple operation. For read locks, there is no notion of a lock owner, so it's a matter of setting the hold count in the lock to reflect the number of readers coming off the turnstile, then issuing the wakeup of each reader.

- An exiting reader always grants the lock to a waiting writer, even if there are higher-priority readers blocked.

  It is possible for a reader freeing the lock to have waiting readers, although it may not be intuitive, given the multiple reader design of the lock. If a reader is holding the lock and a writer comes along, the `wrwant` bit is set to signify that a writer is waiting for the lock. With `wrwant` set, subsequent readers cannot get the lock—we want the holding readers to finish so the writer can get the lock. Therefore, it is possible for a reader to execute `rw_exit_wakeup()` with waiting writers and readers.

The "let's favor writers but be fair to readers" policy described above was first implemented in Solaris 2.6.

3.6.2 Solaris 2.6 RW Lock Differences

Figure 3.10 shows what the RW lock in Solaris 2.6 looks like.

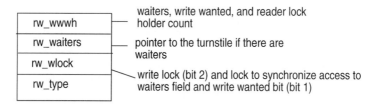

Figure 3.10 Solaris 2.6 Reader/Writer Lock

Note that the lock fields are functionally identical to those in Solaris 7, just implemented differently. `rw_wwwh` provides a `waiter` bit, a write-wanted bit, and a count of readers holding the lock. `rw_waiters` points to the turnstile holding the waiters if any exist. The `rw_wlock` field serves as the actual write lock (bit 2) and a dispatcher lock to synchronize access to the waiters and write-wanted bits. (Dispatcher locks are described in "Dispatcher Locks" on page 96.)

3.6.3 Solaris 2.5.1 RW Lock Differences

The RW lock structure in Solaris 2.5.1 is depicted in Figure 3.11.

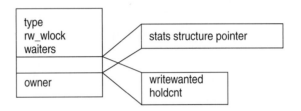

Figure 3.11 Solaris 2.5.1 RW Lock Structure

Solaris 2.5.1 defines several RW lock types, stored in the type field when the lock is initialized. In practice, the RW_DEFAULT type is used almost all the time, except that some device drivers specify an RW_DRIVER lock type. Other types include locks designed to gather statistics. Such locks are only used internally in engineering and are not implemented on production releases. Their enablement requires that a specific compile-time flag be set.

The rw_wlock field is essentially the same as that of the Solaris 2.6 implementation, serving as a dispatcher lock to synchronize access to waiters and writewanted bits and the actual write lock. The owner field contains the address of the kernel thread that owns the write lock. writewanted, when set, signifies that a thread is waiting for a write lock, and holdcnt either represents the number of kernel threads holding the read lock or is set to -1 to signify that the write lock is currently held. Solaris 2.5.1 implements a separate union in the RW lock structure for writewanted and holdcnt.

The RW lock code in Solaris 2.5.1 implements an operations vector array, rwlock_ops, similar to the mutex ops vector array shown in Figure 3.8. The array is populated with rwlock_ops structures that point to lock-type specific functions. As with the mutex array, the rwlock_ops array is indexed, based on the lock type and the offset to the requested function (e.g., init, enter, exit). Entry points into the RW lock functions rw_init(), rw_enter(), and rw_exit() transfer control to the lock-specific function by indexing through the array.

The next most salient differences in the Solaris 2.5.1 RW lock implementation are that the code in Solaris 2.5.1 is written entirely in C (no assembly language entry points), and mutex locks are used to protect the internal data in the RW lock code.

An array of mutex locks, rw_mutex[], is initialized at system boot time with a fixed number (32) of mutex locks. During execution, a hash function indexes into the array, hashing on the address of the RW lock being requested (or released). When the various RW lock functions are entered, a mutex is retrieved from the rw_mutex[] array, based on the address of the RW lock passed in the calling function. The mutex_enter() call is made to acquire the mutex to do an RW lock operation before the code executes, and the mutex is released when the function is ready to exit.

Kernel threads call rw_enter() to acquire an RW lock, passing the address of the lock and a flag that tells whether a reader or writer is required.

Here's the sequence for a read lock request:

- If a read lock is requested, the mutex lock is acquired to protect the RW lock code and a test for either the write lock being held (holdcnt is -1) or a writer waiting (writewanted is set) is made. If neither condition is true, the caller can obtain a read lock.

- The holdcnt is incremented, and the calling thread has its t_kpri_req flag set to tell the dispatcher that a kernel (SYS) priority is requested.

  Setting this flag boosts the priority of the thread holding the lock if it's a timeshare or interactive class thread, with the intent to expedite the thread's execution while it's holding a lock and to minimize the hold time.

- The mutex is released and the code returns to the caller.

- If a writer is holding the lock or a write lock request is pending, the thread is set to block. The mutex is released, and the cpu_sysinfo.rw_rdfails counter is incremented.

  You can examine this counter with mpstat(1M). The srw column displays the sum of the failed reader and failed writer lock attempts.

- The code tests the lock's waiters field, which contains the ID of a turnstile if there are already waiters. No waiters means we must allocate a turnstile from the free pool; one or more waiters means we just need to locate the turnstile holding the other waiters and put the lock on that sleep queue.

- Before putting the thread on the turnstile and changing the thread state to sleep, the code tests the lock again (it may have been released by now). If it's available, the path previously described for an available lock is taken. Otherwise, the turnstile block code is called to place the thread on the sleep queue.

- The priority inversion condition is tested for with the pi_willto() code, and the swtch() function is called for entry to the dispatcher.

The code flow for a writer lock request is similar:

- If the lock is not available, the writewanted bit is set.

- An existing turnstile is fetched if there are already waiters; otherwise, a new one is allocated, and the thread is placed on a sleep queue after the lock is rechecked to make sure it's still unavailable. If it is available or was available when the code was first entered, the `holdcnt` field is set to -1 (the write lock), the `owner` field is set to the kernel thread ID of the caller, and the mutex is released (we grabbed that early on when the write code path was entered).

- An RW lock is released by a call to `rw_exit()`, which acquires the mutex when the function is entered. If a writer is releasing the lock, the `owner` field and `holdcnt` fields in the lock are cleared and we check for any waiters.

  - If there are threads sleeping on the lock, the turnstile is retrieved and the priority of the caller is reset if it was the beneficiary of priority inheritance.

  - If a writer is waiting (`writewanted` is set), the writer thread is woken up. If there is more than one writer, the highest-priority writer gets the wakeup. Otherwise, with no writers waiting, all the readers are woken up.

    This always-favor-the-writer policy was changed in Solaris 2.6 and Solaris 7. For writers, only one thread gets the wakeup, whereas for readers, all waiting readers are woken up. This makes sense because with no writers, all the readers can get the lock (that's how RW locks work, by design). Only one writer at a time can have the lock, so it only makes sense to wake one writer.

- If a reader is releasing the lock, the `holdcnt` field is decremented (one less reader) and writers are again favored for wakeup over readers if both exist. The code first checks to ensure that no other readers are holding the lock (`holdcnt` is 0), as it's certainly possible for other readers to still have a read lock when one thread is releasing it.

Solaris 2.5.1 and earlier releases use a different wakeup policy, which was designed as an "always favor writers" policy. The code path when a thread was releasing an RW lock would basically look for waiting writers first and always grant the lock to a waiting writer, regardless of whether a reader or writer was releasing the lock and regardless of the priority of the readers versus the writers if both were waiting on the lock.

The final point to make here is that not only did the policy change in Solaris 2.6 and 7 with respect to the wakeup selection, but so did the method with which threads coming off the turnstile acquire the lock. In Solaris 2.5.1, the threads, once woken up, are scheduled, executed, and resumed in the `rw_enter()` to get the lock. Solaris 2.6 and Solaris 7 implement a direct handoff mechanism, where threads are given ownership of the lock before sleep queue removal and state change.

3.7   Turnstiles and Priority Inheritance

A turnstile is a data abstraction that encapsulates sleep queues and priority inheritance information associated with mutex locks and reader/writer locks. The mutex and RW lock code use a turnstile when a kernel thread needs to block on a requested lock. The sleep queues implemented for other resource waits do not provide an elegant method of dealing with the priority inversion problem through priority inheritance. Turnstiles were created to address that problem.

Priority inversion describes a scenario in which a higher-priority thread is unable to run because a lower-priority thread is holding a resource it needs, such as a lock. The Solaris kernel addresses the priority inversion problem in its turnstile implementation, providing a *priority inheritance* mechanism, where the higher-priority thread can *will* its priority to the lower-priority thread holding the resource it requires. The beneficiary of the inheritance, the thread holding the resource, will now have a higher scheduling priority and thus get scheduled to run sooner so it can finish its work and release the resource, at which point the original priority is returned to the thread.

In this section, we assume you have some level of knowledge of kernel thread priorities, which are covered in Chapter 6, "Kernel Memory." Because turnstiles and priority inheritance are an integral part of the implementation of mutex and RW locks, we thought it best to discuss them here rather than later. For this discussion, it is important to be aware of these points:

- The Solaris kernel assigns a global priority to kernel threads, based on the scheduling class they belong to.
- Kernel threads in the timeshare and interactive scheduling classes will have their priorities adjusted over time, based on three things: the amount of time the threads spend running on a processor, sleep time (blocking), and the case when they are preempted. Threads in the real-time class are fixed priority; the priorities are never changed regardless of runtime or sleep time unless explicitly changed through programming interfaces or commands.

The Solaris kernel implements sleep queues for the placement of kernel threads blocking on (waiting for) a resource or event. For most resource waits, such as those for a disk or network I/O, sleep queues, in conjunction with condition variables, manage the systemwide queue of sleeping threads. These sleep queues are covered in Chapter 6, "Kernel Memory." This set of sleep queues is separate and distinct from turnstile sleep queues.

The implementation of turnstiles was changed substantially in Solaris 7, although the underlying premise and concepts are the same. We will begin with a look at the turnstile implementation in Solaris 7.

3.7.1 Solaris 7 Turnstiles

Figure 3.12 illustrates the Solaris 7 turnstiles. The rewrite of turnstiles in Solaris 7 resulted in a significant amount of code being removed, and some new, more efficient functions being developed.

Turnstiles are maintained in a systemwide hash table, `turnstile_table[]`, which is an array of `turnstile_chain` structures; each entry in the array (each `turnstile_chain` structure) is the beginning of a linked list of turnstiles. The array is indexed via a hash function on the address of the synchronization object (the mutex or reader/writer lock), so locks that hash to the same array location will have a turnstile on the same linked list. The `turnstile_table[]` array is statically initialized at boot time.

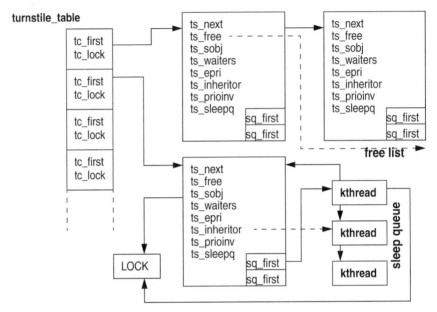

Figure 3.12 Solaris 7 Turnstiles

Each entry in the chain has its own lock, `tc_lock`, so chains can be traversed concurrently. The turnstile itself has a different lock; each chain has an active list (`ts_next`) and a free list (`ts_free`). There are also a count of threads waiting on the sync object (`waiters`), a pointer to the synchronization object (`ts_sobj`), a thread pointer linking to a kernel thread that had a priority boost through priority inheritance, and the sleep queues. Each turnstile has two sleep queues, one for readers and one for writers (threads blocking on a read/write lock are maintained on separate sleep queues). The priority inheritance data is integrated into the turnstile, as opposed to being maintained in a separate data structure (which is what Solaris 2.6 and 2.5.1 do).

In Solaris 7, every kernel thread is *born* with an attached turnstile. That is, when a kernel thread is created (by the kernel `thread_create()` routine), a turnstile is allocated for the kthread and linked to kthread's `t_ts` pointer. A kthread can block on only one lock at a time, so one turnstile is sufficient.

We know from the previous sections on mutex and RW locks that a turnstile is required if a thread needs to block on a synchronization object. Solaris 7 calls `turnstile_lookup()` to look up the turnstile for the synchronization object in the `turnstile_table[]`. Since we index the array by hashing on the address of the lock, if a turnstile already exists (there are already waiters), then we get the correct turnstile. If no kthreads are currently waiting for the lock, `turnstile_lookup()` simply returns a null value. If the blocking code must be called (recall from the previous sections that subsequent tests are made on lock availability before it is determined that the kthread must block), then `turnstile_block()` is entered to place the kernel thread on a sleep queue associated with the turnstile for the lock.

Kernel threads *lend* their attached turnstile to the lock when a kthread becomes the first to block (the lock acquisition attempt fails, and there are no waiters). The thread's turnstile is added to the appropriate turnstile chain, based on the result of a hashing function on the address of the lock. The lock now has a turnstile, so subsequent threads that block on the same lock will donate their turnstiles to the free list on the chain (the `ts_free` link off the active turnstile).

In `turnstile_block()`, the pointers are set up as determined by the return from `turnstile_lookup()`. If the turnstile pointer is null, we link up to the turnstile pointed to by the kernel thread's `t_ts` pointer. If the pointer returned from the lookup is not null, there's already at least one kthread waiting on the lock, so the code sets up the pointer links appropriately and places the kthread's turnstile on the free list.

The thread is then put into a sleep state through the scheduling-class-specific sleep routine (e.g., `ts_sleep()`). The `ts_waiters` field in the turnstile is incremented, the threads `t_wchan` is set to the address of the lock, and `t_sobj_ops` in the thread is set to the address of the lock's operations vectors: the `owner`, `unsleep`, and `change_priority` functions. The kernel `sleepq_insert()` function actually places the thread on the sleep queue associated with the turnstile.

The code does the priority inversion check (now called out of the `turnstile_block()` code), builds the priority inversion links, and applies the necessary priority changes. The priority inheritance rules apply; that is, if the priority of the lock holder is less (worse) than the priority of the requesting thread, the requesting thread's priority is "willed" to the holder. The holder's `t_epri` field is set to the new priority, and the inheritor pointer in the turnstile is linked to the kernel thread. All the threads on the blocking chain are potential inheritors, based on their priority relative to the calling thread.

At this point, the dispatcher is entered through a call to `swtch()`, and another kernel thread is removed from a dispatch queue and context-switched onto a processor.

The wakeup mechanics are initiated as previously described, where a call to the lock exit routine results in a `turnstile_wakeup()` call if threads are blocking on the lock. `turnstile_wakeup()` does essentially the reverse of `turnstile_block()`; threads that inherited a better priority have that priority waived, and the thread is removed from the sleep queue and given a turnstile from the chain's free list. Recall that a thread donated its turnstile to the free list if it was not the first thread placed on the blocking chain for the lock; coming off the turnstile, threads get a turnstile back. Once the thread is unlinked from the sleep queue, the scheduling class wakeup code is entered, and the thread is put back on a processor's dispatch queue.

3.7.2 Solaris 2.5.1 and 2.6 Turnstiles

Figure 3.13 illustrates the turnstile structures and links in Solaris 2.5.1 and 2.6.

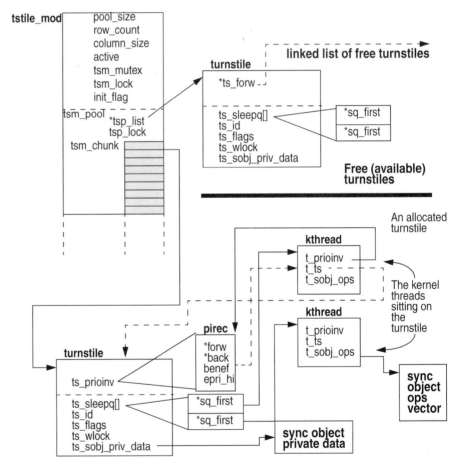

Figure 3.13 Solaris 2.5.1 and Solaris 2.6 Turnstiles

The `tstile_mod` structure is where it all begins. There is one `tstile_mod` systemwide, and it maintains the links to the turnstiles. It also maintains various fields required to support the implementation, such as the number of turnstiles in the pool (pool_size), number of active rows in the tsm_chunk array (active), a link to the pool of turnstiles, and an array of pointers to turnstiles (tsm_chunk[]—these are the active turnstiles).

The tsm_mutex lock is used to protect tstile_mod only when more turnstiles need to be allocated. Other turnstile support functions do not need to acquire tsm_mutex.

The turnstile itself contains a forward link to other turnstiles on the list *or* to a structure with priority inheritance information (pirec). These data items are part of the same union in the structure definition. Thus, a free turnstile will have the forward link, and a used turnstile will contain the pirec structure. Each turnstile has a unique ID, ts_id, that encodes row and column information used to locate the turnstile in the tsm_chunk[] array. (tsm_chunk[] is actually implemented as a two-dimensional array, as we'll see in a minute.)

Additionally, in each turnstile is an array with two sleep queues (ts_sleepq[]). For RW locks, readers and writers are kept on separate sleep queues. For mutex locks, one sleep queue is used. Other links that bind it all together include kernel thread links to the turnstile, set when a kthread is blocking on a synchronization object, and a pointer from the kthread to the pirec structure if the priority of the kernel thread was changed by priority inversion. The benef field of pirec points back to the kernel thread that is the recipient (beneficiary) of a better priority because of inheritance. ts_flags specifies whether the turnstile is either free or active, and ts_wlock is a dispatcher-style lock used by the mutex code to synchronize access to the turnstile.

The kernel creates a small pool of turnstiles at boot time and allocates a turnstile from the pool when a thread needs to block on a mutex or RW lock. The tstile_init() function is called from the startup code during boot to initialize a set of turnstiles with which to get started. The allocation is done in chunks of 128 turnstiles, each chunk (column) attached off a different index in the tsm_chunk[] array (the row). The row/column combination serves as the turnstile ID, determines the placement of the turnstile in the array of active turnstiles, and is established as each chunk is initialized. Figure 3.14 provides the big picture.

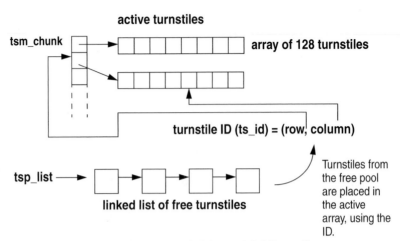

Figure 3.14 Solaris 2.5.1 and 2.6 Turnstiles

Turnstiles are allocated from the free pool (`tsp_list`) and placed in the `tsm_chunk` array when activated. The turnstile is returned to the available pool when no more threads are sleeping on the synchronization object. The kernel attempts to maintain a pool of turnstiles that keeps pace with the number of kernel threads on the system by looking at the turnstile pool every time the internal `thread_create()` function is called to create a new kernel thread. If the number of kernel threads is greater than the number of turnstiles in the pool when a kernel thread is created, then the code dynamically allocates another chunk of turnstiles. This is somewhat different from the Solaris 7 implementation, where a turnstile is created and linked to every kernel thread when the kernel thread is created. Conceptually, it addresses the same problem of having a sufficient number of turnstiles available at all times.

The turnstile functions called by the mutex and RW lock code to put a thread to sleep work as follows. The mutex and RW locks each contain a reference to a turnstile for the synchronization object, which we'll refer to generically as *waiters* in this discussion.

- If the `waiters` field in the lock is 0 (no waiters), then a turnstile is allocated from the pool by `tstile_alloc()`, which simply allocates a turnstile off the `tsp_list` pointer (the free pool link) after setting the pool lock, `tsp_lock`.
- The active counter is incremented, the pool lock is released, and the `pirec` structure associated with the new turnstile is cleared.
- The `waiters` field in the lock is set to the turnstile ID of the turnstile just allocated, and the turnstile's `ts_sobj_priv_data` (turnstile synchronization object private data) field is set to point to the address of the lock structure.

- If threads (at least one other) are already waiting for the mutex, then a turnstile already exists, so the address of the turnstile that has already been allocated for the mutex is retrieved with the `tstile_pointer()` function, which uses the turnstile ID in the `waiters` field of the lock to locate the turnstile in the `tsm_chunk` array.

With a turnstile for the lock now ready, we can proceed with changing the thread state to sleep and setting up the sleep queue associated with the turnstile.

- The kernel `t_block()` function is called and invokes the `CL_SLEEP` macro.
- Scheduling-class-specific functions are invoked by macros that resolve to the proper function, based on the scheduling class of the kernel thread. In the case of a timeshare or interactive class thread, the `ts_sleep()` function is called to set the thread's priority to a `SYS` priority (a priority boost for when it wakes up—it will run before other timeshare and interactive class threads) and to set the thread state to `TS_SLEEP`.
- The kernel thread's `t_wchan` field (wait channel) is set to the address of the lock the thread is waiting for, and the thread's `t_sobj_ops` pointer is set to the lock's synchronization object operations vector. (See "Synchronization Object Operations Vector" on page 70.)
- Finally, the thread's `t_ts` field is set to the address of the turnstile, and the thread is inserted on the turnstile's sleep queue.

  The generic kernel sleep queue functions are invoked indirectly through macros defined in the turnstile header file; for example, insertion of the thread on a sleep queue is done through the `TSTILE_INSERT` macro, which calls the kernel `sleepq_insert()` function.

- When `sleepq_insert()` completes, the kernel thread resides in the sleep queue associated with the turnstile. A kernel thread can be blocked only on one, and no more than one, synchronization object at any time, so `t_ts` will either be a `NULL` pointer or a pointer to one turnstile.

All that remains to be done is the priority inheritance check to determine if the thread holding the lock is at a lower (worse) priority than the thread requesting the lock (the one that was just placed on a turnstile sleep queue).

- The kernel `pi_willto()` function is called to check the priority of the lock owner against the thread waiting.
  - If the owner priority is greater than the waiter priority, we do not have a priority inversion condition and the code just bails out.
  - If the waiter priority is greater (a better priority) than the owner, we do have a priority inversion condition; then, the priority of the lock owner is set to the priority of the waiter.

- The t_epri field of the kernel thread is used for inherited priorities. A non-null value in t_epri results in the inherited priority of the thread being used the next time the lock owner's priority is adjusted (when we enter the dispatcher through an explicit call to the swtch() function).

At this point, the turnstile has been set, with the waiting thread on the turnstile's sleep queue, and a potential priority inversion problem has been checked for a priority inheritance if needed.

- The kernel now enters the dispatcher through the swtch() function to resume scheduling threads.

- When a thread has finished working in the protected data region, it calls the appropriate lock exit routine (mutex_exit() or rw_exit()) to free the lock, which in turn triggers the wakeup mechanism if threads are waiting for the lock.

- The release function checks the waiters field maintained in the synchronization object.

    As with mutex and RW locks, the decision on which thread to wake up or whether to wake all the waiting threads varies depending on the synchronization object and the version of the Solaris kernel. We examined what happens in each circumstance in the sections on mutex and RW locks.

The turnstile support functions used in Solaris 2.5.1 are t_release() for waking a single thread and t_release_all() for waking all the threads. Solaris 2.6 uses macros instead (e.g., TSTILE_WAKEONE), which have the same net effect. That is, the macros result in entering the generic sleep queue code, which has a corresponding function for removing either one thread or all threads from a sleep queue (e.g., sleepq_wakeone() to wake one thread). Prior to issuing the wakeup, the lock code checks for priority inheritance. If the thread releasing the lock was a beneficiary of priority inheritance, then the pi_waive() function is called to change the thread's priority back to what it was before the inheritance.

The wakeup code unlinks the kernel thread (or threads) from the sleep queue and calls the scheduling-class-specific wakeup code (e.g., ts_wakeup() for timeshare and interactive threads). If the thread has been given a SYS class priority (kernel mode priority), the thread is immediately placed on a dispatch queue in the class wakeup function. If not, the thread's global priority is recalculated before the thread is placed on a dispatch queue.

3.8 Dispatcher Locks

The kernel defines lock types that are specific to the kernel dispatcher (threads scheduler), referred to as *dispatcher locks*. Two lock types are implemented for the dispatcher: simple spin locks and locks that raise the interrupt priority level of the processor. These locks are acquired and released by interfaces specific to the lock types (not the previously discussed mutex interfaces). They are also used in a few other areas of the kernel where the requirements for locking warrant the semantics and behavior defined by these locks. We first discuss why the second type of lock, a lock that blocks interrupts, is necessary and then discuss the implementation.

When an interrupt is generated and sent to a processor, the processor must stop what it's doing and execute an interrupt handler. For low-level interrupts (below level 10 on SPARC systems), interrupts are handled on an interrupt thread. Whatever thread was executing when the interrupt is received is pinned, such that the interrupt thread can borrow the running thread's LWP; the interrupt thread executes using its own stack. When the handler is done, the interrupted kernel thread is unpinned and can resume execution. Once executing the interrupt handler, it is possible that the interrupt code could block. If this happens, the dispatcher swtch() function is entered, to determine whether the thread is running as a pinned (interrupt) thread. If it is, the pinned thread is unpinned and selected to resume execution. The kernel implements a resume function, resume_from_intr(), specifically to deal with the special case of restarting a pinned thread when an interrupt thread blocks.

High-level interrupts (interrupts above level 10 on SPARC), on the other hand, *are not* handled on an interrupt thread. When an interrupt above level 10 is received by a processor, the processor is vectored directly into a handler and executes in the context of the thread that was running when the interrupt arrived. The key point here is that low-level interrupts may require a thread context switch; high-level interrupts do not.

A processor will execute at any one of the architecturally defined interrupt levels, and different processors on a multiprocessor system can be executing at different interrupt levels. The interrupt level at which a processor is executing is established by the level set in an internal hardware register. On UltraSPARC processors, the PIL field of the PSTATE register reflects the interrupt level at which the processor is running. The kernel code writes a new PIL value to the hardware PSTATE register to change the interrupt level of the processor. A processor will only receive interrupts that are at a level higher than the level at which it is currently executing. For example, a processor running at PIL 4 will take an interrupt at PIL 5 or higher, but not interrupts at levels 1, 2, or 3. Thus, processors are able to *mask* or *block* interrupts by setting the PIL to the appropriate level, depending on what level of interrupts the processor needs to block.

The kernel dispatcher (threads scheduler) does the selection and context switching of threads and manipulates the dispatch queues. Hence, a protection mechanism is required to prevent the dispatcher from being interrupted while doing queue insertion or removal. Since low-level interrupts may require a context switch, allowing a processor executing in the dispatcher code to take an interrupt and switch to an interrupt handler could result in corruption of the thread state and queue pointers. For this reason, a type of dispatcher lock is implemented. The lock code is called from various places by the dispatcher that not only acquires a spin lock (typically, a lock protecting the dispatch queue) but that also raises the PIL to 10, effectively blocking low-level interrupts. Only high-level interrupts, which are not permitted to require or cause a context switch, are fielded.

The implementation does not define two different lock structures for spin locks and locks that block interrupts. In both cases, the lock definition is a 1-byte data item. The code either acquires a basic spin lock or acquires a lock *and* raises the PIL, based on which interface it calls. A simple `lock_set()` interface is called to acquire a dispatcher spin lock. The code is implemented in assembly language and follows the fundamental algorithm for spin locks.

If the lock is held when an attempt to get the lock is made, a spin loop is used, checking the lock and attempting to acquire it in each pass through the loop. For interrupt protection, the `lock_set_spl()` interface is called. `lock_set_spl()` raises the PIL of the calling processor to 10 and essentially uses the same spin algorithm as the basic spin lock. The PIL of the processor remains elevated until the lock is released. The `lock_set_spl()` code saves the current PIL of the calling process so that when the lock is released, the calling process can be restored to the level at which it was executing.

Areas of the kernel that use dispatcher locks, aside from the dispatcher itself, are the other kernel synchronization primitives: that is, mutex locks, reader/writer locks, turnstiles, and semaphores. The synchronization primitive kernel modules use dispatcher locks when manipulating threads on turnstiles or sleep queues or when protecting access to a particular data item in a lock structure.

As the Solaris releases evolve, improvements are continually made, and the use of dispatcher locks has been reduced with each successive release. For example, Solaris 2.5.1 and 2.6 implement a dispatcher lock in the reader/writer (RW) lock structure to protect access to some fields in the structure. Solaris 7, with a reworking of the RW lock code, no longer requires a dispatcher lock in this area.

3.9   Kernel Semaphores

Semaphores provide a method of synchronizing access to a sharable resource by multiple processes or threads. A semaphore can be used as a binary lock for exclusive access or as a counter, allowing for concurrent access by multiple threads to a finite number of shared resources.

In the counter implementation, the semaphore value is initialized to the number of shared resources (these semaphores are sometimes referred to as counting semaphores). Each time a process needs a resource, the semaphore value is decremented to indicate there is one less of the resource. When the process is finished with the resource, the semaphore value is incremented. A 0 semaphore value tells the calling process that no resources are currently available, and the calling process blocks until another process finishes using the resource and frees it. These functions are historically referred to as semaphore P and V operations—the P operation attempts to acquire the semaphore, and the V operation releases it.

The Solaris kernel uses semaphores where appropriate, when the constraints for atomicity on lock acquisition are not as stringent as they are in the areas where mutex and RW locks are used. Also, the counting functionality that semaphores provide makes them a good fit for things like the allocation and deallocation of a fixed amount of a resource.

The kernel semaphore structure maintains a sleep queue for the semaphore and a count field that reflects the value of the semaphore, shown in Figure 3.15. The figure illustrates the look of a kernel semaphore for all Solaris releases covered in this book.

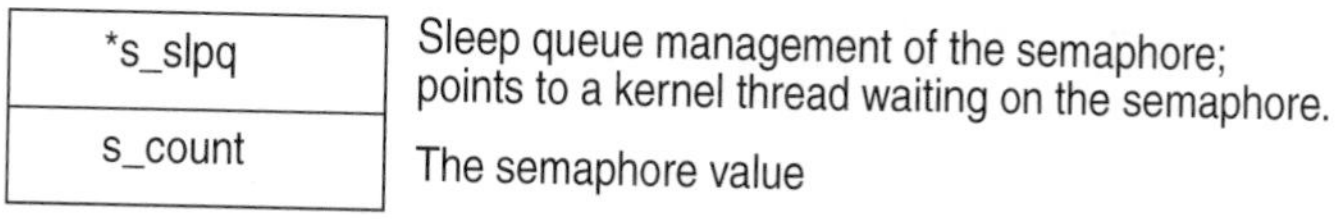

*s_slpq	Sleep queue management of the semaphore; points to a kernel thread waiting on the semaphore.
s_count	The semaphore value

Figure 3.15 Kernel Semaphore

Kernel functions for semaphores include an initialization routine (sema_init()), a destroy function (sema_destroy()), the traditional P and V operations (sema_p() and sema_v()), and a test function (is the semaphore held? sema_held()). There are a few other support functions, as well as some variations on the sema_p() function, which we will discuss later.

The init function simply sets the count value in the semaphore, based on the value passed as an argument to the sema_init() routine. The s_slpq pointer is set to NULL, and the semaphore is initialized. The sema_destroy() function is used when the semaphore is an integral part of a resource that is dynamically created and destroyed as the resource gets used and subsequently released. For example, the bio (block I/O) subsystem in the kernel, which manages buf structures for page I/O support through the file system, uses semaphores on a per-buf structure basis. Each buffer has two semaphores, which are initialized when a buffer is allocated by sema_init(). Once the I/O is completed and the buffer is released, sema_destroy() is called as part of the buffer release code. (sema_destroy() just nulls the s_slpq pointer.)

Kernel threads that must access a resource controlled by a semaphore call the sema_p() function, which requires that the semaphore count value be greater than 0 in order to return success. If the count is 0, then the semaphore is not available and the calling thread must block. If the count is greater than 0, then the count is decremented in the semaphore and the code returns to the caller. Otherwise, a sleep queue is located from the systemwide array of sleep queues, the thread state is changed to sleep, and the thread is placed on the sleep queue. Note that turnstiles are not used for semaphores—turnstiles are an implementation of sleep queues specifically for mutex and RW locks. Kernel threads blocked on anything other than mutexes and RW locks are placed on sleep queues.

Sleep queues are discussed in more detail in Chapter 6, "Kernel Memory." Briefly though, sleep queues are organized as a linked list of kernel threads, and each linked list is rooted in an array referenced through a `sleepq_head` kernel pointer. Some changes were made in Solaris 7 to facilitate faster sleep queue operations: insertion, removal, and queue traversal. In Solaris releases prior to Solaris 7, an entry in the `sleepq_head` array begins a linked list of kernel threads waiting on the same object. The list is singly linked by the kernel thread's `t_link` pointer. In Solaris 7, several additional pointers were added to the kernel thread to support a doubly linked sublist of threads at the same priority. Figure 3.16 illustrates how sleep queues are organized.

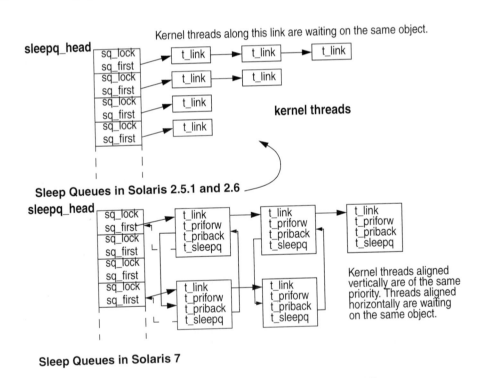

Figure 3.16 Sleep Queues in Solaris 2.5.1, 2.6, and 7

In all pre- and post-Solaris 7 implementations, a hashing function indexes the `sleepq_head` array, hashing on the address of the object. In the pre-Solaris 7 implementations, kernel threads are inserted on the list in descending order based on their priority. In Solaris 7, the singly linked list that establishes the beginning of the doubly linked sublists of kthreads at the same priority is also in ascending order based on priority. The sublist is implemented with a `t_priforw` (forward pointer) and `t_priback` (previous pointer) in the kernel thread. Also, a `t_sleepq` pointer added in Solaris 7 points back to the array entry in `sleepq_head`, identifying which sleep queue the thread is on and providing a quick method to determine if a thread is on a sleep queue at all; if the thread's `t_sleepq` pointer is `NULL`, then the thread is not on a sleep queue.

Inside the `sema_p()` function, if we have a semaphore count value of 0, the semaphore is not available and the calling kernel thread needs to be placed on a sleep queue. A sleep queue is located through a hash function into the `sleep_head` array, which hashes on the address of the object the thread is blocking, in this case, the address of the semaphore. The code also grabs the sleep queue lock, `sq_lock` (see Figure 3.16) to block any further inserts or removals from the sleep queue until the insertion of the current kernel thread has been completed (that's what locks are for!).

The scheduling-class-specific sleep function is called to set the thread wakeup priority and to change the thread state from `ONPROC` (running on a processor) to `SLEEP`. The kernel thread's `t_wchan` (wait channel) pointer is set to the address of the semaphore it's blocking on, and the thread's `t_sobj_ops` pointer is set to reference the `sema_sobj_ops` structure. The thread is now in a sleep state on a sleep queue.

A semaphore is released by the `sema_v()` function, which has the exact opposite effect of `sema_p()` and behaves very much like the lock release functions we've examined up to this point. The semaphore value is incremented, and if any threads are sleeping on the semaphore, the one that has been sitting on the sleep queue longest will be woken up. Semaphore wakeups always involve waking one waiter at a time.

Semaphores are used in relatively few areas of the operating system: the buffer I/O (`bio`) module, the dynamically loadable kernel module code, and a couple of device drivers.

4

KERNEL BOOTSTRAP AND INITIALIZATION

In the previous chapters, we provided a description of the Solaris kernel and an overview of the key features and facilities of the operating system. We emphasized the modular and dynamic nature of the kernel because the Solaris kernel does not originate on disk as a single, monolithic binary object. Rather, the kernel is constructed in memory, during system bootstrap, as major operating system components are loaded.

Kernel objects load both at boot time and while the system is running. In this chapter, we take a look at the directory hierarchy that stores binary kernel objects. We then discuss the kernel bootstrap and initialization process, the dynamic module loading facility, and the kernel runtime linker.

4.1 Kernel Directory Hierarchy

The binary object modules that make up the Solaris kernel exist in a well-defined directory name space in the root and usr file systems. The system directory names are described in Table 4-1.

Table 4-1 System Directories

Directory Name	Description
root (/)	Beginning of the system directory name space
/kernel	Subdirectory tree with platform-independent loadable kernel modules
/platform	Subdirectory tree with platform-dependent loadable kernel modules
The following directories are not subdirectories under root (/). Rather, they are directory names that hold specific types of kernel objects and exist as subdirectories under several top-level directories, such as /kernel, /platform/<arch>) and /usr/kernel. Refer to Figure 4.1.	
sparcv9	*Solaris 7 and later.* The directory name space uses the sparcv9 subdirectory name to store all 64-bit kernel objects
drv	Device drivers
exec	Executable object file routines
fs	File system modules
misc	Miscellaneous modules
sched	Scheduling classes
strmod	STREAMS module support
sys	System calls

The core modules that make up the minimum required for a usable system are split across multiple directories. All kernel modules will be in one of three possible categories that determine their placement in the directory hierarchy: platform and hardware independent, platform dependent, or hardware class dependent. The /kernel directory tree contains operating system modules that are platform independent, including the genunix executable object that is loaded initially at boot time.

The two remaining directory trees are categorized as *hardware-class* dependent and *platform* dependent. The hardware-class is derived from the processor type, in conjunction with the processor-to-memory bus architecture. UltraSPARC-based systems have a *sun4u* hardware class; all such systems use the Ultra Port Architecture (UPA) as the primary processor interconnect. Hardware classes *sun4m* and *sun4d* are systems based on the SuperSPARC (SPARC Version 8), which uses the Mbus (sun4m) interconnect on smaller systems and the XDBus on the larger server systems. You can determine the hardware-class of a system by using the uname(1) command with the -m option.

The platform category is the specific machine type: the type of system, preceded by a SUNW for Sun-based platforms. Examples include SUNW,Ultra-2 and SUNW,Ultra Enterprise-10000. Kernel modules that deal specifically with "box" dependencies, such as environmental controls and interconnect-specific support, reside in the directory tree beginning with /platform/<*platform-name*>. Figure 4.1 shows the directory hierarchy.

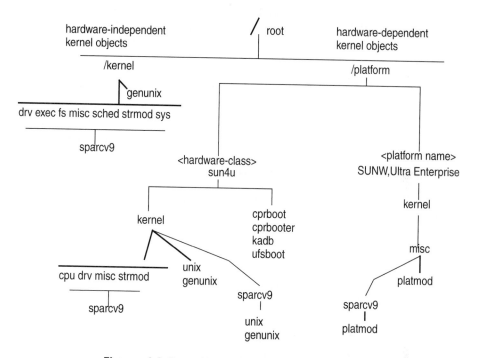

Figure 4.1 Core Kernel Directory Hierarchy

For illustration, we use a specific platform (SUNW,UltraEnterprise) and hardware class (sun4u, which is all UltraSPARC processors) in the example directory tree in Figure 4.1. The modules in these directories make up all the components that are loaded at boot time and are required for a fully functional system.

Other loadable kernel modules are located under the /usr directory tree, which also contains a kernel (/usr/kernel) and platform (/usr/platform) set of subdirectories. The modules under these directories are kernel modules that are loaded as needed: either on demand, as a result of a user or application process requesting a service that requires the loading of one of the modules, or manually with the modload(1M) command. For example, the kernel *exec* support for executing code written in the Java programming language is in /usr/kernel/exec and has the file name javaexec. This module is loaded by the kernel the first time a Java program is started on the system. Note that you can instruct the system to load optional modules at boot time by using the forceload directive in the /etc/system kernel configuration file.

The full path names of the core executable files that form the nucleus of the kernel are listed below.

- `/platform/<arch>/kernel/unix` — The platform-dependent component of the core kernel.

- `/platform/sun4u/kernel/genunix` — A genunix binary optimized for UltraSPARC, but independent of the system (box) type. Only Ultra-SPARC-based systems load this particular binary.

- `/kernel/genunix` — Platform-independent (generic) core kernel code. Only non-UltraSPARC-based systems load this file.

Note that only one genunix binary gets loaded at boot time: either the Ultra-SPARC version on sun4u hardware or the `/kernel/genunix` image on all other SPARC systems. These objects contain all the low-level kernel services and other facilities that need to be memory resident to properly initialize the system and support the dynamic load environment.

Included within the unix and genunix images are the memory management routines, callback and callout facilities, clock and timer support, kernel memory allocator, module load facility, the kernel runtime linker, synchronization primitives, kernel thread and lightweight process code, and device driver interfaces.

The remaining bits load as modules from the directories described in Table 4-1 on page 104. For a listing of the modules currently loaded in a running system, use the modinfo(1M) command.

```
# modinfo
  Id Loadaddr    Size Info Rev  Module Name
   4 f5b28000    3b30    1   1  specfs (filesystem for specfs)
   6 f5b2bb30    2bc8    1   1  TS (time sharing sched class)
   7 f5b2e6f8     4a4    -   1  TS_DPTBL (Time sharing dispatch table)
   8 f5c0e000   23548    2   1  ufs (filesystem for ufs)
  11 f5b63d08     b30    1   1  rootnex (sun4m root nexus)
  13 f5b649c0     530   62   1  dma (Direct Memory Access driver)
  14 f5b64ef0     aeb   59   1  sbus (SBus nexus driver)
  16 f5b67388    14e8   12   1  sad (Streams Administrative driver's)
  44 f5bc2d58    1eed    0   1  elfexec (exec module for elf)
  57 f5eb3000    bb40    8   1  sockfs (filesystem for sockfs)
  63 f5bd7da0    3586  201   1  doorfs (doors)
  64 f5bdb328     c3c   12   1  fdfs (filesystem for fd)
  65 f5f18000     f05   38   1  openeepr (OPENPROM/NVRAM Driver)
  72 f5bdbf68     6c6   90   1  kstat (kernel statistics driver)
  73 f6003000    d3ef   11   1  tmpfs (filesystem for tmpfs)
  91 f625f000    1ce0   52   1  shmsys (System V shared memory)
  92 f5bdefa0     268    -   1  ipc (common ipc code)
  93 f625bac0    1512    -   1  bootdev (bootdev misc module)
 106 f6a19000    587a   40   1  le (Lance Ethernet Driver v1.120)
 107 f5ff1aa8     4d1   78   1  ledma (le dma driver)
```

The sample output above is a partial listing from a running Solaris 7 system. modinfo(1M) provides the name of the kernel object and a brief description. Each kernel module has a unique identifier, shown in the Id column. The kernel virtual address (Loadaddr) and size of the module are also displayed, along with module-specific data in the Info column.

It is from the binary kernel modules that reside within these directories that the in-memory Solaris kernel is constructed.

4.2 Kernel Bootstrap and Initialization

The boot process loads the binary kernel objects that make up the Solaris kernel from a bootable system disk into physical memory, initializes the kernel structures, sets system tuneable parameters, starts system processes (daemons), and brings the system to a known, usable state. The basic steps involved in booting can be summarized as follows:

1. The `boot(1M)` command reads and loads the bootblock into memory.
2. The bootblock locates and loads the secondary boot program, `ufsboot`, into memory and passes control to it.
3. `ufsboot` locates and loads the core kernel images and the required kernel runtime linker into memory and passes control to the loaded kernel.
4. The core kernel locates and loads mandatory kernel modules from the root disk directory tree and executes the main startup code.
5. The kernel startup code executes, creating and initializing kernel structures, resources, and software components.
6. The system executes shell scripts from system directories, bringing the system up to the init state specified in the `/etc/inittab` file.

The preliminary steps shown above are based on a local disk boot. A network boot uses a different secondary boot program: `inetboot` instead of `ufsboot`. Our continuing discussion is based on a local disk boot.

4.2.1 Loading the Bootblock

The initial stage of the boot process requires support from system firmware, typically loaded in a PROM, such that a bootable device can be addressed and that some minimal I/O functionality exists for the reading of a primary bootblock.

Sun SPARC-based systems implement system firmware, known as the Open-Boot PROM (OBP), in the Forth programming language. The OBP firmware provides Power-On Self-Test (POST) functionality for hardware integrity testing, provides a Non-Volatile RAM (NVRAM) space for setting system parameters (e.g., the default boot device), builds a device tree that reflects the hardware configuration of the system, and provides bootstrap support. Intel-based systems use BIOS-based firmware that provides similar functionality. Our coverage here focuses on SPARC-based systems, although much of the initialization process is hardware independent once the secondary boot phase has completed and the kernel is loaded.

On a system that has completed its POST tests, the boot process is initiated either with an explicit boot(1M) command at the OBP prompt or, if the auto-boot? NVRAM variable is set to true, initiating an automatic boot when the system is powered up. The boot(1M) command supports several options, including specifying a boot device and bootfile on the command line (something other than the default), flagging a boot into the kernel debugger (kadb), running the boot in a more verbose mode for more output, etc. Refer to the manual page on boot(1M) for specifics.

On SPARC systems using the default UNIX file system (UFS) for the root file system (a.k.a. the system disk), the bootblock is located on physical disk sectors 1–15, as shown in Figure 4.2. The blocks are labeled as sectors 0 through 16 to distinguish them from file system blocks. Physical sectors on a disk are 512 bytes in size, whereas file system blocks are typically a grouping of some number of physical disk sectors (16 in UFS, for a default file system block size of 8 Kbytes).

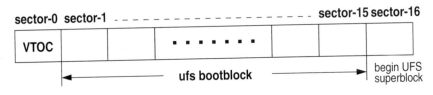

Figure 4.2 Bootblock on a UFS-Based System Disk

Sector 0, the Virtual Table Of Contents (VTOC), contains the disk partition information: the starting and ending block numbers for each of eight possible on-disk partitions. Sector 16 is where a UFS puts the primary superblock (file system metadata).

The Solaris environment provides an installboot(1M) command, which adds or restores a bootblock to a system partition. The bootblock code is maintained in the /usr/platform/<arch>/lib/fs/ufs/bootblk file. The installboot(1M) utility just uses dd(1) to copy this file to the specified disk partition. The size of the bootblock is constrained (it cannot be larger than 7,680 bytes—15 sectors at 512 bytes each), so it is the bare minimum amount of code required to read a directory in a UFS, locate a file, and load it into memory.

4.2.2 Loading ufsboot

The secondary bootfile name, ufsboot, is hardcoded into the bootblock code for a UFS boot; the full path name for ufsboot is /platform/<arch>/ufsboot. (In early Solaris versions, up to and including Solaris 2.4, ufsboot was located in the root directory, /ufsboot.)

Note that the references to <arch> indicate that for this field in the path name, you should substitute the output from uname -m, which displays the hardware class of the system (e.g., sun4u, sun4m, x86, etc.).

4.2.3 Locating Core Kernel Images and Linker

ufsboot, once loaded, locates the kernel image, unix, and the required runtime linker, krtld. The full path name of the first kernel binary loaded by ufsboot is /platform/<arch>/kernel/unix (e.g., /platform/sun4u/kernel/unix on UltraSPARC-based systems). The unix file is an Executable and Linking Format (ELF) binary file, the industry-standard file format for executable binary files on UNIX systems. In an ELF file, specific bits of header information need to be examined to determine things like the execution dependencies. ufsboot knows about ELF files—how to interpret the header information and how to extract the dependencies. Based on information in the unix ELF headers, ufsboot loads the required kernel runtime linker, /kernel/misc/krtld.

4.2.4 Loading Kernel Modules

Control is passed to krtld, which notes dependencies on additional binary object files. Below is the partial output of the dump(1) command on the /platform/sun4u/kernel/unix file, illustrating the dependency listing of the unix binary.

```
# pwd
/platform/sun4u/kernel
# /usr/ccs/bin/dump -Lv unix

unix:

    **** DYNAMIC SECTION INFORMATION ****
.dynamic:
[INDEX] Tag           Value
[1]     NEEDED        genunix
[2]     NEEDED        misc/platmod
[3]     NEEDED        cpu/$CPU
[4]     HASH          0x114
...
```

The dump(1M) flags shown dump the dynamic section of an ELF object file. Not listed is the PT_INTERP entry, which in this case is misc/krtld.

First is the genunix binary, located in /kernel/genunix for all non-Ultra-SPARC-based platforms, or /platform/sun4u/kernel/genunix for all Ultra-SPARC (sun4u) platforms. The remaining dependencies are /platform/<arch>/kernel/misc/platmod and /platform/<arch>/kernel/cpu/$CPU, which are platform- and processor-specific binaries that are part of the core kernel. The $CPU symbol is set to the specific processor type by the OBP firmware and expands properly when krtld resolves the symbol. krtld uses a module search path variable, which is similar to the traditional UNIX shell PATH variable; the module search path specifies the directory names to be searched for dynamically loadable kernel modules. The module search path variable is set by the OBP firmware and differs slightly across different hardware platforms (the search path can be specified by being booted with boot -a). As krtld encounters binary object dependencies, it searches directories specified in the module search path.

Figure 4.3 illustrates the boot flow up to this point, using the sun4u (Ultra-SPARC) directory hierarchy for the example.

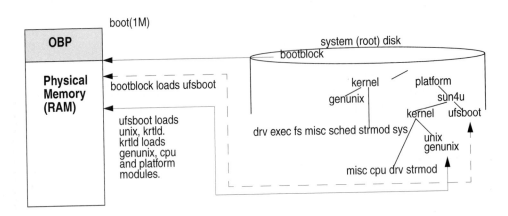

Figure 4.3 Boot Process

4.2.5 Creating Kernel Structures, Resources, and Components

With all the core binary objects (unix, krtld, genunix, platmod, and the $CPU module) loaded into memory and linked, krtld passes control to unix, which is loaded near the top of physical memory space, to take over execution. The Solaris kernel is now running, the Memory Management Unit (MMU) is enabled (the code is generating virtual addresses and working in virtual address space), and the first 16 megabytes of memory are mapped. unix does some low-level setup of processor registers, begins hand-crafting kernel thread 0, and calls an architecture-specific startup function, mlsetup(). mlsetup() completes the initialization of kernel thread 0 and LWP 0, builds the first process (p0), and begins mapping system devices according to device information in the OBP space.

The EEPROM on SPARC systems, which holds the OBP code, is one of the early devices mapped. That is, the eeprom occupies a part of the system's physical address space, much like a physical device. A kernel software layer is initialized, very similar to a device driver, allowing other areas of the kernel to call into the PROM. Calls into the PROM are required during the boot process for a variety of reasons, such as the retrieval of hardware and version information.

With the mlsetup() work done, the kernel main() function is entered, which is where the code begins a sequence of function calls into the higher-level areas of the kernel to continue the initialization process. The main() function is part of the kernel hardware-independent code. It immediately calls into hardware-specific routines for specific initialization steps, then returns to the common code to complete the boot process.

The platform-specific `startup()` function does some preliminary memory initialization: determining available physical memory after the core kernel is loaded, setting up of the kernel address space symbols, and allocating memory page structure. The kernel memory allocation (KVM) subsystem and the kernel `kstat` (kernel statistics) framework are initialized Once these steps are completed, the operating system banner is displayed on the console:

```
SunOS Release 5.7 Version Generic 64-bit [UNIX(R) System V Release 4.0]
Copyright (c) 1983-1998, Sun Microsystems, Inc.
```

Additional platform-specific checking is done on processor types, firmware versions, etc., and the kernel `mod_read_system_file()` function is called to read the `/etc/system` file and populate internal data structures with the parameters and values set in `/etc/system`.

The kernel creates a linked list of `sysparam` data structures, such that each entry on the `/etc/system` file has a corresponding data structure in the list. The `sysparam` structure is defined in `/usr/include/sys/sysconf.h`, and is shown below:

```
/*
 * For each entry in /etc/system a sysparam record is created.
 */
struct sysparam {
        struct sysparam *sys_next; /* pointer to next */
        int        sys_type;       /* type of record */
        int        sys_op;         /* operation */
        char       *sys_modnam;    /* module name (null if param in kernel) */
        char       *sys_ptr;       /* string pointer to device, etc. */
        u_longlong_t    sys_info;  /* additional information */
        char       *sys_config;    /* configuration data */
        int        sys_len;        /* len of config data */
        u_long     *addrp;         /* pointer to valloced config addresses */
};
```

Header File <sys/sysconf.h>

The fields in the `sysparam` structure are generally self-explanatory. Space is defined for parameter-specific information, the parameter type (e.g., a module load entry or an entry to set a value), and the necessary pointer to maintain the linked list. The `mod_read_sys_file()` code walks through each line on `/etc/system`, doing the necessary parsing to determine the entry types and setting the appropriate values in the `sysparam` structure that correspond to the line entry in `/etc/system`. When `mod_read_sys_file()` is finished, a linked list of populated `sysparam` structures is established in kernel memory.

Before `mod_read_sys_file()` returns, the code sets the `maxusers` value. The `maxusers` parameter is calculated on the basis of the amount of physical memory installed on the system, where `maxusers` equals the number of megabytes of RAM, to a maximum value of 1024 (which equates to 1 gigabyte of RAM—on systems with greater than 1 gigabyte of physical memory, maxusers will be 1024). If maxusers is set in /etc/system, that value is used, up to a maximum value of 2048; any /etc/system maxusers value larger than 2048 results in maxusers getting set to 2048. Once maxusers is established, the startup code sets other kernel limits, based on maxusers in the kernel param_calc() function.

- **maxpid** — Maximum process ID value. If pidmax is set in /etc/system, the pidmax value will be tested against a minimum reserved_procs value (5 in Solaris 2.5.1, 2.6, and 7) and a maximum value (30,000 in all three releases). If pidmax is less than reserved_procs or greater than 30,000, it is set to 30,000. Otherwise, the user-defined value is set.

- **max_nprocs** — Maximum number of processes, systemwide, set as (10 + 16 * maxusers).

- **maxuprc** — Maximum processes per non-root user, set as (max_nprocs - reservered_procs). reserved_procs has a default value of 5.

- **ufs_ninode and ncsize** — High limits for the UFS inode cache and directory name cache. (See "The Directory Name Lookup Cache (DNLC)" on page 557.) Both of these caches are set to the same value, (4 * (max_nprocs + maxusers) + 320).

- **ndquot** — The number of UFS disk quota structures, systemwide, set as ((maxusers * 40) / 4) + max_nprocs).

As you can see, maxusers is not really the maximum number of users the system will support. It's simply a parameter that can be set to drive the number of several configurable kernel resources that indirectly affect the load or volume of users the system can handle. Many things factor in to the user load capabilities of the system, not the least of which are what constitutes a user, what a user does, and how a user connects to the system.

Other kernel parameters that are related to the STREAMS subsystem and miscellaneous areas of the system are also set at this time. These parameters use hard-coded default values that are not driven by the maxusers parameter unless a value has been set in /etc/system.

- **nstrpush** — Number of STREAMS modules that can be contained (pushed) on a single STREAM; set to 9.

- **strmsgsz** — Maximum size of a STREAMS message; set to 64 Kbytes.

- **strctlsz** — Maximum size of a STREAMS control message.

- **ngroups_max** — Maximum number of groups a user can belong to; set to 16.

- **rstchown** — A boolean that forces POSIX chown(1) behavior, where a process must have an effective UID of 0 (root) to change file ownership; set to 1 (true) by default.

- **hz, hires_hz, hires_tick** — Clock frequency controls. hz is set to 100, hires_hz to 1000, and hires_tick to 0. hz and hires_hz should not be altered. You can set hires_tick to 1 in /etc/system. Doing so results in an hz value of 1000, causing the system clock to generate a clock interrupt 1000 times a second (every millisecond) versus the default of 100 times a second (every 10 milliseconds).

- **autoup** — Age in seconds of a dirty page before fsflush will write it to disk; set to 30.

- **rlimits** — Per-process resource limits. Default values are set. Per-process file descriptor limits can be set through /etc/system, with rlim_fd_max for the maximum value and rlim_fd_cur for the current value (current can never exceed the maximum).

For a complete listing of kernel tunable parameters, see [5]. See also Appendix A, "Kernel Tunables, Switches, and Limits".

Moving along with the system initialization process: The system device name space is established in the /devices directory, based on the device tree created by the OBP firmware. The system call table is initialized, and the kernel loads the device driver classes file, /etc/driver_classes. System parameters are set in the var data structure; most of these parameters are values that we have previously discussed (e.g., max_nprocs), and others are not used in the Solaris kernel (var is a somewhat outdated SVR4 holdover). You can examine the relevant data stored in the var structure with the sysdef(1M) command or with the var function in crash(1M).

Kernel module loading occurs at various points in the boot process. During the platform-specific startup, several core modules, such as the swap, specfs, procfs and tod (time-of-day clock driver), are loaded. Other module loading occurs when a specific kernel subsystem is initialized. For example, the scheduling classes are loaded during the dispinit() function, which initializes the kernel dispatcher subsystem. These module loads (and dispinit()) occur before the platform-specific startup returns to the kernel main() function. Other loadable modules that are platform specific are loaded a little later in the process. Examples here include modules specific to the UltraEnterprise E3500 (E6500 servers that support environmental monitoring and specific control functions).

Additional virtual memory support is initialized (the HAT layer and segment drivers); the specfs and swapfs file system support modules are loaded and initialized; the root, swap and dump devices are configured; any kernel modules set for forceload in the /etc/system file are loaded; and the kernel trap table is set (traps were handled through the trap table set in the OBP up to this point). The system displays the memory values for actual, installed physical memory and available memory, that is, what's left after the kernel consumes whatever pages it requires.

```
mem = 262144K (0x10000000)
avail mem = 257785856
```

Some additional housekeeping, such as creating the interrupt threads and idle thread, is done for the boot processor, clock interrupts are enabled, and the device configuration process is completed. The code walks through the device tree, reading data from the dev_info structures created for each device and displaying the device information on the console. Several kernel initialization functions for specific subsystems, such as the callout table, buffer I/O subsystem, credentials and file cache, pseudoterminal and STREAMS support, etc., are invoked through an init table array. Several kernel daemon threads are created; the init, pageout, and fsflush processes are created; and any additional processors (MP system) are initialized.

The process creation of init, pageout, and fsflush is done by means of an internal newproc() kernel function, which gets the process table slot and process ID and does some initialization of the proc structure members. An LWP and kernel thread are also created from the newproc() function. The pageout and fsflush processes are actually part of the kernel and execute as kernel threads within the kernel's address space. The process table entries for these processes are simply placeholders, providing a user-visible view of process execution time (the TIME column from the ps(1) command).

The init process, also created with a call to newproc() from the kernel main() function, is the first real user process Solaris creates. Additional work is done by the code path entered when the initial process creation phase (newproc()) is completed. First and foremost, a user address space is allocated for the init process; it does not attach to or execute in the kernel's address space. Second, an on-disk binary file—/sbin/init—is exec'd once the process initialization is completed. The pageout and fsflush processes do not have a distinct user address space; instead, they attach to the kernel's address space. Neither is an explicit exec() function called to overlay the newly created process with a new binary image. pageout and fsflush exist as kernel functions.

Thus, init is the first genuine user process created by the system and the last process the kernel must effectively craft piece-by-piece. All further process creation to get to a running system is done by forking init, and exec'ing the appropriate binary image from disk.

4.2.6 Completing the Boot Process

The remaining phases of the boot process take place under control of the init process, which references the /etc/inittab file to determine the default init level (typically, 3) and controls the serial execution of several shell scripts in the /sbin and /etc directories. The init control and script execution sequence managed through the inittab file is not unique to Solaris and has been used in many System V-based UNIX variants for several years. As such, it is generally well understood and documented in many places.

4.2.7 During the Boot Process: Creating System Kernel Threads

During the boot process, the system creates several kernel threads that are not visible outside the operating system; they cannot be seen by examination of the /proc directory hierarchy or through the ps(1) command. They show up on the systemwide linked list of kernel threads and behave as daemon threads, called by different areas of the operating system when appropriate. These threads are only part of the multithreaded design of the Solaris kernel, and they perform very specific functions. They all execute in the SYS scheduling class and are unique in that they are the only kernel threads in the system that do not have a corresponding LWP. The kernel thread structure provides the necessary support for context information and a stack. Following is a list of the kernel threads created at boot time:

- **thread_reaper** — Cleans up exited (zombie) kernel threads placed on death row.

- **mod_uninstall_daemon** — For checkpoint/resume (CPR) support; unloads kernel modules when the system checkpoints.

- **hotplug_daemon** — Device hotplug support. Adds the dev_info node for an added device to the system device tree.

- **kmem_async_thread** — Garbage collector thread for the kernel slab allocator.

- **seg_pasync_thread** — Reclaims pagelocked pages that have not been referenced for a while.

- **ksyms_update_thread** — Updates the dynamic kernel symbol table, /dev/ksyms, as kernel modules are loaded.

- **callout_thread** — Processes the kernel callout queue by means of the clock interrupt handler.

- **cpu_pause** — Per-processor; for CPU state changes.

- **modload_thread** — Supports dynamic loading of kernel modules.

- **background** — STREAMS-based; services STREAMS queues. One of these threads is created for every CPU on a system at boot time.

- **freebs** — STREAMS-based; manages list of free STREAMS blocks. One of these threads is created for every CPU on a system at boot time.

- **qwriter_outer_thread** — STREAMS-based; processes outer STREAMS syncq messages. One of these threads is created for every CPU on a system at boot time.

All kernel threads, even those threads listed above that are part of the operating system, need a process context to execute, in order to have the required software context state (for example, an address space). Kernel threads created by the operating system are linked to process 0 (PID 0) for contextual information. Process context is discussed in detail in Chapter 5.

4.3 Kernel Module Loading and Linking

Much of the kernel architecture is layered architecture, and many of the kernel's major subsystems call into a common set of lower-level services. In some respects, the kernel architecture is similar to that of a client/server application, except that the interfaces in this case are, for the most part, private to the kernel. That is, many of the callable routines are not public interfaces available for use for general application software development. The other obvious distinction is that the users of the services, or clients, in this context, are other kernel subsystems, as opposed to application code. Exceptions to the private interface generalization are those interfaces defined for device drivers and kernel STREAMS modules, which are documented as the Solaris Device Driver Interface (DDI) specifications, found in section 9 of the manual pages.

The kernel module loading facility serves as a good example of one such service. Several phases are involved in dynamic module loading:

1. Load the module (a binary object file) into memory.
2. Establish kernel address space mappings for module segments.
3. Link the module's segments into the kernel.
4. Perform the module-type-specific *install* function.

The loadable module types are defined in /usr/include/sys/modctl.h; they are device drivers, systems calls, file systems, miscellaneous modules, streams modules, scheduling classes, and exec modules (exec support for executable objects). For each of these module types, some specific kernel installation steps are required to complete the loading process. We will take a look at these shortly.

The steps involved in loading a module into the kernel are similar conceptually to what happens when a dynamically linked program is started under Solaris. That is, shared objects to which a binary is linked are dynamically loaded into memory and linked into the process's address space during execution. The kernel exists in memory as a large, dynamically linked executable, with essentially the same address space segments that exist in any process running on the system: memory mappings for text (instructions), data (initialized and uninitialized), and a stack. Thus, loading a kernel module involves reading the target module into memory and creating the address space mappings in the kernel's address space for the module's text and data. This process is illustrated in Figure 4.4.

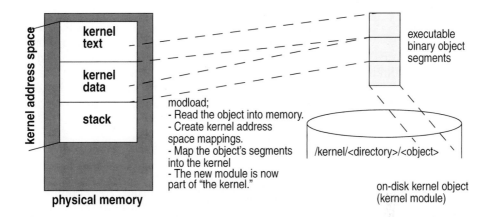

Figure 4.4 Loading a Kernel Module

The illustration in Figure 4.4 is not a precise depiction of the kernel address space or binary object segments but provides a conceptual view. Subsequent chapters describe executable objects and address space mappings in detail.

The system loads the modules required for a functional system at boot time. A path variable that defines the module search path (which directories to search for loadable modules) guides the boot code in locating the appropriate kernel objects. The kernel `modload()` function is the entry point in the code that begins the module load process. The primary data structures used in support of module loading are the `modctl` (module control) structure and `module` structure. You can find the structure definitions for `modctl` and `module` in `/usr/include/sys/modctl.h` and `/usr/include/sys/kobj.h`, respectively.

The kernel maintains a linked list of `modctl` structures for all modules in the kernel, as shown in Figure 4.5.

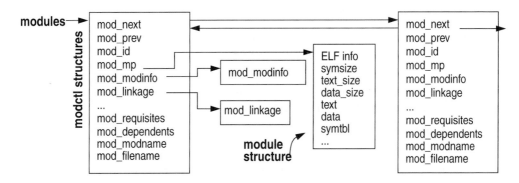

Figure 4.5 Module Control Structures

The kernel `modules` pointer marks the beginning of the doubly linked list of module control structures. Not every structure member is shown in the figure. In addition to the structure links (next and previous pointers), the module identification (`mod_id`) is maintained, along with links to a `mod_modinfo` structure and `mod_linkage` structure. `mod_mp` links to a `module` structure, defined in the kernel object linker code (`/usr/include/sys/kobj.h`) and used by the kernel runtime linker and the module load facility. Other interesting bits include character string pointers to the directory name, `mod_filename`, that holds the module and the module filename, `mod_modname`.

A given kernel module may depend on the existence of other kernel modules in order to function or may have other kernel modules depend on it. For example, the System V Interprocess Communication (IPC) modules for shared memory, semaphores, and message queues all depend on the kernel `ipc` module to function. Such dependencies are defined in the module code and maintained in the `modctl` structure by pointers in `mod_requisites` (other modules this module depends on) and `mod_dependents` (modules that depend on this one).

The kernel module loading facility is threaded. That is, when the kernel `mod_load()` function is called (during bootstrap or by the `modload(1M)` command), it creates a kernel thread to perform the module load function. The benefit here is that concurrent module loads are possible on multiprocessor systems and so provide faster system boot and initialization. Once the kernel thread is created, the following series of events is executed to complete the loading and linking of the module:

1. Create and allocate a `modctl` structure. First, search the linked list of `modctl` structures, looking for a match to the module name (`mod_modname`). If a match is found, return the address of an existing structure; otherwise, create a new one. Add a new `modctl` structure to the linked list.

2. Enter the kernel runtime linker, `krtld`, to create address space segments and bindings, and load the object into memory.

   a) Allocate `module` structure `()`.

   b) Allocate space for the module's symbols in the kernel's `kobj_map` resource map.

   c) Loop through the segments of the module being loaded, and allocate and map space for text and data.

   d) Load the kernel object into memory, linking the object's segments into the appropriate kernel address space segments.

3. Set the `mod_loaded` bit in the module's `modctl` structure, and increment the `mod_loadcnt`.

4. Create a link to the module's `mod_linkage` structure.

5. Execute the module's `mod_install` function indirectly by looking up the module `_init()` routine and calling it.

As the preceding steps indicate, the major kernel subsystems involved in module loading are the module facility and the kernel's runtime linker, krtld, which is loaded very early in the bootstrap procedure. The module subsystem does not free a modctl structure when a module in unloaded. The structure remains on the linked list, and the mod_loaded bit is cleared. This is why step 1 searched the list first; in case the module was loaded and subsequently unloaded, the modctl structure would already exist. This is also why a mod_loaded status bit is maintained—the existence of a modctl structure does not necessarily mean that the module is loaded.

The facts that the Solaris kernel is dynamic in nature and that kernel objects can be loaded and unloaded during the life of a running system require that the kernel's symbol table (step 2) exist as a dynamic entity. All executable object files have a symbol table that holds information required to resolve an object's symbolic references. A symbolic reference is the correlation of the virtual address of a function or variable, and its name. The Solaris kernel's symbol table is maintained through a pseudodevice, /dev/ksyms, and corresponding device driver, /usr/kernel/drv/ksyms. In Solaris 7, the kernel symbol table is updated by a kernel thread created specifically for that purpose. The kernel runtime linker issues a wakeup to the ksyms_update_thread() when a module is loaded (or unloaded), and the kernel symbol table is updated to reflect the current state of loaded kernel objects.

In Solaris 2.5.1 and 2.6, a different update mechanism is used. A kernel variable is updated when a module is loaded or unloaded. Inside the ksyms driver ksyms_open() code, the variable is tested to determine whether a new symbol table image needs to be created. The implication here is that if an open has been issued in the ksyms driver, meaning that a user (or program) is examining the kernel symbol table, and a kernel module is loaded or unloaded, then the currently opened version will not reflect the change. A close and subsequent open must be issued for an updated view. You can use the nm(1) command to examine an object's symbol table; use /dev/ksyms to examine the kernel's table.

```
# nm -x /dev/ksyms | grep modload
[1953]   |0xf011086c|0x000000ac|FUNC |LOCL |0   |ABS   |modctl_modload
[10072]  |0xf011113c|0x000000a0|FUNC |GLOB |0   |ABS   |modload
[1973]   |0xf0111398|0x000000b8|FUNC |LOCL |0   |ABS   |modload_now
[1972]   |0xf01111dc|0x000000c8|FUNC |LOCL |0   |ABS   |modload_thread
[9926]   |0xf0111450|0x000000a4|FUNC |GLOB |0   |ABS   |modloadonly
```

The preceding example searches the symbol table of the running kernel for modload, a kernel function we discussed earlier. The command returned several matches that contain the modload string, including the desired modload function symbol. (For more information on symbol tables and specific information on the columns listed, see the nm(1), a.out(4), and elf(3E) manual pages. Also, refer to any number of texts that describe the Executable and Linking Format (ELF) file, which is discussed in more detail earlier in this chapter.)

In step 5, we indicate that the module install code is invoked indirectly through the module's _init() function. Several functions must be included in any loadable kernel module to facilitate dynamic loading. Device drivers and STREAMS modules *must* be coded for dynamic loading. As such, a loadable driver interface is defined. In general, the required routines and data structures that are documented apply to all loadable kernel modules—not just to drivers and STREAMS modules (although there are components that are specific to drivers)—and do not apply to objects such as loadable system calls, file systems, or scheduling classes.

Within a loadable kernel object, an initialization, information, and finish routine must be coded, as per the definitions in the _init(9E), _info(9E), and _fini(9E) manual pages. A module's _init() routine is called to complete the process of making the module usable after it has been loaded. The module's _info() and _fini() routines also invoke corresponding kernel module management interfaces, as shown in Table 4-2.

Table 4-2 Module Management Interfaces

Kernel Module Routine	Module Facility Interface	Description
_init()	mod_install()	Loads a kernel module.
_info()	mod_info()	Retrieves module information.
_fini()	mod_remove()	Unloads a kernel module.

Module installation is abstracted to define a generic set of structures and interfaces within the kernel. Module operation function pointers for installing, removing, and information gathering (the generic interfaces shown in Table 4-2) are maintained in a mod_ops structure, which is extended to provide a definition for each type of loadable module. For example, there is a mod_installsys() function specific to loading system calls, a mod_installdrv() function specific to loading device drivers, and so forth.

For each of these module types, a module linkage structure is defined; it contains a pointer to the operations structure, a pointer to a character string describing the module, and a pointer to a module-type-specific structure. For example, the linkage structure for loadable system calls, modlsys, contains a pointer to the system entry table, which is the entry point for all system calls. Each loadable kernel module is required to declare and initialize the appropriate type-specific linkage structure, as well as a generic modlinkage structure that provides the generic abstraction for all modules.

Within the module facility is a module type-specific routine for installing modules, entered through the MODL_INSTALL macro called from the generic mod_install() code. More precisely, a loadable module's _init() routine calls mod_install(), which vectors to the appropriate module-specific routine through the MODL_INSTALL macro. This procedure is shown in Figure 4.6.

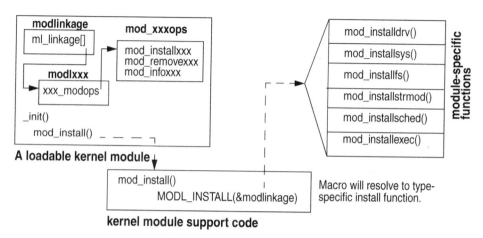

Figure 4.6 Module Operations Function Vectoring

Figure 4.6 shows the data structures defined in a loadable kernel module: the generic modlinkage, through which is referenced a type-specific linkage structure (modlxxx), which in turn links to a type-specific operations structure that contains pointers to the type-specific functions for installing, removing, and gathering information about a kernel module. The MODL_INSTALL macro is passed the address of the module's generic linkage structure and from there vectors in to the appropriate function. The module-specific installation steps are summarized in Table 4-3.

Table 4-3 Module Install Routines

Module Type	Install Function	Summary
Device driver	mod_installdrv	Wrapper for ddi_installdrv(). Installs the driver entry in the kernel devops table.
System call	mod_installsys	Installs the system call's sysent table entry in the kernel sysent table.
File system	mod_installfs	Installs the file system Virtual File System (VFS) switch table entry.
STREAMS modules	mod_installstrmod	Installs the STREAMS entry in the kernel fmodsw switch table.
Scheduling class	mod_installsched	Installs the scheduling class in the kernel sclass array.

Table 4-3 Module Install Routines (Continued)

Module Type	Install Function	Summary
Exec module	`mod_installexec`	Installs the exec entry in the kernel `execsw` switch table.

The summary column in Table 4-3 shows a definite pattern to the module installation functions. In many subsystems, the kernel implements a switch table mechanism to vector to the correct kernel functions for a specific file system, scheduling class, exec function, etc. The details of each implementation are covered in subsequent areas of the book, as applicable to a particular chapter or heading.

As we've seen, the dynamic loading of a kernel module is facilitated through two major kernel subsystems: the module management code and the kernel runtime linker. These kernel components make use of other kernel services, such as the kernel memory allocator, kernel locking primitives, and the kernel ksyms driver, taking advantage of the modular design of the system and providing a good example of the layered model discussed earlier.

Part Two

THE SOLARIS
MEMORY SYSTEM

- Solaris Memory Architecture
- Kernel Memory
- Memory Monitoring

5

SOLARIS MEMORY ARCHITECTURE

The virtual memory system can be considered the core of a Solaris system, and the implementation of Solaris virtual memory affects just about every other subsystem in the operating system. In this chapter, we'll take a look at some of the memory management basics and then step into a more detailed analysis of how Solaris implements virtual memory management. Subsequent chapters in Part Two discuss kernel memory management, and that can be used to monitor and manage virtual memory.

5.1 Why Have a Virtual Memory System?

A virtual memory system offers the following benefits:

- It presents a simple memory programming model to applications so that application developers need not know how the underlying memory hardware is arranged.

- It allows processes to see linear ranges of bytes in their address space, regardless of the physical layout or fragmentation of the real memory.

- It gives us a programming model with a larger memory size than available physical storage (e.g., RAM) and enables us to use slower but larger secondary storage (e.g., disk) as a backing store to hold the pieces of memory that don't fit in physical memory.

A virtual view of memory storage, known as an *address space*, is presented to the application while the VM system transparently manages the virtual storage between RAM and secondary storage. Because RAM is significantly faster than disk, (100 ns versus 10 ms, or approximately 100,000 times faster), the job of the VM system is to keep the most frequently referenced portions of memory in the faster primary storage. In the event of a RAM shortage, the VM system is required to free RAM by transferring infrequently used memory out to the backing store. By so doing, the VM system optimizes performance and removes the need for users to manage the allocation of their own memory.

Multiple users' processes can share memory within the VM system. In a multiuser environment, multiple processes can be running the same process executable binaries; in older UNIX implementations, each process had its own copy of the binary—a vast waste of memory resources. The Solaris virtual memory system optimizes memory use by sharing program binaries and application data among processes, so memory is not wasted when multiple instances of a process are executed. The Solaris kernel extended this concept further when it introduced dynamically linked libraries in SunOS, allowing C libraries to be shared among processes.

To properly support multiple users, the VM system implements memory protection. For example, a user's process must not be able to access the memory of another process; otherwise, security could be compromised or a program fault in one program could cause another program (or the entire operating system) to fail. Hardware facilities in the memory management unit perform the memory protection function by preventing a process from accessing memory outside its legal address space (except for memory that is explicitly shared between processes).

Physical memory (RAM) is divided into fixed-sized pieces called *pages*. The size of a page can vary across different platforms; the common size for a page of memory on an UltraSPARC Solaris system is 8 Kbytes. Each page of physical memory is associated with a file and offset; the file and offset identify the *backing store* for the page. The backing store is the location to which the physical page contents will be migrated (known as a *page-out*) should the page need to be taken for another use; it's also the location the file will be read back in from if it's migrated in (known as a *page-in*). Pages used for regular process heap and stack, known as *anonymous memory,* have the swap file as their backing store. A page can also be a cache of a page-sized piece of a regular file. In that case, the backing store is simply the file it's caching—this is how Solaris uses the memory system to cache files.

If the virtual memory system needs to take a *dirty* page (a page that has had its contents modified), its contents are migrated to the backing store. Anonymous memory is paged out to the swap device when the page is freed. If a file page needs to be freed and the page size piece of the file hasn't been modified, then the page can simply be freed; if the piece has been modified, then it is first written back out to the file (the backing store in this case), then freed.

Rather than managing every byte of memory, we use page-sized pieces of memory to minimize the amount of work the virtual memory system has to do to maintain virtual to physical memory mappings. Figure 5.1 shows how the management and translation of the virtual view of memory (the address space) to physical memory is performed by hardware, known as the *virtual memory management unit* (MMU).

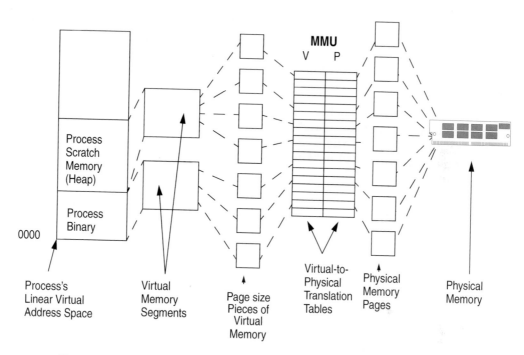

Figure 5.1 Solaris Virtual-to-Physical Memory Management

The Solaris kernel breaks up the linear virtual address space into *segments*, one for each type of memory area in the address space. For example, a simple process has a memory segment for the process binary and one for the scratch memory (known as *heap space*). Each segment manages the mapping for the virtual address range mapped by that segment and converts that mapping into MMU pages. The hardware MMU maps those pages into physical memory by using a platform-specific set of translation tables. Each entry in the table has the physical address of the page of memory in RAM, so that memory accesses can be converted on-the-fly in hardware. We cover more on how the MMU works later in the chapter when we discuss the platform-specific implementations of memory management.

Recall that we can have more virtual address space than physical address space because the operating system can overflow memory onto a slower medium, like a disk. The slower medium in UNIX is known as *swap space*. Two basic types of memory management manage the allocation and migration of physical pages of memory to and from swap space: *swapping* and *demand paging*.

The swapping algorithm for memory management uses a user process as the granularity for managing memory. If there is a shortage of memory, then all of the pages of memory of the least-active process are swapped out to the swap device, freeing memory for other processes. This method is easy to implement, but performance suffers badly during a memory shortage because a process cannot resume execution until all of its pages have been brought back from secondary storage. The demand-paged model uses a *page* as the granularity for memory management. Rather than swapping out a whole process, the memory system just swaps out small, least-used chunks, allowing processes to continue while an inactive part of the process is swapped out.

The Solaris kernel uses a combined demand-paged and swapping model. Demand paging is used under normal circumstances, and swapping is used only as a last resort when the system is desperate for memory. We cover swapping and paging in more detail in "The Page Scanner" on page 178.

The Solaris VM system implements many more functions than just management of application memory. In fact, the Solaris virtual memory system is responsible for managing most objects related to I/O and memory, including the kernel, user applications, shared libraries, and file systems. This strategy differs significantly from other operating systems like earlier versions of System V UNIX, where file system I/O used a separate buffer cache.

One of the major advantages of using the VM system to manage file system buffering is that all free memory in the system is used for file buffering, providing significant performance improvements for applications that use the file system and removing the need for tuning the size of the buffer cache. The VM system can allocate all free memory for file system buffers, meaning that on a typical system with file system I/O, the amount of free memory available is almost zero. This number can often be misleading and has resulted in numerous, bogus, memory-leak bugs being logged over the years. Don't worry; "almost zero" is normal. (Note that free memory is no longer always low with Solaris 8.)

In summary, a VM system performs these major functions:

- It manages virtual-to-physical mapping of memory
- It manages the swapping of memory between primary and secondary storage to optimize performance
- It handles requirements of shared images between multiple users and processes

5.2 Modular Implementation

Early SunOS versions (SunOS 3 and earlier) were based on the old BSD-style memory system, which was not modularized, and thus it was difficult to move the memory system to different platforms. The virtual memory system was completely redesigned at that time, with the new memory system targeted at SunOS 4.0. The new SunOS 4.0 virtual memory system was built with the following goals in mind:

- Use of a new object-oriented memory management framework
- Support for shared and private memory (copy-on-write)
- Page-based virtual memory management

The VM system that resulted from these design goals provides an open framework that now supports many different memory objects. The most important objects of the memory system are segments, vnodes, and pages. For example, all of the following have been implemented as abstractions of the new memory objects:

- Physical memory, in chunks called pages
- A new virtual file object, known as the vnode
- File systems as hierarchies of vnodes
- Process address spaces as segments of mapped vnodes
- Kernel address space as segments of mapped vnodes
- Mapped hardware devices, such as frame buffers, as segments of hardware-mapped pages

The Solaris virtual memory system we use today is implemented according to the framework of the SunOS 4.0 rewrite. It has been significantly enhanced to provide scalable performance on multiprocessor platforms and has been ported to many platforms. Figure 5.2 shows the layers of the Solaris virtual memory implementation.

Physical memory management is done by the hardware MMU and a hardware-specific address translation layer known as the *Hardware Address Translation (HAT) layer*. Each memory management type has its own specific HAT implementation. Thus, we can separate the common machine-independent memory management layers from the hardware-specific components to minimize the amount of platform-specific code that must be written for each new platform.

The next layer is the address space management layer. Address spaces are mappings of segments, which are created with segment device drivers. Each segment driver manages the mapping of a linear virtual address space into memory pages for different device types (for example, a device such as a graphics frame buffer can be mapped into an address space). The segment layers manage virtual memory as an abstraction of a file. The segment drivers call into the HAT layer to create the translations between the address space they are managing and the underlying physical pages.

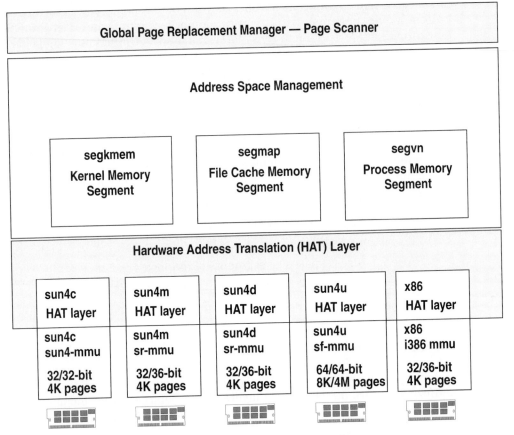

Figure 5.2 Solaris Virtual Memory Layers

5.3   Virtual Address Spaces

The virtual address space of a process is the range of memory addresses that are presented to the process as its environment; some addresses are mapped to physical memory, some are not. A process's virtual address space skeleton is created by the kernel at the time the fork() system call creates the process. (See "Process Creation" on page 289.) The virtual address layout within a process is set up by the dynamic linker and sometimes varies across different hardware platforms. As we saw in Figure 5.1 on page 127, virtual address spaces are assembled from a series of memory segments. Each process has at least four segments:

- Executable text — The executable instructions in the binary reside in the text segment. The text segment is mapped from the on-disk binary and is mapped read-only, with execute permissions.
- Executable data — The initialized variables in the executable reside in the data segment. The data segment is mapped from the on-disk binary and is mapped read/write/private. The private mapping ensures that changes made to memory within this mapping are not reflected out to the file or to other processes mapping the same executable.
- Heap space — Scratch, or memory allocated by `malloc()`, is allocated from anonymous memory and is mapped read/write.
- Process stack — The stack is allocated from anonymous memory and is mapped read/write.

Figure 5.3 illustrates a process's virtual address space.

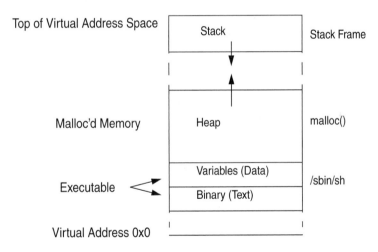

Figure 5.3 Process Virtual Address Space

Figure 5.3 shows how the `/sbin/sh` process has its executable mapped in near the bottom address, with the heap adjoining it, the stack at the top, and a hole between the heap and the stack. The heap grows upward as more memory is allocated through `malloc()`, and the stack grows downward as more frames are placed on the stack. Not all of the virtual address space within a process is mapped, and the process can legally access memory only within the areas mapped by segments; a process's attempt to access memory outside of the mapped segments causes a page fault. A more sophisticated process may have more segments; those that make use of shared libraries or mapped files will have additional segments between the heap and stack.

5.3.1 Sharing of Executables and Libraries

The Solaris kernel supports sharing of memory, files, libraries, and executables. For example, the Solaris kernel shares libraries by dynamically mapping the library file into the address space during program startup. The libraries are mapped into the address space between the stack and the heap, at different positions on different platforms.

When a library file is mapped into a process's address space, it can be mapped *shared* so that all processes share the same physical memory pages. Executable text and data are shared in the same manner, by simply mapping the same executable file into every address space.

We'll see more about how mapping of files and sharing of memory occur when we explore the vnode segment driver, which is responsible for mapping files into address spaces.

5.3.2 SPARC Address Spaces

The process address space on SPARC system varies across different SPARC platforms according to the MMU on that platform. SPARC has three different address space layouts:

- The SPARC V7 combined 32-bit kernel and process address space, found on sun4c, sun4d, and sun4m machines
- The SPARC V9 32-bit separated kernel and process address space model, found on sun4u machines
- The SPARC V9 64-bit separated kernel and process address space model, found on sun4u machines

The SPARC V7 systems use a shared address space between the kernel and process and use the processor's privilege levels to prevent user processes from accessing the kernel's address space. The kernel occupies the top virtual memory addresses, and the process occupies the lower memory addresses. This means that part of the virtual address space available to the process is consumed by the kernel, limiting the size of usable process virtual memory to between 3.5 and 3.75 Gbytes, depending on the size of the kernel's virtual address space. This also means that the kernel has a limited size, ranging between 128 and 512 Mbytes. The SPARC V7 combined 32-bit kernel and process address space is shown in Figure 5.4.

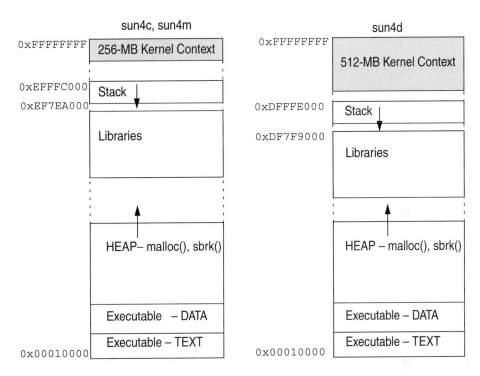

Figure 5.4 SPARC 32-Bit Shared Kernel/Process Address Space

The SPARC V9 (UltraSPARC, sun4u) microprocessor allows the kernel to operate in an address space separate from user processes, so the process can use almost all of the 32-bit address space (a tiny bit is reserved at the top for the Open Boot PROM) and also allows the kernel to have a similar, large address space. This design removes the 512-Mbyte limit for kernel address space, which was a major problem for large machines such as the older SPARCcenter 2000 machines. The process address space looks similar to the shared kernel/process address space, except that the kernel area is missing and the stack and libraries are moved to the top of memory.

The UltraSPARC process also supports the SPARC V9 64-bit mode, which allows a process to have a virtual address space that spans 64 bits. The Ultra-SPARC-I and -II implementations, however, support only 44 bits of the address space, which means that there is a virtual address space hole in the middle of the address space. This area of memory creates a special type of UltraSPARC trap when accessed. Some future generations of SPARC V9 processors will not have the same hole in the address space.

The UltraSPARC V9 32-bit and 64-bit address spaces are shown in Figure 5.5.

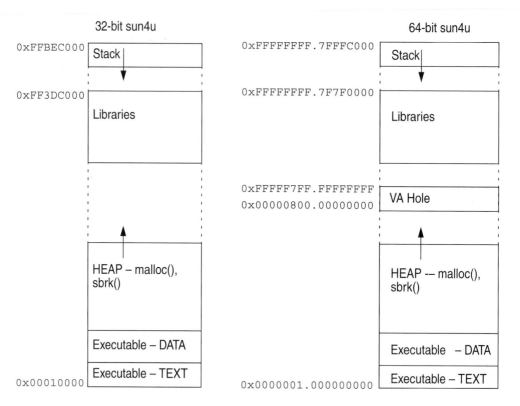

Figure 5.5 SPARC sun4u 32- and 64-Bit Process Address Space

On all SPARC platforms, the bottom of the virtual address space is not mapped. Null pointer references will cause a segmentation fault rather than return spurious contents of whatever was at the bottom of the address space.

5.3.3 Intel Address Space Layout

The Intel x86 address space, like the 32-bit SPARCV7 shared process/kernel address space, shares the same address space for user and kernel. The main difference with the Intel address space is that the stack is mapped underneath the executable binary and grows down toward the bottom. The Intel address space is shown in Figure 5.6.

5.3.4 Process Memory Allocation

Process virtual memory for user data structures is allocated from the heap segment, which resides above the executable data segment. The heap starts out small and then grows as virtual memory is allocated. The heap grows in units of pages and is simply a large area of virtual memory available for reading and writing. A single, large, virtual memory area is difficult to program to, so a general-purpose

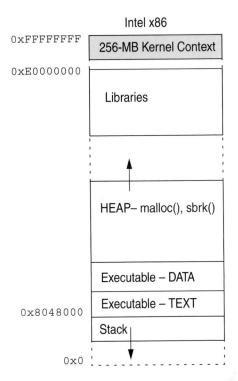

Figure 5.6 Intel x86 Process Address Space

memory allocator manages the heap area; thus, arbitrarily sized memory objects can be allocated and freed. The general-purpose memory allocator is implemented with `malloc()` and related library calls.

A process grows its heap space by making the `sbrk()` system call. The `sbrk()` system call grows the heap segment by the amount requested each time it is called. A user program does not need to call `sbrk()` directly because the `malloc()` library calls `sbrk()` when it needs more space to allocate from. The `sbrk()` system call is shown below.

```
void *sbrk(intptr_t incr);
```

The heap segment is virtual memory, so requesting memory with `malloc` and `sbrk` does not allocate physical memory, it merely allocates the virtual address space. Only when the first reference is made to a page within the allocated virtual memory is physical memory allocated—one page at a time. The memory system transparently achieves this "zero fill on demand" allocation because a page fault occurs the first time a page is referenced in the heap, and then the segment driver recognizes the first memory access and simply creates a page at that location on-the-fly.

Memory pages are allocated to the process heap by zero-fill-on-demand and then remain in the heap segment until the process exits or until they are stolen by the page scanner. Calls to the memory allocator `free()` function do not return physical memory to the free memory pool; `free()` simply marks the area within the heap space as free for later use. For this reason, it is typical to see the amount of physical memory allocated to a process grow, but unless there is a memory shortage, it will not shrink, even if `free()` has been called.

The heap can grow until it collides with the memory area occupied by the shared libraries. The maximum size of the heap depends on the platform virtual memory layout and differs on each platform. In addition, on 64-bit platforms, processes may execute in either 32- or 64-bit mode. As shown in Figure 5.5 on page 134, the size of the heap can be much larger in processes executing in 64-bit mode. Table 5-1 shows the maximum heap sizes and the operating system requirements that affect the maximum size.

Table 5-1 Maximum Heap Sizes

Solaris Version	Maximum Heap Size	Notes
Solaris 2.5	2 Gbytes	
Solaris 2.5.1	2 Gbytes	
Solaris 2.5.1 with patch 103640-08 or greater	3.75 Gbytes	Need to be root to increase limit above 2 GB with `ulimit(1M)`.
Solaris 2.5.1 with patch 103640-23 or greater	3.75 Gbytes	Do not need to be root to increase limit.
Solaris 2.6	3.75 Gbytes	Need to increase beyond 2 GB with `ulimit(1M)`.
Solaris 2.7 32 bit mode	3.75 Gbytes 3.90 Gbytes	(Non-sun4u platform) (sun4u platforms)
Solaris 2.7 64 bit mode	16 Tbytes on UltraSPARC-I and -II	Virtually unlimited.

5.3.5 The Stack

The process stack is mapped into the address space with an initial allocation and then grows downward. The stack, like the heap, grows on demand, but no library grows the stack; instead, a different mechanism triggers this growth.

Initially, a single page is allocated for the stack, and as the process executes and calls functions, it pushes the program counter, arguments, and local variables onto the stack. When the stack grows larger than one page, the process causes a page fault, and the kernel notices that this is a stack segment page fault and grows the stack segment.

5.3.6 Address Space Management

The Solaris kernel is implemented with a central address management subsystem that other parts of the kernel call into. The address space module is a wrapper around the segment drivers, so that subsystems need not know what segment driver is used for a memory range. The address space object shown in Figure 5.7 is linked from the process's address space and contains pointers to the segments that constitute the address space.

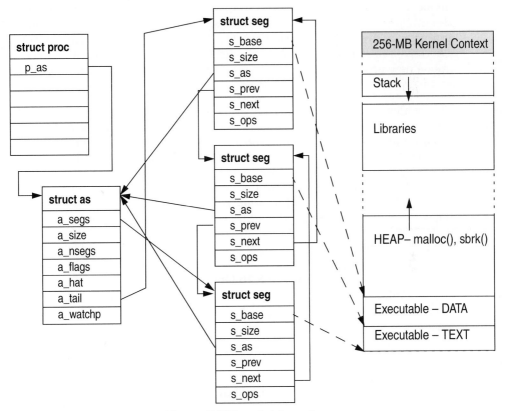

Figure 5.7 The Address Space

The address space subsystem manages the following functions:

- Duplication of address spaces, for `fork()`
- Destruction of address spaces, for `exit()`
- Creation of new segments within an address space
- Removal of segments from an address space
- Setting and management of page protection for an address space
- Page fault routing for an address space
- Page locking and advice for an address space
- Management of watchpoints for an address space

Recall that the process and kernel subsystems call into the address space subsystem to manage their address spaces. The address space subsystem consists of a series of functions, grouped to perform the functions listed above. Although the subsystem has a lot of entry points, the implementation is fairly simple because most of the functions simply look up which segment the operation needs to operate on and then route the request to the appropriate segment driver.

A call to the `as_alloc()` function creates an address space, but `as_alloc()` is invoked only once—when the system boots and the init process is created. After the init process is created, all address spaces are created by duplication of the init process's address space with `fork()`. The `fork()` system call in turn calls the `as_dup()` function to duplicate the address space of the current process as it creates a new process, and the entire address space configuration, including the stack and heap, is replicated at this point.

The behavior of `vfork()` at this point is somewhat different. Rather than calling `as_dup()` to replicate the address space, `vfork()` creates a new process by borrowing the parent's existing address space. The `vfork` function is useful if the fork is going to call `exec()` since it saves all the effort of duplicating the address space that would otherwise have been discarded once `exec()` is called. The parent process is suspended while the child is using its address space, until `exec()` is called. Once the process is created, the address space object is allocated and set up. The Solaris 7 data structure for the address space object is shown below.

```
struct as {
        kmutex_t a_contents;    /* protect certain fields in the structure */
        uchar_t  a_flags;       /* as attributes */
        uchar_t  a_vbits;       /* used for collecting statistics */
        kcondvar_t a_cv;        /* used by as_rangelock */
        struct  hat *a_hat;     /* hat structure */
        struct  hrmstat *a_hrm; /* ref and mod bits */
        caddr_t a_userlimit;    /* highest allowable address in this as */
        union {
                struct seg *seglast;    /* last segment hit on the addr space */
                ssl_spath *spath;       /* last search path in seg skiplist */
        } a_cache;
        krwlock_t a_lock;       /* protects fields below + a_cache */
        int     a_nwpage;       /* number of watched pages */
        struct watched_page *a_wpage;   /* list of watched pages (procfs) */
        seg_next a_segs;        /* segments in this address space. */
        size_t  a_size;         /* size of address space */
        struct  seg *a_tail;    /* last element in the segment list. */
        uint_t  a_nsegs;        /* number of elements in segment list */
        uchar_t a_lrep;         /* representation of a_segs: see #defines */
        uchar_t a_hilevel;      /* highest level in the a_segs skiplist */
        uchar_t a_unused;
        uchar_t a_updatedir;    /* mappings changed, rebuild as_objectdir */
        vnode_t **a_objectdir;  /* object directory (procfs) */
        size_t  a_sizedir;      /* size of object directory */
};
```

Header File <vm/as.h>

Address space fault handling is performed in the address space subsystem; some of the faults are handled by the common address space code, and others are redirected to the segment handlers. When a page fault occurs, the Solaris trap handlers call the `as_fault()` function, which looks to see what segment the page fault occurred in by calling the `as_setat()` function. If the fault does not lie in any of the address space's segments, then `as_fault()` sends a SIGSEGV signal to the process. If the fault does lie within one of the segments, then the segment's fault method is called and the segment handles the page fault.

Table 5-2 lists the segment functions in alphabetical order.

Table 5-2 Solaris 7 Address Space Functions

Method	Description
`as_addseg()`	Creates a new segment and links it into the address space.
`as_alloc()`	Creates a new address space object (only called from the kernel for the init process).
`as_clearwatch()`	Clears all watch points for the address space.
`as_ctl()`	Sends memory advice to an address range for the address space.
`as_dup()`	Duplicates the entire address space.
`as_exec()`	Is a special code for `exec` to move the stack segment from its interim place in the old address to the right place in the new address space.
`as_fault()`	Handles a page fault in the address space.
`as_findseg()`	Finds a segment containing the supplied virtual address.
`as_free()`	Destroys the address space object; called by `exit()`.
`as_gap()`	Finds a hole of at least the specified size within [*base*, *base* + *len*). If the flag supplied specifies AH_HI, the hole will have the highest possible address in the range. Otherwise, it will have the lowest possible address. If the flag supplied specifies AH_CONTAIN, the hole will contain the address *addr*. If an adequate hole is found, *base* and *len* are set to reflect the part of the hole that is within range, and 0 is returned. Otherwise, −1 is returned.
`as_getmemid()`	Calls the segment driver containing the supplied address to find a unique ID for this segment.
`as_getprot()`	Gets the current protection settings for the supplied address.
`as_map()`	Maps a file into the address space.
`as_memory()`	Returns the next range within [*base*, *base* + *len*) that is backed with "real memory."
`as_pagelock()`	Locks a page within an address space by calling the segment page lock function.

Table 5-2 Solaris 7 Address Space Functions (Continued)

Method	Description
as_pagereclaim()	Retrieves a page from the free list for the address supplied.
as_pageunlock()	Unlocks a page within the address space.
as_rangebroadcast()	Wakes up all threads waiting on the address space condition variable.
as_rangelock()	Locks the pages for the supplied address range.
as_rangeunlock()	Unlocks the pages for the supplied address range.
as_rangewait()	Waits for virtual addresses to become available in the specified address space. AS_CLAIMGAP must be held by the caller and is reacquired before returning to the caller.
as_setat()	Finds a segment containing the supplied address.
as_setprot()	Sets the virtual mapping for the interval from [$addr$: $addr + size$) in address space as to have the specified protection.
as_setwatch()	Sets a watchpoint for the address. On a system without watchpoint support, does nothing.
as_swapout()	Swaps the pages associated with the address space to secondary storage, returning the number of bytes actually swapped.
as_unmap()	Unmaps a segment from the address space.

5.3.7 Virtual Memory Protection Modes

We break each process into segments so that we can treat each part of the address space differently. For example, the kernel maps the machine code portion of the executable binary into the process as read-only to prevent the process from modifying its machine code instructions. The virtual memory subsystem does this by taking advantage of the hardware MMU's virtual memory protection capabilities. Solaris relies on the MMU having the following protection modes:

- Read — The mapping is allowed to be read from.
- Write — The mapping is allowed to be written to.
- Executable — The mapping is allowed to have machine codes executed within its address range.

The implementation of protection modes is done in the segment and HAT layers.

5.3.8 Page Faults in Address Spaces

The Solaris virtual memory system uses the hardware MMU's memory management capabilities. MMU-generated exceptions tell the operating system when a memory access cannot continue without the kernel's intervention, by interrupting the executing process with a trap (see "Entering Kernel Mode" on page 28) and then invoking the appropriate piece of memory management code. Three major types of memory-related hardware exceptions can occur: *major page faults*, *minor page faults*, and *protection faults*.

A *major page fault* occurs when an attempt to access a virtual memory location that is mapped by a segment does not have a physical page of memory mapped to it and the page does not exist in physical memory. The page fault allows the virtual memory system to hide the management of physical memory allocation from the process. The virtual memory system traps accesses to memory that the process believes is accessible and arranges to have either a new page created for that address (in the case of the first access) or copies in the page from the swap device. Once the memory system places a real page behind the memory address, the process can continue normal execution. If a reference is made to a memory address that is not mapped by any segment, then a segmentation violation signal (SIG-SEGV) is sent to the process. The signal is sent as a result of a hardware exception caught by the processor and translated to a signal by the address space layer.

A *minor page fault* occurs when an attempt is made to access a virtual memory location that resides within a segment and the page is in physical memory, but no current MMU translation is established from the physical page to the address space that caused the fault. For example, a process maps in the libc.so library and makes a reference to a page within it. A page fault occurs, but the physical page of memory is already present and the process simply needs to establish a mapping to the existing physical page. Minor faults are also referred to as *attaches*.

A *page protection fault* occurs when a program attempts to access a memory address in a manner that violates the preconfigured access protection for a memory segment. Protection modes can enable any of read, write, or execute access. For example, the text portion of a binary is mapped read-only, and if we attempt to write to any memory address within that segment, we will cause a memory protection fault. The memory protection fault is also initiated by the hardware MMU as a trap that is then handled by the segment page fault handling routine.

Figure 5.8 shows the relationship between a virtual address space, its segments, and the hardware MMU.

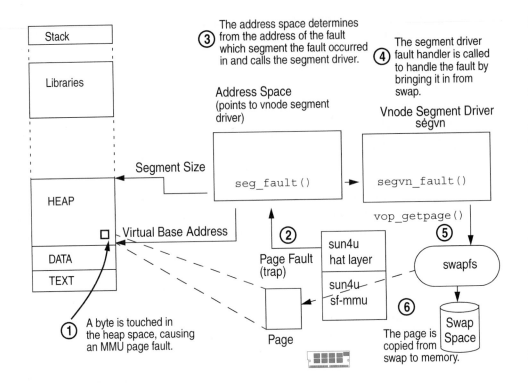

Figure 5.8 Virtual Address Space Page Fault Example

In the figure, we see what happens when a process accesses a memory location within its heap space that does not have physical memory mapped to it. This has most likely occurred because the page of physical memory has previously been stolen by the page scanner as a result of a memory shortage. In the numbered events in the figures we see:

1. A reference is made to a memory address that does not map to a physical page of memory. In this example, the page has been paged out and now resides on the swap device.

2. When the process accesses the address with no physical memory behind it, the MMU detects the invalid reference and causes a trap to occur on the processor executing the code of the running thread. The fault handler recognizes this as a memory page fault and establishes which segment the fault occurred in by comparing the address of the fault to the addresses mapped by each segment.

3. The address space as_fault() routine compares the address of the fault with the addresses mapped by each segment and then calls the page_fault routine of the segment driver for this segment (in this case, the vnode segment driver).

4. The segment driver allocates and maps the page of memory by calling into the HAT layer and then copies the contents of the page from the swap device.

5. The segment driver then reads the page in from the backing store by calling the getpage() function of the backing store's vnode.

6. The backing store for this segment is the swap device, so the swap device getpage() function is called to read in the page from the swap device.

Once this process is completed, the process can continue execution.

5.4 Memory Segments

Another example of the object-oriented approach to memory management is the memory "segment" object. Memory segments manage the mapping of a linear range of virtual memory into an address space. The mapping is between the address space and some type of device. The objective of the memory segment is to allow both memory and devices to be mapped into an address space. Traditionally, this required hard-coding memory and device information into the address space handlers for each device. The object architecture allows different behaviors for different segments.

For example, one segment might be a mapping of a file into an address space (with mmap), and another segment might be the mapping of a hardware device into the process's address space (a graphics framebuffer). In this case, the segment driver provides a similar view of linear address space, even though the file mapping operation with mmap uses pages of memory to cache the file data, whereas the framebuffer device maps the hardware device into the address space.

The flexibility of the segment object allows us to use virtually any abstraction to represent a linear address space that is visible to a process, regardless of the real facilities behind the scenes.

```
struct seg {
        caddr_t s_base;                 /* base virtual address */
        size_t  s_size;                 /* size in bytes */
        struct  as *s_as;               /* containing address space */
        seg_next s_next;                /* next seg in this address space */
        struct  seg *s_prev;            /* prev seg in this address space */
        struct  seg_ops *s_ops;         /* ops vector: see below */
        void *s_data;                   /* private data for instance */
};
```

Header File <vm/seg.h>

To implement an address space, a segment driver implementation is required to provide at least the following: functions to create a mapping for a linear address range, page fault handling routines to deal with machine exceptions within that linear address range, and a function to destroy the mapping. These functions are packaged together into a *segment driver*, which is an instantiation of the segment object interface. Figure 5.9 illustrates the relationship between an address space and a segment and shows a segment mapping the heap space of a process.

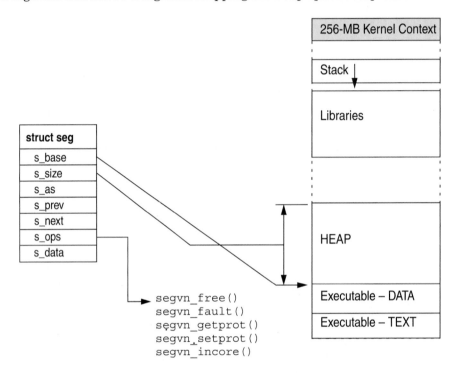

Figure 5.9 Segment Interface

A segment driver implements a subset of the methods described in Table 5-4 on page 146, as well as a constructor function to create the first instance of the object. Functions in the segment operations structure, s_ops, point to functions within the vnode segment driver and are prefixed with segvn. A segment object is created when another subsystem wants to create a mapping by calling as_map() to create a mapping at a specific address. The segment's create routine is passed as an argument to as_map(), a segment object is created, and a segment object pointer is returned. Once the segment is created, other parts of the virtual memory system can call into the segment for different address space operations without knowing what the underlying segment driver is using the segment method operations for.

For example, when a file is mapped into an address space with mmap(), the address space map routine as_map() is called with segvn_create() (the vnode segment driver constructor) as an argument, which in turn calls into the `seg_vn` segment driver to create the mapping. The segment object is created and inserted into the segment list for the address space (struct `as`), and from that point on, the address space can perform operations on the mapping without knowing what the underlying segment is.

The address space routines can operate on the segment without knowing what type of segment is underlying by calling the segment operation macros. For example, if the address space layer wants to call the fault handler for a segment, it calls `SEGOP_FAULT()`, which invokes the segment-specific page fault method, as shown below.

```
#define SEGOP_FAULT(h, s, a, l, t, rw) \
            (*(s)->s_ops->fault)((h), (s), (a), (l), (t), (rw))
```

Header File <vm/seg.h>

The Solaris kernel is implemented with a range of segment drivers for various functions. The different types of drivers are shown in Table 5-3. Most of the process address space mapping—including executable text, data, heap, stack and memory mapped files—is performed with the vnode segment driver, `seg_vn`. Other types of mappings that don't have `vnodes` associated with them require different segment drivers. The other segment drivers are typically associated with kernel memory mappings or hardware devices, such as graphics adapters.

Table 5-3 Solaris 7 Segment Drivers

Segment	Function
seg_vn	The `vnode` mappings into process address spaces are managed with the `seg_vn` device driver. Executable text and data, shared libraries, mapped files, heap and stack (heap and stack are anonymous memory) are all mapped with `seg_vn`.
seg_kmem	The segment from which the bulk of nonpageable kernel memory is allocated. (See Chapter 6, "Kernel Memory".)
seg_kp	The segment from which pageable kernel memory is allocated. Only a very small amount of the kernel is pageable; kernel thread stacks and TNF buffers are the main consumers of pageable kernel memory.
seg_spt	Shared page table segment driver. Fast System V shared memory is mapped into process address space from this segment driver. Memory allocated from this driver is also known as Intimate Shared Memory (ISM).
seg_map	The kernel uses the `seg_map` driver to map files (`vnodes`) into the kernel's address space, to implement file system caching.
seg_dev	Mapped hardware devices.

Table 5-3 Solaris 7 Segment Drivers (Continued)

Segment	Function
seg_mapdev	Mapping support for mapped hardware devices, through the ddi_mapdev(9F) interface.
seg_lock	Mapping support for hardware graphics devices that are mapped between user and kernel address space.
seg_drv	Mapping support for mapped hardware graphics devices.
seg_nf	Nonfaulting kernel memory driver.
seg_mdi	Hardware mapping support for the cgfourteen graphics frame-buffer.
seg_sx	Hardware mapping support for the SPARCstation 20 SX graphics framebuffer.

Table 5-4 describes segment driver methods implemented in Solaris 7.

Table 5-4 Solaris 7 Segment Driver Methods

Method	Description
advise()	Provides a hint to optimize memory accesses to this segment. For example, sequential advice given to mapped files causes read-ahead to occur.
checkprot()	Checks that the requested access type (read, write, exec) is allowed within the protection level of the pages within the segment.
dump()	Dumps the segment to the dump device; used for crash dumps.
dup()	Duplicates the current memory segment, including all of the page mapping entries to the new segment pointer provided.
fault()	Handles a page fault for a segment. The arguments describe the segment, the virtual address of the page fault, and the type of fault.
faulta()	Starts a page fault on a segment and address asynchronously. Used for read-ahead or prefaulting of data as a performance optimization for I/O.
free()	Destroys a segment.
getmemid()	Gets a unique identifier for the memory segment.
getoffset()	Queries the segment driver for the offset into the underlying device for the mapping. (Not meaningful on all segment drivers.)
getprot()	Asks the segment driver for the protection levels for the memory range.
gettype()	Queries the driver for the sharing modes of the mapping.

Table 5-4 Solaris 7 Segment Driver Methods (Continued)

Method	Description
getvp()	Gets the vnode pointer for the vnode, if there is one, behind this mapping.
incore()	Queries to find out how many pages are in physical memory for a segment.
kluster()	Asks the segment driver if it is OK to cluster I/O operations for pages within this segment.
lockop()	Locks or unlocks the pages for a range of memory mapped by a segment.
pagelock()	Locks a single page within the segment.
setprot()	Sets the protection level of the pages with the address range supplied.
swapout()	Attempts to swap out as many pages to secondary storage as possible.
sync()	Syncs up any dirty pages within the segment to the backing store.
unmap()	Unmaps the address space range within a segment.

5.4.1 The vnode Segment: seg_vn

The most widely used segment driver is the vnode segment driver, seg_vn. The seg_vn driver maps files (or vnodes) into a process address space, using physical memory as a cache. The seg_vn segment driver also creates anonymous memory within the process address space for the heap and stack and provides support for System V shared memory. (See "System V Shared Memory" on page 425.)

The seg_vn segment driver manages the following mappings into process address space:

- Executable text
- Executable data
- Heap and stack (anonymous memory)
- Shared libraries
- Mapped files

5.4.1.1 Memory Mapped Files

We can map a file into a process's address space with the mmap system call. (See discussion in "Memory Mapped File I/O" on page 498.) When we map a file into our address space, we call into the address space routines to create a new segment, a vnode segment. A vnode segment handles memory address translation and page faults for the memory range requested in the mmap system call, and the new segment is added to the list of segments in the process's address space. When the segment is created, the seg_vn driver initializes the segment structure with the address and length of the mapping, then creates a seg_vn-specific data structure within the segment structure's s_data field. The seg_vn-specific data structure holds all of the information the seg_vn driver needs to handle the address mappings for the segment.

The seg_vn-specific data structure (struct segvn_data) contains pointers to the vnode that is mapped and to any anonymous memory that has been allocated for this segment. The file system does most of the work of mapped files once the mapping is created. As a result, the seg_vn driver is fairly simple—most of the seg_vn work is done during creation and deletion of the mapping.

The more complex part of the seg_vn driver implementation is its handling of anonymous memory pages within the segment, which we discuss in the sections that follow. When we create a file mapping, we put the vnode and offset of the file being mapped into the segvn_data structure members, vp and offset. The seg_vn data structure is shown below; Figure 5.10 illustrates the seg_vn segment driver vnode relationship.

```
struct  segvn_data {
        krwlock_t lock;         /* protect segvn_data and vpage array */
        uchar_t pageprot;       /* true if per page protections present */
        uchar_t prot;           /* current segment prot if pageprot == 0 */
        uchar_t maxprot;        /* maximum segment protections */
        uchar_t type;           /* type of sharing done */
        u_offset_t offset;      /* starting offset of vnode for mapping */
        struct  vnode *vp;      /* vnode that segment mapping is to */
        ulong_t anon_index;     /* starting index into anon_map anon array */
        struct  anon_map *amp;  /* pointer to anon share structure, if needed */
        struct  vpage *vpage;   /* per-page information, if needed */
        struct  cred *cred;     /* mapping credentials */
        size_t  swresv;         /* swap space reserved for this segment */
        uchar_t advice;         /* madvise flags for segment */
        uchar_t pageadvice;     /* true if per page advice set */
        ushort_t flags;         /* flags - from sys/mman.h */
        ssize_t softlockcnt;    /* # of pages SOFTLOCKED in seg */
};
```

Header File <vm/seg_vn.h>

Creating a mapping for a file is done with the mmap() system call, which calls the map method for the file system that contains the file. For example, calling mmap() for a file on a UFS file system will call ufs_map(), which in turn calls into the seg_vn driver to create a mapped file segment in the address space with the segvn_create() function.

At this point we create an actual virtual memory mapping by talking to the hardware through the hardware address translation functions by using the hat_map() function. The hat_map() function is the central function for creating address space mappings. It calls into the hardware-specific memory implementation for the platform to program the hardware MMU, so that memory address references within the supplied address range will trigger the page fault handler in the segment driver until a valid physical memory page has been placed at the

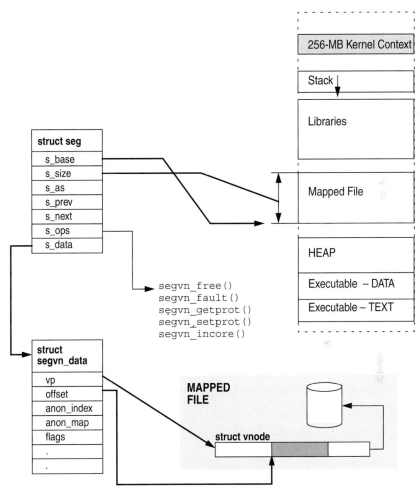

Figure 5.10 The `seg_vn` Segment Driver Vnode Relationship

accessed location. Once the hardware MMU mapping is established, the `seg_vn` driver can begin handling page faults within that segment.

Having established a valid hardware mapping for our file, we can look at how our mapped file is effectively read into the address space. The hardware MMU can generate traps for memory accesses to the memory within that segment. These traps will be routed to our `seg_vn` driver through the `as_fault()` routine. (See "Page Faults in Address Spaces" on page 140.) The first time we access a memory location within our segment, the `segvn_fault()` page fault handling routine is called. This fault handler recognizes our segment as a mapped file (by looking in the `segvn_data` structure) and simply calls into the vnode's file system (in this case, with `ufs_getpage()`) to read in a page-sized chunk from the file system. The subsequent access to memory that is now backed by physical memory simply results in a normal memory access. It's not until a page is stolen from behind the segment (the page scanner can do this) that a page fault will occur again.

Writing to a mapped file is done by updating the contents of memory within the mapped segment. The file is not updated instantly, since there is no software- or hardware-initiated event to trigger any such write. Updates occur when the file system flush daemon finds that the page of memory has been modified and then pushes the page to the file system with the file systems `putpage` routine, in this case, `ufs_putpage()`.

5.4.1.2 Shared Mapped Files

The address space segment architecture makes it easy for two or more processes to map the same file into their address space. When we map files into two or more processes, we create `seg_vn` segments in each process that point to the same vnode. Each process has its own virtual memory mapping to the file, but they all share the same physical memory pages for the files. The first segment to cause a page fault reads a page into physical memory, and then the second and subsequent segments simply create a reference to the existing physical memory page— as *attaching*.

Figure 5.11shows how two processes can map the same file. Each process creates its own segment object, but both segments point to the same file and are mapped to the same physical pages. Notice that the second process need not have all of the pages attached to the segment, even if both segments map the same parts of the file. In this case, the second process would *attach* to these pages when they are referenced. A minor fault is used to describe this event. You can see minor faults by using `vmstat`. (See "Statistics from the vmstat Command" on page 239.)

Several options govern how a file is shared when it is mapped between two or more processes. These options control how changes are propagated across the shared file. For example, if one process wants to modify one of the pages mapped into the process, should the other process see exactly the same change or should the change remain private to the process that made the change? The options allow us to choose which behavior we desire. The options are those that can be passed to the protection and flags argument of `mmap()` when the file is mapped. The behavior for the different flags is listed in Table 5-5.

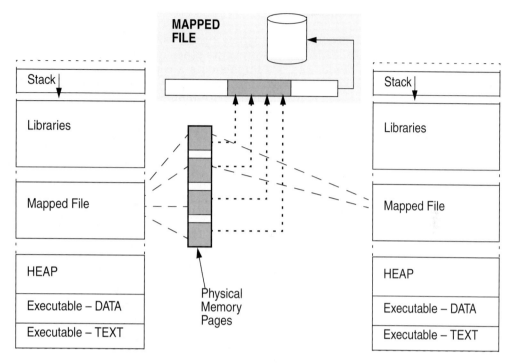

Figure 5.11 Shared Mapped Files

Table 5-5 mmap Shared Mapped File Flags

Flag	Protection Mode	Result
MAP_SHARED	PROT_READ| PROT_WRITE	Modifications are reflected among all processes sharing the mapping.
MAP_PRIVATE	PROT_READ| PROT_WRITE	Modifications are seen only by the process mapping the file. The copy-on-write process creates a page of anonymous memory and gives a private copy to the process.

5.4.2 Copy-on-Write

The copy-on-write process occurs when a process writes to a page that is mapped with MAP_PRIVATE. This process prevents other mappings to the page from seeing changes that are made. seg_vn implements a copy-on-write by setting the hardware MMU permissions of a segment to read-only and setting the segment permissions to read-write. When a process attempts to write to a mapping that is configured this way, the MMU generates an exception and causes a page fault on the page in question. The page fault handler in seg_vn looks at the protection mode for the segment; if it is mapped private and read-write, then the handler initiates a copy-on-write.

The copy-on-write unmaps the shared vnode page where the fault occurred, creates a page of anonymous memory at that address, and then copies the contents of the old page to the new anonymous page. All of this happens in the context of the page fault, so the process never knows what's happening underneath it.

The copy-on-write operation behaves slightly differently under different memory conditions. When memory is low, rather than creating a new physical memory page, the copy-on-write steals the page from the offset of the file underneath and renames it to be the new anonymous page. This only occurs when free memory is lower than the system parameter minfree.

5.4.3 Page Protection and Advice

The seg_vn segment supports memory protection modes on either the whole segment or individual pages within a segment. Whole segment protection is implemented by the segvn_data structure member, prot; its enablement depends on the boolean switch, pageprot, in the segvn_data structure. If pageprot is equal to zero, then the entire segment's protection mode is set by prot; otherwise, page-level protection is enabled.

Page-level protection is implemented by an array of page descriptors pointed to by the vpage structure, shown below. If page-level protection is enabled, then vpage points to an array of vpage structures. Every possible page in the address space has one array entry, which means that the number of vpage members is the segment virtual address space size divided by the fundamental page size for the segment (8 Kbytes on UltraSPARC).

```
struct vpage {
        uchar_t nvp_prot;          /* see <sys/mman.h> prot flags */
        uchar_t nvp_advice;        /* pplock & <sys/mman.h> madvise flags */
};
```

Header File <vm/vpage.h>

The vpage entry for each page uses the standard memory protection bits from Table 5-5. The per-page vpage structures are also used to implement memory advice for memory mapped files in the seg_vn segment. (See "Providing Advice to the Memory System" on page 502.)

5.5   Anonymous Memory

At many points we have mentioned *anonymous memory*. Anonymous memory refers to pages that are not directly associated with a vnode. Such pages are used for a process's heap space, its stack, and copy-on-write pages. In the Solaris kernel, two subsystems are dedicated to managing anonymous memory: the anon layer and the swapfs file system.

The anonymous memory allocated to the heap of a process is a result of a zero-fill-on-demand operation (ZFOD). The ZFOD operation is how we allocate new pages. A ZFOD occurs when we touch a memory address for the first time, and a new page of memory is dynamically allocated at that address. ZFOD is the allocation method used for the heap space and segments created as a map of /dev/zero with segment protection of MAP_PRIVATE. A page fault on a segment of this type will be recognized as ZFOD, and a new zeroed anonymous memory page is created at the fault location. The seg_vn segment fault handler, segvn_fault, handles the fault and creates ZFOD pages.

The seg_vn segment driver allocates anonymous memory to the segment by calling into the anonymous memory layer interfaces and attaching anonymous maps to the amp (anonymous map pointer) member in the segvn_data structure. Figure 5.12 shows a seg_vn segment with the anonymous map structures allocated to it.

Every allocated page-sized piece of virtual memory in the segment is assigned an anonymous map slot. For example, when a segment is first created, there are no anonymous map slots allocated, but the first time a zero fill-on-demand page fault occurs, a slot is allocated for a page, corresponding to the address within the segment where the fault occurred. At that time, a physical page is attached to the slot. Later, the page may be stolen and no page is associated anymore, but an empty slot remains.

5.5.1 The Anonymous Memory Layer

Anonymous pages are created through the anon layer interfaces. The first time a segment receives a page fault, it allocates an anon map structure (which describes where to find the anon header) and puts a pointer to the anon header into the amp field of the anonymous map. It then allocates the slot array, big enough to hold the number of potential pages in the segment. The slot array is either a single or double indirection list, depending on how many slots are required.

32-bit systems require double indirection for segments larger than 16 Mbytes; 64-bit systems, because of larger pointer sizes, require double indirection for segments larger than 8 Mbytes. When we use single indirection, the anon header array_chunk directly references the anon slot array. When we use double indirection, the array is broken into chunks: 2048 slot chunks for 32-bit systems and 1024

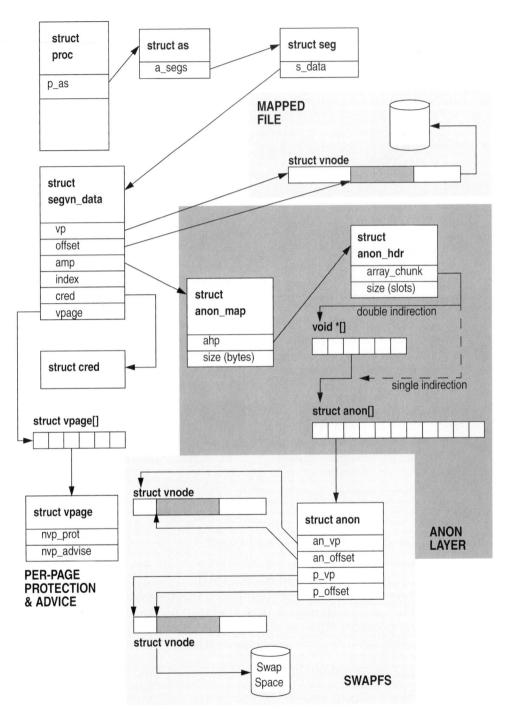

Figure 5.12 Anonymous Memory Data Structures

slot chunks for 64-bit systems. An additional array of pointers is referenced by the `array_chunk` field pointing to each chunk. Figure 5.12 shows the single and double indirection arrays. This allocation process is handled by the anon layer interface, `anonmap_create`. The anon slot is shown below.

```
struct anon {
        struct vnode *an_vp;     /* vnode of anon page */
        struct vnode *an_pvp;    /* vnode of physical backing store */
        anoff_t an_off;          /* offset of anon page */
        anoff_t an_poff;         /* offset in vnode */
        struct anon *an_hash;    /* hash table of anon slots */
        int an_refcnt;           /* # of people sharing slot */
};
```

Header File   <vm/anon.h>

Each `anon` slot points to an `anon` structure, which describes the virtual page of memory corresponding to the page-sized area in the address space. SVR4 implementations simply had a page structure for each slot that had a physical page associated with it, or `NULL` if there was no physical page in memory. However, the Solaris implementation does things differently. Recall that all physical pages have a vnode and offset. The Solaris kernel identifies that physical page, which points to the swap `vnode`, and offset assigned to the page. Note that this is not the swap device *actual* vnode and offset; rather, it's a `vnode` and offset *pointing to* the `swapfs` file system (which we'll discuss shortly). The anon structure also contains space for other information of interest to `swapfs`.

The anon layer functions are listed alphabetically in Table 5-6.

Table 5-6 Anon Layer Functions

Flag	Protection Mode
anon_alloc()	Allocates an anon slot and returns it with the lock held.
anon_copy_ptr()	Copies anon array into a given new anon array.
anon_create()	Creates the list of pointers.
anon_decref()	Decrements the reference count of an anon page. If the reference count goes to zero, frees it and its associated page (if any).
anon_dup()	Duplicates references to *size* bytes worth of anon pages. Used when duplicating a segment that contains private anon pages.
anon_free()	Frees a group of *size* anon pages, *size* in bytes, and clears the pointers to the anon entries.
anon_get_next_ptr()	Returns the anon pointer for the first valid entry in the anon list, starting from the given index.
anon_getpage()	Returns the kept page(s) and protections to the segment driver.

Table 5-6 Anon Layer Functions (Continued)

Flag	Protection Mode
anon_get_ptr()	Returns the pointer from the list for a specified anon index.
anon_pages()	Returns a count of the number of existing anon pages in the anon array in the range.
anon_private()	Turns a reference to an object or shared anon page into a private page with a copy of the data from the original page.
anon_release()	Frees the array of pointers.
anon_resvmem()	Reserves anon space.
anon_set_ptr()	Sets list entry with a given pointer for a specified offset.
anon_unresv()	Gives back an anon reservation.
anon_zero()	Allocates a private zero-filled anon page.
anonmap_alloc()	Allocates and initializes an anon_map structure for segment associating the given swap reservation with the new anon_map.
anonmap_free()	Frees an anon map structure.
anon_map_getpages()	Allocates array of private zero-filled anon pages for empty slots and kept pages for nonempty slots within given range.
non_anon()	Returns true if the array has some empty slots.
set_anoninfo()	Is called from clock handler to sync ani_free value.

5.5.2 The swapfs Layer

Each physical page of memory is identified by its vnode and offset. The vnode and offset identify a backing store that tells where to find the page when it's not in physical memory. For a regular file, the physical page caching the file has a vnode and offset that are simply the file's vnode and offset. Swap space is used as a backing store for anonymous pages of memory, so that when we are short of memory, we can copy a page out to disk and free up a page of memory.

Because swap space is used as the backing store for anonymous memory, we need to ensure we have enough swap space for the pages we may need to swap out. We do that by reserving space upfront when we create writable mappings backed by anonymous memory for heap space, stack, and writable mapped files with MAP_PRIVATE set.

The Solaris kernel allows us to allocate anonymous memory without reserving physical swap space when sufficient memory is available to hold the virtual contents of a process. This means that under some circumstances a system can run with little or no swap.

Traditional UNIX implementations need a page-sized unit of swap space for every page-sized unit of writable virtual memory. For example, a `malloc` request of 8 Mbytes on a traditional UNIX system would require us to reserve 8 Mbytes of swap disk space, even if that space was never used. This requirement led to the old rule of swap space = 2 × memory size—the rough assumption was that processes would, on average, have a virtual size about twice that of the physical pages they consumed. The `swapfs` layer allows Solaris to be much more conservative; you only need swap space for the amount of virtual memory that is larger than the pageable physical memory available in the machine.

The Solaris swap implementation uses `swapfs` to implement space-efficient swap allocation. The `swapfs` file system is a pseudo file system between the anon layer and the physical swap devices. The `swapfs` file system acts as if there is real swap space behind the page, even if no physical swap space was allocated.

5.5.2.1 Swap Allocation

Let's step back for a minute and look at how swap is allocated, and as we move through the process, we can look at how `swapfs` is implemented. We'll refer to swap space as seen by the segment drivers as *virtual swap space*, and real (disk or file) swap space as *physical swap space*.

Swap space allocation goes through distinct stages: reserve, allocate, and swap-out. When we first create a segment, we reserve virtual swap space; when we first touch and allocate a page, we "allocate" virtual swap space for that page; then, if we have a memory shortage, we can "swap out" a page to swap space. Table 5-7 summarizes the swap states.

Table 5-7 Swap Space Allocation States

State	Description
Reserved	Virtual swap space is reserved for an entire segment. Reservation occurs when a segment is created with private/read/write access. The reservation represents the virtual size of the area being created.
Allocated	Virtual swap space is allocated when the first physical page is assigned to it. At that point, a `swapfs` vnode and offset are assigned against the *anon* slot.
Swapped out (used swap)	When a memory shortage occurs, a page may be swapped out by the page scanner. Swap-out happens when the page scanner calls `swapfs_putpage` for the page in question. The page is migrated to physical (disk or file) swap.

Swap space is reserved each time a heap segment is created. The amount of swap space reserved is the entire size of the segment being created. Swap space is also reserved if there is a possibility of anonymous memory being created. For example, mapped file segments that are mapped MAP_PRIVATE (e.g., the executable data segment) reserve swap space because at any time they could create anonymous memory during a copy-on-write operation.

We reserve virtual swap space upfront so that swap space allocation assignment is done at the time of request, rather than at the time of need. That way, an out-of-swap-space error can be reported synchronously during a system call. If we allocated swap space on demand during program execution rather than when we called malloc(), we could run out of swap space during execution and have no simple way to detect the out-of-swap-space condition. For example, in the Solaris kernel, we fail a malloc() request for memory as it is requested rather than when it is needed later, to prevent processes from failing during seemingly normal execution. (This strategy differs from that of operating systems such as IBM's AIX, where lazy allocation is done. If the resource is exhausted during program execution, then the process is sent a SIGDANGER signal.)

The swapfs file system includes all available pageable memory as virtual swap space in addition to the physical swap space. This allows us to "reserve" virtual swap space and "allocate" swap space when we first touch a page. When we reserve swap, rather than reserving disk space, we reserve virtual swap space from the swapfs file system. Disk swap pages are only allocated once a page is paged out.

With swapfs, the amount of virtual swap space available is the amount of available unlocked, pageable physical memory plus the amount of physical (disk) swap space available. If we were to run without swap space, then we would be able to reserve as much virtual memory as there is unlocked pageable physical memory available on the system. This would be fine, except that often our virtual memory requirements are bigger than our physical memory requirements, and this case would prevent us from using all of the available physical memory on the system.

For example, a process may reserve 100 Mbytes of memory and then allocate only 10 Mbytes of physical memory. The process's physical memory requirement would be 10 Mbytes, but it had to reserve 100 Mbytes of virtual swap, thus using 100 Mbytes of virtual swap allocated from our available real memory. If we ran such a process on a 128-Mbyte system, we would likely start only one of these processes before we exhausted our swap space. If we added more virtual swap space by adding a disk swap device, then we could reserve against the additional space, and we would likely get 10 or so of the equivalent processes in the same physical memory.

Another good example of a larger virtual than physical memory requirement is the process data segment. It's mapped MAP_PRIVATE, which means that we need to reserve virtual swap for the whole segment, but we only allocate physical memory for the few pages that we write to within the segment. The amount of virtual swap required is far greater than the physical memory allocated to it, so if we needed to swap pages out to the swap device, we would need only a small amount of physical swap space.

If we had the ideal process that had all of its virtual memory backed by physical memory, then we could run with no physical swap space. Usually, we need something like 0.5 to 1.5 times memory size for physical swap space. It varies, of course, depending on the virtual-to-physical memory ratio of the application.

5.5.2.2 swapfs Implementation

The swapfs file system uses a system global variable, availrmem, to keep track of the available pageable physical memory in the system and adds it to the total amount of swap space available. When we reserve virtual swap, we simply decrement the amount of virtual memory available from the pool. As long as enough available memory and physical swap space are available, then the swap allocations succeed. It's not until later that physical swap space is assigned.

When we create a private segment, we reserve swap and allocate anon structures. At this stage, that's all that happens until a real memory page is created as a result of a ZFOD or copy-on-write (COW). When a physical page is faulted in, it is identified by vnode/offset, which for anonymous memory is the virtual swap device for the page.

Anonymous pages in Solaris are assigned swapfs vnode and offsets when the segment driver calls anon_alloc() to get a new anonymous page. The anon_alloc() function calls into swapfs through swapfs_getvp() and then calls swapfs_getpage() to create a new page with swapfs vnode/offset. The anon structure members, an_vp and an_offset, which identify the backing store for this page, are initialized to reference the vnode and offset within the swapfs virtual swap device.

Figure 5.13 shows how the anon slot points into swapfs. At this stage, we still don't need any physical swap space—the amount of virtual swap space available was decremented when the segment reserved virtual swap space—but because we haven't had to swap the pages out to physical swap, no physical swap space has been allocated.

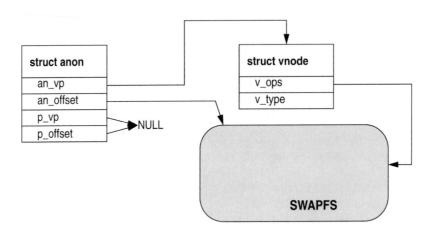

Figure 5.13 Anon Slot Initialized to Virtual Swap Before Page-out

It's not until the first page-out request occurs—because the page scanner must want to push a page to swap—that real swap is assigned. At this time, the page scanner looks up the vnode for the page and then calls its putpage() method. The page's vnode is a swapfs vnode, and hence swapfs_putpage() is called to swap this page out to the swap device. The swapfs_putpage() routine allocates a page-sized block of physical swap and then sets the physical vnode p_vp and p_offset fields in the anon slot to point to the physical swap device. The page is pushed to the swap device. At this point we allocate physical swap space. Figure 5.14 shows the anon slot *after* the page has been swapped out.

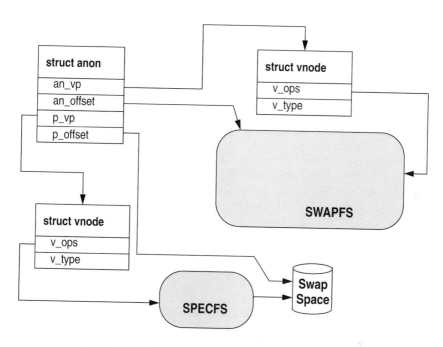

Figure 5.14 Physical Swap After a Page-out Occurs

When we exhaust physical swap space, we simply ignore the `putpage()` request for a page, resulting in memory performance problems that are very hard to analyze. A failure does not occur when physical swap space fills; during reservation, we ensured that we had sufficient available virtual swap space, comprising both physical memory and physical swap space. In this case, the `swapfs_putpage()` simply leaves the page in memory and does not push a page to physical swap. This means that once physical swap is 100 percent allocated, we begin effectively locking down the remaining pages in physical memory. For this reason, it's often a bad idea to run with 100 percent physical swap allocation (swap −1 shows 0 blocks free) because we might start locking down the wrong pages in memory and our working set might not correctly match the pages we really want in memory.

5.5.3 Anonymous Memory Accounting

The amount of anonymous memory in the system is recorded by the `anon` accounting structures. The `anon` layer keeps track of how anonymous pages are allocated in the `kanon_info` structure, shown below, which is defined in the include file `vm/anon.h`.

```
struct k_anoninfo {
        pgcnt_t ani_max;            /* total reservable slots on phys disk swap */
        pgcnt_t ani_free;           /* # of unallocated phys and mem slots */
        pgcnt_t ani_phys_resv;      /* # of reserved phys (disk) slots */
        pgcnt_t ani_mem_resv;       /* # of reserved mem slots */
        pgcnt_t ani_locked_swap;    /* # of swap slots locked in reserved */
                                    /* mem swap */
};
```

Header File <sys/anon.h>

The `k_anoninfo` structure keeps count of the number of slots reserved on physical swap space and against memory. This information is used to populate the data used for the `swapctl` system call. The `swapctl()` system provides the data for the swap command. The swap system call uses a slightly different data structure, the `anoninfo` structure, shown below.

```
struct anoninfo {
        pgcnt_t ani_max;
        pgcnt_t ani_free;
        pgcnt_t ani_resv;
};
```

Header File <sys/anon.h>

The `anoninfo` structure exports the swap allocation information in a platform-independent manner. The `swap` command output, shown below, summarizes information from the `anoninfo` structure.

```
# swap -s
total: 108504k bytes allocated + 13688k reserved = 122192k used, 114880k available
```

The output of `swap -s` can be a little misleading because it confuses the terms used for swap definition. The output is really telling us that 122,192 Kbytes of virtual swap space have been used, 108,504 Kbytes of swap space are allocated to pages that have been touched, and 114,880 Kbytes are free. This information reflects the stages of swap allocation, shown in Figure 5.15. Remember, we reserve swap as we create virtual memory, and then part of that swap is allocated when real pages are assigned to the address space. The balance of swap space remains unused.

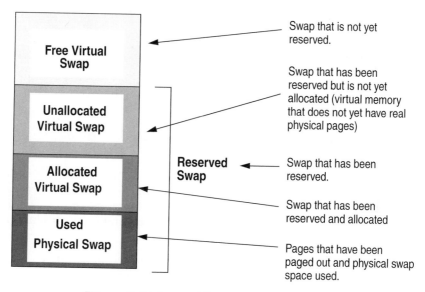

Figure 5.15 Swap Allocation States

You can use the `prtswap` script in MemTool 3.8.1 (see "MemTool: Unbundled Memory Tools" on page 242) to list the states of swap and to find out where the swap is allocated from, as shown below. For just the Swap Allocations summary, use the `prtswap` command.

```
# prtswap -l
Swap Reservations:
---------------------------------------------------------------------------
Total Virtual Swap Configured:                           767MB =
RAM Swap Configured:                                        255MB
Physical Swap Configured:                         +         512MB

Total Virtual Swap Reserved Against:                     513MB =
RAM Swap Reserved Against:                                    1MB
Physical Swap Reserved Against:                   +         512MB

Total Virtual Swap Unresv. & Avail. for Reservation:     253MB =
Physical Swap Unresv. & Avail. for Reservations:           0MB
RAM Swap Unresv. & Avail. for Reservations:       +        253MB


Swap Allocations: (Reserved and Phys pages allocated)
---------------------------------------------------------------------------
Total Virtual Swap Configured:                           767MB
Total Virtual Swap Allocated Against:                    467MB

Physical Swap Utilization: (pages swapped out)
---------------------------------------------------------------------------
Physical Swap Free (should not be zero!):                232MB =
Physical Swap Configured:                                  512MB
Physical Swap Used (pages swapped out):           -        279MB
```

```
# prtswap

Virtual Swap:
---------------------------------------------------------------
Total Virtual Swap Configured:                          767MB
Total Virtual Swap Reserved:                            513MB
Total Virtual Swap Free: (programs will fail if 0)      253MB


Physical Swap Utilization: (pages swapped out)
---------------------------------------------------------------
Physical Swap Configured:                               512MB
Physical Swap Free (programs will be locked in if 0):   232MB
```

The `prtswap` script uses the anonymous accounting structure members to establish how swap space is allocated and uses the `availrmem` counter, the
`swapfsminfree` reserve, and the `swap -l` command to find out how much swap
is used. Table 5-8 shows the anonymous accounting information stored in the kernel.

Table 5-8 Swap Accounting Information

Field	Description
`k_anoninfo.ani_max`	The total number of reservable slots on physical (disk-backed) swap.
`k_anoninfo.ani_phys_resv`	The number of physical (disk-backed) reserved slots.
`k_anoninfo.ani_mem_resv`	The number of memory reserved slots.
`k_anoninfo.ani_free`	Total number of unallocated physical slots + the number of reserved but unallocated memory slots.
`availrmem`	The amount of unreserved memory.
`swapfsminfree`	The `swapfs` reserve that won't be used for memory reservations.

5.6 Virtual Memory Watchpoints

The Solaris kernel implements virtual memory watchpoints within address spaces.
A watchpoint is similar to a breakpoint, except that a watchpoint stops execution
when an address location is read or modified, whereas a breakpoint stops execution when an instruction is executed at a specified location. Watchpoints also provide the ability to implement breakpoints through the watchpoint interface.

You set and clear watchpoints through the `/proc` file system interface, by opening the control file for a process and then sending a `PCWATCH` command. The

PCWATCH command is accompanied by a prwatch structure, which contains the
address, the length of the area to be affected, and the type of watchpoint.

```
typedef struct prwatch {
        uintptr_t pr_vaddr; /* virtual address of watched area */
        size_t    pr_size;  /* size of watched area in bytes */
        int  pr_wflags;     /* watch type flags */
} prwatch_t;
```

Header File   <sys/watchpoint.h>

The pr_vaddr field specifies the virtual address of an area of memory to be
watched in the controlled process; pr_size specifies the size of the area, in bytes,
and pr_wflags specifies the type of memory access to be monitored as a bit-mask
of the flags shown in Table 5-9.

Table 5-9 Watchpoint Flags

Flag	Description
WA_READ	Read access
WA_WRITE	Write access
WA_EXEC	Execution access
WA_TRAPAFTER	Trap after the instruction completes

If pr_wflags is nonzero, then a watched area is established for the virtual
address range specified by pr_vaddr and pr_size. If pr_wflags is zero, then
any previously established watched area starting at the specified virtual address is
cleared; pr_size is ignored.

A watchpoint is triggered when an LWP in the traced process makes a memory
reference that covers at least one byte of a watched area and the memory reference is as specified in pr_wflags. When an LWP triggers a watchpoint, it incurs a
watchpoint trap. If FLTWATCH is being traced, the LWP stops; otherwise, it is sent
a SIGTRAP signal. If SIGTRAP is being traced and is not blocked, then the LWP
stops.

The   watchpoint   trap   occurs   before   the   instruction   completes   unless
WA_TRAPAFTER was specified, in which case it occurs after the instruction completes. If the trap occurs before completion, the memory is not modified. If it occurs
after completion, the memory is modified (if the access is a write access). A minimal example of how a watchpoint is established is shown below. The program creates a watchpoint for read and write access to the bytes occupied by the integer,
test.

```
#include <sys/types.h>
#include <sys/fcntl.h>
#include <procfs.h>

typedef struct {
        long cmd;
        prwatch_t prwatch;
} ctl_t;

main(int argc, char **argv)
{
        int ctlfd;
        ctl_t ctl;
        int test;

        if ((ctlfd = open("/proc/self/ctl", O_WRONLY)) < 0) {
                perror("open /proc");
                exit (1);
        }

        ctl.cmd = PCWATCH;
        ctl.prwatch.pr_vaddr = (uintptr_t)&test;
        ctl.prwatch.pr_size = sizeof(int);
        ctl.prwatch.pr_wflags = WA_READ|WA_WRITE;

        if (write(ctlfd, &ctl, sizeof (ctl)) != sizeof (ctl)) {
                perror("Set PCWATCH");
                exit (1);
        }

        test = 0;
}
```

When we attempt to write to the integer `test`, we trigger a watchpoint and, by default, the process core dumps.

```
$ ./watchpoint
Trace/Breakpoint Trap(coredump)
```

The `/proc` process information file, `prinfo`, contains information pertinent to the watchpoint trap and can be read into a struct `pr_info`. In particular, the `si_addr` field contains the virtual address of the memory reference that triggered the watchpoint, and the `si_code` field contains one of `TRAP_RWATCH`, `TRAP_WWATCH`, or `TRAP_XWATCH`, indicating read, write, or execute access, respectively. The `si_trapafter` field is zero unless `WA_TRAPAFTER` is in effect for this watched area; nonzero indicates that the current instruction is not the instruction that incurred the watchpoint trap. The `si_pc` field contains the virtual address of the instruction that incurred the trap. Figure 5.16 illustrates watchpoint data structures.

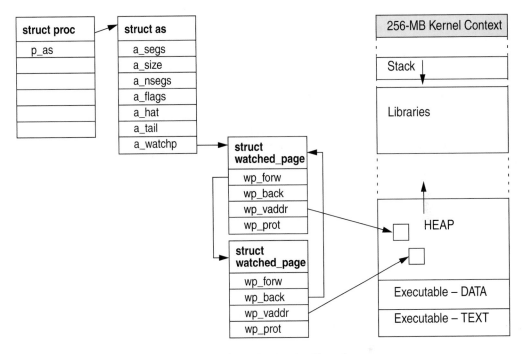

Figure 5.16 Watchpoint Data Structures

5.7 Global Page Management

Pages are the fundamental unit of physical memory in the Solaris memory management subsystem. In this section, we discuss how pages are structured, how they are located, and how free lists manage pools of pages within the system.

5.7.1 Pages—The Basic Unit of Solaris Memory

Physical memory is divided into pages. Every active (not free) page in the Solaris kernel is a mapping between a file (vnode) and memory; the page can be identified with a vnode pointer and the page size offset within that vnode. A page's identity is its vnode/offset pair. The vnode/offset pair is the backing store for the page and represents the file and offset that the page is mapping.

The hardware address translation (HAT) and address space layers manage the mapping between a physical page and its virtual address space (more about that in "The Hardware Address Translation Layer" on page 190). The key property of the vnode/offset pair is reusability; that is, we can reuse each physical page for another task by simply synchronizing its contents in RAM with its backing store (the vnode and offset) before the page is reused.

For example, we can reuse a page of heap memory from a process by simply copying the contents to its vnode and offset, which in this case will copy the contents to the swap device. The same mechanism is used for caching files, and we simply use the vnode/offset pair to reference the file that the page is caching. If we were to reuse a page of memory that was caching a regular file, then we simply synchronize the page with its backing store (if the page has been modified) or just reuse the page if it is not modified and does not need resyncing with its backing store.

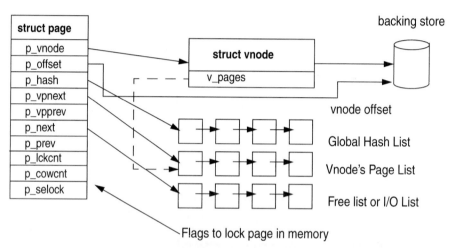

Figure 5.17 The Page Structure

5.7.2 The Page Hash List

The VM system hashes pages with identity (a valid vnode/offset pair) onto a global hash list so that they can be located by vnode and offset. Three page functions search the global page hash list: page_find(), page_lookup(), and page_lookup_nowait(). These functions take a vnode and offset as arguments and return a pointer to a page structure if found.

The global hash list is an array of pointers to linked lists of pages. The functions use a hash to index into the page_hash array to locate the list of pages that contains the page with the matching vnode/offset pair. Figure 5.18 shows how the page_find() function indexes into the page_hash array to locate a page matching a given vnode/offset.

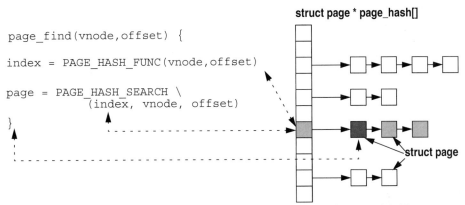

Figure 5.18 Locating Pages by Their Vnode/Offset Identity

`page_find()` locates a page as follows:

1. It calculates the slot in the `page_hash` array containing a list of potential pages by using the `PAGE_HASH_FUNC` macro, shown below.

```
#define PAGE_HASHSZ        page_hashsz
#define PAGE_HASHAVELEN           4
#define PAGE_HASHVPSHIFT          6
#define PAGE_HASH_FUNC(vp, off) \
        ((((uintptr_t)(off) >> PAGESHIFT) + \
                ((uintptr_t)(vp) >> PAGE_HASHVPSHIFT)) & \
                (PAGE_HASHSZ - 1))
```

Header File   <vm/page.h>

2. It uses the `PAGE_HASH_SEARCH` macro, shown below, to search the list referenced by the slot for a page matching vnode/offset. The macro traverses the linked list of pages until it finds such a page.

```
ine PAGE_HASH_SEARCH(index, pp, vp, off) { \
        for ((pp) = page_hash[(index)]; (pp); (pp) = (pp)->p_hash) { \
                if ((pp)->p_vnode == (vp) && (pp)->p_offset == (off)) \
                        break; \
        } \
```

Header File   <vm/page.h>

5.7.3 MMU-Specific Page Structures

The defined `page` structure is the same across different platforms and hence contains no machine-specific structures. We do, however, need to keep machine-specific data about every page, for example, the HAT information that describes how the page is mapped by the MMU. The kernel wraps the machine-independent page structure with a machine-specific page structure, `struct machpage`. The contents of the machine-specific page structure are hidden from the generic kernel—only the HAT machine-specific layer can see or manipulate its contents. Figure 5.19 shows how each page structure is embedded in a machine-dependent `struct machpage`.

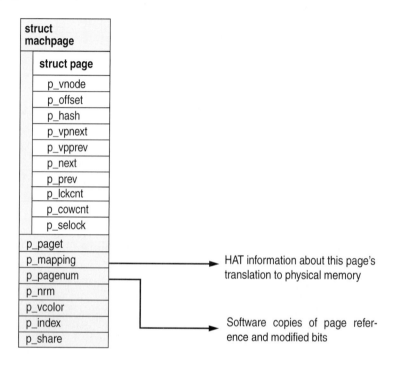

Figure 5.19 Machine-Specific Page Structures: sun4u Example

The machine-specific page contains a pointer to the HAT-specific mapping information, and information about the page's HAT state is stored in the machine-specific `machpage`. The store information includes bits that indicate whether the page has been referenced or modified, for use in the page scanner (covered later in the chapter). Both the machine-independent and machine-dependent page structures share the same start address in memory, so a pointer to a page structure can be cast to a pointer to a machine-specific page structure (see Figure 5.19). Macros for converting between machine-independent pages and machine-dependent page structures make the cast.

5.7.4 Physical Page Lists

The Solaris kernel uses a segmented global physical page list, consisting of segments of contiguous physical memory. (Many hardware platforms now present memory in noncontiguous groups.) Contiguous physical memory segments are added during system boot. They are also added and deleted dynamically when physical memory is added and removed while the system is running. Figure 5.20 shows the arrangement of the physical page lists into contiguous segments.

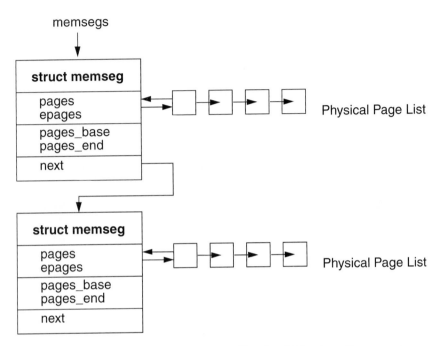

Figure 5.20 Contiguous Physical Memory Segments

5.7.4.1 Free List and Cache List

The free list and the cache list hold pages that are not mapped into any address space and that have been freed by page_free(). The sum of these lists is reported in the *free* column in vmstat. Even though vmstat reports these pages as free, they can still contain a valid page from a vnode/offset and hence are still part of the global page cache. Pages that are caching files in the page cache can appear on the free list. Memory on the cache list is not really free, it is a valid cache of a page from a file. The cache list exemplifies how the file systems use memory as a file system cache.

The free list contains pages that no longer have a vnode and offset associated with them—which can only occur if the page has been destroyed and removed from a vnode's hash list. The free list is generally very small, since most pages that are no longer used by a process or the kernel still keep their vnode/offset information intact. Pages are put on the free list when a process exits, at which point all of the anonymous memory pages (heap, stack, and copy-on-write pages) are freed.

The cache list is a hashed list of pages that still have mappings to valid vnode and offset. Recall that pages can be obtained from the cache list by the page_lookup() routine. This function accepts a vnode and offset as the argument and returns a page structure. If the page is found on the cache list, then the page is removed from the cache list and returned to the caller. When we find and remove pages from the cache list, we are *reclaiming* a page. Page reclaims are reported by vmstat in the "re" column.

5.7.5 The Page-Level Interfaces

The Solaris virtual memory system implementation has grouped page management and manipulation into a central group of functions. These functions are used by the segment drivers and file systems to create, delete, and modify pages. The major page-level interfaces are shown in Table 5-10.

Table 5-10 Solaris 7 Page Level Interfaces

Method	Description
page_create()	Creates pages. Page coloring is based on a hash of the vnode offset. page_create() is provided for backward compatibility only. Don't use it if you don't have to. Instead, use the page_create_va() function so that pages are correctly colored.
page_create_va()	Creates pages, taking into account the virtual address they will be mapped to. The address is used to calculate page coloring.
page_exists()	Tests that a page for vnode/offset exists.
page_find()	Searches the hash list for a page with the specified vnode and offset that is known to exist and is already locked.
page_first()	Finds the first page on the global page hash list.
page_free()	Frees a page. Pages with vnode/offset go onto the cache list; other pages go onto the free list.
page_isfree()	Checks whether a page is on the free list.
page_ismod()	Checks whether a page is modified. This function checks only the software bit in the page structure. To sync the MMU bits with the page structure, you may need to call hat_pagesync() before calling page_ismod().
page_isref()	Checks whether a page has been referenced; checks only the software bit in the page structure. To sync the MMU bits with the page structure, you may need to call hat_pagesync() before calling page_isref().
page_isshared()	Checks whether a page is shared across more than one address space.
page_lookup()	Finds a page representing the specified vnode/offset. If the page is found on a free list, then it will be removed from the free list.

Table 5-10 Solaris 7 Page Level Interfaces (Continued)

Method	Description
page_lookup_nowait()	Finds a page representing the specified vnode/offset that is not locked or on the free list.
page_needfree()	Informs the VM system we need some pages freed up. Calls to page_needfree( ) must be symmetric; that is, they must be followed by another page_needfree( ) with the same amount of memory multiplied by -1,after the task is complete.
page_next()	Finds the next page on the global page hash list.

The page_create_va() function allocates pages. It takes the number of pages to allocate as an argument and returns a page list linked with the pages that have been taken from the free list. page_create_va() also takes a virtual address as an argument so that it can implement page coloring (discussed in Section 5.7.8, "Page Coloring," on page 174). The new page_create_va() function subsumes the older page_create() function and should be used by all newly developed subsystems because page_create() may not correctly color the allocated pages.

5.7.6 The Page Throttle

Solaris implements a page creation throttle so a small core of memory is available for consumption by critical parts of the kernel. The page throttle, implemented in the page_create() and page_create_va() functions, causes page creates to block when the PG_WAIT flag is specified, that is, when available memory is less than the system global, throttlefree. By default, the system global parameter, throttlefree, is set to the same value as the system global parameter minfree. By default, memory allocated through the kernel memory allocator specifies PG_WAIT and is subject to the page-created throttle. (See Section 6.2, "Kernel Memory Allocation," on page 212 for more information on kernel memory allocation.)

5.7.7 Page Sizes

The Solaris kernel uses a fundamental page size that varies according to the underlying hardware. On UltraSPARC and beyond, the fundamental page size is 8 Kbytes. The hardware on which Solaris runs has several different types of memory management units, which support a variety of page sizes, as listed in Table 5-11.

Table 5-11 Page Sizes on Different Sun Platforms

System Type	System Type	MMU Page Size Capability	Solaris 2.x Page Size
Early SPARC systems	sun4c	4K	4K
microSPARC-I, -II	sun4m	4K	4K
SuperSPARC-I, -II	sun4m	4K, 4M	4K, 4M
UltraSPARC-I, -II	sun4u	4K, 64K, 512K, 4M	8K, 4M
Intel x86 architecture	i86pc	4K, 4M	4K, 4M

The optimal MMU page size is a trade-off between performance and memory size efficiency. A larger page size has less memory management overhead and hence better performance, but a smaller page size wastes less memory (memory is wasted when a page is not completely filled). (See "Large Pages" on page 201 for further information on large pages.)

5.7.8 Page Coloring

Some interesting effects result from the organization of pages within the processor caches, and as a result, the page placement policy within these caches can dramatically affect processor performance. When pages overlay other pages in the cache, they can displace cache data that we might not want overlaid, resulting in less cache utilization and "hot spots."

The optimal placement of pages in the cache often depends on the memory access patterns of the application; that is, is the application accessing memory in a random order, or is it doing some sort of strided ordered access? Several different algorithms can be selected in the Solaris kernel to implement page placement; the default attempts to provide the best overall performance.

To understand how page placement can affect performance, let's look at the cache configuration and see when page overlaying and displacement can occur. The UltraSPARC-I and -II implementations use virtually addressed L1 caches and physically addressed L2 caches. The L2 cache is arranged in lines of 64 bytes, and transfers are done to and from physical memory in 64-byte units. Figure 5.27 on page 194 shows the architecture of the UltraSPARC-I and -II CPU modules with their caches. The L1 cache is 16 Kbytes, and the L2 (external) cache can vary between 512 Kbytes and 8 Mbytes. We can query the operating system with adb to see the size of the caches reported to the operating system. The L1 cache sizes are recorded in the vac_size parameter, and the L2 cache size is recorded in the ecache_size parameter.

```
# adb -k
physmem 7a97
vac_size/D
vac_size:
vac_size:        16384
ecache_size/D
ecache_size:
ecache_size:     1048576
```

We'll start by using the L2 cache as an example of how page placement can affect performance. The physical addressing of the L2 cache means that the cache is organized in page-sized multiples of the physical address space, which means that the cache effectively has only a limited number of page-aligned slots. The number of effective page slots in the cache is the cache size divided by the page size. To simplify our examples, let's assume we have a 32-Kbyte L2 cache (much smaller than reality), which means that if we have a page size of 8 Kbytes, there are four page-sized slots on the L2 cache. The cache does not necessarily read and write 8-Kbyte units from memory; it does that in 64-byte chunks, so in reality our 32-Kbyte cache has 1024 addressable slots. Figure 5.21 shows how our cache would look if we laid it out linearly.

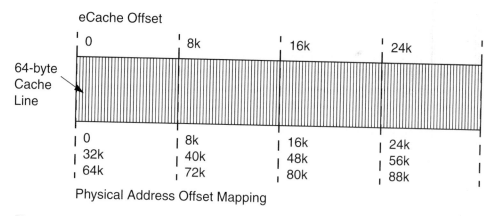

Figure 5.21 Physical Page Mapping into a 64-Kbyte Physical Cache

The L2 cache is direct-mapped from physical memory. If we were to access physical addresses on a 32-Kbyte boundary, for example, offsets 0 and 32678, then both memory locations would map to the same cache line. If we were now to access these two addresses, we cause the cache lines for the offset 0 address to be read, then flushed (cleared), the cache line for the offset 32768 address to be read in, and then flushed, then the first reloaded, etc. This ping-pong effect in the cache is known as cache flushing (or cache ping-ponging), and it effectively reduces our performance to that of real-memory speed, rather than cache speed. By accessing memory on our 32-Kbyte cache-size boundary, we have effectively used only 64 bytes of the cache (a cache line size), rather than the full cache size. Memory is often up to 10–20 times slower than cache and so can have a dramatic effect on performance.

Our simple example was based on the assumption that we were accessing physical memory in a regular pattern, but we don't program to physical memory; rather, we program to virtual memory. Therefore, the operating system must provide a sensible mapping between virtual memory and physical memory; otherwise, effects such as our example can occur.

By default, physical pages are assigned to an address space from the order in which they appear in the free list. In general, the first time a machine boots, the free list may have physical memory in a linear order, and we may end up with the behavior described in our "ping pong" example. Once a machine has been running, the physical page free list will become randomly ordered, and subsequent reruns of an identical application could get very different physical page placement and, as a result, very different performance. On early Solaris implementations, this is exactly what customers saw—differing performance for identical runs, as much as 30 percent difference.

To provide better and consistent performance, the Solaris kernel uses a page coloring algorithm when pages are allocated to a virtual address space. Rather than being randomly allocated, the pages are allocated with a specific predetermined relationship between the virtual address to which they are being mapped and their underlying physical address. The virtual-to-physical relationship is predetermined as follows: The free list of physical pages is organized into specifically colored bins, one color bin for each slot in the physical cache; the number of color bins is determined by the ecache size divided by the page size. (In our example, there would be exactly four colored bins.)

When a page is put on the free list, the `page_free()` algorithms assign it to a color bin. When a page is consumed from the free list, the virtual-to-physical algorithm takes the page from a physical color bin, chosen as a function of the virtual address which to which the page will be mapped. The algorithm requires that when allocating pages from the free list, the page create function must know the virtual address to which a page will be mapped.

New pages are allocated by calling the `page_create_va()` function. The `page_create_va()` function accepts the virtual address of the location to which the page is going to be mapped as an argument; then, the virtual-to-physical color bin algorithm can decide which color bin to take physical pages from. The `page_create_va()` function is described with the page management functions in Table 5-10 on page 172.

Note: The `page_create_va()` function deprecates the older `page_create()` function. We chose to add a new function rather than adding an additional argument to the existing `page_create()` function so that existing third-party loadable kernel modules which call `page_create()` remain functional. However, because `page_create()` does not know about virtual addresses, it has to pick a color at random—which can cause significant performance degradation. The `page_create_va()` function should always be used for new code.

No one algorithm suits all applications because different applications have different memory access patterns. Over time, the page coloring algorithms used in the Solaris kernel have been refined as a result of extensive simulation, benchmarks, and customer feedback. The kernel supports a default algorithm and two optional algorithms. The default algorithm was chosen according to the following criteria:

- Fairly consistent, repeatable results
- Good overall performance for the majority of applications
- Acceptable performance across a wide range of applications

The default algorithm uses a hashing algorithm to distribute pages as evenly as possible throughout the cache. The default and three other available page coloring algorithms are shown in Table 5-12.

Table 5-12 Solaris Page Coloring Algorithms

Algorithm		Description	Solaris Availability		
No.	Name		2.5.1	2.6	7
0	Hashed VA	The physical page color bin is chosen on a hashed algorithm to ensure even distribution of virtual addresses across the cache.	Default	Default	Default
1	P. Addr = V. Addr	The physical page color is chosen so that physical addresses map directly to the virtual addresses (as in our example).	Yes	Yes	Yes
2	Bin Hopping	Physical pages are allocated with a round-robin method.	Yes	Yes	Yes

Table 5-12 Solaris Page Coloring Algorithms (Continued)

Algorithm		Description	Solaris Availability		
No.	**Name**		**2.5.1**	**2.6**	**7**
6	Kessler's Best Bin	Keeps history per process of used colors and chooses least used color; if multiple, use largest bin.	E10000 Only (Default)	E10000 Only (Default)	Not Available

The Ultra Enterprise 10000 has a different default algorithm, which tries to evenly distribute colors for each process's address space so that no one color is more used than another. This algorithm is correct most of the time, but in some cases, the hashed or direct (0 or 1) algorithms can be better.

You can change the default algorithm by setting the system parameter `consistent_coloring`, either on-the-fly with `adb` or permanently in `/etc/system`.

```
# adb -kw
physmem 7a97
consistent_coloring/D
consistent_coloring:
consistent_coloring:            0
consistent_coloring/W 1
consistent_coloring:            0x0            =            0x1
```

So, which algorithm is best? Well, your mileage will vary, depending on your application. Page coloring usually only makes a difference on memory-intensive scientific applications, and the defaults are usually fine for commercial or database systems. If you have a time-critical scientific application, then we recommend that you experiment with the different algorithms and see which is best. Remember that some algorithms will produce different results for each run, so aggregate as many runs as possible.

5.8 The Page Scanner

The page scanner is the memory management daemon that manages systemwide physical memory. The page scanner and the virtual memory page fault mechanism are the core of the demand-paged memory allocation system used to manage Solaris memory. When there is a memory shortage, the page scanner runs to steal memory from address spaces by taking pages that haven't been used recently, syncing them up with their backing store (swap space if they are anonymous pages), and freeing them. If paged-out virtual memory is required again by an address space, then a memory page fault occurs when the virtual address is referenced and the pages are recreated and copied back from their backing store.

The balancing of page stealing and page faults determines which parts of virtual memory will be backed by real physical memory and which will be moved out to swap. The page scanner does not understand the memory usage patterns or working sets of processes; it only knows reference information on a physical page-by-page basis. This policy is often referred to as *global page replacement*; the alternative process-based page management is known as *local page replacement*.

The subtleties of which pages are stolen govern the memory allocation policies and can affect different workloads in different ways. During the life of the Solaris kernel, only two significant changes in memory replacement policies have occurred:

- Enhancements to minimize page stealing from extensively shared libraries and executables

- Priority paging to prevent application, shared library, and executable paging on systems with ample memory

We discuss these changes in more detail when we describe page scanner implementation.

5.8.1 Page Scanner Operation

The page scanner tracks page usage by reading a per-page hardware bit from the hardware MMU for each page. Two bits are kept for each page; they indicate whether the page has been modified or referenced since the bits were last cleared. The page scanner uses the bits as the fundamental data to decide which pages of memory have been used recently and which have not.

The page scanner is a kernel thread, which is awakened when the amount of memory on the free-page list falls below a system threshhold, typically 1/64th of total physical memory. The page scanner scans through pages in physical page order, looking for pages that haven't been used recently to page out to the swap device and free. The algorithm that determines whether pages have been used resembles a clock face and is known as the two-handed clock algorithm. This algorithm views the entire physical page list as a circular list, where the last physical page wraps around to the first. Two hands sweep through the physical page list, as shown in Figure 5.22.

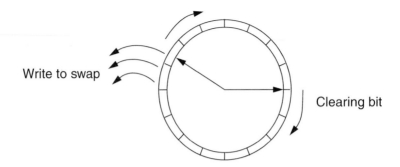

Figure 5.22 Two-Handed Clock Algorithm

The two hands, the front hand and back hand, rotate clockwise in page order around the list. The front hand rotates ahead of the back hand, clearing the referenced and modified bits for each page. The trailing back hand then inspects the referenced and modified bits some time later. Pages that have not been referenced or modified are swapped out and freed. The rate at which the hands rotate around the page list is controlled by the amount of free memory on the system, and the gap between the front hand and back hand is fixed by a boot-time parameter, handspreadpages.

5.8.2 Page-out Algorithm and Parameters

The page-out algorithm is controlled by several parameters, some of which are calculated at system startup by the amount of memory in the system, and some of which are calculated dynamically based on memory allocation and paging activity.

The parameters that control the clock hands do two things: They control the rate at which the scanner scans through pages, and they control the time (or distance) between the front hand and the back hand. The distance between the back hand and the front hand is handspreadpages and is expressed in units of pages. The maximum distance between the front hand and back hand defaults to half of the memory and is capped at 8,192 pages, or 64 Mbytes. Systems with 128 Mbytes or more memory always default this distance to 8,192 pages, or 64 Mbytes.

5.8.2.1 Scan Rate Parameters (Assuming No Priority Paging)

The scanner starts scanning when free memory is lower than lotsfree number of pages free plus a small buffer factor, deficit. The scanner starts scanning at a rate of slowscan pages per second at this point and gets faster as the amount of free memory approaches zero. The system parameter lotsfree is calculated at startup as 1/64th memory, and the parameter deficit is either zero or a small number of pages—set by the page allocator at times of large memory allocation to let the scanner free a few more pages above lotsfree in anticipation of more memory requests.

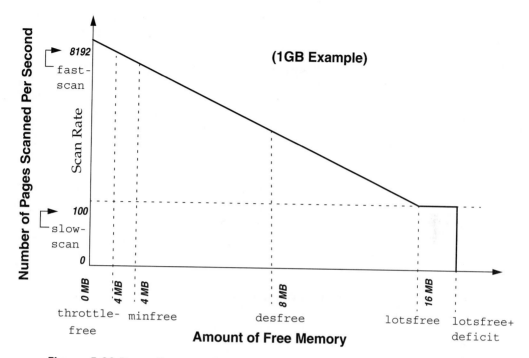

Figure 5.23 Page Scanner Rate, Interpolated by Number of Free Pages

Figure 5.23 shows the rate at which the scanner scans increases linearly as free memory ranges between `lotsfree` and zero. The scanner starts scanning at the minimum rate set by `slowscan` when memory falls below `lotsfree` and then increases to `fastscan` if memory falls low enough.

The number of pages scanned increases from the slowest rate (set by `slowscan` when `lotsfree` pages are free) to a maximum determined by the system parameter `fastscan`. Free memory never actually reaches zero, but for simplicity the algorithm calculates the maximum interpolated rate against the free memory ranging between `lotsfree` and zero. In our example system with 1 Gbyte of physical memory (shown in Figure 5.24 on page 185), we can see that the scanner starts scanning when free memory falls to 16 Mbytes plus the short-term memory deficit.

For this example, we'll assume that the deficit is zero. When free memory falls to 16 Mbytes, the scanner will wake up and start examining 100 pages per second, according to the system parameter `slowscan`. The `slowscan` parameter is 100 by default on Solaris systems, and `fastscan` is set to total *physicalmemory*/2, capped at 8,192 pages per second. If free memory falls to 12 Mbytes (1,536 pages), the scanner scans at a higher rate, according to the page scanner interpolation shown in the following equation:

$$scanrate = \left(\frac{lotsfree - freememory}{lotsfree} \times fastscan\right) + \left(slowscan \times \frac{freemem}{lotsfree}\right)$$

If we convert free memory and `lotsfree` to numbers of pages (free memory of 12 Mbytes is 1,536 pages, and `lotsfree` is set to 16 Mbytes, or 2,048 pages), then we scan at 2,123 pages per second.

$$scanrate = \left(\frac{2048 - 1536}{2048} \times 8192\right) + \left(100 \times \frac{1536}{2048}\right) = 2123$$

By default, the scanner is run four times per second when there is a memory shortage. If the amount of free memory falls below the system parameter `minfree`, the scanner is awoken by the page allocator for each page-create request. This scheme helps the scanner try to keep at least `minfree` pages on the free list.

5.8.2.2 Not Recently Used Time

The time between the front hand and back hand varies according to the number of pages between the front hand and back hand and the rate at which the scanner is scanning. The time between the front hand clearing the reference bit and the back hand checking the reference bit is a significant factor that affects the behavior of the scanner because it controls the amount of time that a page can be left alone before it is potentially stolen by the page scanner. A short time between the reference bit being cleared and checked means that all but the most active pages remain intact; a long time means that only the largely unused pages are stolen. The ideal behavior is the latter because we want only the least recently used pages stolen, which means we want a long time between the front and back hands.

The time between clearing and checking of the reference bit can vary from just a few seconds to several hours, depending on the scan rate. The scan rate on today's busy systems can often grow to several thousand, which means that a very small time exists between the front hand and back hand. For example, a system with a scan rate of 2,000 pages per second and the default hand spread of 8,192 pages has a clear/check time of only 4 seconds. High scan rates are quite normal on systems because of the memory pressure induced by the file system. (We discuss this topic further in "Is All That Paging Bad for My System?" on page 595.)

5.8.3 Shared Library Optimizations

A subtle optimization added to the page scanner prevents it from stealing pages from extensively shared libraries. The page scanner looks at the share reference count for each page; if the page is shared more than a certain amount, then it is skipped during the page scan operation. An internal parameter, po_share, sets the threshold for the amount of shares a page can have before it is skipped. If the page has more than po_share mappings (i.e., it's shared by more than po_share processes), then it is skipped. By default, po_share starts at 8; each time around, it is decremented unless the scan around the clock does not find any page to free, in which case po_share is incremented. The po_share parameter can float between 8 and 134217728.

5.8.4 The Priority Paging Algorithm

Solaris 7 shipped with a new optional paging algorithm—a page-stealing algorithm that results in much better system response and throughput for systems making use of the file systems. The algorithm is also available on older Solaris releases (from 2.5.1 onward) with the addition of a kernel patch. You enable the new algorithm by setting the priority_paging variable to 1 in /etc/system.

```
*
* Enable the Priority Paging Algorithm
*
set priority_paging = 1
```

The new algorithm was introduced to overcome adverse behavior that results from the memory pressure caused by the file system. Back in SunOS 4.0, when the virtual memory system was rewritten, the file system cache and virtual memory system were integrated to allow the entire memory system to be used as a file system cache; that is, the file system uses pages of memory from the free memory pool, just as do processes when they request memory.

The demand paging algorithm allows the file system cache to grow and shrink dynamically as required, by stealing pages that have not been recently used by other subsystems. However, back when this work was done, the memory pressure from the file system was relatively low, as were the memory requests from the processes on the system. Both were in the order of tens to hundreds of pages per second, so memory allocation could be based on who was using the pages the most. When processes accessed their memory pages frequently, the scanner was biased to steal from the file system, and the file system cache would shrink accordingly.

Today, systems are capable of sustaining much higher I/O rates, which means that the file system can put enormous memory pressure on the memory system— so much so that the amount of memory pressure from the file system can completely destroy application performance by causing the page scanner to steal many process pages.

We like to think of the early SunOS 4.0 case as being like a finely balanced set of scales, where the process and file system requests sit on each side of the scale and are reasonably balanced. But on today's system, the scales are completely weighted on the file system side because of the enormous paging rates required to do I/O through the file system. For example, even a small system can do 20 megabytes of I/O per second, which causes the file system to use 2,560 pages per second. To keep up with this request, the scanner must scan at least at this rate, usually higher because the scanner will not steal every page it finds. This typically means a scan rate of 3,000 or higher, just to do some regular I/O.

As we saw earlier, when we scan at this rate, we have as little as a few seconds between the time we clear and the time we check for activity. As a result, we steal process memory that hasn't been used in the last few seconds. The noticeable effect is that everything appears to grind to a halt when we start using the file system for significant I/O, and free memory falls below `lotsfree`. It is important to note that this effect can result even with ample memory in the system—adding more memory doesn't make the situation any better.

To overcome this effect, the page scanner has a new algorithm that puts a higher priority on a process's pages, namely, its heap, stack, shared libraries, and executables. The algorithm permits the scanner to pick file system cache pages only when ample memory is available and hence only steal application pages when there is a true memory shortage.

The new algorithm introduces a new paging parameter, `cachefree`. When the amount of free memory lies between `cachefree` and `lotsfree`, the page scanner steals only file system cache pages. The scanner also now wakes up when memory falls below `cachefree` rather than below `lotsfree`, and the scan rate algorithm is changed accordingly.

$$scanrate = \left(\frac{cachefree - freememory}{cachefree} \times fastscan \right) + \left(slowscan \times \frac{freemem}{cachefree} \right)$$

The scan rate is now interpolated between `cachefree` and zero, rather than between `lotsfree` and zero, as shown in Figure 5.24.

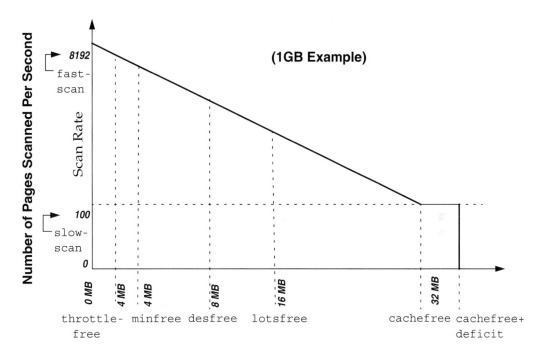

Figure 5.24 Scan Rate Interpolation with the Priority Paging Algorithm

The algorithm pages only against the file system cache when memory is between `cachefree` and `lotsfree` by skipping pages that are associated with the swap device (heap, stack, copy-on-write pages) and by skipping file pages that are mapped into an address space with execute permission (binaries, shared libraries).

The new algorithm has no side effects and should always be enabled on Solaris versions up to Solaris 7. (Note: The algorithm has been replaced in Solaris 8 by a new cache architecture, and priority paging should not be enabled on Solaris 8.) It was not enabled by default in Solaris 7 only because it was introduced very late in the Solaris release cycle.

5.8.4.1 Page Scanner CPU Utilization Clamp

A CPU utilization clamp on the scan rate prevents the page-out daemon from using too much processor time. Two internal limits govern the desired and maximum CPU time that the scanner should use. Two parameters, `min_percent_cpu` and `max_percent_cpu`, govern the amount of CPU that the scanner can use. Like the scan rate, the actual amount of CPU that can be used at any given time is interpolated by the amount of free memory. It ranges from `min_percent_cpu` when free memory is at `lotsfree` (`cachefree` with priority paging enabled) to `max_percent_cpu` if free memory were to fall to zero. The defaults for `min_percent_cpu` and `max_percent_cpu` are 4% and 80% of a single CPU, respectively (the scanner is single threaded).

5.8.4.2 Parameters That Limit Pages Paged Out

Another parameter, `maxpgio`, limits the rate at which I/O is queued to the swap devices. It is set low to prevent saturation of the swap devices. The parameter defaults to 40 I/Os per second on sun4c, sun4m, and sun4u architectures and to 60 I/Os per second on the sun4d architecture. The default setting is often inadequate for modern systems and should be set to 100 times the number of swap spindles.

Because the page-out daemon also pages out dirty file system pages that it finds during scanning, this parameter can also indirectly limit file system throughput. File system I/O requests are normally queued and written by user processes and hence are not subject to `maxpgio`. However, when a lot of file system write activity is going on and many dirty file system pages are in memory, the page-out scanner trips over these and queues these I/Os; as a result, the `maxpgio` limit can sometimes affect file system write throughput. Please refer to the memory parameter appendix for further recommendations.

5.8.4.3 Summary of Page Scanner Parameters

Table 5-13 describes the parameters that control the page-out process in the current Solaris and patch releases.

Table 5-13 Page Scanner Parameters

Parameter	Description	Min	2.7 Default
cachefree	If free memory falls below `cachefree`, then the page-out scanner starts 4 times/second, at a rate of `slowscan` pages/second. Only file system pages are stolen and freed. The `cachefree` parameter is set indirectly by the `priority_paging` parameter. When `priority_paging` is set to 1, `cachefree` is automatically set at twice the value of `lotsfree` during boot.	lotsfree	lotsfree or 2 x lotsfree (with pp.)
lotsfree	The scanner starts stealing anonymous memory pages when free memory falls below `lotsfree`.	512K	1/64th of memory
desfree	If free memory falls below `desfree`, then the page-out scanner is started 100 times/second.	minfree	lotsfree/2

Table 5-13 Page Scanner Parameters (Continued)

Parameter	Description	Min	2.7 Default
minfree	If free memory falls below min-free, then the page scanner is signaled to start every time a new page is created.		desfree/2
throttlefree	The number at which point the page_create routines make the caller wait until free pages are available.	—	minfree
fastscan	The rate of pages scanned per second when free memory = minfree. Measured in pages.	slow-scan	Minimum of 64 MB/s or 1/2 memory size
slowscan	The rate of pages scanned per second when free memory = lotsfree.	—	100
maxpgio	A throttle for the maximum number of pages per second that the swap device can handle.	~60	60 or 90 pages/s
hand-spreadpages	The number of pages between the front hand clearing the reference bit and the back hand checking the reference bit.	1	fastscan

5.8.5 Page Scanner Implementation

The page scanner is implemented as two kernel threads, both of which use process number 2, "pageout." One thread scans pages, and the other thread pushes the dirty pages queued for I/O to the swap device. In addition, the kernel callout mechanism wakes the page scanner thread when memory is insufficient. (The kernel callout scheduling mechanism is discussed in detail in Section 2.5, "The Kernel Callout Table," on page 47.)

The scanner schedpaging() function is called four times per second by a callout placed in the callout table. The schedpaging() function checks whether free memory is below the threshold (lotsfree or cachefree) and, if required, triggers the scanner thread. The page scanner is not only awakened by the callout thread, it is also triggered by the page allocator if memory falls below throttle-free.

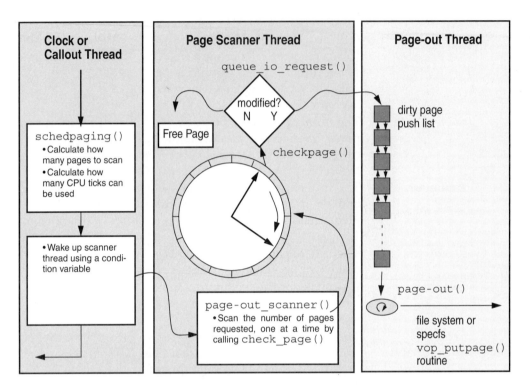

Figure 5.25 Page Scanner Architecture

Figure 5.25 illustrates how the page scanner works.

When called, the `schedpaging` routine calculates two setup parameters for the page scanner thread: the number of pages to scan and the number of CPU ticks that the scanner thread can consume while doing so. The number of pages and cpu ticks are calculated according to the equations shown in "Scan Rate Parameters (Assuming No Priority Paging)" on page 180 and "Page Scanner CPU Utilization Clamp" on page 185. Once the scanning parameters have been calculated, `schedpaging` triggers the page scanner through a condition variable `wakeup`.

The page scanner thread cycles through the physical page list, progressing by the number of pages requested each time it is woken up. The front hand and the back hand each have a page pointer. The front hand is incremented first so that it can clear the referenced and modified bits for the page currently pointed to by the front hand. The back hand is then incremented, and the status of the page pointed to by the back hand is checked by the `check_page()` function. At this point, if the page has been modified, it is placed in the dirty page queue for processing by the page-out thread. If the page was not referenced (it's clean!), then it is simply freed.

Dirty pages are placed onto a queue so that a separate thread, the page-out thread, can write them out to their backing store. We use another thread so that a deadlock can't occur while the system is waiting to swap a page out. The page-out thread uses a preinitialized list of async buffer headers as the queue for I/O requests. The list is initialized with 256 entries, which means the queue can contain at most 256 entries. The number of entries preconfigured on the list is controlled by the async_request_size system parameter. Requests to queue more I/Os onto the queue will be blocked if the entire queue is full (256 entries) or if the rate of pages queued has exceeded the system maximum set by the maxpgio parameter.

The page-out thread simply removes I/O entries from the queue and initiates I/O on it by calling the vnode putpage() function for the page in question. In the Solaris kernel, this function calls the swapfs_putpage() function to initiate the swap page-out via the swapfs layer. The swapfs layer delays and gathers together pages (16 pages on sun4u), then writes these out together. The klust-size parameter controls the number of pages that swapfs will cluster; the defaults are shown in Table 5-14. (See "The swapfs Layer" on page 156.)

Table 5-14 swapfs Cluster Sizes

Platform	Number of Clustered Pages (set by klustsize)
sun4u	16 (128k)
sun4m	31 (124k)
sun4d	31 (124k)
sun4c	31 (124k)
i86	14 (56k)

5.8.6 The Memory Scheduler

In addition to the page-out process, the CPU scheduler/dispatcher can swap out entire processes to conserve memory. This operation is separate from page-out. Swapping out a process involves removing all of a process's thread structures and private pages from memory, and setting flags in the process table to indicate that this process has been swapped out. This is an inexpensive way to conserve memory, but it dramatically affects a process's performance and hence is used only when paging fails to free enough memory consistently.

The memory scheduler is launched at boot time and does nothing unless memory is consistently less than desfree memory (30 second average). At this point, the memory scheduler starts looking for processes that it can completely swap out. The memory scheduler will soft-swap out processes if the shortage is minimal or hard-swap out processes in the case of a larger memory shortage.

5.8.6.1 Soft Swapping

Soft swapping takes place when the 30-second average for free memory is below desfree. Then, the memory scheduler looks for processes that have been inactive for at least maxslp seconds. When the memory scheduler finds a process that has been sleeping for `maxslp` seconds, it swaps out the thread structures for each thread, then pages out all of the private pages of memory for that process.

5.8.6.2 Hard Swapping

Hard swapping takes place when all of the following are true:

- At least two processes are on the run queue, waiting for CPU.
- The average free memory over 30 seconds is consistently less than `desfree`.
- Excessive paging (determined to be true if page-out + page-in > `maxpgio`) is going on.

When hard swapping is invoked, a much more aggressive approach is used to find memory. First, the kernel is requested to unload all modules and cache memory that are not currently active, then processes are sequentially swapped out until the desired amount of free memory is returned. Parameters that affect the Memory Scheduler are shown in Table 5-15.

Table 5-15 Memory Scheduler Parameters

Parameter	Effect on Memory Scheduler
desfree	If the average amount of free memory falls below `desfree` for 30 seconds, then the memory scheduler is invoked.
maxslp	When soft-swapping, the memory scheduler starts swapping processes that have slept for at least `maxslp` seconds. The default for `maxslp` is 20 seconds and is tunable.
maxpgio	When the run queue is greater than 2, free memory is below `desfree`, and the paging rate is greater than `maxpgio`, then hard swapping occurs, unloading kernel modules and process memory.

5.9   The Hardware Address Translation Layer

The hardware address translation (HAT) layer controls the hardware that manages mapping of virtual to physical memory. The HAT layer provides interfaces that implement the creation and destruction of mappings between virtual and physical memory and provides a set of interfaces to probe and control the MMU. The HAT layer also implements all of the low-level trap handlers to manage page faults and memory exceptions. Figure 5.26 shows the logical demarcation between elements of the HAT layer.

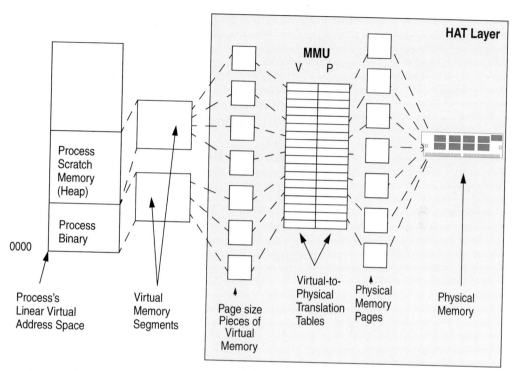

Figure 5.26 Role of the HAT Layer in Virtual-to-Physical Translation

The HAT implementation is different for each type of hardware MMU, and hence there are several different HAT implementations. The HAT layer hides the platform-specific implementation and is used by the segment drivers to implement the segment driver's view of virtual-to-physical translation. The HAT uses the struct hat data structure to hold the top-level translation information for an address space. The hat structure is platform specific and is referenced by the address space structure (see Figure 5.7 on page 137). HAT-specific data structures existing in every page represent the translation information at a page level.

The HAT layer is called when the segment drivers want to manipulate the hardware MMU. For example, when a segment driver wants to create or destroy an address space mapping, it calls the HAT functions specifying the address range and the action to be taken. We can call the HAT functions without knowing anything about the underlying MMU implementation; the arguments to the HAT functions are machine independent and usually consist of virtual addresses, lengths, page pointers, and protection modes.

Table 5-16 summarizes HAT functions.

Table 5-16 Machine-Independent HAT Functions

Function	Description
hat_alloc()	Allocates a HAT structure in the address space.
hat_chgattr()	Changes the protections for the supplied virtual address range.
hat_clrattr()	Clears the protections for the supplied virtual address range.
hat_free_end()	Informs the HAT layer that a process has exited.
hat_free_start()	Informs the HAT layer that a process is exiting.
hat_get_mapped_size()	Returns the number of bytes that have valid mappings.
hat_getattr()	Gets the protections for the supplied virtual address range.
hat_memload()	Creates a mapping for the supplied page at the supplied virtual address. Used to create mappings.
hat_setattr()	Sets the protections for the supplied virtual address range.
hat_stats_disable()	Finishes collecting stats on an address space.
hat_stats_enable()	Starts collecting page reference and modification stats on an address space.
hat_swapin()	Allocates resources for a process that is about to be swapped in.
hat_swapout()	Allocates resources for a process that is about to be swapped out.
hat_sync()	Synchronizes the struct_page software referenced and modified bits with the hardware MMU.
hat_unload()	Unloads a mapping for the given page at the given address.

5.9.1 Virtual Memory Contexts and Address Spaces

A *virtual memory context* is a set of virtual-to-physical translations that maps an address space. We change virtual memory contexts when the scheduler wants to switch execution from one process to another or when a trap or interrupt from user mode to kernel occurs. The Solaris kernel always uses virtual memory context zero to indicate the kernel context. The machine-specific HAT layer implements functions required to create, delete, and switch virtual memory contexts. Different hardware MMUs support different numbers of concurrent virtual memory contexts.

When the number of concurrent address spaces (processes) exceeds the number of concurrent contexts supported by the hardware, the kernel has to steal contexts from peer processes at the time of context switch. Stealing contexts from other address spaces has an indirect effect on performance. However, this issue was only a concern on older systems such as the SPARCstation 1 and 2.

5.9.1.1 Hardware Translation Acceleration

The hardware MMUs convert from virtual-to-physical addresses by looking up entries in a page translation table. All of the platforms on which Solaris runs have a hardware cache of recent translations, known as the translation lookaside buffer (TLB). The number of entries in the TLB is typically 64 on SPARC systems. Some platforms (such as Intel and older SPARC implementations) use hardware to populate the TLB, and others (like the UltraSPARC architecture) use software algorithms.

The characteristics of the MMU hardware for the different Solaris platforms are shown in Table 5-17.

Table 5-17 Solaris MMU HAT Implementations

Platform	No. of Contexts	Size of TLB	TLB Fill	Virtual Bits	Physical Bits
SPARC 1,2	8	64	Hardware	32	32
MicroSPARC	65536	64	Hardware	32	32
SuperSPARC	65536	64	Hardware	32	36
UltraSPARC-I and -II	8192	64 x 2	Software	44	41
Intel Pentium			Hardware	32	36

5.9.2 The UltraSPARC-I and -II HAT

The UltraSPARC-I and -II MMUs do the following:

- Implement mapping between a 44-bit virtual address and a 41-bit physical address

- Support page sizes of 8 Kbytes, 64 Kbytes, 512 bytes, and 4 Mbytes

- Share their implementation with the entire range of UltraSPARC-based desktop and server machines, from the Ultra 1 to the Enterprise Server 10000

The MMU is an integral part of the UltraSPARC chip, which hosts two MMUs: one for instructions and one for data. Figure 5.27 illustrates the topology of the CPU and MMU.

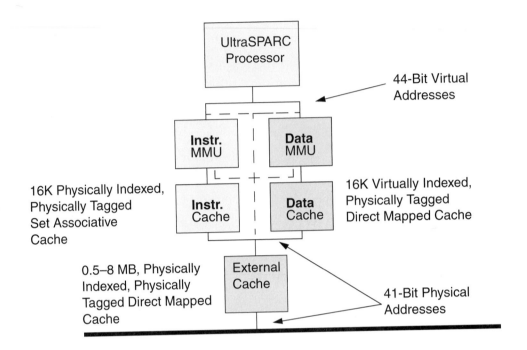

Figure 5.27 UltraSPARC-I and -II MMUs

The UltraSPARC-I and -II MMU supports 44-bit virtual addresses (64 bits with a virtual address hole) and 41-bit physical addresses. During memory access, the MMU translates virtual address to physical addresses by translating a virtual page number into a physical page number and using a common page offset between the virtual and physical pages. The page number of a page is the high-order bits of the address, excluding the page offset. For 8-Kbyte pages, the page number is bits 13 through 63 of the virtual address and bits 13 through 40 of the physical address. For 4-Mbyte pages, the page number is bits 22 through 63 of the virtual address and bits 22 through 40 of the physical address.

8-Kbyte Page

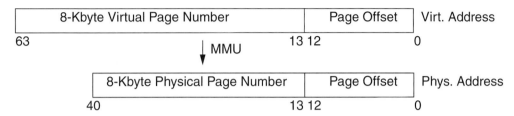

4-Mbyte Page

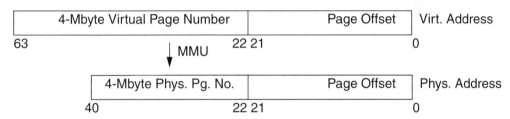

Figure 5.28 Virtual-to-Physical Translation

Figure 5.28 illustrates the relationship between virtual and physical addresses.

We traditionally use page tables to map virtual-to-physical addresses, so that for any given virtual address, the MMU hardware looks up and translates the appropriate physical address. microSPARC and SuperSPARC processors use page tables for address translation to convert virtual page numbers to physical page numbers. The microSPARC and SuperSPARC page table comprises mapping entries, one per page, known as *page table entries*, that map each virtual page to a physical page.

In UltraSPARC-I and -II, we use a translation table to describe the virtual-to-physical translation. A translation table is the functional equivalent of a page table, with some significant differences. For example, unlike the older page table implementation (like that on SuperSPARC), the UltraSPARC-I and -II MMU uses a software-based translation mechanism to fill the hardware TLB translation cache.

The UltraSPARC-I and -II software page table entries are known as *translation table entries* (TTEs), one TTE for each page. The TTE is a translation map entry that contains a virtual address tag and the high bits of the physical address for each page (the physical page number) so that the hardware MMU can convert the virtual page address into a physical address by finding entries matching the virtual page number.

The TTE virtual page tag contains the virtual page number of the virtual address it maps and the address space context number to identify the context to which each TTE belongs. The context information in the TTE allows the MMU to find a TTE specific to an address space context, which allows multiple contexts to be simultaneously active in the TLB. This behavior offers a major performance benefit because traditionally we need to flush all the TTEs for an address space when we context-switch. Having multiple TTE contexts in the TLB dramatically decreases the time taken for a context switch because translations do not need to be reloaded into the TLB each time we context-switch.

The TTEs found in the page structure are a software representation of the virtual-to-physical mapping and must be loaded into the TLB to enable the MMU to perform a hardware translation. Once a TTE is loaded, the hardware MMU can translate addresses for that TTE without further interaction. The hardware MMU relies on the hardware copies of the TTEs in the TLB to do the real translation. The TLB contains the 64 most recent TTEs and is used directly by the hardware to assemble the physical addresses of each page as virtual addresses are accessed.

The MMU finds the TTE entry that matches the virtual page number and current context. When it finds the match, it retrieves the physical page information. The physical page information contains the physical page number (which is the high 13 or 22 bits of the physical address), the size of the page, a bit to indicate whether the page can be written to, and a bit to indicate whether the page can only be accessed in privileged mode.

Figure 5.29 illustrates how TTEs are used.

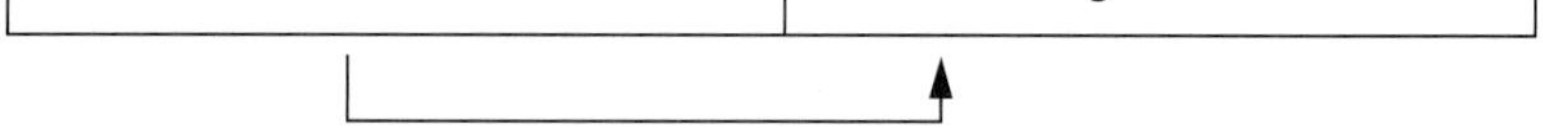

Virtual Page Tag	Physical Page
Virtual Page Number Context Number (0–8191)	Physical Address (Bits 40:13) Page Size Valid Bit Protected Page Bit Writable Page Bit

Figure 5.29 UltraSPARC-I and -II Translation Table Entry (TTE)

Software populates the TLB entries from the `hment` structures in the machine-specific page structure. Since the process of converting a software TTE into a TLB entry is fairly expensive, an intermediate software cache of TTEs is arranged as a direct-mapped cache of the TLB. The software cache of TTEs is the translation software buffer (TSB) and is simply an array of TTEs in regular physical memory. Figure 5.30 shows the relationship between software TTEs, the TSB, and the TLB.

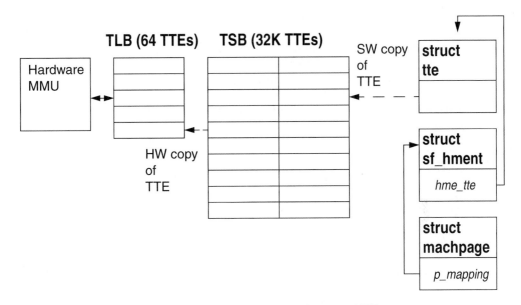

Figure 5.30 Relationship of TLBs, TSBs, and TTEs

The TLB on UltraSPARC-I and -II has 64 entries, and the TSB has between 2,048 and 262,144 entries, depending on the amount of memory in the system. Unlike the previous generation SPARC MMU, the UltraSPARC-I and -II MMU does not use a hardware page tablewalk to access the TSB entries, but it still provides a form of hardware assistance to speed up TSB access: Hardware precomputes TSB table offsets to help the software handler find TTEs in the TSB. When the CPU needs to access a virtual address, the system takes the following steps:

1. The MMU first looks in the TLB for a valid TTE for the requested virtual address.
2. If a valid TTE is not found, then the MMU automatically generates a pointer for the location of the TSB TTE entry and generates a TLB miss trap.
3. The trap handler reads the hardware-constructed pointer, retrieves the entry from the TSB, and places it in the appropriate TLB slot with an atomic write into the TLB.
4. If the TTE is not found in the TSB, then the TLB miss handler jumps to a more complex, but slower, TSB miss handler, which retrieves the TTE from the page structure by using a software hashed index structure.

UltraSPARC-I and -II also provide a separate set of global registers to process MMU traps. This approach dramatically reduces the time taken for the TLB miss handler to locate TSB entries since the CPU does not need to save process state during the trap—it simply locates the entry, atomically stores the entry, and returns to execution of the running process.

To optimize performance, the TSB is sized according to the amount of memory in the system. In addition, if memory is sufficient, a separate TSB is allocated for the kernel context. The maximum size of a TSB on UltraSPARC-I and -II is 512 Kbytes, so to provide a large TSB, multiple 512-Kbyte TSBs are allocated. When multiple TSBs are allocated, they are divided by a mask of the context number, where multiple contexts share the same TSB. An array of TSB base addresses, indexed by the context number, implements the concept. When a context switch is performed, the new TSB base address is looked up in the tsbbase address array and loaded into the MMU TSB base address register.

The memory sizes and the corresponding TSB sizes are shown in Table 5-18.

Table 5-18 Solaris 7 UltraSPARC-I and -II TSB Sizes

Memory Size	Kernel TSB Entries	Kernel TSB Size	User TSB Entries	User TSB Size
< 32 Mbytes	—	—	2,048	128 Kbytes
32 Mbytes–64 Mbytes	4096	256 Kbytes	8,192–16,383	512 Kbytes–1 Mbyte
32 Mbytes–2 Gbytes	4096–262,144	512 Kbytes–16 Mbytes	16,384–524,287	1 Mbyte–32 Mbytes
2 Gbytes–8 Gbytes	262,144	16 Mbytes	524,288–2,097,511	32 Mbytes–128 Mbytes
8 Gbytes ->	262,144	16 Mbytes	2,097,512	128 Mbytes

5.9.3 Address Space Identifiers

SPARC systems use an address space identifier (ASI) to describe the MMU mode and hardware used to access pages in the current environment. UltraSPARC uses an 8-bit ASI that is derived from the instruction being executed and the current trap level. Most of the 50+ different ASIs can be grouped into three different modes of physical memory access, shown in Table 5-19. The MMU translation context used to index TLB entries is derived from the ASI.

Table 5-19 UltraSPARC-I and -II Address Space Identifiers

ASI	Description	Derived Context
Primary	The default address translation; used for regular SPARC instructions.	The address space translation is done through TLB entries that match the context number in the MMU primary context register.

Table 5-19 UltraSPARC-I and -II Address Space Identifiers (Continued)

ASI	Description	Derived Context
Secondary	A secondary address space context; used for accessing another address space context without requiring a context switch.	The address space translation is done through TLB entries that match the context number in the MMU secondary context register.
Nucleus	The address translation; used for TLB miss handlers, system calls, and interrupts.	The nucleus context is always zero (the kernel's context).

The three UltraSPARC ASIs allow an instruction stream to access up to three different address space contexts without actually having to perform a context switch. This feature is used in the Solaris kernel to help place the kernel into a completely separate address space, by allowing very fast access to user space from kernel mode. The kernel can access user space by using SPARC instructions that allow an ASI to be specified with the address of a load/store, and the user space is always available from the kernel in the secondary ASI.

Other SPARC ASIs access hardware registers in the MMU itself, and special ASIs access I/O space. For further details on UltraSPARC ASIs, see the UltraSPARC-I and -II Users Manual [30].

5.9.3.1 UltraSPARC-I and II Watchpoint Implementation

The UltraSPARC-I and -II MMU implementation provides support for watchpoints. Virtual address and physical address watchpoint registers, when enabled, describe the address of watchpoints for the address space. Watchpoint traps are generated when watchpoints are enabled and the data MMU detects a load or store to the virtual or physical address specified by the virtual address data watchpoint register or the physical data watchpoint register, respectively. (See "Virtual Memory Watchpoints" on page 164 for further information.)

5.9.3.2 UltraSPARC-I and -II Protection Modes

Protection modes are implemented by the instruction and data TTEs. Table 5-20 shows the resultant protection modes.

Table 5-20 UltraSPARC MMU Protection Modes

Condition			Resultant Protection Mode
TTE in D-MMU	**TTE in I-MMU**	**Writable Attribute Bit**	
Yes	No	0	Read-only
No	Yes	Don't Care	Execute-only
Yes	No	1	Read/Write
Yes	Yes	0	Read-only/Execute
Yes	Yes	1	Read/Write/Execute

5.9.3.3 UltraSPARC-I and -II MMU-Generated Traps

The UltraSPARC MMU generates traps to implement the software handlers for events that the hardware MMU cannot handle. Such events occur when the MMU encounters an MMU-related instruction exception or when the MMU cannot find a TTE in the TSB for a virtual address. Table 5-21 describes UltraSPARC-I and -II traps.

Table 5-21 UltraSPARC-I and -II MMU Traps

Trap	Description
`Instruction_access_miss`	A TTE for the virtual address of an instruction was not found in the instruction TLB.
`Instruction_access_exception`	An instruction privilege violation or invalid instruction address occurred.
`Data_access_MMU_miss`	A TTE for the virtual address of a load was not found in the data TLB.
`Data_access_exception`	A data access privilege violation or invalid data address occurred.
`Data_access_protection`	A data write was attempted to a read-only page.
`Privileged_action`	An attempt was made to access a privileged address space.
`Watchpoint`	Watchpoints were enabled and the CPU attempted to load or store at the address equivalent to that stored in the watchpoint register.
`Mem_address_not_aligned`	An attempt was made to load or store from an address that is not correctly word aligned.

5.9.4 Large Pages

Large pages, typically 4 Mbytes in size, optimize the effectiveness of the hardware TLB. They were introduced in Solaris 2.5 to map core kernel text and data and have continued to develop into other areas of the operating system. Let's take a look at why large pages help optimize TLB performance.

5.9.4.1 TLB Performance and Large Pages

The memory performance of a modern system is largely influenced by the effectiveness of the TLB because of the time spent servicing TLB misses. The objective of the TLB is to cache as many recent page translations in hardware as possible, so that it can satisfy a process's or thread's memory accesses by performing all of the virtual-to-physical translations on-the-fly. If we don't find a translation in the TLB, then we need to look up the translation from a larger table, either in software (UltraSPARC) or with lengthy hardware steps (Intel or SuperSPARC).

Most TLBs are limited in size because of the amount of transistor space available on the CPU die. For example, the UltraSPARC-I and -II TLBs are only 64 entries. This means that the TLB can at most address 64 pages of translations at any time; on UltraSPARC, 64 x 8 Kbytes, or 512 Kbytes.

The amount of memory the TLB can address concurrently is known as the TLB reach, so we can say the UltraSPARC-I and -II have a TLB reach of 512 Kbytes. If an application makes heavy use of less than 512 Kbytes of memory, then the TLB will be able to cache the entire set of translations. But if the application were to make heavy use of more than 512 Kbytes of memory, then the TLB will begin to miss, and translations will have to be loaded from the larger translation table.

Table 5-22 shows the TLB miss rate and the amount of time spent servicing TLB misses from a study done by Madu Talluri [33] on older SPARC architectures. We can see from the table that only a small range of compute-bound applications fit well in the SuperSPARC TLB (gcc, ML, and pthor), whereas the others spend a significant amount of their time in the TLB miss handlers.

Table 5-22 Sample TLB Miss Data from a SuperSPARC Study

Workload	Total Time (secs)	User Time (secs)	# User TLB Misses	% User Time in TLB Miss Handling	Cache Misses ('000s)	Peak Memory Usage (MB)
coral	177	172	85974	50	71053	19.9
nasa7	387	385	152357	40	64213	3.5
compress	99	77	21347	28	21567	1.4
fftpde	55	53	11280	21	14472	14.7
wave5	110	107	14510	14	4583	14.3
mp3d	37	36	4050	11	5457	4.8
spice	620	617	41923	7	81949	3.6
pthor	48	35	2580	7	6957	15.4
ML	945	917	38423	4	314137	32.0
gcc	118	105	2440	2	9980	5.6

TLB effectiveness has become a larger issue in the past few years because the average amount of memory used by applications has grown significantly—by as much as double per year according to recent statistical data. The easiest way to increase the effectiveness of the TLB is to increase the TLB reach so that the working set of the application fits within the TLB's reach. You can increase TLB reach in two ways:

- Increase the number of entries in the TLB. This approach adds complexity to the TLB hardware and increases the number of transistors required, taking up valuable CPU die space.

- Increase the page size that each entry reflects. This approach increases the TLB reach without the need to increase the size of the TLB.

A trade-off to increasing the page size is this: If we increase the page size, we may boost the performance of some applications at the expense of slower performance elsewhere, and because of larger-size memory fragmentation, we would almost certainly increase the memory usage of many applications. Luckily, a solution is at hand: Some of the newer processor architectures allow us to use two or more different page sizes at the same time. For example, the UltraSPARC microprocessor provides hardware support to concurrently select 8-Kbyte, 64-Kbyte, 512-Kbyte. or 4-Mbyte pages. If we were to use 4-Mbyte pages to map all memory, then the TLB would have a theoretical reach of 64 x 4 Mbytes, or 256 Mbytes. We do, however, need operating system support to take advantage of large pages.

5.9.4.2 Solaris Support for Large Pages

Prior to the introduction of the first UltraSPARC processor, the Solaris kernel did not support multiple page sizes, so significant kernel development effort was required before the kernel could take advantage of the underlying hardware's support for multiple page sizes. This development was phased over several Solaris releases, starting with Solaris 2.5 (the Solaris release with which UltraSPARC was first released).

The page size for Solaris on UltraSPARC is 8 Kbytes, chosen to give a good mix of performance across the range of smaller machines (32 Mbytes) to larger machines (several gigabytes). The 8-Kbyte page size is appropriate for many applications, but those with a larger working set spend a lot of their time in TLB miss handling, and as a result, the 8-Kbyte page size hurts a class of applications, mainly large-memory scientific applications and large-memory databases. The 8-Kbyte page size also hurts kernel performance, since the kernel's working set is in the order of 2 to 3 megabytes.

At Solaris 2.5, the first 4 Mbytes of kernel text and data are mapped with two 4-Mbyte pages at system boot time. This page size significantly reduces the number of TLB entries required to satisfy kernel memory translations, speeding up the kernel code path and freeing up valuable TLB slots for hungry applications. In addition, the Ultra Creator graphics adapter makes use of a large translation to accelerate graphics performance.

However, user applications had no way to take advantage of the large-page support until Solaris 2.6. With that release, Sun enabled the use of 4-Mbyte pages for shared memory segments. This capability primarily benefits databases, since databases typically use extremely large shared memory segments for database data structures and shared file buffers. Shared memory segments ranging from several hundred megabytes to several gigabytes are typical on most database installations, and the 8-Kbyte page size means that very few 8-Kbyte shared memory page translations fit into the TLB. The 4-Mbyte pages allow large contiguous memory to be mapped by just a few pages.

Starting with Solaris 2.6, System V shared memory created with the intimate shared memory flag, `SHM_SHARE_MMU`, is created with as many large 4-Mbyte pages as possible, greatly increasing the performance of database applications. Table 5-23 shows a sample of the performance gains from adding large-page shared memory support.

Table 5-23 Large-Page Database Performance Improvements

Database	Performance Improvement
Oracle TPC-C	12%
Informix TPC-C	1%
Informix TPC-D	6%

6

KERNEL MEMORY

In the last chapter, we looked mostly at process address space and process memory, but the kernel also needs memory to run the operating system. Kernel memory is required for the kernel text, kernel data, and kernel data structures. In this chapter, we look at what kernel memory is used for, what the kernel virtual address space looks like, and how kernel memory is allocated and managed.

6.1 Kernel Virtual Memory Layout

The kernel, just like a process, uses virtual memory and uses the memory management unit to translate its virtual memory addresses into physical pages. The kernel has its own address space and corresponding virtual memory layout. The kernel's address space is constructed of address space segments, using the standard Solaris memory architecture framework.

Most of the kernel's memory is nonpageable, or "wired down." The reason is that the kernel requires its memory to complete operating system tasks that could affect other memory-related data structures and, if the kernel had to take a page fault while performing a memory management task (or any other task that affected pages of memory), a deadlock could occur. Solaris does, however, allow some deadlock-safe parts of the Solaris kernel to be allocated from pageable memory, which is used mostly for the lightweight process thread stacks.

Kernel memory consists of a variety of mappings from physical memory (physical memory pages) to the kernel's virtual address space, and memory is allocated by a layered series of kernel memory allocators. Two segment drivers handle the creation and management of the majority of kernel mappings. Nonpageable kernel memory is mapped with the segkmem kernel segment driver and pageable kernel memory with the segkp segment driver. On platforms that support it, the critical and frequently used portions of the kernel are mapped from large (4-Mbyte) pages to maximize the efficiency of the hardware TLB.

6.1.1 Kernel Address Space

The kernel virtual memory layout differs from platform to platform, mostly based on the platform's MMU architecture. On all platforms except the sun4u, the kernel uses the top 256 Mbytes or 512 Mbytes of a common virtual address space, shared by the process and kernel (see "Virtual Address Spaces" on page 130). Sharing the kernel address space with the process address space limits the amount of usable kernel virtual address space to 256 Mbytes and 512 Mbytes, respectively, which is a substantial limitation on some of the older platforms (e.g., the SPARC-center 2000). On sun4u platforms, the kernel has its own virtual address space context and consequently can be much larger. The sun4u kernel address space is 4 Gbytes on 32-bit kernels and spans the full 64-bit address range on 64-bit kernels.

The kernel virtual address space contains the following major mappings:

- The kernel text and data (mappings of the kernel binary)
- The kernel map space (data structures, caches, etc.)
- A 32-bit kernel map, for module text and data (64-bit kernels only)
- The trap table
- Critical virtual memory data structures (TSB, etc.)
- A place for mapping the file system cache (segmap)

The layout of the kernel's virtual memory address space is mostly platform specific, and as a result, the placement of each mapping is different on each platform. For reference, we show the sun4u 64-bit kernel address space map in Figure 6.1.

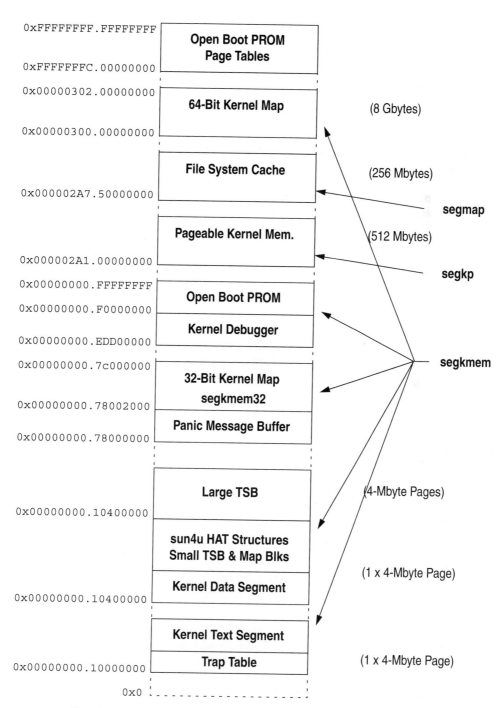

Figure 6.1 Solaris 7 64-Bit Kernel Virtual Address Space

6.1.2 The Kernel Text and Data Segments

The kernel text and data segments are created when the kernel core is loaded and executed. The text segments contain the instructions, and the data segment contains the initialized variables from the kernel/unix image file, which is loaded at boot time by the kernel bootstrap loader.

The kernel text and data are mapped into the kernel address space by the Open Boot PROM, prior to general startup of the kernel, to allow the base kernel code to be loaded and executed. Shortly after the kernel loads, the kernel then creates the kernel address space and the segkmem kernel memory driver creates segments for kernel text and kernel data.

On systems that support large pages, the kernel creates a large translation mapping for the first four megabytes of the kernel text and data segments and then locks that mapping into the MMU's TLB. Mapping the kernel into large pages greatly reduces the number of TLB entries required for the kernel's working set and has a dramatic impact on general system performance. Performance was increased by as much as 10 percent, for two reasons:

1. The time spent in TLB miss handlers for kernel code was reduced to almost zero.
2. The number of TLB entries used by the kernel was dramatically reduced, leaving more TLB entries for user code and reducing the amount of time spent in TLB miss handlers for user code.

On SPARC platforms, we also put the trap table at the start of the kernel text (which resides on one large page).

6.1.3 Virtual Memory Data Structures

The kernel keeps most of the virtual memory data structures required for the platform's HAT implementation in a portion of the kernel data segment and a separate memory segment. The data structures and allocation location are typically those summarized in Table 6-1.

Table 6-1 Virtual Memory Data Structures

Platform	Data Structures	Location
sun4u	The Translation Storage Buffer (TSB). The HAT mapping blocks (HME), one for every page-sized virtual address mapping. (See "The UltraSPARC-I and -II HAT" on page 193.)	Allocated initially from the kernel data-segment large page, and overflows into another large-page, mapped segment, just above the kernel data segment.
sun4m	Page Tables, Page Structures	Allocated in the kernel data-segment large page.

Table 6-1 Virtual Memory Data Structures (Continued)

Platform	Data Structures	Location
sun4d	Page Tables, Page Structures	Allocated in the kernel data-segment large page.
x86	Page Tables, Page Structures	Allocated from a separate VM data structure's segment.

6.1.4 The SPARC V8 and V9 Kernel Nucleus

Required on sun4u kernel implementations is a core area of memory that can be accessed without missing in the TLB. This memory area is necessary because the sun4u SPARC implementation uses a software TLB replacement mechanism to fill the TLB, and hence we require all of the TLB miss handler data structures to be available during a TLB miss. As we discuss in "The UltraSPARC-I and -II HAT" on page 193, the TLB is filled from a software buffer, known as the translation storage buffer (TSB), of the TLB entries, and all of the data structures needed to handle a TLB miss and to fill the TLB from the TSB must be available with wired-down TLB mappings. To accommodate this requirement, SPARC V8 and SPARC V9 implement a special core of memory, known as the nucleus. On sun4u systems, the nucleus is the kernel text, kernel data, and the additional "large TSB" area, all of which are allocated from large pages.

6.1.5 Loadable Kernel Module Text and Data

The kernel loadable modules require memory for their executable text and data. On sun4u, up to 256 Kbytes of module text and data are allocated from the same segment as the kernel text and data, and after the module text and data are loaded from the general kernel allocation area, the kernel map segment. The location of kernel module text and data is shown in Table 6-2.

Table 6-2 Kernel Loadable Module Allocation

Platform	Module Kernel and Text Allocation
sun4u 64 bit	Up to 256 Kbytes of kernel module are loaded from the same large pages as the kernel text and data. The remainder are loaded from the 32-bit kernel map segment, a segment that is specifically for module text and data.
sun4u 32 bit	Up to 256 Kbytes of kernel module are loaded from the same large pages as the kernel text and data. The remainder are loaded from the general kernel memory allocation segment, the kernel map segment.
sun4m	Loadable module text and data are loaded from the general kernel memory allocation segment, the `kernelmap` segment.
sun4d	Loadable module text and data are loaded from the general kernel memory allocation segment, the `kernelmap` segment.

Table 6-2 Kernel Loadable Module Allocation (Continued)

Platform	Module Kernel and Text Allocation
x86	Up to 256 Kbytes of kernel module are loaded from the same large pages as the kernel text and data. The remainder are loaded from an additional segment, shared by HAT data structures and module text/data.

We can see which modules fit into the kernel text and data by looking at the module load addresses with the `modinfo` command.

```
# modinfo
  Id Loadaddr   Size Info Rev Module Name
   5 1010c000   4b63   1   1  specfs (filesystem for specfs)
   7 10111654   3724   1   1  TS (time sharing sched class)
   8 1011416c    5c0   -   1  TS_DPTBL (Time sharing dispatch table)
   9 101141c0  29680   2   1  ufs (filesystem for ufs)
                 .
                 .
                 .
  97 10309b38   28e0  52   1  shmsys (System V shared memory)
  97 10309b38   28e0  52   1  shmsys (32-bit System V shared memory)
  98 1030bc90    43c   -   1  ipc (common ipc code)
  99 78096000   3723  18   1  ffb (ffb.c 6.42 Aug 11 1998 11:20:45)
 100 7809c000   f5ee   -   1  xfb (xfb driver 1.2 Aug 11 1998 11:2)
 102 780c2000   1eca   -   1  bootdev (bootdev misc module)
```

Using the `modinfo` command, we can see on a sun4u system that the initial modules are loaded from the kernel-text large page. (Address 0x1030bc90 lies within the kernel-ext large page, which starts at 0x10000000.)

On 64-bit sun4u platforms, we have an additional segment for the spillover kernel text and data. The reason for having the segment is that the address at which the module text is loaded must be within a 32-bit offset from the kernel text. That's because the 64-bit kernel is compiled with the ABS32 flag so that the kernel can fit all instruction addresses within a 32-bit register. The ABS32 instruction mode provides a significant performance increase and allows the 64-bit kernel to provide similar performance to the 32-bit kernel. Because of that, a separate kernel map segment (`segkmem32`) within a 32-bit offset of the kernel text is used for spillover module text and data.

Solaris does allow some portions of the kernel to be allocated from pageable memory. That way, data structures directly related to process context can be swapped out with the process during a process swap-out operation. Pageable memory is restricted to those structures that are not required by the kernel when the process is swapped out:

* Lightweight process stacks
* The TNF Trace buffers

- Special pages, such as the page of memory that is shared between user and kernel for scheduler preemption control

Pageable memory is allocated and swapped by the `seg_kp` segment and is only swapped out to its backing store when the memory scheduler (swapper) is activated. (See "The Memory Scheduler" on page 189.)

6.1.6 The Kernel Address Space and Segments

The kernel address space is represented by the address space pointed to by the system object, `kas`. The segment drivers manage the manipulation of the segments within the kernel address space (see Figure 6.2).

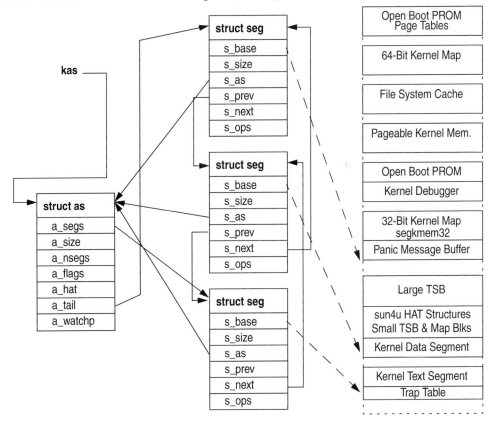

Figure 6.2 Kernel Address Space

The full list of segment drivers the kernel uses to create and manage kernel mappings is shown in Table 6-3. The majority of the kernel segments are manually calculated and placed for each platform, with the base address and offset hard-coded into a platform-specific header file. See Appendix B, "Kernel Virtual Address

Maps" for a complete reference of platform-specific kernel allocation and address maps.

Table 6-3 Solaris 7 Kernel Memory Segment Drivers

Segment	Function
seg_kmem	Allocates and maps nonpageable kernel memory pages.
seg_kp	Allocates, maps, and handles page faults for pageable kernel memory.
seg_nf	Nonfaulting kernel memory driver.
seg_map	Maps the file system cache into the kernel address space.

6.2   Kernel Memory Allocation

Kernel memory is allocated at different levels, depending on the desired allocation characteristics. At the lowest level is the page allocator, which allocates unmapped pages from the free lists so the pages can then be mapped into the kernel's address space for use by the kernel.

Allocating memory in pages works well for memory allocations that require page-sized chunks, but there are many places where we need memory allocations smaller than one page; for example, an in-kernel inode requires only a few hundred bytes per inode, and allocating one whole page (8 Kbytes) would be wasteful. For this reason, Solaris has an object-level kernel memory allocator in addition to the page-level allocator to allocate arbitrarily sized requests, stacked on top of the page-level allocator. The kernel also needs to manage where pages are mapped, a function that is provided by the resource map allocator. The high-level interaction between the allocators is shown in Figure 6.3.

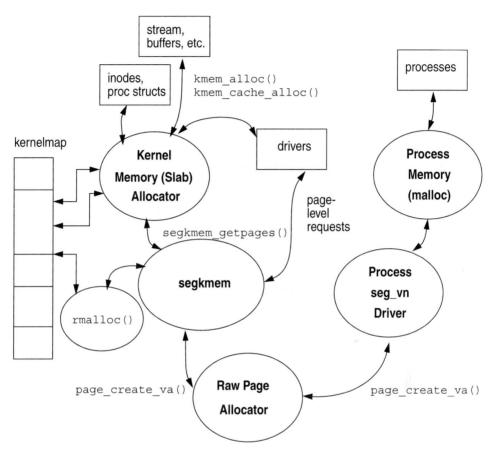

Figure 6.3 Different Levels of Memory Allocation

6.2.1 The Kernel Map

We access memory in the kernel by acquiring a section of the kernel's virtual address space and then mapping physical pages to that address. We can acquire the physical pages one at a time from the page allocator by calling `page_create_va()`, but to use these pages, we first need to map them. A section of the kernel's address space, known as the *kernel map*, is set aside for general-purpose mappings. (See Figure 6.1 for the location of the sun4u kernelmap; see also Appendix B, "Kernel Virtual Address Maps" for kernel maps on other platforms.)

The kernel map is a separate kernel memory segment containing a large area of virtual address space that is available to kernel consumers who require virtual address space for their mappings. Each time a consumer uses a piece of the kernel map, we must record some information about which parts of the kernel map are free and which parts are allocated, so that we know where to satisfy new requests. To record the information, we use a general-purpose allocator to keep track of the start and length of the mappings that are allocated from the kernel map area. The allocator we use is the resource map allocator, which is used almost exclusively for managing the kernel map virtual address space.

The kernel map area is large, up to 8 Gbytes on 64-bit sun4u systems, and can quickly become fragmented if it accommodates many consumers with different-sized requests. It is up to the resource map allocator to try to keep the kernel map area as unfragmented as possible.

6.2.2 The Resource Map Allocator

Solaris uses the resource map allocator to manage the kernel map. To keep track of the areas of free memory within the map, the resource map allocator uses a simple algorithm to keep a list of start/length pairs that point to each area of free memory within the map. The map entries are sorted in ascending order to make it quicker to find entries, allowing faster allocation. The map entries are shown in the following map structure, which can be found in the `<sys/map.h>` header file.

```
struct map {
        size_t  m_size;         /* size of this segment of the map */
        ulong_t m_addr;         /* resource-space addr of start of segment */
};
```

Header File <vm/rm.h>

The area managed by the resource map allocator is initially described by just one map entry representing the whole area as one contiguous free chunk. As more allocations are made from the area, more map entries are used to describe the area, and as a result, the map becomes even more fragmented over time.

The resource map allocator uses a first-fit algorithm to find space in the map to satisfy new requests, which means that it attempts to find the first available slot in the map that fits the request. The first-fit algorithm provides a fast find allocation at the expense of map fragmentation after time. For this reason, it is important to ensure that kernel subsystems do not perform an excessive amount of map allocation and freeing. The kernel slab allocator (discussed next) should be used for these types of requests.

Map resource requests are made with the `rmalloc()` call, and resources are returned to the map by `rmfree()`. Resource maps are created with the `rmalloc-map()` function and destroyed with the `rmfreemap()` function. The functions that implement the resource map allocator are shown in Table 6-4.

Table 6-4 Solaris 7 Resource Map Allocator Functions from <sys/map.h>

Function	Description
`rmallocmap()`	Dynamically allocates a map. Does not sleep. Driver-defined basic locks, read/write locks, and sleep locks can be held across calls to this function. DDI-/DKI-conforming drivers may only use map structures that have been allocated and initialized with `rmallocmap()`.
`rmallocmap_wait()`	Dynamically allocates a map. It *does* sleep. DDI-/DKI-conforming drivers can only use map structures that have been allocated and initialized with `rmallocmap()` and `rmallocmap_wait()`.
`rmfreemap()`	Frees a dynamically allocated map. Does not sleep. Driver-defined basic locks, read/write locks, and sleep locks can be held across calls to this function. Before freeing the map, the caller must ensure that nothing is using space managed by the map and that nothing is waiting for space in the map.
`rmalloc()`	Allocates *size* units from the given map. Returns the base of the allocated space. In a map, the addresses are increasing and the list is terminated by a 0 size. Algorithm is first-fit.
`rmalloc_wait()`	Like `rmalloc`, but waits if necessary until space is available.
`rmalloc_locked()`	Like `rmalloc`, but called with lock on map held.
`rmfree()`	Frees the previously allocated space at *addr* of *size* units into the specified map. Sorts *addr* into map and combines on one or both ends if possible.
`rmget()`	Allocates *size* units from the given map, starting at address *addr*. Returns *addr* if successful, 0 if not. This may cause the creation or destruction of a resource map segment. This routine returns failure status if there is not enough room for a required additional map segment.

6.2.3 The Kernel Memory Segment Driver

The segkmem segment driver performs two major functions: It manages the creation of general-purpose memory segments in the kernel address space, and it also provides functions that implement a page-level memory allocator by using one of those segments—the kernel map segment.

The segkmem segment driver implements the segment driver methods described in Section 5.4, "Memory Segments," on page 143, to create general-purpose, nonpageable memory segments in the kernel address space. The segment driver does little more than implement the segkmem_create method to simply link segments into the kernel's address space. It also implements protection manipulation methods, which load the correct protection modes via the HAT layer for segkmem segments. The set of methods implemented by the segkmem driver is shown in Table 6-5.

Table 6-5 Solaris 7 segkmem Segment Driver Methods

Function	Description
segkmem_create()	Creates a new kernel memory segment.
segkmem_setprot()	Sets the protection mode for the supplied segment.
segkmem_checkprot()	Checks the protection mode for the supplied segment.
segkmem_getprot()	Gets the protection mode for the current segment.

The second function of the segkmem driver is to implement a page-level memory allocator by combined use of the resource map allocator and page allocator. The page-level memory allocator within the segkmem driver is implemented with the function kmem_getpages(). The kmem_getpages() function is the kernel's central allocator for wired-down, page-sized memory requests. Its main client is the second-level memory allocator, the *slab* allocator, which uses large memory areas allocated from the page-level allocator to allocate arbitrarily sized memory objects. We'll cover more on the slab allocator later in this chapter.

The kmem_getpages() function allocates page-sized chunks of virtual address space from the kernelmap segment. The kernelmap segment is only one of many segments created by the segkmem driver, but it is the only one from which the segkmem driver allocates memory.

The resource map allocator allocates portions of virtual address space within the kernelmap segment but on its own does not allocate any physical memory resources. It is used together with the page allocator, page_create_va(), and the hat_memload() functions to allocate physical mapped memory. The resource map allocator allocates some virtual address space, the page allocator allocates pages, and the hat_memload() function maps those pages into the virtual address space provided by the resource map. A client of the segkmem memory allocator can acquire pages with kmem_getpages and then return them to the map with kmem_freepages, as shown in Table 6-6.

Pages allocated through kmem_getpages are not pageable and are one of the few exceptions in the Solaris environment where a mapped page has no logically asso-

Table 6-6 Solaris 7 Kernel Page Level Memory Allocator

Function	Description
kmem_getpages()	Allocates *npages* pages worth of system virtual address space, and allocates wired-down page frames to back them. If *flag* is KM_NOSLEEP, blocks until address space and page frames are available.
kmem_freepages()	Frees *npages* (MMU) pages allocated with kmem_getpages().

ciated vnode. To accommodate that case, a special vnode, kvp, is used. All pages created through the segkmem segment have kvp as the vnode in their identity—this allows the kernel to identify wired-down kernel pages.

6.2.4 The Kernel Memory Slab Allocator

In this section, we introduce the general-purpose memory allocator, known as the slab allocator. We begin with a quick walk-through of the slab allocator features, then look at how the allocator implements object caching, and follow up with a more detailed discussion on the internal implementation.

6.2.4.1 Slab Allocator Overview

Solaris provides a general-purpose memory allocator that provides arbitrarily sized memory allocations. We refer to this allocator as the slab allocator because it consumes large slabs of memory and then allocates smaller requests with portions of each slab. We use the slab allocator for memory requests that are:

- Smaller than a page size
- Not an even multiple of a page size
- Frequently going to be allocated and *freed*, so would otherwise fragment the kernel map

The slab allocator was introduced in Solaris 2.4, replacing the *buddy* allocator that was part of the original SVR4 UNIX. The reasons for introducing the slab allocator were as follows:

- The SVR4 allocator was slow to satisfy allocation requests.
- Significant fragmentation problems arose with use of the SVR4 allocator.
- The allocator footprint was large, wasting a lot of memory.
- With no clean interfaces for memory allocation, code was duplicated in many places.

The slab allocator solves those problems and dramatically reduces overall system complexity. In fact, when the slab allocator was integrated into Solaris, it resulted in a net reduction of 3,000 lines of code because we could centralize a great deal of the memory allocation code and could remove a lot of the duplicated memory allocator functions from the clients of the memory allocator.

The slab allocator is significantly faster than the SVR4 allocator it replaced. Table 6-7 shows some of the performance measurements that were made when the slab allocator was first introduced.

Table 6-7 Performance Comparison of the Slab Allocator

Operation	SVR4	Slab
Average time to allocate and free	9.4 µs	3.8 µs
Total fragmentation (wasted memory)	46%	14%
Kenbus benchmark performance (number of scripts executed per second)	199	233

The slab allocator provides substantial additional functionality, including the following:

- General-purpose, variable-sized memory object allocation
- A central interface for memory allocation, which simplifies clients of the allocator and reduces duplicated allocation code
- Very fast allocation/deallocation of objects
- Low fragmentation / small allocator footprint
- Full debugging and auditing capability
- Coloring to optimize use of CPU caches
- Per-processor caching of memory objects to reduce contention
- A configurable back-end memory allocator to allocate objects other than regular wired-down memory

The slab allocator uses the term *object* to describe a single memory allocation unit, *cache* to refer to a pool of like objects, and *slab* to refer to a group of objects that reside within the cache. Each object type has one cache, which is constructed from one or more slabs. Figure 6.4 shows the relationship between objects, slabs, and the cache. The example shows 3-Kbyte memory objects within a cache, backed by 8-Kbyte pages.

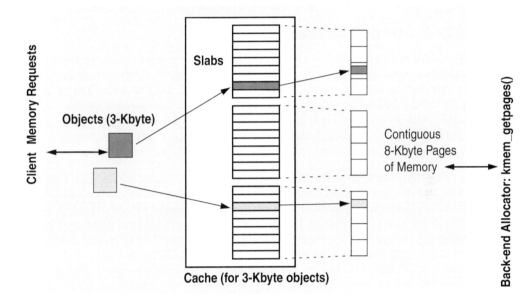

Figure 6.4 Objects, Caches, Slabs, and Pages of Memory

The slab allocator solves many of the fragmentation issues by grouping different-sized memory objects into separate caches, where each object cache has its own object size and characteristics. Grouping the memory objects into caches of similar size allows the allocator to minimize the amount of free space within each cache by neatly packing objects into slabs, where each slab in the cache represents a contiguous group of pages. Since we have one cache per object type, we would expect to see many caches active at once in the Solaris kernel. For example, we should expect to see one cache with 440 byte objects for UFS inodes, another cache of 56 byte objects for file structures, another cache of 872 bytes for LWP structures, and several other caches.

The allocator has a logical front end and back end. Objects are allocated from the front end, and slabs are allocated from pages supplied by the back-end page allocator. This approach allows the slab allocator to be used for more than regular wired-down memory; in fact, the allocator can allocate almost any type of memory object. The allocator is, however, primarily used to allocate memory objects from physical pages by using kmem_getpages as the back-end allocator.

Caches are created with kmem_cache_create(), once for each type of memory object. Caches are generally created during subsystem initialization, for example, in the init routine of a loadable driver. Similarly, caches are destroyed with the kmem_cache_destroy() function. Caches are named by a string provided as an argument, to allow friendlier statistics and tags for debugging. Once a cache is created, objects can be created within the cache with kmem_cache_alloc(), which creates one object of the size associated with the cache from which the object is created. Objects are returned to the cache with kmem_cache_free().

6.2.4.2 Object Caching

The slab allocator makes use of the fact that most of the time objects are heavily allocated and deallocated, and many of the slab allocator's benefits arise from resolving the issues surrounding allocation and deallocation. The allocator tries to defer most of the real work associated with allocation and deallocation until it is really necessary, by keeping the objects alive until memory needs to be returned to the back end. It does this by telling the allocator what the object is being used for, so that the allocator remains in control of the object's true state.

So, what do we really mean by keeping the object *alive*? If we look at what a subsystem uses memory objects for, we find that a memory object typically consists of two common components: the header or description of what resides within the object and associated locks; and the actual payload that resides within the object. A subsystem typically allocates memory for the object, constructs the object in some way (writes a header inside the object or adds it to a list), and then creates any locks required to synchronize access to the object. The subsystem then uses the object. When finished with the object, the subsystem must deconstruct the object, release locks, and then return the memory to the allocator. In short, a subsystem typically allocates, constructs, uses, deallocates, and then frees the object.

If the object is being created and destroyed often, then a great deal of work is expended constructing and deconstructing the object. The slab allocator does away with this extra work by caching the object in its constructed form. When the client asks for a new object, the allocator simply creates or finds an available constructed object. When the client returns an object, the allocator does nothing other than mark the object as free, leaving all of the constructed data (header information and locks) intact. The object can be reused by the client subsystem without the allocator needing to construct or deconstruct—the construction and deconstruction is only done when the cache needs to grow or shrink. Deconstruction is deferred until the allocator needs to free memory back to the back-end allocator.

To allow the slab allocator to take ownership of constructing and deconstructing objects, the client subsystem must provide a constructor and destructor method. This service allows the allocator to construct new objects as required and then to deconstruct objects later, asynchronously to the client's memory requests. The kmem_cache_create() interface supports this feature by providing a constructor and destructor function as part of the create request.

The slab allocator also allows slab caches to be created with no constructor or destructor, to allow simple allocation and deallocation of simple raw memory objects.

The slab allocator moves a lot of the complexity out of the clients and centralizes memory allocation and deallocation policies. At some points, the allocator may need to shrink a cache as a result of being notified of a memory shortage by the

VM system. At this time, the allocator can free all unused objects by calling the destructor for each object that is marked free and then returning unused slabs to the back-end allocator. A further callback interface is provided in each cache so that the allocator can let the client subsystem know about the memory pressure. This callback is optionally supplied when the cache is created and is simply a function that the client implements to return, by means of `kmem_cache_free()`, as many objects to the cache as possible.

A good example is a file system, which uses objects to store the inodes. The slab allocator manages inode objects; the cache management, construction, and deconstruction of inodes are handed over to the slab allocator. The file system simply asks the slab allocator for a "new inode" each time it requires one. For example, a file system could call the slab allocator to create a slab cache, as shown below.

```
inode_cache = kmem_cache_create("inode_cache",
          sizeof (struct inode), 0, inode_cache_constructor,
          inode_cache_destructor, inode_cache_reclaim,
          NULL, NULL, 0);

struct inode *inode = kmem_cache_alloc(inode_cache, 0);
```

The example shows that we create a cache named `inode_cache`, with objects of the size of an inode, no alignment enforcement, a constructor and a destructor function, and a reclaim function. The back-end memory allocator is specified as `NULL`, which by default allocates physical pages from the `segkmem` page allocator.

We can see from the statistics exported by the slab allocator that the UFS file system uses a similar mechanism to allocate its inodes. We use the `netstat -k` function to dump the statistics. (We discuss allocator statistics in more detail in "Slab Allocator Statistics" on page 228.)

```
# netstat -k ufs_inode_cache
ufs_inode_cache:
buf_size 440 align 8 chunk_size 440 slab_size 8192 alloc 20248589
alloc_fail 0 free 20770500 depot_alloc 657344 depot_free 678433
depot_contention 85 global_alloc 602986 global_free 578089
buf_constructed 0 buf_avail 7971 buf_inuse 24897 buf_total 32868
buf_max 41076 slab_create 2802 slab_destroy 976 memory_class 0
hash_size 0 hash_lookup_depth 0 hash_rescale 0 full_magazines 0
empty_magazines 0 magazine_size 31 alloc_from_cpu0 9583811
free_to_cpu0 10344474 buf_avail_cpu0 0 alloc_from_cpu1 9404448
free_to_cpu1 9169504 buf_avail_cpu1 0
```

The allocator interfaces are shown in Table 6-8.

Table 6-8 Solaris 7 Slab Allocator Interfaces from `<sys/kmem.h>`

Function	Description
`kmem_cache_create()`	Creates a new slab cache with the supplied *name*, aligning objects on the boundary supplied with alignment. The constructor, destructor, and reclaim functions are optional and can be supplied as NULL. An argument can be provided to the constructor with *arg*. The back-end memory allocator can also be specified or supplied as NULL. If a NULL back-end allocator is supplied, then the default allocator, `kmem_getpages()`, is used. Flags can supplied as be KMC_NOTOUCH, KMC_NODEBUG, KMC_NOMAGAZINE, and KMC_NOHASH.
`kmem_cache_destroy()`	Destroys the cache referenced by *cp*.
`kmem_cache_alloc()`	Allocates one object from the cache referenced by *cp*. Flags can be supplied as either KM_SLEEP or KM_NOSLEEP.
`kmem_cache_free()`	Returns the buffer *buf* to the cache referenced by *cp*.
`kmem_cache_stat()`	Returns a named statistic about a particular cache that matches the string name. Finds a name by looking at the kstat slab cache names with `netstat -k`.

Caches are created with the `kmem_cache_create()` function, which can optionally supply callbacks for construction, deletion, and cache reclaim notifications. The callback functions are described in Table 6-9.

Table 6-9 Slab Allocator Callback Interfaces from `<sys/kmem.h>`

Function	Description
`constructor()`	Initializes the object *buf*. The arguments *arg* and *flag* are those provided during `kmem_cache_create()`.
`destructor()`	Destroys the object *buf*. The argument *arg* is that provided during `kmem_cache_create()`.
`reclaim()`	Where possible, returns objects to the cache. The argument is that provided during `kmem_cache_create()`.

6.2.4.3 General-Purpose Allocations

In addition to object-based memory allocation, the slab allocator provides backward-compatible, general-purpose memory allocation routines. These routines allocate arbitrary-length memory by providing a method to malloc(). The slab allocator maintains a list of various-sized slabs to accommodate kmem_alloc() requests and simply converts the kmem_alloc() request into a request for an object from the nearest-sized cache. The sizes of the caches used for kmem_alloc() are named kmem_alloc_*n*, where *n* is the size of the objects within the cache (see Section 6.2.4.9, "Slab Allocator Statistics," on page 228). The functions are shown in Table 6-10.

Table 6-10 General-Purpose Memory Allocation

Function	Description
kmem_alloc()	Allocates *size* bytes of memory. Flags can be either KM_SLEEP or KM_NOSLEEP.
kmem_zalloc()	Allocates *size* bytes of zeroed memory. Flags can be either KM_SLEEP or KM_NOSLEEP.
kmem_free()	Returns to the allocator the buffer pointed to by *buf* and *size*.

6.2.4.4 Slab Allocator Implementation

The slab allocator implements the allocation and management of objects to the front-end clients, using memory provided by the back-end allocator. In our introduction to the slab allocator, we discussed in some detail the virtual allocation units: the object and the slab. The slab allocator implements several internal layers to provide efficient allocation of objects from slabs. The extra internal layers reduce the amount of contention between allocation requests from multiple threads, which ultimately allows the allocator to provide good scalability on large SMP systems.

Figure 6.5 shows the internal layers of the slab allocator. The additional layers provide a cache of allocated objects for each CPU, so a thread can allocate an object from a local per-CPU object cache without having to hold a lock on the global slab cache. For example, if two threads both want to allocate an inode object from the inode cache, then the first thread's allocation request would hold a lock on the inode cache and would block the second thread until the first thread has its object allocated. The per-CPU cache layers overcome this blocking with an object cache per CPU to try to avoid the contention between two concurrent requests. Each CPU has its own short-term cache of objects, which reduces the amount of time that each request needs to go down into the global slab cache.

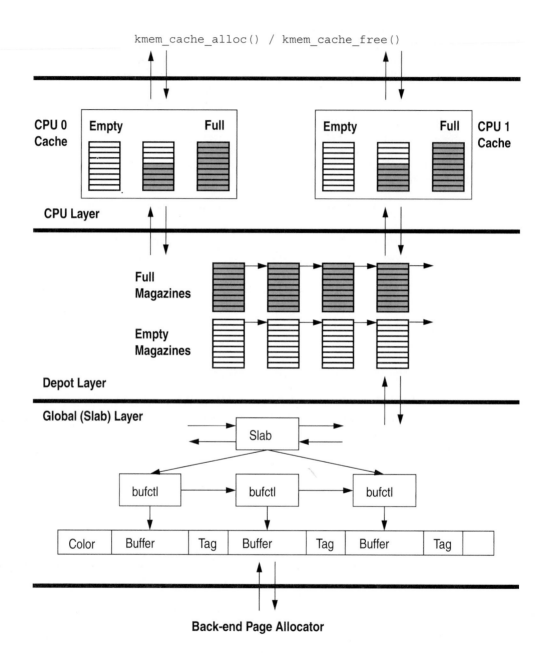

Figure 6.5 Slab Allocator Internal Implementation

The layers shown in Figure 6.5 are separated into the slab layer, the depot layer, and the CPU layer. The upper two layers (which together are known as the magazine layer) are caches of allocated groups of objects and use a military analogy of allocating rifle rounds from magazines. Each per-CPU cache has magazines of allocated objects and can allocate objects (rounds) from its own magazines without having to bother the lower layers. The CPU layer needs to allocate objects from the lower (depot) layer only when its magazines are empty. The depot layer refills magazines from the slab layer by assembling objects, which may reside in many different slabs, into full magazines.

6.2.4.5 The CPU Layer

The CPU layer caches groups of objects to minimize the number of times that an allocation will need to go down to the lower layers. This means that we can satisfy the majority of allocation requests without having to hold any global locks, thus dramatically improving the scalability of the allocator.

Continuing the military analogy: Three magazines of objects are kept in the CPU layer to satisfy allocation and deallocation requests—a full, a half-allocated, and an empty magazine are on hand. Objects are allocated from the half-empty magazine, and until the magazine is empty, all allocations are simply satisfied from the magazine. When the magazine empties, an empty magazine is returned to the magazine layer, and objects are allocated from the full magazine that was already available at the CPU layer. The CPU layer keeps the empty and full magazine on hand to prevent the magazine layer from having to construct and deconstruct magazines when on a full or empty magazine boundary. If a client rapidly allocates and deallocates objects when the magazine is on a boundary, then the CPU layer can simply use its full and empty magazines to service the requests, rather than having the magazine layer deconstruct and reconstruct new magazines at each request. The magazine model allows the allocator to guarantee that it can satisfy at least a magazine size of rounds without having to go to the depot layer.

6.2.4.6 The Depot Layer

The depot layer assembles groups of objects into magazines. Unlike a slab, a magazine's objects are not necessarily allocated from contiguous memory; rather, a magazine contains a series of pointers to objects within slabs.

The number of rounds per magazine for each cache changes dynamically, depending on the amount of contention that occurs at the depot layer. The more rounds per magazine, the lower the depot contention, but more memory is consumed. Each range of object sizes has an upper and lower magazine size. Table 6-11 shows the magazine size range for each object size.

Table 6-11 Magazine Sizes

Object Size Range	Minimum Magazine Size	Maximum Magazine Size
0–63	15	143
64–127	7	95
128–255	3	47
256–511	1	31
512–1023	1	15
1024–2047	1	7
2048–16383	1	3
16384–	1	1

A slab allocator maintenance thread is scheduled every 15 seconds (controlled by the tunable `kmem_update_interval`) to recalculate the magazine sizes. If significant contention has occurred at the depot level, then the magazine size is bumped up. Refer to Table 6-12 on page 227 for the parameters that control magazine resizing.

6.2.4.7 The Global (Slab) Layer

The global slab layer allocates slabs of objects from contiguous pages of physical memory and hands them up to the magazine layer for allocation. The global slab layer is used only when the upper layers need to allocate or deallocate entire slabs of objects to refill their magazines.

The slab is the primary unit of allocation in the slab layer. When the allocator needs to grow a cache, it acquires an entire slab of objects. When the allocator wants to shrink a cache, it returns unused memory to the back end by deallocating a complete slab. A slab consists of one or more pages of virtually contiguous memory carved up into equal-sized chunks, with a reference count indicating how many of those chunks have been allocated.

The contents of each slab are managed by a `kmem_slab` data structure that maintains the slab's linkage in the cache, its reference count, and its list of free buffers. In turn, each buffer in the slab is managed by a `kmem_bufctl` structure that holds the freelist linkage, the buffer address, and a back-pointer to the controlling slab.

For objects smaller than 1/8th of a page, the slab allocator builds a slab by allocating a page, placing the slab data at the end, and dividing the rest into equal-sized buffers. Each buffer serves as its own `kmem_bufctl` while on the freelist. Only the linkage is actually needed, since everything else is computable. These are essential optimizations for small buffers; otherwise, we would end up allocating almost as much memory for `kmem_bufctl` as for the buffers themselves. The free-list linkage resides at the end of the buffer, rather than the beginning, to facilitate debugging. This location is driven by the empirical observation that the beginning of a data structure is typically more active than the end. If a buffer is modified after being freed, the problem is easier to diagnose if the heap structure (free-list linkage) is still intact. The allocator reserves an additional word for constructed objects so that the linkage does not overwrite any constructed state.

For objects greater than 1/8th of a page, a different scheme is used. Allocating objects from within a page-sized slab is efficient for small objects but not for large ones. The reason for the inefficiency of large-object allocation is that we could fit only one 4-Kbyte buffer on an 8-Kbyte page—the embedded slab control data takes up a few bytes, and two 4-Kbyte buffers would need just over 8 Kbytes. For large objects, we allocate a separate slab management structure from a separate pool of memory (another slab allocator cache, the `kmem_slab_cache`). We also allocate a buffer control structure for each page in the cache from another cache, the `kmem_bufctl_cache`. The `slab/bufctl/buffer` structures are shown in the slab layer in Figure 6.5 on page 224.

The slab layer solves another common memory allocation problem by implementing slab coloring. If memory objects all start at a common offset (e.g., at 512-byte boundaries), then accessing data at the start of each object could result in the same cache line being used for all of the objects. The issues are similar to those discussed in "The Page Scanner" on page 178. To overcome the cache line problem, the allocator applies an offset to the start of each slab, so that buffers within the slab start at a different offset. This approach is also shown in Figure 6.5 on page 224 by the color offset segment that resides at the start of each memory allocation unit before the actual buffer. Slab coloring results in much better cache utilization and more evenly balanced memory loading.

6.2.4.8 Slab Cache Parameters

The slab allocator parameters are shown in Table 6-12 for reference only. We recommend that none of these values be changed.

Table 6-12 Kernel Memory Allocator Parameters

Parameter	Description	2.7 Def.
`kmem_reap_interval`	The number of ticks after which the slab allocator update thread will run.	15000 (15s)
`kmem_depot_contention`	If the number of times depot contention occurred since the last time the update thread ran is greater than this value, then the magazine size is increased.	3
`kmem_reapahead`	If the amount of free memory falls below `cachefree` + `kmem_reapahead`, then the slab allocator will give back as many slabs as possible to the back-end page allocator.	0

6.2.4.9 Slab Allocator Statistics

Two forms of slab allocator statistics are available: global statistics and per-cache statistics. The global statistics are available through the crash utility and display a summary of the entire cache list managed by the allocator.

```
# crash
dumpfile = /dev/mem, namelist = /dev/ksyms, outfile = stdout
> kmastat
                          buf    buf   buf    memory    #allocations
cache name                size avail total   in use    succeed fail
----------                ----- ----- -----  --------   ------- ----
kmem_magazine_1             16    483   508      8192       6664    0
kmem_magazine_3             32   1123  1270     40960      55225    0
kmem_magazine_7             64    584   762     49152      62794    0
kmem_magazine_15           128    709   945    122880     194764    0
kmem_magazine_31           256     58    62     16384      24915    0
kmem_magazine_47           384      0     0         0          0    0
kmem_magazine_63           512      0     0         0          0    0
kmem_magazine_95           768      0     0         0          0    0
kmem_magazine_143         1152      0     0         0          0    0
kmem_slab_cache             56    308  2159    139264      22146    0
kmem_bufctl_cache           32   2129  6096    196608      54870    0
kmem_bufctl_audit_cache    184     24 16464   3211264      16440    0
kmem_pagectl_cache          32    102   254      8192     406134    0
kmem_alloc_8                 8   9888 31527    253952  115432346    0
kmem_alloc_16               16   7642 18288    294912  374733170    0
kmem_alloc_24               24   4432 11187    270336   30957233    0
     .
     .
kmem_alloc_12288         12288      2     4     49152        660    0
kmem_alloc_16384         16384      0    42    688128       1845    0
     .
     .
streams_mblk                64   3988  5969    385024   31405446    0
streams_dblk_32            128    795  1134    147456   72553829    0
streams_dblk_64            160    716  1650    270336  196660790    0
     .
     .
streams_dblk_8096         8192     17    17    139264  356266482    0
streams_dblk_12192       12288      8     8     98304   14848223    0
streams_dblk_esb            96      0     0         0     406326    0
stream_head_cache          328     68   648    221184     492256    0
queue_cache                456    109  1513    729088    1237000    0
syncq_cache                120     48    67      8192        373    0
qband_cache                 64    125   635     40960       1303    0
linkinfo_cache              48    156   169      8192         90    0
strevent_cache              48    153   169      8192    5442622    0
as_cache                   120     45   201     24576     158778    0
seg_skiplist_cache          32    540  1524     49152    1151455    0
anon_cache                  48   1055 71825   3481600    7926946    0
anonmap_cache               48    551  4563    221184    5805027    0
segvn_cache                 88    686  6992    622592    9969087    0
flk_edges                   48      0     0         0          1    0
physio_buf_cache           224      0     0         0   98535107    0
snode_cache                240     39   594    147456    1457746    0
ufs_inode_cache            440   8304 32868  14958592   20249920    0
     .
     .
----------                ----- ----- -----  --------   ------- ----
permanent                   -      -     -     98304        501    0
oversize                    -      -     -   9904128     406024    0
----------                ----- ----- -----  --------   ------- ----
Total                       -      -     -  58753024 2753193059    0
```

The `kmastat` command shows summary information for each statistic and a systemwide summary at the end. The columns are shown in Table 6-13.

Table 6-13 kmastat Columns

Parameter	Description
Cache name	The name of the cache, as supplied during `kmem_cache_create()`.
`buf_size`	The size of each object within the cache in bytes.
`buf_avail`	The number of free objects in the cache.
`buf_total`	The total number of objects in the cache.
Memory in use	The amount of physical memory consumed by the cache in bytes.
Allocations succeeded	The number of allocations that succeeded.
Allocations failed	The number of allocations that failed. These are likely to be allocations that specified `KM_NOSLEEP` during memory pressure.

A more detailed version of the per-cache statistics is exported by the `kstat` mechanism. You can use the `netstat -k` command to display the cache statistics, which are described in Table 6-14.

```
# netstat -k ufs_inode_cache
ufs_inode_cache:
buf_size 440 align 8 chunk_size 440 slab_size 8192 alloc 20248589
alloc_fail 0 free 20770500 depot_alloc 657344 depot_free 678433
depot_contention 85 global_alloc 602986 global_free 578089
buf_constructed 0 buf_avail 7971 buf_inuse 24897 buf_total 32868
buf_max 41076 slab_create 2802 slab_destroy 976 memory_class 0
hash_size 0 hash_lookup_depth 0 hash_rescale 0 full_magazines 0
empty_magazines 0 magazine_size 31 alloc_from_cpu0 9583811
free_to_cpu0 10344474 buf_avail_cpu0 0 alloc_from_cpu1 9404448
free_to_cpu1 9169504 buf_avail_cpu1 0
```

Table 6-14 Slab Allocator Per-Cache Statistics

Parameter	Description
`buf_size`	The size of each object within the cache in bytes.
`align`	The alignment boundary for objects within the cache.
`chunk_size`	The allocation unit for the cache in bytes.
`slab_size`	The size of each slab within the cache in bytes.

Table 6-14 Slab Allocator Per-Cache Statistics (Continued)

Parameter	Description
`alloc`	The number of object allocations that succeeded.
`alloc_fail`	The number of object allocations that failed. (Should be zero!)
`free`	The number of objects that were freed.
`depot_alloc`	The number of times a magazine was allocated in the depot layer.
`depot_free`	The number of times a magazine was freed to the depot layer.
`depot_contention`	The number of times a depot layer allocation was blocked because another thread was in the depot layer.
`global_alloc`	The number of times an allocation was made at the global layer.
`global_free`	The number of times an allocation was freed at the global layer.
`buf_constructed`	Zero or the same as `buf_avail`.
`buf_avail`	The number of free objects in the cache.
`buf_inuse`	The number of objects used by the client.
`buf_total`	The total number of objects in the cache.
`buf_max`	The maximum number of objects the cache has reached.
`slab_create`	The number of slabs created.
`slab_destroy`	The number of slabs destroyed.
`memory_class`	The ID of the back-end memory allocator.
`hash_size`	Buffer hash lookup statistics.
`hash_lookup_depth`	Buffer hash lookup statistics.
`hash_rescale`	Buffer hash lookup statistics.
`full_magazines`	The number of full magazines.
`empty_magazines`	The number of empty magazines.
`magazine_size`	The size of the magazine.
`alloc_from_cpu`N	Object allocations from CPU N.
`free_to_cpu`N	Objects freed to CPU N.
`buf_avail_cpu`N	Objects available to CPU N.

6.2.4.10 Slab Allocator Tracing

The slab allocator includes a general-purpose allocation tracing facility that tracks the allocation history of objects. The facility is switched off by default and can be enabled by setting the system variable `kmem_flags`. The tracing facility captures the stack and history of allocations into a slab cache, named as the name of the cache being traced, with .DEBUG appended to it. Audit tracing can be enabled by the following:

- Setting kmem_flags to indicate the type of tracing desired, usually 0x1F to indicate all tracing
- Booting the system with kadb -d and setting kmem_flags before startup

The following simple example shows how to trace a cache that is created on a large system, after the flags have been set. To enable tracing on all caches, the system must be booted with kadb and the kmem_flags variable set. The steps for such booting are shown below.

```
ok boot kadb -d
Resetting ...

Sun Ultra 1 UPA/SBus (UltraSPARC 167MHz), No Keyboard
OpenBoot 3.1, 128 MB memory installed, Serial #8788108.
Ethernet address 8:0:20:86:18:8c, Host ID: 8086188c.


Rebooting with command: boot kadb -d
Boot device: /sbus/SUNW,fas@e,8800000/sd@0,0  File and args: kadb -d
kadb: <return>
kadb[0]: kmem_flags/D
kmem_flags:
kmem_flags:     0
kadb[0]: kmem_flags/W 0x1f
kmem_flags:     0x0       =       0x1f
kadb[0]: :c

SunOS Release 5.7 Version Generic 64-bit
Copyright 1983-2000 Sun Microsystems, Inc.  All rights reserved.
\
```

Note that the total number of allocations traced will be limited by the size of the audit cache parameters, shown in Table 6-12 on page 227. Table 6-15 shows the parameters that control kernel memory debugging.

Table 6-15 Kernel Memory Debugging Parameters

Parameter	Description	2.7 Def.
kmem_flags	Set this to select the mode of kernel memory debugging. Set to 0x1F to enable all debugging, or set the logical AND of the following: 0x1 transaction auditing 0x2 deadbeef checking 0x4 red-zone checking 0x8 freed buffer content logging	0

Table 6-15 Kernel Memory Debugging Parameters (Continued)

Parameter	Description	2.7 Def.
`kmem_log_size`	Maximum amount of memory to use for slab allocator audit tracing.	2% of mem.
`kmem_content_maxsave`	The maximum number of bytes to log in each entry.	256

7

MEMORY MONITORING

In the preceding chapters we covered design and implementation of the Solaris virtual memory system. This chapter is more practical in nature and covers the tools available to monitor the VM system.

7.1 A Quick Introduction to Memory Monitoring

In Chapter 5, "Solaris Memory Architecture" we saw that Solaris memory is used for several major functions, including the kernel, processes, and the file system cache. The first step to understanding Solaris memory utilization is to summarize, at the global level, the following categories:

- Total physical memory available
- Memory allocated internally within the Solaris kernel
- Memory used for the file system page cache
- Memory used by processes
- Memory free

Several different Solaris utilities are required for derivation of the global summary, and we will see how we can use these tools to build our summary. We later discuss MemTool, a downloadable toolset you can load into the Solaris kernel to provide even more detailed information.

7.1.1 Total Physical Memory

From the output of the Solaris `prtconf` command, we can ascertain the amount of total physical memory.

```
# prtconf

System Configuration:  Sun Microsystems   sun4u
Memory size: 384 Megabytes
System Peripherals (Software Nodes):
```

7.1.2 Kernel Memory

We find the amount of kernel memory by using the Solaris `sar` command and summing the three pool columns. The output is in bytes; in this example, the kernel is using 55, 361, 536 bytes of memory.

```
# sar -k 1 1

SunOS devhome 5.7 SunOS_Development sun4u    02/07/00

18:12:28 sml_mem   alloc  fail  lg_mem   alloc  fail  ovsz_alloc  fail
18:12:31 8732672 7658792      0 37380096 30195320     0    9248768     0
```

7.1.3 Free Memory

Free memory is almost always zero because the buffer cache grows to consume free memory. Use the `vmstat` command to measure free memory. The first line of output from `vmstat` is an average since boot, so the real free memory figure is available on the second line. The output is in kilobytes. Note that this has changed in Solaris 8—free memory now contains the majority of the file system cache.

```
# vmstat 3
 procs     memory            page            disk          faults      cpu
 r b w   swap  free  re  mf pi po fr de sr f0 s6 sd sd   in   sy   cs us sy id
 1 0 0  29008 38456   1   4 17  0  6  0  0  0  0  0  0  209 1755  399  5  1 94
 0 0 0 514952 12720   0   8  0  0  0  0  0  0  0  0  0  232  482  330  1  0 98
 0 0 0 514952 12720   0   0  0  0  0  0  0  0  0  0  0  214  432  307  0  0 100
 1 0 0 514952 12720   0   0  0  0  0  0  0  0  0  0  0  192  409  271  0  0 100
```

7.1.4 File System Caching Memory

The file system cache uses available free memory to cache files on the file system. On most systems, the amount of free memory is almost zero because the file system cache is occupying all of the memory not being used by processes. We typically see free memory (reported in `vmstat`) start high when a system is booted, then slowly drop to almost zero after time. Free memory typically stays at or almost at zero until either a file system is unmounted or the system is rebooted. This behavior is completely normal. In Solaris 8, the file system cache *is included* in free memory, so the free memory value is interpreted differently.

To look at the amount of file buffer cache, use the MemTool package. We can use the MemTool `memps` command to dump the contents of the buffer cache, and we can get a summary of the buffer cache memory with the MemTool `prtmem` command.

```
# prtmem

Total memory:             241 Megabytes
Kernel Memory:             39 Megabytes
Application:              106 Megabytes
Executable & libs:         36 Megabytes
File Cache:                59 Megabytes
Free, file cache:           3 Megabytes
Free, free:                 0 Megabytes
```

7.1.5 Memory Shortage Detection

A critical component of performance analysis is ascertaining where the bottlenecks are. Detecting memory bottlenecks is not quite as straightforward as measuring processor and disk bottlenecks and requires a few more steps to arrive at a conclusion. To determine if there is a memory shortage, we need to determine the following:

- Whether the applications are paging excessively because of a memory shortage
- Whether the system could benefit by making more memory available for file buffering

The paging activity reported by the Solaris `vmstat` command includes both file system activity and application paging and is not a fail-safe method of identifying memory shortages. We can, however, use `vmstat` to rule out any question of a memory shortage in some circumstances. We recommend the following steps:

- Use `vmstat` to see if the system is paging. If it is not, then there is no chance of a memory shortage. Excessive paging activity is evident by activity in the scan-rate (sr) and page-out (po) columns, where values are constantly nonzero. However, if the system is paging heavily, this is not necessarily a sign of a memory shortage.
- Look at the activity reported for the swap device. If application paging is occurring, then the swap device will have I/Os queued to it. Any significant I/O to the swap device is a sure sign of memory shortage.
- Use the MemTool to measure the distribution of memory in the system. If an application memory shortage exists, then the file system buffer cache size will be very small (i.e., less than 10 percent of the total memory available).

7.1.6 Swap Space

Solaris swap space has two important states that we must observe: swap reservation and physical swap allocation. (See "The swapfs Layer" on page 156 for details about the Solaris swap implementation.) Two important measures of Solaris swap space are these:

- The amount of virtual swap space that is configured and available for swap reservations
- The amount of physical swap space that is configured and available for physical page-outs

We need to ensure that neither of these two types of swap space is exhausted. When we exhaust virtual space, `malloc()` and related calls fail, which means our programs start to fail. When we exhaust physical swap space, programs do not fail, but since there is no longer any space left to page them out to, the Solaris kernel begins locking down pages of memory that would normally be paged out.

7.1.6.1 Virtual Swap Space

The amount of virtual swap space configured is the sum of the amount of physical swap space (disk swap space) plus the amount of memory that Solaris can use for swap. We can use the `swap -s` command to see if enough virtual swap space is configured. When the "available" column falls to zero, programs will start to fail. We can add virtual swap by simply adding more physical swap space.

```
# swap -s
total: 251232k bytes allocated + 25544k reserved = 276776k used, 514992k available
```

7.1.6.2 Physical Swap Space

The amount of physical swap space configured is simply the amount of physical disk or file-based swap configured through `/etc/vfstab` or by the `swap` command. The amount of physical swap space affects the amount of virtual swap space available for reservations, as just discussed, but it also affects the amount of physical space available that pages can be paged out to. Even if there is sufficient total virtual space for reservations, we may still have insufficient space for physical page-outs. The physical swap configuration and the amount of physical swap available for pages to be paged out to can be seen with the `-l` option of the `swap` command. The amount of physical swap space available for paging out to is shown in the free column (note that the free column is not the amount of physical swap available for reservations, it's the amount of space available for physical page-outs). If free physical swap is zero, then pages will no longer be paged out to swap and memory will effectively start being locked down.

```
# swap -l
swapfile              dev  swaplo blocks    free
/dev/dsk/c1t2d3s1    118,105     16 1048784 47024
```

Ensure that both `swap -s` "available" and `swap -l` "free" are nonzero.

7.2 Memory Monitoring Tools

To understand the memory behavior and requirements of a particular system, we need to be able to measure the activity and operation of the virtual memory system. In this section, we look at the current tools bundled with the Solaris kernel, and we discuss some other unbundled tools that allow us to look a little deeper into the virtual memory system.

We have two basic objectives in looking at Solaris memory: to find out where all of the memory is allocated and to look at memory (or paging) activity. Table 7-1 lists the tools we discuss and the capabilities of each.

Table 7-1 Solaris Memory Monitoring Commands

Tool	Location of Tool	Capabilities for Memory Utilization Reporting	Paging Activity Reporting
vmstat	/usr/bin	Basic	Systemwide only
ps	/usr/bin	Process size	—
swap	/usr/bin	Swap allocation	—
wsm	Engineering/free	Working set size	—
ipcs	/usr/bin	SysV shared memory	—
MemTool	Engineering/download	Process/file system cache	—
memstat	Engineering/download	Same as vmstat	Breakout of paging for file systems, applications, and libraries
pmap	/usr/proc/bin	Process address map	—
pmap -x	/usr/proc/bin	Process physical memory utilization, including the amount of memory shared among processes	—
crash	/usr/bin/crash	Kernel memory utilities	—
dbx	SPARCworks	Memory leaks	—

7.3   The vmstat Command

The Solaris `vmstat` utility summarizes various functions within the virtual memory system, including systemwide free memory, paging counters, disk activity, system calls, and CPU utilization. The output of `vmstat` is shown below with explanations of the various fields. Let's take a look at how we can use `vmstat` to get a quick summary of what is happening on our system. Note that the first line of output from `vmstat` shows a summary since boot, followed by the output over the last 3 seconds for each additional line.

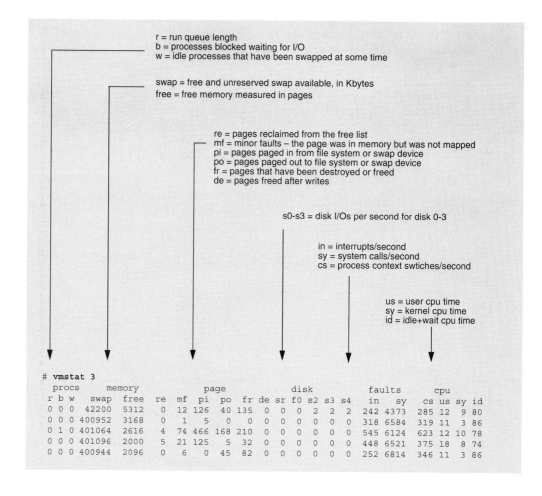

```
# vmstat 3
 procs     memory            page            disk          faults      cpu
 r b w   swap  free  re   mf   pi  po   fr de sr f0 s2 s3 s4   in   sy    cs us sy id
 0 0 0  42200  5312   0   12  126  40  135  0  0  0  2  2  2  242 4373  285 12  9 80
 0 0 0 400952  3168   0    1    5   0    0  0  0  0  0  0  0  318 6584  319 11  3 86
 0 1 0 401064  2616   4   74  466 168  210  0  0  0  0  0  0  545 6124  623 12 10 78
 0 0 0 401096  2000   5   21  125   5   32  0  0  0  0  0  0  448 6521  375 18  8 74
 0 0 0 400944  2096   0    6    0  45   82  0  0  0  0  0  0  252 6814  346 11  3 86
```

r = run queue length
b = processes blocked waiting for I/O
w = idle processes that have been swapped at some time

swap = free and unreserved swap available, in Kbytes
free = free memory measured in pages

re = pages reclaimed from the free list
mf = minor faults – the page was in memory but was not mapped
pi = pages paged in from file system or swap device
po = pages paged out to file system or swap device
fr = pages that have been destroyed or freed
de = pages freed after writes

s0-s3 = disk I/Os per second for disk 0-3

in = interrupts/second
sy = system calls/second
cs = process context swtiches/second

us = user cpu time
sy = kernel cpu time
id = idle+wait cpu time

7.3.1 Free Memory

Our `vmstat` example shows that we have 2,096 Kbytes of memory free, which seems low for a system with 128 Mbytes. Recall from the introduction that free memory is low because the VM system has used all of it for file system caching, which means that free memory has fallen to approximately the value of `lotsfree`. (See "The Page Scanner" on page 178 for the meaning of `lotsfree`.) Although free memory is almost zero, plenty of memory may still be available for applications. We will look at how to observe how much of our memory is being used for file system caching later when we discuss MemTool in detail.

7.3.2 Swap Space

The `vmstat` command reports the amount of virtual swap space that is free and available for reservation. This is the sum of the total amount of physical swap space available plus the amount of memory swap space. It is equivalent to the "available" column in `swap -s`.

7.3.3 Paging Counters

The `vmstat` paging counters show us the systemwide virtual memory paging activity. The counters include paging activity to/from program memory (anonymous memory) and to/from file systems. The fields are shown in Table 7-2.

Table 7-2 Statistics from the `vmstat` Command

Counter	Description
re	Page reclaims — The number of pages reclaimed since the last sample. Some of the file system cache is in the free list, and when a file page is reused and removed from the free list, a reclaim occurs. File pages in the free list can be either regular files or executable/library pages.
mf	Minor faults — The number of pages attached to an address space since the last sample. If the page is already in memory, then a minor fault simply reestablishes the mapping to it.
pi	Page-ins — The number of pages paged in since the last sample. A page-in occurs whenever a page is brought back in from the swap device or brought from a file system into the file system cache.
po	Page-outs — The number of pages paged out and freed. A page-out is counted whenever a page is written *and* freed. Often, this is as a result of the pageout scanner, fsflush, or file close.
fr	Page frees — The number of pages that have been freed by either the page scanner or by the file system (free behind).

Table 7-2 Statistics from the `vmstat` Command (Continued)

Counter	Description
`de`	The precalculated, anticipated, short-term memory shortfall. Used by the page scanner to free ahead enough pages to satisfy requests.
`sr`	The number of pages scanned by the page scanner per second.

7.3.4 Process Memory Usage, ps, and the pmap Command

The memory usage of a process can be categorized into two classes: its virtual memory usage and its physical memory usage. The virtual memory size is the amount of virtual address space that has been allocated to the process, and the physical memory is the amount of real memory pages that has been allocated to a process. We refer to the physical memory usage of a process as its resident set size, often abbreviated RSS. We can use the `ps` command to display a process's virtual and physical memory usage.

```
# ps -e -opid,vsz,rss,args
  PID  VSZ  RSS COMMAND
11896 1040  736 ps -a -opid,vsz,rss,args
11892 1032  768 sh
 3603 1032  768 sh
 2695 1896 1432 telnet donan
 2693 1920 1456 telnet donan
 2433 1920 1440 telnet firefly
 3143 1920 1456 telnet devnull
 2429 1920 1440 telnet firefly.eng
 2134 1920 1440 telnet devnull
```

From the `ps` example, we can see that the `/bin/sh` shell uses 1,032 Kbytes of virtual memory, 768 Kbytes of which have been allocated from physical memory. We can also see that two shells are running. `ps` reports that both shells are using 768 Kbytes of memory each, but in fact, because each shell uses dynamic shared libraries, the total amount of physical memory used by both shells is much less than 768K x 2.

To ascertain how much memory is really being used by both shells, we need to look more closely at the address space within each process. Figure 7.1 shows how the two shells share both the `/bin/sh` binary and their shared libraries. The figure shows each segment of memory within the shell's address space. We've separated the memory use into three categories:

- **Private** — Memory that is mapped into each process and that is not shared by any other processes.

- **Shared** — Memory that is shared with all other processes on the system, including read-only portions of the binary and libraries, otherwise known as the "text" segments.

- **Partially shared** — A segment that is partly shared with other processes. The data segments of the binary and libraries are shared this way because they are shared but writable and within each process are private copies of pages that have been modified. For example, the /bin/sh data segment is mapped shared between all instances of /bin/sh but is mapped read/write because it contains initialized variables that may be updated during the execution of the process. Variable updates must be kept private to the process, so a private page is created by a "copy on write" operation. (See "Copy-on-Write" on page 152 for further information.)

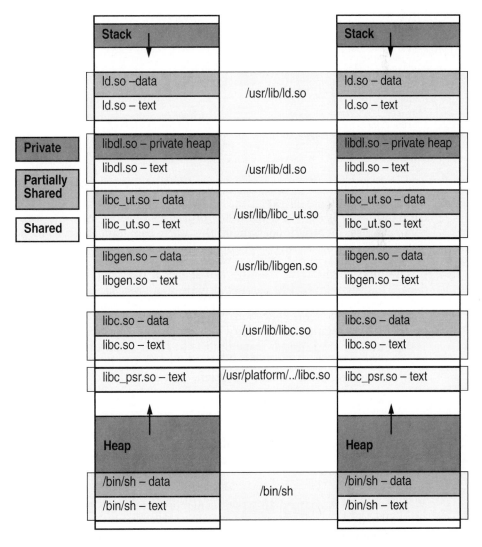

Figure 7.1 Process Private and Shared Mappings (/bin/sh Example)

The `pmap` command provides a mechanism for a detailed look at a process's memory utilization. The `pmap` command can show how much memory is resident, how much of that is shared, and how much private memory a process has.

```
# /usr/proc/bin/pmap -x 1069

pmap -x $$
4285:   sh
Address   Kbytes Resident Shared Private Permissions      Mapped File
00010000      88       88     88       - read/exec        sh
00034000      16       16      -      16 read/write/exec   sh
00038000       8        8      -       8 read/write/exec   [ heap ]
FF270000      16       16     16       - read/exec         libc_psr.so.1
FF280000     656      608    600       8 read/exec          libc.so.1
FF332000      32       32      -      32 read/write/exec    libc.so.1
FF350000      24       24     24       - read/exec          libgen.so.1
FF364000      16       16      -      16 read/write/exec    libgen.so.1
FF370000       8        8      -       8 read/exec          libc_ut.so
FF380000       8        8      -       8 read/write/exec    libc_ut.so
FF390000       8        8      8       - read/exec          libdl.so.1
FF3A0000       8        8      -       8 read/write/exec    [ anon ]
FF3B0000     120      120    120       - read/exec          ld.so.1
FF3DC000       8        8      -       8 read/write/exec    ld.so.1
FFBEC000      16       16      -      16 read/write/exec    [ stack ]
--------  ------   ------ ------  ------
total Kb    1032      984    856     128
```

The example output from `pmap` shows the memory map of the `/bin/sh` command. At the top of the output are the executable text and data segments. All of the executable binary is shared with other processes because it is mapped read-only into each process. A small portion of the data segment is shared; some is private because of copy-on-write (COW) operations.

The next segment in the address space is the heap space, or user application data. This segment is 100 percent private to a process.

Following the heap space are the shared libraries. Each shared library has a text and data segment, which are like the executable text and data. Library text is 100 percent shared, and library data is partially shared. At the bottom of the process dump is the stack, which, like the heap, is 100 percent private. A summary of the total virtual size, resident portion, and private memory is printed at the bottom.

7.4 MemTool: Unbundled Memory Tools

MemTool was developed to provide a more in-depth look at where memory has been allocated on a Solaris system. Using these tools, we can find out where every page of memory is, and in what proportions. MemTool is available as a downloadable, unsupported package from Sun Engineering. Note that these tools are not supported by the normal Sun support channels. The latest version of MemTool can be found at `http://www.solarisinternals.com`.

7.4.1 MemTool Utilities

The MemTool package provides command-line, GUI, and character tools, as listed in Table 7-3.

Table 7-3 MemTool Utilities

Tool	Interface	Description
memps	CLI	Dumps process summary and file system cache memory (-m).
prtmem	CLI	Displays a systemwide summary of memory allocation.
prtswap	CLI	Displays a systemwide detailed description of swap allocation. Both virtual and physical swap allocation are shown.
memtool	GUI	Is a comprehensive GUI for UFS and process memory.
mem	CUI	Is a Curses interface for UFS and process memory.

7.4.2 Command-Line Tools

MemTool provides three command-line tools: `prtmem`, `memps`, and `prtswap`.

7.4.2.1 System Memory Summary: prtmem

The `prtmem` command shows a systemwide summary of memory utilization, categorized into seven major groups. The output from the `prtmem` command is shown below; the rows are described in Table 7-4.

```
# prtmem

Total memory:            241 Megabytes
Kernel Memory:            39 Megabytes
Application:             106 Megabytes
Executable & libs:        36 Megabytes
File Cache:                3 Megabytes
Free, file cache:         58 Megabytes
Free, free:                0 Megabytes
```

Table 7-4 `prtmem` Rows

Row	Description
Total memory	The total amount of usable memory in the system minus that used for low-level memory management.

Table 7-4 prtmem Rows (Continued)

Row	Description
Kernel Memory	Memory used for the kernel executable, data structures, and kernel allocations, internal to the operating system.
Application	Anonymous memory used by processes, typically heap, stack, and copy-on-write pages.
Executable & libs	Executable and shared library pages that are mapped into process address space.
File Cache	File cache that is not on the free list.
Free, file cache	File system cache that has been placed on the free list. This file cache memory still contains valid cache but will be consumed from the free list when memory is needed.
Free, free	Memory that is free and not associated with any files.

7.4.2.2 File System Cache Memory: memps -m

Memtool provides a list showing where the pool of filesystem cache memory has been allocated, sorted by vnode. The list summarizes the size of each vnode in the file system cache and, if possible, gives the real file name. If the real file name cannot be determined, then the device and inode number are printed for that vnode.

We can display the list of vnodes in file system cache with the memps -m command. Table 7-5 describes the columns.

```
# memps -m

SunOS devhome 5.7 SunOS_Development sun4u     02/08/100

00:23:12
  Size E/F Filename
 10232k E  /export/ws/local/netscape/netscape
  5648k E  /export/ws/dist/share/framemaker,v5.5.3/bin/sunxm.s5.sparc/maker5X.e
  2944k F  /home/rmc/.netscape/history.dat
  2888k E  /ws/on998-tools/SUNWspro/SC5.x/contrib/XEmacs20.3-b91/bin/sparc-sun-
  2000k E  /export/ws/dist/share/acroread,v3.01/Reader/sparcsolaris/lib/libXm.s
  1648k E  /usr/dt/lib/libXm.so.4
  1400k E  /usr/dt/lib/libXm.so.3
  1392k E  /usr/openwin/server/lib/libserverdps.so.5
   928k E  /export/ws/dist/share/acroread,v3.01/Reader/sparcsolaris/lib/libread
   824k E  /export/ws/dist/share/acroread,v3.01/Reader/sparcsolaris/bin/acrorea
     .
     .
     .
```

Table 7-5 memps Columns

Column	Description
Size	The amount of physical memory in the file system cache for this file.
E/F	If the VM system sees this file as an executable or library, then E for *executable* is shown; otherwise, F for *file* is shown.
Filename	The filename if known; otherwise, the file system mount point and inode number are shown.

7.4.2.3 The prtswap Utility

The prtswap utility shows the three main states of swap and the way in which that state affects the virtual and physical swap configured.

```
# prtswap -l

Swap Reservations:
------------------------------------------------------------------
Total Virtual Swap Configured:                     336MB =
RAM Swap Configured:                                      159MB
Physical Swap Configured:                          +      177MB

Total Virtual Swap Reserved Against:               289MB =
RAM Swap Reserved Against:                                111MB
Physical Swap Reserved Against:                    +      177MB

Total Virtual Swap Unresv. & Avail. for Reservation:  47MB =
Physical Swap Unresv. & Avail. for Reservations:          0MB
RAM Swap Unresv. & Avail. for Reservations:        +     47MB


Swap Allocations: (Reserved and Phys pages allocated)
------------------------------------------------------------------
Total Virtual Swap Configured:                     336MB
Total Virtual Swap Allocated Against:              254MB

Physical Swap Utilization: (pages swapped out)
------------------------------------------------------------------
Physical Swap Free (should not be zero!):           42MB =
Physical Swap Configured:                                177MB
Physical Swap Used (pages swapped out):            -     135MB
```

7.4.3 The MemTool GUI

The MemTool GUI provides an easy method for invoking most of the functionality of the MemTool command line interfaces. Invoke the GUI as the root user to see all of the process and file information.

```
# /opt/RMCmem/bin/memtool &
```

The MemTool GUI offers three basic modes: buffer cache memory, process memory, and a process/buffer cache mapping matrix.

7.4.3.1 File System Cache Memory

The initial screen shows the contents of the file system cache. The file system cache display shows each entry in the UFS file system cache. Figure 7.2 shows the fields; Table 7-6 describes them.

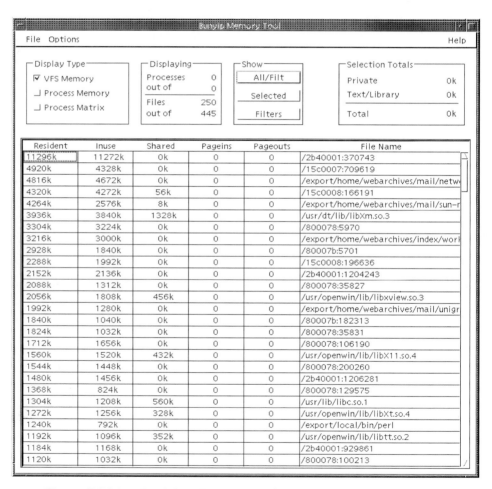

Figure 7.2 MemTool GUI: File System Cache Memory

The GUI displays only the largest 250 files. A status panel at the top of the display shows the total number of files and the number that have been displayed.

Table 7-6 MemTool Buffer Cache Fields

Field	Description
Resident	The amount of physical memory that this file has associated with it.
Used	The amount of physical memory that this file has mapped into a process segment or SEGMAP. Generally, the difference between this and the resident figure is what is on the free list associated with this file.
Shared	The amount of memory that this file has in memory that is shared with more than one process.
Pageins	The amount of minor and major page-ins for this file.
Pageouts	The amount of page-outs for this file.
Filename	The filename if known; otherwise, the file system mount point and inode number are shown.

7.4.3.2 Process Memory

The second mode of the MemTool GUI is the process memory display. Click on the Process Memory checkbox at the left of the GUI to select this mode. The process memory display shows the process table with a memory summary for each process. Each line of the process table is the same as the per-process summary from the pmap command. Figure 7.3 shows the fields; Table 7-7 describes them.

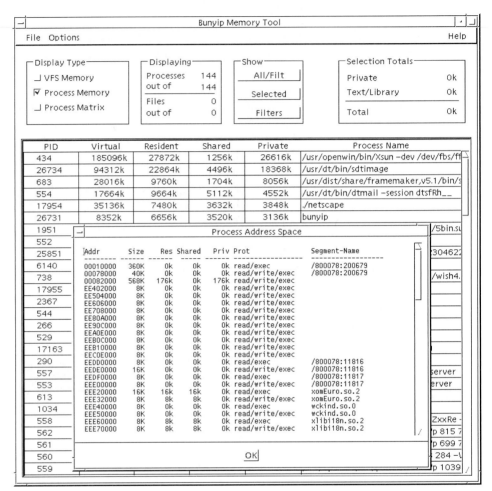

Figure 7.3 MemTool GUI: Process Memory

Table 7-7 MemTool Process Table Field

Field	Description
PID	Process ID of the process.
Virtual	The virtual size of the process, including swapped-out and unallocated memory.
Resident	The amount of physical memory that this process has, including shared binaries, libraries, etc.

Table 7-7 MemTool Process Table Field (Continued)

Field	Description
Shared	The amount of memory that this process is sharing with another process, that is, shared libraries, shared memory, etc.
Private	The amount of resident memory this process has that is not shared with other processes. This figure is essentially *Resident—Shared*.
Process	The full process name and arguments.

To select the individual process map for a process, click on one of the process entries.

7.4.3.3 Process Matrix

The process matrix, Figure 7.4, shows the relationship between processes and mapped files. Across the top of the display is the list of processes that we viewed in the process memory display, and down the side is a list of the files that are mapped into these processes. Each column of the matrix shows the amount of memory mapped into that process for each file, with an extra row for the private memory associated with that process.

The matrix can be used to show the total memory usage of a group of processes. By default, the summary box at the top right-hand corner shows the memory used by all of the processes displayed. We can select a group of processes with the left mouse button and then summarize by pressing the Selection button at the top-middle of the display. Selecting the All/Filt button returns the full display.

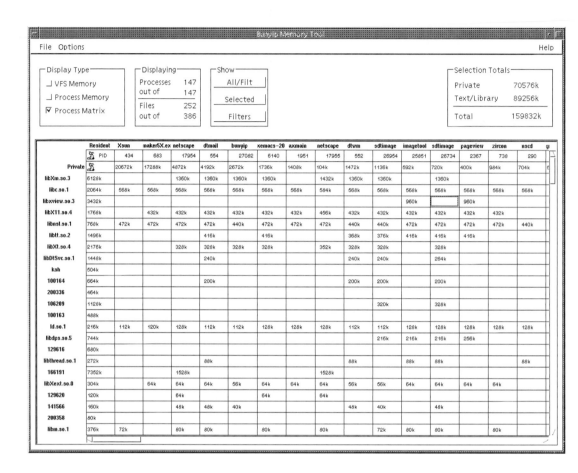

Figure 7.4 MemTool GUI: Process/File Matrix

7.5 Other Memory Tools

Two other memory tools—Workspace Monitor (wsm) and memstat (an extended vmstat)—provide additional information.

7.5.1 The Workspace Monitor Utility: WSM

Another good utility for monitor memory usage is the workspace monitor. It shows a live status of a process's memory map and lists the amount of memory that has been read or written to in the sampled interval. This information is particularly useful for determining how much memory a process is using at any given instant. The wsm command is invoked against a single process.

```
# wsm -p 732 -t 10

 Read  Write  Mapped  PROT  Segment    maker5X.exe(pid 683)  Mon Jul 21 15:44:10 1997
  235      0     782  (R-X) maker
   10     11      36  (RWX) maker
  207    384    2690  (RWX) Bss & Heap
   14      0      74  (R-X) /usr/lib/libc.so.1
    2      1       3  (RWX) /usr/lib/libc.so.1
    0      1       1  (RWX) /dev/zero <or other device>
    0      0       1  (R-X) /usr/lib/straddr.so
    0      0       1  (RWX) /usr/lib/straddr.so
    1      0       2  (R-X) /usr/platform/SUNW,Ultra-2/lib/libc_psr.so.1
    1      0       1  (RWX) /dev/zero <or other device>
    0      0      56  (R-X) /usr/lib/libnsl.so.1
    0      0       4  (RWX) /usr/lib/libnsl.so.1
    0      0       3  (RWX) /dev/zero <or other device>
    0      0       2  (R-X) /usr/lib/libmp.so.2
    0      0       1  (RWX) /usr/lib/libmp.so.2
    0      0       9  (R-X) /usr/openwin/lib/libXext.so.0
    0      0       1  (RWX) /usr/openwin/lib/libXext.so.0
   26      0      54  (R-X) /usr/openwin/lib/libX11.so.4
    2      1       3  (RWX) /usr/openwin/lib/libX11.so.4
    0      0       4  (R-X) /usr/lib/libsocket.so.1
    0      0       1  (RWX) /usr/lib/libsocket.so.1
    0      0       1  (RWX) /dev/zero <or other device>
    0      0       1  (R-X) /usr/lib/libdl.so.1
    0      0      14  (R-X) /usr/lib/ld.so.1
    2      0       2  (RWX) /usr/lib/ld.so.1
    0      3       6  (RWX) Stack
  500    401    3753        Totals
```

The counters in the wsm utility are in units of pages.

7.5.2 An Extended vmstat Command: memstat

Additional paging statistics are provided in the Solaris 7 kernel. Later, in Solaris 8, a new vmstat option (-p) was added to examine these statistics. The statistics can be observed on Solaris 7 with a simple command-line utility: memstat.

memstat shows the paging activity, page-ins, page-outs, and page-frees separated into three classes: file system paging, anonymous memory paging, and executable/shared library paging.

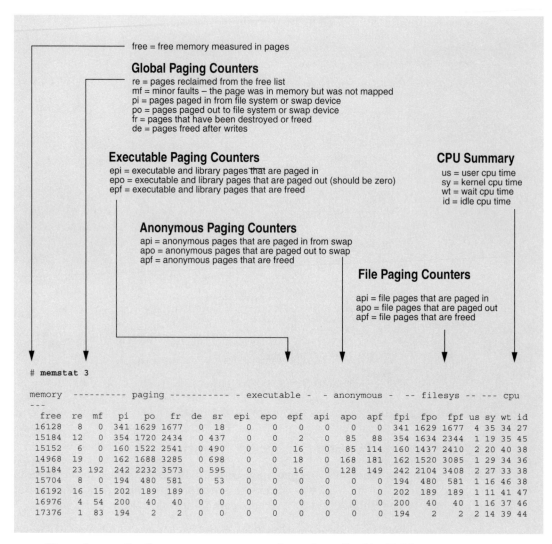

The columns for the `memstat` command are described in Table 7-8.

Table 7-8 Statistics from the `memstat` Command

Counter	Description
free	The amount of free memory as reported by `vmstat`, which reports the combined size of the cache list and free list. Free memory on Solaris 7 may contain some of the file system cache.

Table 7-8 Statistics from the `memstat` Command (Continued)

Counter	Description
re	Page reclaims — The number of pages reclaimed since the last sample. Some of the file system cache is in the free list, and when a file page is reused and removed from the free list, a reclaim occurs. File pages in the free list can be either regular files or executable/library pages.
mf	Minor faults — The number of pages attached to an address space since the last sample. If the page is already in memory, then a minor fault simply reestablishes the mapping to it
pi	Page-ins — The number of pages paged in since the last sample. A page-in occurs whenever a page is brought back in from the swap device or brought from a file system into the file system cache.
po	Page-outs — The number of pages paged out and freed. A page-out will be counted whenever a page is written *and* freed, often as a result of the pageout scanner, fsflush, or file close.
fr	Page-frees — The number of pages that have been freed by either the page scanner or by the file system (free-behind).
de	The precalculated anticipated short-term memory shortfall. Used by the page scanner to free ahead enough pages to satisfy requests.
sr	The number of pages scanned by the page scanner per second.
epi	Executable and library page-ins — The number of pages from executable or shared library files paged in since the last sample. An executable/library page-in occurs whenever a page for the executable binary or shared library is brought back in from the file system.
epo	Executable and library page-outs. Should be zero.
epf	Executable and library page-frees — The number of executable and library pages that have been freed by the page scanner.
api	Anonymous memory page-ins — The number of anonymous (application heap and stack) pages paged in from the swap device since the last sample.
apo	Anonymous memory page-outs — The number of anonymous (application heap and stack) pages paged out to the swap device since the last sample.
apf	Anonymous memory page-frees — The number of anonymous (application heap and stack) pages that have been freed, after they have been paged out.

Table 7-8 Statistics from the `memstat` Command (Continued)

Counter	Description
fpi	Regular file page-ins — The number of pages from regular files paged in since the last sample. A file page-in occurs whenever a page for a regular file is read in from the file system (part of the normal file system read process).
fpo	Regular file page-outs — The number of regular file pages that were paged out and freed, usually as a result of being paged out by the page scanner or by write free-behind (when free memory is less than `lotsfree` + `pages_before_pager`).
fpf	Regular file page-frees — The number of regular file pages that were freed, usually as a result of being paged out by the page scanner or by write free-behind (when free memory is less than `lotsfree` + `pages_before_pager`).

Part Three

THREADS, PROCESSES, AND IPC

- The Solaris Multithreaded Process Architecture
- The Solaris Kernel Dispatcher
- Interprocess Communication

8

THE SOLARIS MULTITHREADED PROCESS ARCHITECTURE

T he *process* was one of the two fundamental abstractions on which the original UNIX system was built (the other was the *file*). Processes were the basic unit of scheduling and execution on UNIX systems. Traditional implementations provided facilities for the creation, prioritization, scheduling, managing, and termination of processes. Some primitive commands and utilities existed for process monitoring (e.g., the ps(1) command), and cryptic debugging facilities allowed for setting breakpoints and stepping through process execution.

In this chapter, we discuss the Solaris process model, the process execution environment, and the multithreaded process architecture, including processes, lightweight processes, and kernel threads. We also cover other topics directly related to the kernel's process model: procfs, signals, process groups, and session management.

8.1 Introduction to Solaris Processes

The Solaris kernel provides support for an entity known as a *process,* and the kernel maintains a systemwide *process table*, whereby each process is uniquely identified by a positive integer called the process identification number (PID). The ps(1) command provides a point-in-time snapshot, taken as specified by the ps(1) command options, of the kernel's process table, providing process names, PIDs, and other relevant data about the processes.

The Solaris process model is in some ways similar to the traditional UNIX process model. At a high level, processes include the basic abstractions required for execution, such as a hardware state and operating-system-maintained software context. The Solaris kernel considerably extends the traditional implementation of operating system process support by providing support for multiple threads of execution within a single process, and each thread shares much of the process *state* and can be scheduled and run on a processor independently of other threads in the same process.

The current model is a two-level threads model that provides thread abstractions at the kernel and user level. The goal of this two-level model is to allow for the creation of hundreds or thousands of user threads within a single process with a minimum of overhead in the kernel. On multiprocessor hardware, this approach provides the potential for fine-grained application concurrency that previously required multiple processes, which incur considerably more operating system overhead.

The process priority scheme and scheduling have been completely redesigned from prior implementations. The original UNIX model provided a timesharing scheduling policy that essentially applied a round-robin approach to scheduling processes on processors so that there was a fairly even distribution of CPU time for all processes. The Solaris environment, however, implements *scheduling classes,* which define the policies and algorithms that the kernel applies to scheduling and execution. For each *scheduling class*, there exists a table of values and parameters the dispatcher code uses for selecting a thread to run on a processor; these tables, known as the *dispatch tables*, are discussed further in Chapter 9, "The Solaris Kernel Dispatcher".

In addition to the architectural changes, the level of sophistication of utilities and tools related to process management, monitoring, and debugging have evolved considerably, due largely to the implementation and evolution of the process file system, procfs. Procfs is a pseudo file system that emerged with AT&T UNIX System V Release 4 (SVR4). Procfs exports the kernel's process model and underlying abstractions to users, providing a file-like interface for the extraction of process data, and facilities for process control and debugging. Procfs is covered in "Procfs — The Process File System" on page 302.

8.1.1 Architecture of a Process

Each process has a context and various items of state information that define the execution environment of the process. All processes require memory in order to store instructions (text), data, temporary processing space (heap), and stack. Thus, every process has an *address space,* which is a kernel abstraction for managing the memory pages allocated to the process. A process's context can be further divided into a hardware and software context. The hardware context comprises the platform-specific components that define the process execution environment, such as the hardware registers (general registers, stack pointer, stack frame pointer, etc.). The software context includes the process's credentials (owner, group), opened files, identifiers, the address space, signal dispositions, signal handlers, and so forth. The basic process execution environment, minus the thread abstractions, is shown in Figure 8.1.

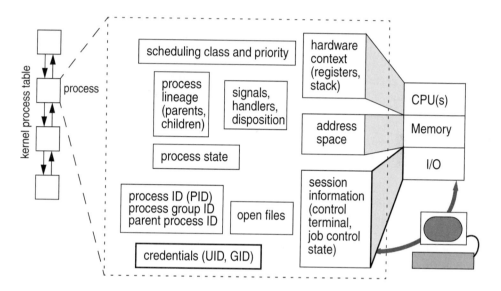

Figure 8.1 Process Execution Environment

Figure 8.1 shows the major components that establish the execution environment for a process. We introduce these abstractions here and discuss them in detail later in the chapter.

The address space defines the mapped memory pages for a process's various address space segments. The identifiers maintained for each process include the process's PID, the PID of its parent process, and the ID of the process group the process belongs to. Process groups provide a linkage for processes under control of the same terminal and facilitate things like job control signal delivery and management, which are part of the session management abstraction.

Most processes have at least three opened files—commonly referred to as standard input (stdin), standard output (stdout), and standard error (stderr)—that define the source and destination of input and output character streams for the process. These file descriptors may link to device information for a controlling terminal or window or may represent a file in a file system. Signals provide a means by which a process can be notified of an event or condition that may alter the execution environment. All processes maintain signal masks, can alter the disposition of one or more signals, and can define signal handlers for particular signals. Finally, there exists a means by which processes are assigned an execution priority and scheduling class, which determine how much processor time the process will get relative to other processes executing on the system.

The process we show in Figure 8.1 is single threaded. In the Solaris kernel, such a process has exactly one *lightweight process* (LWP) and *kernel thread* (kthread) in its address space. These are the kernel-level thread abstractions that are part of the two-level threads model. We didn't show these structures in the figure because we wanted to illustrate the core abstractions that define the execution environment, and the LWP and kthread are effectively transparent in a nonthreaded process. Now, we'll add the additional components that are an integral part of the kernel's multithreaded process architecture.

The actual implementation of lightweight processes and kernel threads are in the form of kernel data structures that are linked to the process structure, forming the foundation for the threads design. This model isolates the kernel from *user threads*, which are separate and distinct from kernel threads and LWPs. User threads are not visible to the kernel. More specifically, user threads are not visible to the kernel as an executable entity that can be scheduled.

User threads are threads created explicitly as a result of a program calling the thr_create(3T) or pthread_create(3T) library routines (Solaris ships with 2 thread's libraries; libthread.so for Solaris threads, and libpthread.so for POSIX threads). User threads have their own priority scheme that is separate and distinct from the priority mechanism implemented by the kernel scheduler. User threads essentially schedule themselves by calling into the thread library dispatcher and switch routines periodically at predefined preemption points. A user thread is scheduled from the thread library's point of view by getting linked on to an available LWP. Recognizing this behavior is essential to understanding the potential level of concurrency in a multithreaded program: *The availability of an LWP is required for a user thread to execute, and LWPs are not created automatically when user threads are created. Instead the thread create call must explicitly ask the kernel to create an LWP.*

In some texts, the LWP is referred to as a "virtual CPU," by way of describing the relationship of the LWP and the user thread. From a user thread's point of view, getting an LWP is as good as getting a CPU (which is not exactly the case, but it is one step closer).

The LWP and kernel thread are visible to the kernel; every LWP has a corresponding kernel thread. The reverse, however, is not always so; not every kernel thread has a corresponding LWP. The kernel itself is multithreaded and will create kernel threads that perform various operating-system-specific tasks—memory management, STREAMS queue processing, scheduling, etc.—that execute as kernel threads not bound to a user process. However, all user and application processes (any process seen by means of the ps(1) command), that are not system (kernel) created processes, have the one-to-one relationship between kthreads and LWPs, without exception. Hence, some authors use "LWP" and "kthread" interchangeably. More frequently, the term LWP is used to describe the LWP/kthread component of the process model, for brevity and simplicity. However, in this book, we differentiate between the terms.

Programmers can drive the ratio of LWPs to user threads in a couple of different ways. First, they can have the operating system create an LWP when the thread is created, by setting the appropriate flag, THR_NEW_LWP, in the thr_create(3T) call. Programmers can also bind the user thread to an LWP by using the THR_BOUND flag, as discussed later in this chapter.

The POSIX pthread_create(3T) equivalent is to set the contentionscope attribute to PTHREAD_SCOPE_SYSTEM. A bound user thread retains its binding to the LWP for its entire existence, in such a way that the LWP is not available to the user threads scheduler for linking to a different user thread. Binding user threads to LWPs offers a more predictable execution model for multithreaded programs because the user thread is linked to the kernel-level resource (an LWP) it requires for execution. The downside to the binding approach is longer thread create times, since the kernel creates an LWP/kthread along with the user thread in the thread create call. Moreover, the kernel has a larger pool of LWPs and kthreads to manage. For threaded processes with a great many threads, creating all bound threads may have a negative performance impact.

The Solaris threads interface also provides a thr_setconcurrency(3T) routine, which advises the kernel as to the number of concurrent threads the programmer wishes to be executed. The POSIX library provides an equivalent pthread_setconcurrency(3T) interface. In the absence of the explicit creation of LWPs or concurrency advice from the programmer, the threads library attempts to maintain a reasonable number of LWPs such that user threads have the resources they need to execute. The system attempts to maintain a balance between keeping too many idle LWPs around and not having enough LWPs. The former requires additional kernel overhead to manage; the latter results in runnable user threads waiting for a resource so they can execute. Solaris 2.5.1 (and prior releases) used a signal mechanism to manage the LWP pool and create more LWPs for a process with runnable user threads (more on this in "Signals" on page 320). Beginning in Solaris 2.6, a facility known as *scheduler activations* provides a bidirectional communication channel between the user threads library and the kernel; this facility greatly improves the management of the LWP-to-user thread problem.

Processes that are not explicitly multithreaded, meaning the code does not call one of the thread create interfaces, have a single LWP/kthread as part of their address space, created by the kernel when the process is created. Users and developers need not necessarily be aware of the multithreaded architecture of the Solaris environment and the additional kernel abstractions. The system provides the traditional process model view in which the standard interfaces are used for process creation: the fork/exec model. In fact, all processes on a Solaris system today are created through the fork and exec interfaces. The kernel silently creates the LWP and kthread in new processes to support the low-level infrastructure for process scheduling and management.

In the multithreaded process model, most of the process state and context is shared by all threads within a process. That is, the address space (mapped memory pages), credentials, open files, signal handlers, etc., are shared. However, each thread has its own hardware context or machine state. The general registers, stack pointer, program counter, and frame pointer are specific to the thread of execution. Specifically, the LWP maintains a control structure that stores the hardware context (the registers) when a thread is context-switched off a processor, and provides the register state loaded into the hardware registers when a thread is context-switched onto a processor for execution. Figure 8.2 illustrates the multithreaded model.

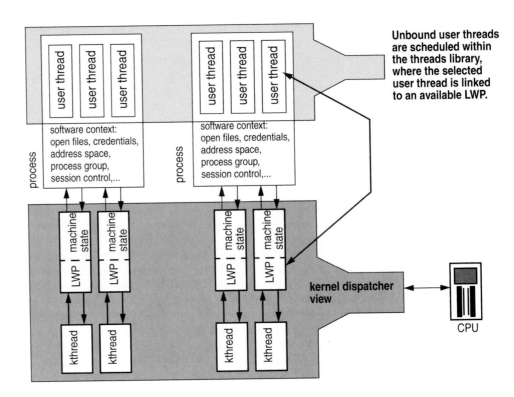

Figure 8.2 The Multithreaded Process Model

The key point to be derived from examining Figure 8.2 is that the two-level threads design in the Solaris kernel offers thread abstractions at two levels. User threads are created with specific programming interfaces and are scheduled by a per-process scheduling thread in the threads library. The kernel dispatcher (scheduler) schedules kernel threads. The linking of a user thread to a kernel thread (LWP—in this context, they can be thought of as a single entity) is required before the user thread becomes an executable entity that the kernel can schedule. When the kernel thread/LWP the user thread is linked to is scheduled, the user thread executes.

8.1.2 Process Image

We discuss the process image briefly before we dive into the discussion of data structures and other kernel process-related topics, to provide a foundation that the subsequent topics build on and to help keep the big picture in focus. The process image, in this context, is the definition of what a process looks like when it is loaded in memory and ready for execution on a Solaris system. We also talk about the format of the binary object file, the file's on-disk image.

All processes begin life as programs, and programs are simply text files written in a computer programming language (that statement may seem something of an oversimplification these days, but it's generally accurate). The program is compiled and linked by the appropriate language-specific compiler. A successful compilation process results in the creation of an executable binary file on disk. This file becomes a process in the Solaris environment through invocation of the exec(2) system call.

Once an executable object file is exec'd, the runtime linker, ld.so.1(1), is invoked to manage linking to other shared objects required for execution, typically a shared object library such as libc.so.1. This sequence of events is known as *dynamic linking*, where references in the program to shared object library functions (e.g., printf(3), read(2), etc.) are resolved at runtime by ld.so.1. It is possible to build *statically linked* executables through a compilation flag (-B static on the compile command line); this flag forces the inclusion of all referenced library functions in the executable object at build time. This technique requires that an archive version of the library be available (e.g., libc.a for static linking and libc.so.1 for dynamic linking). The building of applications using static linking is discouraged; in fact, it is not possible to build 64-bit executables in Solaris 7 that statically link to system libraries because no archive versions (.a files) of the 64-bit objects ship with the release.

The format of the object file complies with the ELF file format, or Executable and Linking Format. There are two class definitions for the ELF file format, one for 32-bit and one for 64-bit executables (ELFCLASS32 and ELFCLASS64); Solaris 7 provides support for both types of executables. Prior Solaris versions support 32-bit executables only.

ELF provides format definitions for both the on-disk and execution (in-memory) image, shown in Figure 8.3. The ELF format is an industry standard, part of the System V Application Binary Interface (ABI) that defines an operating system interface for compiled, executable programs. Since the ABI defines the binary interface for several implementations of UNIX System V across a variety of different hardware platforms, the ELF definition must be divided into two components: a platform-independent piece and a specification that is specific to a processor (e.g., Sun SPARC V8, Sun SPARC V9, Intel x86, etc.). Areas of the ABI that are processor specific include the definition of the function-calling sequence (system calls, stack management, etc.) and the operating system interface (signals, process initialization). Our focus for the remainder of this section is on the object file format, or ELF, as it applies to an *executable* file. The ABI also provides for ELF definitions for *relocatable* and *shared object* files.

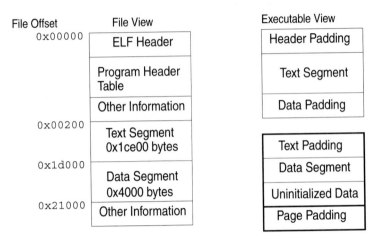

Figure 8.3 ELF Object Views

The main body of ELF files comprises various *sections*. Sections are the smallest indivisible unit that can be relocated within an ELF file. They fall into two main categories: program data (text, data, etc.) and link-editor information (e.g., symbol table information). A *segment* on the executable side is a grouping of related information. File image sections do not necessarily map one-to-one to executable view segments. As we will see shortly, a process's address space can be broken up into several text and data segments. ELF sections are defined by the ELF file's Section Header Table, or SHT. ELF files also implement structures defined by a Program Header Table, or PHT, which is used when the file is exec'd to create the memory image of program.

For further information on ELF file formats and specifics on the various data structures that define the ELF header, see the SHT and PHT tables in the *Linkers and Libraries Guide* that ships as part of the Solaris documentation set. See also the /usr/include/sys/elf.h file for the structure definitions. Also, Solaris ships with a library, libelf(3E), for developing code that can manipulate ELF files. Refer to the *Linker and Libraries Guide* for information on using the libelf(3E) interfaces.

Figure 8.4 provides a conceptual view of a process. Various data items relating to processes, some of which are shown in Figure 8.4, can be extracted with the commands in the /usr/proc/bin directory (reference proc(1)).

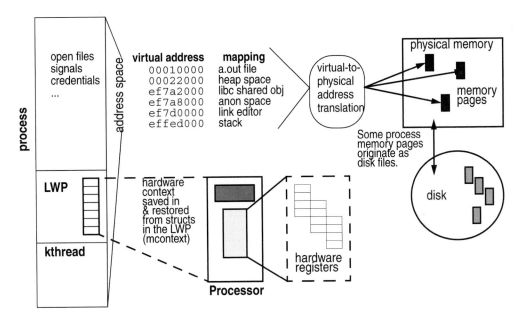

Figure 8.4 Conceptual View of a Process

To summarize the previous paragraphs: It is through the ELF file definition and format that the kernel and associated tools (compiler and linker) create a disk file that is an executable object which can be properly loaded into memory and turned into a process for scheduling and execution.

All of the process context, both hardware and software, is maintained in the data structures described in the sections that follow.

8.2 Process Structures

In this section, we take a look at the major data structures that make up the multithreaded process model in the Solaris kernel.

8.2.1 The Process Structure

The process structure, or *proc* structure, provides the framework for the creation and management of processes and threads in the Solaris environment. Figure 8.5 illustrates the big picture, showing the process structure with most of the structure members, along with all the other components that provide the entire process execution environment.

the process structure

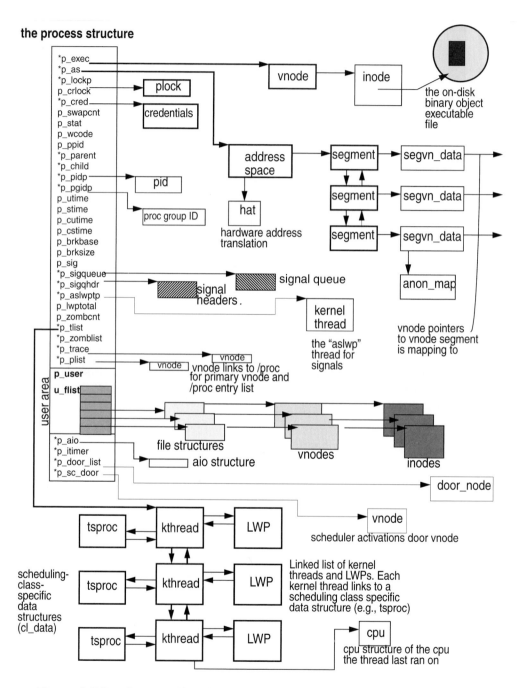

Figure 8.5 The Process Structure and Associated Data Structures

Like any kernel data structure, the members of the proc structure cover the full range of data types, including a great many pointers to support structures that, in total, make up the entire process picture in the Solaris environment. In the following pages, we describe the major structure members and associated links. See also the header file /usr/include/sys/proc.h.

- **p_exec** — Pointer to a vnode. A process is often referred to as the executable form of a program. As such, all processes originate as binary files in a file system. When the file is exec'd, the kernel loads the binary ELF file into memory. The p_exec pointer points to a vnode that ultimately links to the on-disk image of the file. The vnode structure is defined in /usr/include/sys/vnode.h.

- **p_as** — Address space structure pointer. All of the memory pages mapped to a process make up that process's address space. The as structure, a kernel abstraction for managing the memory pages allocated to a process, defines the process's virtual address space (see Figure 8.6). You can dump the address space mappings of a process by using /usr/proc/bin/pmap.

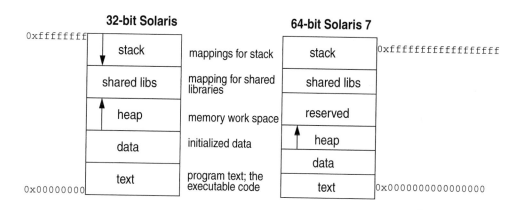

Figure 8.6 Process Virtual Address Space

Below is sample output of the /usr/proc/bin/pmap command (with the -x flag), which dumps all the segments that make up a process's virtual address space. The pmap(1) display provides the virtual address of the mapping (Address), the size of the mapping in Kbytes, how much of the mapping is resident in physical memory, how much is mapped shared, how much is mapped private, the permissions to the mapping, and the mapped filename. Note that the stack is mapped read/write/exec, as required for compliance with the SPARC V8 Application Binary Interface.

There is a security exposure to mapping stack pages with exec permissions because a system is subject to buffer overflow attacks, where rogue code positions itself on a process's stack, sets the program counter, and begins executing instructions. You can set an /etc/system variable, called no_exec_user_stack, to pre-

vent the mapping of stack pages with execute permissions on Solaris 2.6 and
Solaris 7. The entry in the /etc/system file will look like:

```
set no_exec_user_stack = 1
```

Note that Solaris 2.5.1 does not include this tunable parameter. Here is an
address space dump of a process on Solaris 2.6.

```
$ /usr/proc/bin/pmap -x 25639
25639: tp
Address   Kbytes Resident Shared Private Permissions          Mapped File
00010000       8        8      8       - read/exec            dev:193,2 ino:1089162
00020000       8        8      8       - read/write/exec      dev:193,2 ino:1089162
00022000    1032     1032      -    1032 read/write/exec       [ heap ]
EF580000    1024     1024      -    1024 read/write/exec/shared [shmid=0x12d]
EF6E0000       8        8      -       8 read/write/exec       [anon]
EF6F0000      16       16     16       - read/exec            libc_psr.so.1
EF700000     592      552    544       8 read/exec            libc.so.1
EF7A2000      24       24      8      16 read/write/exec      libc.so.1
EF7A8000       8        8      -       8 read/write/exec       [anon]
EF7A8000       8        8      -       8 read/write/exec       [anon]
EF7F8000       8        8      8       - read/write/exec      ld.so.1
EF7D0000     104      104    104       - read/exec            ld.so.1
EF7F8000       8        8      8       - read/write/exec      ld.so.1
EFBFE000    4104     4104      -    4104 read/write/exec       [stack]
--------  ------   ------ ------  ------
total Kb    6944     6904    704    6200
```

Here's a pmap(1) dump of a 64-bit executable on a Solaris 7 system, complete
with 64-bit addresses. For 64 bits, the SPARC V9 Application Binary Interface
defines stack pages as read/write only, to block buffer overflow attacks.

```
$ /usr/proc/bin/pmap -x 9964
9964:   mem 1048576
Address     Kbytes Resident Shared Private Permissions        Mapped File
0000000100000000      8        8      8       - read/exec          mem
0000000100100000      8        8      -       8 read/write/exec    mem
0000000100102000   1040     1032      -    1032 read/write/exec     [ heap ]
FFFFFFFF7F400000    696      576    416     160 read/exec          libc.so.1
FFFFFFFF7F5AC000     64       64      -      64 read/write/exec    libc.so.1
FFFFFFFF7F5BC000      8        8      -       8 read/write/exec     [ anon ]
FFFFFFFF7F680000    112      112    112       - read/exec          ld.so.1
FFFFFFFF7F79A000     16       16      -      16 read/write/exec    ld.so.1
FFFFFFFF7F7C0000     16        8      8       - read/exec          libc_psr.so.1
FFFFFFFF7F7E0000      8        8      -       8 read/write/exec     [ anon ]
FFFFFFFF7F7F0000      8        8      8       - read/exec          libdl.so.1
FFFFFFFF7FFFC000     16       16      -      16 read/write          [ stack ]
----------------  ------   ------ ------  ------
       total Kb    2000     1864    552    1312
```

- **p_lockp** — Process lock structure pointer. The p_lock is a kernel mutex
  (mutual exclusion) lock that synchronizes access to specific fields in the process structure (see Chapter 2, "Kernel Services"). This level of granularity of
  kernel lock increases parallelism because there is not a single lock on the
  entire process table. Instead, there is per-table entry locking, such that multiple kernel threads can concurrently access different proc structures.

- **p_nwpage** — Count of watched pages. This count is used when a process issues a vfork(2) and is also used in conjunction with p_wpage, which points to a watched_page structure. Watched pages are part of a debug facility that provides for the triggering of a debugger event if a watched page is referenced or written to.

- **p_cred** — Pointer to the credentials structure, which maintains the user credentials information such as user identification (UID) and group identification (GID), etc. Every user on a Solaris system has a unique UID as well as a primary GID, although a user can belong to multiple groups.

A user's UID and GID are established through fields in the /etc/passwd file when the user's account is set up. You can use the id(1M) command to see what your UID and GID are. Use the su(1) command to change user identities. Use the newgrp(1) command to change your real and effective GID. The UID and GID of the user that started the process have their credentials maintained here in the credentials structure, and *effective* UID and GID are maintained here as well.

Solaris supports the notion of *effective* UID and GID, which allow for the implementation of the setuid and setgid mode bits defined in a file's inode (remember, the process started life as an executable file on a file system). A process could have an effective UID that is different from the UID of the user that started the process.

A common example is a program that requires root (UID 0) privileges to do something, for example, the passwd(1) command, which writes to protected files (/etc/passwd and /etc/shadow). Such a program is owned by root (aka superuser), and with the setuid bit set on the file, the effective UID of the process is 0. During process execution, the kernel checks for effective UID and GID during permission checks, which will be the same as the UID and GID of the user if neither the setuid nor setgid mode bit has been set. The specific contents of the credentials structure are shown in Table 8-1.

Table 8-1 Credentials Structure Members

Member	Description
cr_ref	Reference count on the credentials structure
cr_uid	Effective UID
cr_gid	Effective GID
cr_ruid	Real UID (from the user's /etc/passwd file entry)
cr_rgid	Real GID (from the user's /etc/passwd file)
cr_suid	Saved UID (in case UID changes across exec)

Table 8-1 Credentials Structure Members

Member	Description
cr_sgid	Saved GID, as above
cr_ngroups	Number of supplementary groups
cr_groups[]	Array of supplementary groups; the size of the array is maintained in cr_ngroups, and the maximum number of groups a user can belong is limited to 16

- **p_crlock** — Kernel mutex to synchronize access to the credentials structure.

- **p_swpcnt** — Counter of LWPs linked to the process that have been swapped out. Under severe memory shortfalls, the memory scheduler (PID 0, the sched process) will swap out entire LWPs to free up some memory pages.

- **p_stat** — The process status, or state. The notion of process states is somewhat misleading in the Solaris environment, since the kernel thread, not the process, is the entity that gets a scheduling class, is prioritized, and is put on a dispatch queue for scheduling. Kernel threads change state in the Solaris environment much more frequently than do processes. For a nonthreaded process, the process state is essentially whatever the state of the kthread is. For multithreaded processes, several kthreads that belong to the same process can be in different states (e.g., running, sleeping, runnable, zombie, etc.).

In a few areas in the kernel, the process state (p_stat) is used explicitly. In the fork() code, during process creation, the SIDL state is set, and later in fork, p_stat is set to SRUN—the process has been created and is runnable. In the exit() code, pstat is set to ZOMB when a process is terminated. Those three exceptions aside, all other state changes during the lifetime of a process occur in the kthread and are reflected in the state field in the kthread structure. In fact, the state (S) column from the ps(1) command is derived from the kthread state field, not the process p_stat data. If a process has more than one LWP and the -L flag has not been specified on the ps(1) command line, then the state field is derived from LWP 1 (the -L flag to ps(1) will print information about each LWP in each selected process). A process can be in one of the following possible states:

- SLEEP — Process is sleeping (waiting for an event)

- RUN — Process is runnable, waiting to be scheduled

- ZOMB — Process is a zombie, that is, it has exited but a wait has not yet executed on its behalf

- STOP — Process is stopped, typically because of debugger activity

- SIDL — Process is being created and is assigned this interim state

- ONPROC — Process is running on a processor

Process states and state transitions are shown in Figure 8.7.

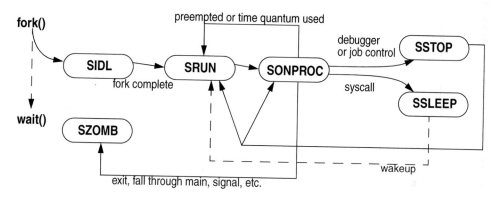

Figure 8.7 Process State Diagram

- **p_wcode** — Defined as current wait code. A synchronization field that contains data to support SIGCLD (child signal) information. A process is sent a SIGCLD signal when the status of one of its child processes has changed. The p_wcode holds a status bit that identifies the reason for the status change (e.g., child has exited, stopped, coredumped, was killed, or has continued).

- **p_pidflag** — Another field used to support synchronization via signals. Status bits to indicate a SIGCLD signal is pending or a SIGCLD was sent to notify the parent that the child process has continued (see "Signals" on page 320).

- **p_wdata** — Also used for process synchronization with signals and used in conjunction with p_wcode; contains status bits that provide a reason for an event. For example, if a process is killed by a SIGKILL signal, the p_wcode will indicate the child was killed and the p_wdata will indicate a SIGKILL signal was the reason (see "Signals" on page 320).

- **p_ppid** — The process's parent process ID.

Many of the process structure fields defined above are covered in more detail as we move through other process-related information in the remainder of this chapter.

The process model in the Solaris kernel maintains a lineage for all the processes running on the system. That is, every process has a parent process and may have child processes. The process creation model, in which a new process begins life as the result of an existing process issuing some variant of the fork(2) system call, means that, by definition, there will minimally be a parent process to the newly created process. Not only will a process have a parent, but it may also have siblings—processes that have been created by the same parent. Every process in the Solaris environment can reside on as many as a dozen or so linked lists maintained by the kernel; the proc structure stores the various pointers required. All of the process structure members described below are pointers to a process structure.

- **p_parent** — Pointer to the parent process.

- **p_child** — Pointer to the first child process. Subsequent children are linked by means of the sibling pointers in the child processes.

- **p_sibling** — Pointer to the first sibling (next child created by parent).

- **p_psibling** — Pointer to previous sibling. Back pointer in support of a doubly linked list of related processes.

- **p_sibling_ns** — Pointer to a sibling process that has changed state.

- **p_child_ns** — Pointer to a child process that has changed state.

- **p_next** — Next process in the active process list. The kernel maintains a doubly linked list of active processes in the system, pointed to by the kernel *practive* pointer.

- **p_prev** — Previous process in the active process list (see above).

- **p_nextofkin** — Link maintained back to parent process. Used in process exit code to gather accounting information (accumulated user time and system time). Also used to set orphan pointers when a process exits. The orphan links of an exiting process are linked to the nextofkin process, which is the parent.

- **p_orphan** — Orphan pointer. An orphan process lost its parent; that is, an orphan process continues executing after its parent has exited. In the fork code, the p_orphan pointer in the parent is set to point to the newly created child. Processes without children have a NULL p_orphan pointer. If child processes spawn other child processes, p_orphan will link to the "grandchildren" should the parent terminate.

- **p_nextorph** — Next orphan pointer. In fork, the newly created child process's p_nextorph pointer is set to the p_orphan pointer in the parent. Essentially, p_nextorph links siblings.

- **p_pglink** — Process group link. Forward link to a hash chain of processes in the same process group. Processes are linked in a group when they are controlled by the same controlling terminal. See "Sessions and Process Groups" on page 337.

- **p_ppglink** — Previous process group link. Back link to hash chain of processes in the same process group.

Figure 8.8 illustrates how the process lineage pointers are set up with a test program, *bd*, written for that purpose. The processes shown depict process *bd*, which fork/execs three child processes, *c1*, *c2*, and *c3*. The *c2* process fork/execs its own child (process *cc2*), as does the *c3* process (child name *cc3*). The *cc3* child process also fork/execs a child, *ccc3*. So, we end up with a reasonably realistic process hierarchy that we can use for illustration.

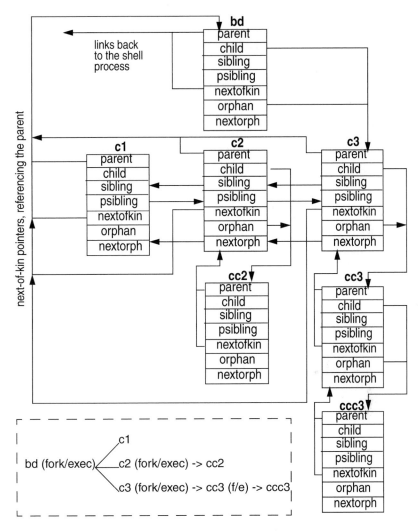

Figure 8.8 Process Lineage Pointers

In Figure 8.8, pointers without connecting lines are NULL. The linked pointers can be summarized as follows. The parent and child pointers are (we hope) straightforward. The *bd* process `parent` pointer links to the shell that spawned it (not shown), the `child` pointer links to *c3*, the last child created (chronologically), `nextofkin` links to the parent, and `orphan` links to the last child created, *c3*. The three children, *c1*, *c2*, and *c3*, of the *bd* process link to each other through the `sibling` and `psibling` pointers, forming a linked list of all the children spawned by the same parent (*bd*). The `nextofkin` pointer in all three child processes links to the parent, *bd*.

The *cc2*, *cc3*, and *ccc3* processes have no siblings; thus, the `sibling` pointers are `NULL`. They link back to the parent through the `parent` and `nextofkin` pointers. And, of course, the parent/child links between the *cc3* and *ccc3* processes round out the picture.

The way the picture changes if a process dies is due in part to how the code is constructed. In this example, the *bd* process was blocking in a `waitpid(2)` call, waiting on the PID of the *c3* process. We killed process *c3*, which resulted in *bd* and *c3* both terminating, leaving *c1, c2, cc2, cc3,* and *ccc3*. The `parent` and `nextofkin` pointers in *c1, c2,* and *cc3* linked to the init process, which inherits orphan processes. The `sibling` pointers in *c1* and *c2* changed, where `sibling` in *c1* linked to *c2*, and `psibling` in *c2* linked back to *c1*.

Additional pointers maintained in the proc structure include the following:

- **`p_sessp`** — Pointer to a session structure, which contains information for managing the process's control terminal. See "Sessions and Process Groups" on page 337.

- **`p_pidp`** — Pointer to a `pid` structure, for process ID (PID) information. The process's actual PID is stored in one of the fields in the `pid` structure.

- **`p_pgpidp`** — Another `pid` structure pointer, for process group information (process group ID).

The Solaris kernel maintains a data structure for managing PIDs and process group IDs (Figure 8.9).

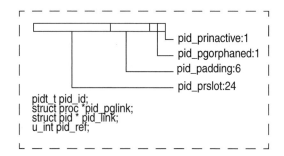

Figure 8.9 PID Structure

The first 4 bytes of the PID structure store 2 status bits, `pid_prinactive` and `pid_pgorphaned`, followed by 6 pad bits (unused bits) and 24 bits to store the slot number of the /proc table entry for the process, `pid_prslot`. Since we use 24 bits to store the unique /proc table entry for processes, we have a limit of 16 million possible /proc table entries. This limit will never actually be reached in Solaris versions up to and including Solaris 7 because the kernel defines a `MAXPID` value of 30,000. The limit of 30,000 processes is imposed by the use of a 2-byte data type in the `utmp` structure.

The kernel maintains a /var/adm/utmp and /var/adm/wtmp file for the storage of user information used by the who(1), write(1), and login(1) commands (the accounting software and commands use utmp and wtmp as well). The PID data is maintained in a signed short data type, which has a maximum value of 32,000. This "limit" should in no way be construed as a problem; 30,000 is a great many processes and our largest installations today do not have anywhere near that many processes running. See "The Kernel Process Table" on page 286 for a description of how the actual systemwide process limits are established.

The PID structure links to other PID structures in the kernel through pid_link, which maintains a hashed list of active PIDs in the kernel, and pid_pglink, which links back to the process structure. Finally, the prinactive bit flags the structure as being free or used, and pgorphaned indicates whether the process is orphaned (the parent has exited or died—orphaned processes are adopted by the init process).

Several condition variables are maintained in the proc structure. Condition variables are a kernel synchronization mechanism used to notify a process or thread if a specific event, such as the completion of an I/O, has occurred. Condition variables are used in the Solaris environment to implement sleep and wakeup. One such condition variable is *p_holdlwps*, a special condition variable for holding process LWPs. In a fork(), the LWPs must be suspended at some point so their kernel stacks can be cloned for the new process.

In the process structure, the kernel maintains time totals that reflect the amount of user time and system time the process accumulated, as well as summations for all the child processes' system time and user time. The child information is summed when a child process exits. The p_utime and p_stime fields maintain the process's user and system time, respectively; the p_cutime and p_cstime fields maintain the child process's user and system time.

The process maintains several bits of information on LWPs and kernel threads, including a total of all LWPs linked to the process (p_lwpcnt) and all LWPs created, p_lwptotal. The latter may be different from p_lwpcnt because the kernel may have allocated LWPs to the process from the systemwide pool. Such LWPs will not have been explicitly created by the process. Counters are maintained for the number of blocked LWPs (p_lwpblocked), runnable LWPs (p_lwprcnt), and zombie LWPs (p_zombcnt). A pointer rooted in the proc structure references a linked list of kernel threads (p_tlist) and a linked list of zombie threads (p_zomblist). (A zombie process is a process that has exited but whose parent process did not issue a *wait* call to retrieve the exit status.)

The remaining members of the process structure can be grouped into several categories. Per-process signal handling support involves linking to signal queue structures, supporting the signal mask and signal posting structures. The Solaris signal model has undergone significant work to support the multithreaded architecture and is discussed beginning on page 326. Support for the /proc file system requires the inclusion of various pointers and data types in the proc structure. Also, the

Solaris kernel includes a facility called Doors, which provides a fast cross-process call interface for procedure calling.

Process-level resource usage and microstate accounting information are maintained within the process structure, as well as on a per-LWP basis. We discuss the details in "The Kernel Process Table" on page 286.

Process profiling is supported by the inclusion of a prof structure (p_prof) and is enabled when the program is compiled (i.e., before it becomes a "process"). During the execution of the process, process profiling gathers statistical data that tells the programmer which routines the process was spending time executing in and how much time was spent in each function relative to the total execution time of the process.

You can use the /etc/crash(1M) utility to examine the contents of a proc structure on a running system. First, use the p function with no arguments to dump the process table. Determine the process table slot of the process you're interested in, then use p -f slot_number to dump the contents. To save space, we're showing a partial listing of the process table and structure.

```
# ps
   PID TTY       TIME CMD
 24676 pts/6     0:00 sh
 25170 pts/6     0:00 ps
# /etc/crash
dumpfile = /dev/mem, namelist = /dev/ksyms, outfile = stdout
> p
PROC TABLE SIZE = 1962
SLOT ST  PID  PPID  PGID   SID  UID PRI   NAME      FLAGS
   0 t     0     0     0     0    0  96 sched      load sys lock
   1 s     1     0     0     0    0  58 init       load
   2 s     2     0     0     0    0  98 pageout    load sys lock nowait
   3 s     3     0     0     0    0  60 fsflush    load sys lock nowait
  66 s 24676   719 24676   719    0  58 sh         load
  67 s 21238 21218 21218   716 20821 59 netscape   load jctl
  75 s 21218   716 21218   716 20821 59 cam        load
  76 s 24529   729 24529   729    0  59 sh         load
> p -f 66
PROC TABLE SIZE = 1962
SLOT ST  PID  PPID  PGID   SID  UID PRI   NAME      FLAGS
  66 s 24676   719 24676   719    0  58 sh         load

        Session: sid: 719, ctty: vnode(60abe884) maj( 24) min(    6)
        Process Credentials: uid: 0, gid: 1, real uid: 0, real gid: 1
        as: 60022910
        wait code: 0, wait data: 0
        sig: efffeb18   link 0
        parent: 60a31470       child: 60b72f80
        sibling: 0 threadp: 60832840
        utime: 3        stime: 5        cutime: 24      cstime: 15
        trace: 0        sigmask: efffeb10      class: 2
        lwptotal: 1     lwpcnt: 1      lwprcnt: 1
        lwpblocked: -1
```

In the above example, we used ps(1), determined the PID of our shell process, invoked the crash utility, and used the p function to get the process table slot (66, in this case). Then, to dump the proc structure for process PID 24676, we again used the p utility, with the -f flag and the process table slot number.

8.2.2 The User Area

The role of the user area (traditionally referred to as the *uarea)*, has changed somewhat in the Solaris environment when compared with traditional implementations of UNIX. The uarea was linked to the proc structure through a pointer and thus was a separate data structure. The uarea was swappable if the process was not executing and memory space was tight. Today, the uarea is embedded in the process structure—it is not maintained as a separate structure. The process kernel stack, which was traditionally maintained in the uarea, is now implemented in the LWP (see "The Lightweight Process (LWP)" on page 281). The interesting bits in the uarea are listed below in the relative order in which they appear in the /usr/include/sys/user.h).

- **u_execid** — The magic number (file type) of the on-disk executable that was loaded with an exec(2) system call.

- **u_execsz** — The size of the executable file.

- **u_tsize** — Size of the text segment of the process address space.

- **u_dsize** — Size of the data segment of the process address space.

- **u_start** — Time when the process started, set when the process is first created, just after the start time is set in p_mstart.

- **u_ticks** — Total execution time in clock ticks of the process. When accounting is turned on, written to the accounting file on exit. A clock tick varies across processor types. On UltraSPARC-based systems, there are 100 ticks per second.

- **u_exdata** — Embedded exdata structure. Executable file information, such as text, data, heap, shared library size, magic number, etc.

- **u_psargs[]** — Array of arguments passed to exec.

- **u_comm[]** — User command string when process was invoked.

- **u_argc, u_argv, u_envp** — The number of command-line arguments (u_argc), a pointer to the array of command-line arguments (u_argv), and a pointer to the array of environmental variables (u_envp). These are the variables passed to the main() program function; they must be declared in every program written to execute on the Solaris system, as set up by the compiler when code is generated to run.

- **u_cdir** — Pointer to the vnode for the current directory.

- **u_rdir** — Pointer to the root vnode. Not used unless chroot(2) is called.

- **u_ttyvp** — Pointer to vnode for controlling tty.

- **u_cmask** — File creation mask. Defines default file modes when files are created.

- **u_mem** — Memory usage. Updated in the clock handler for the active thread on each processor.

- **u_nshmseg** — Number of attached shared memory segments.

- **u_rlimit[]** — Array of `rlimit` structures that defines the resource limits for the process. The system imposes a total of seven resource limits. Each resource limit has a current value and maximum value (also referred to as a soft limit and a hard limit), maintained as `rlim_cur` and `rlim_max` in the `rlimit` structure. In Solaris releases up to and including Solaris 2.5.1, `rlim_cur` and `rlim_max` are 32-bit data types. Beginning in Solaris 2.6, there's a 64-bit version of the `rlimit` structure, and `rlim_cur` and `rlim_max` are 64-bit data types.

The system defines a maximum value for each type, which is effectively the maximum attainable value for the data types. The actual value isn't really significant in most cases because the value is sufficiently large that an "infinite" resource limit is implied, which is essentially no limit. When we use the term "infinite" in describing resource limits below, we mean the maximum value for a 64-bit data type. (In case you're interested, the max value for a *signed* 64-bit data type is 9,223,372,036,854,775,807, or 9 *exabytes*. An *unsigned* 64-bit data type has a maximum value of 18,446,744,073,709,551,615, or 18 *exabytes*. Now you know why we consider limits set at these values "virtually unlimited"!)

In Solaris releases up to and including Solaris 2.6, a process's resource limits were changed with `limit(1)` or `ulimit(2)`, which affected only the running process (a shell, typically) and whatever children were spawned. In Solaris 7, a `plimit(1)` command was added, which allows you to change resource limits in other processes by specifying a PID on the command line. The following list describes each of the resource limits.

- CPU – Maximum CPU time in seconds. Default soft and hard limit is the same; 4 billion for pre-2.6 releases, infinite for release 2.6 and beyond. The clock interrupt handler tests for this limit, and sends a SIGXCPU signal if the limit is reached.

- FSIZE – Maximum file size, in 512 byte blocks. Same default values as CPU. The file system write code (the `wrip()` function in UFS) tests for this limit and sends a SIGXFSZ signal to the process if the limit is reached.

- DATA – Maximum size of the process data segment. Default soft limit is 2 Gbytes, hard limit is 4 billion for pre-2.6 releases. In Solaris 2.7, infinite for soft and hard limit. Hitting this limit can cause a ENOMEM error if a memory allocation routine (e.g., `malloc()`) is called.

- STACK – Maximum size of the process stack segment. Default soft limit is 8 Mbytes, hard limit is 2 Gbytes in Solaris 2.6. In Solaris 2.7, the hard limit is infinite on UltraSPARC-based systems, 2 Gbytes on all others.

- CORE – Maximum core file size. Soft and hard limit is infinite. A value of 0 here prevents the creation of a core file.

- NOFILE – Maximum number of open files. Default soft limit is 64, hard limit is 1024.

- VMEM – Maximum address space. Infinite soft and hard limit. In reality, 4 Gbytes is the maximum virtual address space attainable on all Solaris releases up to and including Solaris 2.6. Solaris 7 provides a 64-bit address space when booted as a 64-bit kernel, running a 64-bit binary. The Sun UltraSPARC-I and UltraSPARC-II 64-bit processors implement a 44-bit virtual address, allowing for a maximum virtual address space of 16 terabytes.

The uarea is where process open file information is maintained, in the form of an array of uf_entry structures. Each structure contains three elements: a pointer (uf_ofile) to the file's file structure, a 2-byte member for file flag bits (uf_pofile), and a reference count (uf_refcnt). A pointer, u_flist, is set to point to the first element in the array (the first uf_entry structure), and the array is indexed with the file descriptor number, or fd. An open file in a process is uniquely identified with an fd, which is a positive integer value returned by a successful call to open(2). Allocations of uf_entry structures are done in groups of 24 (the NFPCHUNK variable in /usr/include/sys/user.h).

Solaris 7 (SunOS 5.7) adds a structure pointer to the uf_entry structure: uf_fpollinfo, which is a pointer to an fpollinfo structure. Solaris 7 also adds new functionality in the form of a *poll cache* to enhance support of the poll(2) system call. The kernel uses the poll cache to track process file descriptors that are being polled. The fpollinfo structure supports the poll cache implementation.

The following members of the uarea support management of the process's open file table:

- **u_flock** — A kernel mutex lock to synchronize access to the process open file list.

- **u_nofiles** — Number of open file slots (i.e., number of open files in the process).

- **u_flist** — Pointer to the first uf_entry structure. Structure storage is implemented as an array, indexed by the fd (file descriptor) number.

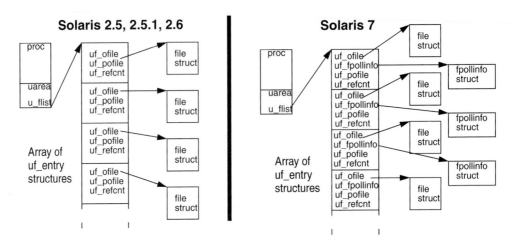

Figure 8.10 Process Open File Support Structures

Figure 8.10 illustrates `uf_entry` support structures

To obtain a list of a process's open files, use the `/usr/proc/bin/pfiles` command.

```
$ /usr/proc/bin/pfiles 490
490:    /bin/ksh /usr/dt/bin/Xsession
  Current rlimit: 64 file descriptors
    0: S_IFDIR mode:0777 dev:32,24 ino:2 uid:0 gid:0 size:1024
       O_RDONLY|O_LARGEFILE
    1: S_IFREG mode:0644 dev:32,8 ino:1026 uid:19821 gid:10 size:996
       O_WRONLY|O_APPEND|O_LARGEFILE
    2: S_IF       O_WRONLY|O_APPEND|O_LARGEFILE
       O_WRONLY|O_APPEND|O_LARGEFILE
    3: S_IFCHR mode:0666 dev:32,24 ino:143524 uid:0 gid:3 rdev:13,12
       O_RDWR
    5: S_IFREG mode:0644 dev:32,24 ino:22740 uid:0 gid:0 size:4
       O_WRONLY|O_LARGEFILE
       advisory write lock set by process 308
    7: S_IFSOCK mode:0666 dev:166,0 ino:27432 uid:0 gid:0 size:0
       O_RDWR
   62: S_IFREG mode:0555 dev:32,24 ino:294581 uid:2 gid:2 size:18792
       O_RDONLY|O_LARGEFILE FD_CLOEXEC
```

The command lists the process name and PID (in this example, we dumped the open files for the windowing system session-manager process). Note that various bits of information are provided on each open file, including the file type, file flags, mode bits, and size.

Like the process structure, the `uarea` contains supporting data for signals, including an array that defines the disposition for each possible signal. The signal disposition tells the operating system what to do in the event of a signal: ignore it, catch it and invoke a user-defined signal handler, or take the default action. See "Signals" on page 320.

The /etc/crash utility provides a function, shown below, for dumping a process's uarea.

```
# /etc/crash
dumpfile = /dev/mem, namelist = /dev/ksyms, outfile = stdout
> u 67
PER PROCESS USER AREA FOR PROCESS 67
PROCESS MISC:
        command: crash, psargs: /etc/crash
        start: Fri May  5 21:37:41 2000
        mem: 4cf9, type: exec
        vnode of current directory: f64769c0
OPEN FILES, POFILE FLAGS, AND THREAD REFCNT:
        [0]: F 0xf6407cd0, 0, 0 [1]: F 0xf6407cd0, 0, 0
        [2]: F 0xf6407cd0, 0, 0 [3]: F 0xf65695a8, 0, 0
        [4]: F 0xf65696c0, 0, 0 [5]: F 0xf6569300, 0, 1
        [6]: F 0xf6569b98, 0, 0
 cmask: 0022
RESOURCE LIMITS:
        cpu time: 18446744073709551613/18446744073709551613
        file size: 18446744073709551613/18446744073709551613
        swap size: 2147479552/18446744073709551613
        stack size: 8388608/2147479552
        coredump size: 18446744073709551613/18446744073709551613
        file descriptors: 64/1024
        address space: 18446744073709551613/18446744073709551613
SIGNAL DISPOSITION:
            1:  default    2: ef638914    3:  default    4:  default
            5:  default    6:  default    7:  default    8:  default
            9:  default   10:  default   11:  default   12:  default
           13:  default   14:  default   15:  default   16:  default
           17:  default   18:  default   19:  default   20:  default
           21:  default   22:  default   23:  default   24:  default
           25:  default   26:  default   27:   ignore   28:  default
           29:  default   30:  default   31:  default   32:  default
           33:  default   34:  default   35:  default   36:  default
           37:  default   38:  default   39:  default   40:  default
           41:  default   42:  default   43:  default   44:  default
           45:  default
```

In the preceding example, we omitted the upfront dumping of the process table (the p function) to select a process's uarea to dump. The u function takes a process table slot number as an argument, slot 19 in this case (the Xsession process, the same one we used in the previous pfiles example). Note the rather large values in the resource limits. This example was done on a Solaris 2.6 system, which included 64-bit data types for the rlimits.

8.2.3 The Lightweight Process (LWP)

The LWP structure is defined in /usr/include/sys/klwp.h. The kernel maintains resource utilization counters and microstate accounting information for every LWP. The sum total of all LWPs resource usage is stored in the process when the LWP exits. See "The Kernel Process Table" on page 286.

Other interesting information maintained in the LWP include the following:

- **lwp_pcb** — The hardware context data for the LWP, called a process control block (pcb). It contains various bits of machine state information that are saved when the LWP is switched out and restored when it is switched back in. This is the machine state represented in Figure 8.2.
- **lwp_ap** — Pointer to the arglist passed in a system call.
- **lwp_errno** — Error number for current system call.
- **lwp_error** — Returns value for current system call.
- **lwp_eosys** — End-of-syscall action. Used for post-system-call handling and for special conditions, such as profiling and process tracing.
- **lwp_watchtrap** — Supports debugger single-step operations.
- **lwp_regs** — Pointer to registers saved on the stack.
- **lwp_fpu** — Pointer to floating point unit (fpu) registers.

Most of the above LWP structure members exist to support system calls and to maintain hardware context information. Remember, system calls are function calls into the kernel—a process's way of asking the operating system to do something on its behalf (e.g., open/read/write a file, get my PID, etc). Since LWPs can be scheduled on processors (along with their corresponding kernel thread) independently of other LWPs in the same process, they need to be able to execute system calls on behalf of the thread they're bound to. An LWP blocked on a system call does not cause the entire process to block (as long as it's a multithreaded process). See Chapter 2 for details on system call processing.

The following LWP fields handle signals and debugging through the /proc interfaces.

- **lwp_cursig** — Current signal.
- **lwp_asleep** — LWP sleeping in system call.
- **lwp_sigaltstack** — Alternate signal stack specified.
- **lwp_curinfo** — Pointer to a sigqueue, signal information for current signal.
- **lwp_siginfo** — Signal information for stop-on-fault.
- **lwp_sigoldmask** — Snapshot of signal mask for sig-suspend.
- **lwp_scall_start** — Start time of system call.
- **lwp_utime** — Time LWP spent running in user mode.
- **lwp_stime** — Time LWP spent running in system (kernel) mode.
- **lwp_thread** — Pointer to the associated kernel thread. Every LWP has a corresponding kernel thread.
- **lwp_procp** — Pointer to the proc structure.

8.2.4 The Kernel Thread (kthread)

The kernel thread is the entity that actually gets put on a dispatch queue and scheduled. This fact is probably the most salient departure from traditional UNIX implementations, where processes maintain a priority and processes are put on run queues and scheduled. It's the kthread, not the process, that is assigned a scheduling class and priority. You can examine this on a running system by using the -L and -c flags to the ps(1) command. The columns in the ps(1) output below provide the process ID (PID), the LWP number within the process (LWP), the scheduling class the LWP is in (CLS), and the priority (PRI).

```
$ ps -eL
   PID  LWP TTY      LTIME CMD
     0    1 ?         0:01 sched
     1    1 ?         0:00 init
     2    1 ?         0:00 pageout
     3    1 ?         1:40 fsflush
   235    1 ?         0:00 sendmail
   260    1 ?         0:00 vold
   260    2 ?         0:00 vold
   260    3 ?         0:00 vold
   260    4 ?         0:00 vold
   260    5 ?         0:00 vold
   319    1 ?         0:00 sac
   121    1 ?         0:00 in.route
   133    1 ?         0:00 keyserv
   133    2 ?         0:00 keyserv
   133    3 ?         0:00 keyserv
   133    6 ?         0:00 keyserv
   100    1 ?         0:00 aspppd
   131    1 ?         0:00 rpcbind
   158    1 ?         0:00 inetd
   184    1 ?         0:00 syslogd
   184    2 ?         0:00 syslogd
   184    3 ?         0:00 syslogd
   184    4 ?         0:00 syslogd
   184    5 ?         0:00 syslogd
```

It is interesting to note that the output indicates that the LWP has a priority and scheduling class, when technically it's the kthread associated with the LWP that actually maintains this information.

The kernel thread structure is defined in /usr/include/sys/thread.h. The significant fields in the kthread include the following:

- **t_link** — Pointer to a kthread structure. Linked list support, links the kthread with other kthreads on the same queue: dispatch queue, sleep queue, and free queue.
- **t_stack** — Kernel stack pointer (address).
- **t_bound_cpu** — Pointer to a CPU structure. Data to manage binding to a processor, and data to support a processor set.
- **t_affinitycnt** — Maintains CPU affinity (loose coupling to a specific processor, a best effort to keep a thread on the same CPU).

- **t_bind_cpu** — User-specified CPU binding (i.e., pbind(2)).
- **t_flag** — Thread flag bits. Thread flags provide the kernel with a method of setting and tracking necessary bits of information about the thread, such as whether the thread is an interrupt thread, whether it is blocking, whether its corresponding LWP is in a zombie state, etc.
- **t_proc_flag** — Additional thread flag bits. The distinction between these bits and the ones in t_flag above are locking requirements. Only the T_WAKEABLE flag in t_flag requires a synchronization lock for setting or checking since it must coincide with the thread state. The bits in t_proc_flag are set and checked under protection of the p_lock, the kernel mutex that synchronizes access to the proc structure.
- **t_schedflag** — Flags the dispatcher uses for scheduling. They indicate conditions such as the thread is in memory, the thread should not be swapped, or the thread is on a swap queue. The dispatcher also uses these flags to change the thread's state to runnable.
- **t_preempt** — Flag used to specify that thread should not be preempted.
- **t_state** — Thread state. Any one of the following:
    - TS_FREE – Free thread structure.
    - TS_SLEEP – Sleeping on an event.
    - TS_RUN – Runnable, waiting for a processor.
    - TS_ONPROC – Thread is running on a processor.
    - TS_ZOMB – Thread has exited, but not yet been reaped.
    - TS_STOPPED – Thread is stopped. Initial thread state; possible through a debugger as well.

The description of the process table showed that a process state field is maintained in the process structure along with the kernel thread. The kernel thread, not the process, changes during execution. There is, for the most part, a correlation between states defined for the process and kernel thread states, as shown in Table 8-2.

Table 8-2 Kernel Thread and Process States

Process	Kernel Thread	Description
SIDL		State during fork(2) (creation).
SRUN	TS_RUN	Runnable.
SONPROC	TS_ONPROC	Running on a processor.
SSLEEP	TS_SLEEP	Sleeping (blocked).
SSTOP	TS_STOPPED	Stopped.
SZOMB	TS_ZOMB	Kthread/process has terminated.
	TS_FREE	Thread is waiting to be reaped.

The disparities in the state of a process and kernel thread have to do with process creation (process SIDL state) and the state of a kernel thread following termination (TS_FREE). We discuss this subject in the sections on process creation and termination.

- **t_pri** — The thread's scheduling priority.
- **t_epri** — The thread's inherited priority. Used for the implementation of priority inheritance, which addresses the priority inversion problem.
- **t_wchan0, t_wchan** — Wait channel. What the thread is blocking on.
- **t_cid** — Scheduling class ID (e.g., TS, RT).
- **t_cldata** — Pointer to a scheduling-class-specific data structure.
- **t_clfuncs** — Pointer to scheduling-class operations vector.
- **t_cpu** — Pointer to a CPU structure for the CPU that the thread last ran on.
- **t_sigqueue** — Pointer to a siginfo structure. Root pointer of siginfo queue.
- **t_sig** — Signals pending to this thread.
- **t_hold** — Signal hold bit mask.
- **t_forw** — Kthread pointer, forward link for linked list, processwide.
- **t_back** — Kthread pointer, backward pointer for above.
- **t_lwp** — Pointer to the LWP structure.
- **t_procp** — Pointer to the proc structure.
- **t_next** — Forward pointer for systemwide linked list of kernel threads.
- **t_prev** — Back pointer for above.
- **t_cred** — Pointer to current credentials structure.
- **t_sysnum** — System call number.

The following kernel thread members are used by the dispatcher code for thread scheduling.

- **t_lockp** — Pointer to dispatcher lock.
- **t_oldspl** — The previous priority level.
- **t_pre_sys** — Flag for system call preprocessing.
- **t_disp_queue** — Pointer to the thread's dispatch queue.
- **t_disp_time** — Last time this thread was running.
- **t_kpri_req** — Kernel priority required for this thread.

The next group of kthread members deals with post-system-call or post-trap handling. The kthread members are embedded in the kthread structure as a union. A bit set in any of these members prevents a direct return to user mode of the thread until the condition has been satisfied.

- `_t_astflag` — Flag to indicate post-trap processing required, such as signal handling or a preemption.
- `_t_sig_check` — Signal pending.
- `_t_post_syscall` — Some post-system-call processing is required.
- `_t_trapret` — Invokes the scheduling class-specific trap return code.

Figure 8.11 provides the big picture. Obviously, not every pointer implemented is shown. We wanted to provide a visual representation of how the major data structures link together and in general to illustrate what a subsection of a typical process/lwp/kthread list looks like from a coarse-grained view.

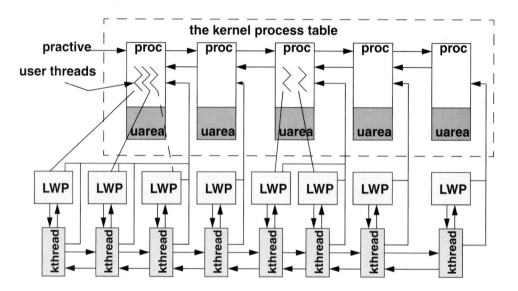

Figure 8.11 The Process, LWP, and Kernel Thread Structure Linkage

8.3 The Kernel Process Table

Every process occupies a slot in the kernel process table, which maintains a process structure (commonly abbreviated as *proc structure*) for the process. The process structure is relatively large, about 900 bytes in size, and contains all the information the kernel needs to manage the process and schedule the LWPs and kthreads for execution. As processes are created, kernel memory space for the process table is allocated dynamically by the kmem cache allocation and management routines.

8.3.1 Process Limits

At system boot time, the kernel initializes a `process_cache`, which begins the allocation of kernel memory for storing the process table. Initially, space is allocated for one proc structure. The table itself is implemented as a doubly linked list, such that each proc structure contains a pointer to the next process and previous processes on the list. The maximum size of the process table is based on the amount of physical memory (RAM) in the system and is established at boot time. During startup, the kernel sets a tunable parameter, `maxusers`, to the number of megabytes of memory installed on the system, up to a maximum of 2,048. Thus, systems with more than 2 Gbytes of physical memory will have a `maxusers` value of 2,048. Systems with less than 2 Gbytes set `maxusers` to the amount of physical memory in megabytes; for example, a system with 512 Mbytes of RAM will have a `maxusers` value of 512. The `maxusers` value subsequently determines the amount of several major kernel resources, such as the maximum process table size and the maximum number of processes per user.

The formula is quite simple:

```
max_nprocs = (10 + 16 * maxusers)
maxuprc = (max_nprocs - 5)
```

The `max_nprocs` value is the maximum number of processes systemwide, and `maxuprc` determines the maximum number of processes a non-root user can have occupying a process table slot at any time. The system actually uses a data structure, the `var` structure, which holds generic system configuration information, to store these values in. There are three related values:

- `v_proc`, which is set equal to `max_nprocs`.
- `v_maxupttl`, which is the maximum number of process slots that can be used by all non-root users on the system. It is set to `max_nprocs` minus some number of reserved process slots (currently `reserved_procs` is 5).
- `v_maxup`, the maximum number of process slots a non-root user can occupy. It is set to the `maxuprc` value. Note that `v_maxup` (an individual non-root user) and `v_maxupttl` (total of all non-root users on the system) end up being set to the same value, which is `max_nprocs` minus 5.

You can use adb(1) to examine the values of maxusers, max_nprocs, and max-uprc on a running system.

```
# adb -k /dev/ksyms /dev/mem
physmem bdde
maxusers/D
maxusers:
maxusers:        189
max_nprocs/D
max_nprocs:
max_nprocs:      3034
maxuprc/D
maxuprc:
maxuprc:         3029
```

You can also use crash(1M) or the system var structure to dump those values.

```
# /etc/crash
> od -d maxusers
f0274dc4: 0000000253
> od -d max_nprocs
f027126c: 0000004058
> od -d maxuprc
f0270f28: 0000004053
> var
v_buf: 100
v_call: 0
v_proc: 4058
v_nglobpris: 110
v_maxsyspri: 99
v_clist: 0
v_maxup: 4053
v_hbuf: 256
v_hmask: 255
v_pbuf: 0
v_sptmap: 0
v_maxpmem: 0
v_autoup: 30
v_bufhwm: 5196
```

Note that the /etc/crash var utility does not dump the v_maxupttl value; it just dumps v_proc and v_maxup. The hexadecimal value to the left of the parameter value is the kernel virtual address of the variable. For example, f0274dc4 is the address of the maxusers kernel variable (in this example).

Finally, sar(1M) with the -v flag gives you the maximum process table size and the current number of processes on the system.

```
$ sar -v 1 1

SunOS sunsys 5.6 Generic sun4m      05/05/00

22:27:47  proc-sz    ov  inod-sz    ov  file-sz    ov   lock-sz
22:27:48   63/3034     0 2480/13212   0   392/392    0    0/0
```

Under the `proc-sz` column, the 72/1962 values represent the current number of processes (72) and the maximum number of processes (1962).

The kernel does impose a maximum value in case `max_nprocs` is set in `/etc/system` to something beyond what is reasonable, even for a large system. In Solaris releases 2.4, 2.5, 2.5.1, 2.6, and 7, the maximum is 30,000, which is determined by the `MAXPID` macro in the `param.h` header file (available in `/usr/include/sys`).

In the kernel `fork` code, the current number of processes is checked against the `v_proc` parameter. If the limit is reached, the system produces an "out of processes" message on the console and increments the proc table overflow counter maintained in the `cpu_sysinfo` structure. This value is reflected in the ov column to the right of `proc-sz` in the `sar(1M)` output. For non-root users, a check is made against the `v_maxup` parameter, and an "out of per-user processes for uid (UID)" message is logged. In both cases, the calling program would get a `-1` return value from `fork(2)`, signifying an error.

8.3.2 LWP Limits

Now that we've examined the limits the kernel imposes on the number of processes systemwide, let's look at the limits on the maximum number of LWP/kthread pairs that can exist in the system at any one time.

Each LWP has a kernel stack, allocated out of the `segkp` kernel address space segment. The size of the kernel `segkp` segment and the space allocated for LWP kernel stacks vary according to the kernel release and the hardware platform. On UltraSPARC (sun4u)-based systems running a 32-bit kernel, the `segkp` size is limited to 512 Mbytes and the kernel stacks are 16 Kbytes. Thus, the maximum number of LWPs systemwide is 32,768 (32K) (512-Mbyte `segkp` segment size and 16-Kbyte stack size). On 64-bit Solaris 7, the larger (24-Kbyte) LWP kernel stack allocation reduces the total number of LWPs on an UltraSPARC-based system to 21,845.

On non-UltraSPARC-based systems, the stack allocation is slightly smaller—12 Kbytes. The kernel `segkp` segment is also smaller; the total size is based on the hardware architecture and amount of physical memory on the system.

8.4   Process Creation

All processes in Solaris are created with the traditional `fork/exec` UNIX process creation model that was part of the original UNIX design and is still implemented in virtually every version of UNIX in existence today. The only exceptions in the Solaris environment are the creation of four system daemons at startup, PIDs 0 through 3: the memory scheduler (sched, PID 0), `init` (PID 1), the pageout daemon (PID 2), and `fsflush` (PID 3). These processes are created by an internal kernel `newproc()` function. The mechanics of process creation are illustrated in Figure 8.12.

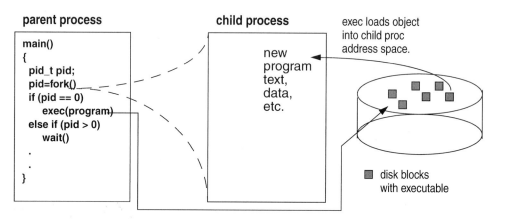

Figure 8.12 Process Creation

The `fork(2)` and `exec(2)` system calls are used extensively in the various software components that come bundled with Solaris as well as in hundreds of applications that run on Solaris. (However, more and more Solaris daemons and applications are being threaded with each release, which means that the programs use threads as an alternative to multiple processes.)

The `fork(2)` system call creates a new process. The newly created process is assigned a unique process identification (PID) and is a child of the process that called `fork`; the calling process is the parent. The `exec(2)` system call overlays the process with an executable specified as a path name in the first argument to the `exec(2)` call. The model, in pseudocode format, looks like this:

```
main(int argc, char *argv[], char *envp[])
{
        pid_t child_pid;
        child_pid = fork();
        if (child_pid == -1)
                perror(RforkS); /* fork system call failed */
        else if (child_pid == 0)
                execv(R/path/new_binaryS,argv); /* in the child, so exec */
        else
                wait()  /* pid > 0, weUre in the parent */
}
```

The pseudocode above calls `fork(2)` and checks the return value from `fork(2)` (pid). Remember, once `fork(2)` executes successfully, there are two processes: `fork` returns a value of 0 to the child process and returns the PID of the child to the parent process. In the example, we called `exec(2)` to execute `new_binary` once in the child. Back in the parent, we simply wait for the child to complete (we'll get back later to this notion of "waiting").

A couple of different flavors of fork(2) that are available take different code paths in the process creation flow. The traditional fork(2) call duplicates the entire parent process, including all the threads and LWPs that exist within the process when the fork(2) is executed.

With Solaris 2.X and threads support came a variant of fork(2): fork1(2). In the fork1(2) call, only the thread that issues the fork1(2) call and its associated support structures are replicated. This call is extremely useful for multithreaded programs that also do process creation because it reduces the overhead of replicating potentially tens or hundreds of threads in the child process. If an exec(2) call is planned following the fork(2), as is typically the case, the exec(2) code will free all but one LWP/kthread, which makes the use of fork(2) somewhat superfluous in a multithreaded process. Note that linking fork to a particular threads library modifies fork's behavior. Linking with the Solaris threads library (-lthread compilation flag) results in the described replicate-all fork(2) behavior. Linking with the POSIX threads library (-lpthread) results in a call to fork(2) replicating only the calling thread. In other words, linking with -lpthread (POSIX threads library) and calling fork(2) results in fork1(2) behavior.

Finally, there's vfork(2), which is described as a "virtual memory efficient" version of fork. A call to vfork(2) results in the child process "borrowing" the address space of the parent, rather than the kernel duplicating the parent's address space for the child, as it does in fork(2) and fork1(2). The child's address space following a vfork(2) is the same address space as that of the parent. More precisely, the physical memory pages of the new process's (the child) address space are the same memory pages as for the parent. The implication here is that the child must not change any state while executing in the parent's address space until the child either exits or executes an exec(2) system call—once an exec(2) call is executed, the child gets its own address space. In fork(2) and fork1(2), the address space of the parent is copied for the child by means of the kernel address space duplicate routine (the kernel as_dup()).

For some applications, the use of vfork(2) instead of fork(2) can improve application efficiency noticeably. Applications that fork/exec a lot of processes (e.g., mail servers, Web servers) do not incur the overhead of having the kernel create and set up a new address space and all the underlying segments with each fork(2) call. Rather, address spaces are built as needed following the exec(2) call.

The kernel code flow for process creation is represented in the following pseudocode.

```
fork() or fork1() or vfork()
cfork()
getproc()
        Get proc structure (via kmem_cache_alloc(process_cache)).
        Set process state (p_stat) to SIDL.
        Set process start time (p_mstart).
        Call pid_assign() to get PID.
        pid_assign().
                Get a pid structure.
                Get a /proc directory slot.
                Get an available PID.
                init the PID structure.
                        Set reference count.
                        Set PID.
                        Set proc slot number.
                        Return pid to getproc().
Check for process table overflow (procs > v.v_nprocs).
Check for per-user process limit reached.
Put new process on process table linked list.
Set new process p_ignore and p_signal from parent.
Set the following fields in new (child) process from parent.
        Session stucture pointer p_sessp.
        Executable vnode pointer p_exec.
        Address space fields p_brkbase, p_brksize, p_stksize.
        Set child parent PID.
        Set parent-child-sibling pointers.
        Copy profile state from parent to child, p_prof.
Increment reference counts in open file list
(child inherits these).
Copy parent's uarea to child (includes copying open file list).
if (child inherits /proc tracing flag (SPRFORK set in p_flag)
        Set p_sigmask in child from parent.
        Set p_fltmask in child from parent.
else
        Clear p_sigmask and p_fltmask in child (set to emtpy).
if (inherit microstate accounting flag in parent)
        Enable microstate accounting in child
Return from getproc() to cfork().
if (vfork())
        Set child address space to parent (child p_as = parent p_as).
        Set child SVFORK in p_flag.
else (not a vfork())
        Duplicate copy of parent's address space for child (as_dup())
        Duplicate parent's shared memory for child.
Duplicate parent LWPs and kthreads.
                if (fork1())
                        Just duplicate the current thread.
                        forklwp()
                                lwp_create()
                else (walk the process thread list - p_tlist; for each thread)
                        forklwp()
                                lwp_create() - create an LWP
                                        Replicate scheduling class from parent
                                thread_create() - create a kernel thread
Add the child to the parent's process group (pgjoin())
Set the child process state (p_stat) to SRUN
if (vfork())
        Increment cpu_sysinfo vfork count (cpu_sysinfo.sysvfork)
        Call continuelwps() for child execution before parent
else
        Increment cpu_sysinfo fork count (cpu_sysinfo.sysfork)
        Place child in front of parent on dispatch queue
        (so it runs first).
Set return values: PID to parent, 0 to child
```

As the preceding pseudocode flow indicates, when the fork(2) system call is entered, a process table slot is allocated in kernel memory: the *process_cache*, which was first implemented in Solaris 2.6. (In prior Solaris versions, the kernel simply grabbed a chunk of kernel memory for a process structure.) The process start-time field (p_mstart) is set, and the process state is set to SIDL, which is a state flag to indicate the process is in an intermediate "creation" state. The kernel then assigns a PID to the process and allocates an available slot in the /proc directory for the procfs entry. The kernel copies the process session data to the child, in the form of the session structure; this procedure maintains the session leader process and controlling terminal information. The kernel also establishes the process structure pointer linkage between the parent and child, and the uarea of the parent process is copied into the newly created child process structure.

The Solaris kernel implements an interesting throttle here in the event of a process forking out of control and thus consuming an inordinate amount of system resources. A failure by the kernel pid_assign() code, which is where the new process PID is acquired, or a lack of an available process table slot indicates a large amount of process creation activity. In this circumstance, the kernel implements a delay mechanism by which the process that issued the fork call is forced to sleep for an extra clock tick (a tick is every 10 milliseconds). By implementing this mechanism, the kernel ensures that no more than one fork can fail per CPU per clock tick.

The throttle also scales up, in such a manner that an increased rate of fork failures results in an increased delay before the code returns the failure and the issuing process can try again. In that situation, you'll see the console message "out of processes," and the ov (overflow) column in the sar -v output will have a non-zero value. You can also look at the kernel fork_fail_pending variable with adb. If this value is nonzero, the system has entered the fork throttle code segment. Below is an example of examining the fork_fail_pending kernel variable with adb(1).

```
# adb -k /dev/ksyms /dev/mem
physmem bdde
fork_fail_pending/D
fork_fail_pending:
fork_fail_pending:              0
```

When a vfork(2) is issued and the child is using the parent's address space, the kernel takes some extra steps to prevent the parent from executing until the child has either exited or issued an exec(2) call to overlay the new process space with a new program. The kernel uses the t_post_syscall flag in the thread structure, causing the post_syscall() kernel routine to be invoked when the calling thread returns from the vfork(2) call. The post_syscall() code checks the t_sysnum in the thread structure, which holds the system call type issued (set by the kernel in the pre-system-call handling). In this case, t_sysnum reflects SYS_vfork and causes the thread to issue a vfwait() call; that action keeps the parent waiting until the child has issued an exit(2) or exec(2) call. At that point, the virtual memory the child was holding can be released (relvm()) and the parent can safely resume execution.

The final important point to make about process creation and fork concerns inheritance. Specifically, the bits of the parent process that are inherited by the child are the credentials structure (real and effective UID and GID), open files, the parent's environment (the environment list includes typical environmental variables such as HOME, PATH, LOGNAME, etc.), mode bits for set UID or set GID, the scheduling class, the nice value, attached shared memory segments, current working and root directories, and the file mode creation mask (umask).

With a newly created process/LWP/kthread infrastructure in place, most applications will invoke exec(2). The exec(2) system call overlays the calling program with a new executable image. (Not following a fork(2) with an exec(2) results in two processes executing the same code; the parent and child will execute whatever code exists after the fork(2) call.)

There are several flavors of the exec(2) call; the basic differences are in what they take as arguments. The exec(2) calls vary in whether they take a path name or filename as the first argument (which specifies the new executable program to start), whether they require a comma-separated list of arguments or an argv[] array, and whether the existing environment is used or an envp[] array is passed.

Because Solaris supports the execution of several different file types, the kernel exec code is split into object file format-dependent and object file format-independent code segments. Most common is the previously discussed ELF format. Among other supported files is a.out, which is included to provide a degree of binary compatibility that enables executables created on SunOS 4.X system to run on SunOS 5.X. Other inclusions are a format-specific exec routine for programs that run under an interpreter, such as shell scripts and awk programs, and an exec routine for COFF (Common Object File Format) under x86 architectures. Lastly, support code for programs in the Java programming language is included in Solaris releases since 2.5, with a Java-specific exec code segment.

Calls into the object-specific exec code are done through a switch table mechanism. During system startup, an execsw[] array is initialized with the magic number of the supported object file types. (Magic numbers uniquely identify different object file types on UNIX systems. See /etc/magic and the magic(4) manual page.) Each array member is an execsw structure, and each structure contains the following four structure members:

- **exec_magic** — A pointer to the magic number that uniquely identifies the type of object file.

- **exec_func** — A function pointer; points to the exec function for the object file type.

- **exec_core** — A function pointer; points to the object-file-specific core dump routine.

- **exec_lock** — A pointer to a kernel read/write lock, to synchronize access to the exec switch array.

The object file exec code is implemented as dynamically loadable kernel modules, found in the /kernel/exec directory (aoutexec, elfexec, intpexec) and /usr/kernel/exec (javaexec). The elf and intp modules will load through the normal boot process, since these two modules are used minimally by the kernel startup processes and startup shell scripts. The a.out and java modules will load automatically when needed as a result of exec'ing a SunOS 4.X binary or a Java program. When each module loads into RAM (kernel address space in memory), the mod_install() support code loads the execsw structure information into the execsw[] array.

Figure 8.13 illustrates the flow of exec, with ELF file-type functions illustrating object-file-specific calls.

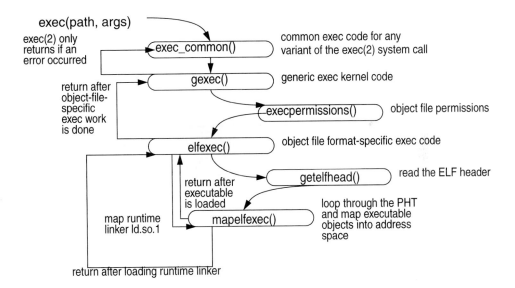

Figure 8.13 exec Flow

All variants of the exec(2) system call resolve in the kernel to a common routine, exec_common(), where some initial processing is done. The path name for the executable file is retrieved, exitlwps() is called to force all but the calling LWP to exit, any POSIX4 interval timers in the process are cleared (p_itimer field in the proc structure), and the sysexec counter in the cpu_sysinfo structure is incremented (counts exec system calls, readable with sar(1M)). If scheduler activations have been set up for the process, the door interface used for such purposes is closed (i.e., scheduler activations are not inherited), and any other doors that exist within the process are closed. The SPREXEC flag is set in p_flags (proc structure field), indicating an exec is in the works for the process. The SPREXEC flag blocks any subsequent process operations until exec() has completed, at which point the flag is cleared.

The kernel generic exec code, gexec() is now called; here is where we switch out to the object-file-specific exec routine through the execsw[] array. The correct array entry for the type of file being exec'd is determined by a call to the kernel vn_rdwr() (vnode read/write) routine and a read of the first four bytes of the file, which is where the file's magic number is stored. Once the magic number has been retrieved, the code looks for a match in each entry in the execsw[] array by comparing the magic number of the exec'd file to the exec_magic field in each structure in the array. Prior to entering the exec switch table, the code checks permissions against the credentials of the process and the permissions of the object file being exec'd. If the object file is not executable or the caller does not have execute permissions, exec fails with an EACCESS error. If the object file has the set-uid or setgid bits set, the effective UID or GID is set in the new process credentials at this time.

Figure 8.14 illustrates the basic flow of an exec call through the switch table.

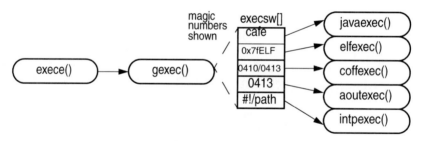

Figure 8.14 exec Flow to Object-Specific Routine

Note that Solaris 7 implements two ELF entries, one for each data model supported: 32-bit ILP32 ELF files and 64-bit LP64 ELF files. Let's examine the flow of the elfexec() function, since that is the most common type of executable run on Solaris systems.

Upon entry to the elfexec() code, the kernel reads the ELF header and program header (PHT) sections of the object file (see "The Multithreaded Process Model" on page 262 for an overview of the ELF header and PHT). These two main header sections of the object file provide the system with the information it needs to proceed with mapping the binary to the address space of the newly forked process. The kernel next gets the argument and environment arrays from the exec(2) call and places both on the user stack of the process, using the exec_args() function. The arguments are also copied into the process uarea's u_psargs[] array at this time.

32-bit binary stack offsets _____ **64-bit binary stack offsets**

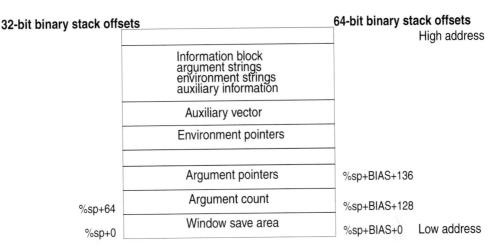

Figure 8.15 Initial Process Stack Frame

A quick Solaris 7 implementation note: Before actually setting up the user stack with the `argv[]` and `envp[]` arrays, Solaris 7, if booted as a 64-bit kernel, must first determine if a 32-bit or 64-bit binary is being exec'd (a 32-bit Solaris 7 system can only run 32-bit binaries). This information is maintained in the ELF header, where the system checks the `e_ident[]` array for either an `ELFCLASS32` or `ELFCLASS64` file identity. With the data model established, the kernel sets the initial size of the exec file sections to 4 Kbytes for the stack, 4 Kbytes for stack growth (stack increment), and 1 Mbyte for the argument list (ELF32) or 2-Mbyte argument list size for an ELF64.

Once the kernel has established the process user stack and argument list, it calls the `mapelfexec()` function to map the various program segments into the process address space. `mapelfexec()` walks through the Program Header Table (PHT), and for each `PT_LOAD` type (a loadable segment), `mapelfexec()` maps the segment into the process's address space. `mapelfexec()` bases the mapping on the `p_filesz` and `p_memsz` sections of the header that define the segment, using the lower-level, kernel address space support code. Once the program loadable segments have been mapped into the address space, the dynamic linker (for dynamically linked executables), referenced through the PHT, is also mapped into the process's address space. The `elfexec` code checks the process resource limit `RLIMIT_VMEM` (max virtual memory size) against the size required to map the object file and runtime linker. An `ENOMEM` error is returned in the event of an address space requirement that exceeds the limit.

All that remains for `exec(2)` to complete is some additional housekeeping and structure initialization, which is done when the code returns to `gexec()`. This last part deals with clearing the signal stack and setting the signal disposition to default for any signals that have had a handler installed by the parent process. The kernel thread ID is set to 1, and the `p_lwptotal` is set to 1 in the new process. Finally, all open files with the close-on-exec flag set are closed, and the exec is complete. A call made into `procfs` clears the `SPREXEC` flag and unlocks access to the process by means of `/proc`.

As we'll see in the next chapter, threads inherit their scheduling class and priority from the parent. Some scheduling-class-specific fork code executes at the tail end of the fork process that takes care of placement of the newly created kthread on a dispatch queue. This practice gets the child executing before the parent in anticipation that the child will immediately execute an `exec(2)` call to load in the new object file. In the case of a `vfork(2)`, where the child is mapped to the address space of the parent, the parent is forced to wait until the child executes and gets its own address space.

8.5   Process Termination

The termination of a process results from one of three possible events. First, the process explicitly calling `exit(2)` or `_exit(2)` causes all the threads in a multithreaded process to exit. (The threads libraries include `thr_exit(3T)` and `pthread_exit(3T)` interfaces for programmatically terminating an individual user thread without causing the entire process to exit.) Second, the process simply completes execution and falls through to the end of the `main()` function—which is essentially an implicit exit. Third, a signal is delivered, and the disposition for the signal is to terminate the process. This disposition is the default for some signals (see "Signals" on page 320). There is actually one other possibility: a process can explicitly call the `abort(3C)` function and cause a `SIGABRT` signal to be sent to the process. The default disposition for `SIGABRT` is to terminate the process and create a core file.

Regardless of which event causes the process to terminate, the kernel exit function is ultimately executed, freeing whatever resources have been allocated to the process, such as the address space mappings, open files, etc., and setting the process state to `SZOMB`, or the *zombie* state. A zombie process is one that has exited and that requires the parent process to issue a `wait(2)` system call to gather the exit status. The only kernel resource that a process in the zombie state is holding is the process table slot. Successful execution of a `wait(2)` call frees the process table slot. Orphaned processes are inherited by the init process solely for this purpose.

An exception to the above scenario is possible if a parent process uses the `sigaction(2)` system call to establish a signal handler for the `SIGCLD` signal and sets the `SA_NOCLDWAIT` flag (no child wait) in the `sa_flags` field of the `sigaction` structure. A process is sent a `SIGCLD` signal by the kernel when one of its child processes terminates. If a process installs a `SIGCLD` handler as described, the kernel sets the `SNOWAIT` bit in the calling (parent) process's `p_flag` field, signifying that the parent process is not interested in obtaining status information on child processes that have exited. The actual mechanics happens in two places:

when the signal handler is installed and when the kernel gets ready to post a SIG-CLD signal.

First, when the sigaction() call is executed and the handler is installed, if SA_NOCLDWAIT is true, SNOWAIT is set in p_flags and the code loops through the child process list, looking for child processes in the zombie state. For each such child process found, the kernel freeproc() function is called to release the process table entry. (The kernel exit code, described below, will have already executed, since the process must have terminated—otherwise, it would not be in the zombie state.) In the second occurrence, the kernel calls its internal sigcld() function to post a SIGCLD signal to a process that has had a child terminate. The sigcld() code calls freeproc() instead of posting the signal if SNOWAIT is set in the parent's p_flags field.

Having jumped ahead there for a second, let's turn our attention back to the kernel exit() function, starting with a summary of the actions performed.

```
exit()
        Exit all but 1 LWP (exitlwps())
        Clean up any doors created by the process
        Clean up any pending async I/Os
        Clean up any realtime timers
        Flush signal information (set ignore for all signals, clear posted signals)
        Set process LWP count to zero (p_lwpcnt = 0)
        NULL terminate the process kernel thread linked list
        Set process termination time (p_mterm)
        Close all open file descriptors
        if (process is a session leader)
                Release control terminal
        Clean up any semaphore resources being held
        Release the processUs address space
        Reassign orphan processes to next-of-kin
        Reassign child processes to init
        Set process state to zombie
        Set process p_wdata and p_wcode for parent to interrogate
        Call kernel sigcld() function to send SIGCLD to parent
                if (SNOWAIT flag is set in parent)
                        freeproc() /* free the proc table slot - no zombie */
                else
                        post the signal to the parent
```

The sequence of events outlined above is pretty straightforward. It's a matter of walking through the process structure, cleaning up resources that the process may be holding, and reassigning child and orphan processes. Child processes are handed over to init, and orphan processes are linked to the next-of-kin process, which is typically the parent. Still, we can point out a few interesting things about process termination and the LWP/kthread model as implemented in Solaris.

8.5.1 The LWP/kthread Model

The `exitlwps()` code is called immediately upon entry to the kernel `exit()` function, which, as the name implies, is responsible for terminating all but one LWP in the process. If the number of LWPs in the process is 1 (the `p_lwpcnt` field in the proc structure) and there are no zombie LWPs (`p_zombcnt` is 0), then `exitlwps()` will simply turn off the `SIGWAITING` signal and return. `SIGWAITING` is used to create more LWPs in the process if runnable user threads are waiting for a resource. We certainly do not want to catch `SIGWAITING` signals and create LWPs when we're terminating.

If the process has more than one LWP, the LWPs must be stopped (quiesced) so they are not actively changing state or attempting to grab resources (file opens, stack/address space growth, etc.). Essentially what happens is this:

1. The kernel loops through the list of LWP/kthreads in the process, setting the `t_astflag` in the kernel thread. If the LWP/kthread is running on a processor, the processor is forced to enter the kernel through the cross-call interrupt mechanism.

2. Inside the trap handler, which is entered as a result of the cross-call, the kernel tests the `t_astflag` (which is set) and tests for what condition it is that requires post-trap processing. The `t_astflag` specifically instructs the kernel that some additional processing is required following a trap.

3. The trap handler tests the process `HOLDFORK` flag and if it is set in `p_flags` (which it will be in this case), calls a `holdlwp()` function that, under different circumstances, would suspend the LWP/kthread.

4. During an exit, with `EXITLWPS` set in `p_flags`, the `lwp_exit()` function is called to terminate the LWP. If the LWP/kthread is in a sleep or stopped state, then it is set to run so it can ultimately be quiesced as described.

The kernel `lwp_exit()` function does per-LWP/kthread cleanup, such as timers, doors, signals, and scheduler activations. Finally, the LWP/kthread is placed on the process's linked list of zombie LWPs, `p_zomblist`. Once all but one of the LWP/kthreads in the process have been terminated and placed on the process zombie list, the `exit()` code moves on to execute the functions summarized on the previous page.

The pseudocode below summarizes the `exitlwps()` function.

```
exitlwps()
        if (process LWP count == 1)
                nuke SIGWAITING
                return
        else
                for (each LWP/kthread on the process linked list)
                        if (LWP/kthread is sleeping or stopped)
                                make it runnable
                        if (LWP/kthread is running on a processor)
                                t_astflag = 1;
                                poke_cpu() /* cross-call, to trap into the kernel */
                                        holdlwp()
                                                lwp_exit()
                                                place kthread/LWP on zombie list
                done (loop)
        place zombie threads on deathrow
        return to kernel exit()
```

Once the `exit()` code has completed, the process is in a zombie state, occupying only a process table entry and PID structure. When a `wait()` call is issued on the zombie, the kernel `freeproc()` function is called to free the process and PID structures.

8.5.2 Deathrow

`exitlwps()` does one last bit of work before it returns to `exit()`. It places a zombie's kernel threads on *deathrow*.

The kernel maintains a list, called deathrow, of LWPs and kernel threads that have exited, in order to reap a terminated LWP/kthread when a new one needs to be created (`fork()`). If an LWP/kthread is available on the list of zombies, the kernel does not need to allocate the data structures and stack for a new kthread; it simply uses the structures and stack from the zombie kthread and links the kthread to the process that issued the `fork(2)` (or `thread_create()`).

In the process creation flow, when the `forklwp()` code calls `lwp_create()`, `lwp_create()` first looks on deathrow for a zombie thread. If one exists, the LWP, kthread, and stack are linked to the process, and the kernel is spared the need to allocate new kthread, LWP, and stack space during the `fork()` process. The kernel simply grabs the structures from the deathrow list, links the pointers appropriately, and moves on. `thread_create()` (kernel thread create, not the user thread API), called from `lwp_create()`, is passed the LWP data and stack and thus avoids doing any kernel memory allocations.

A kernel thread, `thread_reaper()`, runs periodically and cleans up zombie threads that are sitting on deathrow. The list of zombie threads on deathrow is not allowed to grow without bounds (no more than 32 zombies), and the zombies are not left on deathrow forever.

8.6   Procfs — The Process File System

The process file system, procfs, is a pseudo file system. Pseudo file systems provide file-like abstractions and file I/O interfaces to something that is not a file in the traditional sense. Procfs abstracts the Solaris kernel's process architecture such that all processes running on the system appear in the root directory name space under the /proc directory; every process in the system exists as a file under /proc, with the process's PID serving as the filename. The PID filename under /proc is actually a directory, containing other files and subdirectories that, combined, make up the complete /proc directory space. The many kernel data structures that provide process data and control points appear as files within the /proc/<PID> directory hierarchy, and multithreaded processes have a subdirectory for each LWP in the process. Per-LWP data and control structures exist as files under the /proc/<PID>/lwp/<LWP_ID>. The objects that appear under /proc are not on-disk files; they are objects that exist in kernel memory. When a user executes an ls(1) command in /proc or any /proc subdirectory, the system is reading kernel memory.

This file-like abstraction for processes provides a simple and elegant means of extracting information about processes, their execution environment, and kernel resource utilization. Simple things, such as opening a /proc file object to read bits of information about a process, are relatively easy to do with procfs. Process control is powerful and relatively straightforward; processes can be stopped and started, and event-driven stops can be established for things like signals, traps, and system calls. In general, process management and debugging is greatly simplified. It is worth noting that the original design goal of procfs was to provide a set of interfaces for writing debuggers; it has evolved considerably since the original implementation.

The Solaris system ships with several commands that implement /proc for extracting information and issuing control directives. These commands reside in the /usr/proc/bin directory and are described in the proc(1) manual page. We use some of these commands throughout the book to provide examples of different kernel abstractions, such as opened files or a process's address space. The process status command, ps(1), is also built on top of the procfs interfaces.

The control and informational data made available through the /proc file system are maintained in a hierarchy of files and subdirectories. The files and subdirectories implemented in /proc are listed below. See the proc(4) manual page for additional information on these files and their uses.

- **/proc** — The top-level directory for procfs.

- **/proc/<pid>** — The top-level directory for a specific process, where the process's PID is the directory name.

- **/proc/<pid>/as** — The process's address space, as defined by the p_as link to an address space structure (struct as) in the process's proc structure. In other words, the process's address space as represented by the /proc/<pid>/as file is not a /proc-specific representation of the address space. Rather, /proc provides a path to address space mappings through the proc structure's p_as pointer.

- **/proc/<pid>/ctl** — A process control file. Can be opened for write-only, and can be used to send control messages to a process to initiate a specific event or to enable a particular behavior. Examples include stopping or starting a process, setting stops on specific events, or turning on microstate accounting.

  This file exemplifies the power and elegance of procfs; you can accomplish process control and event tracing by opening the control file for the target process and writing a control message (or multiple control messages) to inject desired behavior. See the proc(4) man page for a detailed list of control messages and functions.

- **/proc/<pid>/status** — General state and status information about the process. The specific contents are defined in the pstatus structure, defined in /usr/include/sys/procfs.h. pstatus is also described in proc(4).

  Note that pstatus embeds an lwpstatus structure (the pr_lwp field of pstatus). This structure is described as a representative LWP. A non-threaded process has only one LWP, so selecting a representative LWP is simple. For threaded processes with multiple LWPs, an internal kernel routine loops through all the LWPs in the process and selects one on the basis of its state. First choice is an executing LWP. If an executing LWP is not available, selection criteria look for runnable, sleeping, or stopped.

- **/proc/<pid>/lstatus** — An array of lwpstatus structures, one for each LWP in the process.

- **/proc/<pid>/psinfo** — Process information as provided by the ps(1) command. Similar to the status data as described above, in that a representative LWP is included with an embedded lwpsinfo structure.

- **/proc/<pid>/lpsinfo** — Per-LWP ps(1) information.

- **/proc/<pid>/map** — Address space map information. The data displayed by the pmap(1) command.

- **/proc/<pid>/rmap** — Reserved address space segments of the process.

- **/proc/<pid>/xmap** — Extended address space map information. The data displayed when the pmap(1) command is run with the -x flag.

- **/proc/<pid>/cred** — Process credentials, as described in the prcred structure (/usr/include/sys/procfs.h).

- **/proc/<pid>/sigact** — Array of `sigaction` structures, each representing the signal disposition for all signals associated with the process.

- **/proc/<pid>/auxv** — An array of `auxv` (auxiliary vector, defined in `/usr/include/sys/auxv.h`) structures, with the initial values as passed to the dynamic linker when the process was `exec`'d.

- **/proc/<pid>/ldt** — Local descriptor table. Intel x86 architecture only.

- **/proc/<pid>/usage** — Process resource usage data. See "Process Resource Usage" on page 314.

- **/proc/<pid>/lusage** — Array of LWP resource usage data. See "Process Resource Usage" on page 314.

- **/proc/<pid>/pagedata** — Another representation of the process's address space. Provides page-level reference and modification tracking.

- **/proc/<pid>/watch** — An array of `prwatch` structures (defined in `/usr/include/sys/procfs.h`), as created when the kernel sets a `PCWATCH` operation by writing to the control file. Allows for monitoring (watching) one or more address space ranges, such that a trap is generated when a memory reference is made to a watched page.

- **/proc/<pid>/cwd** — Symbolic link to the process's current working directory.

- **/proc/<pid>/root** — Symbolic link to the process's root directory.

- **/proc/<pid>/fd** — Directory that contains references to the process's open files.

- **/proc/<pid>/fd/nn** — The process's open file descriptors. Directory files are represented as symbolic links.

- **/proc/<pid>/object** — Subdirectory containing binary shared object files the process is linked to.

- **/proc/<pid>/object/nn** — Binary object files. The process's executable binary (`a.out`), along with shared object files the process is linked to.

In addition to the file objects and subdirectories maintained at the process level, each /proc/<pid>/ directory has an `lwp` subdirectory, which contains several file objects that contain per-LWP data. Subdirectories are described below.

- **/proc/<pid>/lwp** — Subdirectory containing files that represent all the LWPs in the process.

- **/proc/<pid>/lwp/<lwpid>** — Subdirectory containing the procfs files specific to an LWP.

- **/proc/<pid>/lwp/<lwpid>/lwpctl** — Control file for issuing control operations on a per-LWP basis.

- `/proc/<pid>/lwp/<lwpid>/lwpstatus` — LWP state and status information, as defined in the `lwpstatus` structure in `/usr/include/sys/procfs.h`.

- `/proc/<pid>/lwp/<lwpid>/lwpsinfo` — LWP ps(1) command information, as defined in `lwpsinfo`, also in `/usr/include/sys/procfs.h`.

- `/proc/<pid>/lwp/<lwpid>/lwpusage` — LWP resource usage data. See "Process Resource Usage" on page 314.

- `/proc/<pid>/lwp/<lwpid>/xregs` — Extra general state registers; this file is processor-architecture specific and may not be present on some platforms. On SPARC-based systems, the data contained in this file is defined in the `prxregset` structure, in `/usr/include/sys/procfs_isa.h`.

- `/proc/<pid>/lwp/<lwpid>/gwindows` — General register windows. This file exists on SPARC-based systems only and represents the general register set of the LWP (part of the hardware context), as defined in the `gwindows` structure in `/usr/include/sys/regset.h`.

- `/proc/<pid>/lwp/<lwpid>/asrs` — Ancillary register set. SPARC V9 architecture (UltraSPARC) only. An additional set of hardware registers defined by the SPARC V9 architecture. This file, representing the ancillary registers, is present only on sun4u-based systems running a 64-bit kernel (Solaris 7 or later), and only for 64-bit processes. (Remember, a 64-bit kernel can run 32-bit processes. A 32-bit process will not have this file in its lwp subdirectory space.)

That completes the listing of files and subdirectories in the procfs directory space. Once again, please refer to the proc(4) manual page for more detailed information on the various files in `/proc` and for a complete description of the control messages available.

8.6.1 Procfs Implementation

Procfs is implemented as a dynamically loadable kernel module, `/kernel/fs/procfs`, and is loaded automatically by the system at boot time. `/proc` is mounted during system startup by virtue of the default `/proc` entry in the `/etc/vfstab` file. The mount phase causes the invocation of the procfs `prinit()` (initialize) and `prmount()` file-system-specific functions, which initialize the `vfs` structure for procfs and create and initialize a `vnode` for the top-level directory file, `/proc`.

The kernel memory space for the `/proc` files is, for the most part, allocated dynamically, with an initial static allocation for the number of directory slots required to support the maximum number of processes the system is configured to support (see "The Kernel Process Table" on page 286).

A kernel `procdir` (procfs directory) pointer is initialized as a pointer to an array of `procent` (procfs directory entry) structures. The size of this array is derived from the `v.v_proc` variable established at boot time, representing the maximum number of processes the system can support. The entry in `procdir` maintains a pointer to the process structure and maintains a link to the next entry in the array. The `procdir` array is indexed through the `pr_slot` field in the process's `pid` structure. The `procdir` slot is allocated to the process from the array and initialized at process creation time (`fork()`), as shown in Figure 8.16.

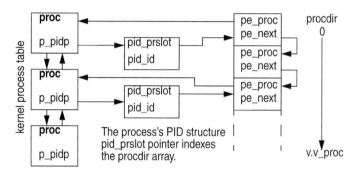

Figure 8.16 procfs Kernel Process Directory Entries

The specific format of the procfs directory entries is described in the procfs kernel code. It is modeled after a typical on-disk file system: Each directory entry in the kernel is described with a directory name, and offset into the directory, a length field, and an inode number. The inode number for a /proc file object is derived internally from the file object type and process PID. Note that /proc directory entries are not cached in the directory name lookup cache (dnlc); by definition they are already in physical memory.

Because procfs is a file system, it is built on the Virtual File System (VFS) and vnode framework. In Solaris, an instance of a file system is described by a `vfs` object, and the underlying files are each described by a `vnode`. The `vfs/vnode` architecture is described in "Solaris File System Framework" on page 531. Procfs builds the `vfs` and `vnode` structures, which are used to reference the file-system-specific functions for operations on the file systems (e.g., mount, unmount), and file-system-specific functions on the /proc directories and file objects (e.g., open, read, write).

Beyond the `vfs` and `vnode` structures, the procfs implementation defines two primary data structures used to describe file objects in the /proc file system. The first, `prnode`, is the file-system-specific data linked to the vnode. Just as the kernel UFS implementation defines an `inode` as a file-system-specific structure that describes a UFS file, procfs defines a `prnode` to describe a procfs file. Every file in the /proc directory has a vnode and prnode. A second structure, `prcommon`, exists at the directory level for /proc directory files. That is, the /proc/<pid> and /proc/<pid>/lwp/<lwpid> directories each have a link to a prcommon structure. The underlying nondirectory file objects within /proc/<pid> and /proc/<pid>/lwp/<lwpid> do not have an associated prcommon structure. The reason is that prcommon's function is the synchronization of access to the file objects associated with a process or an LWP within a process. The prcommon structure provides procfs clients with a common file abstraction of the underlying data files within a specific directory (see Figure 8.17).

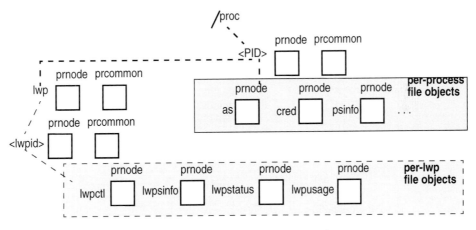

Figure 8.17 procfs Directory Hierarchy

Refer to /usr/include/sys/proc/prdata.h for definitions for the prnode and prcommon structures.

Structure linkage is maintained at the proc structure and LWP level, which reference their respective /proc file vnodes. Every process links to its primary /proc vnode (that is, the vnode that represents the /proc/<pid> file), and each LWP in the process links to the vnode that represents its /proc/<pid>/lwp/<lwpid> file, as shown in Figure 8.18.

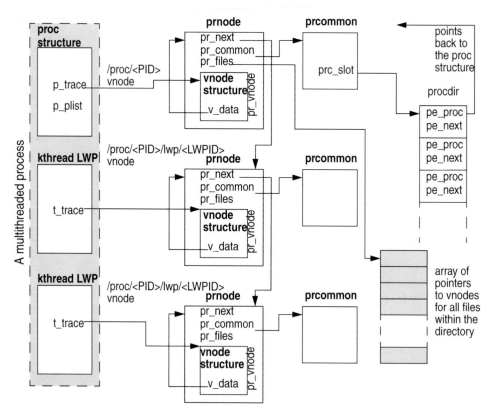

Figure 8.18 procfs Data Structures

Figure 8.18 provides a partial view of what the procfs data structures and related links look like when a procfs file is opened for reading or writing. Note that all of the vnodes associated with a process are linked through the pr_next pointer in the prnode. When a reference is made to a procfs directory and underlying file object, the kernel dynamically creates the necessary structures to service a client request for file I/O. More succinctly, the procfs structures and links are created and torn down dynamically. They are not created when the process is created (aside from the procdir procfs directory entry and directory slot allocation). They appear to be always present because the files are available whenever an open(2) request is made or a lookup is done on a procfs directory or data file object. (It is something like the light in your refrigerator—it's always on when you look, but not when the door is closed.)

The data made available through procfs is, of course, always present in the kernel proc structures and other data structures that, combined, form the complete process model in the Solaris kernel. This model, shown in Figure 8.5 on page 266, represents the true source of the data extracted and exported by procfs. By hiding the low-level details of the kernel process model and abstracting the interesting information and control channels in a relatively generic way, procfs provides a ser-

vice to client programs interested in extracting bits of data about a process or
somehow controlling the execution flow. The abstractions are created when
requested and are maintained as long as necessary to support file access and
manipulation requests for a particular file.

File I/O operations through procfs follow the conventional methods of first opening a file to obtain a file descriptor, then performing subsequent read/write operations and closing the file when completed. The creation and initialization of the
`prnode` and `prcommon` structures occur when the procfs-specific `vnode` operations are entered through the `vnode` switch table mechanism as a result of a client (application program) request. The actual procfs `vnode` operations have
specific functions for the lookup and read operations on the directory and data files
within the `/proc` directory.

The implementation in procfs of lookup and read requests through an array of
function pointers that resolve to the procfs file-type-specific routine is accomplished through the use of a lookup table and corresponding lookup functions. The
file type is maintained at two levels. At the `vnode` level, procfs files are defined as
`VPROC` file types (`v_type` field in the `vnode`). The `prnode` includes a type field
(`pr_type`) that defines the specific procfs file type being described by the pnode.
The procfs file types correspond directly to the description of `/proc` files and directories that are listed at the beginning of this section ("Procfs — The Process File
System" on page 302). Examples include the various directory types (a process PID
directory, an LWPID directory, etc.) and data files (status, psinfo, address space,
etc.).

The basic execution flow of a procfs file open is shown in Figure 8.19.

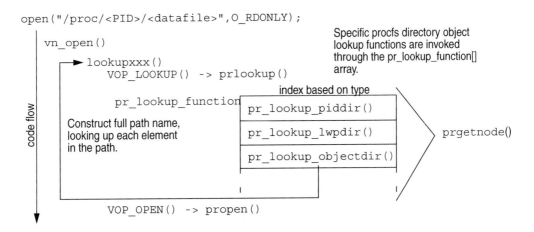

Figure 8.19 procfs File Open

The function flow in Figure 8.19 starts at the application program level, where an
`open(2)` system call is issued on a procfs file. The `vnode` kernel layer is entered

(vn_open()), and a series of lookups is performed to construct the full path name of the desired /proc file. Macros in the vnode layer invoke file-system-specific operations. In this example, VOP_LOOKUP() will resolve to the procfs pr_lookup() function. pr_lookup() will do an access permissions check and vector to the appropriate procfs function based on the directory file type, for example, pr_lookup_piddir() to perform a lookup on a /proc/<PID> directory. Each of the pr_lookup_xxx() directory lookup functions does some directory-type-specific work and calls prgetnode() to fetch the prnode.

prgetnode() creates the prnode (which includes the embedded vnode) for the /proc file and initializes several of the prnode and vnode fields. For /proc PID and LWPID directories (/proc/<PID>, /proc/<PID>/lwp/<LWPID>), the prcommon structure is created, linked to the prnode, and partially initialized. Note that for /proc directory files, the vnode type will be changed from VPROC (set initially) to VDIR, to correctly reflect the file type as a directory (it is a procfs directory, but a directory file nonetheless).

Once the path name is fully constructed, the VOP_OPEN() macro invokes the file-system-specific open() function. The procfs propen() code does some additional prnode and vnode field initialization and file access testing for specific file types. Once propen() completes, control is returned to vn_open() and ultimately a file descriptor representing a procfs file is returned to the caller.

The reading of a procfs data file object is similar in flow to the open scenario, where the execution of a read system call on a procfs file will ultimately cause the code to enter the procfs prread() function. The procfs implementation defines a data-file-object-specific read function for each of the file objects (data structures) available: pr_read_psinfo(), pr_read_pstatus(), pr_read_lwpsinfo(), etc. The specific function is entered from prread() through an array of function pointers indexed by the file type—the same method employed for the previously described lookup operations.

The Solaris 7 implementation of procfs, where both 32-bit and 64-bit binary executables can run on a 64-bit kernel, provides 32-bit versions of the data files available in the /proc hierarchy. For each data structure that describes the contents of a /proc file object, a 32-bit equivalent is available in a 64-bit Solaris 7 kernel (e.g., lwpstatus and lwpstatus32, psinfo and psinfo32). In addition to the 32-bit structure definitions, each of the pr_read_xxx() functions has a 32-bit equivalent in the procfs kernel module, more precisely, a function that deals specifically with the 32-bit data model of the calling program. Procfs users are not exposed to the multiple data model implementation in the 64-bit kernel. When prread() is entered, it checks the data model of the calling program and invokes the correct function as required by the data model of the caller. An exception to this is a read of the address space (/proc/<PID>/as) file; the caller must be the same data model. A 32-bit binary cannot read the as file of a 64-bit process. A 32-bit process can read the as file of another 32-bit process running on a 64-bit kernel.

The pr_read_xxxx() functions essentially read the data from their original source in the kernel and write the data to the corresponding procfs data structure fields, thereby making the requested data available to the caller. For example, pr_read_psinfo() will read data from the targeted process's proc structure, credentials structure, and address space (as) structure and will write it to the corresponding fields in the psinfo structure. Access to the kernel data required to satisfy the client requests is synchronized with the proc structure's mutex lock, plock. This approach protects the per-process or LWP kernel data from being accessed by more than one client thread at a time.

Writes to procfs files are much less frequent. Aside from writing to the directories to create data files on command, writes are predominantly to the process or LWP control file (ctl) to issue control messages. Control messages (documented in proc(1)) include stop/start messages, signal tracing and control, fault management, execution control (e.g., system call entry and exit stops), and address space monitoring.

Note: We've discussed I/O operations on procfs files in terms of standard system calls because currently those calls are the only way to access the /proc files from developer-written code. However, there exists a set of interfaces specific to procfs that are used by the proc(1) commands that ship with Solaris. These interfaces are bundled into a libproc.so library and are not currently documented or available for public use. The libproc.so library is included in the /usr/lib distribution in Solaris 7, but the interfaces are evolving and not yet documented. Plans are under way to document these libproc.so interfaces and make them available as a standard part of the Solaris APIs.

The interface layering of the kernel procfs module functions covered in the previous pages is shown in Figure 8.20.

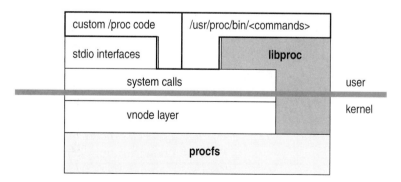

Figure 8.20 procfs Interface Layers

The diagram in Figure 8.20 shows more than one path into the procfs kernel routines. Typical developer-written code makes use of the shorter system call path, passing through the vnode layer as previously described. The proc(1) command is built largely on the `libproc.so` interfaces. The need for a set of library-level interfaces specific to procfs is twofold: An easy-to-use set of routines for code development reduces the complexity of using a powerful kernel facility; the complexity in controlling the execution of a process, especially a multithreaded process, requires a layer of code that really belongs at the application programming interface (as opposed to kernel) level.

The developer controls a process by writing an operation code and (optional) operand to the first 8 bytes of the control file (or 16 bytes if it's an LP64 kernel). The control file write path is also through the `vnode` layer and ultimately enters the procfs `prwritectl()` function. The implementation allows multiple control messages (operations and operands) to be sent to the control file in a single write. The `prwritectl()` code breaks multiple messages into distinct operation/operand pairs and passes them to the kernel `pr_control()` function, where the appropriate flags are set at the process or LWP level as a notification that a control mechanism has been injected (e.g., a stop on an event).

Table 8-3 lists the possible control messages (operations) that are currently implemented. We include them here to provide context for the subsequent descriptions of control functions, as well as to illustrate the power of procfs. See also the `proc`(1) manual page and `/usr/include/sys/procfs.h`.

Table 8-3 procfs Control Messages

Control Message	Operand (arg)	Description
PCSTOP	n/a	Requests process or LWP to stop; waits for stop.
PCDSTOP	n/a	Requests process or LWP to stop.
PCWSTOP	n/a	Waits for the process or LWP to stop. No timeout implemented.
PCTWSTOP	timeout value	Waits for stop, with millisecond timeout arg.
PCRUN	long	Sets process or LWP runnable. Long arg can specify clearing of signals or faults, setting single step mode, etc.
PCCSIG	n/a	Clears current signal from LWP.
PCCFAULT	n/a	Clears current fault from LWP.
PCSSIG	siginfo_t	Sets current signal from `siginfo_t`.
PCKILL	long	Posts a signal to process or LWP.
PCUNKILL	long	Deletes a pending signal from the process or LWP.
PCSHOLD	sigset_t	Sets LWP signal mask from arg.
PCSTRACE	sigset_t	Sets traced signal set from arg.
PCSFAULT	fltset_t	Sets traced fault set from arg.
PCSENTRY	sysset_t	Sets tracing of system calls (on entry) from arg.
PCSEXIT	sysset_t	Sets tracing of system calls (on exit) from arg.
PCSET	long	Sets mode(s) in process/LWP.

Table 8-3 procfs Control Messages (Continued)

Control Message	Operand (arg)	Description
PCUNSET	`long`	Unsets mode(s) in process/LWP.
PCSREG	`prgregset_t`	Sets LWP's general registers from arg.
PCSFPREG	`prfpregset_t`	Sets LWP's floating-point registers from arg.
PCSXREG	`prxregset_t`	Sets LWP's extra registers from arg.
PCNICE	`long`	Sets `nice` value from arg.
PCSVADDR	`long`	Sets PC (program counter) to virtual address in arg.
PCWATCH	`prwatch_t`	Sets or clears watched memory area from arg.
PCAGENT	`prgregset_t`	Creates agent LWP with register values from arg.
PCREAD	`priovec_t`	Reads from the process address space through arg.
PCWRITE	`priovec_t`	Writes to process address space through arg.
PCSCRED	`prcred_t`	Sets process credentials from arg.
PCSASRS	`asrset_t`	Sets ancillary state registers from arg.

As you can see from the variety of control messages provided, the implementation of process/LWP control is tightly integrated with the kernel process/LWP subsystem. Various fields in the process, user (`uarea`), LWP, and kernel thread structures facilitate process management and control with procfs. Establishing process control involves setting flags and bit mask fields to track events that cause a process or thread to enter or exit the kernel. These events are signals, system calls, and fault conditions. The entry and exit points for these events are well defined and thus provide a natural inflection point for control mechanisms.

The system calls, signals, and faults are set through the use of a *set* data type, where `sigset_t`, `sysset_t`, and `fltset_t` operands have values set by the calling (controlling) program to specify the signal, system call, or fault condition of interest. A stop on a system call entry occurs when the kernel is first entered (the system call trap), before the argument list for the system call is read from the process. System call exit stops have the process stop after the return value from the system call has been saved. Fault stops also occur when the kernel is first entered; fault conditions generate traps, which force the code into a kernel trap handler. Signal stops are tested for at all the points where a signal is detected, on a return from a system call or trap, and on a wakeup (see "Signals" on page 320).

Address space watch directives allow a controlling process to specify a virtual address, range (in bytes), and access type (e.g., read or write access) for a segment of a process's virtual address space. When a watched event occurs, a watchpoint trap is generated, which typically causes the process or LWP to stop, either through a trace of a FLTWATCH fault or by an unblocked SIGTRAP signal.

In some cases, the extraction of process information and process control requires the controlling process to have the target process perform specific instructions on its behalf. For example, the pfiles(1) command, which lists the open files of a process and provides information about each opened file, requires the target process to issue a stat(2) system call on each of its open file descriptors. Since the typical process running on a Solaris system spends a fair amount of its time blocking on a system call (not related to procfs), getting control of the target process to perform a specific task requires grabbing the process while it is blocked and preserving the system call state, so it can be restored and resume properly when the controlling process has had its request satisfied.

Procfs implements an agent LWP for this purpose. Rather than complicating state preservation and restoration by using an existing LWP in the target process, procfs provides a facility for creating an agent LWP (note the PCAGENT control message). When an agent LWP is created, it remains the only runnable LWP in the process for the duration of its existence. The agent LWP controls the execution of the target process as required to satisfy the controlling process's request (e.g., executes system calls within the target process). When completed, the agent LWP is destroyed and the process/LWP state is restored. The proc structure maintains a pointer, p_agenttp, that is linked to the agent LWP when one is created. A test on this pointer in various areas of the kernel determines whether an agent LWP exists for the process.

The finer details of the process control directives, how to use them, and the subtleties of the behavior they create are well documented in the proc(4) manual page.

Among its many benefits, procfs enables us to track and extract information about process resource utilization and state changes—the subject of the next section.

8.6.2 Process Resource Usage

The kernel supports the gathering of relatively fine-grained resource-utilization information in the process framework. Resource usage data is a collection of counters, embedded in a structure called lrusage. Both the process and LWP contain an lrusage structure. Data is collected (the counters incremented) during LWP execution. When an LWP terminates, the lrusage data is copied from the LWP to the process-level lrusage structure. Thus, the data reflected at the process level represent the sum total for all the LWPs in the process. Table 8-4 describes the lrusage counters.

Table 8-4 lrusage Fields

Field	Description
minflt	Minor page faults (a page fault resolved without a disk I/O).
majflt	Major page faults (disk I/O required). Incremented in the kernel block I/O pageio_setup() routine, which sets up a buf struct for a page.

Table 8-4 Irusage Fields (Continued)

Field	Description
nswap	Number of times the LWP was swapped out. Incremented in the LWP swapout() code.
inblock	Number of input blocks. Incremented in the kernel block I/O subsystem (bio.c) for block device reads.
outblock	Number of output blocks. As above, incremented in bio.c for block device writes.
msgsnd	STREAMS messages sent. Incremented in the STREAMS common code for putmsg().
msgrcv	STREAMS messages received. Incremented in the STREAMS common code for getmsg().
nsignals	Number of signals received. Incremented in the kernel psig() code, where the LWP is set up to run the signal handler.
nvcsw	Number of voluntary context switches. Incremented when an LWP blocks (is put to sleep), waiting for an I/O or synchronization primitive.
nivcsw	Number of involuntary context switches. Incremented when an LWP is context-switched because it uses up its allotted time quantum or is preempted by a higher-priority kthread.
sysc	Number of system calls. Incremented in the system call trap handler.
ioch	Characters read and written. Incremented in the read/write system call code.

The resource utilization counters do not require enabling microstate accounting for the process or LWP. They are accessible through the usage structure maintained by procfs, where /proc/<PID>/usage represents the process level usage and /proc/<PID>/lwp/<LWP_ID>/lwpusage represents the per-LWP usage data. See the source code in Appendix C, "A Sample Procfs Utility".

Within the process, the operating system maintains a high-resolution time-stamp that marks process start and terminate times. A p_mstart field, the process start time, is set in the kernel fork() code when the process is created, and the process termination time, p_mterm, is set in the kernel exit() code. Start and termination times are also maintained in the LWP when microstate accounting is enabled. The associated process's p_mlreal field contains a sum of the LWP's elapsed time, as derived from the start and terminate times.

The system uses an internal gethrtime() routine, get_high_resolution_time (there is an equivalent gethrtime(3C) API). When get_high_resolution_time is called, it returns a 64-bit value expressed in nanoseconds. The value is not related to current time and thus is only useful when used in conjunction with a subsequent call to gethrtime(). In that case, the difference in the return values from the first call and the second call yields a high-resolution measurement of elapsed time in nanoseconds. This is precisely how it is used when microstate accounting is enabled. For example, the difference between the value of p_mstart, which is set during process creation, and p_mterm, which is set when the process terminates, yields the elapsed time of the process. p_mlreal is the sum total elapsed time, taken in a similar fashion, for the process's LWPs. The fine-grained, nanosecond-level values are derived from a hardware register in the processor that maintains a count of CPU clock cycles (on UltraSPARC processors, it's the TICK register). Processor-specific conversion routines convert the register value to nanoseconds, based on processor clock speeds.

8.6.3 Microstate Accounting

The kernel also supports the notion of microstate accounting, that is, the timing of low-level processing states when microstate accounting is explicitly enabled. Appendix C, "A Sample Procfs Utility", contains the source code for a simple program that turns microstate accounting on for a process and dumps the microstate accounting state times and resource usage counters (described above).

Microstate accounting is the fine-grained retrieval of time values taken during one of several possible state changes that can occur during the lifetime of a typical LWP. The timestamps are maintained in arrays at the LWP and process level. As was the case with resource utilization, the LWP microstates are recorded during execution, and the array in the process is updated when the LWP terminates. The microstate accounting (and resource usage structures) for the process and LWP are shown below.

```
Process level usage and microstate accounting (from /usr/include/sys/proc.h):

        /*
         * Microstate accounting, resource usage, and real-time profiling
         */
        hrtime_t p_mstart;              /* hi-res process start time */
        hrtime_t p_mterm;              /* hi-res process termination time */
        hrtime_t p_mlreal;             /* elapsed time sum over defunct lwps */
        hrtime_t p_acct[NMSTATES];     /* microstate sum over defunct lwps */
        struct lrusage p_ru;           /* lrusage sum over defunct lwps */

LWP level usage and microstate accounting data (from /usr/include/sys/klwp.h):

        struct mstate {
                int ms_prev;                    /* previous running mstate */
                hrtime_t ms_start;              /* lwp creation time */
                hrtime_t ms_term;               /* lwp termination time */
                hrtime_t ms_state_start;        /* start time of this mstate */
                hrtime_t ms_acct[NMSTATES];     /* per mstate accounting */
        } lwp_mstate;

        /*
         * Per-lwp resource usage.
         */
        struct lrusage lwp_ru;
```

By default, microstate accounting is disabled to keep overhead down to a minimum. Turning microstate accounting on must be done programmatically by means of /proc. The process control file, /proc/<pid>/ctl, must be opened and a control message sent in the form of a write(2) to the control file, which requires an operator (PCSET) and an operand (PR_MSACCT). Here is a partial code example of how to enable microstate accounting in a process.

```
int control[2];
int cfd; /* control_file_descriptor */
control[0] = PCSET;
control[1] = PR_MSACCT;
cfd=open("/proc/<pid>/ctl",O_WRONLY);
write(cfd, control, sizeof(control));
```

Once microstate accounting is enabled, it is reflected in a flag at the process level (SMSACCT in the proc structure's p_flag field) and at the LWP/kthread level (TP_MSACCT in the t_proc_flag field). The kernel lwp_create() code tests the process level SMSACCT flag to determine if microstate accounting has been enabled. If it has, then lwp_create() sets the TP_MSACCT flag in the kernel thread. Also lwp_create() initializes the microstate accounting structure, lwp_mstate, regardless of the state of the SMSACCT flag. This allows the kernel to set the start time (ms_start in the LWP's lwp_mstate structure) and initialize the ms_acct[] array.

The kernel implementation of microstate accounting requires only four kernel functions:

- The initialization function init_mstate()
- An update function, new_mstate(), called during state changes
- A function, term_mstate(), to update the process-level data when an LWP terminates
- A function, restore_mstate(), called from the dispatcher code when an LWP/kthread has been selected for execution

At various points, the kernel code tests the TP_MSACCT flag to determine if microstate accounting is enabled; if it is, the code updates the current microstate by a call into the new_mstate() function, which is passed as an argument flag indicating the new microstate.

The microstates defined by the kernel can be found in /usr/include/sys/msacct.h. They reflect the basic execution states of an LWP/kthread: running, sleeping, or stopped. What they provide is finer-grained information about a particular state, such as why an LWP/kthread was sleeping, what mode it was running in, etc. Table 8-5 describes the microstates, as maintained in the procfs process prusage structure.

Table 8-5 Microstates

prusage Field	Flag	Description
pr_utime	LMS_USER	User mode execution time.
pr_stime	LMS_SYSTEM	System (kernel) mode execution time.
pr_ttime	LMS_TRAP	Other system trap time (*other* meaning aside from system call traps, which are accounted for in pr_stime).
pr_tftime	LMS_TFAULT	Time sleeping while waiting for a page fault on a text page to be resolved.
pr_dftime	LMS_DFAULT	Time sleeping while waiting for a page fault on a data page to be resolved.
pr_kftime	LMS_KFAULT	Time sleeping while waiting for a kernel page fault to be resolved.
pr_ltime	LMS_USER_LOCK	Time sleeping while waiting for a user lock (e.g., user-defined mutex lock).
pr_slptime	LMS_SLEEP	Any sleep time not accounted for in the above fields.
pr_wtime	LMS_WAIT_CPU	Time spent waiting for an available CPU.
pr_stoptime	LMS_STOPPED	Time spent stopped (e.g., job control or debug).

The microstate measurements are taken as follows: init_mstate() initializes the microstate date of a new LWP/kthread when the LWP/kthread is created. The init_mstate() function performs the following actions (see the previous page).

- Set the previous microstate, ms_prev, to LMS_SYSTEM.
- Set ms_start to return value of the gethrtime() call.
- Set ms_state_start to return the value of gethrtime() call.
- Set t_mstate in the kernel thread to LMS_STOPPED.
- Set t_waitrq in the kernel thread to zero.
- Zero the msacct[] array.

The LWP/kthread microstate data is thus initialized prior to executing for the first time. The above initialization steps show two additional microstate-related fields not yet discussed. In the kernel thread structure, the current microstate is maintained in t_mstate, and t_waitrq calculates CPU wait time. We will see where this comes into play in a moment.

During execution if TP_MSACCT is set, calls are made to the new_mstate() routine when a state transition occurs. The caller passes new_mstate() a state flag (LMS_USER, LMS_SYSTEM, etc.) that stipulates the new state. The system calculates the time spent in the previous state by finding the difference between the current return value of gethrtime() and the ms_state_start field, which was set during initialization and is reset on every pass through new_mstate(), marking the start time for a new state transition. The ms_acct[] array location that corresponds to the previous microstate is updated to reflect elapsed time in that state. Since the time values are summed, the current value in the ms_acct[] location is added to the new elapsed time just calculated. Thus, the ms_acct[] array contains the elapsed time in the various microstates, updated dynamically when state changes occur. Lastly, the kernel thread's t_mstate is set to reflect the new microstate.

The calls into new_mstate() for the tracked microstates come from several areas in the kernel. Table 8-6 lists the kernel functions that call new_mstate() for specific state changes.

Table 8-6 Microstate Change Calls into new_mstate()

New state	Called from
LMS_USER	System call handler, on return from a system call.
LMS_SYSTEM	System call handler, when a system call is entered.
LMS_TRAP	Trap handler, when a trap occurs (including floating point traps).
LMS_TFAULT	Trap handler (text page fault).
LMS_DFAULT	Trap handler (data page fault).
LMS_KFAULT	Trap handler (kernel page fault).
LMS_USER_LOCK	LWP support code, when a mutex lock is acquired.
LMS_SLEEP	Turnstile code, when an LWP/kthread is about to block.
LMS_WAIT_CPU	Dispatcher code. Not updated in new_mstate(), but updated in restore_mstate() (see text below).
LMS_STOPPED	Signal code, when a job control stop signal is sent.

The last function to discuss apropos of microstate accounting is restore_mstate(), which is called from a few places in the dispatcher code to restore the microstate of an LWP just selected for execution. restore_mstate() calculates the microstate time value spent in the previous state (typically a sleep) by using the same basic algorithm described for the new_mstate() function, and the previous state is restored from the ms_prev field (lwp_mstate structure).

When LWP/kthreads terminate, the microstate accounting data in the ms_acct[] array, along with the resource usage counters, is added to the values in the corresponding locations in the proc structure. Again, the process level resource counters and microstate accounting data reflect all LWP/kthreads in the process.

8.7   Signals

Signals are a means by which a process or thread can be notified of a particular event. Signals are often compared with hardware interrupts, when a hardware subsystem, such as a disk I/O interface (e.g., a SCSI host adapter), generates an interrupt to a processor as a result of an I/O being completed. The interrupt causes the processor to enter an interrupt handler, so subsequent processing, based on the source and cause of the interrupt, can be done in the operating system. The hardware interrupt analogy maps pretty well to what signals are all about. Similarly, when a signal is sent to a process or thread, a signal handler may be entered (depending on the current *disposition* of the signal), analogous to the system entering an interrupt handler as the result of receiving an interrupt.

Quite a bit of history attaches to signals and design changes in the signal code across various implementations of UNIX. These changes in the implementation and interfaces to signals were due in part to some deficiencies in the early implementation of signals, as well as the parallel development work done on different versions of UNIX, primarily BSD UNIX and AT&T System V. This history is summarized in [25] and [10] and is not repeated here.

What does warrant mention here is that early implementations of signals were deemed *unreliable*. The unreliability stemmed from the fact that, in the old days, the kernel would reset the signal handler to its default if a process caught a signal and invoked its own handler but the kernel's reset occurred before the process's handler was invoked. Attempts to address this issue in user code by having the signal handler first reinstall itself did not always solve the problem, because successive occurrences of the same signal resulted in race conditions, where the default action was invoked before the user-defined handler was reinstalled. For signals that had a default action of terminating the process, this behavior created some severe problems. This problem (and some others) were addressed in the mid-1980s in 4.3BSD UNIX and SVR3. The implementation of *reliable* signals— where an installed signal handler remains persistent and is not reset by the kernel—has been in place for many years now. The POSIX standards provide a fairly well-defined set of interfaces for using signals in code, and today the Solaris implementation of signals is fully POSIX compliant. Note that reliable signals require the use of the newer sigaction(2) interface, as opposed to the traditional signal(3C) call. The signal(3C) library does not keep the handler persistent, resulting in the unreliable signal behavior.

The occurrence of a signal may be *synchronous* or *asynchronous* to the process or thread, depending on the source of the signal and the underlying reason or cause. Synchronous signals occur as a direct result of the executing instruction stream, where an unrecoverable error such as an illegal instruction or illegal address reference requires an immediate termination of the process. Such signals are directed to the thread whose execution stream caused the error. Because an error of this type causes a trap into a kernel trap handler, synchronous signals are sometimes referred to as traps.

Asynchronous signals are, as the term implies, external (and in some cases unrelated) to the current execution context. An obvious example is a process or thread sending a signal to another process by means of a kill(2), _lwp_kill(2), or sigsend(2) system call or by invocation of the thr_kill(3T), pthread_kill(3T), or sigqueue(3R) library. Asynchronous signals are also referred to as interrupts.

Every signal has a unique signal name: an abbreviation that begins with SIG, such as SIGINT (interrupt signal), SIGILL (illegal instruction signal), etc., and a corresponding signal number. For all possible signals, the system defines a default *disposition*, or action to take, when a signal occurs. There are four possible default dispositions.

- **Exit** — Terminate the process.
- **Core** — Create a core image of the process and terminate.
- **Stop** — Suspend process execution (typically, job control or debug).
- **Ignore** — Discard the signal and take no action, even if the signal is blocked.

A signal's disposition within a process's context defines what action the system will take on behalf of the process when a signal is delivered. All threads and LWPs within a process share the signal disposition—it is processwide and cannot be unique among threads within the same process. (This is generally true; however, [14] provides an example of setting up a per-thread signal handler based on the process handler. We do not explore that subject in this text). In the process uarea, a u_signal[MAXSIG] array is maintained, with an array entry for every possible signal that defines the signal's disposition for the process. The array will contain either a 0, indicating a default disposition, a 1, which means ignore the signal, or a function pointer if a user-defined handler has been installed.

Table 8-7 describes all signals and their default action.

Table 8-7 Signals

Name	Number	Default action	Description
SIGHUP	1	Exit	Hang up (ref termio(7I))
SIGINT	2	Exit	Interrupt (ref termio(7I))
SIGQUIT	3	Core	Quit (ref termio(7I))
SIGILL	4	Core	Illegal instruction
SIGTRAP	5	Core	Trace or breakpoint trap
SIGABRT	6	Core	Abort
SIGEMT	7	Core	Emulation trap
SIGFPE	8	Core	Floating-point arithmetic exception

Table 8-7 Signals *(Continued)*

Name	Number	Default action	Description
SIGKILL	9	Exit	Kill (cannot be caught or ignored)
SIGBUS	10	Core	Bus error; actually, a misaligned address error
SIGSEGV	11	Core	Segmentation fault; typically, an out-of-bounds address reference
SIGSYS	12	Core	Bad system call
SIGPIPE	13	Exit	Broken pipe
SIGALRM	14	Exit	Alarm clock – `setitimer(2)`, `ITIMER_REAL`, `alarm(2)`
SIGTERM	15	Exit	Terminated
SIGUSR1	16	Exit	User-defined signal 1
SIGUSR2	17	Exit	User-defined signal 2
SIGCHLD	18	Ignore	Child process status changed
SIGPWR	19	Ignore	Power fail or restart
SIGWINCH	20	Ignore	Window size change
SIGURG	21	Ignore	Urgent socket condition
SIGPOLL	22	Exit	Pollable event (ref `streamio(7I)`)
SIGIO	22	Exit	`aioread`/`aiowrite` completion
SIGSTOP	23	Stop	Stop (cannot be caught/ignored)
SIGTSTP	24	Stop	Stop (job control, e.g., ^z))
SIGCONT	25	Ignore	Continued
SIGTTIN	26	Stop	Stopped – tty input (ref `termio(7I)`)
SIGTTOU	27	Stop	Stopped – tty output (ref `termio(7I)`)
SIGVTALRM	28	Exit	Alarm clock – `setitimer(2)`, `ITIMER_VIRTUAL`
SIGPROF	29	Exit	Profiling alarm – `setitimer(2)`, `ITIMER_PROF`, and `ITIMER_REALPROF`
SIGXCPU	30	Core	CPU time limit exceeded (ref `getrlimit(2)`)
SIGXFSZ	31	Core	File size limit exceeded (ref `getrlimit(2)`)
SIGWAITING	32	Ignore	Concurrency signal used by threads library
SIGLWP	33	Ignore	Inter-LWP signal used by threads library
SIGFREEZE	34	Ignore	Checkpoint suspend
SIGTHAW	35	Ignore	Checkpoint resume
SIGCANCEL	36	Ignore	Cancellation signal used by threads library
SIGLOST	37	Ignore	Resource lost
SIGRTMIN	38	Exit	Highest-priority real-time signal
SIGRTMAX	45	Exit	Lowest-priority real-time signal

SIGLOST first appeared in Solaris release 2.6. Releases 2.5. and 2.5.1 do not define this signal and have SIGRTMIN and SIGRTMAX at signal numbers 37 and 44, respectively. The kernel defines MAXSIG (available for user code in /usr/include/sys/signal.h) as a symbolic constant used in various places in kernel signal support code. MAXSIG is 44 in Solaris 2.5 and 2.5.1, and 45 in Solaris 2.6 and Solaris 7. Also, SIGPOLL and SIGIO are both defined as signal number 22. SIGIO is generated as a result of a process issuing an asynchronous read or write through aioread(3) or aiowrite(3) (or the POSIX equivalent aio_read(3R) or aio_write(3R)), to notify the process that the I/O is complete or that an error occurred. SIGPOLL is a more generic indicator that a pollable event has occurred.

The disposition of a signal can be changed from its default, and a process can arrange to catch a signal and invoke a signal handling routine of its own or can ignore a signal that may not have a default disposition of ignore. The only exceptions to this are SIGKILL and SIGSTOP—the default disposition of these two signals cannot be changed. The interfaces for defining and changing signal disposition are the signal(3C) and sigset(3C) libraries and the sigaction(2) system call.

Signals can also be blocked, which means the process or thread has temporarily prevented delivery of a signal. The generation of a signal that has been blocked results in the signal remaining pending to the process until it is explicitly unblocked or until the disposition is changed to ignore. Signal masks for blocking signals exist within the kthread and at the user thread level; the t_hold structure member (the same name is used in both the kernel and user thread) is a sigset_t data type, using set bits to represent signal that are blocked. The sigprocmask(2) system call sets or gets a signal mask for the calling kthread. A non-threaded process has one LWP/kthread pair; thus, t_hold in the kthread becomes the processwide signal mask. An equivalent interface—thr_setsigmask(3T) and pthread_sigmask(3T)—sets and retrieves the signal mask at the user-threads level (t_hold in the *user* thread structure).

The psig(1) command lists the signal actions for a process. The example below dumps the signal actions for our ksh process; we omitted lines to save space.

```
$ /usr/proc/bin/psig 448
448:      -ksh
HUP     caught  RESTART
INT     caught  RESTART
QUIT    caught  RESTART
ILL     caught  RESTART
TRAP    caught  RESTART
ABRT    caught  RESTART
EMT     caught  RESTART
FPE     caught  RESTART
KILL    default
BUS     caught  RESTART
SEGV    default
SYS     caught  RESTART
PIPE    caught  RESTART
ALRM    caught  RESTART
TERM    ignored
USR1    caught  RESTART
USR2    caught  RESTART
CLD     default NOCLDSTOP
PWR     default
            .
            .
            .
RTMAX   default
```

Recall that a signal can originate from several different places, for a variety of reasons. SIGHUP, SIGINT, and SIGQUIT, are typically generated by a keyboard entry from the controlling terminal (SIGINT and SIGQUIT) or if the control terminal is disconnected, which generates a SIGHUP. Note that use of the nohup(1) command makes processes "immune" from hangups by setting the disposition of SIGHUP to ignore. Other terminal I/O-related signals include SIGSTOP, SIGTTIN, SIGTTOU, and SIGTSTP. For those signals that originate from a keyboard command, the actual key sequence that results in the generation of these signals is defined within the parameters of the terminal session, typically, by stty(1). For example, ^c [Control-C] is usually the interrupt key sequence and results in a SIGINT being sent to a process, which has a default disposition of forcing the process to exit.

Signals generated as a direct result of an error encountered during instruction execution start with a hardware trap on the system. Different processor architectures define various traps that result in an immediate vectored transfer of control to a kernel trap-handling function. The Solaris kernel builds a trap table and inserts trap handling routines in the appropriate locations, based on the architecture specification of the processors that the Solaris environment supports: SPARC V7 (early sun4 architectures), SPARC V8 (SuperSPARC— sun4m and sun4d architectures), SPARC V9 (UltraSPARC—sun4u architectures), and Intel x86. (In Intel parlance the routines are called Interrupt Descriptor Tables, or IDTs. On SPARC, they're called trap tables). The kernel-installed trap handler ultimately generates a signal to the thread that caused the trap. The signals that result from hardware traps are SIGILL, SIGFPE, SIGSEGV, SIGTRAP, SIGBUS, and SIGEMT. Table 8-8 lists traps and signals for UltraSPARC.

Table 8-8 UltraSPARC Traps and Resulting Signals

Trap Name	Signal
instruction_access_exception	SIGSEGV, SIGBUS
instruction_access_MMU_miss	SIGSEGV
instruction_access_error	SIGBUS
illegal_instruction	SIGILL
privileged_opcode	SIGILL
fp_disabled	SIGILL
fp_exception_ieee_754	SIGFPE
fp_exception_other	SIGFPE
tag_overflow	SIGEMT
division_by_zero	SIGFPE
data_access_exception	SIGSEGV, SIGBUS
data_access_MMU_miss	SIGSEGV
data_access_error	SIGBUS
data_access_protection	SIGSEGV
mem_address_not_aligned	SIGBUS
privileged_action	SIGILL
async_data_error	SIGBUS

Signals can originate from sources other than terminal I/O and error trap conditions; process-induced (e.g., SIGXFSZ) and external events (kill()) can also generate signals. For example:

- Applications can create user-defined signals as a somewhat crude form of interprocess communication by defining handlers for SIGUSR1 or SIGUSR2 and sending those signals between processes. The kernel sends SIGXCPU if a process exceeds its processor time resource limit or sends SIGXFSZ if a file write exceeds the file size resource limit. A SIGABRT is sent as a result of an invocation of the abort(3C) library. If a process is writing to a pipe and the reader has terminated, SIGPIPE is generated.

- kill(2), sigsend(2), or thr_kill(3T) does an explicit, programmatic send. The kill(1) command sends a signal to a process from the command line; sigsend(2) and sigsendset(2) programmatically send signals to processes or groups of processes. The kernel notifies parent processes of a status change in a child process by SIGCHLD. The alarm(2) system call sends a SIGALRM when the timer expires.

A complete list can be found in any number of texts on UNIX programming (see [32]).

In terms of actual implementation, a signal is represented as a bit (binary digit) in a data structure (several data structures actually, as we'll see shortly). More precisely, the posting of a signal by the kernel results in a bit getting set in a structure member at either the process or thread level. Because each signal has a unique signal number, we use a structure member of sufficient width, such that we can represent every signal by simply setting the bit that corresponds to the signal number of the signal we wish to post. For example, set the 17th bit to post signal 17, `SIGUSR1` (which is actually bit number 16, because they start with 0, and the signal numbers start with 1).

Since more than 32 signals are now possible in the Solaris environment, a `long` or `int` data type is not wide enough to represent each possible signal as a unique bit, so we need a data structure. (In 64-bit Solaris 7, a `long` is a 64-bit data type, but the signal code was developed prior to the implementation of 64-bit data types.) Several of the process data structures use the `k_sigset_t` data structure, defined in `/usr/include/signal.h`, to store the posted signal bits. `k_sigset_t` is an array of two unsigned long data types (array members 0 and 1), providing a bit width of 64 bits, as shown in Figure 8.21. `sigset_t`, defined in `signal.h`, is essentially the same thing as a `k_sigset_t`, except that it is twice the size (four arrays in `sigset_t` as opposed to two in `k_sigset_t`).

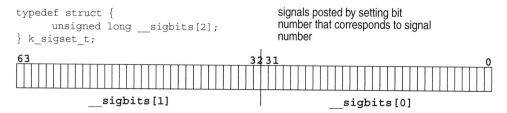

Figure 8.21 Signal Representation in `k_sigset_t` Data Type

8.7.1 Signal Implementation

Our discussion of the signal implementation in Solaris reflects code that first appeared in Solaris 2.5. The discussion is applicable to all releases from Solaris 2.5 up to and including Solaris 7.

The multithreaded architecture of the Solaris environment made for some interesting challenges in developing a means of supporting signals that comply with the UNIX signal semantics as defined by industry standards such as POSIX. Signals traditionally go through two well-defined stages: *generation* and *delivery*. Signal *generation* is the point of origin of the signal—the sending phase. A signal is said to be *delivered* when whatever disposition has been established for the signal is invoked, even if it is to be ignored. If a signal is being blocked, thus postponing delivery, it is considered *pending*.

User threads in the Solaris environment, created by explicit calls to either `thr_create(3T)` or `pthread_create(3T)`, each have their own signal mask. Threads can choose to block signals independently of other threads executing in the same process; thus, different threads may be available to take delivery of different signals at various times during process execution. The threads libraries (POSIX and

Solaris threads) provide the `thr_sigsetmask`(3T) and `pthread_sigmask`(3T) interfaces for establishing per-user thread signal masks. The disposition and handlers for all signals are shared by all the threads in a process, such that a `SIGINT` (for example), with the default disposition in place, will cause the entire process to exit. Signals generated as a result of a trap (`SIGFPE`, `SIGILL`, etc.) are sent to the thread that caused the trap. Asynchronous signals, which are all signals not defined as traps, are delivered to the first thread that is found not blocking the signal.

The difficulty in implementing semantically correct signals in the Solaris environment arises from the fact that user-level threads are not visible to the kernel; thus, the low-level kernel signal code has no way of knowing which threads have which signals blocked and, therefore, no way of knowing which thread a signal should be sent to. Some sort of intermediary phase needed to be implemented: something that had visibility both to the user thread signal masks and to the kernel. The solution came in the form of a special LWP that the threads library creates for programs that are linked to `libthread`; this LWP is called the *aslwp* (it's actually an LWP/kthread pair; remember, they always travel in pairs). The implementation of the aslwp extends the traditional signal generation and delivery phases, by adding two additional steps: *notification* and *redirection*.

Generation -> Notification -> Redirection -> Delivery

Sending a signal (*generation*) to a process causes the aslwp to be *notified*, at which point the aslwp looks for a thread that can take delivery of the signal. Once such a thread is located, the signal is *redirected* to that thread and can then be *delivered*. The exception to this rule is the sending of synchronous or trap signals (listed in Table 8-8). A trap signal, such as a `SIGSEGV`, is not channeled through the aslwp, but rather is delivered to the LWP/kthread that caused the trap, and from there up to the user thread.

Before we delve into the mechanics of signal delivery, we should look at the data types used to support signals in the process, LWP/kthread, and user thread structures.

Figure 8.22 illustrates all the structures, data types, and linked lists required to support signals in Solaris. There are, of course, differences between a multithreaded process and a nonthreaded process. The figure shows a multithreaded process (with only one user thread, for simplicity). Nonthreaded processes are a little easier to deal with because they do not require the use of the aslwp for signal redirection. The major data structures shown in Figure 8.22 are described in Table 8-9 and Table 8-10.

Table 8-9 `sigqueue` Structure

Field Name	Data Type	Description
`sq_next`	pointer	Pointer to `sigqueue` structure for linked list
`sq_info`	`siginfo` struct	Embedded `siginfo` structure (see below)

Table 8-9 sigqueue Structure (Continued)

Field Name	Data Type	Description
sq_func	pointer	Function pointer—references destructor function
sq_backptr	pointer	Points to data structure related to above

The sigqueue structure provides a framework for a linked list of siginfo structures, maintained at the process level, and for multithreaded processes at the LWP/kthread level. siginfo stores various bits of information for many different types of signals. Within the structure are several unions (and in some cases, nested unions), so the available datum depends on how the structure is instantiated during runtime. In the interest of readability, not all union declarations are shown.

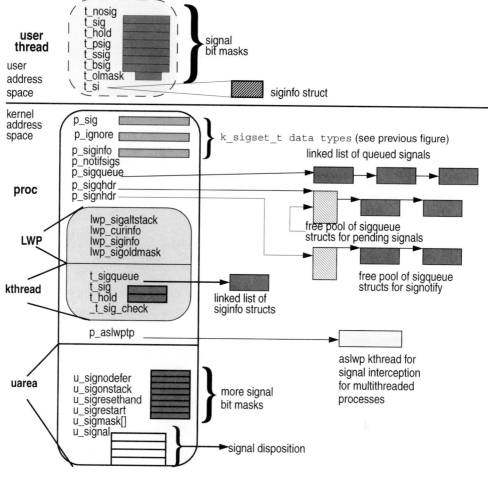

Figure 8.22 Signal-Related Structures

The `siginfo` data is available to processes (well, programs really) that need to know more about the reason a signal was generated. The `sigaction(2)` system call programmatically provides this information. An optional `SA_SIGINFO` flag (in the `sa_flags` field of the `sigaction` structure) results in two additional arguments being passed to the signal handler (assuming of course that the signal disposition has been set up to be caught). The first argument is always the signal number. A non-`NULL` second argument is a pointer to a `siginfo` structure (described in Table 8-10), and a third argument is a pointer to a `ucontext_t` data structure, which contains hardware context information (stack pointer, signal mask, and general register contents) about the receiving process when the signal was delivered. The `siginfo` data can be useful for debugging when a trap signal is generated; for example, in the case of a `SIGILL` or `SIGFPE`, more specific information about the underlying reason for the trap can be gleaned from the data the kernel plugs into `siginfo` when getting ready to send a signal. (See the `sigaction(2)`, `siginfo(5)`, and `ucontext(5)` manual pages.)

Table 8-10 siginfo Structure

Structure or Union	Field Name	Data Type	Description
struct siginfo	si_signo	integer	Signal number
	si_code	integer	A code related to the signal
	si_errno	integer	System call `errno`
union _proc			Proc union datum instantiated in `kill(2)`, `SIGCLD`, and `sigqueue()`
	pid	pid_t	PID
	status	int	SIGCLD–child exit status
	stime	clock_t	child system time
	utime	clock_t	child user time
	uid	uid_t	UID, kill
	value	int	
union _fault			Fault union for `SEGV`, `BUS`, `ILL`, `TRAP`, `FPE`
	addr	caddr_t	fault address
	trapno	int	trap number
	pc	caddr_t	program counter
union _file			File union for `POLL`, `XFSZ`
	fd	int	file descriptor
	band	int	band
union _prof			
	faddr	caddr_t	last fault address
	tstamp	timestruct	timestamp
	syscall	short	system call number

Table 8-10 siginfo Structure (Continued)

Structure or Union	Field Name	Data Type	Description
	nsysarg	char	number of sys call args
	fault	char	last fault code

At the process level, there are three k_sigset_t structures (see Figure 8.22 on page 328):

- The p_sig field has a bit set for each signal pending for the process

- p_ignore represents signals with the disposition set to ignore

- p_siginfo indicates there is information in a siginfo structure about the signal.

The siginfo data structure is embedded in the sigqueue structure, a linked list of which is rooted in the process p_sigqueue pointer for any signals queued to the process. siqueue structures are allocated from a pool pointed to by p_sigqhdr. The pool of sigqueue structures is allocated the first time a sigqueue(2) system call is executed by the process. Thirty-two (the default) sigqueue structures are linked to form the available pool. An additional pool is rooted at the p_signhdr for signotify calls. (The signotify(2) system call is not currently exposed as an API in Solaris—it's used internally from within the POSIX message queue facility.) Signals that have reached the notification phase—they've been generated but not yet delivered—are represented in the p_notifsigs field, along with a condition variable, p_notifcv, for synchronization between the aslwp and the process.

In the embedded uarea, several bit maps are maintained for flagging various signal-related events or forcing a particular behavior, settable by the sigaction(2) system call. An array of pointers exists to signal dispositions: u_signal[MAXSIG], which contains one array entry per signal. The entries in the array may indicate the signal is to be ignored (SIG_IGN) or the default action is set (SIG_DEF). If the signal is to be caught, with a handler installed by signal(3C) or sigaction(2), the array location for the signal points to the function to be invoked when the signal is delivered. The uarea signal fields are described in the following list. The described behavior occurs when a signal corresponding to a bit that is set in the field is posted.

- **u_sigonstack** — Flags an alternate signal stack for handling the signal. Assumes sigaltstack(2) has been called to set up an alternate stack. If one has not been set up, the signal is handled on the default stack. Set by sigaction(2), with the SA_ONSTACK flag in sa_flags field of sigaction structure.

- **u_sigresethand** — Resets the disposition to default (SIG_DEF) when the handler is entered for the signal. The signal will not be blocked when the handler is entered. As above, set by SA_RESETHAND in sa_flags.

- **u_sigrestart** — If inside a system call when the signal is received, restarts the system call. This behavior does not work for all system calls, only those that are potentially "slow" (e.g., I/O-oriented system calls—read(2), write(2), etc.). Interrupted system calls typically result in an error, with the errno being set to EINTR. Set by SA_RESTART in sa_flags.
- **u_signodefer** — Does not block subsequent occurrences of the signal when it is caught. Normally, a signal is blocked when it has been delivered and a handler is executed. Set by SA_NODEFER in sa_flags.
- **u_sigmask[]** — Signals that have been caught and are being held while a handler is executing.
- **u_signal[]** — Signal dispositions.

The LWP stores the current signal in lwp_cursig and stores a pointer to a sig-queue struct with the siginfo data for the current signal in lwp_curinfo, which is used in the signal delivery phase.

Other fields include a stack pointer if an alternate signal stack, lwp_sigaltstack, is set up by a call to sigaltstack(2). It is sometimes desirable for programs that do their own stack management to handle signals on an alternate stack, as opposed to the default use of the thread's runtime stack (SA_ONSTACK through sigaction(2) when the handler is set). The kernel thread maintains two k_sigset_t members: t_sig and t_hold. t_sig has the same meaning as p_sig at the process level, that is, a mask of pending signals; t_hold is a bit mask of signals to block.

In addition, t_sigqueue points to a sigqueue for siginfo data. A signal's siginfo structure will be placed either on the process p_sigqueue or the kthread's t_sigqueue. The kthread t_sigqueue is used in the case where a non-NULL kthread pointer has been passed in the kernel signal code, indicating a directed signal, for example, a multithreaded process with more than one LWP.

Finally, for multithreaded processes, the user thread (not to be confused with the kernel thread) maintains signal masks for pending signals (t_psig), sent signals (t_ssig), bounced signals (t_bsig—more on bounced signals later), and signals to be blocked (t_hold). There is also a siginfo structure for deferred signals, referenced as t_si.

Clearly, there appears to be more than a little redundancy in the signal support structure members spread throughout the various entities that exist within the context of a process. This redundancy is due to the requirements for support of the multithreaded model and the fact that different signals get posted to different places, depending on the signal itself and the source. Earlier in the discussion, we provided several examples of why some signals are sent and where they originate. Asynchronous signals could originate from a user or from various places in the kernel. Signals that are sent from userland (e.g., kill(1), kill(2), sigqueue(2)) are sent to the process. Some signals that originate in the kernel are directed to a particular LWP/kthread; for example, the kernel clock interrupt handler may send a SIGPROF or SIGVTALRM directly to a LWP/kthread. The pthread_kill(3T) and thr_kill(3T) threads library interfaces provide for sending asynchronous signals to a specific *user* thread. The STREAMS subsystem sends `SIGPOLL` and `SIGURG` to the process when appropriate (e.g., polled event occurs or urgent out-of-band message is received).

Regardless of the source of the signal, the ultimate delivery mechanism through the operating system is the kernel `sigtoproc()` function, which takes up to four arguments: a process pointer, a kernel thread pointer, the signal number, and an optional flag, `fromuser`, which indicates whether the source of the signal was the kernel or user. Signals that should be directed to a kthread/LWP call `sigtoproc()` with a valid kthread pointer. A `NULL` kthread pointer indicates the signal should be posted to the process. Let's take a look at the code flow of `sigtoproc()`.

```
sigtoproc(proc pointer, kthread pointer, int signal, fromuser flag)
      if (signal == SIGKILL) /* kill signal */
            Set SKILLED in p_flags
            Set kthread pointer to NULL
      else if (signal == SIGCONT) /* continue - job control */
            Delete queued siginfo structs for pending STOP signals
            (SIGSTOP, SIGTSTP, SIGTTOU, SIGTTIN)
            if (process has an aslwp thread) /* multithreaded processes */
                  Clear SIGSTOP, SIGTSTP, SIGTTOU, SIGTTIN in aslwp t_sig
                  Clear SIGSTOP, SIGTSTP, SIGTTOU, SIGTTIN in p_notifsigs
            if (process has more than one kthread)
                  Loop through kthread linked list
                        Delete siginfo structs for STOP, TSTP, TTOU, TTIN
                  End loop
            else /* process has one kthread */
                  Clear STOP, TSTP, TTOU, TTIN in p_sig
      Clear p_stopsig
      if (process is multithreaded)
            Loop through kthread linked list
                  if (thread is stopped due to job control)
                        Set kthread t_schedflag to TS_XSTART
                        Call setrun /* get the thread running */
            End loop
      if (signal is STOP or TSTOP or TTOU or TTIN)
            Set kthread pointer to the process aslwp thread
            Delete any siginfo structures for queued SIGCONT
            if (process is multithreaded)
                  Clear pending SIGCONT in aslwp
                  Clear pending SIGCONT in p_notifsigs
                  Loop through linked list of kernel threads
                        Delete queued SIGCONT siginfo structures
                        Clear pending SIGCONT in t_sig
                  End loop
            else /* process is not multithreaded */
                  Clear pending SIGCONT in p_sig
      if (signal is discardable)
            return
      if (process has an aslwp kernel thread)
            Set signal bit in aslwp t_sig
            Call eat_signal()
      else if (process is multithreaded)
            Set the signal bit in process p_sig
            Loop through linked list of kernel threads
                  if (eat signal)
                        break out of loop
            if (signal is SIGKILL)
                  Try to run a kthread so signal can be delivered
            End Loop
End sigtoproc
```

Before moving on, we want to reiterate a few key points: a refresher on what the forest looks like before we examine the trees.

First, a high-level view of what `sigtoproc()` does. The `sigtoproc()` kernel function posts a signal to a process or kthread, which simply means "set the bit in the process's `p_sig` field that corresponds to the signal." If `sigtoproc()` is passed a non-`NULL` kernel thread pointer and the signal is directed, the signal is posted to the LWP/kthread, meaning the correct bit gets set in the kthread `t_sig` field. Non-directed asynchronous signals are channeled through the aslwp for redirection to the first user thread it can find that's not masking the signal. Clearly, that's an oversimplification, as the previous pseudocode flow of the function indicates, but it's a good place to start.

The second key point to keep in mind is the different phases involved in processing signals. We mentioned earlier how the Solaris implementation extends the traditional UNIX model of signal generation and delivery by imposing a notification and redirection phase, to support the multithreaded model while maintaining a semantically correct signal implementation. Once a signal has reached its final destination—meaning that the `siginfo` structure has been placed on the queue and the correct bit has been set in the process, LWP/kthread, or user thread—the existence of a signal must be made known to the process/thread so action can be taken. When you consider that a signal is represented by the setting of a bit in a data structure, it seems intuitive that the kernel must periodically check for set bits (i.e., pending signals). This is, in fact, precisely how delivery is done. The kernel checks for posted signals at several points during the typical execution flow of a process:

- Return from a system call
- Return from a trap
- Wake up from a sleep

In essence, the determination of the existence of a signal is a polling process, where the signal fields in the process `p_sig` and kthread `t_sig` fields are examined frequently for the presence of a set bit. Once it is determined that a signal is posted, the kernel can take appropriate action, based on the signal's current disposition in the context of the process that received it.

Figure 8.23 illustrates the process.

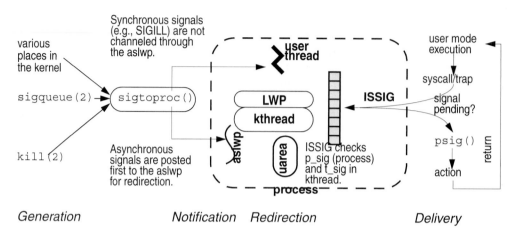

Figure 8.23 High-Level Signal Flow

This signal flow explains why zombie processes cannot be killed (any horror movie fan knows you can't kill a zombie). A process must be executing in order to take delivery of a signal. A zombie process is, by definition, a process that has terminated. It exists only as a process table entry, with all of its execution state having been freed by the kernel.

A lot of the upfront work in `sigtoproc()` deals with job control and the terminal I/O signals. In compliance with the POSIX specifications, this behavior is documented in the `signal(5)` manual page, which we summarize here: Any pending SIGCONT signals are discarded upon receipt of a SIGSTOP, SIGTSTP, SIGTTIN, or SIGTTOU signal, regardless of the disposition. The inverse is also true; if any of those four signals are pending when a SIGCONT is received, they are discarded, again regardless of the disposition. In both cases, the posted signal will be delivered following the flow described in "Synchronous Signals," below.

8.7.1.1 Synchronous Signals

Synchronous signals, or trap signals, originate from within the kernel trap handler. When an executing instruction stream causes one of the events described in Table 4.2, it is detected by the hardware, and execution is redirected to a kernel trap handler. The trap handler code populates a `siginfo` structure with the appropriate information about the trap and invokes the `trap_cleanup()` function, where the function determines whether to stop the kthread/LWP because of a debugger "stop on fault" flag. The entry point into the kernel signal subsystem is through the `trapsig()` function, which is executed next. If the signal is masked or the disposition has been set to ignore, then `trapsig()` unmasks the signal and sets the disposition to default. The `siginfo` structure is placed on the kthread's `t_sigqueue` list, and `sigtoproc()` is called to post the signal.

With reference to the `sigtoproc()` pseudocode flow on page 332, the posting of a trap signal occurs at the segment shown below.

```
/* sigtoproc was passed a non-NULL kthread pointer,
 * indicating a directed signal
 */
Set signal bit in aslwp kernel threadUs t_sig (sigaddset())
Call eat_signal()
```

The signal will be added to the `t_sig` field in the kthread, and the `eat_signal()` function is invoked. The job of `eat_signal()` is to make sure the kthread is going to take delivery of the signal quickly—a sleeping thread is made runnable, taken off the sleep queue, and put on a dispatch queue, and the `t_astflag` in the kthread structure is set. The `t_astflag` will force the thread to check for a signal when execution resumes. With the signal now posted, `sigtoproc()` is done, and the code returns to `trap_cleanup()`. The cleanup code invokes the `ISSIG_PENDING` macro, which will determine from the bit set in the `t_sig` field that a signal has been posted. Once the macro establishes the presence of the signal, it invokes the kernel `psig()` function to handle actual delivery.

The system defines several macros for speeding up the examination of the proc `p_sig` and kthread `t_sig` fields for the presence of a posted signal. The definitions below are from `/usr/include/sys/proc.h`.

```
#define ISSIG(t, why)ISSIG_FAST(t, ttolwp(t), ttoproc(t), why)

/*
 * Fast version of ISSIG.
 *1. uses register pointers to lwp and proc instead of reloading them.
 *2. uses bitwise OR of tests, since the usual case is that none of them
 *    are true; this saves orcc's and branches.
 *    are true; this saves orcc's and branches.
 *3. loads the signal flags instead of using sigisempty() macro which does
 *    a branch to convert to boolean.
 */
#define ISSIG_FAST(t, lwp, p, why)\
(ISSIG_PENDING(t, lwp, p) && issig(why))

#define ISSIG_PENDING(t, lwp, p)\
((lwp)->lwp_cursig |\
    (p)->p_sig.__sigbits[0] |\
    (p)->p_sig.__sigbits[1] |\
    (t)->t_sig.__sigbits[0] |\
    (t)->t_sig.__sigbits[1] |\
    (p)->p_stopsig |\
    ((t)->t_proc_flag & (TP_PRSTOP|TP_HOLDLWP|TP_CHKPT|TP_PAUSE)) | \
    ((p)->p_flag & (EXITLWPS|SKILLED|HOLDFORK1|HOLDWATCH)))
```

Header File <sys/proc.h>

As you can see, `ISSIG` and `ISSIG_FAST` resolve to `ISSIG_PENDING`, which performs a logical OR on the `p_sig` and `t_sig` fields, logically ANDing that result with the return value of `issig(why)`.

The issig() function is the last bit of work the kernel does before actual signal delivery. The "why" argument passed to issig will be one of JUSTLOOKING or FORREAL. The JUSTLOOKING flag causes issig() to return if a signal is pending but does not stop the process if a debugger requests a stop. In the case of a trap signal, issig() is passed FORREAL, which causes the process to be stopped if a stop has been requested or a traced signal is pending. Assuming no special debugger flags or signal tracing, the kernel invokes the psig() signal delivery function to carry out the delivery phase, based on the current disposition of the signal.

8.7.1.2 Asynchronous Signals

Asynchronously generated (interrupt) signals can originate from a user command or program or from somewhere inside the kernel. Such signals are channeled through the aslwp in multithreaded programs. For nonthreaded code, the signal is delivered to the kernel thread within the process.

The aslwp essentially loops forever in an internal call to a function similar to the sigwait(2) system call. When a signal is generated by kill(1), kill(2), thr_kill(3T), sigqueue(2), etc., or from within the kernel, the sigtoproc() function is invoked to post the signal. After sigtoproc() completes the upfront work for dealing with the tty and job control signals, it determines whether an aslwp exists within the process and sets the correct signal bit in the aslwp's t_sig signal mask.

This action wakes up the aslwp, which is looping on an internal sigwait function. When the aslwp first enters its wait function, it unmasks all signals (clears all the bits in the kernel-thread signal mask t_hold). It checks for any pending signals in the notification mask, maintained at the process level in p_notifsigs. Recall that notification follows signal generation and precedes redirection and delivery. Once the aslwp detects the posted signal, it adds it to the notification mask, signifying that it has been notified but that the signal has not yet been delivered. The internal sigwait code moves a new signal from the t_sig field in the aslwp's kernel thread to the p_notifsigs bit mask.

With the signal set in the notification mask, it's time for the aslwp to look for a thread that isn't masking the signal so it can be delivered. An internal thr_sigredirect function conducts this procedure by adding the signal to the user thread's t_bsig field (a "bounced" signal; it was bounced from the aslwp to the user thread).

That done, the signal must be moved to the kthread/LWP to be detected by the ISSIG macro. Remember, the kernel examines the kthread t_sig and the process p_sig fields for a posted signal. The kernel cannot "see" user threads, so an additional function call is invoked to move the signal to the kthread's t_sig field. The function itself is a kernel-level redirect routine; it redirects the signal based on the lwpid, which is maintained in the user thread structure. If the user thread isn't currently running on an LWP/kthread, then the signal remains pending in the user thread's t_bsig mask. The user-level threads library scheduler detects the pending signal when the user thread is scheduled on an LWP/kthread and invokes the redirect function to post the signal at the LWP/kthread level.

Summarizing the sequence of events, we have a thread (aslwp) looping in a function waiting for signals. Signal generation causes the wait function to move the signal to a notification set, which completes the notification phase. The signal is then redirected, first at the user-thread level to the thread's t_bsig field, and then down to the LWP/kthread through a couple of redirect functions. Once posted at the kthread level, the signal is detected by means of the ISSIG macro calls, which are invoked on returns from system calls, traps, and on wakeups from a sleep. If a signal is present, the macro calls the kernel psig() function, which is where signal delivery takes place.

psig() sets up the correct state (stack, registers) for the handling of the signal in two cases: if a handler has been set up by sigaction(2) or signal(3) or if the default disposition of the signal requires something other than ignoring the signal (like stopping the process, terminating the process, or terminating and generating a core file). Remember, signal disposition is processwide—whatever signal handler code runs potentially affects all the threads in a multithreaded process.

8.7.2 SIGWAITING: A Special Signal

The execution of a user-level thread requires the availability of an LWP/kthread for the user thread to get scheduled onto. That part is done by a dedicated scheduling thread in the threads library. (User threads have their own priority scheme and a threads library dispatcher that selects the next user thread to execute. There are quite a few similarities architecturally between the threads library dispatcher and the kernel dispatcher.) Threads do not need to be bound to an LWP when created, and it is not uncommon in multithreaded programs to have many unbound threads scheduled onto a smaller pool of LWPs. Deciding on the optimal ratio of LWPs to user threads is not always straightforward, and suboptimal performance can result from having either too many or too few LWPs. Excess LWPs are more work for the kernel to manage; not enough LWPs can result in runnable user threads hanging around waiting for an LWP to become available, slowing overall execution.

The thr_setconcurrency(3T) interface enables a programmer to provide hints to the operating system as to how many LWPs it should make available for the process. LWPs can also be created in the thr_create(3T) call (THR_NEW_LWP flag), and a user thread can be bound to an LWP with the THR_BOUND flag set.

8.8   Sessions and Process Groups

The kernel creates several groupings of processes representing different abstractions by which it manages various aspects of process control. In addition to the family hierarchy of process parent/child, the kernel implements *process groups* and links processes associated with the same terminal *session*. Both sessions and process groups are collections of one or more processes that have a common relationship or ancestry. The two abstractions, sessions and process groups, are intimately related to each other and tied closely to the signal and terminal (tty) subsystems.

Historically, process groups and sessions arose from the desire to increase the power and flexibility available to UNIX users: developers, systems administrators, and end users. The groups and sessions enable users to run multiple, concurrent jobs from a single login session, to place jobs in the background, bring them into the foreground, suspend and continue jobs, and toggle which job is actively connected to the control terminal (the foreground job).

The kernel maintains process groups and session links to establish an event notification chain in support of job control shells. The signal facility starts and stops processes (or *jobs* in this context), puts processes in the background, and brings them into the foreground. Using the process group linkage makes signal delivery to multiple, related processes much easier to implement. Adding the sessions abstraction puts a boundary between the process group jobs and the interactive login session.

Every process belongs to a process group, identified by the p_pgidp pointer in the process structure, and is established in the kernel fork code when the process is created. Thus, processes in the same parent/child/sibling chain, by default belong to the same process group. The process group ID (PGID) is the process PID of the process group leader. That is, every process group has a process group leader, where the PID and PGID are the same. Sibling processes are assigned the PGID of the parent process; thus, the PGID of siblings will be the PID of the process group leader.

When a standalone process is started from a shell, it is placed in its own process group with the setpgid(2) system call, invoked from the shell code after the process is created with fork(2). Processes grouped on a command line (e.g., a pipeline) will all be part of the same process group. The first process created becomes the process group leader of the new process group, and subsequent processes in the pipeline are added to the group. Here's a quick example:

```
ksh> cat report_file | sort -1 +2 | lp &
```

The shell in the above example is the Korn shell. Three processes will be created, one each for cat(1), sort(1), and lp(1), and all placed in the same process group. That group will be put in the background, where the above *job* crunches away while an interactive user session continues. In this context, a job refers to processes in the same process group working toward a common goal and connected by pipes. The proper job control keystrokes (Control-Z in /bin/ksh) could stop all the processes in the group, sending a SIGTSTP signal to all the processes in the process group. The setpgid(2) system call places the processes in the same process group. Although process groups are most commonly created from the user's shell, an application program can use the setpgid(2) or setpgrp(2) system calls to create new process groups.

Process groups can be in the foreground or the background. The foreground process group is the process group that has access to the controlling terminal, meaning that input characters are sent to the foreground process group and output characters (writes to stdout and stderr) are sent to the controlling terminal. Background process groups cannot read from or write to the controlling terminal. An attempt to read from or write to the controlling terminal by a process in a background process group results in a SIGTTIN (read) or SIGTTOU (write) signal from the kernel to the processes in the background process group. The default disposition for these signals is to stop the processes.

Processes belonging to the same process group are linked on a doubly linked list by pointers in the process structure: p_pglink (points to the next process in the process group), and p_ppglink (points to the previous process). Figure 8.24 illustrates the process group links and the ID name space links (pointers to the PID structures).

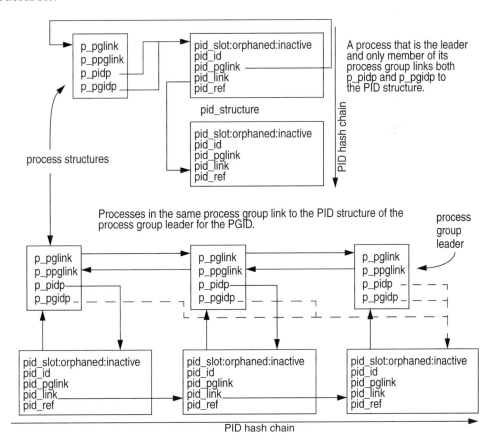

Figure 8.24 Process Group Links

Figure 8.24 illustrates a process as the only member of a process group (upper diagram), and three processes in the same process group (lower diagram). The processes in the lower diagram that are not the process group leader obtain their PGID by linking to the PID structure of the process group leader.

Process groups are a subset of *sessions*; a session has one or more process groups associated with it. A session abstracts a process and the process's control terminal and extends the abstraction to include process groups. All the process groups within a session have a common controlling terminal. Thus, all processes belong to a process group and are associated with a session. Sessions are abstracted by the session data structure, which the process links to through its p_sessp pointer. As with process groups, sessions are inherited through the fork() code.

The control terminal is typically the login terminal the user connects to when logging in to a Solaris system. The phrase *control terminal* is more an abstraction these days (as opposed to an actual, physical terminal) because most login sessions are network based and the *terminal* is a window on the screen of a workstation, implemented by one of many terminal emulation utilities (xterm, dtterm, shelltool, cmdtool, etc.). Network logins (rlogin(1), telnet(1), etc.) are supported through the use of pseudoterminals, which are software abstractions that provide terminal I/O semantics over a network link or through a window manager running under the X Window System. (X windows is the network-transparent windowing system that virtually all UNIX vendors on the planet use for their Graphical User Interface (GUI)-based workstation environments).

A control terminal is associated with a session, and a session can have only one control terminal associated with it. A control terminal can be associated with only one session. We sometimes refer to a session leader, which is the foreground process or process group that has established a connection to the control terminal. The session leader is usually the login shell of the user. It is the session leader that directs certain input sequences (job control keystrokes and commands) from the control terminal to generate signals to process groups in the session associated with the controlling terminal. Every session has a session ID, which is the PGID of the session leader.

The session abstraction is implemented as a data structure, the session structure, and some support code in the kernel for creating sessions and managing the control terminal. The session structure includes the following:

- The device number of the control terminal device special file
- A pointer to the vnode for the control terminal device, which links to the snode, since it's a device
- UID and GID of the process that initiated the session
- A pointer to a credentials structure, which describes the credentials of the process that initiated the session
- A reference count

- A link to a PID structure

The session ID is derived in the same way as the PGID for a process. That is, the session structure will link to the PID structure of the process that is attached to the control terminal, the login shell in most cases. Note that daemon processes, which do not have a control terminal, will have a NULL vnode pointer in the session structure. All processes will thus link to a session structure, but processes without control terminals will not have the vnode link; that is, they have no connection to a control device driver.

Figure 8.25 provides the big picture, illustrating a login session with a process group and showing the links to the related data structures.

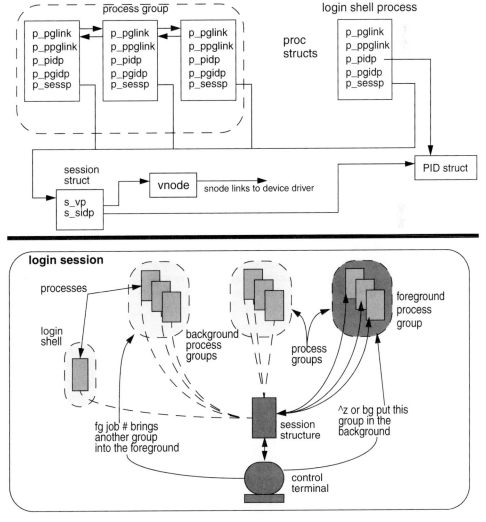

Figure 8.25 Process and Session Structure Links

Figure 8.25 provides two illustrations. The top diagram shows some detail of the data structures and links for a simple case of a login session with two process groups. One process group has only one process, the login shell. The other process group has three processes. They all link to the session structure, which connects to the device and device driver through the s_vp vnode pointer. The session leader is the login shell, and the session ID is the PID of the login shell.

The lower illustration is a broader view, encapsulating a login session (a session) with a shell process in its own process group, plus three additional process groups. One process group is in the foreground, thus attached to the control terminal, receiving characters typed and able to write to the terminal screen. Job control shells use a ^Z (Control-Z) key sequence to place a foreground process/process group in the background. A SIGTSTP signal is sent to all the processes in the group, and the processes are stopped. If a process sets up a signal handler and catches SIGTSTP, the handler is invoked and governs the process behavior.

The session leader (e.g., the shell) handles the communication link to the control terminal by using library calls that translate to ioctl() routines into the STREAMS subsystem. (The character device drivers in Solaris for serial terminals and pseudoterminals are STREAMS based.) The standard C library includes tcsetpgrp(3) and tcgetpgrp(3) interfaces for setting and getting the process group ID for a control terminal.

When processes or process groups are moved from the background into the foreground, the session leader issues a tcsetpgrp(3) call to direct the control terminal to the new foreground process. The tcsetpgrp(3) call results in an ioctl() call into the tty/pty driver code with the TIOCSPGRP flag, which in turn enters the STREAMS subsystem, calling the strsetpgrp() function (STREAM set process group). The data structures associated with the control terminal include a STREAM header structure, stdata, which contains a pointer to a PID structure for the foreground process group. When a new process or process group is placed into the foreground, the sd_pgidp pointer is set to reference the PID structure of the process group leader in the new foreground process group. In this way, the control terminal is dynamically attached to different process groups running under the same session.

The signal mechanism in the kernel that delivers signals to groups of processes is the same code used for other signal delivery. A pgsignal() (process group signal) interface is implemented in the kernel. The function follows the pointers that link processes in a process group and calls the generic sigtoproc() function in each pass through the loop, causing the signal to be posted to each process in the process group.

9

THE SOLARIS KERNEL DISPATCHER

In the previous chapter, we discussed (among other things) the creation and termination of processes and the LWPs and kernel threads within the process. Now we'll talk about what happens in between creation and termination: the scheduling and execution phase, managed by the Solaris kernel dispatcher (a.k.a. scheduler).

The framework on which the Solaris 2.X scheduler is built is rooted in the Unix SVR4 scheduler, which represents a complete rework of the traditional Unix scheduler. The rework incorporated the notion of a *scheduling class*, which defines the scheduling policies and systemwide priority range for kernel threads in a particular scheduling class. The implementation of dispatcher tables for storing the parameters used by the scheduler code was introduced. For each scheduling class, there exists a table of values and parameters the dispatcher code uses for establishing the priority of a kernel thread, which ultimately drives the thread's placement on a dispatch queue—the Solaris queues of runnable threads waiting for an available processor.

In this chapter, we examine the implementation of the kernel scheduler, or dispatcher, in Solaris. We discuss the scheduling classes, the dispatch tables, and the kernel functions that provide the dispatcher infrastructure, including the kernel thread priority scheme and priority algorithms. We take a look at sleep queues and the kernel sleep/wakeup facilities. Finally, we discuss innovative features in the kernel, such as scheduler activations.

9.1   Overview

The Solaris kernel scheduler provides a rich set of features and innovations that contribute significantly to the speed and scalability of the operating system. The Solaris kernel is preemptive; that is, the execution of an operating system kernel thread, or user thread, can be preempted if a higher priority thread becomes runnable. This feature minimizes dispatch latency and is a key component to the implementation of the real-time scheduling class. The preemption mechanism is applied across the entire range of system priorities. In general, if a thread of a higher (better) priority than all threads currently executing becomes runnable, a preemption will occur, forcing the executing thread to relinquish the processor so the higher priority thread can run.

The process of moving a kernel thread on and off a processor (CPU) is referred to as *context switching*, and the Solaris kernel tracks both *involuntary* context switches and *voluntary* context switches. An involuntary context switch occurs when a thread is preempted (because a better priority thread has transitioned to the runnable state) or when an executing kernel thread uses up its allotted time quantum. Voluntary context switches result from a thread executing a blocking system call, such as a file read, where the thread will be context-switched off the processor and placed on a sleep queue. When the event a thread is sleeping (blocking) for occurs, a wakeup mechanism notifies the thread and places it back on a run queue, where it will be scheduled onto a processor, based on its global priority as compared to other runnable threads.

Additionally, a scalable queueing mechanism is employed for runnable threads. Rather than implementing a single, monolithic queue to hold all runnable threads systemwide, the Solaris kernel creates a set of dispatch queues for every processor on a system. Access to the per-processor queues is synchronized by means of locks that exist at the queue level (as opposed to a single dispatch queue lock), providing concurrency on queue manipulation functions.

The Solaris kernel dispatcher implements additional features that enhance the overall usability and flexibility of the operating system:

- **Scheduling classes.** Kernel threads have a scheduling class and priority. Different scheduling classes provide different scheduling policies and priority boundaries.

- **Intuitive priority scheme.** Higher priorities are better priorities (the traditional Unix implementation was so designed that lower priorities were better priorities). The kernel defines a range of global priorities, 0–169. Within that global priority range, a given scheduling class is assigned a subset of the total number of global priorities, as shown in Figure 9.1.

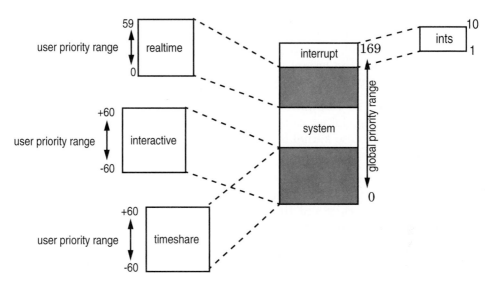

Figure 9.1 Global Priority Scheme and Scheduling Classes

The priority assignments for each scheduling class are shown in Table 9-1.

Table 9-1 Scheduling Class Priority Ranges

Class Priority Range	Global Priority Range	Scheduling Class
0 – 59	000 – 059	Timeshare (TS) and Interactive (IA)
0 – 39	060 – 099	System (SYS)
0 – 9	100 – 109	Interrupt threads (not really a scheduling class) *if* the RT class is *not* loaded
0 – 59	100 – 159	Real-time (RT)
0-9	160 – 169	Interrupt threads if the RT class is loaded

- **Real-time support.** Solaris now provides support for real-time applications, which require a predictable, bounded dispatch latency (the elapsed time between the time when a thread needs to run and the time when it actually begins executing on a processor).

- **Table-driven scheduler parameters.** You can now "tune" the dispatcher for specific application requirements by altering the values in the dispatch table for a particular scheduling class. Note that the altering of the dispatch table values can dramatically affect the behavior of an application, sometimes for the worse if the user or administrator does not understand what the values mean. The SYS class is not implemented by a dispatch table—it exists to allow user threads to execute at a higher priority under certain conditions and to enable execution of non-user-related kernel threads. There is no tuning to be done because SYS class execution does not do time slicing; there is no time quantum.

- **Object-like implementation with loadable module support.** Additional scheduling classes can be created and added to the system without the need for a complete kernel build (e.g., a batch scheduling class was created by Sun Customer Engineering for specific use).

- **Scheduler activations.** Innovative design features address several areas of kernel scheduling, including improved communication between the user-level threads library and the kernel. There is much more on this in "Scheduler Activations" on page 407.

- **Priority inversion addressed.** The issue of a higher-priority thread being blocked from execution because a lower-priority thread is holding a resource (e.g., a lock) needed to run is described as priority inversion. The Solaris dispatcher addresses this problem through priority inheritance.

- **Scalable design.** The major areas of the dispatcher and related data structures implement fine-grained locking, providing excellent scalability on multiprocessor platforms. For example, the kernel implements per-processor dispatcher queues (run queues—queues of runnable kernel threads) with per-queue locking.

9.1.1 Scheduling Classes

Beginning with Solaris 2.0, the system shipped with three scheduling classes by default: system (SYS), timesharing (TS), and real-time (RT). Somewhere around the Solaris 2.4 time frame, the Interactive (IA) scheduling class was added to provide snappier interactive desktop performance. The TS class provides the traditional resource sharing behavior, such that all kernel threads on the system get their share of execution time, based on priority, time spent running, and time spent waiting to run. Priorities are recalculated regularly, so threads that have had more processor time have their priorities worsened and threads that have waited longest have their priorities improved. The IA class implements the same basic scheduling policies as TS (the same dispatch table is used, and most of the same code). IA-class threads are kernel threads that are created under a windowing system (e.g., CDE or OpenWindows) and get a priority boost advantage over TS class threads.

The SYS class exists mostly for operating system kernel threads, such as the threads created at boot time to provide various operating systems services (STREAMS processing, the thread reaper, etc.). SYS class threads are not time sliced and the priorities are fixed. A kernel thread in the SYS class runs until it voluntarily surrenders the processor or is preempted when a higher-priority thread becomes runnable. TS/IA threads can also be placed in the SYS class for a short time if the thread is holding a critical resource; a RW lock, or a page lock on a memory page.

The RT class provides real-time scheduling behavior through a fixed priority scheduling policy that has kernel preemption capabilities. RT class threads have a higher global priority than that of TS and SYS threads. Real-time applications require a minimum, consistent, and deterministic *dispatch latency*, so when an event occurs that a real-time thread needs to process, the thread gets priority over most other threads (all but interrupt threads) on the system for execution on a processor.

Other kernel enhancements were needed to provide real-time application support. The kernel had to be made preemptable, such that a real-time thread that needed a processor could cause the kernel to be preempted from what it was doing in order to allow the real-time thread to run. Most of the kernel is preemptable; a few critical code paths are non-preemptable, for example, when critical state information is saved or manipulated, as during a context switch.

The second thing that needed to be addressed was memory locking. A real-time thread cannot usually afford to be exposed to the latency involved in resolving a page fault, which causes thread execution to be suspended. This problem was addressed by addition of a memory locking facility, so that the developer of a real-time application can use the memcntl(2) system call or mlock(3C) library function to lock a range of pages in physical memory, thus keeping the memory pages resident in RAM.

These features, combined with *processor sets, exclusive thread-to-processor set binding* (see Chapter 1, "System Overview"), and the ability to *take a processor out of the interrupt pool*, combine to make Solaris an outstanding choice for a great many real-time applications. A properly configured system, that is, a system with sufficient number of processors and memory, can provide a dispatch latency on the order of 1 millisecond or less. For absolute minimum dispatch latency for a real-time process or thread, we recommend that you take the following steps.

- Size the system appropriately so the Solaris processor requirements for running kernel threads for memory management, STREAMS processing, network and disk I/O, etc., can be met without impeding system performance. Remember, such processing is done by the kernel on behalf of the applications it is running, which determine the load.

- Configure a processor set (Solaris 2.6 or later). The processor set can have one processor if that meets the real-time application requirements.

- Disable interrupts to the processor set dedicated to running the RT process(es).

- Place your process or processes in the RT scheduling class, and bind them to the processor set.

- If you have more than one RT thread or process, consider whether it needs to be prioritized in terms of one thread or process getting processor time over another, and use priocntl(1) to adjust RT priorities accordingly.

The preceding recommendations give your RT application exclusive access to a processor, or processors, depending on requirements and how many are configured into the processor set. You can add and remove processors from a processor set dynamically while the system and application are running.

Figure 9.2 shows the various scheduling classes supported by Solaris, in their relative positions with respect to global (systemwide) priorities. The range of interrupt priorities depends on whether or not the realtime class has been loaded.

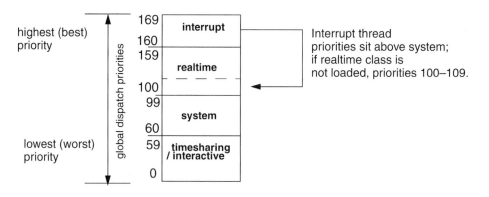

Figure 9.2 Solaris Scheduling Classes and Priorities

The TS, IA, and RT scheduling classes are implemented as dynamically loadable kernel modules. The kernel binaries for the TS class are located in the /kernel/sched directory; the IA and RT classes reside in the /usr/kernel/sched directory. Note that most of the support functions for IA class threads are handled by the TS class code. There are only a few IA-class-specific routines. The SYS class is an integral part of the kernel and thus is not built as a dynamically loadable module. The core dispatcher code is also an integral part of the kernel and is loaded with the initial unix and genunix objects at boot time.

From an architectural perspective, the scheduling class implementation follows an object-oriented design similar to the vfs/vnode architecture described in Chapter 10. Just as the vfs/vnode implementation defined file-system-dependent and file-system-independent routines and used macro calls that resolved to the file-system-specific code (e.g., VFS_OPEN() -> ufs_open() for a UFS file), the kernel dispatcher comprises scheduling-class-specific and scheduling-class-independent functions; it also uses system-defined macros to resolve to a class-specific routine.

In Solaris, a system class array is initialized at boot time, where each entry in the array is an `sclass` structure, one for each of the loaded scheduling classes. The `sclass` structure, shown in Figure 9.3 on page 356, contains the following structure members:

- `cl_name` — Pointer to the class name (e.g., TS for timeshare).
- `cl_init` — Pointer to the class-specific initialization function (e.g., `ts_init()` for initialization of the timesharing class).
- `cl_funcs` — Pointer to a class functions structure; a kernel structure containing pointers to the class-specific functions (e.g., fork, stop, sleep, preempt, etc.).
- `cl_lock` — A kernel lock for synchronized access to the class structure.
- `cl_count` — A counter maintaining a count of the number of threads attempting to load the class.
- `cl_size` — The size in bytes of the class data maintained on a per-thread basis. The size of the structure referenced through the kernel threads `t_cldata` pointer.

The class init routine is called at boot time for all the preloaded scheduling classes. By default, the timeshare and system classes are loaded. The interactive class is dynamically loaded when an X server and Window Manager are started. Only the real-time class is not loaded in a default environment. When a thread is set to the real-time class, with the `priocntl(1)` command or `priocntl(2)` system call, the real-time class module is dynamically loaded by the operating system. You can examine which scheduling classes are currently loaded on the running system with the `dispadmin(1M)` command, as shown below.

```
# dispadmin -l
CONFIGURED CLASSES
==================

SYS      (System Class)
TS       (Time Sharing)
IA       (Interactive)
```

Or, for a bit more information, there's a `class` function in the `crash(1M)` utility.

```
# /etc/crash
dumpfile = /dev/mem, namelist = /dev/ksyms, outfile = stdout
> class
SLOT     CLASS    INIT FUNCTION    CLASS FUNCTION

0        SYS      100fdd10         1042c5a0
1        TS       10137c2c         1045ef90
2        IA       10137d0c         1045f080
```

Now, let's put a process in the real-time scheduling class; process PID 833 is a test program which just sleeps for a minute, then exits.

```
# priocntl -s -c RT -i pid 833
```

Then, we'll take another look at which scheduling classes are loaded on the system:

```
# dispadmin -l
CONFIGURED CLASSES
==================

SYS     (System Class)
TS      (Time Sharing)
IA      (Interactive)
RT      (Real Time)
# /etc/crash
dumpfile = /dev/mem, namelist = /dev/ksyms, outfile = stdout
> class
SLOT    CLASS   INIT FUNCTION   CLASS FUNCTION

0       SYS     100fdd10        1042c5a0
1       TS      10137c2c        1045ef90
2       IA      10137d0c        1045f080
3       RT      102045b8        7802f6e8
```

The class function in crash(1M) provides the class name, the kernel virtual address of the init function for that class, and the address of the class operations table, also known as the class functions structure or class operations vector table. (Operations vector table is a generic term that describes an array of pointers to functions, which is precisely what the class functions [cl_funcs] structure is.)

The class functions structure bundles together function pointers for all of the class-specific (scheduling-class-dependent) kernel routines. They essentially fall into one of two categories: class management and thread control. The kernel switches in to the appropriate routine for a specific scheduling class, using essentially the same method used in the vfs/vnode subsection. A set of macros is defined; the macros resolve to the class-specific function by indexing through either the current kernel thread pointer or the system class array. Both the system class array and kthread structure maintain a pointer to the class functions structure. For example, the class-specific enterclass and exitclass functions are indexed through the system class array. (The functions must be called to enable a thread to enter or exit the scheduling class because the kernel thread link to the class operations table would not yet be in place.) The macro for the enterclass function is shown below.

```
#define CL_ENTERCLASS(t, cid, clparmsp, credp, bufp) \
        (sclass[cid].cl_funcs->thread.cl_enterclass) (t, cid, \
            (void *)clparmsp, credp, bufp)
```

Header File <sys/class.h>

The argument list for the enterclass routine follows the macro name CL_ENTERCLASS. On the second line, the system class array, sclass[], is indexed, using the class ID (cid: each loaded scheduling class has a unique class ID). From there, the pointer to the class functions table, cl_funcs, gets us to the class-specific cl_enterclass code. An example of a macro that uses the kernel thread clfuncs pointer is the preempt routine.

```
#define CL_PREEMPT(tp) (*(tp)->t_clfuncs->cl_preempt)(tp)
```

Header File <sys/class.h>

Here, *tp* is a pointer to the current kernel thread, and the cl_preempt code is entered through the thread's t_clfuncs pointer to the class functions table.

Below is a complete list of the kernel scheduling-class-specific routines and a description of what they do. More details on many of the functions described below follow in the subsequent discussions on thread priorities and the dispatcher algorithms. Each routine name is listed to indicate which scheduling class provides code for a given function. The first five functions fall into the class management category and, in general, support the priocntl(2) system call, which is invoked from the priocntl(1) and dispadmin(1M) commands. priocntl(2) can, of course, be called from an application program as well.

- **ts_admin, rt_admin** — Retrieve or alter values in the dispatch table for the class.
- **ts_getclinfo, ia_getclinfo, rt_getclinfo** — Get information about the scheduling class. Currently, only the max user priority (*xx_maxupri*) value is returned.
- **ts_parmsin, ia_parmsin, rt_parmsin** — Validate user-supplied priority values to ensure they fall within range. Also check permissions of caller to ensure the requested operation is allowed. For the TS and IA classes, a limit check is done against the max user priority (maxupri). For the RT class, the notion of a user priority does not exist, so a range check is made against the max RT priority. The functions support the PC_SETPARMS command in priocntl(2).
- **ts_parmsout, rt_parmsout** — Support PC_GETPARMS command in priocntl(2). Retrieve the class-specific scheduling parameters of a kthread.
- **ts_getclpri, rt_getclpri, sys_getclpri** — Get class priority ranges. For each scheduling class, return the minimum (lowest) and maximum (highest) global priority.

The following functions are for thread support and management.

- **ts_enterclass, rt_enterclass, sys_enterclass** — Allocate the resources needed for a thread to enter a scheduling class. For the TS class, a tsproc structure is allocated. If the requested class ID is IA (remember, IA

class threads use a `tsproc` structure and most of the `TS` support code), make
sure the caller is either root or a member of the windowing system process
group. Initialize the `tsproc` structure members with either user-supplied
values (after validating values and permissions) or default values, and add it
to the linked list of `tsproc` structures. Follow the same procedures as for `RT`
class. The `SYS` class routine is just a stub that returns 0; since there is no sys-
tem-class-specific data structure, there's nothing to allocate or initialize.

- **ts_exitclass, rt_exitclass** — Remove the class-specific data structure
  (`tsproc` or `rtproc`) from the linked list and free it.

- **ts_fork, rt_fork, sys_fork** — Process fork support code. Allocate a
  class-specific data structure (`tsproc` or `rtproc`), initialize it with values
  from the parent thread, and add it to the linked list. The `SYS` fork is a no-op.
  It is called from the `lwpcreate()` and `lwpfork()` kernel functions as part
  of the `fork(2)` system call kernel code when a new process is created.

- **ts_forkret, rt_forkret, sys_forkret** — Called from the kernel
  `cfork()` (common fork) code in support of a `fork(2)` system call. It is the last
  thing done before the `fork(2)` returns to the calling parent and the newly created child process. The `xx_forkret` functions resolve the run order of the
  parent and child, since it is desired that the child run first so the new object
  can be `exec`'d and can set up its own address space mappings to prevent the
  kernel from needlessly having to duplicate copy-on-write pages. In the TS
  class, the child is placed at the back of the dispatch queue and the parent
  gives up the processor. This is handled in another class routine, `ts_setrun`.

- **ts_parmsget, ia_parmsget, rt_parmsget** — Get the current priority and
  max user priority for a thread. The functions are called from the `prio-`
  `cntl(2)` system call. `ts_upri` and `ts_uprilim` from the class-specific structure (`tsproc`, `iaproc`) are returned. `IA` class threads also return the
  `ia_nice` field. For `RT` threads, the `rt_pri` and `rt_pquantum` from the
  `rtproc` structure are returned.

- **ts_parmsset, ia_parmsset, rt_parmsset** — Set the priority of a thread
  on the basis of passed input arguments. A user parameter data structure is
  defined for each scheduling class: `iaparms`, `tsparms`, and `rtparms`. For the
  `IA` and `TS` class, a user priority limit and user priority value can be set. The
  support code checks the user priority or priority limit when a `priocntl()` is
  executed to ensure the values fall within the boundary values for the class
  and also checks credentials to ensure the caller has permission to alter the
  thread's priority. Valid user-supplied priorities for `TS/IA` class threads are set
  in the `ts_upri` field in the `tsproc` structure and factor in to priority adjustments on the thread.

RT class threads do not support the notion of user-supplied priorities in the
same manner as do TS/IA class threads. Where user-supplied priorities for
TS/IA threads nudge the actual thread priority in one direction or another, a
user-supplied priority for RT class threads directly maps to the RT thread's
global priority. Details are provided in "Thread Priorities" on page 369.

- **ts_swapin** — Calculate the effective priority of a thread to determine the eligibility of its associated LWP for swapping in. (Kernel threads are not swappable; LWPs are.) ts_swapin is called by the memory scheduler (sched()). The sched() function might be called from the clock interrupt handler if memory is tight.

  Basically, the scheduler (which should really be called the swapper) loops through all the active processes and, for each active process, executes an inner loop, which walks the linked list of kernel threads, calling swapin for each thread. The effective priority for each kernel thread is based on the amount of time the thread has been swapped out, the user mode priority of the thread, and the address space size. Smaller address spaces are more desirable to swap in, since, if we're running the memory scheduler at all, memory must be tight. The address space is based on the process p_swrss (resident set size before last swap), which is, of course, processwide.

  ts_swapin returns the effective priority of the thread back to the caller, sched(), which then sets a process-level priority that is based on the best kthread effective priority in the list. Note that RT and SYS class threads do not get swapped out, so there's no need for a swap-in function.

- **ts_swapout** — Calculate the effective priority of a thread for swapping out of its associated LWP. Called by the memory scheduler (sched()), the swapout function is passed a pointer to a kthread and a flag to indicate whether the memory scheduler is in hardswap or softswap mode (called from a similar loop in sched(), as described above). Softswap means *avefree* < *desfree*, (average free memory is less than desired free), so only threads sleeping longer than maxslp (20) seconds are marked for swapout. Hardswap mode means *avefree* has been less than *minfree* and *desfree* for an extended period of time (30 seconds), an average of two runnable threads are on the dispatch queues, and the paging (pagein + pageout) rate is high. (See Chapter 12 for discussions about *avefree*, *minfree*, *desfree*, etc.)

  The code is relatively simple; if in softswap mode, set effective priority to 0. If in hardswap mode, calculate an effective priority in a similar fashion as for swap-in, such that threads with a small address space that have been in memory for a relatively long amount of time are swapped out first. A time field in the kthread structure, t_stime, is set by the swapper when a thread is marked for swap-out, as well as swap-in. The timestamp maintained in this field is compared to the current time in both ts_swapin and ts_swapout to determine how long a thread has been either swapped in or swapped out.

- **rt_swapri, sys_swappri** — Stub functions, designed to establish an effective swap priority for RT and SYS class threads. They are not called from anywhere in the kernel.

- **ts_trapret** — Trap return code, called on return to user mode from a system call or trap and designed to readjust the thread's priority.

- **ts_preempt, rt_preempt** — Called when a kernel thread needs to be preempted and must be placed on a dispatch queue. A TS class thread interrupted in kernel mode is given a SYS class priority so it returns to execution quickly. Preemption is discussed in more detail shortly.

- **ts_setrun, rt_setrun** — Set a kernel thread runnable, typically called when a thread is removed from a sleep queue. Place the thread on a dispatch queue. For TS threads, readjust the global dispatch priority if the thread has been waiting (sleeping) an inordinate amount time.

- **ts_sleep** — Prepare a thread for sleep. Set the thread's priority on the basis of wait time or if a kernel priority is requested (the kernel thread's t_kpri_req flag). A kernel priority (SYS class priority) is set if the thread is holding an exclusive lock on a memory page or an RW write lock.

- **ts_tick, rt_tick** — Tick processing for the thread, called from the clock interrupt handler (see "System Clocks and Timers" in Chapter 1). CPU execution time for TS and IA class threads is tracked in the scheduling-class-specific data structure linked to the kernel thread, tsproc (see Figure 9.3 on page 356). ts_timeleft in the tsproc structure is decremented in the ts_tick function for an executing thread that is *not* running at a SYS class priority. TS and IA class threads will sometimes have their priority elevated for a short time by getting a SYS class priority. A thread's execution time for threads running in the SYS class is not tracked because SYS class threads, by definition, run until they voluntarily surrender the processor.

  The ts_timeleft value is tested to determine if the thread has used up its CPU time quantum. If it has, the thread's priority is recalculated and the thread is placed on the appropriate dispatch queue. If it has not, a check is made to determine if a higher-priority thread is waiting for a processor; if that condition is true, then the thread surrenders the processor. If both conditions are false, then the code simply returns, leaving the thread to continue executing on the processor. The kernel also tests for a scheduler activation, known as preemption control, in the tick handler; that topic is discussed shortly.

  The rt_tick handler for RT class threads is similar. If an RT class thread does not have an infinite time quantum and has used its allotted CPU time or if a thread with a higher priority is sitting on a dispatcher queue, the RT class thread is forced to surrender the CPU. Preemption control is not implemented for RT threads.

- **ts_wakeup, rt_wakeup** — Called when a thread is coming off a sleep queue and must be placed on a dispatch queue. TS/IA class threads at a SYS priority are placed on the appropriate queue; otherwise, the priority is recalculated before queue placement. RT class threads are simply placed on a queue.

- **ts_donice, rt_donice, sys_donice** — Called when a nice(1) command is issued on the thread to alter the priority. Adjust the priority according to the nice value for TS/IA class threads. nice(1) is not supported for RT and SYS class threads; the kernel functions for SYS and RT return an invalid operation error. The nice(1) command exists in Solaris for compatibility. Thread priority adjustments should be done with priocntl(1).

- **ts_globpri, rt_globpri** — Return the global dispatch priority that a thread would be assigned, for a given user mode priority. The calculation of the actual dispatch priority of a thread is based on several factors, including the notion of a user priority. See "Thread Priorities" on page 369 for details.

- **ia_set_process_group** — Establish the process group associated with the window session for IA class threads.

- **ts_yield, rt_yield** — Called from the yield(2) system call when a thread is yielding (surrendering) the processor. The kernel thread is placed at the back of a dispatch queue.

The scheduling-class-related structures are depicted in Figure 9.3. The system class array is shown, with pointers to the class operations vector array, the class name, and class-specific init routine. Also shown is a coarse-grained view of the systemwide linked list of kernel threads, each of which is linked to its own class-specific data structure. That structure maintains bits of information used by the dispatcher to manage the execution time and scheduling of the kthread; the structure also maintains a pointer to the class operations array.

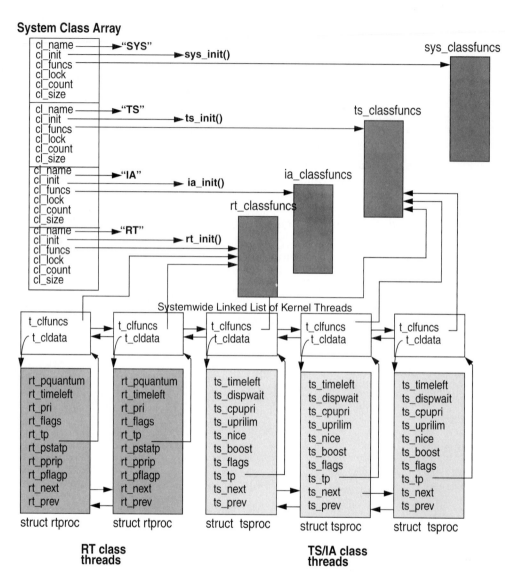

Figure 9.3 Scheduling Class Data Structures

9.1.2 Dispatch Tables

Each scheduling class, except the SYS class, loads with a corresponding dispatch table containing default values for priorities and priority readjustment; in the SYS class, the priorities are defined in a simple array and interrupt, which is not really a scheduling class. You can examine and modify the dispatch tables with the disp_admin(1M) command, for example, dispadmin -c TS -g will dump the current timeshare (TS) and interactive (IA) class dispatch table on your Solaris system. (TS and IA use the same dispatch table.)

```
# dispadmin -g -c TS
# Time Sharing Dispatcher Configuration
RES=1000

# ts_quantum  ts_tqexp  ts_slpret  ts_maxwait  ts_lwait  PRIORITY LEVEL
     200         0         50          0          50       #    0
     200         0         50          0          50       #    1

     .............................................................

      40        48         58          0          59       #   58
      20        49         59        32000        59       #   59
```

Table 9-2 shows the default values for a selected group of timeshare/interactive priorities. In the interest of space and readability, we don't list all 60 (0–59) priorities since we only need a representative sample for this discussion.

Table 9-2 Timeshare and Interactive Dispatch Table

RES	ts_globpri	ts_quantum	ts_tqexp	ts_slpret	ts_maxwait	ts_lwait	PRI
1000	0	200	0	50	0	50	0
	5	200	0	50	0	50	5
	10	160	0	51	0	51	10
	11	160	1	51	0	51	11
	15	160	5	51	0	51	15
	20	120	10	52	0	52	20
	25	120	15	52	0	52	25
	30	80	20	53	0	53	30
	35	80	25	54	0	54	35
	40	40	30	55	0	55	40
	45	40	35	56	0	56	45
	50	40	40	58	0	59	50
	55	40	45	58	0	59	55
	59	20	49	59	32000	59	59

Each entry in the TS/IA dispatch table (each row) is defined by the tsdpent (time-share dispatch entry) data structure (from /usr/include/sys/ts.h), as shown below.

```
 * time-sharing dispatcher parameter table entry
 */
typedef struct tsdpent {
        pri_t   ts_globpri;      /* global (class independent) priority */
        int     ts_quantum;      /* time quantum given to procs at this level */
        pri_t   ts_tqexp;        /* ts_umdpri assigned when proc at this level */
                                 /*   exceeds its time quantum */
        pri_t   ts_slpret;       /* ts_umdpri assigned when proc at this level */
                                 /*   returns to user mode after sleeping */
        short   ts_maxwait;      /* bumped to ts_lwait if more than ts_maxwait */
                                 /*   secs elapse before receiving full quantum */
        short   ts_lwait;        /* ts_umdpri assigned if ts_dispwait exceeds   */
                                 /*   ts_maxwait */
} tsdpent_t;
```

Header File   <sys/ts.h>

The RES and PRI columns are not defined in tsdpent. Those fields, along with the defined members in the structure table, are described below.

- **RES** — (resolution value) Interprets the ts_quantum column in the dispatch table. The reciprocal of RES determines the level of granularity in which the ts_quantum field will be displayed. As the value of RES increases, the ts_quantum column values also increase by the same order of magnitude. See ts_quantum below for more information.

- **PRI** — The class-dependent priority, not the systemwide global priority. The PRI column is derived as the row number in the dispatch table. The dispatch table is like any other generic table—it has rows and columns. Every row corresponds to a unique priority level within the scheduling class, and each column in the row contains values that determine the priority adjustments made on the thread running at that particular priority. This is not the same as ts_globpri.

- **ts_globpri** — The only table parameter (tsdpent structure member) that is not displayed in the output of the dispadmin(1M) command and also the only value that is not tunable. ts_globpri is the class-independent global priority that corresponds to the timeshare priority (column farthest to the right).

  A given scheduling class within Solaris has a range of priorities beginning with 0, which represents the lowest priority for that class. The TS and IA classes have 60 priorities, range 0–59. The kernel implements a global priority scheme, such that every priority level available in every scheduling class can be uniquely identified with an integer value. Refer to Figure 9.2 on page 348 for a list of global priorities when all the bundled scheduling classes are loaded.

  Since TS/IA is the lowest class, the kernel global priorities 0–59 correspond to the TS/IA class priorities 0–59. The kernel computes global priorities at boot time and will recompute if necessary if a new class is loaded into a running system. For example, referring again to Figure 9.2, if the RT class is not loaded, global priorities for interrupt threads will be 100–109, just above system (SYS). If the RT class gets loaded, the global priorities for RT become 100–159, and interrupts are bumped up to 160–169. ts_globpri sets the t_pri field for a timeshare kernel thread when priorities are set and readjusted.

- **ts_quantum** — The time quantum; the amount of time that a thread at this priority is allowed to run before it must relinquish the processor. Be aware that the ts_dptbl(4) manual page, as well as other references, indicate that the value in the ts_quantum field is in ticks. A tick is a unit of time that can vary from platform to platform. On all UltraSPARC-based systems, there are 100 ticks per second, so a tick occurs every 10 milliseconds. The value in ts_quantum is in ticks only if RES is 100. If RES is any other value, including the default value of 1000, then ts_quantum represents some fraction of a second, the fractional value determined by the reciprocal value of RES. With a default value of RES = 1000, the reciprocal of 1000 is.001, or milliseconds. Thus, by default, the ts_quantum field represents the time quantum for a given priority in milliseconds.

  From Table 9-2 on page 357, we see that priority 0 kthreads get 200 milliseconds (20 ticks), priority 10 kthreads get 160 milliseconds, etc. As a kthread's priority gets better (higher global priority integer value), its time quantum is less. Lower (worse) priorities get larger time quantums, since they are scheduled to run less frequently. Changing the RES value by using the -r flag with dispadmin(1M)

  ```
  dispadmin -c TS -g -r 100
  ```

  causes the values in the ts_quantum column to change. For example, at priority 0, instead of a quantum of 200 with a RES of 1000, we have a quantum of 20 with a RES of 100. The fractional unit is different. Instead of 200 milliseconds with a RES value of 1000, we get 20 tenths-of-a-second, which is the same amount of time, just represented differently [$20 \times .010 = 200 \times .001$]. In general, it makes sense to simply leave the RES value at the default of 1000, which makes it easy to interpret the ts_quantum field as milliseconds.

- **ts_tqexp** — Time quantum expired. The new priority thread is set to when it has exceeded its time quantum. From the default values in the TS dispatch table, threads at priorities 0–10 will have their priority set to 0 if they burn through their allotted time quantum of 200 milliseconds (160 milliseconds for priority 10 threads). As another example, threads at priority 50 have a 40-millisecond time quantum and will have their priority set to 40 if they use up their time.

- **ts_slpret** — The sleep return priority value. A thread that has been sleeping has its priority set to this value when it is woken up. These are set such that the thread will be placed at a higher priority (in some cases, substantially higher) so the thread gets some processor time after having slept (waited for an event, which typically is a disk or network I/O).

- **ts_maxwait** — Used in conjunction with ts_lwait. They attempt to compensate threads that have been preempted and have waited a (relatively) long time before using up their time quantum. When a thread begins execution, a field, called ts_dispwait, in the class-specific structure linked to the thread (Figure 9.3 on page 356) counts the number of seconds that have elapsed since the thread began executing. This value is not reset if the thread is preempted (must involuntarily relinquish the processor). Once per second, a kernel routine executes to increment the ts_dispwait field for all TS and IA class threads. If the value of the ts_dispwait for the thread is greater than that of ts_maxwait, the thread priority is set to the value of ts_lwait, a higher priority for the thread since in this circumstance it must have been preempted and never had a chance to use its time quantum.

- **ts_lwait** — The new priority for a thread that has waited longer than ts_maxwait to use its time quantum. Interesting to note is that the default values in the TS and IA dispatch tables inject a 0 value in ts_maxwait for every priority except the highest priority (59). So, just one increment in the ts_dispwait field will cause the thread priority to be readjusted to ts_lwait, except for priority 59 threads. The net effect is that all but the highest priority (59) timeshare threads have their priority bumped to the 50–59 range (ts_lwait) every second.

This process has the desirable effect of not penalizing a thread that is CPU-bound for an extended period of time. Threads that are CPU hogs will, over time, end up in the low 0–9 priority range as they keep using up their time quantum because of priority readjustments by ts_tqexp. Once a second, they'll get bumped back up to the 50–59 range and will only migrate back down if they sustain their cpu-bound behavior.

Priority 59 threads are handled differently. These threads are already at the maximum (highest/best) priority for a timeshare thread, so there's no way to bump their priority with ts_maxwait and make it better. The ts_update() routine, which is the kernel code segment that increments the ts_dispwait value and readjusts thread priorities by means of ts_lwait, reorders the linked list of threads on the dispatch queues after adjusting the priority. The reordering after the priority adjustment puts threads at the front of their new dispatch queue for that priority. The threads on the priority 59 linked list would end up reordered but still at the same priority.

Experimentation has shown that this approach has two results: some percentage of priority 59 threads never get processor time, and the threads that ts_update() puts on the front of the dispatch queue following adjustment get scheduled more frequently. When the ts_maxwait value is set to 32000 for priority 59, the queue is never reordered by ts_update() and every thread has a fair shot at getting scheduled.

You can apply user-supplied values to the dispatch tables by using the dispadmin(1M) command or by compiling a new /kernel/sched/TS_DPTBL loadable module and replacing the default module. The ts_dptbl(4) manual page provides the source and the instructions for doing this. Either way, any changes to the dispatch tables should be done with extreme caution and should be tested extensively before going into production—we've seen dispatch table "tweaks" drastically affect the performance of a system, not always for the better.

The interactive class (IA) uses the timeshare dispatch table. This is not necessarily intuitive; you can specify the TS or IA table to the dispadmin(1M) command, and the command output header will indicate either "Interactive Dispatcher Configuration" or "Time Sharing Dispatcher Configuration," depending on what was specified on the command line. Both classes use the same dispatch table; thus, any changes made for one class affect the other. The IA class was added to make the Solaris window-based desktop environment provide snappier performance. To enhance performance, all processes that started under the windowing system (either OpenWindows or CDE) are put in the IA class, and the priority of processes attached to the window that has the current input focus (the active window—the one being used by the user) is boosted. The procedure uses most of the TS class infrastructure with just a few IA-specific routines, which we discuss in the next section.

For the SYS class (kernel mode priorities), an array is built within the TS class framework to define the kernel mode priorities available to TS/IA class threads when they warrant a priority boost into the SYS class. The config_ts_kmdpris[] array is an array of 40 priorities, values 60–99, and is defined in the tsdptbl (timeshare dispatch table) loadable module that can be modified, compiled, and loaded into the system. (See ts_dptbl(4) for instructions and the module template.) The array is referenced through a ts_kmdpris pointer that points to the first element in the array.

```
/* Array of global priorities used by ts procs sleeping or
 * running in kernel mode after sleep. Must have at least
 * 40 values.
 */

pri_t config_ts_kmdpris[] = {
      60,61,62,63,64,65,66,67,68,69,
      70,71,72,73,74,75,76,77,78,79,
      80,81,82,83,84,85,86,87,88,89,
      90,91,92,93,94,95,96,97,98,99
};
```

The real-time (RT) dispatch table is quite simple, since RT threads run at fixed priorities. The kernel does not change the priority of an RT thread unless explicitly instructed to do so as a result of a priocntl(1) command or priocntl(2) system call. Each entry in the RT dispatch table is defined by the rtdpent data structure in /usr/include/sys/rt.h.

```
 * Real-time dispatcher parameter table entry
 */
typedef struct rtdpent {
      pri_t     rt_globpri;     /* global (class independent) priority */
      int       rt_quantum;     /* default quantum associated with this level */
} rtdpent_t;
```

Header File <sys/rt.h>

The RT dispatch table contains two columns: the rt_quantum field, which is the time quantum for processor execution time, and rt_globpri, which is the system-wide global priority, calculated dynamically when the RT scheduling class is loaded. The rt_quantum field has the same meaning as the ts_quantum field in the TS table, that is, the amount of time a thread at this priority is allowed to run before being scheduled off the processor. Also, just as with the TS table, when the dispatch table is dumped by means of the dispadmin(1M) command, the value is dependent on the RES value. With a default RES value of 1000, rt_quantum is in milliseconds. Also as with the TS table, the PRIORITY column produced by dis-padmin(1M) equates to the row number of the dispatch table entry, which is the same as the class-specific priority level and is *not* the same as rt_globpri, the global priority.

```
# dispadmin -g -c RT
# Real Time Dispatcher Configuration
RES=1000

# TIME QUANTUM                          PRIORITY
# (rt_quantum)                          LEVEL
     1000                      #            0
     1000                      #            1

     . . . . . . . . . . . . . . . . . . . . . . . . . . . .

      100                      #           58
      100                      #           59
```

9.2   The Kernel Dispatcher

The dispatcher is the kernel code segment that manages queues of runnable kernel threads, called dispatch queues; places the highest-priority runnable thread on a processor for execution; and manages the recalculation of thread priorities that are based on execution time, sleep time, and time spent on the queue waiting for a processor. The context switching of threads on and off processors is driven by the dispatcher code.

Early versions of Solaris 2 implemented a simple, global dispatch queue that was shared by all processors on a multiprocessor system. Scalability and dispatch latency, especially for real-time threads, was less than optimal because of the coarse-grained locking. A single scheduling lock for the dispatch queue needed to be acquired for a processor to insert or remove a kthread from the queue, which became a point of contention on busy multiprocessor systems. A new design was done for Solaris 2.3, and since that release, Solaris implements multiple dispatch queues, one for each processor, and a global queue for threads that run at a priority high enough to cause kernel preemption. Such threads are real-time and interrupt threads (although interrupt threads are not placed on a dispatch queue—they live on a linked list off every CPU structure). Solaris 2.5 saw an algorithmic change to the thread selection process (which thread gets execution time next). We go through the *select and ratify* process of thread selection in our discussion of the dispatcher algorithm.

Another change came with the introduction of processor sets in Solaris 2.6. Processor sets can be configured through psrset(1M), where some number of processors are configured into the set, and processes and kernel threads can be bound to a processor set. The bound processes and threads are scheduled only on processors in the set; other threads and processes running on the system that are not bound to the processor set will not be scheduled on processors in the set. Multiple processor sets can be configured, with multiple bindings. (Processor sets are also discussed in Chapter 1, "System Overview.") The addition of processor sets added a new data structure, cpupart, and a modification to the kernel preempt dispatch queues. Prior to Solaris 2.6, only one kernel preempt queue maintained runnable RT class threads. Beginning in Solaris 2.6, there is a kernel preempt queue for each processor set or one queue systemwide if processor sets have not been configured.

The dispatcher uses data stored in different areas of the kernel to maintain scheduling information such as priorities, thread execution time, dispatch queue utilization and state, thread wait and sleep time, per-processor queue data and state, etc. The dispatch tables described in the previous section are just one area of the kernel where scheduling-specific information is stored. In addition to the tables, a scheduling-class-specific data structure is linked to every kthread on the system. These structures, illustrated in Figure 9.3 on page 356, are used by the dispatcher for maintaining bits of information on each thread's execution time, state, and priority.

The class-specific data structures are linked not only to the kthread but also to each other. That is, the class-specific structures are linked on a linked list maintained by the dispatcher code. Many of the fields in the class-specific structures have the same name and meaning across all three scheduling classes (TS, IA, and RT; there is no structure for the SYS class). Hence, we describe each structure in Table 9-3 by using a single row where a structure member has a common name and meaning for more than one scheduling class. The structures take the name of *xxproc*, where *xx* is *ts, rt,* or *ia*.

Table 9-3 Scheduling-Class-Specific Data Structure Members

tsproc	iaproc	rtproc	Meaning
ts_timeleft	ia_timeleft	rt_timeleft	Time remaining in thread's time quantum
ts_dispwait	ia_dispwait	N/A	Wall clock elapsed time since quantum began. Not reset if thread is preempted
ts_cpupri	ia_cpupri	N/A	Priority
ts_uprilim	ia_uprilim	N/A	User priority limit
ts_upri	ia_upri	N/A	User priority

Table 9-3 Scheduling-Class-Specific Data Structure Members (Continued)

tsproc	iaproc	rtproc	Meaning
ts_umdpri	ia_umdpri	N/A	User priority within class
ts_nice	ia_nice	N/A	Nice value
N/A	N/A	rt_pquantum	Time quantum for the thread
N/A	N/A	rt_pri	Priority within RT class
ts_flags	ia_flags	rt_flags	State flags
ts_boost	N/A	N/A	Priority boost value
N/A	ia_pstatp	rt_pstatp	Pointer to pstat
N/A	ia_pprip	rt_pprip	Pointer to thread priority
N/A	ia_pflagp	rt_pflagp	Pointer to p_flag
N/A	ia_mode	N/A	IA on/off flag
ts_tp	ia_tp	rt_tp	Pointer back to kthread
ts_next	ia_next	rt_next	Forward link
ts_prev	ia_prev	rt_prev	Backward link

As we mentioned earlier, the kernel maintains doubly linked lists of the class-specific structures—separate lists for each class. Current implementations of Solaris, up to and including Solaris 7, do not actually use the iaproc for interactive class threads (it's declared in the sys/ia.h header file but not defined anywhere in the kernel code). Threads in the IA class link to a tsproc structure, and most of the class supporting code for interactive threads is handled by the TS routines. IA threads are distinguished from TS threads by a flag in the ts_flags field, the TSIA flag.

Maintaining the linked lists for the class structures greatly simplifies the dispatcher supporting code that updates different fields in the structures (such as time quantum) during the clock-driven dispatcher code. Since most Solaris systems have considerably more TS threads than any other scheduling class, the tsproc lists are managed differently from the RT list.

The kernel builds an array of 16 tsproc structures (array name ts_plisthead) that anchor up to 16 doubly linked lists of the tsproc structures systemwide. The code implements a hash function, based on the thread pointer, to determine which list to place a thread on, and each list is protected by its own kernel mutex (ts_list_lock is an array of 16 kernel mutexes). Implementing multiple linked lists in this way makes for faster traversal of all the tsproc structures in a running system, and the use of a lock per list allows multiple kernel routines to traverse different lists at the same time (see Figure 9.4).

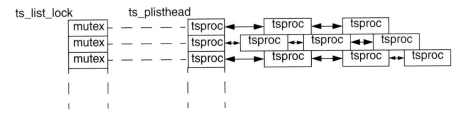

Figure 9.4 `tsproc` Structure Lists

9.2.1 Dispatch Queues

Every processor on the system has its own dispatch queue (actually, a queue of queues), and per-processor scheduling information is maintained in the data structures that describe the processors in the kernel (the CPU structures). Data structures make up the actual dispatch queues, which provide the linkage to the lists of runnable kthreads on the system and state information for each queue. Threads in the TS, IA, and SYS classes are placed on the per-processor dispatch queues.

A separate queue is maintained for threads that are runnable at a priority high enough to cause a kernel preemption. The Solaris kernel is, for the most part, preemptable, such that a processor executing in kernel (system) mode can be preempted so a higher-priority thread can run. Currently, the global dispatch priorities for RT class threads and interrupt threads are above SYS and can generate a kernel preemption. Since interrupt threads do not actually go on a dispatch queue, only unbound RT class threads are placed on the kernel preempt (kp_preempt) queue. There is one such queue systemwide on systems that do not have processor sets configured. A kernel preempt queue is created when a processor set is configured, so there is a per-processor set kp_preempt queue, plus one for the default processor set. Since the kernel will not allow every available processor on a system to be placed in a processor set, the number of kernel preempt queues on a system will always be the number of processor sets configured, plus 1. Without processor sets configured, there is one kp_preempt queue systemwide. We discuss preemption later in more detail.

The creation of the dispatch queues occurs at boot time during the Solaris system initialization. A kernel dispatcher initialization routine, dispinit(), is called from the architecture-specific startup code, which builds the kernel preemption queue and the per-cpu dispatch queues. The kernel data structures that make up the complete dispatch queue picture are the cpu, disp_queue_info, _disp, and dispq structures, as shown in Figure 9.5 on page 368. It is during the dispatcher initialization that the default processor partition is created, which is where the kernel preempt queue (cp_kp_queue) is maintained. In Solaris 2.5.1, which does not have processor sets, the global kernel preempt queue was maintained in a separate disp_t structure, disp_kp_queue.

A quick note on terminology before we proceed. A processor *partition* is essentially the same thing as a processor *set*. A user's view of a processor set is what the kernel references as a processor partition. A different abstraction exists for a possible future implementation, where some processor partitions are visible to the kernel but not visible to the user, so what users see as available processor sets may be different from the kernel's view of usable processor partitions. A default processor partition, which includes all available processors on the system, is created at boot time. As processor sets are created, processors configured into a user processor set are removed from the default partition and added to the configured set. (Processor sets are discussed in "Kernel Processor Control and Processor Sets" on page 411.)

The kernel retains at least one processor for the default partition and does not allow all available processors to be configured into user-created processor sets. Kernel threads that are part of the operating system, such as the daemon threads created at boot time (Chapter 2), pageout, NFS server threads, etc., will not run on a user processor set. That's why a default partition is created at boot time and at least one processor is retained for the default partition. In practice, it is always prudent to assess processor requirements before allocating processor resources by means of processor sets. A system with sufficient processing power for bound application processes may run poorly if CPU resources for the kernel are inadequate.

Several dispatcher-related variables are embedded in each cpu structure.

- **cpu_disp** — An embedded _disp structure; the dispatch queue data for the processor, which contains the link to the actual per-processor queues.
- **cpu_runrun** — A preemption flag indicating that the thread currently running on the CPU will be preempted before switching back to user mode. The user preemption flag.
- **cpu_kprunrun** — Another preemption flag, kernel preemption, indicating that the thread should be preempted immediately or as soon as possible (e.g., return from an interrupt). The kernel preemption flag.
- **cpu_chosen_level** — The priority at which the CPU was chosen for scheduling a kthread. Used by the dispatcher when selecting the next thread for execution.
- **cpu_dispthread** — A pointer to the kthread selected for execution on the CPU.
- **cpu_thread_lock** — A dispatcher lock on the current thread.
- **cpu_last_switch** — A time value: the last time the CPU switched execution to a new thread.

The dispatcher queue structure embedded in the cpu structure is where the per-CPU dispatch queue is rooted. It links to the per-priority dispatch queues maintained for each processor. Within each processor dispatch queue, separate linked lists of runnable kthreads are maintained for every priority level, except real-time lists. Unbound real-time threads are maintained on the global kp_queue. If processor sets are configured, then a kernel preempt queue is configured for each processor set.

Other data the dispatcher needs for queue management and thread scheduling maintained in the dispatch queue structure includes the following.

- `disp_lock` — A synchronization lock to protect fields in the structure.
- `disp_npri` — The number of priority levels in the queue.
- `disp_q` — The pointer to the dispatch queue (pointer to a `dispq_t` structure).
- `disp_q_limit` — Another pointer to a `dispq_t` structure, set to point to the end of the queue.
- `disp_qactmap` — A bitmap indicating which queues actually have runnable threads in them. Using the bitmap in conjunction with `disp_maxrunpri` and `disp_nrunnable`, the dispatcher code can traverse the queues with extreme speed and efficiency, searching for the best runnable thread.
- `disp_maxrunpri` — The priority of the highest-priority thread on the queue.
- `disp_max_unbound_pri` — The priority of the highest-priority unbound thread on the queue.
- `disp_nrunnable` — Total number of runnable threads on the queue.
- `disp_cpu` — A pointer back to the `cpu` structure that owns this queue.

The dispatch queue entry itself is a small, three-member data structure, defined as a `dispq_t` structure. It contains a pointer to the first kthread on the queue (`dq_first`), a pointer to the last kthread on the queue (`dq_last`), and a count of kthreads on the queue (`dq_sruncnt`). Each per-priority queue maintains a count of threads on the queue, and the sum of all per-priority queues is represented in `disp_nrunnable`.

Finally, there's the `disp_queue_info` structure. An array of these structures is created at boot time, one for each processor on the system. Each array member (`disp_queue_info` structure) contains a pointer to one per-process dispatch queue (`disp_t`) embedded in the `cpu` structure. There are two additional `disp_t` pointers, `olddispq` and `newdispq`, and storage space for an old and new queue bitmap field, `oldqactmap` and `newqactmap`, for queue manipulation and maintenance. The number of global priorities in the queue is also maintained in `oldnglobpris`. As we move through the algorithmic flow of the dispatcher code, we'll see how these structures and members are used. Figure 9.5 provides the big picture.

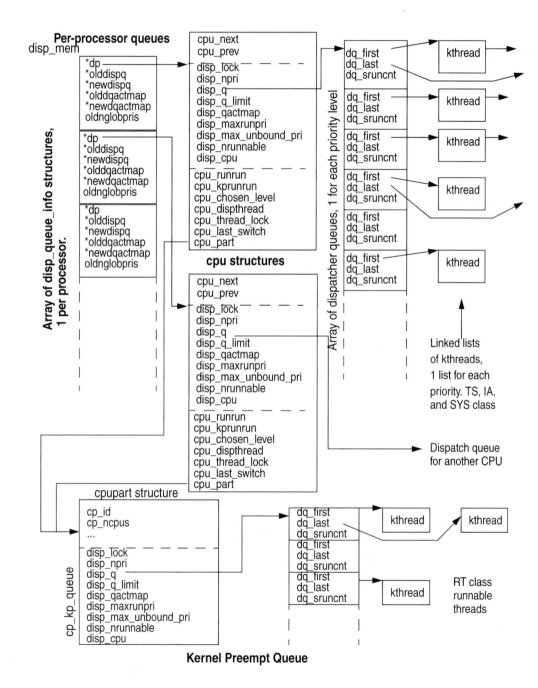

Figure 9.5 Solaris Dispatch Queues

9.2.2 Thread Priorities

The operating system uses a global priority scheme to assign priorities to kernel threads; the priorities are derived from a dispatch table according to the scheduling class the thread belongs to. As we saw, each scheduling class has a range of priorities assigned to it. As scheduling classes load into the system, the kernel must ensure that every priority level across all loaded scheduling classes has a unique priority number.

The range of priorities for the TS/IA class is 0–59, which corresponds to global priorities 0–59 since the TS/IA class is the lowest class on the system. SYS priorities range from 0–39 and are assigned global priorities 60–99 since the SYS class sits directly above the TS/IA class. If the RT class is not loaded, interrupt priorities, range 0–9, occupy global priorities 100–109. Thus, without the RT class loaded, there is a total of 110 (0–109) global priorities. When the RT class (range 0–39) loads, the interrupt thread priorities are bumped up to global priorities 160–169, and the RT global priority range is 100–159. This protocol is represented in Figure 9.2 on page 348 and Table 9-1 on page 345.

During dispatcher initialization, the kernel calculates the maximum SYS global priority value and the total number of global priorities as scheduling classes are loaded. These values are recalculated if scheduling classes are loaded following initialization, for example, if the RT class is loaded sometime after the system has been booted. The calculated values are stored in the system var structure's v_nglobpris and v_maxsyspri field.

```
# /etc/crash
dumpfile = /dev/mem, namelist = /dev/ksyms, outfile = stdout
> v
 .
 .
v_nglobpris: 170
v_maxsyspri:  99
 .
 .
```

Newly created threads inherit their priority and scheduling class from the parent process (parent thread, actually—remember, nonthreaded processes have one LWP/kthread pair). Recall from the previous chapter, the forklwp() kernel routine calls lwp_create(), which in turn calls thread_create(). thread_create() is passed as arguments a thread state (TS_STOPPED—the initial state of a kthread) and priority, which is established from the calling thread. The other applicable kthread structure members are initialized toward the end of the forklwp() code, including the allocation of the class-specific data structure (e.g., tsproc). Entry into the class-specific fork routine through CL_FORK() completes the setup of the dispatcher data for the new thread, initializing the class data structure for the thread and putting it on the linked list of class structures.

The kernel thread structure fields relevant to thread priorities are t_pri, which is the actual global dispatcher priority for the thread, t_epri, which

reflects an inherited priority, and t_kpri_req, which is a flag to indicate to the
dispatcher that a SYS priority is requested for the thread. Other per-thread prior-
ity-related data is maintained in the class-specific data structure linked to the
kthread: tsproc for TS/IA threads, rtproc for RT threads. For TS/IA threads, the
kernel provides a facility for user-level priority adjustments, similar in concept to
the traditional nice(1) command. Unix systems provided a nice(1) command that
allowed users to adjust the priority of the processes they owned. Non-root users
could only make their own process priorities worse (they could be *nice* to the other
users of the system), and root could make priorities better with nice(1). Solaris
supports nice(1) today for compatibility, but the proper way to apply user-level
priorities to threads is to use the priocntl(1) command. Issuing priocntl(1)
with the -l (lowercase l) flag displays the range of user priorities.

```
# priocntl -l
CONFIGURED CLASSES
==================

SYS (System Class)

TS (Time Sharing)
        Configured TS User Priority Range: -60 through 60

IA (Interactive)
        Configured IA User Priority Range: -60 through 60

RT (Real Time)
        Maximum Configured RT Priority: 59
```

The user priority ranges shown in the preceding priocntl(1) command output
clearly do not reflect the range of priorities for the TS/IA class from a kernel perspective. The user priority facility allows a user to move a process or thread priority in a positive (better) or negative (worse) direction. The priority value specified
on the command line can be as high as 60 (maximum potential priority) or as low
as –60 (lowest possible priority). A priority value specified on a priocntl(1) command line does not become the process's or thread's actual global dispatch priority
(as seen with ps(1), e.g., ps -Lc), but rather is used by the dispatcher code to
adjust a kernel thread's priority. A user-supplied priority will alter the global dispatcher priority of the thread in one direction or another, depending on the value
specified.

   For RT class threads or processes, the valid range of priorities is 0–59; the
priocntl(1) output shown above indicates a maximum value of 59. The RT class
does not support the notion of user mode priorities. Priority tweaking of RT
threads involves simply specifying a priority value in the RT class range; then,
that value will be directly reflected in the global dispatch priority of the process.
For example, the global priority range for RT is 100–159, where global priority
100 corresponds to RT priority 0, global priority 120 corresponds to RT priority
19, and so on. So, below, we used priocntl(1) to start a program in real time
and specified a priority.

```
# priocntl -e -c RT -p 59 ./hog &
1016
# ps -Lc
   PID   LWP  CLS PRI TTY      LTIME CMD
  1016     1   RT 159 pts/2    0:03 hog
  1015     1   TS  48 pts/2    0:00 sh
  1017     1   TS  48 pts/2    0:00 ps
```

We specified a priority value of 59 on the command line. Note the actual global dispatch priority of the process we started is 159. This value results from the kernel turning the specified priority into a global dispatch priority. In the case of RT processes and threads, the kernel uses the user-supplied RT priority value as an index into the RT dispatch table to retrieve the corresponding global dispatch priority, as illustrated in Figure 9.6.

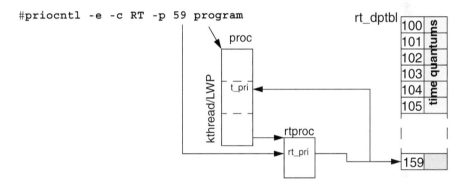

Figure 9.6 Setting RT Priorities

An invocation of the priocntl(1) command to execute a process as a real-time process defaults to the base RT class priority, which is 0, resulting in a global dispatch priority of 100—the value in the 0th entry in the real-time dispatch table (rt_dptbl). The example in Figure 9.6 specifies a value of 59, which the kernel will plug into the rt_pri field of the thread's rtproc structure and use as an index in the dispatch table, rt_dbtbl. The corresponding value is used to set the thread's actual global dispatch priority, 159, in this example. A kernel thread_change_pri() function is called to set the dispatcher priority in the kthread's t_pri field.

User-settable priorities for RT threads is the easy case, which is why we talked about that first. The SYS class is even easier: user-level tweaking of SYS class thread priorities does not exist, period. Which brings us back to TS/IA class threads. First, a quick note before we move on. Kernel threads in the same process can run at different scheduling classes and priorities. A multithreaded process can have LWP/kthread pairs in the TS, IA, SYS, and RT class. The priocntl(1) command, however, does not provide that level of granularity for control. priocntl(1) provides for scheduling class and priority control only on a per-process level, not per LWP/kthread. The priocntl(2) system call has facilities for specifying an LWP ID versus a PID, so code can alter scheduling classes and priorities at the LWP/kthread level.

Several fields in the tsproc structure support the implementation of user mode priorities for TS threads: ts_umdpri, the user priority within the TS class range; ts_upri, the user priority value; ts_uprilim, a boundary (limit) on user priority values; and ts_cpupri, the kernel component of user priorities. ts_cpupri exists essentially to give the kernel some control over user-adjusted priorities (think of it as a throttle). It is used in conjunction with the user priority, ts_umdpri, to index into the TS dispatch table to set new values for both ts_cpupri and the thread's actual priority, t_pri. The ts_uprilim field exists to enable users to place their own throttle on user mode priorities.

The dispatcher uses these values in the kernel for boundary checking on user-supplied priorities and for adjusting a thread's priority as a result of the priocntl() call. Once user priorities are set, they remain in use for subsequent thread priority adjustments. ts_cpupri is set to 29 when the LWP/kthread is initialized; ts_upri and ts_uprilim are initialized to 0. Without an explicit priocntl(1) or priocntl(2) command issued on a process or kthread, the user mode priorities do not factor in to the normal priority adjustments done during the execution life of a kernel thread. If an LWP/kthread has a user priority set and issues a fork(), then the new process LWP/kthread inherits the user-supplied values from the parent thread.

RT class thread priorities are fixed, as oppsed to TS/IA thread priorities, which are adjusted in many places during the life of a thread: after initialization on return from a fork(), when a thread is made runnable by ts_setrun(), upon sleep and wakeup, upon return from a trap, during clock tick processing, prior to a context switch, and during a regular thread update that is executed through the callout queue feature from the clock interrupt handler. The actual priority adjustment is, in some cases, contingent on a conditional test in the code, for example, has a thread been waiting to get on a dispatch queue for an inordinate amount of time? We'll look at some examples to illustrate the mechanics of establishing a thread's priority, starting with TS and IA class threads.

Refer to Figure 9.7, which illustrates the following sequence.

1. After the creation and initialization of the LWP/kthread (fork()), a fork return function is called to set the kthread's priority and place it on a dispatch queue. The inherited ts_cpupri value indexes into the TS dispatch table (1).

2. It creates a new ts_cpupri value that is based on the ts_tqexp value in the indexed table location.

3. The ts_timeleft value is set on the basis of the allotted time quantum for the priority level.

4. ts_dispwait is set to 0. A user mode priority is calculated, setting the ts_umdpri value, which is then used as an index into the TS/IA dispatch table to establish the thread's actual dispatch priority,

5. `t_pri` is determined by the `ts_globpri` (global priority) value in the indexed table location (5).

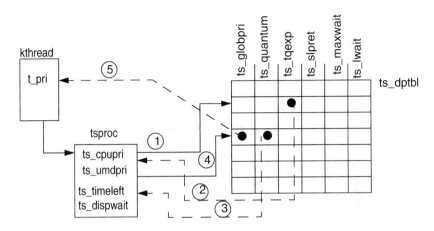

Figure 9.7 Setting a Thread's Priority Following `fork()`

The calculation of the user mode priority (between steps 2 and 3), which is done whenever a TS/IA thread priority adjustment is required, is simple arithmetic, summing the `ts_cpupri`, `ts_upri`, and `ts_boost` values. `ts_boost` is used for IA class threads as a means of boosting the priority by a value of 10. `ts_umdpri` is set to the sum of `ts_cpupri`, `ts_upri`, and `ts_boost` and is tested against some boundary values; it cannot be greater than the maximum TS/IA class priority, 59, or less than 0.

The other relevant step taken in the fork return code is the setting of the `ts_timeleft` and `ts_dispwait` fields in the kthread's `tsproc` structure. `ts_timeleft` tracks execution time when the kthread is running on a processor and is decremented in the clock tick handler (if the thread is actually running on a processor, of course). When `ts_timeleft` counts down to 0, the kthread has used its time quantum and is context-switched off the processor. `ts_dispwait` tracks how much time the thread has spent sitting on a dispatch queue, waiting to get context-switched onto a processor for execution. For all threads on a dispatch queue, `ts_dispwait` is updated once a second by the `ts_update()` thread, which is run out of the callout queue from the clock interrupt handler (more on this in a minute).

When the priority work has been done and `t_pri` in the kernel thread has a valid dispatch priority, the thread is ready to be placed on a dispatch queue; such placement is ultimately done by one of the dispatcher queue management functions, `setfrontdq()` or `setbackdq()`. How these functions work and whether a kthread ends up at the front or back of a queue are matters we'll get into in just a bit.

Once a kthread is off and running, it can go through potentially many state changes that determine how and where priority adjustments are made. A typical thread spends time executing, gets interrupted, gets preempted, issues a blocking system call causing the thread to be placed on a sleep queue, and so forth. Class-specific functions are called and act appropriately as dictated by the transition and the dispatcher-related values in the thread's `tsproc` structure for priority adjustment. For example, if a thread burns through its allotted time quantum (as set from the `ts_quantum` value in the dispatch table, Figure 9.7, step 3), the kthread is switched off the processor and given a new dispatch priority.

The scheduling-class-specific clock tick handler is called from the system clock interrupt handler for each CPU that has a noninterrupt thread running on it. When the `ts_tick()` function is entered, the `ts_timeleft` value is decremented and tested. If `ts_timeleft` reaches 0, the time quantum has expired for the kthread. This is the case for TS/IA threads that are not at a SYS class priority—threads running at a SYS class priority are not time sliced. Assuming an expired time quantum, the code tests to see if a *scheduler activation* has been turned on for the thread, in the form of *preemption control*.

Solaris provides an innovative facility, called preemption control, for stretching a thread's time quantum for a short time. Preemption control does not require altering priorities or dispatcher table values. Using a simple API— `schedctl_init(3X)`, `schedctl_start(3X)`, `schedctl_stop(3X)`—programmers can develop code that initializes and turns on a preemption control for a kthread. What this does is effectively give the kthread a few extra clock ticks of execution time on a processor, beyond its time quantum, before it is switched off. This feature addresses situations where a thread is holding a critical resource, such as a mutex lock (an application-level mutex lock, not a kernel mutex lock) and a few extra ticks of execution time will allow the kthread to complete its task and free the lock. Otherwise, if the thread is taken off the processor before releasing the resource, other threads that need the same resource will begin to block, waiting for the resource to be freed. This behavior requires that the thread holding the resource work its way up the dispatch queue for rescheduling.

The use of preemption control in application code is illustrated in the following pseudocode, showing preemption control being turned on and then off around the acquisition and freeing of a mutex lock.

```
mutex_t mylock;
mutex_init(&mylock);
schedctl_init();
  .
  .
schedctl_start();
mutex_lock(&mylock);

        do work while holding the mutex

mutex_unlock(&mylock);
schedctl_stop();
```

Without the activation turned on to enable preemption control, there's a greater possibility that the kthread will be forced to surrender the processor before it is able to free the lock. Think of preemption control as a means of telling the dispatcher "I'm about to grab a critical resource, so grant me a little extra execution time."

Getting back to the `ts_tick()` code, we've entered the main processing segment of `ts_tick()` because the kthread was *not* running at a SYS class priority *and* its time quantum has expired. If preemption control has been turned on for the kthread, it is allowed an extra couple of clock ticks to execute, no priority tweaks are done, and `ts_tick()` is finished with the thread. There is a limit to how many additional clock ticks a kthread with preemption control turned on will be given. If that limit has been exceeded, the kernel sets a flag such that the thread will get one more time slice and on the next pass through `ts_tick()`, the preemption control test will fail and normal tick processing will be done. In this way, the kernel does not allow the scheduler activation to keep the thread running indefinitely. If the requirement is that the thread must stay on the processor indefinitely, the RT class should be used.

Regular TS/IA tick processing involves adjusting the thread priority in the same way the priority is set in the fork return code (Figure 9.7 on page 373). `ts_cpupri` is used as an index into the TS dispatch table and is assigned a new value that is based on `ts_tqexp` from the indexed location. The user mode priority is calculated, `ts_dispwait` is set to 0, and a new dispatcher priority is derived from the TS/IA dispatch table. The new priority is based on the global priority value in the table row corresponding to `ts_umdpri`, which is used as the dispatch table array index. What's different between the `ts_tick()` handler and the fork return scenario is that the thread's priority is not set directly in `ts_tick()`, but rather in a `thread_change_pri()` kernel function. A change in a thread's priority may warrant a change in its position on a queue; `thread_change_pri()` handles such a case. In the fork return, we are dealing with a new thread that has not yet been on a queue, so it's not an issue.

By design for TS/IA class threads, the adjusted priority in the preceding scenario will end up being something worse than the thread was previously. If a thread consumed its entire time quantum, it gets a worse priority to allow other threads a better opportunity to obtain processor time. You can test this behavior by plugging in some actual values, walking through the adjustment sequence as we described it, and figuring out where the thread's priority lands after the thread uses a full time quantum.

Here's a quick example, assuming a simple case of no user mode priority.

- A kthread starts with a `ts_cpupri` value of 29, which puts it right in the middle of the TS/IA priority range (which we're assuming is why the default value of 29 was chosen). The `ts_tqexp` value at table location 29 (the 28th row, because the count starts at 0) is 18.

- Thus, the new `ts_cpupri` value is 18, which also becomes the `ts_umdpri` value when the user mode priority is calculated—since `ts_upri` and `ts_boost` are zero values (no user priority, and it's a TS class thread, so no priority boost).
- The global dispatch priority at index location 18 is 17, so the kthread's initial priority (`t_pri`) is 17, with a 120 clock tick time quantum (derived by using `ts_cpupri` as an index).
- When 120 ticks are gone and `ts_timeleft` has clicked down to 0, we'll essentially repeat the steps to get the new priority.
- `ts_cpupri` is now 18, the `ts_tqexp` value at the corresponding table location is 7, so the new `ts_cpupri` value is 7, which again becomes `ts_umdpri` after the user mode priority is calculated.
- The global dispatch priority at the 7th array location is 6, so the kthread's priority after the kthread uses its time quantum will go from 17 to 6, a worse priority. Its time quantum is larger, at 160 clock ticks, so it will wait longer to run but will get more clock ticks when it does execute. The behavior is consistent with the targeted behavior of timeshare class threads. As threads get more execution time, their priority is worsened; as threads spend more time waiting to run, their priority is improved.

The second case we'll look at centers around kthread sleep and wakeup. Specifics of the sleep queue implementation and wakeup mechanism are discussed in the next section, but we can still examine the priority component of those state changes without detracting from either discussion.

- The `ts_sleep()` function handles the preparation of a TS/IA class thread for sleep. The code tests the `t_kpri_req` flag (kernel priority requested), which will be set if the thread is holding a kernel RW lock or an exclusive page lock on a memory page when the sleep function is invoked. If `t_kpri_req` is set, the thread priority, `t_pri`, is set to 100, the lowest SYS class priority, which puts it above all TS/IA class priorities.
- The kthreads TSKPRI flag is set to indicate that thread is at a SYS priority.

  If a kernel priority has not been requested for the thread, the `ts_sleep()` code tests the `ts_dispwait` value (how long the thread has been waiting on a dispatcher queue) against the `ts_maxwait` value in the dispatch table, as indexed by `ts_umdpri`, which will index the same row used to retrieve the global priority the last time it was set. The test looks something like this.

```
if (kthread->tsproc.ts_dispwait > ts_dptbl[ts_umdpri].ts_maxwait)
```

  That condition is `true` if the thread has been waiting a relatively long time for processor cycles.

- The priority is recomputed, as previously described, with one significant difference. The `ts_cpupri` value is set from the `ts_slpret` (sleep return priority) column in the TS/IA dispatch table, not the `ts_tqexp` column, as was the case in the previous example. The `ts_slpret` priorities give the thread a high priority so they are scheduled sooner than most other TS/IA threads sitting on the dispatch queues.

- The final scenario in the `ts_sleep()` code is entered *if* the thread has *not* had a kernel priority requested and *if* the thread has *not* been waiting longer than `ts_maxwait` (the first two scenarios just described).

  If those two conditions are not `true` and if the thread is already at a SYS priority, the thread's priority is set back to a TS/IA class priority, with `ts_umdpri` used as an index into the TS/IA dispatch table and `t_pri` set to the corresponding global priority.

  If none of the three conditions is true—which means the thread is not at a SYS priority, is not required to be assigned a SYS priority, and has not been waiting an inordinate amount of time—then the `ts_sleep()` code essentially does nothing and simply returns to the caller without having altered any of the thread's dispatcher properties. The thread will get another shot at having its priority tweaked in the wakeup code.

- The wakeup function places the kthread on a dispatch queue and adjusts the thread priority only if the thread wait test described previously is `true`; that is, the thread's `ts_dispwait` value was greater than `ts_maxwait`, again using `ts_umdpri` to retrieve the `ts_maxwait` value from the dispatch table.

  The wakeup code also resets the `ts_dispwait` value back to 0 after adjusting the thread's priority, before calling the dispatcher queue functions for queue insertion. The actual priority adjustment is done by use of the `ts_slpret` dispatch table value to set `ts_cpupri`, as was the case in the `ts_sleep()` code for a long-waiting thread.

  `ts_timeleft` is set to `ts_quantum`, and `t_pri` is assigned a dispatch priority after the user priority arithmetic is done, with the `ts_umdpri` value determining from which row the dispatch table the global priority is retrieved, as shown in the sequence in Figure 9.8.

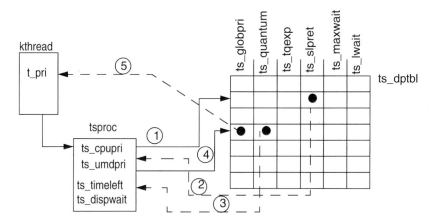

Figure 9.8 Priority Adjustment with `ts_slpret`

- The kernel runs a `ts_update()` routine once per second with the callout facility. `ts_update()` walks through a linked list of kernel threads and updates the thread's `ts_dispwait` value for TS/IA class threads (RT and SYS class threads are not updated).

  The update code alternates across the multiple linked lists of `tsproc` structures (see Figure 9.4 on page 365), starting at `ts_listhead`, traversing one list at a time. If the thread's updated `ts_dispwait` is greater than `ts_maxwait`, the thread's priority is bumped by the methods already described but with a different column in the dispatch table to reset `ts_cpupri`.

  `ts_lwait` in the dispatch table is fetched from the indexed row to set the new `ts_cpupri` value, the user mode priority is calculated, and `ts_dispwait` is reset to 0.

  The `ts_update()` function calls `ts_change_pri()`, which does a little extra work on behalf of the update process.

- If the thread is currently running on a processor (thread state is ONPROC), then a new global priority is set in `t_pri`: the new `ts_umdpri` value derived in the `ts_update()` function grabs the global priority from the dispatch table.
- If the thread's new priority is greater than the highest-priority thread sitting on the processor's dispatch queue (the dispatcher structure `disp_maxrunpri`, which is always updated when a thread in placed on a dispatch queue, is used for the test), then the thread has its `ts_timeleft` parameter reset from `ts_quantum` (in the dispatch table) and continues to run.
- If a higher-priority thread is sitting on the dispatch queue, the thread is forced to surrender the processor.
  - The other possible condition in `ts_change_pri` is that the thread is not running on a processor, in which case `thread_change_pri()` is called to set the new priority. A thread in the SLEEP state (sitting on a sleep queue) will have its priority changed by a synchronization object-specific function.

    For example, if the thread is sleeping on a mutex lock, the `mutex_change_pri()` code is invoked to change the priority and reposition the thread on the sleep queue if necessary (more on this in "The Kernel Sleep/Wakeup Facility" on page 396). Otherwise, the thread must be sitting on a dispatch queue. The priority is set, and one of the dispatcher queue insertion functions is called to set the thread's position on the dispatch queue.

This entire process is illustrated in the pseudocode listed below.

```
ts_update()
        set list from ts_plisthead[] /* lists of tsproc structures */
        ts_update_list()
                while (not at the end of the current list)
                        if (thread is not in TS or IA class)
                                bail out
                        if (thread has preemption control turned on)
                                bail out
                        if (thread is not sitting on a dispatch queue)
                                    set thread flags for post trap processing
                                bail out
                        kthread->tsproc.ts_cpupri = ts_dptbl[ts_cpupri].ts_lwait
                        calculate new user mode priority (ts_umdpri)
                        kthread->tsproc.ts_dispwait = 0
                        if (the threadUs priority will change based on new ts_umdpri)
                                        ts_change_priority()
                end while loop
ts_change_priority()
        if (thread is running on a processor) /* state is ONPROC */
                kthread.t_pri = ts_dptbl[ts_umdpri].ts_globpri
                if (threadUs priority > max runnable priority on dispatch queue)
                            kthread->tsproc.ts_timeleft = ts_dptlb[ts_umdpri].ts_quantum
                else
                            set flag for back of dispatch queue
                            surrender cpu
        else /* thread is not running */
                set front dispatch queue flag if IA class thread
                thread_change_pri()
                if (thread was on a run queue)
                            kthread->tsproc.ts_timeleft = ts_dptbl[ts_umdpri].ts_quantum
                else
                            set dispatch back queue flag
thread_change_pri()
        if (thread is not on a sleep queue or run queue)
                set new priority and return
        if (thread is on a sleep queue)
                call synchronization object specific priority change code
        else
                take the thread of the dispatch queue
                set the new priority
                call a dispatcher queue insertion function /* put it back on a queue */
```

Having examined a couple TS/IA-specific functions that occur at regular intervals—ts_tick() and ts_update(), both driven from the clock interrupt handler—we need to ensure that the distinction is clear between what each function is intended to do. ts_tick() is designed to process threads *running* on a processor. ts_update() is designed to process threads that are *not running* on a processor but rather are sitting on a dispatch queue or sleep queue. In case you got lost in some of the detail of the preceding discussions, we thought it a good idea to drive this salient point home.

As we pointed out earlier, IA class threads are, for the most part, processed by the TS class functions just described. The class-specific functions defined for the IA class include code to initialize the IA class and retrieve class-specific information and support code for setting and fetching class parameters. The ia_init() code is minimal, as most of the IA class work is done in the TA class code. ia_init() sets its scheduling class ID, a pointer to its class functions table, and its maximum global priority (which is 59, same as with TS). The user mode priority support functions, ia_parmsin(), ia_parmsset(), and ia_parmsget(), track the equivalent TS support code in flow and function.

Processes are put in the IA class by an IA class-specific routine, ia_set_process_group(), which is called from a STREAMS ioctl() (strioctl()—ioctls are I/O control calls, supported by all character device drivers) when a TTY is taken over by a new process group. It is rooted in the STREAMS-based terminal driver code in the kernel. If you were to boot your Solaris desktop system and not start a windowing system, you would not have any IA processes running (just TS and the SYS class Solaris daemons). When the windowing system starts, it takes over control of the "terminal," which in the case of a desktop is a keyboard, mouse, and the graphics card interface to the monitor.

The takeover generates the set-process-group ioctl call, which ultimately calls the CL_SET_PROCESS_GROUP macro. This macro resolves to the ia_set_process_group() IA-class-specific function since the caller is an interactive process (the windowing system software sees to that). All the processes associated with the windowing system are put in the IA class. And since processes and threads inherit their scheduling class from the parent, newly created processes (terminal windows, applications) are also put in the IA class. IA class threads are given a priority boost value of 10, which is factored in to the thread's user mode priority when that calculation is done, that is, every time a thread's priority is adjusted. Recall that the user priority is the sum of ts_cpupri, ts_upri, and ts_boost. (ts_boost has a fixed value of 10 for IA class threads.)

Processing for an RT class thread is much simpler; since RT priorities are fixed, they do not get better or worse during the execution life of the thread. The only way the priority of an RT class thread changes is if it is explicitly changed as the result of a priocntl() command or system call. When a thread enters the RT scheduling class (rt_enterclass()) through priocntl(), the thread RT class priority, rt_pri in the rtproc structure, is set to the default of 0 unless a priority has been specified; in that case, rt_pri will reflect the requested priority (provided it falls within the valid range for the class). rt_pquantum (also in rtproc) is set to the rt_quantum value from the RT dispatch table corresponding to the row number, as indexed by the priority. For example, the default RT class priority of 0 defines a time quantum of 1000, which translates to 1000 milliseconds, or 100 clock ticks (see the description of RES in "Dispatch Tables" on page 356).

If the thread is currently running on a processor, the thread's global priority is set in t_pri, and the code looks at the dispatch queue to determine whether the current thread has a priority greater than the highest-priority thread sitting on a dispatch queue. If it does, rt_timeleft is set to rt_pquantum, and the thread is allowed to continue to run; otherwise, it is forced to surrender the processor. If the thread is not currently running, the thread_change_pri() code is called (the same function described in the TS/IA examples), and the thread is placed on the appropriate dispatch queue. The following pseudocode illustrates this sequence of events.

```
rt_enterclass()
        if (not superuser)
                return  /* must be root to use RT class */
        if (no user-supplied priority)
                rtproc->rt_pri = 0;
                rtproc->rt_pqunatum = rt_dbtbl[0].rt_qunatum;
        else
                rtproc->rt_pri = user-supplied priority;
                if (user-supplied time quantum) /* -t flag in priocntl */
                        rtproc->rt_pqunatum = user-supplied time quantum
                else
                        rtproc->rt_pquantum = rt_dptbl[rt_pri].rt_quantum;
        if (thread is running)
                kthread->t_pri = rt_dptbl[rt_pri].rt_globpri;
                if (thread priority > highest-priority thread on a queue)
                        rtproc->rt_timeleft = rtproc->rt_pquantum
                else
                        surrender the processor
        else /* thread is not running */
                thread_change_pri(new_priority)
```

Other housekeeping work—initializing the other members of rtproc and setting the pointers in rtproc and the kthread structure—done in rt_enterclass() is not shown above.

A thread will also enter the RT class if it is forked from another RT thread, because child threads inherit their scheduling class from the parent. The child thread inherits the parent priority and time quantum in the rt_fork() code. The execution order of parent and child threads in the RT class is different from that of TS/IA class threads. The child executes first, by design, when a TS/IA class thread is forked (this is especially true in the case of vfork(), as discussed in the previous chapter). RT child threads end up on the dispatch while the parent continues to run, unless, of course, the application code is written explicitly to do otherwise.

The rt_tick() code, called from the clock tick handler for an RT class thread, determines if the thread's time quantum has expired. If it has, the thread is forced to surrender the processor; otherwise, it continues. RT class threads decrement a time counter, rt_timeleft, in the rtproc structure to track processor time clicks (as is the case with TS threads). A zero rt_timeleft means the time quantum has been used. It's possible to set an infinite time quantum for RT class threads. An rt_quantum value of –2 in the RT dispatch table is interpreted by the kernel as an infinite time quantum, in which case an RT class thread will continue to run unless it voluntarily surrenders the processor as a result of a sleep (e.g., issuing a blocking system call).

The RT code does not index the RT dispatch table to fetch the rt_quantum data every time a test is necessary. Once the RT thread is established, the time quantum from the RT table is stored in rt_pquantum in the thread's rtproc structure. Subsequent tests are done with rt_pquantum, which will get a new value should a priocntl() be issued on the thread, giving it a new priority and time quantum. Once an RT thread is initialized and begins execution, the priority never changes unless explicitly changed with priocntl().

9.2.3 Dispatcher Functions

The dispatcher's primary functions are to decide which runnable thread gets executed next, to manage the context switching of threads on and off processors, and to provide a mechanism for inserting kthreads that become runnable into a dispatch queue. Support code for the initialization process (loading scheduling classes, setting up dispatch queues, etc.) and support of the dispadmin(1M) and priocntl(1) commands are also defined within the dispatcher subsystem.

The heart of the dispatcher is the disp() function, which selects the next thread for execution. disp() is called primarily from the context-switching function, swtch(), which is the main entry point into the dispatcher and which is called from many areas of the kernel. Queue insertion is handled by the setfrontdq() and setbackdq() code, which place a kthread on a dispatch queue according to the thread's priority. Whether the kthread is placed at the front or the back of the queue is determined before the queue insertion function is called; we'll take a look at how that is decided as we move through the function descriptions.

9.2.3.1 Dispatcher Queue Insertion

In the previous section on thread priorities, we mentioned queue insertion following the priority setting from several class-specific routines. When a thread is created, the fork return code calls the class-specific setrun() function after setting the thread's priority. The queue insertion code is invoked from setrun() as the final step in the thread creation process. The class wakeup functions call into the dispatcher to insert a newly awakened kernel thread, moving it from a sleep queue to a dispatch queue. The preemption code must have the preempted thread placed on a dispatch queue, and thread_change_pri() also calls setfrontdq() or setbackdq(). Figure 9.9 illustrates the execution phases of a typical kernel thread as it is moved to and from dispatch queues and sleep queues.

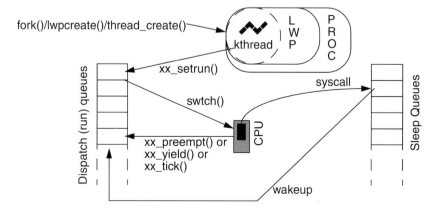

Figure 9.9 Kernel Thread Queue Insertion

The thread yield (xx_yield) scenario occurs only when a yield call is issued programmatically in application code through thr_yield(3T). Preemption, as we mentioned earlier, means a thread is involuntarily context-switched off a processor in favor of a higher-priority thread. Once the code segments shown in Figure 9.9 have completed the priority work, it's time for queue selection and insertion. Basically, four possible scenarios drive queue selection:

- An unbound thread whose priority is less than kpreemptpri
- An unbound thread whose priority is greater than or equal to kpreemptpri
- A bound thread whose priority is less than kpreemptpri
- A bound thread whose priority is greater than or equal to kpreemptpri

kpreemptpri, kernel preemption priority, is a global variable set by the kernel during initialization. The kernel sets the kpreemptpri value as scheduling classes are loaded, either during boot or when a class is loaded at some point while the system is running. By default, kpreemptpri is set to a value of 100, which is the maximum system priority (99) plus 1. Any thread with priority equal to or greater than kpreemptpri will cause a kernel preemption.

The basic, simplified logic of queue selection goes like this.

```
if (unbound AND priority < kpreemptpri)
        insert on dispatcher queue for t_cpu processor
if (unbound AND priority >= kpreemptppri)
        insert in cp_kp_queue /* systemwide kernel preempt queue */
if (bound AND priority < kpreemptpri)
        insert in dispatch queue of CPU thread is bound to
if (bound AND priority >- kpreemptpri)
        insert in dispatch queue of CPU thread is bound to
```

When a thread is switched onto a processor for execution, the thread's t_cpu pointer points to the CPU structure of the selected processor. Unbound TS/IA threads are placed on the dispatch queue of the processor they ran on last, in the hopes of hitting a warm processor cache and thus maximizing performance. This loose affinity maintained by the dispatcher has a time limit in the form of the kernel rechoose_interval parameter, which by default is 3 clock ticks. If more than rechoose_interval ticks have transpired since the thread ran last, the likelihood of the thread getting a cache hit has diminished, and the next available processor is selected. rechoose_interval can be set to a higher value in /etc/system and for some loads can provide some measurable improvement in performance, especially on loads that have a lot of threads with short execution times and processors with relatively large caches. However, as with anything else, you must take great care if you alter the default value. *Never do such a thing on a production system without having first tested extensively.*

Unbound RT threads are placed on the systemwide kernel preempt queue, cp_kp_queue. If processor sets are configured and the thread has been bound to a processor set, the cp_kp_queue for the processor set is used. If processor sets

have been configured and the thread has not been bound to a set, the
cp_kp_queue for the default partition is selected. Bound threads in any scheduling class, even RT class threads, are placed on the dispatch queue or the processor
they've been bound to.

The insertion of a thread on a dispatch queue is accomplished with the set-
frontdq() and setbackdq() routines for the per-processor dispatch queues, and
setkpdq() for the kernel preemption queue (or queues). The algorithm for set-
frontdq(), whose job it is to place a thread at the front of a dispatch queue, is
represented in the following pseudocode.

```
setfrontdq()
if (thread is swapped out or on swap queue)
        call disp_swapped_setrun()
        return
if (uniprocessor system)
        selected_cpu = t_cpu
if (MP system with 1 online CPU)
        selected_cpu = t_cpu
else if (thread is not bound)
        if (thread priority >= kpreemptpri)
                call setkpdq()
                return
        selected_cpu = t_cpu
        if (thread was running on the same partition that selected CPU belongs to)
                if (thread priority < highest-priority thread sitting on the queue)
                        selected_cpu = cpu_choose()
                else
                        selected_cpu = disp_lowpri_cpu()
/*
* at this point, the processor and associated dispatch queue have been selected
*/
set thread state to TS_RUN /* thread is runnable */
increment runnable thread count on dispatch queue structure - disp_nrunnable
place thread on the processorUs dispatch queue
set the disp_qactmap queue bitmap to reflect added thread
if (priority of thread placed on queue > disp_maxrunpri)
                dispatch_queue->disp_maxrunpri = threadUs priority
                call cpu_resched();
```

The selection of a dispatch queue for a TS/IA thread is essentially the selection of a
processor, since each processor has its own dispatch queue. That is why we reference *selected_cpu* in the preceding pseudocode. For a uniprocessor system or a
multiprocessor system with one online processor, processor selection becomes triv-
ial, which is why the code tests for those conditions up-front, immediately following the swapped thread test. A thread that is either swapped out or sitting on the
swap queue needs to be reloaded before it can be placed on a dispatch queue.

To nudge the memory scheduler (PID 0), disp_swapped_setrun() will set
one of two possible flags: either wake_sched or wake_sched_sec, depending on
the priority of the thread. These flags are tested in the clock interrupt handler,
where wake_sched is tested every clock interrupt and wake_sched_sec is tested
every 100 clock interrupts, or once every second. Threads at a priority greater than
99 (highest SYS class priority) wake up the scheduler right away—the next clock

interrupt (`wake_sched`); lower-priority threads result in `wake_sched_sec` getting set and thus wait a little longer.

The next test in `setfrontdq()` is for bound threads and uses `t_bound_cpu` in the thread structure. A bound thread will have its `t_bound_cpu` pointer pointing to the processor it is bound to. If the thread is *not* bound and its priority is greater than `kpreemptpri`, call `setkpri()` to place the thread on the kernel preempt queue and return. Otherwise (not bound, priority less than `kpreemptpri`), a cpu is selected initially from the threads `t_cpu` pointers (the loose affinity discussed earlier) and the processor partition test is done. Intuitively, it would seem that a processor set from the thread's `t_cpu` structure would belong to the processor partition referenced by the same thread's `t_cpupart` pointer, but it's possible some processor set configuration changes were made since they last ran, so the test is necessary.

If the selected processor is in the same partition on which the thread last ran, and if the thread's priority is greater than or equal to the highest-priority thread sitting on the processor's dispatch queue, stick with the selected processor. Otherwise, call `cpu_choose()` and find another processor queue in the same partition on which to place the thread. If the partition test fails, meaning the partition that the selected processor belongs to is different from the partition on which the thread last ran, then `setfrontdq()` calls `disp_lowpri_cpu()` to find a processor in the thread's `t_cpupart` partition. This code deals with situations where processor set configuration changes were made since the thread was last placed on a dispatch queue.

The `cpu_choose()` routine looks for the best processor on which to put the thread. In `cpu_choose()`, the kernel compares the amount of time (clock ticks) that has transpired since the thread last ran against `rechoose_interval`. The thread's `t_disp_time` field is incremented (by the `ts_update` thread) in the clock tick handler if the thread is not on a queue, and the kernel compares this value against `rechoose_interval`. If `t_disp_time` is less than `rechoose_interval`, the thread is kept on the processor it ran on last. Otherwise, `disp_lowpri_cpu()` is called to find a processor. `disp_lowpri_cpu()` searches the linked list of online processors in the partition for the processor with the lowest-priority thread. Once found, the thread is inserted in the selected processor's dispatch queue.

Bound threads, as we mentioned earlier, are placed on the queue of the processor they are bound to; or, if bound to a processor set, a processor within the set is selected, applying the loose affinity rule with `rechoose_interval`. Once the processor dispatch queue has been selected, the thread's priority is used to determine the correct priority queue. Recall that the per-processor queues are a queue of queues, and within each processor queue are linked lists of threads on individual queues, one for each priority. The `disp_nrunnable` counter in the processor queue is incremented, as is the `dq_sruncnt` counter for the priority queue on which the thread is placed. The thread is inserted at the front of the selected priority queue (remember, we are going through `setfrontdq()`), and the `disp_qactmap` (dispatcher queue active map) bitmap is updated. The priority of the newly inserted thread is tested against the queue's `disp_maxrunpri` value. If it is greater, `disp_maxrunpri` is set to the thread's priority to reflect the highest-priority thread sitting on the queue, and `cpu_resched()` is called to determine if a preemption condition exists.

`cpu_resched()` checks the priority of the thread currently executing on the processor against the priority of the thread just inserted onto the processor dispatch queue and also tests for a user or kernel preemption. A user preemption means the thread has a greater priority than the currently running thread, but not greater than `kpreemptpri`. More succinctly, if the thread's priority is less than 100 but greater than the currently running thread, the code sets up a user preemption. A kernel preemption is the result of the thread having a priority greater than the currently running thread and greater than `kpreemptpri`. The `cpu_resched()` work is represented in the following pseudocode.

```
cpu_resched()
        if (CPU is NOT IDLE AND thread priority > current thread priority)
                if (thread priority >= upreemptpri AND cpu_runrun == 0)
                        set cpu_runrun in CPU structure
                        set t_astflag in currently executing thread
                        if (thread priority < kpreemptpri AND selected cpu is not CPU)
                                poke_cpu()
                if (thread priority >= kpreemptpri AND cpu_kprunrun == 0)
                        set cpu_kprunrun in CPU structure
                        if (selected cpu is not CPU)
                                poke_cpu()
```

A couple of additional points to make on `cpu_resched()`. First, on a multiprocessor system, the processor that owns the dispatch queue selected for the thread may be a different processor than the one currently executing the code being examined: the `setfrontdq()` routine. The uppercase `CPU` reference is a kernel macro that always resolves to the currently executing processor. Thus, the tests described above are testing to see if the selected processor is different from the current processor. If it is not, a cross-call is generated by `poke_cpu()` to get the attention of the selected processor and force it to enter the kernel via a cross-call trap handler so the preemption will happen. If it is the same processor, the cross-call is not necessary since the current processor is already in the kernel and will detect the preemption flag when it returns to the code that originated the `setfrontdq()` call.

The last thing that `setfrontdq()` does is to set the dispatch queue's `disp_max_unbound_pri` variable, which, as the name implies, maintains the priority value of the highest-priority unbound thread on the queue. If the newly inserted thread's priority is greater than the current `disp_max_unbound_pri` and the thread is not bound, the value will be updated. That done, the kernel `setfrontdq()` queue insertion process is completed. The thread is now sitting on a dispatch queue and will be scheduled on the basis of its priority and position in the queue when the dispatcher `disp()` and `swtch()` code executes next. We're going to walk through that process in just a moment.

The `setbackdq()`, which puts a thread at the back of a dispatch queue, is similar from an algorithmic point of view to `setfrontdq()`, with just a few differences. First, in `setbackdq()` the kernel attempts to maintain a balance in queue depths across processors. Once a CPU has been selected with `cpu_choose()`, the number of runnable threads on the processor queue for the corresponding thread priority is examined. If it is greater than `MAX_RUNQ_DIFF`, which has a value of 2, then the kernel tries the next CPU in the same partition. That behavior aside, `setbackdq()` is essentially the same as `setfrontdq()`, except, of course, the thread is inserted at the back of the selected queue.

The decision as to whether `setfrontdq()` or `setbackdq()` is called from the various points in the kernel where queue insertion is called is driven by factors such as how long a thread has been waiting to run, whether or not the thread is in the IA class, etc. IA class threads are put on the front of a dispatch queue, for an additional edge on getting scheduled. A preempted thread with a scheduler activation is always placed at the front of a queue. RT class threads are always placed at the back of the kernel preempt queue. Threads that have waited a while (relatively speaking) to run (as determined by the thread's `t_disp_time` value) are placed at the front of a queue.

9.2.3.2 Thread Preemption

We talked a bit about thread preemption in the `setfrontdq()` code description and referred to it in the thread priority section. To complete the picture, we'll tie up some loose ends on the subject here. First, a quick review of what preemption is.

The kernel will preempt a thread running on a processor when a higher-priority thread is inserted onto a dispatch queue. The thread is effectively forced to reschedule itself and surrender the processor before having used up its time quantum. Two types of preemption conditions are implemented—a *user* preemption and a *kernel* preemption—distinguished by the priority level of the preempted thread, which drives how quickly the preemption will take place.

A user preemption occurs if a thread is placed on a dispatch queue and the thread has a higher priority than the thread currently running on the processor associated with the queue but has a lower priority than the minimum required for a kernel preemption. A kernel preemption occurs when a thread is placed on a dispatch queue with a priority higher than `kpreemptpri`, which is set to 100, representing the lowest global dispatch priority for an RT class thread. RT and interrupt threads have global priorities greater than `kpreemptpri`.

User preemption provides for higher-priority TS/IA threads getting processor time expediently. Kernel preemption is necessary for support of real-time threads. Traditional real-time support in Unix systems was built on a kernel with various preemption points, allowing a real-time thread to displace the kernel at a few well-defined preemptable places. The Solaris implementation goes the next step and implements a *preemptable* kernel with a few *non-preemption* points. In critical code paths, Solaris will temporarily disable kernel preemption for a short period and reenable it when the critical path has completed. Kernel preemption is disabled for very short periods in the `thread_create()` code, during the `pause_cpus()` routine, and in a few memory management (MMU) code paths, such as when a hardware address translation (HAT) is being set up.

Preemptions are flagged through fields in the per-processor `cpu` structure: `cpu_runrun` and `cpu_kprunrun`. `cpu_runrun` flags a user preemption; it is set when a thread inserted into a dispatch queue is a higher priority than the one running but a lower priority than `kpreemptpri`. `cpu_kprunrun` flags a kernel preemption. We saw in the `cpu_resched()` code one example of where these flags get set. The runrun flags can also get set in the following kernel routines.

- **`cpupart_move_cpu()`.** When a processor set configuration is changed and a processor is moved from a processor set, the runrun flags are set to force a preemption so the threads running on the processor being moved can be moved to another processor in the set they've been bound to. Note that if only one processor is left in the set and there are bound threads, the processor set cannot be destroyed until any bound threads are first unbound.

- **`cpu_surrender()`.** A thread is surrendering the processor it's running on, called from the TS/IA clock tick handler, sleep code, and trap return code. The RT class routines for `enterclass`, setting parameters, and clock tick handler can also call `cpu_surrender()`. Recall from the section on thread priorities that `cpu_surrender()` is called following a thread's priority change and a test to determine if preemption conditions exist. Entering `cpu_surrender()` means a preemption condition has been detected and is the first step in a kthread giving up a processor in favor of a higher-priority thread.

Two other areas of the kernel that potentially call `cpu_surrender()` are the priority inheritance code and the processor support code that handles the binding of a thread to a processor. The conditions under which the priority inheritance code calls `cpu_surrender()` are the same as previously described, that is, a priority test determined that a preemption is warranted. The thread binding code will force a preemption through `cpu_surrender()` when a thread is bound to a processor in a processor set and the processor the thread is currently executing on is not part of the processor set the thread was just bound to. This is the only case when a preemption is forced that is not the result of a priority test.

`cpu_surrender()` will set the `cpu_runrun` flag and will set `cpu_kprunrun` if the preemption priority is greater than `kpreemptpri`. On a multiprocessor system, if the processor executing the `cpu_surrender()` code is different from the processor that needs to preempt its thread, then a cross-call is sent to the processor that needs to be preempted, forcing it into a trap handler. At that point the runrun flags are tested. The other possible condition is one in which the processor executing the `cpu_surrender()` code is the same processor that must preempt the current thread, in which case it will test the runrun flags before returning to user mode; thus, the cross-call is not needed. In other words, the processor is already in the kernel by virtue of the fact that it is running the `cpu_surrender()` kernel routine, so a cross-call would be superfluous.

Once the preemption condition has been detected and the appropriate runrun flag has been set in the processor's CPU structure, the kernel must enter a code path that tests the runrun flags before the actual preemption occurs. This happens in different areas of the kernel for user versus kernel preemptions. User preemptions are tested for (`cpu_runrun`) when the kernel returns from a trap or interrupt handler. Kernel preemptions are tested for (`cpu_kprunrun`) when a dispatcher lock is released.

The trap code that executes after the main trap or interrupt handler has completed tests `cpu_runrun`, and if it is set, calls the kernel `preempt()` function. `preempt()` tests two conditions initially. If the thread is not running on a processor (thread state is not `ONPROC`) *or* if the thread's dispatch queue pointer is referencing a queue for a processor other than the processor currently executing, then no preemption is necessary and the code falls through and simply clears a dispatcher lock.

Consider the two test conditions. If the thread is not running (the first test), then obviously it does not need to be preempted. If the thread's `t_disp_queue` pointer is referencing a dispatch queue for a different processor (different from the processor currently executing the `preempt()` code), then clearly the thread has already been placed on another processor's queue, so that condition also obviates the need for a preemption.

If the conditions just described are not true, `preempt()` increments the LWP's `lrusage` structure `nicsw` counter, which counts the number of involuntary context switches. The processor's `inv_switch` counter is also incremented in the `cpu_sysinfo` structure, which counts involuntary context switches processor-wide, and the scheduling-class-specific preempt code is called. The per-processor counters are available with `mpstat(1M)`, reflected in the icsw column. The LWP `lrusage` data is not readily available with a bundled command, but you can develop code that uses `procfs` and reads the data by means of `/proc/<PID>/lwp/<LWPID>/lwpusage`.

The class-specific code for TS/IA threads prepares the thread for placement on a dispatch queue and calls either `setfrontdq()` or `setbackdq()` for actual queue insertion. `ts_preempt()` checks whether the thread is in kernel mode and whether the kernel-priority-requested flag (`t_kpri_req`) in the thread structure is set. If it is set, the thread's priority is set to the lowest SYS class priority (typically 60). The `t_trapret` and `t_astflag` kthread flags are set, causing the `ts_trapret()` function to run when the thread returns to user mode (from kernel mode). At that point, the thread's priority is set back to something in the TS/IA priority range. `ts_preempt()` tests for a scheduler activation on the thread. If an activation has been enabled *and* the thread has not avoided preemption beyond the threshold of two clock ticks *and* the thread is not in kernel mode, then the thread's priority is set to the highest user mode priority (59) and is placed at the front of a dispatch queue with `setfrontdq()`.

If the thread's TSBACKQ flag is set, indicating the thread should be placed in the back of a dispatch queue with setbackdq(), the thread preemption is due to time-slice expiration. (Recall that ts_tick() will call cpu_surrender().) The thread's t_dispwait field is zeroed, and a new time quantum is set in ts_timeleft from the dispatch table (indexed with ts_cpupri, as previously discussed) prior to setbackdq() being called. Otherwise, if TSBACKQ is not set, a real preemption occurred (higher-priority thread became runnable) and the thread is placed at the front of a dispatch queue.

The rt_preempt() code is much less complex. If RTBACKQ is true, the preemption was due to a time quantum expiration (as was the case previously), and setbackdq() is called to place the thread at the back of a queue after setting the rt_timeleft value from rt_pquantum. Otherwise, the thread is placed at the front of a dispatch queue with setfrontdq().

The class-specific preempt code, once completed, returns to the generic preempt() routine, which then enters the dispatcher by calling swtch(). We look at the swtch() code in the next section.

Kernel preemption, as we said earlier, is detected when a dispatcher lock is released. It is also tested for in kpreempt_enable(), which reenables kernel preemption after kpreempt_disable() blocked preemptions for a short time. The goal is to have kernel preemptions detected and handled more expediently (with less latency) than user preemptions. A dispatcher lock is a special type of mutex lock that not only provides mutual exclusion semantics for access to a specific dispatch queue, but does so at a raised priority level, protecting the queue from access from an interrupt handler for a low-priority interrupt. Dispatcher locks are acquired and held at priority level 10 on SPARC systems, blocking all low-priority interrupts. Interrupts above level 10 are high priority, and handlers for high-priority interrupts are not permitted to execute code that may require entering the dispatcher (e.g., causing a sleep and context switch). Every dispatch queue has a disp_lock, maintained in the dispatch queue structure that describes the queue (see Figure 9.5 on page 368).

Because the test for a kernel preemption, cpu_kprunrun, is put in the disp_lock_exit() code, the detection happens synchronously with respect to other thread scheduling and queue activity. The dispatcher locks are acquired and freed at various points in the dispatcher code, either directly through the dispatcher lock interfaces or indirectly through macro calls. For example, each kernel thread maintains a pointer to a dispatcher lock, which serves to lock the thread *and* the queue during dispatcher functions. The THREAD_LOCK and THREAD_UNLOCK macros use the dispatcher lock entry and exit functions. The key point is that a kernel preemption will be detected before a processor running a thread flagged for preemption completes a pass through the dispatcher.

When disp_lock_exit() is entered, it tests whether cpu_kprunrun is set; if so, then disp_lock_exit() calls kpreempt(). A clear cpu_kprunrun flag indicates a kernel preemption is not pending, so there is no need to call kpreempt().

Kernel preemptions are handled by the kpreempt() code, represented here in pseudocode.

```
kpreempt()
        if (current_thread->t_preempt)
                do statistics
                return
        if (current_thread NOT running) OR (current_thread NOT on this CPUs queue)
                return
        if (current PIL >= LOCK_LEVEL)
                return
        block kernel preemption (increment current_thread->t_preempt)
        call preempt()
        enable kernel preemption (decrement current_thread->t_preempt)
```

The preceding pseudocode basically summarizes at a high level what happens in kpreempt(). Kernel threads have a t_preempt flag, which, if set, signifies the thread is not to be preempted. This flag is set in some privileged threads, such as a processor's idle and interrupt threads. Kernel preemption is disabled by incrementing t_preempt in the current thread and is reenabled by decrementing t_preempt. kpreempt() tests t_preempt in the current thread; if t_preempt is set, kpreempt() increments some statistics counters and returns. If t_preempt is set, the code will not perform a kernel preemption.

The second test is similar in logic to what happens in the preempt() code previously described. If the thread is not running or is not on the current processor's dispatch queue, there's no need to preempt. The third test checks the priority level of the processor. If we're running at a high PIL, we cannot preempt the thread, since it may be holding a spin lock. Preempting a thread holding a lock could result in a deadlock situation.

Any of the first three test conditions evaluating true will cause kpreempt() to return without actually doing a preemption. Assuming the kernel goes ahead with the preemption, kernel preemptions are disabled (to prevent nested kernel preemptions) and the preempt() function is called. Once preempt() completes, kernel preemption is enabled and kpreempt() is done.

The kernel statistical data maintained for kernel preemption events is not accessible with a currently available Solaris command. The data is maintained in a `kpreempt_cnts` (kernel preemption counts) data structure and can be interrogated with adb(1).

```
# adb -k /dev/ksyms /dev/mem
physmem fdde
kpreempt_cnts/D
kpreempt_cnts:
kpreempt_cnts:                          0 <- Idle thread
kpreempt_cnts+4:                        3 <- Interrupt thread
kpreempt_cnts+8:                        0 <- Clock thread
kpreempt_cnts+0xc:                      37<- Blocked *t_preempt is set)
kpreempt_cnts+0x10:                     32<- Not on Proc
kpreempt_cnts+0x14:                     0<- Inv Switch
kpreempt_cnts+0x18:                     15<- Priority to High
kpreempt_cnts+0x1c:                     35<- Async Preempts
kpreempt_cnts+0x20:                     593759<- Sync Preempts
```

In the example, we inserted a short description of the event each counter correlates to. Most of the descriptions are comprehensible when examined in conjunction with the preceding text. The last two counters, async preempts and sync preempts, count each of the possible methods of kernel preemption. The `kpreempt()` function is passed one argument, `asyncspl`. For async preempts, `asyncspl` is a priority-level argument, and the `kpreempt()` code will raise the PIL, as dictated by the value passed. Sync preempts pass a −1 argument and do not change the processor's priority level.

Thread preemption is a relatively simple concept to understand, but as with many other things, it's easy to get lost in the details of implementation. Figure 9.10 summarizes thread preemption at a high level.

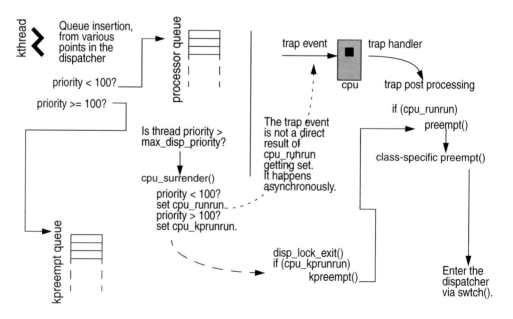

Figure 9.10 Thread Preemption Flow

In the case of both user and kernel preemption, the code ultimately executes the `preempt()` function, which as a last step, enters the dispatcher `swtch()` routine—the topic of the next section.

9.2.3.3 The Heart of the Dispatcher: swtch()

The kernel `swtch()` routine initiates the context switching of a thread off a processor, figures out which thread should run next, and context-switches the selected thread onto a processor for execution. It's called from many places within the operating system: in the class fork return function (a thread has just been created), from the idle thread (executed by processors if there are no runnable threads on a dispatch queue), by interrupt and trap handlers (to reenter the dispatcher), for thread sleep management, in kernel synchronization support code (mutexes, reader/writer locks, condition variables, etc.), and, of course, from the `preempt()` function. The various entry points to `swtch()` are listed in Table 9-4.

Table 9-4 Sources of Calls to swtch()

Kernel Subsystem	Kernel Function	Description
Dispatcher	idle	Per-processor idle thread
	preempt	Last phase of a preemption
Kthread	`release_interrupt`	Called from an interrupt thread
TS/IA class	`ts_forkret`	After kthread is created
Sleep/wakeup	`cv_xxxx`	Various conditional variable functions
CPU	`force_migrate`	Thread migration to another processor
	`cpu_pause`	Processor state change to pause
Mutex	`mutex_vector_enter`	Mutex lock acquisition
RWlock	`rw_enter_sleep`	RW lock acquisition
Memory scheduler	`sched`	PID 0
Semaphore	`sema_p`	Semaphore "p" operation
Signal	`stop`	Thread stop function
Sleep/wakeup	`slp_cv_wait`	Thread to sleep state
Interrupt	`intr_thread_exit`	Exit of an interrupt handler

Entering the `swtch()` routine causes the `cpu_sysinfo.pswtch` counter to be incremented, as reported in `mpstat(1M)` in the csw column, and reflects the number of context switches per second, on a per-processor basis.

The `swtch()` function first checks to see if the current thread is an interrupt thread. When interrupts happen, the thread stack is switched to that of an interrupt thread, from the linked list of interrupt threads in the processor's cpu structure. If `swtch()` was entered with an interrupt thread as the current thread, the kernel must restore the interrupted thread's state so it can be resumed. The interrupted thread is unpinned (a thread that has been preempted for an interrupt is considered pinned), and the kernel `resume_from_interrupt()` assembly routine is called to restore the state of the interrupted thread.

If the thread is not an interrupt thread, the code tests the handoff pointer in the kernel thread (`t_handoff`). A non-`NULL` `t_handoff` pointer indicates the processor should be handed off to another thread, in support of scheduler activations. (Scheduler activations were first introduced in Solaris 2.6 and are discussed in "Scheduler Activations" on page 407.)

Briefly, one of the goals of scheduler activations is to provide a framework for communication between the kernel dispatcher and the user-level threads library. Such communication improves the scheduling of user threads and reduces the latency of a runnable user thread getting an LWP if all the LWPs in a process are blocked. Recall from an earlier discussion that a user-level thread, that is, a thread created through a `thr_create(3T)` or `pthread_create(3T)` call, is mapped onto an LWP by the user thread's scheduler. If all the LWPs in a process are blocked and there are runnable user threads, the user thread's scheduler does not have the resource it needs, an LWP, to schedule a user thread. Prior to Solaris 2.6, the kernel implemented a signal mechanism, using `SIGWAITING` in conjunction with a signal handler for `SIGWAITING`, to increase the pool of available LWPs for the process.

With scheduler activations, a communication path is established between the kernel and the user threads library. If an activation has been established for the process, a pool of LWPs might be readily available, in which case the `t_handoff` pointer would be non-`NULL`. If that is the case, a kernel handoff function is called, and ultimately the kernel `resume()` code is entered to context-switch the kernel thread referenced with `t_handoff` onto the processor.

If the current thread is *not* an interrupt thread and a handoff is *not* required, `swtch()` calls the `disp()` function, which is the code segment that looks for the highest-priority thread to run, sets the thread's state to running (`TS_ONPROC`), and arranges for it to be switched onto a processor. At a high level, the `disp()` function searches the dispatch queues for the best-priority kernel thread, starting with the kernel preempt queue and then searching the queue of the current processor—that is, the processor executing the `disp()` code. If those searches come up blank, then the code searches the dispatch queues of other processors on a multiprocessor system, looking for a runnable kernel thread. If no threads are found on the dispatch queues, the processor executes its idle thread, which executes a tight loop, testing for runnable threads on each pass through the loop and entering `swtch()` if the run count is greater than 0.

The search for the highest-priority thread begins with the kernel preempt queue, as referenced by the current processor through its `cpu_part` structure, where the preempt queue is linked to `cp_kp_queue`. In this case, on a system with multiple processor partitions (user processor sets—recall there is a kernel preempt queue per processor set), the preempt queue for the processor partition that the executing processor belongs to is searched first. The `cp_kp_queue` search is represented in the following pseudocode.

```
kpq = pointer to kernel preempt queue
dq = pointer to processor's dispatch queue
while ( priority = kpq->dispmaxrunpri >= 0 ) AND
                ( priority >= dq->dispmaxrunpri) AND
                ( the current CPU is NOT offline) AND
                ( thread_pointer = disp_getbest(kpq) != NULL )
                        if (disp_ratify(thread_pointer, kpq) != NULL)
                                return(thread_pointer)
```

The preceding queue search loop validates the priority value according to the queue's `disp_maxrunpri`, which reflects the highest-priority thread sitting on the queue, makes sure the current processor is not offline, and calls the dispatcher `disp_getbest()` code to fetch the best-priority thread from the kernel preempt queue. `disp_getbest()` finds the highest-priority unbound thread, calls `disp-deq()` to have the thread removed from the dispatch queue, and returns the thread pointer back to `disp()`. If nothing is found, a `NULL` value is returned.

```
disp_getbest()
        dpq = dispatch queue pointer (cp_kp_queue in this example)
        priority = dpq->disp_max_unbound_pri
        if (priority == -1)
                return(NULL)
        queue = dpq->disp_q[pri];
        thread_pointer = queue->dq_first;
        loop through linked list of threads on queue, skip bound threads
        if (no unbound threads)
                return NULL
        else
                thread_pointer = thread found
        dispdeq(thread_pointer)
        set thread t_disp_queue, processorUs cpu_dispthread, thread state to ONPROC
        return (thread_pointer)
```

If an unbound thread is found in `disp_getbest()`, the thread is dequeued with `dispdeq()`, the thread's `t_disp_queue` pointer is set to reference the processor's `cpu` structure `cpu_disp` queue pointer, the processor's `cpu_dispthread` pointer is set to the selected thread pointer, and the thread state is set to `ONPROC`.

`dispdeq()` deals with updating the dispatch queue data structures with the selected thread removed from the queue. It decrements `disp_nrunnable`, which is the total count for all the queues, and `dq_sruncnt`, which maintains the count of runnable threads at the same priority (refer to Figure 9.5 on page 368). If the per-priority queue count, `dq_sruncnt`, is 0, then the queue bitmap is updated to reflect an empty queue. The `disp_qactmap` bitmap uses a set bit to reflect the presence of runnable threads on a per-priority queue; thus, the bit that corresponds to the zeroed queue is cleared. The `disp_maxrunpri` and `disp_max_unbound_pri` fields are also updated to reflect the new highest-priority thread on the queue if it is different from the thread that has just been removed from the queue.

Once the thread selection has been made and the thread dequeued, the code returns to `disp()`, which calls `disp_ratify()` to ensure that the selected thread was, in fact, the best candidate to run next. The fine-grained locking used within the dispatcher routines allows for simultaneous changes to be made to the queues and the queue state by potentially many processors. For this reason, a *select-and-ratify* algorithm was chosen for implementation. The select phase of the algorithm now completed, `disp_ratify()` is entered to complete the ratify phase. The ratify code simply compares the priority of the selected thread to the `disp_maxrunpri` values of the processor and kernel preempt queue. If the selected thread priority is greater than `maxrunpri`, the selection is ratified and the context switch is done. If not, we reenter the code loop to find the best runnable thread. More precisely, if a higher-priority thread appears on the queue when `disp_ratify()` executes, the selected thread is placed back on the dispatch queue with a call to `setfrontdq()` and `disp_ratify()` returns NULL to `disp()`.

If a thread is not found on the kernel preempt queue, then the per-processor queue `disp_maxrunpri` is tested. A value of –1 means that nothing is on the queue. In that case, the code searches the queues of the other processors on the system, beginning with the `disp_getwork()` code, which finds a processor with the highest-priority thread. Then, the code uses the `disp_getbest()` and `disp_ratify()` functions previously described.

If the current processor's `disp_maxrunpri` indicates runnable threads, the first thread from the highest priority queue is removed, the queue data is updated (`disp_nrunnable`, `dq_nruncnt`, `disp_qactmap`, `disp_max_unbound_pri`, and `disp_maxrunpri`), the selection is ratified, and `disp()` returns the thread pointer to `swtch()`.

If no work is found on any of the dispatch queues, the processor's idle thread is selected by setting the thread pointer to the `cpu_idle_thread`, referenced from the processor's `cpu` structure. The pointer to the idle thread is returned to the `swtch()` code.

Back in `swtch()`, with a thread pointer for the selected thread (or idle thread), the kernel `resume()` code is called to handle the switching of the thread on the processor. `resume()` is implemented in assembly language because the process of context switching requires low-level contact with processor hardware, for two reasons: to save the hardware context of the thread being switched off; and to set up the hardware registers and other context information so the new thread can begin execution.

9.3   The Kernel Sleep/Wakeup Facility

The typical lifetime of a kernel thread includes not only execution time on a processor but also time spent waiting for requested resources to become available. An obvious example is a read or write from disk, when the kernel thread will issue the `read(2)` or `write(2)` system call, then sleep so another thread can make use of the processor while the I/O is being processed by the kernel. Once the I/O has been completed, the kernel will wake up the thread so it can continue its work.

Kernel threads that are runnable and waiting for a processor reside on dispatch queues. Kernel threads that must block, waiting for an event or resource, are placed on sleep queues. A kernel thread is placed on a sleep queue when it needs to sleep, awaiting availability of a resource (e.g., a mutex lock, reader/writer lock, etc.) or awaiting some service by the kernel (e.g., a system call). A few sleep queues implemented in the kernel vary somewhat, although they all use the same underlying sleep queue structures. Turnstiles are implemented with sleep queues and are used specifically for sleep/wakeup support in the context of priority inheritance, mutex locks, and reader/writer locks. Kernel threads put to sleep for something other than a mutex or reader/writer lock are placed on the system's sleep queues. Turnstiles and priority inheritance are discussed in Chapter 2, "Kernel Synchronization Primitives."

9.3.1 Condition Variables

The underlying synchronization primitive used for sleep/wakeup in Solaris is the *condition variable*. Condition variables are always used in conjunction with mutex locks. A condition variable call is issued on the basis of a specific condition being either true or false. The mutex ensures that the tested condition cannot be altered during the test and maintains state while the kernel thread is being set up to block on the condition. Once the condition variable code is entered and the thread is safely on a sleep queue, the mutex can be released. This is why all entry points to the condition variable code are passed the address of the condition variable and the address of the associated mutex lock.

In implementation, condition variables are data structures that identify an event or a resource for which a kernel thread may need to block and are used in many places around the operating system. The structure itself is quite small (see Figure 9.11) and can be examined in `/usr/include/sys/condvar.h` and `/usr/include/sys/condvar_impl.h`.

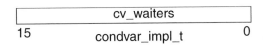

Figure 9.11 Condition Variable

The condition variable itself is simply a 2-byte (16-bit) data type with one defined field, `cv_waiters`, that stores the number of threads waiting on the specific resource the condition variable has been initialized for. The implementation is such that the various kernel subsystems that use condition variables declare a condition variable data type with a unique name either as a standalone data item or embedded in a data structure. Try doing a `grep(1)` command on `kcondvar_t` in the `/usr/include/sys` directory, and you'll see dozens of examples of condition variables. A generic kernel `cv_init()` function sets the condition variable to all zeros during the initialization phase of a kernel module. Other kernel-level condition variable interfaces are defined and called by different areas of the operating system to set up a thread to block a particular event and to insert the kernel thread on a sleep queue.

At a high level, the sleep/wakeup facility works as follows. At various points in the operating system code, conditional tests are performed to determine if a specific resource is available. If it is not, the code calls any one of several condition variable interfaces, such as `cv_wait()`, `cv_wait_sig()`, `cv_timedwait()`, `cv_wait_stop()`, etc., passing a pointer to the condition variable and mutex. This sequence is represented in the following small pseudocode segment.

```
kernel_function()
        mutex_init(resource_mutex);
        cv_init(resource_cv);
        mutex_enter(resource_mutex);
        if (resource is not available)
                cv_wait(&resource_cv, &resource_mutex);
        consume resource
        mutex_exit(resource_mutex);
```

These interfaces provide some flexibility in altering behavior as determined by the condition the kernel thread must wait for. Ultimately, the `cv_block()` interface is called; the interface is the kernel routine that actually sets the `t_wchan` value in the kernel thread and calls `sleepq_insert()` to place the thread on a sleep queue. The `t_wchan`, or *wait channel*, contains the address of the conditional variable that the thread is blocking on. This address is listed in the output of a `ps -efl` command, in the WCHAN column.

The notion of a wait channel or `wchan` is something that's familiar to folks that have been around Unix for a while. Traditional implementations of Unix maintained a `wchan` field in the process structure, and it was always related to an event or resource the process was waiting for (why the process was sleeping). Naturally, in the Solaris multithreaded model, we moved the wait channel into the kernel thread, since kernel threads execute independently of other kernel threads in the same process and can execute system calls and block.

When the event or resource that the thread was sleeping on is made available, the kernel uses the condition variable facility to alert the sleeping thread (or threads) and to initiate a wakeup, which involves moving the thread from a sleep queue to a processor's dispatch queue.

Figure 9.12 illustrates the sleep/wake process.

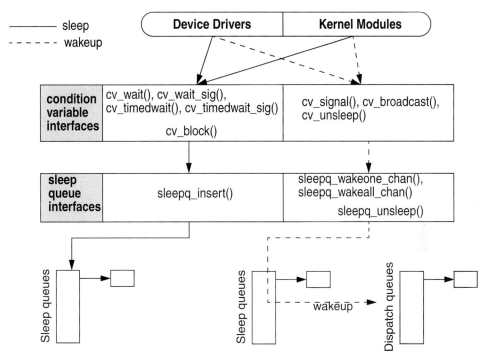

Figure 9.12 Sleep/Wake Flow Diagram

9.3.2 Sleep Queues

Sleep queues are organized as a linked list of kernel threads, each linked list rooted in an array referenced via a `sleepq_head` kernel pointer. Some changes were made in Solaris 7 to facilitate faster sleep queue operations (insertion, removal, and queue traversal). In Solaris releases prior to Solaris 7, an entry in the `sleepq_head` array begins a linked list of kernel threads waiting on the same condition variable. The list is singly linked by the kernel thread's `t_link` pointer. In Solaris 7, several additional pointers were added to the kernel thread to support a doubly linked sublist of threads at the same priority.

Figure 9.13 illustrates sleep queues.

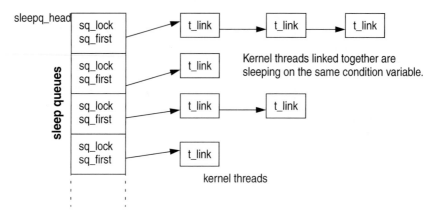

Figure 9.13 Solaris 2.5.1 and Solaris 2.6 Sleep Queues

In all implementations (pre- and post-Solaris 7, that is), a hashing function indexes the `sleepq_head` array, hashing on the address of the condition variable. In the pre-Solaris 7 implementation, kernel threads are inserted on the list in order of descending priority. In Solaris 7, the singly linked list that establishes the beginning of the doubly linked sublists of kthreads at the same priority is also in ascending order of priority. The sublist is implemented by `t_priforw` (forward pointer) and `t_priback` (previous pointer) in the kernel thread. Also, a `t_sleepq` pointer was added to point back to the array entry in `sleepq_head`, identifying which sleep queue the thread is on and also providing a quick method to determine if a thread is on a sleep queue at all. (If `t_sleepq == NULL`, the thread is not on a sleep queue.)

Figure 9.14 illustrates priority order on sleep queues.

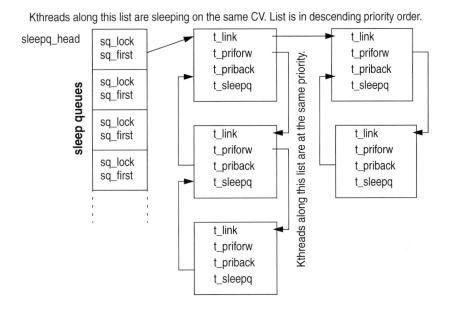

Figure 9.14 Solaris 7 Sleep Queues

The number of kernel interfaces to the sleep queue facility is minimal. Only a few operations are performed on sleep queues: the insertion of a kernel thread on a sleep queue (putting a thread to sleep), the removal of a thread from a sleep queue (waking a thread up), and traversing the sleep queue in search of a kernel thread. There are interfaces that provide for waking up only one thread or all threads sleeping on the same condition variable.

Insertion of a kthread simply involves indexing into the `sleepq_head` array to find the appropriate sleep queue specified by the condition variable address, then traversing the list, checking thread priorities along the way to determine the proper insertion point. Once the appropriate sublist has been found (at least one kernel thread at the same priority) or it has been determined that no other threads on the sleep queue have the same priority, a new sublist is started, the kernel thread is inserted, and the pointers are set up properly.

The removal of a kthread either involves searching for and removing a specific thread that has been specified by the code calling into `sleepq_dequeue()` or `sleepq_unsleep()`, or waking up all the threads blocking on a particular condition variable. Waking up all threads or a specified thread is relatively straightforward: hash into the `sleepq_head` array specified by the address of the condition variable, and walk the list, either waking each thread up or searching for a particular kthread and waking the targeted thread. In case a single, unspecified kthread needs to be removed, the code implements the list as a FIFO (First In, First Out), so the kthread that has been sleeping the longest on a condition variable will be selected for wakeup first.

9.3.3 The Sleep Process

Now that we've introduced condition variables and sleep queues, let's tie them together to form the complete sleep/wakeup picture in Solaris. The interfaces to the sleep queue (sleepq_insert(), etc.) are, for the most part, called only from the condition variables and turnstiles subsystems. From a hierarchical perspective, you could view the sleep/wakeup implementation, as depicted in Figure 9.12 on page 399, where a well-defined and limited set of interfaces manipulate kernel threads on the sleep queues.

The process of putting a thread to sleep begins with a call into the condition variable code wait functions, one of cv_wait(), cv_wait_sig(), cv_wait_sig_swap(), cv_timedwait(), or cv_timedwait_sig(). Each of these functions is passed the condition variable and a mutex lock. They all ultimately call cv_block() to prepare the thread for sleep queue insertion. cv_wait() is the simplest condition variable sleep interface; it grabs the dispatcher lock for the kthread and invokes the class-specific sleep routine (e.g., ts_sleep()). The *timed* variants of the cv_wait() routines take an additional time argument, ensuring that the thread will be woken up when the time value expires if it has not yet been removed from the sleep queue. cv_timedwait() and cv_timedwait_sig() use the kernel callout facility for handling the timer expiration. The realtime_timeout() interface is used and places a high-priority timeout on the kernel callout queue. The setrun() function is placed on the callout queue, along with the kernel thread address and time value. When the timer expires, setrun(), followed by the class-specific setrun function (e.g., rt_setrun()), executes on the sleeping thread, making it runnable and placing it on a dispatch queue.

The *sig* variants of the condition variable code, cv_wait_sig(), cv_timedwait_sig(), etc., are designed for potentially longer-term waits, where it is desirable to test for pending signals before the actual wakeup event. They return 0 to the caller if a signal has been posted to the kthread. The swap variant, cv_wait_sig_swap(), can be used if it is safe to swap out the sleeping thread while it's sleeping. The various condition-variable routines are summarized below. Note that all functions described below release the mutex lock after cv_block() returns, and they reacquire the mutex before the function itself returns.

- **cv_wait()** — Calls cv_block(). Then, cv_wait() enters the dispatcher with swtch() when cv_block() returns.

- **cv_wait_sig()** — Checks for SC_BLOCK scheduler activation (last LWP in the process is blocking). If false, cv_wait_sig() calls cv_block_sig(). On return from cv_block_sig(), it tests for a pending signal. If a signal is pending, cv_wait_sig() calls setrun(); otherwise, it calls swtch(). If an SC_BLOCK activation is true, cv_wait_sig() removes the thread timeout and returns –1, unless a signal is pending; then, it returns 0.

- **cv_wait_sig_swap()** — Essentially the same as cv_wait_sig() but flags the thread as swappable.

- `cv_timedwait()` — Tests for timer expiration on entry. If the timer has expired, `cv_timedwait()` returns –1. It calls `realtime_timeout()` to set callout queue entry, calls `cv_block()`, and checks the timer on return from `cv_block()`. If the timer has expired, `cv_timedwait()` calls `setrun()`; otherwise, it calls `swtch()`.

- `cv_timedwait_sig()` — Tests for time expiration. If the timer has expired, `cv_timedwait_sig()` returns –1 unless a signal is pending; then, it returns 0. If neither condition is true, then `cv_timedwait_sig()` calls `realtime_timeout()` to set the callout queue entry and tests for an `SC_BLOCK` activation. If false, `cv_timedwait_sig()` calls `cv_block_sig()`. On return from `cv_block_sig()`, it tests for a pending signal. If a signal is pending, `cv_timedwait_sig()` calls `setrun()`; otherwise, it calls `swtch()`. If an `SC_BLOCK` activation is true, `cv_timedwait_sig()` removes the thread timeout and returns –1 unless a signal is pending; then, it returns 0.

All of the above entry points into the condition variable code call `cv_block()` or `cv_block_sig()`, which just sets the `T_WAKEABLE` flag in the kernel thread and then calls `cv_block()`. `cv_block()` does some additional checking of various state flags and invokes the scheduling-class-specific sleep function through the `CL_SLEEP()` macro, which resolves to `ts_sleep()` for a `TS` or `IA` class thread. The intention of the `ts_sleep()` code is to boost the priority of the sleeping thread to a `SYS` priority if such a boost is flagged. As a result, the kthread is placed in an optimal position on the sleep queue for early wakeup and quick rescheduling when the wakeup occurs. Otherwise, the priority is reset according to how long the thread has been waiting to run.

The assignment of a `SYS` priority to the kernel thread is not guaranteed every time `ts_sleep()` is entered. Flags in the kthread structure, along with the kthread's class-specific data (`ts_data` in the case of a `TS` class thread), specify whether a kernel mode (`SYS`) priority is required. A `SYS` class priority is flagged if the thread is holding either a reader/writer lock or a page lock on a memory page. For most other cases, a `SYS` class priority is not required and thus will not be assigned to the thread. `RT` class threads do not have a class sleep routine; because they are fixed-priority threads, there's no priority adjustment work to do. The `ts_sleep()` function is represented in the following pseudocode.

```
ts_sleep()
        if (SYS priority requested) /* t)_kpri_req flag */
                set TSKPRI flag in kthread
                set t_pri to requested SYS priority /* tpri = ts_kmdpris[arg] */
                set kthread trap return flag /* t_trapret */
                set thread ast flag      /* t_astflag */
        else if (ts_dispwait > ts_maxwait) /* has the thread been waiting long */
                calculate new user mode priority
                set ts_timeleft = ts_dptbl[ts_cpupri].ts_quantum
                set ts_dispwait = 0
                set new global priority in thread (t_pri)
                if (thread priority < max priority on dispatch queue)
                        call cpu_surrender() /* preemption time */
        else if (thread is already at a SYS priority)
                set thread priority to TS class priority
                clear TSKPRI flag in kthread
                if (thread priority < max priority on dispatch queue)
                        call cpu_surrender() /* preemption time */
```

The thread priority setting in `ts_sleep()` in the second code segment above is entered if the thread has been waiting an inordinate amount of time to run, as determined by `ts_dispwait` in the `ts_data` structure, and by the `ts_maxwait` value from the dispatch table, as indexed by the current user mode priority, `ts_umdpri`. The sequence is represented graphically in Figure 9.15.

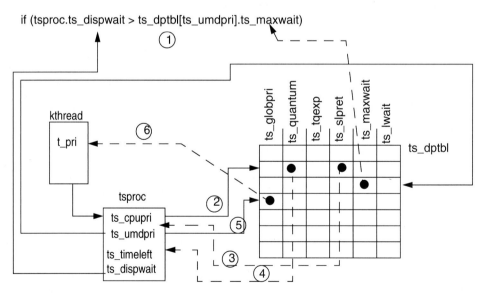

Figure 9.15 Setting a Thread's Priority in `ts_sleep()`

The code will return to `cv_block()` from `ts_sleep()`, where the kthreads `t_wchan` is set to the address of the condition variable and the kthreads `t_sobj_ops` is set to the address of the condition variable's operations structure.

If you take a look at `/usr/include/sys/sobject.h`, you'll find a definition for a synchronization object operations structure.

```
typedef struct _sobj_ops {
                syncobj_t sobj_type;
                kthread_t *(*sobj_owner)();
                void (*sobj_unsleep)(kthread_t *);
                void (*sobj_change_pri)(kthread_t *, pri_t, pri_t *);
} sobj_ops_t;
```

Header File <sys/sobject.h>

This is a generic structure that is used for all types of synchronization objects supported by the operating system. Note the enumerated types in the same header file; they describe mutex locks, reader/writer locks, semaphores, condition variables, etc. Essentially, this object provides a placeholder for a few routines specific to the synchronization object that may require invocation while the kernel thread is sleeping. In the case of condition variables (our example), the sobj_ops structure is populated with the address of the cv_owner(), cv_unsleep(), and cv_change_pri() functions, with the sobj_type field set to SOBJ_CV. The address of this structure is what the kthread's t_sobj_ops field is set to in the cv_block() code.

With the kthread's wait channel and synchronization object operations pointers set appropriately, the correct sleep queue is located by use of the hashing function on the condition variable address to index into the sleepq_head array. Next, the cv_waiters field in the condition variable is incremented to reflect another kernel thread blocking on the object, and the thread state is set to TS_SLEEP. Finally, the sleepq_insert() function is called to insert the kernel thread into the correct position (based on priority) in the sleep queue. The kthread is now on a sleep queue in a TS_SLEEP state, waiting for a wakeup.

9.3.4 The Wakeup Mechanism

For every cv_wait() (or variant) call on a condition variable, a corresponding wakeup call uses cv_signal(), cv_broadcast(), or cv_unsleep(). In practice, cv_unsleep() is not called in current versions of Solaris. cv_signal() wakes up one thread, and cv_broadcast() wakes up all threads sleeping on the same condition variable. Here is the sequence of wakeup events.

- The cv_broadcast() function simply locates the address of the sleep queue by invoking the hash function on the address of the condition variable, which was passed to cv_broadcast() as an argument, clears the cv_waiters field in the condition variable (all the threads are getting a wakeup, so the condition variable should reflect zero threads waiting on the condition variable), and calls sleepq_wakeall_chan().

- In Solaris 7, `sleepq_wakeall_chan()` traverses the linked list of kernel threads waiting on that particular condition variable and, for each kthread, calls `sleepq_unlink()`. `sleepq_unlink()` removes the kthread from the sleep queue linked list, adjusts the pointers (the `t_priforw`, `t_priback` pointers) and returns to `sleepq_wakeall_chan()`.

- On the return to `sleepq_wakeall_chan()`, the kthread's `t_wchan` and `t_sobj_ops` fields are cleared, and the scheduling-class-specific wakeup code is called.

  For TS/IA threads, the code is `ts_wakeup()`; for RT class threads, it is `rt_wakeup()`. In Solaris 2.5.1 and Solaris 2.6, the queue is a singly linked list, linked with the `t_link` pointer in the kthread.

  Solaris 2.5.1 and Solaris 2.6 do not have a `sleepq_unlink()` function, so `sleep_wakeall_chan()` removes each thread from the list and sets the thread's `t_link`, `t_wchan`, and `t_sobj_ops` fields to NULL.

- `cv_signal()` locates the correct index into the `sleepq_head` array by hashing on the address of the condition variable, decrements the `cv_waiters` field in the condition variable by 1, since only one thread is getting a wakeup, and calls `sleepq_wakeone_chan()`.

- The `ts_wakeup()` code puts the kernel thread back on a dispatch queue so it can be scheduled for execution on a processor.

  Threads that have a kernel mode priority (as indicated by the TSKPRI flag in the class-specific data structure, which is set in `ts_sleep()` if a SYS priority is assigned) are placed on the front of the appropriate dispatch queue. IA class threads will also result in `setfrontdq()` being called; otherwise, `setbackdq()` is called to place the kernel thread at the back of the dispatch queue.

- Threads that are not at a SYS priority are tested to see if they've waited longer for a shot at getting scheduled than the time value set in the `ts_maxwait` field in the dispatch table for the thread's priority level.

  If the thread has been waiting an inordinate amount of time to run (if `dispwait > dispatch_table[priority]dispwait`), then the thread's priority is recalculated, using the `ts_slpret` value from the dispatch table. This is essentially the same logic used in `ts_sleep()` and gives a priority boost to threads that have spent an inordinate amount of time on the sleep queue.

It is in the dispatcher queue insertion code (`setfrontdq()`, `setbackdq()`) that the thread state is switched from TS_SLEEP to TS_RUN. It's also in these functions that we determine if the thread we just placed on a queue is of a higher priority than the currently running thread and if so, force a preemption. At this point, the kthread has been woken up and is sitting on a dispatch queue, ready to get context-switched onto a processor when the dispatcher `swtch()` function runs again and the newly inserted thread is selected for execution.

9.4 Scheduler Activations

We made several references to scheduler activations in the preceding text and highlighted the preemption control feature in the thread priority descriptions. Scheduler activations were added to Solaris 2.6 to address several deficiencies in the two-level threads architecture of Solaris and to provide a facility for short-term preemption control by a process. (This section and any previous references to scheduler activations do not apply to Solaris 2.5.1; they apply only to Solaris 2.6 and Solaris 7).

The two levels in the design refer to user-level threads and the underlying kthread/LWP. We use the term LWP from this point forward when discussing the kernel level, and we use threads to refer to a user thread created from the threads library. User-level threads are scheduled within the framework of the threads library—the user threads actually participate in their own scheduling through preemption points and internal threads library routines. User threads are, by design, not visible to the kernel. The priority of a user thread has no bearing on the scheduling or priority of an LWP linked to the thread for execution.

Prior to Solaris 2.6, there was no facility for communication between the user threads scheduler and the kernel dispatcher (see Figure 9.16), and thus no correlation between the priority of a user thread and the priority of the underlying LWP. This problem could be circumvented to some extent by the use of bound threads, where every user thread was bound to an LWP, and priority control facilities (priocntl(1M)) managed execution priorities at the LWP level.

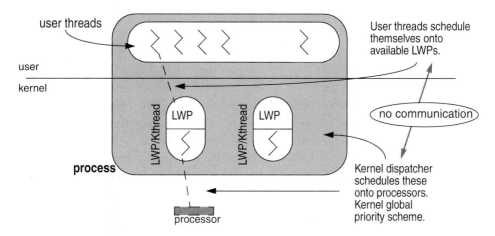

Figure 9.16 Two-Level Threads Model

Other problems existed in the area of synchronization primitives used by threaded programs. At the user threads level, the use of mutex locks and other synchronization mechanisms were prone to priority inversion problems. We described how priority inheritance addressed this problem in the kernel for kernel synchronization primitives. There was no means by which an inheritance scheme could be implemented at the user threads level, since the priority information of the LWP was not readily available to the library code. This lack of LWP state information at the threads library level also made the implementation of adaptive locks impossible.

Finally, keeping a sufficient pool of LWPs available to a threaded process such that runnable user threads would have the resource they needed to execute when they needed it was not easily solved. Solaris 2.5.1 and previous releases use a special SIGWAITING signal generated by the kernel when all the LWPs in a process are blocked and a special signal handler creates more LWPs for the process. In Solaris 2.5.1 (and previous releases), the sleep/wakeup subsystem calls a sigwaiting_check() routine, which compares the total number of LWPs in the process, p_lwpcnt, with the total number of blocked LWPs, p_lwpblocked. If the values are the same, all the LWPs in the process are blocked. The kernel generates a SIGWAITING signal, caught by a special signal handler in the threads library, and the SIGWAITING handler creates a new LWP for the process. This solution works reasonably well for many applications, but the management of keeping the correct number of LWPs available for a threaded process in general required improvement.

9.4.1 User Thread Activation

Scheduler activations provide a very fast communication facility between the kernel and user-level threads library, based on shared memory pages (*not* System V IPC Shared Memory, but the same conceptually) and the kernel Doors framework. State information can be shared between the threads library and the kernel through the shared memory pages, and the kernel can generate an upcall into the threads library when an event of interest to the threads scheduler occurs. Note that the use of scheduler activations for multithreaded programs does not change the API—the activations are done by the library and the kernel and do not require code changes.

The preemption control component of scheduler activations (discussed earlier) has an associated API, schedctl_init(3X), for initializing, turning on, and turning off preemption control. These interfaces can be used with nonthreaded and multithreaded applications, but threaded applications *require* that the calling user thread be *bound* to an LWP. Because the preemption control code works at the kthread/LWP level, the only way a user thread can be assured of predictable results is through LWP binding. Calling the preemption control interfaces from unbound threads is not supported.

The primary infrastructure for scheduler-activations support in the kernel is the creation and management of shared memory pages for the kernel's threads library, and the upcall mechanism, which is built on Solaris Doors. You may recall from

Chapter 1 that Doors provides a process-to-process procedure call facility, where a server process can establish a door to a function in the process and client processes can make door calls into the server door. Essentially, a process can execute a function call to a function that is part of another process's address space, pass the function arguments, and get a return value as if the function was part of the calling process. Doors provide a very fast and efficient method of interprocess communication, making them ideal for use in scheduler activations as a facility for the kernel calling up into the user threads library (upcall).

These facilities are put in place when a multithreaded process first begins execution. The initialization of a multithreaded process begins with the creation of the primordial thread, t0 (thread zero), which triggers the creation of several threads required to support threaded processes, such as the SIGWAITING signal handler, dynamiclwps(). The t0 initialization code calls an sc_init() routine that sets up the shared memory pages and the upcall door. sc_init() calls door_create() to establish a door for kernel-to-user upcalls, then calls sc_setup() to complete the initialization of the scheduler-activations support structures.

Most of the setup work and support for scheduler activations in the kernel is done in the lwp_schedctl() system call, a new system call created specifically for scheduler activations. Note that lwp_schedctl() is *not* a public interface; the invocation of lwp_schedctl() by an application program is *not* supported. The call itself is not documented in the section 2 manual pages for that reason. When invoked from sc_setup(), lwp_schedctl() creates the shared memory pages, which are mapped to the kernel and the user process and locked in memory so they cannot be paged out.

9.4.2 LWP Pool Activation

LWP pool activation refers to the fast and efficient replenishing of LWPs to a threaded process that has all LWPs in a blocking or sleeping state, potentially leaving runnable user threads without an execution resource. This condition is tested for and handled when the condition variables code is entered to put an LWP/kthread to sleep. The cv_wait_sig(), cv_timedwait(), and cv_wait_sig_swap() routines issue a call to schedctl_check(), with the SC_BLOCK flag set as an argument, to determine if an activation exists for the LWP/kthread. This is done in conjunction with a subsequent call to schedctl_block(), which determines if all LWPs in the process are blocked.

schedctl_check() tests the kernel thread's t_schedctl pointer and the passed flag, SC_BLOCK in this case. If an activation has been established, the kthread's t_schedctl pointer references an sc_data structure, which contains links to the shared memory page pool and state flags. For a threaded application, t_schedctl will have been set during the initialization process, and sc_flags (in sc_data as referenced by t_schedctl) will have the SC_BLOCK flag set.

The `schedctl_block()` code will determine if this LWP/kthread is the last one in the process. At the process level, `p_sc_unblocked` in the `proc` structure maintains a count of unblocked LWPs in the process. That count is decremented since another LWP is about to block. If `p_sc_unblocked` drops to zero after being decremented, `schedctl_block()` looks in the activations door pool for an LWP that it can hand off to the dispatcher and issues a `door_get_activation()` call. `door_get_activation()` returns a pointer to an LWP/kthread and plugs it into the `t_handoff` field of the calling kthread if an LWP is available in the pool. If an LWP is not available in the pool, `schedctl_block()` uses the old-fashioned method and calls `sigwaiting_send()` to send a `SIGWAITING` signal, which results in a new LWP being created through the `SIGWAITING` signal handler in the threads library.

If we retrieved an LWP/kthread from the activations pool, the calling kernel thread's `t_handoff` field will be pointing to the LWP/kthread fetched from the pool. Recall from our discussion of the `swtch()` code in the dispatcher that an early test in `swtch()` is for a non-NULL `t_handoff` pointer. Thus, when the dispatcher is entered from the condition variable code, it will find a valid LWP/kthread pointer in `t_handoff`. The presence of a valid pointer causes `swtch()` to call a shuttle routine to prepare the LWP/kthread from the pool for execution and ultimately calls `resume()` to context-switch the LWP/kthread onto the processor. The switched-in LWP from the door pool executes a short code segment that essentially tests for any runnable user threads in the process. If runnable user threads exist, the user threads dispatcher is entered so a user thread can be scheduled on the new LWP.

To summarize: an activation for blocked LWPs is initialized when a threaded process begins execution. When an LWP is about to be put to sleep (block), the kernel tests for an activation enabled and an available LWP from a pool created at initialization time. If an LWP is found from the pool, the dispatcher hands off the processor to the new LWP, effectively keeping the process running on the processor.

The preemption control feature of scheduler activations was discussed in the dispatcher section in this chapter. Scheduler activations provide the infrastructure to support other very useful facilities in the Solaris kernel, such as adaptive locks at the user threads level, better priority management and control for user threads, and affinity scheduling for better hardware cache utilization. These features will be added to future versions of Solaris.

Kernel thread execution, context switching and affinity (binding to a specific processor) is tied very closely with the processor support mechanism implemented in the operating system. In the next section, we discuss how the Solaris kernel manages processors and how processor sets, a feature added in Solaris 2.6, are implemented.

9.5   Kernel Processor Control and Processor Sets

Every operating system requires intimate knowledge of the hardware processors it supports and has low-level kernel code to manage things like processor state, trap and interrupt handling, clock tick processing, thread context switching, memory management, stack management, etc. The Solaris kernel extends the notion of processor control considerably beyond traditional implementations. The current model in the Solaris kernel was driven by several requirements of two goals:

- **Multiprocessor system efficiency.** Sun leads the industry in building scalable multiprocessor server systems based on the Symmetric Memory Processor (SMP) architecture. This architecture is defined as some number of processors that share a single image of the operating system, the system's physical address space (physical memory and I/O space), and the kernel's virtual address space. Building an operating system that manages processor resources effectively and efficiently is key to system scalability and management.

- **Resource management and control.** The ability to manage the hardware resources of a system effectively, such that applications or groups of users can be guaranteed some percentage of available processor resources, has become a mainstream requirement in all facets of computing. Other control mechanisms such as dynamically taking processors offline without affecting the entire system, bringing processors online, redirecting interrupts, and even powering processors down are also features that are much in demand.

The Solaris kernel delivers on these requirements with a kernel implementation built around per-processor data structures and kernel code functions for processor management and integration into related areas of the operating system, primarily the kernel threads scheduler, or dispatcher.

Every processor on a Solaris system has a corresponding data structure, the cpu structure, which maintains various bits of information, such as the state of the processor, and links to resources used by the processor, such as its dispatch queues, an idle thread, and interrupt threads. The cpu structure members can be categorized by function.

- **General information** — The CPU identification number, a sequential ID number, and state flags.

- **Kernel thread pointers** — Pointers to the currently executing kernel thread, an idle kernel thread, and a pause kernel thread; a pointer to the current LWP.

- **CPU structure linked lists** — A CPU appears on one or more linked lists maintained in the kernel; a list of existing (installed and configured) CPUs, a list of online CPUs, and a list of other CPUs in the same processor set; a pointer to a cpupart structure (CPU partition) for processor set support.

- **Scheduling variables** — The per-processor dispatch queue (queue of runnable kernel threads), scheduling flags to manage thread preemption, and per-kernel thread scheduling information.

- **Interrupt information** — The CPU's interrupt stack, a pointer to a linked list of interrupt threads, a flag to indicate the CPU in running on the interrupt stack, and interrupt-level information.
- **Statistics** — Statistical data, mostly in the form of counters, on CPU activity (used by sar(1M), vmstat(1M), and mpstat(1M)).
- **Configuration and control data** — Processor information such as the CPU type, Floating Point Unit (FPU) information, and clock speed; control for state changes and checkpoint/resume support.
- **Architecture-specific data** — Processor architecture-specific control and information, such as fine-grained clock tick data, architecture-specific interrupt data, and processor control block for saving hardware state (general registers, floating-point registers, etc.).

The structure, defined in /usr/include/sys/cpuvar.h, is illustrated in Figure 9.17.

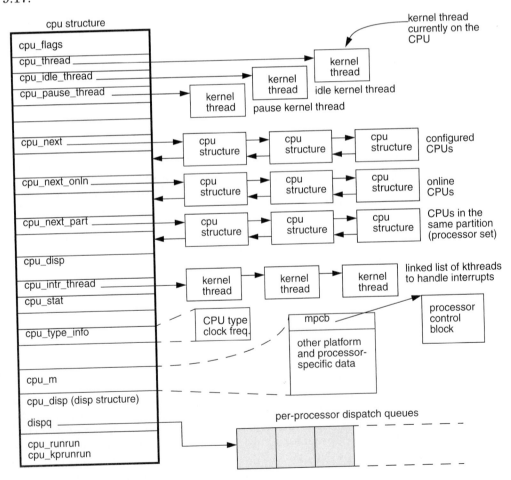

Figure 9.17 CPU Structure and Major Links

Most of the fields in the CPU structure are machine independent and thus apply to all platforms supported by the Solaris environment. As we indicated earlier, the data that is architecture specific is referenced through the cpu_m field in the structure, which contains the machine-dependent data and links to the processor-specific processor control block (PCB). The cpu_stat field is an embedded data structure that combines most of the kernel-maintained counters defined in /usr/include/sys/sysinfo.h. Per-processor statistical information is maintained and reported by utilities like mpstat(1M). Other bundled tools, vmstat(1M) and sar(1M), provide systemwide statistics by summing the per-processor data.

The linked lists of CPU structures are all doubly linked, with a forward and backward pointer. The diagram in Figure 9.17 shows only the forward pointer names (e.g., cpu_next_*xxx*), but every forward link also has a corresponding cpu_prev_*xxx* back pointer. The primary linked list is all configured processors, linked by cpu_next/cpu_prev. All online processors are linked by cpu_next_onln/cpu_prev_onln. A processor taken offline by the psradm(1M) command or p_online(2) system call is removed from the online linked list and taken out of the dispatcher—kernel threads will not be placed on an offline processor's dispatch queues. Offline processors *can* still field interrupts.

9.5.1 Processor Control

The system creates several kernel threads that serve a specific purpose for CPU control or general operating system activity. The interrupt threads are designed to facilitate fast switching to and from an interrupt handler by having a thread ready to execute interrupt handling code. The linked list is created at boot time, one thread for each interrupt level—10 on the Ultra Enterprise Server systems. (There are actually 15 interrupt levels, but levels above 10 do not require an interrupt thread.) The idle thread is executed if there are no runnable threads on any of the dispatch queues when the scheduler runs. The idle thread essentially loops, calling the dispatcher function to examine the queues, looking for the highest (best) priority runnable thread. The pause thread exists as part of the processor control facilities and keeps the CPU in a safe place in the interim between state changes (e.g., online to offline).

A CPU in Solaris can be in one of several possible states, as defined by the bits set in the cpu_flags field.

- **CPU_RUNNING.** The CPU is running, able to execute kernel threads, handle interrupts, etc.
- **CPU_READY.** The CPU will take cross-calls and directed interrupts.
- **CPU_QUIESCED.** The CPU is not running kernel threads or interrupt threads.
- **CPU_EXISTS.** All installed CPUs when the system initializes (boots) will minimally be in the EXISTS state.
- **CPU_ENABLE.** The CPU is enabled to take interrupts, but it is not part of the dispatcher's pool of online CPUs to schedule kernel threads. With this flag off,

the CPU may still take *directed* interrupts and cross-calls, but not interrupts
that can be directed to another CPU.

- **CPU_OFFLINE.** The processor was taken offline by psradm(1M) or
  p_online(2) and is no longer scheduling kernel threads. The CPU will still
  take interrupts. (That's the difference between the offline state and quiesced
  state—a CPU in the quiesced state will not take interrupts.) A CPU with
  bound threads cannot be taken offline.

- **CPU_POWEROFF.** (Solaris 2.6 and Solaris 7 only.) The CPU has been powered
  off.

You can examine the CPU structures on a running system by using an available
adb macro, cpu. (adb macros can be found in the /usr/lib/adb directory.) The
kernel maintains the address of the first CPU structure in the linked list in a kernel variable called cpu_list.

```
# adb -k
physmem 3b5f
cpu_list/K
cpu_list:
cpu_list:      1041ad20
1041ad20$<cpu

cpu0:
cpu0:          id               seqid            flags
               0                0                1b
cpu0+0x10:     thread           idle_thread      pause_thread
               30000ab8fe0      2a10001fd40      2a10000fd40
cpu0+0x28:     lwp              fpowner          part
               30000a70070      0                1041bc88
cpu0+0x48:     next             prev             next_onln
               300003d2010      300003d2010      300003d2010
cpu0+0x60:     prev_onln        next_part        prev_part
               300003d2010      300003d2010      300003d2010
cpu0+0x78:     disp

cpu0+0x78:     lock     npri    queue
               0        170     3000048a000
cpu0+0x88:     limit            actmap           maxrunpri
               3000048aff0      30000a40840      -1
cpu0+0x9a:     max_unb_pri      nrunnable
               -1               0

cpu0+0xa8:     runrun   kprunrun         chosen_level
               0        0                -1
cpu0+0xb0:     dispthread       thread_lock      last_swtch
               30000ab8fe0      0                12e9f54
cpu0+0xc8:     intr_stack       on_intr          intr_thread
               2a10001bf50      0                2a10007dd40
cpu0+0xe0:     intr_actv        base_spl         profile_cyclic_id
               0                0                0
cpu0+0x278:    profile_pc       profile_pil      profile_when
               syscall_trap+0x28                 0                0
cpu0+0x290:    profile_ilate    cyc_cpu
               53               300000678c8
```

To look at structures for the remaining processors, feed the next value into the adb cpu macro.

Note the flags field, which is the cpu_flags member. This example represents the state after bootstrap of a CPU that has not had its state altered explicitly. Following initialization, the set cpu_flags bits are CPU_RUNNING, CPU_READY, CPU_EXISTS, and CPU_ENABLE. Below is an example of the use of psrinfo(1M) and psradm(1M) to display CPU status and take a CPU offline.

```
# psrinfo
0        on-line    since 04/26/00 14:39:27
1        on-line    since 04/26/00 14:39:31
# psradm -f 1
# psrinfo
0        on-line    since 04/26/00 14:39:27
1        off-line   since 04/28/00 21:48:51
```

Another look at the CPU structures with adb(1), specifically the structure for CPU ID 2 (the CPU taken offline), shows that the CPU states (cpu_flags) are CPU_RUNNING, CPU_READY, CPU_QUIESCED, CPU_EXISTS, and CPU_OFFLINE. Taking the CPU offline results in the CPU_QUIESCED and CPU_OFFLINE flags getting set and the CPU_ENABLE flag getting cleared. This example demonstrates that the CPU state flags may not always appear as expected if examined online or with a kernel debugger. You might expect that taking the CPU offline would result in CPU_RUNNING or CPU_READY to be cleared, but they are not cleared. The macro the kernel uses to determine if a CPU is active tests for the CPU_OFFLINE state, and the dispatcher looks at CPU_QUIESCED and CPU_OFFLINE bits to determine if a CPU should participate in running kernel threads.

Solaris 7 added the ability to remove a CPU from the interrupt pool, meaning that an administrator can issue a psradm(1M) command that tells the kernel not to send the specified processor interrupts; instead, the kernel should keep the processor online so it will continue to schedule kernel threads. This functionality is mostly useful when used in conjunction with processor binding (binding a process or kernel thread to processor) for real-time applications that require some predictable, bounded dispatch latency for thread scheduling. Using psradm(1M) to disable interrupts on a processor results in the CPU_ENABLE flag being cleared; the other flags set during initialization remain set. Table 9-5 summarizes the CPU state flags following some state changes.

Table 9-5 CPU State Flags

State	Flags Set
After boot/initialization	RUNNING, READY, EXISTS, ENABLE
Interrupts disabled	RUNNING, READY, EXISTS
Offline	RUNNING, READY, QUIESCED, EXISTS, OFFLINE
Offline and interrupts disabled	RUNNING, READY, QUIESCED, EXISTS, OFFLINE

Note that there is no difference in the CPU state if the CPU is taken offline (psradm -f) or if the CPU is taken offline and interrupts are disabled (psradm -f, and -i). Offline implies that interrupts are disabled for a CPU.

Processor control can happen at one of several levels. Under normal circumstances, the kernel initializes existing processors at boot time, and those processors participate in interrupt handling, cross-call activity, and kernel thread scheduling and execution. Processor state changes, online-to-offline and interrupt enable/disable, are driven by a command set or can be done programmatically by system calls. Additionally, processor management, the creation and management of processor sets, thread-to-processor binding, etc., are also done at either the command or programming level. The commands and APIs used for processor control and management are summarized in Table 9-6.

Table 9-6 Processor Control Interfaces

Command (1M) or Interface (2)	Description
psrinfo(1M)	Displays processor status and information.
processor_info(2)	Gets processor type and status.
psradm(1M)	Changes processor state (offline/online, disable/enable interrupt processing).
p_online(2)	Programmatically changes processor state (online/offline, disable/enable interrupts).
pbind(1M)	Binds (or unbinds) a process to a CPU.
processor_bind(2)	Binds (or unbinds) a process to a CPU from a program.
psrset(1M)	Creates, manages processor sets. Binds/unbinds processes to/from a processor set.
pset_bind(2)	Binds/unbinds a process or LWP to/from a processor set.
pset_info(2)	Gathers information about a processor set.
pset_create(2), pset_destroy(2), pset_assign(2)	Creates or destroys a processor set. Assigns a CPU to a processor set.

The commands listed in Table 9-6 are built on the system calls created for processor control and management, listed in the same table. The state changes discussed in the previous pages are driven by psradm(1M) or the p_online(2) system call.

9.5.2 Processor Sets

The Solaris kernel enables processor sets to be configured, where some number of processors (one or more) are grouped into a processor set for resource management and application binding. Processes can be bound to a processor set or to a single processor. Internally, processor sets are referred to as CPU *partitions*. Some future release may possibly distinguish between a processor partition in the kernel and a processor set as seen by users of the system. As of right now (up to and including Solaris 7), processor sets and processor partitions are the same thing.

Processor binding can happen in two ways: using the traditional bind commands or interfaces for processors that have not been configured into a processor set, or using processor sets and the associated bind methods specific to processor sets.

The original (and still supported) method of binding a process to a CPU was through the pbind(1M) command and processor_bind(2) system call. Bindings created with either method result in all the LWPs of the process getting scheduled only on the CPU that the process is bound to. It is not an exclusive binding; other LWPs in the system may get scheduled on the CPU. It is also possible that other CPUs will do some processing on behalf of the bound LWPs. If an LWP issues an I/O, the I/O may be processed on another CPU, including the interrupt processing when the I/O is complete. Using the command interface, pbind(1M), we can only bind at the process level. The kernel supports LWP-level binding, where different LWPs in the same process could be bound to different CPUs. This binding can be done programmatically with processor_bind(2), by which you can specify an LWP ID.

Solaris 2.6 added processor sets, and with processor sets comes another method of binding processes to CPUs. Recall that a processor set is a user-level abstraction of a grouping of processors. In the kernel, all processors in the same set are part of the same CPU partition. Once a processor set is created (psrset -c cpu_id), the processors in the set are no longer available for running all kernel threads systemwide. Rather, they will only run kernel threads (LWPs) that have been bound to the processor set with psrset(1M) or pset_bind(2). Once a process is bound, the binding is exclusive—only threads bound to the processor set are scheduled and executed on CPUs in the set. CPUs in a processor set are not available as targets of pbind(1M) requests—you cannot use pbind(1M) (or processor_bind(2)) to bind processes or LWPs to a CPU that is part of a user processor set. If a process has been bound to a CPU with pbind(1M), that processor cannot be placed in a processor set until the binding is undone.

Not every processor on a system can be placed in a processor set. The kernel will not allow all the processors to be configured into a user processor set; at least one CPU must remain in the default system partition (created at boot time). Support for processor binding, either to a single processor or to a processor set, exists at the kernel thread level (or LWP, as it is referred to in the reference manual pages; in this context, the kernel thread and LWP can be thought of as the same thing). A few kernel thread structure fields link to CPU structures if the thread is bound, or they reference the processor set in the case of a partition binding. These fields are discussed in more detail in Chapters 3 and 4.

The implementation of processor sets is built on the cpupart data structure (/usr/include/sys/cpupart.h) and support code in the kernel. The cpupart structure has links to processors in the partition, maintains links to other partitions in the system, and maintains some general housekeeping data, such as the partition ID, the type of partition (public or private), number of online CPUs in the partition, and a kernel priority dispatch queue.

Figure 9.18 shows two partitions, glued together by the `cpupart` structure. The list of CPUs that are part of the partition are linked by `cp_cpulist` and from there are linked through the `cpu_next_part/cpu_prev_part` links in the `cpu` structure (see Figure 9.17 on page 412). All partitions configured in the system are linked through the `cp_next` and `cp_prev` links (doubly linked list), and a pointer to the base or "parent" partition is maintained in `cp_base`. The `cp_list_head` pointer is set up in the kernel to point to the first `cpupart` structure in the system.

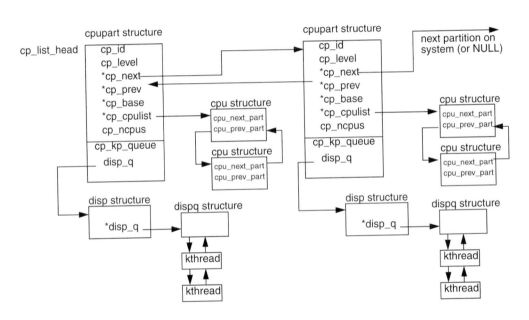

Figure 9.18 Processor Partition (Processor Set) Structures and Links

We alluded earlier to a *default* partition, created at system initialization (boot) time. All installed processors are placed in this default partition during the initialization process, and if no other partitions (processor sets) are explicitly created by `psrset(1M)` or `pset_create(2)`, the system simply maintains the internal default set, which is not made visible to users. `psrset(1M)` will show all processors on the system as unassigned; available to be configured into a processor set. The kernel defines three possible levels for partitions (`cp_level`): CP_DEFAULT, CP_SYSTEM, CP_PRIVATE. The default partition created at boot time is, of course, CP_DEFAULT and will be the only default partition systemwide (only one such partition is allowed). Additional partitions created on the system are set to CP_PRIVATE. The CP_PRIVATE level is not currently used but will likely be implemented in the future as a means of creating internal (kernel only) partitions.

We show a dispatch queue for each partition. To summarize our earlier discussion of dispatch queues; the Solaris kernel maintains several dispatch queues: queues of runnable kernel threads waiting for a processor. Every CPU has its own set of dispatch queues for runnable threads below real-time priorities. For real-time threads, a systemwide queue, known as the *kernel preempt queue*, is maintained. Threads placed on this queue are at a high enough priority to force a kernel preemption, hence the name. If processor sets are created, then each processor set (partition) manages its own kernel preempt queue. This per-partition queue is part of the `cpupart` structure, which integrates a `disp` structure (dispatcher—the `cp_kp_queue` member of `cpupart`). This is where the queue link is maintained, by a `disp_q` pointer.

Kernel support functions for CPU control are split between CPU partition management functions and per-CPU control functions, several of which are executed during system boot to build and initialize the required kernel data structures, plug in all the links, and bring all the processors online. Once the system is up and running, any subsequent state changes to a CPU will likely be the result of a user-initiated procedure, such as a dynamic reconfiguration operation, thread binding, or processor set management.

10

INTERPROCESS COMMUNICATION

Interprocess communication (IPC) encompasses facilities provided by the operating system to enable the sharing of data (shared memory segments), the exchange of information and data (message queues), and synchronization of access to shared resources (semaphores) between processes and threads on the same system. Contrast IPC to networking-based facilities, such as sockets and RPC interfaces, which enable communication over a network link between distributed systems. Early IPC facilities originated in AT&T Unix System V, which added support for shared memory, semaphores, and message queues around 1983. This original set of three IPC facilities is generally known as System V IPC. Over time, a similar set of IPC features evolved from the POSIX standards, and we now have POSIX semaphores, shared memory, and message queues. The System V and POSIX IPCs use different APIs and are implemented differently in the kernel, although for applications they provide similar functionality.

Other facilities for interprocess communication include memory mapped files (mmap(2)), named pipes (also known as FIFOs), Unix domain sockets, and recently added Solaris Doors, which provide an RPC-like facility for threads running on the same system. Each method by which an application can do interprocess communication offers specific features and functionality which may or may not be useful for a given application. It's up to the application developer to determine what the requirements are and which facility best meets those requirements.

Our goal here is not to provide a tutorial on programming with these interfaces, although some mention of the APIs is necessary when we describe a feature or functional component. Several texts discuss programming and interprocess communication, most notably, *UNIX Network Programming—Interprocess Communication*, 2nd edition, Volume II, by W. Richard Stevens.

10.1 Generic System V IPC Support

Several data structures and low-level kernel routines are common to all three System V IPC facilities. In this section, we cover those common areas, and then we get into the specifics of each IPC implementation. Common interfaces and structures include:

- ***xxxid_ds* data structures.** Each facility has a data structure that contains various bits of information about the resource. The naming convention used for the data structure is the same across all three sets of interfaces (see Table 10-1).

- **Keys and identifiers.** To share IPC resources across processes (which is the whole point of interprocess communication), a process must be able to uniquely identify a resource when it issues a get call. The IPC facilities require a key value in the *xxx*get(2) call and return an identifier based on the passed key value.

- `ipcget()` **and** `ipcaccess()`. These common kernel routines are used by the IPC facilities to get the identifier and to check access permissions.

10.1.1 Module Creation

The System V IPC kernel modules are implemented as dynamically loadable modules. Each facility has a corresponding loadable module in the /kernel/sys directory (shmsys, semsys, and msgsys). In addition, all three methods of IPC require loading of the /kernel/misc/ipc module, which provides two low-level routines shared by all three facilities. The ipcaccess() routine is called to verify access permissions to a particular IPC resource, for example, a shared memory segment, a semaphore, or a message queue. The ipcget() code fetches a data structure associated with a particular IPC resource that generated the call, based on a *key* value that is passed as an argument in the shmget(2), msgget(2), and semget(2) system calls.

When an IPC resource is initially created, a positive integer, known as an *identifier*, is assigned to identify the IPC object. The identifier is derived from a *key* value. The kernel IPC *xxx*get(2) system call will return the same identifier to processes or threads, using the same key value, which is how different processes can be sure to access the desired message queue, semaphore, or shared memory segment. An ftok(3C), or file-to-key interface, is the most common method of having different processes obtain the correct key before they call one of the IPC *xxx*get() routines.

Associated with each IPC resource is an *id* data structure, which the kernel allocates and initializes the first time an *xxx*get(2) system call is invoked with the appropriate flags set. The *xxx*get(2) system call for each facility returns the identifier to the calling application, again based on arguments passed in the call and permissions. The structures are similar in name and are defined in the header file for each facility (see Table 10-1).

Table 10-1 IPC ID Structure Names

Facility Type	`xxxget(2)`	ID Structure Name
semaphores	`semget(2)`	`semid_ds`
shared memory	`shmget(2)`	`shmid_ds`
message queues	`msgget(2)`	`msgid_ds`

The number of `xxxid_ds` structures available in the kernel is static and is determined by each facility's `xxxmni` kernel tunable parameter, that is, `msgmni`, `semmni`, and `shmmni` determine the maximum number of `msgid_ds`, `semid_ds`, and `shmid_ds` structures available, respectively. Kernel memory for these structures is allocated during the initialization phase of the IPC facility, based on the structure size and `xxxmni` value.

Most fields in the ID structures are unique for each IPC type, but they all include as the first structure member a pointer to an `ipcperm` data structure, which defines the access permissions for that resource, much as access to files is defined by permissions maintained in each file's inode. The `ipcperm` structure is defined in `/usr/include/sys/ipc.h`; it contains the members listed in Table 10-2.

Table 10-2 ipc_perm Data Structure

Member Name	Data Type	Description
`uid`	`uid_t`	Owner's user ID
`gid`	`gid_t`	Owner's group ID
`cuid`	`uid_t`	Creator's user ID
`cgid`	`gid_t`	Creator's group ID
`mode`	`mode_t`	Access modes (permission bits)
`seq`	`ulong`	Slot usage sequence number
`key`	`key_t`	IPC key value

For each IPC resource, the UID and GID of the owner and creator will be the same. Ownership could subsequently be changed through a control system call, but the creator's IDs never change. The access mode bits are similar to file access modes, differing in that there is no execute mode for IPC objects; thus, the mode bits define read/write permissions for the owner, group, and all others. The `seq` field, described as the slot usage sequence number, is used by the kernel to establish the unique identifier of the IPC resource when it is first created.

The kernel `ipcget()` routine is invoked from each of the IPC *xxx*get(2) system calls; its behavior is determined by whether the object already exists and by flags set by the programmer making the *xxx*get(2) call. It's up to the programmer to pass a *key* value along as one of the arguments to the *xxx*get(2) system call. The key value provides a means by which different processes can access the IPC object they wish to share; callers using the same key value will have the same IPC object identifier returned to them (assuming permissions allow access). The following pseudocode illustrates how the process works.

```
ipcget(...,args,...)
        if (key == IPC_PRIVATE)
            loop through each xxxid_ds structure
            if (allocated)
                    continue through loop
            if (not allocated)
                    init xxxid_ds structure and return
            reached end of loop and all are allocated, return ENOSPC
        else (key is not IPC_PRIVATE)
        loop through each xxxid_ds structure
        if (allocated)
            if (key passed matches key in ipc_perm structure)
                    if (IPC_EXCL /* exclusive flag */)
                            return error EEXIST
                    if (access not allowed)
                            return error EACCESS
                      else (it's allocated, key matches, not exclusive, access allowed)
            else /* it's allocated but key does not match */
            continue through loop
        else (not allocated)
            set pointer
        if (IPC_CREATE is NOT set)
            return error ENOENT /* there is no corresponding entry */
        if (end of loop, everything is allocated and no key match)
            return error ENOSPC
```

Summarizing the preceding pseudocode flow: a new *xxxid_ds* structure (where *xxx* is *sem*, *shm*, or *msg*) is initialized on behalf of the caller if there is a free slot and if there is no entry with a matching key, and if the caller specified `IPC_CREATE` or `IPC_EXCL` (or both). A pointer to an *existing* object is returned if the key does match and if the mode bits grant permission and if it's not an exclusive object (i.e., it was not created with `IPC_EXCL`).

The `ipcaccess()` code is called at various points by the IPC support code in the kernel to verify access permissions to the IPC resource being requested. The code is straightforward: it verifies access permissions set for the UID and GID of the caller against the mode bits in the `ipc_perm` structure. The initial mode of an IPC object is determined when the object is first created by an IPC get call, specified by the *flag* argument in the call, which represents access mode permission expressed in numeric form, similar to file access modes, as in:

```
shmget(key, size, IPC_CREAT | 0644);
```

The preceding example shows a shmget(2) system call, with the third argument setting the CREATE flag and setting the access modes to read/write for the owner and read-only for group and other. With no access mode bits specified in the *get* call, no mode bits are set, disallowing access for everyone except root. The kernel returns an EACCESS error if the permission test fails on an *xxx*get(2) call.

10.1.2 Resource Maps

Two of the three IPC facilities—message queues and semaphores—use a low-level kernel memory allocation scheme known as resource maps. Resource maps are a means by which small units of kernel memory can be allocated and freed from a larger pool of kernel pages that have been preallocated. Message queues and semaphores are relatively dynamic in nature since applications tend to move messages on and off a queue frequently, and messages can vary in size from a few bytes to several Kbytes (or more). System V IPC supports the notion of semaphore sets, and the number of semaphores per set can vary during execution. For this reason, the kernel code is called upon to allocate space for new messages or semaphores and to free the space when a message is removed or a semaphore deleted. Because these objects are stored in kernel memory, this approach would result in potentially frequent calls to the kernel memory allocator. It makes more sense to allocate a large chunk up-front and use a lighter-weight interface to manage the preallocated space. Resource maps fill that function and are used in Solaris to manage kernel space for storing semaphores and the data portion of messages.

The amount of space allocated for resource maps for the IPC facilities is determined by kernel tunable parameters, one parameter each for message queues and semaphores. The semmap parameter (default value of 10) and msgmap parameter (default value of 100) can be tuned in the /etc/system according to application requirements. Setting the values larger results in more kernel memory allocated up-front. Each facility uses its own resource map, meaning that the resource map space allocated for semaphores is not available for use by message queues, and vice versa. Shared memory does not use resource maps—shared memory segments are part of the process's address space. Only the shdmid_ds structure is in the kernel, and space for those structures is allocated up-front as specified by the shmmni tunable parameter.

10.2 System V Shared Memory

Shared memory provides an extremely efficient means of sharing data between multiple processes on a Solaris system, since the data need not actually be moved from one process's address space to another. As the name implies, shared memory is exactly that: the sharing of the same physical memory (RAM) pages by multiple processes, such that each process has mappings to the same physical pages and can access the memory through pointer dereferencing in code. The use of shared memory in an application requires implementation of just a few interfaces bundled into the standard C language library, /usr/lib/libc.so, as listed in Table 10-3. Consult the manual pages for more detailed information. In the following sections, we examine what these interfaces do from a kernel implementation standpoint.

Table 10-3 Shared Memory APIs

System Call	Arguments Passed	Returns	Description
shmget(2)	key, size, flags	Identifier	Creates a shared segment if one with a matching key does not exist, or locates an existing segment based on the key.
shmat(2)	Identifier, address, flags	Pointer	Attaches shared segment to processes address space.
shmdt(2)	Address	0 or 1	Detaches a shared segment from a process's address space.
shmctl(2)	Identifier, command, status structure	0 or 1 (success or failure)	Control call—gets/sets permissions, gets stats, destroys identifier, etc.

The shared memory kernel module is not loaded automatically by Solaris at boot time; none of the System V IPC facilities are. The kernel will dynamically load a required module when a call that requires the module is made. Thus, if the shmsys and ipc modules are not loaded, then the first time an application makes a shared memory system call (e.g., shmget(2)), the kernel loads the module and executes the system call. The module remains loaded until it is explicitly unloaded by the modunload(1M) command or until the system reboots. This behavior explains an FAQ on shared memory: why, when the ipcs(1M) command is executed, it sometimes comes back with this status:

```
sel> ipcs
IPC status from <running system> as of Mon May  1 17:15:56 2000
Message Queue facility not in system.
T         ID       KEY         MODE         OWNER      GROUP
Shared Memory:
m          0    0x50110705  --rw-r--r--      root       root
Semaphores:
```

The facility not in system message means the module is not loaded. You can tell the operating system to load the module during bootup by using the forceload directive in the /etc/system file.

```
forceload: sys/msgsys
```

Also, you can use the modload(1M) command, which allows a root user to load any loadable kernel module from the command line. You can use the modinfo(1M) command to see which loadable modules are currently loaded in the kernel. Note that Solaris is smart enough not to allow the unloading (modunload(1M)) of a loadable module that is in use. Note also that the code is written to be aware of dependencies, such that loading the shmsys module also causes the ipc module to be loaded.

The kernel maintains certain resources for the implementation of shared memory. Specifically, a shared memory identifier, shmid, is initialized and maintained by the operating system whenever a shmget(2) system call is executed successfully. The shmid identifies a shared segment that has two components: the actual shared RAM pages and a data structure that maintains information about the shared segment, the shmid_ds data structure, detailed in Table 10-4.

Table 10-4 shmid_ds Data Structure

Name	Data Type	Corresponding ipcs(1M) Column	Description
shm_perm	struct	see ipc perm table	Embedded ipc_perm structure. Generic structure for IPC facilities that maintains permission information
shm_segsz	unsigned int	SEGSZ	Size in bytes of the shared segment
shm_amp	pointer	none	Pointer to corresponding anon map structure
shm_lkcnt	unsigned short	none	Lock count; number of locks on the shared segment
shm_lpid	long	LPID	Last PID; PID of last process to do a shared memory operation on the segment
shm_cpid	long	CPID	Creator PID; PID of the process that created the shared segment
shm_nattch	unsigned long	NATTCH	Number of attaches to the shared segment
shm_cnattch	unsigned long	none	Creator attaches? *Not currently used*
shm_atime	long	ATIME	Time of last attach
shm_dtime	long	DTIME	Time of last detach
shm_ctime	long	CTIME	Time of last change to shmid_ds structure
shm_cv	cond var	none	Condition variable. *Not used*
shm_sptas	pointer	none	Pointer to address space structure

The system allocates kernel memory for some number of shmid_ds structures at boot time, as determined from the shared memory tunable parameter shmmni. All together, only four tunable parameters are associated with shared memory. They are described in Table 10-5.

Table 10-5 Shared Memory Tunable Parameters

Name	Default Value	Minimum Value	Maximum Value	Data Type	Description
shmmax	1048576	1	4,294,967,295 (4 GB)	unsigned int	Maximum size in bytes of a shared memory segment
shmmin	1	1	4,294,967,295 (4 GB)	unsigned int	Minimum size for a shared segment
shmmni	100	1	2147483648 (2 GB)	int	Maximum number of shmid_ds structures, systemwide.
shmseg	6	1	32767 (32K)	short	Max segments per process

When the system first loads the shared memory module, it allocates kernel memory to support the shmid_ds structures and other required kernel support structures. Each shmid_ds structure is 112 bytes in size and has a corresponding kernel mutex lock, which is an additional 8 bytes. Thus, the amount of kernel memory required by the system to support shared memory can be calculated as ((shmmni * 112) + (shmmni * 8)). The default value of 100 for shmmni requires the system to allocate 112.8 Kbytes of kernel memory for shared memory support. The system makes some attempt to protect itself against allocating too much kernel memory for shared memory support by checking for the maximum available kernel memory, dividing that value by 4, and using the resulting value as a limit for allocating resources for shared memory. Simply put, the system will not allow more than 25 percent of available kernel memory be allocated.

The preceding description applies to Solaris 2.5, 2.5.1, and 2.6. Prior releases, up to and including Solaris 2.4, did not impose a 25 percent limit check. Nor did they require the additional 8 bytes per shmid_ds for a kernel mutex lock, since shared memory used very coarse-grained locking in the earlier releases and only implemented one kernel mutex in the shared memory code. Beginning in Solaris 2.5, finer-grained locking was implemented, allowing for greater potential parallelism of applications using shared memory.

It should be clear that one should not set shmmni to an arbitrarily large value simply to ensure sufficient resources. There are limits as to how much kernel memory the system supports. On sun4m-based platforms, the limits are on the order of 128 Mbytes for releases prior to Solaris 2.5, and 256 Mbytes for Solaris 2.5, 2.5.1, and 2.6. On sun4d systems (SS1000 and SC2000), the limits are about 576 Mbytes in Solaris 2.5 and later. On UltraSPARC (sun4u)-based systems, the kernel has its own 4-Gbyte address space, so it is much less constrained. Still, keep in mind that the kernel is not pageable, and thus whatever kernel memory is needed remains resident in RAM, reducing available memory for user processes. Given that Sun ships systems today with very large RAM capacities, this characteristic of the kernel may not be an issue, but it should be considered nonetheless.

Note that the maximum value for shmmni listed in Table 10-5 is 2 Gbytes. This is a theoretical limit, based on the data type (a signed integer), and should not be construed as something configurable today. Applying the math from above, you see that 2 billion shared memory identifiers would require over 200 Gbytes of kernel memory! Assess to the best of your ability the number of shared memory identifiers required by the application, and set shmmni to that value plus 10 percent or so for headroom.

The remaining three shared memory tunable parameters are defined quite simply.

shmmax defines the maximum size a shared segment can be. The size of a shared memory segment is determined by the second argument to the shmget(2) system call. When the call is executed, the kernel checks to ensure that the size argument is not greater than shmmax. If it is, an error is returned. Setting shmmax to its maximum value does not affect the kernel size—no kernel resources are allocated on the basis of shmmax, so this variable can be tuned to its maximum value of 4 Gbytes (0xffffffff) on a 32-bit Solaris system, and larger on a 64-bit Solaris 7 system. The /etc/system entry examples that follow illustrate two ways of setting the 4-Gbyte limit for a 32-bit system and setting something larger on a 64-bit Solaris 7 system, in this case, a 10-Gbyte maximum shared segment.

```
set shmsys:shminfo_shmmax=0xffffffff       /* hexadecimal - 4GB limit */
set shmsys:shminfo_shmmax=4294967295       /* decimal - 4GB limit */
set shmsys:shminfo_shmmax=10000000000      /* decimal - 10GB, 64-bit example */
```

The shmmin tunable defines the smallest possible size a shared segment can be, as per the size argument passed in the shmget(2) call. There's no compelling reason to set this tunable from the default value of 1.

Lastly, shmseg defines the number of shared segments a process can attach (map pages) to. Processes can attach to multiple shared memory segments for application purposes, and this tunable determines how many mapped shared segments a process can have attached at any one time. Again, the 32-Kbyte limit (maximum size) in Table 10-5 is based on the data type (short) and does not necessarily reflect a value that will provide application performance that meets business requirements if some number of processes attach to 32,000 shared memory segments. Things like shared segment size, system size (amount of RAM, number and speed of processors, etc.) all factor in to determining the extent to which you can push the boundaries of this facility.

10.2.1 Shared Memory Kernel Implementation

In this section we look at the flow of kernel code that executes when the shared
memory system calls are called.

Applications first call shmget(2) to get a shared memory identifier. The kernel
uses a key value passed in the call to locate (or create) a shared segment.

```
[application code]
shmget(key, size, flags [PRIVATE or CREATE])

[kernel]
shmget()
        ipcget() /* get an identifier - shmid_ds */
        if (new shared segment)
                check size against min and max tunables
                get anon_map and anon array structures
                initialize anon structures
                initialize shmid_ds structure
        else /* existing segment */
                check size against existing segment size
        return shmid (or error) back to application
ipcget()
        if (key == IPC_PRIVATE)
                loop through shmid_ds structures, looking for a free one
                        if (found)
                                goto init
                        else
                                return ENOSPC /* tough cookies */
        else /* key is NOT IPC_PRIVATE */
                loop through shmid_ds structures, for each one
                if (structure is allocated)
                        if (the key matches)
                                if (CREATE or EXCLUSIVE flags set as passed args)
                                        return EEXIST error /* segment with matching key
exists */
                                if (permissions do NOT allow access)
                                        return EACCESS error
                        set status
                        set base address of shmid_ds
                        return 0 /* that's a good thing */

        set base address of shmid_ds /* if we reach this, we have an unallocated shmid_ds
structure */
        if (do not CREATE)
                return ENOENT error /*we're through them all, and didn't match keys */
        if (CREATE and no space)
                return ENOSPC error
        do init
        return 0 /* goodness */
```

shmget(), when entered, calls ipcget() to fetch the shmid_ds data structure.
Remember, all possible shmid_ds structures are allocated up-front when /ker-
nel/sys/shmsys loads, so we need to either find an existing one that matches the
key value or initialize an unallocated one if the flags indicate we should and a
structure is available. The final init phase of ipcget() sets the mode bits, creator
UID, and creator GID. When ipcget() returns to shmget(), the anon page mappings are initialized for a new segment or a simple size check is done. (The size

argument is the argument passed in the shmget(2) call, not the size of the existing segment.)

Once a shmget(2) call returns success to an application, the code has a valid shared memory identifier. The program must call shmat(2) to create the mappings (attach) to the shared segment.

```
[application]
shmat(shmid, address, flags)

[kernel]
shmat()
        ipc_access() /* check permissions */
        /* ipc_access() will return EACCESS if permission tests fail */
        /* and cause shmat() to bail out */
        if (kernel has ISM disabled)
                clear SHM_SHARE_MMU flag
        if (ISM and SHM_SHARE_MMU flag)
                calculate number pages
                find a range of pages in the address space and set address
                if (user-supplied address)
                        check alignment and range
                map segment to address
                create shared mapping tables
        if (NOT ISM)
                if (no user-supplied address)
                        find a range of pages in the address space and set address
                else
                        check alignment and range
return pointer to shared segment, or error
```

Much of the work done in shmat() requires calls into the lower-level address space support code and related memory management routines. The details on a process's address space mappings are covered in Chapter 10. Remember, attaching to a shared memory segment is essentially just another extension to a process's address space mappings.

At this point, applications have a pointer to the shared segment that they use in their code to read or write data. The shmdt(2) interface allows a process to unmap the shared pages from its address space (detach itself). Unmapping does not cause the system to remove the shared segment, even if all attached processes have detached themselves. A shared segment must be explicitly removed by the shmctl(2) call with the IPC_RMID flag set or from the command line with the ipcrm(1) command. Obviously, permissions must allow for the removal of the shared segment.

We should point out that the kernel makes no attempt at coordinating concurrent access to shared segments. The software developer must coordinate this access by using shared memory to prevent multiple processes attached to the same shared pages from writing to the same locations at the same time. Coordination can be done in several ways, the most common of which is the use of another IPC facility, semaphores, or mutex locks.

The shmctl(2) interface can also be used to get information about the shared segment (returns a populated shmid_ds structure), to set permissions, and to lock the segment in memory (processes attempting to lock shared pages must have an effective UID of root).

You can use the ipcs(1) command to look at active IPC facilities in the system. When shared segments are created, the system maintains permission flags similar to the permission bits used by the file system. They determine who can read and write the shared segment, as specified by the user ID (UID) and group ID (GID) of the process attempting the operation. You can see extended information on the shared segment by using the -a flag with the ipcs(1) command. The information is fairly intuitive and is documented in the ipcs(1) manual page. We also listed in Table 10-4 on page 427 the members of the shmid_ds structures that are displayed by ipcs(1) output and the corresponding column name. The permissions (mode) and key data for the shared structure are maintained in the ipc_perm data structure, which is embedded in (a member of) the shmid_ds structure and described in Table 10-2 on page 423.

10.2.2 Intimate Shared Memory (ISM)

Intimate shared memory (ISM) is an optimization introduced first in Solaris 2.2. It allows for the sharing of the low-level kernel data and structures involved in the virtual-to-physical address translation for shared memory pages, as opposed to just sharing the actual physical memory pages. Typically, non-ISM systems maintain per-process mapping information for the shared memory pages. With many processes attaching to shared memory, this scheme creates a lot of redundant mapping information to the same physical pages that the kernel must maintain.

Figure 10.1 illustrates the difference between ISM and non-ISM shared segments.

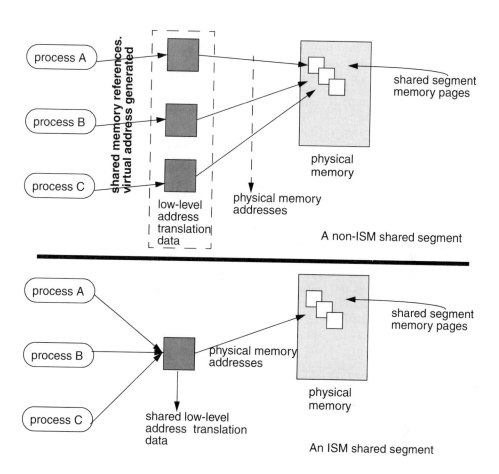

Figure 10.1 Shared Memory: ISM versus Non-ISM

The actual mapping structures differ across processors. That is, the low-level address translation structures and functions are part of the hardware-specific kernel code, known as the Hardware Address Translation (HAT) layer. The HAT layer is coded for a specific processor's Memory Management Unit (MMU), which is an integral part of the processor design, and responsible for translating virtual addresses generated by running processes to physical addresses generated by the system hardware to fetch the memory data.

In addition to the translation data sharing, ISM provides another useful feature: when ISM is used, the shared pages are locked down in memory and will never be paged out. This feature was added for the RDBMS vendors. As we said earlier, shared memory is used extensively by commercial RDBMS systems to cache data (among other things, such as stored procedures). Non-ISM implementations treat shared memory just like any other chunk of anonymous memory—it gets backing store allocated from the swap device, and the pages themselves are fair game to be paged out if memory contention becomes an issue. The effects of paging out shared memory pages that are part of a database cache would be disastrous from a performance standpoint—RAM shortages are never good for performance. Since a vast majority of customers that purchase Sun servers use them for database applications and since database applications make extensive use of shared memory, addressing this issue with ISM was an easy decision.

Solaris implements memory page locking by setting some bits in the memory page's page structure. Every page of memory has a corresponding page structure that contains information about the memory page. Page sizes vary across different hardware platforms. UltraSPARC-based systems implement an 8-Kbyte memory page size, which means that 8 Kbytes is the smallest unit of memory that can be allocated and mapped to a process's address space.

The page structure contains several fields, among which are two fields called p_cowcnt and p_lckcnt, that is, page copy-on-write count and page lock count. Copy-on-write tells the system that this page can be shared as long as it's being read, but once a write to the page is executed, the system is to make a copy of the page and map it to the process that is doing the write. Lock count maintains a count of how many times page locking was done for this page. Since many processes can share mappings to the same physical page, the page can be locked from several sources. The system maintains a count to ensure that processes that complete and exit will not result in the unlocking of a page that has mappings from other processes. The system's pageout code, which runs if free memory gets low, checks the status to the page's p_cowcnt and p_lckcnt fields. If either of these fields is nonzero, the page is considered locked in memory and thus not marked as a candidate for freeing. Shared memory pages using the ISM facility do not use the copy-on-write lock (that would make for a nonshared page after a write). Pages locked through ISM implement the p_lckcnt page structure field.

Even though ISM locks pages in memory so that they'll never be paged out, Solaris still treats ISM shared segments the same way it treats non-ISM shared segments and other anonymous memory pages: it ensures that there is sufficient backing store in swap before completing the page mapping on behalf of the requesting process. While this seems superfluous for ISM pages (allocating disk swap space for pages that can't be swapped out), it made the implementation cleaner. Solaris 2.6 changes this somewhat, and in Solaris 2.6 swap is not allocated for ISM pages. The net effect is that allocation of shared segments using ISM requires sufficient available swap space for the allocation to succeed, at least until Solaris 2.6. Using ISM requires setting a flag in the shmat(2) system call. Specifically, the SHM_SHARE_MMU flag must be set in the shmflg argument passed in the shmat(2) call, to instruct the system to set up the shared segment as intimate shared memory. Otherwise, the system will create the shared segment as a non-ISM shared segment.

In Solaris releases up to and including Solaris 7, there is not an easy way to tell whether or not a shared segment is an ISM shared segment. It can be done but requires root permission and use of the crash(1M) utility.

In the example below, we start a program called shm1, which creates and attaches to a 1-Mbyte shared segment, and we use a key value of 10 (the command-line arguments). The program prints the process virtual address of the shared segment and touches all the pages in the shared segment, printing a message indicating how many bytes have been touched. The test program then just sits in a loop, doing nothing.

The PID of the test process is 20179. The crash(1M) utility is started, and the p function dumps the process table (most of the table output is deleted). The process is located in table slot 73, as verified with the p 73 command. Finally, a full listing of the address space is dumped with the as -f command.

Looking at the address space listing, matching the address of the shared segment, ed000000, we can determine which segment driver is used for that address space segment. In this case, the segment driver is the segspt_shm driver, which is a driver specifically for ISM shared memory. Any address space segment mapped that shows this segment driver is an ISM segment. If the mapping represents a shared segment that is not an ISM segment, the segment driver will be the standard segvn_ops driver.

```
# shm1 1048576 10 &
[1]     20179
sunsys>
Attached, shmptr: ed000000
touching pages
bytes touched: 1048576
sunsys> su
# /etc/crash
dumpfile = /dev/mem, namelist = /dev/ksyms, outfile = stdout
> p
PROC TABLE SIZE = 4058
SLOT ST  PID  PPID  PGID   SID   UID PRI   NAME           FLAGS
   0 t    0     0     0     0     0  96 sched          load sys lock
   1 s    1     0     0     0     0  58 init           load
       .
       .
       .
  72 z 19821  5234 19821 19821     0  99 zombie         load
  73 r 20179   533 20179   533 19821   0 shm1           load
  74 s 17199   490 17199   490     0  45 sh             load
  75 z 19809  5234 19809 19809     0  99 zombie         load
  79 s 20180   533 20180   533     0  54 sh             load
> p 73
PROC TABLE SIZE = 4058
SLOT ST  PID  PPID  PGID   SID   UID PRI   NAME           FLAGS
  73 p 20179   533 20179   533 19821   0 shm1           load
> as -f 73

PROC         PAGLCK   CLGAP  VBITS HAT        HRM         RSS
  SEGLST     LOCK          SEGS      SIZE      LREP TAIL     NSEGS
  73         0        0       0x0   0xf59cfb58  0x0
0xf69af3c0 0xefffed58 0xf69775a0 17563648  0       0xf69afb20   11
  BASE       SIZE       AS       NEXT        PREV        OPS       DATA
  0x00010000   2000 0xf591eba0 0xf65d4500 0x00000000   segvn_ops 0xf69b9d68
  0x00021000   1000 0xf591eba0 0xf69aff20 0xf69775a0   segvn_ops 0xf65f1288
  0xed000000 1000000 0xf591eba0 0xf69af3c0 0xf65d4500   segspt_shm 0xf653a480
  0xef700000  93000 0xf591eba0 0xf69afb40 0xf69aff20   segvn_ops 0xf65d1a60
       .
       .
  0xefffe000   2000 0xf591eba0 0x00000000 0xf69aff00   segvn_ops 0xf69a4dd0
```

10.3 System V Semaphores

A semaphore, as defined in the dictionary, is a mechanical signalling device or a means of doing visual signalling. The analogy typically used is the railroad mechanism of signalling trains, where mechanical arms would swing down to block a train from a section of track that another train was currently using. When the track was free, the arm would swing up, and the waiting train could then proceed.

The notion of using semaphores as a means of synchronization in computer software was originated by a Dutch mathematician, E. W. Dijkstra, in 1965. Dijkstra's original work defined two semaphore operations, wait and signal (which correlate nicely to the railroad example). The operations were referred to as P and V operations. The P operation was the wait, which decremented the value of the semaphore if it was greater than zero, and the V operation was the signal, which incremented the semaphore value. The terms P and V originate from the Dutch terms for try and increase. P is from *Probeer,* which means *try* or *attempt*, and V is from *Verhoog*, which means *increase*. P(robeer) decreases the semaphore count and V(erhoog) increases the count. (Thanks to henk-jan_van_scherpenseel@stratus.com for sharing that bit of trivia with us.)

Semaphores provide a method of synchronizing access to a sharable resource by multiple processes. They can be used as a binary lock for exclusive access or as a counter; they manage access to a finite number of shared resources, where the semaphore value is initialized to the number of shared resources. Each time a process needs a resource, the semaphore value is decremented. When the process is done with the resource, the semaphore value is incremented. A zero semaphore value conveys to the calling process that no resources are currently available, and the calling process blocks until another process finishes using the resource and frees it.

The semaphore implementation in Solaris (System V semaphores) allows for semaphore sets, meaning that a unique semaphore identifier can contain multiple semaphores. Whether a semaphore indentifier contains one semaphore or a set of semaphores is determined when the semget(2) system call creates the semaphore. The second argument to semget(2) determines the number of semaphores that will be associated with the semaphore identifier returned by semget(2). The semaphore system calls allow for some operations on the semaphore set, such that the programmer can make one semctl(2) or semop(2) system call and touch all the semaphores in the semaphore set. This approach makes dealing with semaphore sets programmatically a little easier.

10.3.1 Semaphore Kernel Resources

The tunable kernel parameters that apply to semaphores are summarized in Table 10-6. We next take a closer look at each one and discuss how kernel resources are allocated.

Table 10-6 Semaphore Kernel Tunables

Name	Default Value	Maximum Value	Data Type	Description
semmap	10	2 billion	signed int	Size of semaphore resource map
semmni	10	65536	signed int	Number of semaphore identifiers
semmns	60	2 billion	signed int	Total semaphores, system-wide
semmnu	30	2 billion	signed int	Total undo structures, systemwide
semmsl	25	65536	unsigned short	Maximum number semaphores per identifier
semopm	10	2 billion	signed int	Maximum operations per semop(2) call
semume	10	2 billion	signed int	Maximum undo entries per process
semusz	96	2 billion	signed int	Total bytes required for undo structures, system-wide
semvmx	32767	65536	unsigned short	Maximum value of a semaphore
semaem	16384	32767	signed short	Maximum adjust on exit value

- **semmap** — Determines the maximum number of entries in a semaphore map. The memory space given to the creation of semaphores is taken from the semmap, which is initialized with the number of map entries fixed by the value of semmap. The implementation of allocation maps is generic within UNIX SVR4 and Solaris, supported with a standard set of kernel routines (rmalloc(), rmfree(), etc.).

The use of allocation maps by the semaphore subsystem is just one example of their implementation. They basically prevent the kernel from having to deal with allocating and deallocating additional kernel memory as semaphores are initialized and freed. By initialization and use of allocation maps, kernel memory is allocated up-front, and map entries are allocated and freed dynamically from the semmap allocation maps. Given that semmns limits the total number of semaphores systemwide and that semaphore space is allocated from the resource map, it makes sense to set semmap equal to semmns.

- **semmni** — Establishes the maximum number of systemwide semaphore sets. Every semaphore set in the system has a unique identifier and control structure, the semid_ds data structure. During init, the system allocates kernel memory for semid_ds control structures as determined from the semmni tunable. Each control structure is 84 bytes, so as with the shared memory shmmni tunable, you should avoid making this value arbitrarily large.

- **semmns** — Defines the maximum number of semaphores in the system. A semaphore set can have more than one semaphore associated with it, and each semaphore has a corresponding sem data structure. Each sem structure is only 16 bytes, but you still shouldn't go over the edge with this (do not make it arbitrarily a very large value). Actually, this number should really be calculated as semmns = semmni × semmsl. Since semmsl defines the maximum number of semaphores per semaphore set and semmni defines the maximum number of semaphore sets, the total number of semaphores systemwide can never be greater than the product of semmni and semmsl. semmns and semmap should be the same value.

- **semmnu** — Defines the systemwide maximum number of semaphore undo structures. Semaphore undo structures are maintained in the event of termination of a process that has made some semaphore value adjustments. If the SEM_UNDO bit is true in the semaphore flag value (sem_flg) when the semaphore operation is done (the semop(2) system call), then the kernel undoes changes made to the semaphore(s) when the process terminates. Seems intuitive to make this equal to semmni, which would provide for an undo structure for every semaphore set. Each semaphore undo structure is 16 bytes.

- **semmsl** — Maximum number of semaphores per semaphore set. Each semaphore set can have one or more semaphores associated with it; this tunable defines the maximum number per set.

- **semopm** — Maximum number of semaphore operations that can be performed per semop(2) call. This tunable takes us back to the notion of semaphore sets and the ability to do operations on multiple semaphores by means of the semop(2) system call. The semaphores in the set will all be associated with the same semaphore ID (semid_ds structure). You should probably set this value equal to semmsl so you'll always be able to do an operation on every semaphore in a semaphore set.

  When a semop(2) call is executed, the kernel checks to ensure that the third argument to semop(2), which is the size of the semaphore set array, is not larger than the semopm tunable. If it is, an error is returned to the calling code.

- **semume** — Determines the maximum allowable per process undo structures, or, put another way, the maximum number of semaphore undo operations that can be performed per process. The kernel maintains information on changes that processes make to semaphores (semaphore value adjustments). In the event of a process exiting prematurely, the kernel can set the semaphore values back to what they were before the process changed them. This is what undo structures are used for: to undo semaphore alterations in the event of abnormal process termination.

- `semusz` — Size in bytes for undo structures. We don't know why this is even documented as a tunable. During initialization of the semaphore code, the kernel sets `semusz` to `(sizeof(undo) + (semume × sizeof(undo))`, so setting it in `/etc/system` is pointless. Leave it alone; it should be removed as a tunable.

- `semvmx` — Maximum value of a semaphore. Because of the interaction with undo structures and `semaem` (more details below), this tunable should not exceed a maximum of its default value of 32767 unless you can guarantee that `SEM_UNDO` is never being used. The actual value of a semaphore is stored as an unsigned short (2 bytes) in its semaphore structure, implying that the maximum semaphore value can be 65535 (64 Kbytes), the maximum value of an unsigned short data type. The next bullet explains why the limit should really be 32767.

- `semaem` — Maximum adjust-on-exit value. This value is stored as an integer in the `seminfo` structure that the kernel uses to maintain the tunable values, but it is implemented as a signed short in the undo structure. It needs to be signed because semaphore operations can increment or decrement the value of a semaphore, and thus the system might need to apply a negative or positive adjustment value to the semaphore to do a successful adjust-on-exit operation.

  The actual value of a semaphore can never be negative. The maximum value for a signed short, which is 2 bytes (16 bits), is 32767 (32 Kbytes). If `semvmx` were set to 65535 and the application actually set semaphore values that high, the system would not be able to undo the entire range of semaphore value changes, because `semaem` can never be greater than 32767. This is why `semvmx` should never be greater than 32767, unless you don't care about undo operations.

10.3.2 Kernel Implementation of System V Semaphores

During initialization of the semaphore code, when `/kernel/sys/semsys` is first loaded, the value of `semmni` is checked to ensure it is not greater than the maximum allowable value of 65536 (64 Kbytes). If it is, it gets set to 65536 and a console message is printed stating that the value of `semmni` was too large. Following that, the tunable parameters, with the exception of `semusz`, from the `/etc/system` file are plugged into the internal `seminfo` data structure.

Just as with shared memory, the system checks for the maximum amount of available kernel memory and divides that number by 4, to prevent semaphore requirements from taking more than 25 percent of available kernel memory. Actual memory requirements for semaphores are calculated as follows.

```
total_kernel_memory_required =
            (semmns * (sem structure size)) +
            (semmni * (semid_ds structure size)) +
            (semmni * (kernel mutex size)) +
            (max_nprocs * (undo structure size)) +
            (semusz * semmnu * (integer size))
```

The structure sizes are given in the previous section. Pointers and integers are 4 bytes, and a kernel mutex is 8 bytes. The maximum process value is determined during startup and is based on the amount of RAM in the system. You can determine the actual value on your system with the sysdef(1M) command.

```
# sysdef | grep v_proc
1962 maximum number of processes (v.v_proc)
```

Doing the actual arithmetic is left as an exercise for the reader. If the required memory is more than 25 percent of available kernel memory, a message so stating is displayed on the console.

Assuming everything fits, kernel memory is allocated as follows. Resource map allocation is done, based on semmap, and a kernel semmap pointer is set. Space is allocated for the following:

- All the sem structures (one for every semaphore); based on semmns
- All the semaphore identifiers (semid_ds); based on the size of that structure
- All the undo structure pointers; based on the max processes and pointer size
- All the undo structures themselves; based on semmnu and the size of an undo structure
- All the kernel mutex locks required, one for every unique semaphore identifier; based on semmni and the size of a kernel mutex

A kernel mutex lock is created for each semaphore set. This practice results in fairly fine-grained parallelism on multiprocessor hardware, since it means that multiple processes can do operations on different semaphore sets concurrently. For operations on semaphores in the same set, the kernel needs to ensure atomicity for the application. Atomicity guarantees that a semaphore operation initiated by a process will complete without interference from another process, whether the operation is on a single semaphore or multiple semaphores in the same set.

10.3.3 Semaphore Operations Inside Solaris

The creation of a semaphore set by an application requires a call to semget(2). Every semaphore set in the system is described by a semds_id data structure, which contains the following elements.

```
/*
 * There is one semaphore id data structure (semid_ds) for each set of
 * semaphores in the system.
 */

struct semid_ds {
        struct ipc_perm sem_perm;       /* operation permission struct */
        struct sem      *sem_base;      /* ptr to first semaphore in set */
        ushort_t        sem_nsems;      /* # of semaphores in set */
        time_t          sem_otime;      /* last semop time */
        long            sem_pad1;       /* reserved for time_t expansion */
        time_t          sem_ctime;      /* last change time */
        long            sem_pad2;       /* time_t expansion */
        long            sem_binary;     /* flag indicating semaphore type */
        long            sem_pad3[3];    /* reserve area */
};
```

Header File <sys/sem.h>

The system checks to see if a semaphore already exists by looking at the key value passed to semget(2) and checks permissions by using the ipc support routine, ipcaccess(). Semaphore permissions differ slightly from permission modes we're used to seeing in things like Solaris files. They're defined as READ and ALTER, such that processes can either read the current semaphore value or alter it (increment/decrement). Permissions are established with arguments passed to the semget(2) call, following the owner, group, and other conventions used for Solaris file permissions.

Assuming a new semaphore, space is allocated from the resource map pool as needed for the number of semaphores in the set requested, and the elements in the semid_ds data structure are initialized, with the sem_base pointer being set to point to the first semaphore in the set.

Once the semaphore is created, typically the next step is initializing the semaphore values. Initialization is done with the semctl(2) call, using either SETVAL to set the value of each semaphore in the set one at a time (or if there is but one semaphore in the set) or SETALL to set the value of all the semaphores in the set in one operation. The actual kernel flow is relatively straightforward, with the expected permission and value checks against the maximum allowable values, and the setting of the user-defined values if everything checks out.

Actual semaphore use by application code involves the semop(2) system call. semop(2) takes the semaphore ID (returned by semget(2)), a pointer to a sembuf structure, and the number of semaphore operations as call arguments. The sembuf structure contains the following elements.

```
struct sembuf {
        ushort_t        sem_num;        /* semaphore # */
        short           sem_op;         /* semaphore operation */
        short           sem_flg;        /* operation flags */
};
```

Header File <sys/sem.h>

The programmer must create and initialize the `sembuf` structure, setting the `semaphore` number (specifying which semaphore in the set), the operation (more on that in a minute), and the flag. The value of `sem_op` determines whether the semphore operation will alter or read the value of a semaphore. A nonzero `sem_op` value either negatively or positively alters the semaphore value. A zero `sem_op` value will simply do a read of the current semaphore value.

The semop(2) manual page contains a fairly detailed flow in the DESCRIPTION section on what the operation will be for a given `sem_op` value and a given flag value.

10.4 System V Message Queues

Message queues provide a means for processes to send and receive messages of various size in an asynchronous fashion on a Solaris system. As with the other IPC facilities, the initial call when message queues are used is an `ipcget` call, in this case, msgget(2). The msgget(2) system call takes a key value and some flags as arguments and returns an identifier for the message queue. Once the message queue has been established, it's simply a matter of sending and receiving messages. Applications use msgsnd(2) and msgrcv(2) for those purposes. The sender simply constructs the message, assigns a message type, and calls msgsnd(2). The system will place the message on the appropriate message queue until a msgrcv(2) is successfully executed. Sent messages are placed at the back of the queue, and messages are received from the front of the queue; thus the queue is implemented as a FIFO (First In, First Out).

The message queue facility implements a message type field, which is user (programmer) defined. So, programmers have some flexibility, since the kernel has no embedded or predefined knowledge of different message types. Programmers typically use the `type` field for priority messaging or directing a message to a particular recipient.

Lastly, applications use the msgctl(2) system call to get or set permissions on the message queue and to remove the message queue from the system when the application is finished with it. For example, msgct(2) offers a clean way to implement an application shutdown procedure, because the system will not remove an empty and unused message queue unless it is explicitly instructed to do so or the system is rebooted.

10.4.1 Kernel Resources for Message Queues

Like the IPC facilities previously discussed, the message queue facility comes in the form of a dynamically loadable kernel module, `/kernel/sys/msgsys`, and depends on the IPC support module, `/kernel/misc/ipc`, to be loaded in memory.

The number of resources that the kernel allocates for message queues is tunable. Values for various message queue tunable parameters can be increased from their default values so more resources are made available for systems running applications that make heavy use of message queues. Table 10-7 summarizes the tunable parameters and lists their default and maximum values.

Table 10-7 Message Queue Tunable Parameters

Name	Default	Max	Data Type	Description
msgmap	100	2 billion	signed int	Number of message map entries
msgmni	50	2 billion	signed int	Maximum number of message queue identifiers
msgmax	2048	2 billion	signed int	Maximum message size
msgmnb	4096	2 billion	signed int	Maximum number of bytes on a message queue
msgtql	40	2 billion	signed int	Maximum number of message headers
msgssz	8	2 billion	signed int	Maximum message segment size
msgseg	1024	32 Kbytes	unsigned short	Maximum number of message segments

- **msgmap** — Number of entries in the message map; essentially the same as the semmap parameter used for semaphores. Both IPC facilities use resource allocation maps in the kernel. A kernel resource map is simply an array of map structures used for the allocation and deallocation of segments of an address space. They provide a convenient means of managing small segments of kernel memory where there is frequent allocation and deallocation, such as the case with message queues (and semaphores). The system grabs message map entries when it needs space to store new messages to place on a message queue.

- **msgmni** — Number of message queue identifiers. Like shared memory segments and semaphores, message queues have an identifier associated with them, with a corresponding ID data structure, the msqid_ds structure. The value of msgmni determines the maximum number of message queues the kernel can maintain. As we'll see below, the system allocates kernel memory based on the value of msgmni, so don't set this value arbitrarily high. With luck, the system software engineers will have a sense for how many message queues are needed by the application and can set msgmni appropriately, adding 10 percent or so for headroom.

- **msgmax** — Maximum size a message can be, in bytes. The kernel does not allocate resources up-front on the basis of msgmax, but it is something that the application developer needs to be aware of. The system will not allow messages that have a size larger than msgmax on the message queue and will return an error to the calling code, stating the message is too large.

  Even with a theoretical size limit of 2 Gbytes for the maximum message size, message queues are probably not the most efficient way to move large blocks of data between processes. If the data requirements are relatively large, software engineers should consider using shared memory instead of message queues for data sharing among processes. Or, programmers could use one of the more recent additions to Unix, such as a FIFO (named pipe). By *more recent*, we mean recent relative to message queues—FIFOs have actually been around for quite a while, but not as long as message queues.

- **msgmnb** — Maximum number of bytes on a message queue. Rephrased, the sum total of all the bytes of all the messages on the queue cannot exceed msgmnb. When the message queue is initialized (the first msgget(2) call executed with the IPC_CREAT flag set), the kernel sets a member of the msgid_ds structure, the msg_qbytes field, to the value of msgmnb. This value makes the information available to programmers, who can use msgctl(2) to retrieve the msgid_ds data. More importantly, code executed with an effective UID of root (typically 0) can programmatically increase this variable, in case the queue needs to hold more message bytes than originally allocated at boot time.

  If an application attempts to put a new message on a message queue that will result in the total bytes being greater then msgmnb, the msgsnd(2) call either returns an error or the process blocks, waiting for the message to be pulled off the queue, depending on whether the IPC_WAIT flag is true.

- **msgtql** — Maximum number of message headers. Each message on a message queue requires a message header, which is defined in the kernel by the msg structure (more on that in the next section). Basically, this tunable should reflect the maximum number of messages (message queues times messages per queue) the application will need, plus a little headroom.

- **msgssz** — Maximum message segment size. Determines the maximum number of message segments. msgseg is stored as a signed short data type in the kernel and thus cannot be greater then 32768 (32 Kbytes) bytes in size. The kernel creates a pool of memory to hold the message data, and the size of that pool is the product of msgssz and msgseg parameters. Described more clearly: the number of units of allocation from the data space is msgseg, and the size of each allocation unit from the space is msgssz.

- **msgseg** — As above, the number of units of space that can be allocated from the memory map segment described previously.

When the /kernel/sys/msgsys module is first loaded, an initialization routine executes. The routine does much the same sort of work that is done for shared memory and semaphore initialization. That is, it checks the amount of kernel memory that will be required for resources, as determined by the tunable parameters. Then, provided the required amount is no greater than 25 percent of available kernel memory, the system allocates the resources.

The amount of kernel memory required is calculated as follows.

```
kernel_memory_required =
    ((msgseg * msgssz) * sizeof char data type) +
    (msgmap * sizeof map structure) +
    (msgmni * sizeof msqds_id structure) +
    (msgtql * sizeof msg structure) +
    (msgmni * sizeof msglock structure)
```

In the next few paragraphs, we give you the sizes of the structures in bytes, and once again the arithmetic with either the default or custom values is left as an exercise for the reader. The `char` data type on SPARC/Solaris systems is 1 byte in size.

The kernel sets several pointers in the message queue that will be referenced in the subsequent text when the resources are initialized. An `msg` pointer is set to point to the beginning of the pool of memory used to store message data, described earlier. `msgmap` points to the beginning of the map structures used for maintaining resource allocation maps. A map structure is 8 bytes in size and contains the size of the mapped segment and the base address.

The kernel data structure that describes each message queue is the `msqid_ds` structure.

```
struct msqid_ds {
        struct ipc_perm msg_perm;       /* operation permission struct */
        struct msg      *msg_first;     /* ptr to first message on q */
        struct msg      *msg_last;      /* ptr to last message on q */
        ulong           msg_cbytes;     /* current # bytes on q */
        ulong           msg_qnum;       /* # of messages on q */
        ulong           msg_qbytes;     /* max # of bytes on q */
        pid_t           msg_lspid;      /* pid of last msgsnd */
        pid_t           msg_lrpid;      /* pid of last msgrcv */
        time_t          msg_stime;      /* last msgsnd time */
        long            msg_pad1;       /* reserved for time_t expansion */
        time_t          msg_rtime;      /* last msgrcv time */
        long            msg_pad2;       /* time_t expansion */
        time_t          msg_ctime;      /* last change time */
        long            msg_pad3;       /* time expansion */
        kcondvar_t      msg_cv;
        kcondvar_t      msg_qnum_cv;
        long            msg_pad4[3];    /* reserve area */
};
```

Header File <sys/msg.h>

The preceding structure field descriptions are basically self-explanatory. The permissions are established by the process that creates the shared segment, and they can be changed with the `msgctl(2)` system call. The kernel pointer `msgque` points to the beginning of the kernel space allocated to hold all the system msqid_ds structures. It is simply an array of msqid_ds structures, with msgque pointing to the first structure in the array; the total number of structures in the array is equal to the msgmni tunable. Each structure is 112 bytes in size.

The messages in a message queue are maintained in a linked list, with the root of the list in the msqid_ds data structure (the msg_first pointer), which points to the message header for the message. The kernel also maintains a linked list of message headers, rooted in the kernel pointer.

```
struct msg {
        struct msg      *msg_next;      /* ptr to next message on q */
        long            msg_type;       /* message type */
        ushort_t        msg_ts;         /* message text size */
        short           msg_spot;       /* message text map address */
};
```

Header File <sys/msg.h>

The kernel message structure (actually, message *header* structure would be a more accurate name) is 12 bytes in size, and, as we said, one exists for every message on every message queue (the msgtql tunable). The last chunk of kernel memory allocated is for the message queue synchronization locks. The method of synchronization is a condition variable protected by a mutex (mutual exclusion) lock, defined in the msglock structure, created for every message queue (one per message queue identifier).

Condition variables are a means of allowing a process (thread) to test whether a particular condition is true under the protection of a mutex lock. The mutex ensures that the condition can be checked for atomically, and no other thread can change the condition while the first thread is testing the condition. The thread will block, holding the mutex until the condition changes state (becomes true), at which point the thread can continue execution. A good example is a message on a queue. If none exists, the thread blocks (sleeps) on the condition variable. When a message appears on the queue, the system sends a broadcast and the thread is awakened, ready to pull the message off the queue.

A final note on kernel locking. All versions of the Solaris, up to and including Solaris 2.5.1, do very coarse-grained locking in the kernel message queue module. Specifically, one kernel mutex is initialized to protect the message queue kernel code and data. As a result, applications running on multiprocessor platforms using message queues do not scale well. This situation is changed in Solaris 2.6, which implements a finer-grained locking mechanism, allowing for greater concurrency. The improved message queue kernel module has been backported and is available as a patch for Solaris 2.5 and 2.5.1.

Figure 10.2 illustrates the general layout of things after initialization of the message queue module is complete, along with the kernel pointers described above.

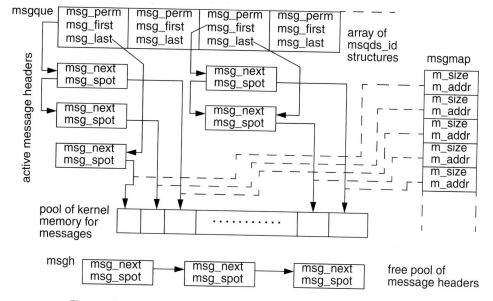

Figure 10.2 System V Message Queue Structures

10.4.2 Kernel Implementation of Message Queues

We'll walk through the kernel flow involved in the creation of a message queue and the sending and receiving of messages, since these represent the vast majority of message queue activities.

- The creation of a message on behalf of an application calling the `msgget(2)` system call starts with a call to the kernel `ipcget()` routine. An `ipc_perm` structure will be available for every message queue identifier (`msgmni`).

- Once a structure has been allocated, the system initializes the structure members as specified by the UID and GID of the calling process and the permission mode bits passed by the calling code, then sets the `IPC_ALLOC` bit to signify the `ipc_perm` structure has been allocated. (The `ipcget()` code is the same as illustrated previously—it's the same function!—so we won't revisit it here.)

  If `ipcget()` returns successfully, the application code has a valid message queue identifier, can send and receive messages, and can run message control (`msgctl(2)`) operations.

A message send (`msgsnd(2)`) call requires the application to construct a message, setting a message type field and creating the body of the message (e.g., a text message).

- When the code path for the message send kernel support code is first entered, the code does some general housekeeping—such as incrementing the processor statistics to announce a message queue system call is being executed. The cpu_sysinfo structure maintains a msg counter that reflects the total number of message queue system calls executed.

- The code verifies the calling process's access permissions to the message queue and tests the message size against the msgmax tunable.

- Next, the code copies the message type field from the user address space to a designated area in the kernel.

The rest of the message send flow is best represented in pseudocode.

```
if (message queue no longer exists)
        return EIDRM error
if (current bytes on queue + bytes in new msg > msgmax)
        if (IPC_NOWAIT is set)
                return EAGAIN
        else
                set MSGWAIT flag in msqid_ds.msg_perm.mode
                call cv_wait_sig() /* put the caller to sleep until space is
                                      available on the queue */
/* on wakeup, code will validate msqid, and set EDIRM if itUs
        been removed */
        allocate space for message from resource map (msgmap)
        if (space not available)
                if (IPC_NOWAIT)
                        return EAGAIN error
        else
                call cv_wait_sig() /* sleep waiting for space */
/* once the wakeup is issued, the necessary resources are
        available for putting the message on the queue */
        copy message data from user space to kernel space (map area)
        increment msqid_ds.qnum
        msqid_ds.msg_cbytes += new message size
        msqid_ds.mds_lspid = PID of caller
        msqid_ds.msg_stime = current time

        update message header msg_type, msg_ts (text size) and msg_spot (map location
pointer)
        adjust the queue pointers (msg_first, msg_next, msg_last)
return success to calling program
```

The msgrcv support code is a little less painful, since now we're looking for a message on the queue (as opposed to putting one on the queue). Kernel resources do not need to be allocated for a msgrcv. The general flow of the kernel code path for receiving messages involves checking permissions for operation in a loop through all the messages on the queue.

- If the requested message type matches a message on the queue, the code copies the message type to the user-supplied location and copies the message data to the user-supplied location.

- Next, the code updates the `msqid_ds` structure fields, subtracts the message size from `msg_cbytes`, sets PID in `msg_lrpid`, sets time in `msg_rtime`, frees the message resources, frees the message header (`msg` structure), and frees the resource map entry.

- If the code looped through all messages and found no matching type, it returns a No Message error.

When the sequence is completed, the application code will have the message type and data in a buffer area supplied in the `msgrcv(2)` system call.

The only remaining callable routine for applications to use is the `msgctl(2)` system call. The control functions are straightforward; they typically involve either retrieving or setting values in a message queue's `ipc_perm` structure.

- When `msgctl(2)` is invoked with the `IPC_RMID` flag, meaning the caller wishes to remove the message queue from the system, the kernel walks the linked list of messages on the queue, freeing up the kernel resources associated with each message.

- The kernel sends a wakeup signal to processes (threads) sleeping on the message queue. The processes ultimately end up with an `EIDRM` error (ID removed).

- The system simply marks the `msqid_ds` structure as being available, and returns.

10.5 POSIX IPC

The evolution of the POSIX standard and associated application programming interfaces (APIs) resulted in a set of industry-standard interfaces that provide the same types of facilities as the System V IPC set: shared memory, semaphores, and message queues. They are quite similar in form and function to their System V equivalents but very different in implementation.

The POSIX implementation of all three IPC facilities is built on the notion of POSIX IPC names, which essentially look like file names but need not be actual files in a file system. This POSIX name convention provides the necessary abstraction, a file descriptor, to use the Solaris file memory mapping interface, `mmap(2)`, on which all the POSIX IPC mechanisms are built. This is very different from the System V IPC functions, where a key value was required to fetch the proper identifier of the desired IPC resource. In System V IPC, a common method used for generating key values was the `ftok(3C)` (file-to-key) function, where a key value was generated based on the path name of a file. POSIX eliminates the use of the key, and processes acquire the desired resource by using a file-name convention.

No kernel tunable parameters are required (or available) for the POSIX IPC code. The per-process limits of the number of open files and memory address space are the only potentially limiting factors in POSIX IPC.

Table 10-8 lists the POSIX APIs for the three IPC facilities.

Table 10-8 POSIX IPC Interfaces

Semaphores	Message Queues	Shared Memory
sem_open	mq_open	shm_open
sem_close	mq_close	shm_unlink
sem_unlink	mq_unlink	
sem_init	mq_getattr	
sem_destroy	mq_setattr	
sem_wait	mq_send	
sem_trywait	mq_receive	
sem_post	mq_notify	
sem_getvalue	mq_getvalue	

The POSIX interfaces require linking with the libposix4.so shared object library when building and running code that uses any of the POSIX IPC facilities on Solaris. Within the POSIX library are several common routines that are called by the public interfaces to support the POSIX IPC object name convention. These routines are *not* public interfaces and must *not* be called directly by an application program.

- **__pos4obj_open()**. Opens/creates a POSIX named object. If the O_CREAT flag was set in the *xxx*_open(3R) call, creates the file if it does not exist. If O_EXCL is set along with O_CREAT, the open will fail if the object name exists.

- **__pos4obj_name()**. Qualifies the path name of a POSIX object name. The POSIX standard requires that the name argument to the *xx*_open(3R) routines begin with a / (slash) character and that no other slash characters exist in the path name. This routine ensures that the passed argument follows the rules and then strips off the slash. It is called by __pos4obj_open() and returns the path string minus the slash to the open code.

- **__open_nc()**. Called from __pos4obj_open(), defined as noncancel open. Essentially, __open_nc() is the POSIX library wrapper around the open(2) system call, with thread cancellation protection set before open(2) is called and cleared when open(2) returns.

- **__close_nc()**. Closes a POSIX named object. Similar to __open_nc() above, __close_nc() calls the close(2) system call, disabling thread cancellation before calling close(2).

- **__pos4obj_lock()**. Locks a POSIX named object for exclusive access. Uses the lockf(3C) interface and advisory (versus mandatory) locks.

- **__pos4obj_unlock()**. Unlocks a POSIX named object. Calls lockf(3C) with the F_UNLOCK flag and closes the file.

All of the POSIX IPC functions are either directly or indirectly based on memory mapped files. The message queue and semaphore functions make direct calls to mmap(2), creating a memory mapped file based on the file descriptor returned from the *xx*_open(3R) call. Using POSIX shared memory requires the programmer to make the mmap(2) call explicitly from the application code.

The details of mmap(2) and memory mapped files are covered in subsequent chapters, but, briefly, the mmap(2) system call maps a file or some other named object into a process's address space, as shown in Figure 10.3.

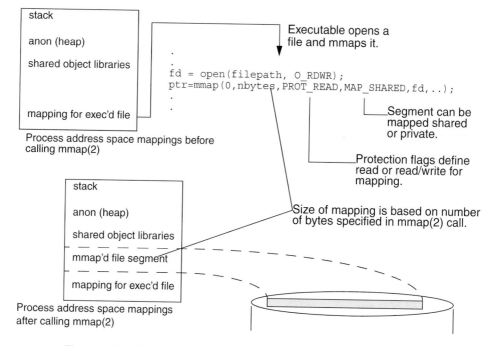

Figure 10.3 Process Address Space with mmap(2)

As shown in Figure 10.3, the address space mapping created by mmap(2) can be private or shared. It is the shared mapping capability that the POSIX IPC implementation relies on.

10.5.1 POSIX Shared Memory

The POSIX shared memory interfaces provide an API for support of the POSIX IPC name abstraction. The interfaces, shm_open(3R) and shm_unlink(3R), do not allocate or map memory into a calling process's address space. The programmer using POSIX shared memory must create the address space mapping with an explicit call to mmap(2). Different processes that wish to access the same shared segment will execute shm_open(2) on the same object, for example, shm_open("/tmp/seg1",...,), and then execute mmap(2) on the file descriptor returned from shm_open(3R). Any writes to the shared segment are directed to the underlying file and thus made visible to processes that run mmap(2) on the same file descriptor or, in this case, POSIX object name.

Under the covers, the shm_open(3R) call directly invokes __pos4obj_open(), which uses __pos4obj_name() to qualify the name and __open_nc() to open the named object (file). shm_unlink(3R) also uses __pos4obj_name() and issues the unlink(2) system call to remove the directory entry. That is, the file (object) is removed.

10.5.2 POSIX Semaphores

The POSIX specification provides for two types of semaphores that can be used for the same purposes as System V semaphores, but are implemented differently. POSIX *named* semaphores follow the POSIX IPC name convention discussed earlier and are created with the sem_open(3R) call. POSIX also defines *unnamed* semaphores, which do not have a name in the file system space and are memory based. Additionally, a set of semaphore interfaces that are part of the Solaris threads library provides the same level of functionality as POSIX unnamed semaphores but uses a different API. Table 10-9 lists the different semaphore interfaces that currently ship with Solaris.

Table 10-9 Solaris Semaphore APIs

Origin or Type	Interfaces	Library	Manual Section
System V	semget(), semctl(), semop()	libc	section (2)
POSIX named	sem_open(), sem_close(), sem_unlink(), sem_wait(), sem_trywait(), sem_post(), sem_getvalue()	libposix4	section (3R)

Table 10-9 Solaris Semaphore APIs (Continued)

Origin or Type	Interfaces	Library	Manual Section
POSIX unnamed	`sem_init()`, `sem_destroy()`, `sem_wait()`, `sem_trywait()`, `sem_post()`, `sem_getvalue()`	`libposix4`	section (3R)
Solaris threads	`sema_init()`, `sema_destroy()`, `sema_wait()`, `sema_trywait()`, `sema_post()`	`libthread`	section (3T)

Note the common functions for named and unnamed POSIX semaphores: the actual semaphore operations—sem_wait(3R), sem_trywait(3R), sem_post(3R) and sem_getvalue(3R)—are used for both types of semaphores. The creation and destruction interfaces are different. The Solaris implementation of the POSIX sem_init(3R), sem_destroy(3R), sem_wait(3R), sem_trywait(3R), and sem_post(3R) functions actually invokes the Solaris threads library functions of the same name through a jump-table mechanism in the Solaris POSIX library. The jump table is a data structure that contains function pointers to semaphore routines in the Solaris threads library, libthread.so.1.

POSIX defines two system-imposed limits specific to POSIX semaphores: SEM_NSEMS_MAX, the maximum number of semaphores per process; and SEM_VALUE_MAX, the maximum value of a semaphore. In Solaris 2.6 and Solaris 7, both of these limits are set to 2147483647 (2 billion). This does not mean that applications will work well (or at all) opening 2 billion semaphores (the usual caveats apply with respect to limits on resources). The sem_open(3R) code requires an available file descriptor for a very short period, but the file descriptor is closed once the semaphore is acquired, so file descriptor limits should not be an issue.

The use of POSIX named semaphores begins with a call to sem_open(3R), which returns a pointer to an object defined in the /usr/include/semaphore.h header file, sem_t. The sem_t structure defines what a POSIX semaphore looks like, and subsequent semaphore operations reference the sem_t object. The fields in the sem_t structure include a count (sem_count), a semaphore type (sem_type), and magic number (sem_magic). sem_count reflects the actual semaphore value. sem_type defines the scope or visibility of the semaphore, either USYNC_THREAD, which means the semaphore is only visible to other threads in the same process, or USYNC_PROCESS, which means the semaphore is visible to other processes running on the same system. sem_magic is simply a value that uniquely identifies the synchronization object type as a semaphore rather than a condition variable, mutex lock, or reader/writer lock (see /usr/include/synch.h).

Semaphores within the same process are maintained by the POSIX library code on a linked list of `semaddr` structures. The structure fields and linkage are illustrated in Figure 10.4.

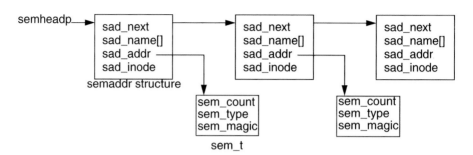

Figure 10.4 POSIX Named Semaphores

The linked list exists within the process's address space, not in the kernel. `sem-headp` points to the first `semaddr` structure on the list, and `sad_next` provides the pointer for support of a singly linked list. The character array `sad_name[]` holds the object name (file name), `sad_addr` points to the actual semaphore, and `sad_inode` contains the inode number of the file that was passed in the `sem_open(3R)` call. Here is the sequence of events.

- When entered, `sem_open(3R)` obtains a file lock on the passed file argument, using the `pos4obj_lock()` internal interface.
- Once the lock is acquired, `pos4obj_open()` and underlying routines open the file and return a file descriptor.
  - If this is a new semaphore, the file is truncated with `ftruncate(3C)` to the size of a `sem_t` structure (it does not need to be any larger than that).
  - If it's not a new semaphore and the process is opening an existing semaphore, then the linked list is searched, beginning at `semheadp`, until the inode number of the file argument to `sem_open(3R)` matches the `sad_inode` field of one of the `semaddr` structures, which means the code found the desired semaphore.

Once the semaphore is found, the code returns `sad_addr`, a pointer to the semaphore, to the calling program.

The POSIX semaphore code uses the `/tmp` file system for the creation and storage of the files that the code memory maps based on the name argument passed in the `sem_open(3R)` call. For each semaphore, a lock file and a data file are created in `/tmp`, with the file name prefix of `.SEML` for the lock file, and `.SEMD` for the data file. The full file name is prefix plus the strings passed as an argument to `sem_open(3R)`, without the leading slash character. For example, if a sem_open(3R) call was issued with "/sem1" and the first argument, the resulting file names in /tmp would be .SEMLsem1 and .SEMDsem1. This file name convention is used in the message queue code as well, as we'll see shortly.

If a new semaphore is being created, the following events occur.

- Memory for a semaddr structure is malloc'd, the passed file descriptor is mmap'd, the semaphore (sem_t) fields and semaddr fields are initialized, and the file descriptor is closed.

  Part of the initialization process is done with the jump table and a call to sema_init(). (sema_init() is used for semaphore calls from the Solaris threads library, libthread, and also used for POSIX unamed semaphores.) sema_init() is passed a pointer to a sem_t (either from the user code or when invoked from sem_open(3R), as is the case here), an initial semaphore value, and a type.

- The fields in sem_t are set according to the passed arguments, and the code returns. If a type is not specified, the type is set to USYNC_PROCESS.

The sem_t structure contains two additional fields not shown in the diagram. In semaphore.h, they are initialized as extra space in the structure (padding). The space stores a mutex lock and condition variable used by the library code to synchronize access to the semaphore and to manage blocking on a semaphore that's not available to a calling thread.

The remaining semaphore operations follow the expected, documented behavior for using semaphores in code.

- sema_close(3R) frees the allocated space for the semaddr structure and unmaps the mmap'd file.

  Once closed, the semaphore is no longer accessible to the process, but it still exists in the system—similar to what happens in a file

- close. sem_unlink(3R) removes the semaphore from the system.

10.5.3 POSIX Message Queues

POSIX message queues are constructed on a linked list built by the internal libposix4 library code. Several data structures are defined in the implementation, as shown in Figure 10.5. We opted not to show every member of the message queue structure, in the interests of space and readability.

The essential interfaces for using message queues are mq_open(3R) which opens, or creates and opens, a queue, making it available to the calling process, mq_send(3R) and mq_receive(3R), for sending and receiving messages. Other interfaces (see Table 10-8 on page 450) manage queues and set attributes, but our discussion focuses on the message queue infrastructure, built on the open, send, and receive functions.

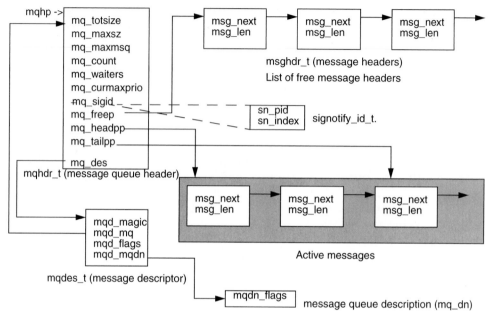

Figure 10.5 POSIX Message Queue Structures

A POSIX message queue is described by a message queue header, a data structure created and initialized when the message queue is first created. The message queue header contains information on the queue, such as the total size in bytes (mq_totsize), maximum size of each message (mq_maxsz), maximum number of messages allowed on the queue (mq_maxmsq), current number of messages (mq_current), current number of threads waiting to receive messages (mq_waiters), and the current maximum message priority (mq_curmaxprio).

Some attributes are tunable with mq_setattr(3R). The library code sets default values of 128 for the maximum number of messages, 1024 for the maximum size of a single message, and 32 for maximum number of message priorities. If necessary, you can increase the message size and number of messages by using msg_setattr(3R), or you can increase them initially when the queue is created, by populating an attributes structure and passing it on the mq_open(3R) call.

The message pointers, mq_headpp and mq_tailpp, in the header do not point directly to the messages on the linked list. That is, they do not contain the address of the message headers. Since the shared mapping can result in the different processes referencing the message queue so each has a different virtual address within their address space for the mapping, mq_headpp and mq_tailpp are implemented as offsets into the shared region.

A message descriptor maintains additional information about the queue, such as the file permission flags (read-only or read/write), and the magic number identifying the type of POSIX named object. A second structure (mq_dn) maintains per-process flags on the message, allowing different processes to specify either blocking or nonblocking behavior on the message queue files. This is analogous to regular file flags, where a file descriptor for an open file is maintained at the process level, and different processes can have different flags set on the same file. (For example, one process could have the file opened for read/write and another process could have the same file opened read-only.)

With the big picture in place (Figure 10.5), let's take a look at what happens when a message queue is created and opened.

- When `mq_open()` is entered, it creates the lock file and acquires a file lock. All the message queue files use the `/tmp` directory and follow a file name convention similar to that described in the semaphore section. That is, file names begin with a prefix— `.MQD` (data file), `.MQL` (lock file), `.MQP` (permission file), or `.MQN` (description file)—and end with the appended file name passed as an argument to `mq_open`(3R) minus the slash character.

- If a new message queue is being created, the maximum message size and messages per queue sizes are set, either with the default values or from a passed attributes structure in the `mq_open`(3R) call.

  - The permission file is opened, permissions are verified, and the file is closed.

  - The total amount of space needed for messages, based on the limits and structure size, is calculated, and the data file is created, opened, and set to the appropriate size with `ftruncate`(3C).

- If a new message queue is not being created, then an existing queue is being opened, in which case the permission test is done and the queue data file is tested to ensure the queue has been initialized.

The steps described next apply to a new or existing message queue; the latter case is a queue being opened by another process.

- Space for a message queue descriptor is `malloc`'d (`mqdes_t`), and the data file is `mmap`'d into a shared address space, setting the `mqhp` pointer (Figure 10.5) as the return address from the `mmap`(2) call.

- The message queue descriptor file is created, opened, `mmap`'d (also into a shared address space), and closed.

- For new message queues, the `mq_init()` function (not part of the API) is called to complete the initialization process. Each message queue header has several semaphores (not shown in Figure 10.5) used to synchronize access to the messages, the header structure, and other areas of the queue infrastructure.

  `mq_init()` initializes the semaphores with calls to `sem_init()`, which is part of the `libposix4.so` library.

- The queue head (`mq_headpp`), tail (`mq_tailpp`), and free (`mq_freep`) pointers are set on the message header structure, and `mq_init()` returns to `mq_open()`, completing the open process.

Once a queue is established, processes insert and remove messages by using `mq_send`(3R) and `mq_receive`(3R).

- `mq_send`(3R) does some up-front tests on the file type (`mqd_magic`) and tests the `mq_notfull` semaphore for space on the queue.

  - If the process's queue flag is set for nonblocking mode, `sem_trywait()` is called and returns to the process if the semaphore is not available, meaning there's no space on the queue.

  - Otherwise, `sem_wait()` is called, causing the process to block until space is available.

- Once space is available, `sem_wait()` is called to acquire the `mq_exclusive` mutex, which protects the queue during message insertions and removals.

POSIX message queues offer an interesting feature that is not available with System V message queues: automatic notification to a process or thread when a message has been added to a queue. An `mq_notify`(3R) interface can be issued by a process that needs to be notified of the arrival of a signal. To continue with the sequence for the next code segment:

- `mq_send()` checks to determine if a notification has been set up by testing the `mq_sigid` structure's `sn_pid` field. If it is non-NULL, the process has requested notification, and a notification signal is sent if no other processes are already blocked, waiting for a message.

- Finally, the library's internal `mq_putmsg()` function is called to locate the next free message block of the free list (`mq_freep`) and to place the message on the queue.

For receiving messages:

- `mq_receive()` issues a `sem_trywait()` call on the `mq_notempty` semaphore.

  - If the queue is empty and the descriptor has been set to nonblock, `sem_trywait()` returns with an EAGAIN error to the caller.

  - Otherwise, the `mq_rblocked` semaphore is incremented (`sem_post`), and `sem_wait()` is called.

- Once a message shows up on the queue, the `mq_exclusive` semaphore is acquired, and the internal `mq_getmsg()` function is called.

- The next message is pulled off the head of the queue, and the pointers are appropriately adjusted.

Our description omits some subtle details, mostly around the priority mechanism available for POSIX message queues. A message priority can be specified in the mq_send(3R) and mq_receive(3R) calls. Messages with better priorities (larger numeric values) are inserted into the queue before messages of lower priority, so higher-priority messages are kept at the front of the queue and will be removed first. The use and behavior of message priorities is well documented in the manual pages, as well as in Steven's *UNIX Network Programming—Interprocess Communication* [25].

10.6 Solaris Doors

Doors provide a facility for processes to issue procedure calls to functions in other processes running on the same system. Using the APIs, a process can become a door server, exporting a function through a door it creates by using the door_create(3X) interface. Other processes can then invoke the procedure by issuing a door_call(3X), specifying the correct door descriptor. Our goal here is not to provide a programmer's guide to doors but rather to focus on the kernel implementation, data structures, and algorithms. Some discussion of the APIs is, of course, necessary to keep things in context, but we suggest that you refer to the manual pages and to Steven's book [25] to understand how to develop applications with doors.

The door APIs were available in Solaris 2.5.1 but not documented and, at that point, subject to change. Solaris 2.6 was the first Solaris release that included a relatively stable set of interfaces (*stable* in the sense that they were less likely to change). The Solaris kernel ships with a shared object library, libdoor.so, that must be linked to applications using the doors APIs. Table 10-10 describes the door APIs available in Solaris 2.6 and Solaris 7. During the course of our coverage of doors, we refer to the interfaces as necessary for clarity.

Table 10-10 Solaris Doors Interfaces

Interface	Description
door_create(3X)	Creates a door. Called from a door server to associate a procedure within the program with a door descriptor. The door descriptor, returned by door_create(3X), is used by client programs that wish to invoke the procedure.
door_revoke(3X)	Revokes client access to the door. Can only be called by the server.
door_call(3X)	Invokes a function exported as a door. Called from a client process.

Table 10-10 Solaris Doors Interfaces

Interface	Description
door_return(3X)	Returns from a door function. Typically used as the last function call in a routine exported as a door.
door_info(3X)	Fetches information about a door.
door_server_create(3X)	Specifies a door thread create function.
door_cred(3X)	Fetches client credential information.
door_bind(3X)	Associates the calling thread with a door thread pool.
door_unbind(3X)	Removes current thread from door pool.

10.6.1 Doors Overview

Figure 10.6 illustrates broadly how doors provide an interprocess communication mechanism.

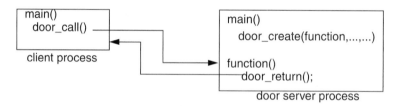

Figure 10.6 Solaris Doors

The file abstraction used by doors is the means by which client kernel threads retrieve the proper door handle required to issue a door_call(3X). It is similar to the methodology employed when POSIX IPC facilities are used; a path name in the file system name space is opened, and the returned file descriptor is passed as an argument in the door_call(3X) to call into the desired door. An argument structure, door_arg_t, is declared by the client code and used for passing arguments to the door server function being called. The address of the door_arg_t structure is passed as the second argument by the client in door_call(3X).

On the server side, a function defined in the process can be made available to external client processes by creation of a door (door_create(3X)). The server must also bind the door to a file in the file system name space. This is done with fattach(3C), which binds a STREAMS-based or door file descriptor to a file system path name. Once the binding has been established, a client can issue an open to the path name and use the returned file descriptor in door_call(3X).

10.6.2 Doors Implementation

Doors are implemented in the kernel as a pseudofile system, `doorfs`, which is loaded from the `/kernel/sys` directory during boot. Within a process, a door is referenced through its door descriptor, which is similar in form and function to a file descriptor, and, in fact, the allocation of a door descriptor in a process uses an available file descriptor slot.

The major data structures required for doors support are illustrated in Figure 10.7

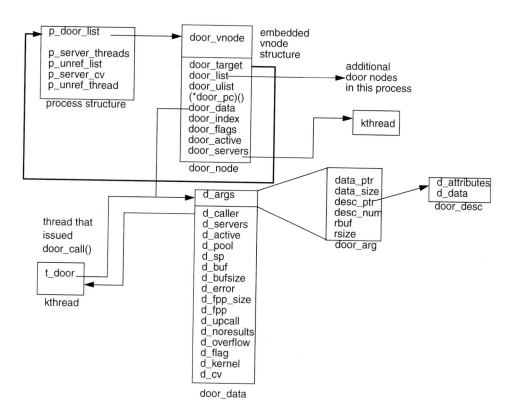

Figure 10.7 Solaris Doors Structures

The two main structures are `door_node`, linked to the process structure with the `p_door_list` pointer, and `door_data`, linked to the `door_node` with the `door_data` pointer. A process can be a door server for multiple functions (multiple doors). Each call to `door_create(3X)` creates another `door_node`, which links to an existing `door_node` (if one already exists) through the `door_list`. `door_data` is created as part of the setup of a server thread during the create process, which we're about to walk through. `door_data` includes a `door_arg` structure, which manages the argument list passed in `door_call(3X)`, and a link to a door descriptor (door_desc), used for passing door descriptors when a door function is called.

To continue: A call to door_create(3X) enters the libdoor.so library door_create() entry point (as is the case with any library call).

- The kernel door_create() is invoked from the library and performs the following actions:
    - Allocates kernel memory for door_node and initializes several fields of door_node and the door vnode (part of the door_node structure).
    - Links the door_target field to the process structure of the calling kernel thread.
    - Sets door_pc, a function pointer, to the address of the function being served by the door (the code that will execute when a client calls door_call(3X)).
    - Sets door_flags as directed by the attributes passed by the caller.
    - Initializes the vnode mutex lock (v_lock) and condition variable (v_cv). Initializes several other fields in the vnode to specify the vnode type (VDOOR) and references to the vnode operations and virtual file system (VFS) switch table entries of the doorfs file system.
    - Adds the door_node to the process's door list (p_door_list) and allocates a file descriptor for the door descriptor by means of the kernel falloc() function, which allocates a file structure and user file descriptor.
- The kernel door_create() now completed, the code returns to the libdoor.so door_create() code.
- The library code makes sure that the calling process has been linked with the Solaris threads library, libthread.so and returns an error if the link has not been made.

  A door server requires linking with libthread.so because the door code uses the threads library interfaces to create and manage a pool of door server threads.
- The last thing the library-level door_create() code does is call thr_create(3T) to create a server thread for the door server, as an execution resource for calls into the function being exported by the door server.
- thr_create(3T) creates a detached, bound thread that executes the library door_create_func() routine, which disables cancellation of the current thread (pthread_setcancelstate(3T)) and enters the kernel door_return() code.

door_return(3X) is part of the doors API and is typically called at the end of the function being exported by the door_create(3X) call.

- door_return(3X) returns processor control to the thread that issued door_call(3X) and causes the server thread to sleep, waiting for another invocation of the door function.
- When entered (remember, we're in the kernel now, not in the doors library), door_return() allocates a door_data structure for the calling thread and links it to the kernel thread's t_door pointer.

    This sequence is done if the current thread's t_door pointer is NULL, signifying a door_data structure has not yet been allocated.

The next bit of code in door_return() applies to argument handling, return data, and other conditions that need to be dealt with when a kernel thread issues door_call(3X). We're still in the door create phase, so a bit later we'll revisit what happens in door_return() as a result of door_call(3X).

Continuing with the door create in the door_return() kernel function:

- The kernel door_release_server() code is called to place the current thread on the list of threads available to execute on behalf of door calls into the server.
- The kernel thread is linked to the process's p_server_thread link, and cv_broadcast() is done on the door condition variable, door_cv, causing any threads blocked in door_call(3X) to wake up.

    At this point, the door create is essentially completed.

- A call into the shuttle code to place the kernel thread to sleep on a shuttle synchronization object is made (shuttle_swtch()); the thread is thus placed in a sleep state and enters the dispatcher through swtch().

We now digress slightly to explain shuttle synchronization objects. Typically, execution control flow is managed by the kernel dispatcher (Chapter 5), using condition variables and sleep queues. Other synchronization primitives, mutex locks, and reader/writer locks are managed by turnstiles, an implementation of sleep queues that provides a priority inheritance mechanism.

Shuttle objects are a relatively new (introduced in Solaris 2.5, when doors first shipped) synchronization object that essentially allows very fast transfer of control of a processor from one kernel thread to another without incurring the overhead of the dispatcher queue searching and normal kernel thread processing. In the case of a door_call(), control can be transferred directly from the caller (or client in this case), to a thread in the door server pool, which executes the door function on behalf of the caller. When the door function has completed, control is transferred directly back to the client (caller), all using the kernel shuttle interfaces to set thread state and to enter the dispatcher at the appropriate places. This direct transfer of processor control contributes significantly to the IPC performance attainable with doors. Shuttle objects are currently used only by the doors subsystem in Solaris.

Kernel threads sleeping on shuttle objects have a 0 value in their wait channel field (t_wchan) and a value of 1 in t_wchan0. The thread's t_sobj_ops (synchronization object operations table) pointer is set to the shuttle object's operations structure (shuttle_sops); the thread's state is, of course, TS_SLEEP, and the thread's T_WAKEABLE flag is set.

Getting back to door creation:

- A default of one server thread is created unless there are concurrent invocations, in which case a thread will be created for each door call. The API allows for programs creating their own separate, private pool of door threads that have different characteristics than the default thread properties.
- The doors library will create a bound, detached thread with the default thread stack size and signal disposition by default.

  This completes the creation of a door server. A server thread in the door pool is left sleeping on a shuttle object (the call to shuttle_swtch()), ready to execute the door function.

Application code that creates a door to a function (becomes a door server) typically creates a file in the file system to which the door descriptor can be attached, using the standard open(2) and fattach(3C) APIs, to make the door more easily accessible to other processes.

The fattach(3C) API has traditionally been used for STREAMS code, where it is desirable to associate a STREAM or STREAMS-based pipe with a file in the file system name space, for precisely the same reason one would wish to associate a door descriptor with a file name; that is, to make the descriptor easily accessible to other processes on the system so application software can take advantage of the IPC mechanism. The door code can leverage from the fact that the binding of an object to a file name, when that object does not meet the traditional definition of what a file is, has already been solved.

fattach(3C) is implemented with a pseudo file system called namefs, the name file system. namefs allows the mounting of file systems on nondirectory mount points, as opposed to the traditional mounting of a file system that requires the selected mount point to be a directory file. Currently, fattach(3C) is the only client application of namefs; it calls the mount(2) system call, passing namefs as the file system name character string and a pointer to a namefs file descriptor. The mount(2) system call enters the VFS switch table through the VFS_MOUNT macro and enters the namefs mount code, nm_mount().

With the door server in place, client processes are free to issue a door_call(3X) to invoke the exported server function.

- The kernel `door_call()` code (nothing happens at the doors library level in `door_call()`) allocates a `door_data` structure from kernel memory and links it to the `t_door` pointer in the calling kernel thread.

  - If a pointer to an argument structure (`door_arg`) was passed in the `door_call(3X)`, the arguments are copied from the passed structure in user space to the `door_arg` structure embedded in door_data.

  - If no arguments were passed, the `door_arg` fields are zeroed and the `d_noresults` flag in `door_data` is set to indicate no results can be returned.

  The `door_call(3X)` API defines that a NULL argument pointer means no results can be returned. A lookup is performed on the passed door descriptor and returns a pointer to the `door_node`. Typically, file descriptor lookups return a vnode pointer. In this case, the vnode pointer and the `door_node` pointer are one and the same because the vnode is embedded in the `door_node`, located at the top of the structure.

- The kernel `door_get_server()` function retrieves a server kernel thread from the pool to execute the function.

  - The thread is removed from the list of available server threads (`p_server_threads`) and changed from TS_SLEEP to TS_ONPROC state (this kernel thread was sleeping on a shuttle object, not sitting on a sleep queue).

  - The arguments from the caller are copied to the server thread returned from `door_get_server()`. The `door_active` counter in the `door_node` is incremented, the calling (client) thread's d_error field (in `door_data`) is set to DOOR_WAIT, the door server thread's `d_caller` field (`door_data` structure for the server thread) is set to the client (caller), and a pointer to the `door_node` is set in the server thread's `door_data` d_active field.

  With the necessary data fields set up, control can now be transferred to the server thread; this transfer is done with a call to `shuttle_resume()`.

- `shuttle_resume()` is passed a pointer to the server thread removed from the door pool.

Just to get back to the forest for a moment (in case you're lost among the trees), we're into `shuttle_resume()` as a result of a kernel thread issuing `door_call(3X)`. The `door_call()` kernel code up to this point essentially allocated or initialized the necessary data structures for the server thread to have the exported function executed on behalf of the caller. The `shuttle_resume()` function is entered from `door_call()`, so the kernel thread now executing in `shuttle_resume()` is the door client. So, what needs to happen is really pretty simple (relatively speaking)—the server thread, which was passed to `shuttle_resume()` as an argument, needs to get control of the processor, and the current thread executing the `shuttle_resume()` code needs to be put to sleep on a shuttle object, since the current thread and the door client thread are one and the same. So:

- `shuttle_resume()` sets up the current thread to sleep on a shuttle object in the same manner described previously (t_wchan0 set to 1, state set to TS_SLEEP, etc.); the server thread has its T_WAKEABLE flag, t_wchan0 field, and t_sobj_ops field cleared.

- The code tests for any interesting events that may require attention, such as a hold condition on the thread, and checks for posted signals. If any signals are posted, `setrun()` is called with the current (client) thread.

- Finally, the dispatcher `swtch_to()` function is called and is passed the server thread address. `swtch_to()` updates the per-processor context-switch counter in the `cpu_sysinfo` structure (pswitch) and calls `resume()` to have the server thread context-switched onto the processor. The general flow is illustrated in Figure 10.8.

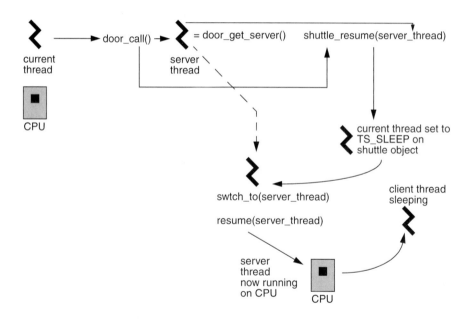

Figure 10.8 `door_call()` Flow with Shuttle Switching

- The server thread executes the function associated with the `door_node`, as specified by the first argument passed when the server executed `door_create`(3X).

- The last call made by the server function is `door_return`(3X), which returns results and control to the calling thread (client) and blocks in the server, waiting for another `door_call`(3X).

- The kernel `door_return()` code copies the return data back to the caller and places the server thread back in the door server pool. The calling (client) thread, which we left in a sleep state back in `door_call()`, is set back to an `T_ONPROC` state, and the shuttle code (`shuttle_resume()`) is called to give the processor back to the caller and have it resume execution.

Some final points to make regarding doors. There's a fair amount of code in the kernel `doorfs` module designed to deal with error conditions and the premature termination of the calling thread or server thread. In general, if the calling thread is awakened early, that is, before `door_call()` has completed, the code figures out why the wakeup occurred (signal, exit call, etc.) and sends a cancel signal (`SIGCANCEL`) to the server thread. If a server thread is interrupted because of a signal, exit, error condition, etc., the `door_call()` code bails out. In the client, an `EINTR` (interrupted system call) error will be set, signifying that `door_call()` terminated prematurely.

Part Four

FILES AND FILE SYSTEMS

- Files and File I/O
- File System Overview
- File System Framework
- The UFS File System
- File System Caching

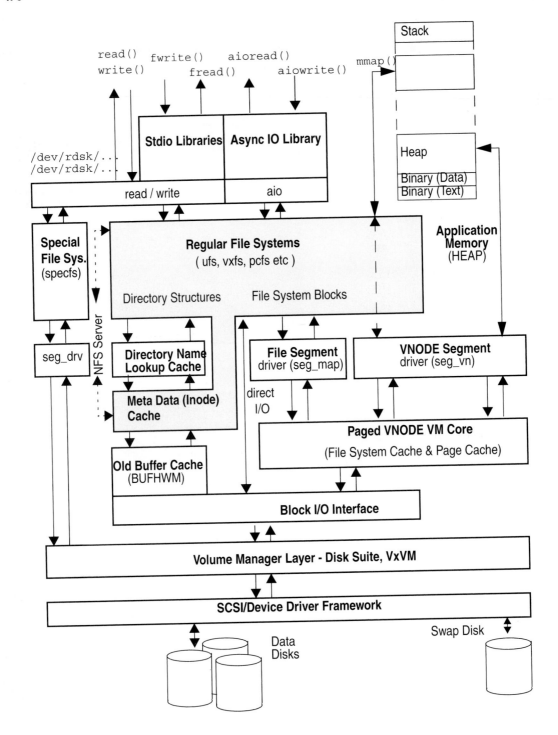

The Solaris File I/O System

11

SOLARIS FILES AND FILE I/O

From its inception, Unix has been built around two fundamental entities: *processes* and *files*. Everything that is executed on the system is a process, and all process I/O is done to a file. We saw in previous chapters how the process model has evolved and how the kernel thread is the unit of execution in the Solaris kernel. The implementation of files and file I/O facilities has also seen some changes since the early versions of UNIX. The notion of a file now includes more abstract types, and the interfaces available for doing file I/O have expanded.

In this chapter, we look at the implementation of files in Solaris and discuss some of the abstract file types and the file I/O facilities.

11.1 Files in Solaris

Generically defined, a file is an entity that stores data as an array of bytes, beginning at byte zero and extending to the end of the file. The contents of the file (the data) can take any number of forms: a simple text file, a binary executable file, a directory file, etc. Solaris supports many types of files, several of which are defined at the kernel level, meaning that some component of the kernel has intimate knowledge of the file's format by virtue of the file type. An example is a directory file on a UFS file system—directory files have a specific format that is known to the UFS kernel routines designed for directory I/O.

The number of file types in the kernel has increased over the last several years with the addition new kernel abstractions in the form of pseudofiles. Pseudofiles provide a means by which the kernel can abstract as a file a binary object, like a data structure in memory. Users and programmers view the object as a file, in that the traditional file I/O operations are supported on it (for the most part). It's a pseudofile because it is not an on-disk file; it's not a real file in the traditional sense.

Under the covers, the operations performed on the object are managed by the file system on which the file resides. A specific file type often belongs to an underlying file system that manages the storage and retrieval of the file and defines the kernel functions for I/O and control operations on the file. (See Chapter 14, "The UNIX File System", for details about file systems.) Table 11-1 lists the various types of files implemented in Solaris.

Table 11-1 Solaris File Types

File Type	File System	Character Designation	Description
Regular	UFS	—	A traditional on-disk file. Can be a text file, binary shared object, or executable file.
Directory	UFS	d	A file that stores the names of other files and directories. Other file systems can implement directories within their own file hierarchy.
Symbolic Link	UFS	l	A file that represents a link to another file, potentially in another directory or on another file system.
Character Special	specfs	c	A device special file for devices capable of character mode I/O. Device files represent I/O devices on the system and provide a means of indexing into the device driver and uniquely identifying a specific device.
Block Special	specfs	b	As above, a device special file for devices capable of block-mode I/O, such as disk and tape devices.
Named Pipe (FIFO)	fifofs	p	A file that provides a bidirectional communication path between processes running on the same system.
Door	doorfs	D	Part of the door interprocess communication facility. Doors provide a means of doing very fast interprocess procedure calling and message and data passing.

Table 11-1 Solaris File Types (Continued)

File Type	File System	Character Designation	Description
Socket	sockfs	s	A communication endpoint for network I/O, typically used for TCP or UDP connections between processes on different systems. UNIX domain sockets are also supported for interprocess communication between processes on the same system. The "s" character designation appears only for AF_UNIX sockets.

The character designation column in Table 11-1 refers to the character produced in the lefthand column of an `ls -l` command. When a long file listing is executed, a single character designates the type of file in the listing.

Within a process, a file is identified by a *file descriptor*: an integer value returned to the process by the kernel when a file is opened. An exception is made if the standard I/O interfaces are used. In that case, the file is represented in the process as a pointer to a `FILE` structure, and the file descriptor is embedded in the `FILE` structure. The file descriptor references an array of per-process file entry (`uf_entry`) structures, which form the list of open files within the process. These per-process file entries link to a file structure, which is a kernel structure that maintains specific status information about the file on behalf of the process that has the file opened. If a specific file is opened by multiple processes, the kernel maintains a file structure for each process; that is, the same file may have multiple file structures referencing it. The primary reason for this behavior is to maintain a per-process read/write file pointer for the file, since different processes may be reading different segments of the same file.

The kernel implements a virtual file abstraction in the form of a `vnode`, where every opened file in Solaris is represented by a `vnode` in the kernel. A given file has but one `vnode` that represents it in the kernel, regardless of the number of processes that have the file opened. The `vnode` implementation is discussed in detail in "The vnode" on page 533. In this discussion, we allude to the `vnode` and other file-specific structures as needed for clarity.

Beyond the `vnode` virtual file abstraction, a file-type-specific structure describes the file. The structure is implemented as part of the file system on which the file resides. For example, files on the default Unix File System (UFS) are described by an inode that is linked to the `v_data` pointer of the `vnode`.

Figure 11.1 illustrates the relationships of the various file-related components, providing a path from the file descriptor to the actual file. The figure shows how a file is viewed at various levels. Within a process, a file is referenced as a file descriptor. The file descriptor indexes the per-process `u_flist` array of `uf_entry` structures, which link to the kernel file structure. The file is abstracted in the kernel as a virtual file through the vnode, which links to the file-specific structures (based on the file type) through the v_data pointer in the vnode.

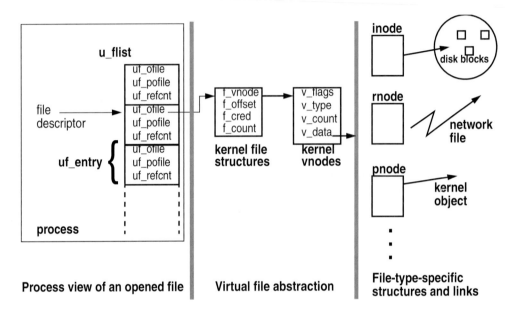

Figure 11.1 File-Related Structures

The process-level uf_entry structures are allocated dynamically in groups of 24 as files are opened, up to the per-process open file limit. The uf_entry structure contains a pointer to the file structure (uf_ofile) and a uf_pofile flag field used by the kernel to maintain file state information. The possible flags are FRESERVED, to indicate that the slot has been allocated, FCLOSING, to indicate that a file-close is in progress, and FCLOSEXEC, a user-settable close-on-exec flag, which instructs the kernel to close the file descriptor if an exec(2) call is executed. uf_entry also maintains a reference count in the uf_refcnt member. This count provides a means of tracking multiple references to the file in multithreaded processes.

The kernel establishes a default hard and soft limit for the number of files a process can have opened at any time. rlim_fd_max is the hard limit, and rlim_fd_cur is the current limit (or soft limit). A process can have up to rlim_fd_cur file descriptors and can increase the number up to rlim_fd_max. You can set these parameters systemwide by placing entries in the /etc/system file:

```
set rlim_fd_max=8192
set rlim_fd_cur=1024
```

You can alter the per-process limits either directly from the command line with the limit(1) or ulimit(1) shell commands or programmatically with setrlimit(2). The actual number of open files that a process can maintain is driven largely by the file APIs used. For 32-bit systems, if the stdio(3S) interfaces are used, the limit is 256 open files. This limit results from the data type used in the FILE structure for the actual file descriptor. An unsigned 8-bit data type, which has a range of values of 0–255, is used. Thus, the maximum number of file descriptors is limited to 256 for 32-bit stdio(3S)-based programs. For 64-bit systems (and 64-bit processes), the stdio(3S) limit is 64 Kbytes.

The select(3C) interface, which provides a mechanism for file polling, imposes another API limit. select(3C) limits the number of open files to 1 Kbyte on 32-bit systems, with the exception of 32-bit Solaris 7. In 32-bit Solaris 7, select(3C) can poll up to 64-Kbyte file descriptors. If you use file descriptors greater than 1-Kbyte with select(3C) on 32-bit Solaris 7, then you must declare FD_SETSIZE in the program code. On 64-bit Solaris 7, a 64-bit process has a default file descriptor set size (FD_SETSIZE) of 64 Kbytes. Table 11-2 summarizes file descriptor limitations.

Table 11-2 File Descriptor Limits

Interface (API)	Limit	Notes
stdio(3S)	256	All 32-bit systems.
stdio(3S)	64K (65536)	64-bit programs only (Solaris 7 and later).
select(3C)	1K (1024)	All 32-bit systems. Default value for 32-bit Solaris 7.
select(3C)	64K (65536)	Attainable value on 32-bit Solaris 7. Requires you to add: #define FD_SETSIZE 65536 to program code before inclusion on additional system header files.
select(3C)	64K (65536)	Default for 64-bit Solaris 7 (and beyond).

Those limitations aside, there remain only the practical limits that govern the number of files that can be opened on a per-process and systemwide basis. A practical limit from a per-process perspective really comes down to two things: how the application software is designed; and what constitutes a manageable number of file descriptors within a single process, such that the maintenance, performance, portability, and availability requirements of the software can be met. The file descriptors and uf_entry structures do not require a significant amount of memory space, even in large numbers, so per-process address space limitations are typically not an issue when it comes to the number of open files.

11.1.1 Kernel File Structures

The Solaris kernel does not implement a system file table in the traditional sense. That is, the systemwide list of file structures is not maintained in an array or as a linked list. A kernel object cache segment is allocated to hold file structures, and they are simply allocated and linked to the process and vnode as files are created and opened.

We can see in Figure 11.1 that each process uses file descriptors to reference a file. The file descriptors ultimately link to the kernel file structure, defined as a file_t data type, shown below.

```
typedef struct file {
        kmutex_t         f_tlock;        /* short-term lock */
        ushort_t         f_flag;
        ushort_t         f_pad;          /* Explicit pad to 4-byte boundary */
        struct vnode     *f_vnode;       /* pointer to vnode structure */
        offset_t         f_offset;       /* read/write character pointer */
        struct cred      *f_cred;        /* credentials of user who opened it */
        caddr_t          f_audit_data;   /* file audit data */
        int              f_count;        /* reference count */
} file_t;
```

Header File   <sys/file.h>

The fields maintained in the file structure are, for the most part, self-explanatory. The f_tlock kernel mutex lock protects the various structure members. These include the f_count reference count, which lists how many threads have the file opened, and the f_flag file flags, described in "File Open Modes and File Descriptor Flags" on page 485.

Solaris allocates file structures for opened files as needed, growing the open file count dynamically to meet the requirements of the system load. Therefore, the maximum number of files that can be opened systemwide at any time is limited by available kernel address space, and nothing more. The actual size to which the kernel can grow depends on the hardware architecture of the system and the Solaris version the system is running. The key point is that a fixed kernel limit on a maximum number of file structures does not exist.

The system initializes space for file structures during startup by calling file_cache(), a routine in the kernel memory allocator code that creates a kernel object cache. The initial allocation simply sets up the file_cache pointer with space for one file structure. However, the kernel will have allocated several file structures by the time the system has completed the boot process and is available for users, as all of the system processes that get started have some opened files. As files are opened/created, the system either reuses a freed cache object for the file entry or creates a new one if needed. You can use /etc/crash as root to examine the file structures.

```
# crash
dumpfile = /dev/mem, namelist = /dev/ksyms, outfile = stdout
> file
ADDRESS        RCNT      TYPE/ADDR              OFFSET    FLAGS
3000009e008    1         FIFO/300009027e0            0    read write
3000009e040    1         UFS /3000117dc68          535    write appen
3000009e078    1         SPEC/300008ed698         3216    write appen
3000009e0b0    1         UFS /300010d8c98            0    write
3000009e0e8    1         UFS /30001047ca0            4    read write
3000009e120    2         DOOR/30000929348           0    read write
3000009e158    1         SPEC/30000fb45d0           0    read
3000009e1c8    1         UFS /300014c6c98          106    read write
3000009e200    1         SPEC/30000c376a0           0    write
3000009e238    2         DOOR/30000929298           0    read write
3000009e270    3         SPEC/300008ecf18           0    read
3000009e2a8    1         UFS /30000f5e0f0            0    read
3000009e2e0    1         SPEC/30000fb46c0           0    read write
3000009e318    1         UFS /300001f9dd0            0    read
3000009e350    1         FIFO/30000902c80           0    read write
```

The ADDRESS column is the kernel virtual memory address of the file structure. RCNT is the reference count field (f_count). TYPE is the type of file, and ADDR is the kernel virtual address of the vnode. OFFSET is the current file pointer, and FLAGS are the flags bits currently set for the file.

You can use sar(1M) for a quick look at how many files are opened systemwide.

```
# sar -v 3 3

SunOS devhome 5.7 Generic sun4u    08/01/99

11:38:09  proc-sz      ov  inod-sz      ov  file-sz   ov  lock-sz
11:38:12  100/5930      0 37181/37181    0  603/603    0  0/0
11:38:15  100/5930      0 37181/37181    0  603/603    0  0/0
11:38:18  101/5930      0 37181/37181    0  607/607    0  0/0
```

This example shows 603 opened files. The format of the sar output is a holdover from the early days of static tables, which is why it is displayed as 603/603. Originally, the value on the left represented the current number of occupied table slots, and the value on the right represented the maximum number of slots. Since file structure allocation is completely dynamic in nature, both values will always be the same.

For a specific process, you can use the pfiles(1) command to create a list of all the files opened.

```
$ pfiles 585
585:    /space1/framemaker,v5.5.3/bin/sunxm.s5.sparc/maker -xrm *iconX:0 -xrm
  Current rlimit: 64 file descriptors
   0: S_IFCHR mode:0666 dev:32,24 ino:143523 uid:0 gid:3 rdev:13,2
      O_RDONLY|O_LARGEFILE
   1: S_IFCHR mode:0666 dev:32,24 ino:143523 uid:0 gid:3 rdev:13,2
      O_WRONLY|O_APPEND|O_LARGEFILE
   2: S_IFCHR mode:0666 dev:32,24 ino:143523 uid:0 gid:3 rdev:13,2
      O_WRONLY|O_APPEND|O_LARGEFILE
   3: S_IFIFO mode:0666 dev:176,0 ino:4132162568 uid:0 gid:0 size:0
      O_RDWR|O_NONBLOCK FD_CLOEXEC
   4: S_IFDOOR mode:0444 dev:176,0 ino:4127633624 uid:0 gid:0 size:0
      O_RDONLY|O_LARGEFILE FD_CLOEXEC  door to nscd[202]
   5: S_IFREG mode:0644 dev:32,9 ino:3643 uid:19821 gid:10 size:297984
      O_RDONLY FD_CLOEXEC
   6: S_IFREG mode:0644 dev:32,8 ino:566 uid:19821 gid:10 size:29696
      O_RDWR FD_CLOEXEC
   7: S_IFREG mode:0644 dev:32,8 ino:612 uid:19821 gid:10 size:0
      O_RDWR FD_CLOEXEC
   8: S_IFREG mode:0644 dev:32,8 ino:666 uid:19821 gid:10 size:0
      O_RDWR FD_CLOEXEC
   9: S_IFCHR mode:0000 dev:32,24 ino:360 uid:0 gid:0 rdev:41,104
      O_RDWR FD_CLOEXEC
  10: S_IFREG mode:0644 dev:32,9 ino:38607 uid:19821 gid:10 size:65083
      O_RDONLY
  11: S_IFREG mode:0644 dev:32,8 ino:667 uid:19821 gid:10 size:4096
      O_RDWR
```

In the preceding example, the pfiles command is executed on PID 585. The PID and process name are dumped, followed by a listing of the process's opened files. For each file, we see a listing of the file descriptor (the number to the left of the colon), the file type, file mode bits, the device from which the file originated, the inode number, file UID and GID, and the file size.

11.2 File Application Programming Interfaces (APIs)

Several different APIs perform file I/O in Solaris. These include standard I/O—the generic C buffered I/O mechanism—and several flavors of low-level operating system file I/O.

The traditional C buffered interfaces are known as the Standard I/O functions, abbreviated as stdio. They are the buffered I/O interfaces that were added to Unix V6 by Bell Laboratories in 1976; they appear as a standard file I/O mechanism in nearly all C runtime environments. These stdio library interfaces exist as a layer above the lower-level system calls.

Of the several different types of system I/O, the most basic are the read and write system calls. The more advanced (and more recent) are POSIX I/O through pread and pwrite system calls and scatter/gather I/O through the readv and writev system calls. Asynchronous I/O is done through either the aio_read(3R) and aio_write(3R) interfaces, which are part of the posix4 library, or aioread(3) and aiowrite(3), which are part of the libaio library. Both sets of asynchronous I/O interfaces provide similar functionality; they differ in how they are used in application code.

Figure 11.2 shows the general relationships among the various file-related APIs and the underlying kernel subsystems.

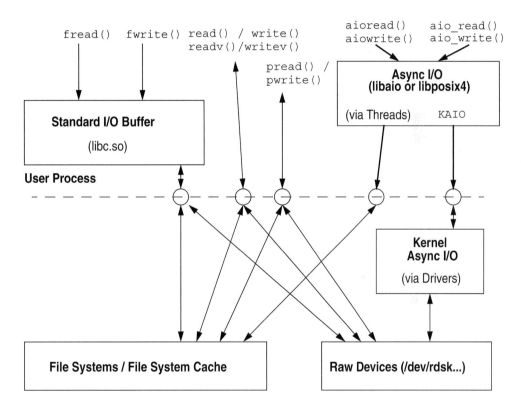

Figure 11.2 Kernel File I/O Interface Relationships

11.2.1 Standard I/O (stdio)

The standard I/O functions allow a file to be opened as a "stream" of bytes, known as a file stream. This approach allows a C program to access the file by reading and writing characters and arbitrary length strings, while the underlying libraries deal with the system calls necessary to implement the real I/O operations. This design has the advantage that it is completely portable, even across different operating systems, and the programmer does not need to consider any underlying machine-dependent characteristics, such as alignment with the file system block size.

For example, a C program can read a file one byte at a time, and rather than reading from disk in 1-byte I/Os, the standard I/O library will buffer the I/O so that the file system and I/O subsystem can read in large efficient sizes. Standard I/O file buffering does come at the cost of additional processing overhead for each I/O.

The basic handle for a standard I/O file stream is the FILE handle, which is acquired by a call to fopen. Once a file handle is established, a suite of standard I/O routines is available to perform stream I/O on the handle.

The traditional Unix definition for a file handle defines the FILE structure in <stdio.h>, which is also true for Solaris versions up to and including Solaris 2.6. Beginning with Solaris 7, the FILE structure is defined in stdio_impl.h, a form of the standard I/O header. There are now different definitions for the FILE structure for 32- and 64-bit implementations.

```
#ifdef  _LP64

struct __FILE_TAG {
        long      __pad[16];
};

#else

struct __FILE_TAG       /* needs to be binary-compatible with old versions */
{
#ifdef _STDIO_REVERSE
        unsigned char   *_ptr;  /* next character from/to here in buffer */
        ssize_t         _cnt;/* number of available characters in buffer */
#else
        ssize_t         _cnt;/* number of available characters in buffer */
        unsigned char   *_ptr;  /* next character from/to here in buffer */
#endif
        unsigned char   *_base; /* the buffer */
        unsigned char   _flag;  /* the state of the stream */
        unsigned char   _file;  /* UNIX System file descriptor */
        unsigned        __orientation:2; /* the orientation of the stream */
        unsigned        __filler:6;
};

#endif /*        _LP64    */
```

Header File <stdio_impl.h>

The members of the 32-bit FILE structure are defined as follows:

- **_cnt** — Count of the number of characters in the buffer.

- **_ptr** — Pointer to the current character position in the buffer.

- **_base** — Pointer to the buffer (a char * array).

- **_flag** — Flag field that stores status bits about the state of the file. Examples of flag bits are indications that the file is currently being read or written, the file pointer is at EOF (end-of-file), or an I/O error occurred on the file.

- **_file** — The file descriptor itself is stored as an unsigned char data type in this member. The file descriptor is, as we said, the data member that limits the number of open files to 256 for 32-bit programs using stdio(3S).

The 64-bit definition for the FILE structure is similarly defined internally, but it is publicly defined as an array of long to prevent users of the standard I/O interface from accessing the internal members, so that binary compatibility can be retained if the internal members change. The only differences in the 64-bit FILE structure are 64-bit pointers and the use of an integer for the file descriptor.

The 64-bit Solaris 7 implementation effectively makes the FILE structure opaque to application code. Programs that made explicit references to the FILE structure members in code (e.g., to read the _cnt field to determine the number of bytes in the buffer) can use a portable set of routines created to provide access to the stdio(3C) FILE structure members. These interfaces are documented in the __fbufsize(3C) manual page.

Table 11-3 describes the standard I/O functions.

Table 11-3 Standard I/O Functions

Function	Definition
clearerr()	Resets the error indicator and EOF indicator to 0 on the named stream.
fclose()	Closes a FILE stream.
feof()	Returns a nonzero value when EOF has previously been detected during reading from the named input stream. Otherwise, returns 0.
ferror()	Returns a nonzero value when an error has previously occurred during reading from or writing to the named stream. Otherwise, returns 0.
fflush()	Flushes the contents of the file stream to the operating system for writing asynchronously. Note that the file stream contents are not immediately flushed to disk.
fgetc()	Gets a single character from a file stream.
fgetpos()	Gets the position within a file stream.
fgets()	Gets a string from a file stream.
fileno()	Returns the integer file descriptor associated with the named stream.
flockfile()	Locks the file stream, and blocks other file stream operations until funlockfile is called.
fopen()	Opens the file path name and returns a file stream handle.
fprintf()	Prints formatted strings to the file stream.
fputc()	Puts a single character onto the file stream.

Table 11-3 Standard I/O Functions (Continued)

Function	Definition
fputs()	Puts a string onto the file stream.
fread()	Reads a given number of bytes from a file stream.
freopen()	Flushes a file stream, closes the file, and reopens a new file on the given file stream handle.
fscanf()	Interprets bytes specified by the given format on the file stream.
fseek()	Seeks to a given position in the file stream.
fsetpos()	Seeks to a position given by fgetpos.
ftrylockfile()	Locks the file stream only if it is unlocked; otherwise, returns 0.
funlockfile()	Unlocks the file stream.
fwrite()	Writes the given number of bytes onto the stream.
getc()	Gets a single character from the stream.
getc_unlocked()	Gets a single character from the file stream without locking the file stream. Use flockfile to lock the file stream.
getw()	Gets a word from the file steam.
pclose()	Closes a pipe on the given file stream.
popen()	Forks and executes a new process, and redirects its input and output to a file stream.
putc()	Puts a single character onto the file stream.
rewind()	Rewinds the file stream to the beginning.
setbuf()	Sets the buffer size used for the stream.
setvbuf()	Sets the buffer type and size used for the stream.
ungetc()	Returns a character to the file stream.

For more information on each standard I/O function, see the Solaris stdio(3S) manual page.

11.2.2 C Runtime File Handles

The standard I/O environment is part of the C runtime environment shipped with Solaris. By default, each C program that is linked to the default C library (libc.so) is started with three open file streams, corresponding to the terminal input and output. These file streams can be used to write characters and read characters to and from the controlling terminal for the C program. Table 11-4 describes the file streams.

Table 11-4 File Streams

File Stream	Description
stdin	Terminal input stream.
stdout	Terminal output stream.
stderr	Terminal error output stream.

By default, the standard I/O library functions such as printf and scanf write to stdout and read from stdin.

11.2.3 Standard I/O Buffer Sizes

Standard I/O buffers are configured by default when the file is first opened with fopen(3C). The buffer size is chosen according to the characteristics of the underlying file and the following criteria:

- If the file is a terminal, then a buffer of 128 bytes is chosen.

- If the file is a regular file, then the standard I/O library queries the file system for the suggested I/O size for this file and sets the standard I/O buffer to that size.

- If the underlying file system does not indicate a preferred I/O size, then a 1024-byte size is chosen.

11.3 System File I/O

System file I/O involves the use of systems calls and some library routines for reading and writing files and doing control functions such as file locking or altering file flags. These I/O interfaces do not abstract the target of the I/O as a file stream, nor do they provide the extra level of buffering as the standard I/O (stdio) interfaces. From a layering perspective, the stdio interfaces sit above the file I/O system calls. The fopen(3S) library interface ultimately calls the open(2) system call, fread(3S) calls read(2), fwrite(3S) calls write(2), and so on.

11.3.1 File I/O System Calls

Once a file descriptor is established, a number of system calls can operate on the open file descriptor. The most basic system calls are the open(), close(), read(), and write() calls. These provide the basic mechanics to perform low-level I/O to a file. For implementation specifics of the file system calls, see "The vnode" on page 533.

11.3.1.1 The open() and close() System Calls

The open system call does the work of converting a path name into an open file descriptor. The target file can be opened with a variety of flags, controlling how the underlying file system will perform I/O for that file descriptor. We discuss the flags controlling open modes in "File Open Modes and File Descriptor Flags" on page 485.

11.3.1.2 The read() and write() System Calls

The read() and write() system calls allow us to do I/O on a file by reading and writing data to and from a user process's address space, as shown below. See "read() and write() System Calls" on page 549 for details.

```
ssize_t read(int fildes, void *buf, size_t nbyte);

ssize_t write(int fildes, const void *buf, size_t nbyte);
```

Header File   <unistd.h>

How data is read or written is implemented by the underlying file system, whether it be a regular disk-based file system (such as UFS) or a special file system (such as specfs for the device of a terminal). Table 11-5 lists all the file I/O system calls.

Table 11-5 File I/O System Calls

Function	Definition
close()	Closes the given file descriptor.
creat()	Creates a file of a name given by the supplied path name.
dup()	Duplicates the given file descriptor handle.
fcntl()	Performs control functions on a file, such as file locking.
fstat()	Retrieves file attributes for the file corresponding to the given file descriptor.
lseek()	Seeks to a given location within a file. The offset may be relative to the start, end, or current position within the file.
lstat()	Retrieves file attributes for the symbolic link corresponding to the given path name.
open()	Opens a file of a given path name and returns a file descriptor.
poll()	Polls the file descriptor for an event.
pread()	Reads a fixed number of bytes from the given file descriptor, starting at the given offset, into a byte array.

Table 11-5 File I/O System Calls (Continued)

Function	Definition
pwrite()	Writes a fixed number of bytes to the given file descriptor, starting at the given offset from a byte array.
read()	Reads a fixed number of bytes from the given file descriptor into the given byte array.
readv()	Equivalent to read() but places the input data into the buffers specified by the members of the supplied array of pointers. This is a way of initiating multiple reads from a single system call.
select()	From an array of file descriptors, selects the next file descriptor that has pending I/O.
stat()	Retrieves file attributes for the file corresponding to the given path name.
write()	Writes a fixed number of bytes to the given file descriptor from the given byte array.
writev()	Equivalent to write() but writes data from the buffers specified by the members of the supplied array of pointers. Provides a way of initiating multiple write operations from a single system call.

11.3.2 File Open Modes and File Descriptor Flags

The Solaris kernel maintains several file flags at different layers in the file code. Within the file structure, flags can be set when the file is opened (open(2) system call). Subsequent file operations using the fcntl(2) (file control) system call allow for setting and clearing file flags after the file has been opened. Some of these flags get pushed down to the file's vnode, so that file manipulation at the vnode layer has the information available without referencing the file structure. Finally, some flags maintained in the inode are not exported to the process (application) level.

The system begins looking at file flags in the very early stages of opening a file. When the open system call is entered, the system checks to ensure that either the read or write flag is set, and the kernel looks at the O_NDELAY and O_NONBLOCK flags, which the programmer can set (see open(2)). O_NDELAY and O_NONBLOCK have the same meaning—they specify nonblocking I/O. Two flags exist because of evolving standards: the O_NDELAY flag emerged as a Unix SVR4 standard, and the O_NONBLOCK flag comes from the POSIX.1 specification. The Solaris environment supports both standards for compatibility. New applications should use the POSIX.1 standard (NONBLOCK), which is what the system chooses if both are set.

To see which flags are set, use the fcntl(2) system call with the F_GETFD flag, which retrieves the flags from the file descriptor.

11.3.2.1 Nonblocking I/O

Nonblocking I/O, as the term implies, instructs the system to prevent a read or write to the file from blocking if the operation cannot be done right away. The specific conditions under which the kernel implements this functionality vary, depending on the file type.

For regular files, nonblocking I/O is possible when used in conjunction with mandatory file locking. If a read or write is attempted on a regular file and a record lock exists on the section of the file (the "record") to be read or written, then the read or write blocks until the I/O can be completed. However, if the O_NDELAY or O_NONBLOCK flag is set, then the read or write fails and the kernel sets the errno (error number) to EAGAIN (a hint to the programmer to try again later). Blocking simply means that the kernel puts the process or thread to sleep. When an event occurs that the process or thread is waiting for, in this case, a file lock being released, the kernel issues a wakeup and places the process on a dispatch queue so the scheduler can schedule it for execution on a processor.

For other file types, such as sockets, FIFOs, and device-special files, data may not be available for a read (e.g., read from a named pipe or socket when data has not been written yet). Without the O_NONBLOCK or O_NDELAY flag set, the read or write would simply block until data becomes available as a result of a write to a FIFO or socket.

As documented in the open(2) man page, if both flags are set in the open(2) call, the O_NONBLOCK flag takes precedence and the O_NDELAY flag is cleared in the kernel open code. To maintain the blocking (or nonblocking) requirements for read/write operations to the file, the FNDELAY flag is set in the file structure. The NONBLOCK/NDELAY flags do not have corresponding flags at the vnode or inode layers because there is no need for the kernel to push this information down to those structures.

11.3.2.2 Exclusive open

The O_EXCL flag, exclusive open, can be used in conjunction with the O_CREAT flag to request that the system return an error if the file already exists. If the file does not already exist and both flags are set, the file creation and return of a file descriptor to the calling process are guaranteed to be atomic. Atomic means that the steps involved are guaranteed to complete entirely or not at all. The system does not allow an operation to partially complete and have its state altered by something else. Atomicity enables applications to reliably create lock files, which are often implemented by applications as a means of persistent synchronization. For example, some applications create a lock file during startup to ensure another instance of the application is not running.

The O_CREAT flag instructs the system to create the file if it does not already exist. The following pseudocode demonstrates the results of a file open under different conditions. The information below assumes all other permission conditions are such that they would not result in an error, for example, read/write permission to the working directory is good.

```
if (file exists)
        if (O_CREAT is clear and O_EXCL is clear)
                return file descriptor (open succeeds)
        if (O_CREAT is clear and O_EXCL is set)
                return file descriptor (open succeeds)
        if (O_CREAT is set and O_EXCL is clear)
                return file descriptor (open succeeds)
        if (O_CREAT is set and O_EXCL is set)
                return "file exists" error (open fails)
if (file does not exist)
        if (O_CREAT is clear and O_EXCL is clear)
                return "no such file" error (open fails)
        if (O_CREAT is clear and O_EXCL is set)
                return "no such file" error (open fails)
        if (O_CREAT is set and O_EXCL is clear)
                create file
                return file descriptor (open succeeds)
        if (O_CREAT is set and O_EXCL is set)
                create file
                return file descriptor (open succeeds)
```

The O_CREAT and O_EXCL flags have no meaning beyond the open operation and are not preserved in any of the underlying file support structures.

File modes are established as a result of the (optional) mode bits that can be passed in the open system call, along with the process file creation mask. The file creation mask is set with the umask(1) command or programmatically with the umask(2) system call. It allows users to define default permissions for files they create. Once set, the value is stored in the user area of the process structure, in the variable u_cmask. See the umask(1) manual page for specifics. Briefly, the umask value represents the file-mode bits the user wants unset when a file is created. Put another way, the umask value determines which file permission bits will be turned off by default. The kernel simply uses standard C language bitwise operators to turn off whatever bits are defined in the u_cmask value for the file's permission modes when a file is created. Note that u_cmask applies only to newly created files.

An open(2) can, of course, be issued on an existing file, in which case the permission checks are done to ensure that the calling process has proper permissions. If the open(2) has a mode value defined as an optional third argument, the permission bits of an existing file are not changed. Such a change requires use of chmod(1) or chmod(2).

11.3.2.3 File Append Flag

If the file is opened with the O_APPEND flag set in the open(2) call, the kernel sets the corresponding FAPPEND flag in the file structure. This flag instructs the system to position the file pointer (offset) to the end of the file prior to every write. This positioning is implemented fairly simply—inside the file-system-specific write code (e.g., `ufs_write()` for UFS files); the kernel sets the file offset to the file size value maintained in the file's inode before doing the write.

11.3.2.4 Data Integrity and Synchronization Flags

Solaris provides file flags that set different levels of data synchronization and file integrity. Thus, application developers have some flexibility when designing applications that read and write files, albeit at increasing cost as the level of integrity is increased.

Three applicable flags can be set in the open system call: O_SYNC, O_RSYNC, and O_DSYNC. The file structure that is allocated when the file is opened has three corresponding flags that will be set in the structure's f_flag field, based on what is passed in the open(2) call. Table 11-6 defines the flags. Any of these flags can be set on an open file by a fcntl(2) system call on the file descriptor with the appropriate arguments.

Table 11-6 File Data Integrity Flags

Flag in open(2)	Correcsponding flag in file structure	Definition
O_SYNC	FSYNC	Data and inode integrity when writing
O_DSYNC	FDSYNC	Data integrity when writing
O_RSYNC	FRSYNC	Read data synchronization

The O_SYNC flag tells the operating system that file data and inode integrity must be maintained. That is, when the O_SYNC flag is set on a file descriptor and a write is done to the file, the write system call does not return to the calling process or thread until the data has been written to the disk and the file inode data has been updated. Without the O_SYNC flag, the write will return when the data has been committed to a page into the buffer cache (physical memory), with the inode information being cached as well. This is the default behavior, which is essentially asynchronous in nature. Better overall file I/O throughput is achieved with the default because nonsynchronous writes take advantage of the caching mechanisms implemented in the Solaris environment. The O_SYNC flag provides optional functionality for applications that require file integrity (e.g., to commit file data to nonvolatile storage—either the disk platters or a nonvolatile disk I/O cache) for every write.

The O_DSYNC flag also provides synchronous write functionality, meaning that the write system call does not return to the calling process until the write data has been committed to the disk storage. Unlike O_SYNC, however, O_DSYNC does not require that the file inode data be committed to the disk. The data-only synchronization implementation comes as part of support for POSIX.4, which is why the Solaris system defines two levels of integrity—synchronized I/O file integrity and synchronized I/O data integrity—for file I/O operations. File integrity has to do with data and inode information; data integrity covers just file data. For each of the flags available, one or the other level of synchronized I/O integrity is guaranteed. See the `fcntl(5)` manual page for the documented definitions of file and data integrity.

The `O_RSYNC` flag provides for read synchronization and is used in conjunction with the `O_SYNC` or `O_DSYNC` flag. With the `O_SYNC` flag, file integrity (data and inode) is enforced. With the `O_DSYNC` flag, data integrity is enforced, meaning that any pending writes to the file are completed before the read is done. If `O_RSYNC` and `O_SYNC` are both set, then pending write I/Os are completed and the inode information is updated before the kernel processes the read request. Note that all read operations are guaranteed not to return stale data. A read issued on a file without any of the `O_SYNC` flags set simply implies that a read from a buffer may be reading data that has not yet been written to the disks. The open(2) and `fcntl(2)` manual pages do not state explicitly that `O_RSYNC` must be used along with either `O_SYNC` or `O_DSYNC`, though it is somewhat implied.

The various data integrity flags have no corresponding flags at the vnode layer. The inode maintains flags to indicate synchronous inode operations. These flags are set in the read/write code path in the kernel file system code (e.g., `ufs_read()`, `ufs_write()`), based on the status of the `O_SYNC` flags in the file structure for the file. They're used by the kernel in the lower-level I/O routines. Solaris also provides two library routines—fdatasync(3R) and fsync(3C)—that applications can call, for file or data integrity synchronization, before issuing a read or write. These calls allow for per-file synchronization of data to disk, and they return only when the write to nonvolatile storage has been completed.

11.3.2.5 Other File Flags

Other flags are maintained in the per-process file descriptor and are not pushed down to the file structure. The flags that are used at the file descriptor level are mostly for the operating system to use—they are not user settable.

One such flag is `FCLOEXEC`: the close-on-exec flag. This flag notifies the operating system to close the file descriptor in the new process if a process executes an exec(2) call. Normally, all open files are inherited by child processes, which is not always the desired behavior. The kernel implements `FCLOEXEC` with a simple `close_exec()` kernel routine called from exec(2). `close_exec()` walks through the file descriptor array and closes any file with the `FCLOEXEC` flag set. The `fcntl(2)` call sets, clears, and examines the file descriptor's flag field. Currently, `FCLOEXEC` is the only flag that can be set, cleared, or examined.

11.3.2.6 The dup System Call

The `dup(2)` system call allows us to duplicate a file descriptor, such that two file descriptors point to the same file structure entry. We indicated earlier that an open(2) call will fetch a new file descriptor and result in a new file structure getting allocated, even if the process already has the same file opened. dup(2) duplicates a file descriptor and will result in a new `uf_entry` structure for the file descriptor. The difference is that the `uf_ofile` pointer, which points to file structure, will point to the same file structure as the dup'ed file descriptor. A new file structure is not created, as would be the case with a second open(2) of the same file.

dup(2) is useful for situations where the programmer wants multiple references to the same file to share the same view of the current file offset. Since the current file pointer (byte offset) is maintained in the file structure, dup'd file descriptors share a common view of the file's offset.

Consider a test program, ofd (code not shown), that does two opens of the same file. The second open sets the O_SYNC flag (which we added only to demonstrate how these file structure flags can be examined). After the two opens, a dup(2) is executed to duplicate the second file descriptor. Below is some output and an example of using /usr/proc/bin/pfiles to look at a process's open files.

```
$ ofd &
[1]     24788
fawlty>
fd1: 3, fd2: 4,dfd: 5
$ /usr/proc/bin/pfiles 24788
24788:  ofd
  Current rlimit: 64 file descriptors
    0: S_IFCHR mode:0620 dev:32,0 ino:324208 uid:20821 gid:7 rdev:24,1
       O_RDWR
    1: S_IFCHR mode:0620 dev:32,0 ino:324208 uid:20821 gid:7 rdev:24,1
       O_RDWR
    2: S_IFCHR mode:0620 dev:32,0 ino:324208 uid:20821 gid:7 rdev:24,1
       O_RDWR
    3: S_IFREG mode:0755 dev:32,8 ino:18 uid:20821 gid:30 size:0
       O_RDWR
    4: S_IFREG mode:0755 dev:32,8 ino:18 uid:20821 gid:30 size:0
       O_RDWR|O_SYNC
    5: S_IFREG mode:0755 dev:32,8 ino:18 uid:20821 gid:30 size:0
       O_RDWR|O_SYNC
```

On the first line, we can see that the test program prints the three open file descriptor values after the open(2) and dup(2) calls have executed. Every process already has file descriptors 0, 1, and 2 allocated, and as a result, the two open files and dup'ed file are file descriptors 3, 4, and 5. The pfiles command dumps some information on process open files, and we see that fd 4 and fd 5 have the O_SYNC flag set, which is logical because they're both referencing the same file structure.

Now, we use crash(1M) to illustrate the file structure sharing in our test program.

```
# /etc/crash
dumpfile = /dev/mem, namelist = /dev/ksyms, outfile = stdout
> p 59
PROC TABLE SIZE = 1962
SLOT ST  PID  PPID  PGID   SID   UID PRI   NAME           FLAGS
  59  r 24774 24716 24774 24716 20821   0  ofd             load
> u 59
PER PROCESS USER AREA FOR PROCESS 59
PROCESS MISC:
        command: ofd, psargs: ofd
        start: Tue Apr 21 21:55:51 1998
        mem: 43449, type: exec
        vnode of current directory: 60025394
OPEN FILES, POFILE FLAGS, AND THREAD REFCNT:
        [0]: F 0x60b6eca8, 0, 0 [1]: F 0x60b6eca8, 0, 0
        [2]: F 0x60b6eca8, 0, 0 [3]: F 0x60824c58, 0, 0
        [4]: F 0x60824870, 0, 0 [5]: F 0x60824870, 0, 0
> f 60824c58
ADDRESS   RCNT    TYPE/ADDR       OFFSET   FLAGS
60824c58   1      UFS /608ba0e8        0   read write
> f 60824870
ADDRESS   RCNT    TYPE/ADDR       OFFSET   FLAGS
60824870   2      UFS /608ba0e8        0   read write sync
```

The u utility in crash dumps the uarea of a process. For each open file, crash provides the address of the corresponding file structure. As you can see, fd 3 and 4 reference different file structures, even though we opened the same file in the same process. File descriptors 4 and 5 show the same file structure address (60824870), because 5 is a dup of 4. Finally, the f (file) utility dumps file structure information. We first dump the file structure for fd 3 (f 60824c58) and then for fd 4 (f 60824870). You can see that the file structure has a reference count of 2, because two file descriptors are referencing it, and you can also see that the sync flag is set in the file structure, as set in the original open(2) system call. The TYPE/ADDR column in the f utility output provides the file type and kernel address of the vnode. Note that the vnode is the same, as any open file in the system will have one and only one vnode, despite the number of opens and file structures.

11.3.2.7 The pread and pwrite System Calls

The POSIX standard provides two more interfaces, shown below, for performing basic read and write I/O. These interfaces are similar to the read() and write() system calls but allow a file offset to be specified as part of the system call.

```
ssize_t pread(int fildes, void *buf,  size_t  nbyte,  off_t offset);

ssize_t pwrite(int fildes, const void *buf,  size_t  nbyte, off_t offset);
```

Header File <unistd.h>

With `pread(2)` and `pwrite(2)`, a read or write can be initiated at a specific offset with only one system call, rather than the traditional method that uses both the `lseek()` and `read()` system calls.

11.3.2.8 The readv and writev System Calls

The `readv()` and `writev()` system calls, shown below, are similar to the `read()` and `write()` system calls, but allow the transfer to occur to and from a range of memory addresses, rather than from a single memory buffer. This technique is often referred to as *scatter/gather* I/O.

```
ssize_t readv(int  fildes,  const  struct  iovec  *iov,  int iovcnt);

ssize_t writev(int fildes,  const  struct  iovec  *iov,  int iovcnt);
```

Header File   <unistd.h>

Each I/O request supplies an array of `iovec` structures and a count of the number of `iovec` structures. The total size of the I/O is the sum of the size of all of the `iovec` structures. The `iovec` structure is shown below.

```
struct  iovec {
        caddr_t iov_base;
        int     iov_len;
};
```

Header File   <unistd.h>

Each `iovec` structure provides the base address of the memory buffer and the length in bytes of the buffer. As a result, the I/O transfer is read or written to the process's memory address space in the specified pattern and to or from the file in a sequential manner.

11.4 Asynchronous I/O

Asynchronous I/O interfaces have been available in Solaris for some time. A specific set of interfaces in the Solaris libraries provides a means by which applications can issue I/O requests and not have to block or cease working until the I/O has completed. (Don't confuse that behavior with the behavior of an I/O request if the file data integrity flags are not set in the file descriptor. See "Data Integrity and Synchronization Flags" on page 488.)

Two sets of interfaces do asynchronous I/O in Solaris: the `aioread(3)` and `aiowrite(3)` routines; and the POSIX-equivalent routines, `aio_read(3R)` and `aio_write(3R)`, which are based on the POSIX standards for real-time extensions. Real-time applications must, by definition, deal with an unpredictable flow of external interrupt conditions that require predictable, bounded response times.

Hence, they need a complete nonblocking I/O facility. Asynchronous I/O interfaces meet the requirements of most real-time applications.

The POSIX and Solaris asynchronous I/O interfaces are functionally identical. The real differences exist in the semantics of using one interface or the other, and the system libraries that must be linked in. Using the Solaris asynchronous I/O interfaces requires linking to `libaio`, whereas using the POSIX asynchronous I/O interfaces requires linking to `libposix4`.

The Solaris interface definitions are shown below.

```
int aioread(int fildes, char *bufp, int bufs, off_t  offset, int whence,
        aio_result_t *resultp);

int aiowrite(int fildes, const char *bufp, int  bufs,  off_t offset, int whence,
        aio_result_t *resultp);
```

Header File   <sys/async.h>

The routines enable the calling process or thread to continue processing after it issues a read or write. The thread that issues the asynchronous read or write receives notification through a signal (SIGIO) either upon completion of the I/O operation or upon occurrence of an error condition. The implementation is based on the calling thread passing a data structure to the asynchronous I/O read or write call. The call result is set in one of the structure members; the calling program must test the result to determine if the I/O was successful or if an error was encountered. The passed structure provides space for storing the error number in the event of an error.

11.4.1 File System Asynchronous I/O

Asynchronous I/O is implemented by means of a user-land thread library for regular file systems and a private kernel interface (kernel asynchronous I/O) for some raw disk devices. The implementation of the aioread(3) and aiowrite(3) routines creates a queue of I/O requests and processes them through user-level threads. When the aioread(3) or aiowrite(3) is entered, the system puts the I/O in a queue and creates an LWP (a thread) to do the I/O. The LWP returns when the I/O is complete (or when an error occurs), and the calling process is notified by a special signal, SIGIO. The programmer must put a signal handler in place to receive the SIGIO and take appropriate action. Such action must minimally include checking the return status of the read or write by reading the appropriate structure members (the structures are different between the libaio and libposix4 interfaces).

As an alternative to the signal-based SIGIO notification, you can call aiowait(3) after issuing an aioread(3) or aiowrite(3). This call causes the calling thread to block until the pending async I/O has completed. You can set a time-value and pass it as an argument to aiowait(3) so that the system only waits for a specified amount of time, as shown below.

```
aio_result_t *aiowait(const struct timeval *timeout);
```

11.4.2 Kernel Asynchronous I/O

Although the threads library implementation of asynchronous I/O worked well
enough for many applications, it didn't necessarily provide optimal performance
for applications that made heavy use of the async I/O facilities. Commercial rela-
tional database systems, for example, use the async I/O interfaces extensively.
Overhead associated with the creation, management, and scheduling of user
threads motivated the design of an implementation that required less overhead
and provided better performance and scalability. A review of the existing async I/O
architecture and subsequent engineering effort resulted in an implementation
called kernel asynchronous I/O, or kaio.

Kaio first appeared in Solaris 2.4 (with a handful of required patches) and has
been available, with some restrictions, in every Solaris release since. The restrictions have to do with which devices and software include kaio support and which
ones do not. The good news for applications is that the presence or absence of kaio
support for a given combination of storage devices, volume managers, and file systems is transparent. If kaio support exists, it will be used. If it doesn't, the original library-based async I/O will be used. Applications do not change in order to
take advantage of kaio. The system figures out what is available and enters the
appropriate code path.

What kaio does, as the name implies, is implement async I/O inside the kernel
rather than in user-land with user threads. The I/O queue is created and managed
in the operating system. The basic sequence of events is as follows:

- When an application calls aioread(3) or aiowrite(3), the corresponding
  library routine is entered.

- Once entered, the library routine first tries to process the request with kaio.
  A kaio initialization routine is executed and creates a "cleanup" thread, which
  is intended to ensure that no remaining memory segments have been allocated but not freed during the async I/O process.

- Once that is complete, kaio is called, at which point a test is made to determine if kaio is supported for the requested I/O.

Support for kaio requires specific async I/O read and write routines at the
device-driver level. The Solaris kernel provides this support in the SCSI driver for
all currently shipping Sun storage products and the Solstice DiskSuite (SDS)
device drivers. These products include the fiber-based storage products, which
implement the SCSI protocol over the Fibre Channel connect.

Kaio only works when the target of the async I/O is a character device-special file.
In other words, kaio works only on raw disk device I/O. Additional support has been
added with the host-based volume management software used for creating RAID
volumes on SPARC/Solaris servers: Sun Enterprise Volume Manager, based on Veritas, and Solstice DiskSuite. RAID devices created with either Veritas or DiskSuite

have raw device entry points through the /dev/vx/rdsk and /dev/md/rdsk
device-special files, and the pseudodrivers implemented for these volume managers
include async I/O routines for kaio support. You can also use the kaio test described
below to establish whether your underlying device supports kaio.

If kaio support is available, here's what happens:

- The kernel allocates an aio_req structure from the queue (or creates a new
  one in kernel memory with kmem_alloc) and calls the async I/O routine in
  the appropriate device driver.
- Inside the driver, the required kernel data structures are set up to support
  the I/O, and an async-I/O-specific physical I/O routine, aphysio, is entered.
- Synchronous raw device I/O uses the kernel physio function, whereby kernel buffers are set up, and the driver strategy routine is called to do the
  actual device I/O.
- The physio routine waits for the driver strategy routine to complete through
  the buffer I/O biowait() kernel code.
- The aphysio routine sets up the async I/O support structures and signal
  mechanism, then calls the driver strategy routine without waiting for the I/O
  to complete.

The presence of an ENOTSUP error signals that kaio support is unavailable. That is,
when the libaio routine (or libposix4 if the POSIX interfaces are used) makes
a kaio system call, the kaio call returns an ENOTSUP error if kaio is not supported. If kaio support isn't available, the code path taken is very different.

- Basically, the original user-thread async I/O facility puts the I/O in an async
  I/O queue and hands off the aioread or aiowrite to a worker thread that
  was created when the libaio library was initialized (more on this after the
  example below).
- The thread assigned to do the I/O on behalf of the calling process uses the
  pread(2) and pwrite(2) system calls to enter the kernel.

  Essentially, the user-thread implementation of async I/O makes the I/O
  appear asynchronous to the calling process by creating a thread to do the I/O
  and allowing the caller to return to do other work without waiting. The implementation actually uses the traditional synchronous Solaris system calls
  (pread(2) and pwrite(2)) to do the I/O.

In either case (kaio or non-kaio), the underlying mechanics of doing the actual
physical I/O are no different than if the I/O was initiated through a simple read(2)
or write(2) system call. Once the read or write has been completed, the result
(error or success) is set in a data structure that was passed by the code that initiated the I/O, and a signal (SIGIO) is sent to the calling process to indicate the I/O
has either completed or cannot be completed because of an error condition. It is up
to the programmer to write a signal handler for the SIGIO signal and deal with
the condition as required by the application.

Internal benchmarking and testing at Sun have shown that the implementation of kaio was truly a worthwhile effort. The reductions in overhead and dedi-

cated device driver-level support yield overall faster and more efficient async I/C operations. On relatively small, lightly loaded systems, the improvement is less dramatic, with typical performance improvements on the order of 5 to 6 percent. As the size of the system (number of processors and amount of RAM) increases and the number of async I/O requests (load) grows, the kaio approach delivers much more scalable performance, with improvements measuring up to 30 percent under some benchmarks. Your mileage will, of course, vary.

Kaio is implemented as a loadable kernel module, /kernel/sys/kaio, and is loaded the first time an async I/O is called. You can determine if the module is loaded with modinfo(1M).

```
# modinfo | grep kaio
105 608c4000   2efd 178   1  kaio (kernel Async I/O)
```

If the preceding command returns nothing, it simply means the kaio kernel module hasn't yet been loaded. The system loads it automatically as needed.

There's a relatively simple test you can run to determine whether or not you have kaio support available for a given file. It involves compiling and running a small program that calls aioread(3) and then uses truss(1) on the program to watch the system-call activity. First, here's the C language source code.

```c
/*
 * Quick kaio test. Read 1k bytes from a file using async I/O.
 * To compile:
 * cc -o aio aio.c -laio
 *
 * To run:
 * aio file_name
 */
#include <sys/stdio.h>
#include <sys/types.h>
#include <sys/fcntl.h>
#include (sys/aio.h>

#define BSIZE 1024

main(int argc, char *argv[])
{
        aio_result_t res;
        char buf[BSIZE];
        int fd;

        if ((fd = open(argv[1], O_RDONLY)) == -1) {
                perror("open");
                exit(-1);
        }
        aioread(fd, buf, BSIZE, 0L, SEEK_SET, &res);
        aiowait(0);
        if (res.aio_return == BSIZE) {
                printf("aio succeeded\n");
                close(fd);
                exit(0);
        }
        perror("aio");
}
```

Once you have the test program compiled, use the truss(1) command to do a system-call trace of the execution path.

```
# truss -t kaio,lwp_create aio /dev/rdsk/c0t3d0s0
kaio(5, 0xFFFFFFE8, 0xFFFFFFFF, 0xEF68FB50, 0x00000000, 0x00000000, 0x00000000) = 0
lwp_create(0xEFFFEE10, 0, 0xEF68FF44)           = 2
lwp_create(0x00000000, 0, 0x00000000)           = 0
kaio(AIOREAD, 3, 0xEFFFF190, 1024, 0, 0xEFFFF590) = 0
kaio(AIOWAIT, 0x00000000)                        = -268438128
aio succeeded
```

Note that you run this test as root because it's reading directly from a raw device-special file. On the command line, the -t flag is specified with truss to instruct truss to trace only the kaio and lwp_create system calls.

The example used a raw device-special file as the argument to the aio program. (You have to specify a full path name for a file when you invoke aio.) The truss(1) output shows a kaio system call, followed by two lwp_create calls, and finally two more entries into the kaio routine to do the actual read, followed by the aiowait. The last line is the output from the aio program (aio succeeded). In this example, kaio is in fact a supported facility for this I/O operation—the kaio call with the AIOREAD flag did not return an error.

In the example below, kaio is not supported for the I/O.

```
# truss -t kaio,lwp_create aio /junkfile
kaio(5, 0xFFFFFFE8, 0xFFFFFFFF, 0xEF68FB50, 0x00000000, 0x00000000, 0x00000000) = 0
lwp_create(0xEFFFEE08, 0, 0xEF68FF44)           = 2
lwp_create(0x00000000, 0, 0x00000000)           = 0
kaio(AIOREAD, 3, 0xEFFFF188, 1024, 0, 0xEFFFF588) Err#48 ENOTSUP
lwp_create(0xEFFFFEDA8, 0, 0xEF686F44)          = 3
lwp_create(0x00000000, 0, 0x00000000)           = -278369456
lwp_create(0xEFFFFEDA8, 0, 0xEF67DF44)          = 4
lwp_create(0x00000000, 0, 0x00000000)           = -278406320
lwp_create(0xEFFFFEDA8, 0, 0xEF674F44)          = 5
lwp_create(0x00000000, 0, 0x00000000)           = -278443184
lwp_create(0xEFFFFEDA8, 0, 0xEF66BF44)          = 6
lwp_create(0x00000000, 0, 0x00000000)           = -278480048
lwp_create(0xEFFFFEDA8, 0, 0xEF662F44)          = 7
lwp_create(0x00000000, 0, 0x00000000)           = -278516912
lwp_create(0xEFFFFEDA8, 0, 0xEF659F44)          = 8
lwp_create(0x00000000, 0, 0x00000000)           = -278553776
lwp_create(0xEFFFFEDA8, 0, 0xEF650F44)          = 9
lwp_create(0x00000000, 0, 0x00000000)           = -278590640
lwp_create(0xEFFFFEDA8, 0, 0xEF647F44)          = 10
lwp_create(0x00000000, 0, 0x00000000)           = -278627504
lwp_create(0xEFFFFEDA8, 0, 0xEF63EF44)          = 11
lwp_create(0x00000000, 0, 0x00000000)           = -278664368
kaio(AIOWAIT, 0x00000000)                        Err#22 EINVAL
kaio(AIOWAIT, 0x00000000)                        Err#22 EINVAL
kaio(AIONOTIFY, 170560)                          = 0
aio succeeded
```

In this example, we are reading a file in the file system. The trace shows that our example entered the kernel with a kaio system call, created a couple of LWPs, and attempted to do the async I/O through the kaio facility. The second `kaio` call failed with the `ENOTSUP` (not supported) error, and the system dropped back to the library implementation, resulting in the creation of a bunch of threads (LWPs) up to the completion of the I/O. Note that the last line from the program output, `aio succeeded`, indicates that the `aioread`(3) was indeed successful—we just didn't use the kaio facility to do it.

It's clear that the user-threads implementation results in a lot more thread/LWP creation and management, which adds overhead and reduces efficiency. So why does the Solaris environment create 11 LWPs for a single async I/O request? The answer has to do with the initialization of the async I/O library.

The first time an `aioread`(3) or `aiowrite`(3) is called, an async I/O library initialization routine is called and creates several worker threads to do async I/Os. The system is simply getting ready to process several async I/Os and thus creates four reader LWPs and four writer LWPs, along with one thread to do file syncs. That accounts for the nine successful `lwp_create` calls you see above. If you were to add a second `aioread`(3) or `aiowrite`(3) to the test program and rerun it with the `truss`(1) command, you wouldn't see all the `lwp_creates` for the second async I/O. The library handles subsequent async I/O requests with the worker threads created during initialization (though it will, of course, create more worker threads to keep up with the level of incoming async I/O requests).

Although the creation of a pool of worker threads up-front helps provide better scalability for the user-threads async I/O facility, it still involves more overhead and a longer code path than does kernel async I/O.

11.5 Memory Mapped File I/O

File I/O discussed so far is done with the `read`, `write`, and `lseek` system calls to perform I/O on behalf of a process and to copy the data to or from the process's address space. The I/O is performed into a kernel buffer and then copied to or from the process's address space, as illustrated in Figure 11.3.

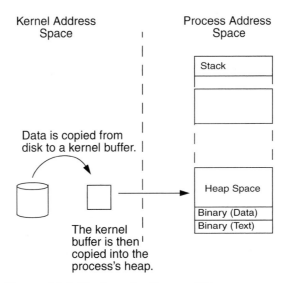

Kernel Address Space

Process Address Space

Stack

Data is copied from disk to a kernel buffer.

Heap Space

Binary (Data)

Binary (Text)

The kernel buffer is then copied into the process's heap.

Figure 11.3 File Read with read(2)

The new memory architecture first introduced with SunOS 3.2 allows a new way of doing file I/O, that is, by mapping a file directly into the process's address space. The mmap system call allows us to map a range of a file into a process's address space; then, the file can be accessed by references to memory locations with C pointers. This approach allows us to do I/O on the file without the overhead of the read and write system calls and without the overhead of handling the data twice. Figure 11.4 illustrates the process.

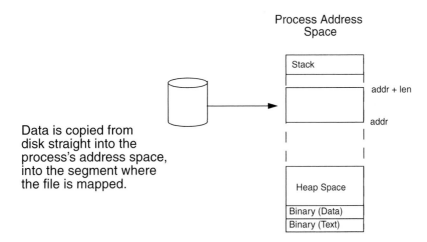

Process Address Space

Stack

addr + len

addr

Data is copied from disk straight into the process's address space, into the segment where the file is mapped.

Heap Space

Binary (Data)

Binary (Text)

Figure 11.4 Memory Mapped File I/O

The function definition for the mmap(2) system call is shown below.

```
void *mmap(void *addr, size_t len, int prot, int flags,  int fildes, off_t off);
```

Header File   <sys/mman.h>

The mmap system call is called with an open file handle, the offset and length of the file being mapped, the address and length at which the file should be mapped in a process's address space, a flag for options, and a protection type indicating what memory protection should be used for the mapping, as shown below.

```
if ((addr = mmap64((caddr_t)0, length, PROT_READ,
    MAP_SHARED, fd, offset)) == NULL) {
        perror("mmap failed");
        exit(1);
}
```

The operating system uses the memory map function to map executable files and shared libraries into a process's address space. You can list the mappings for a process with the pmap(1) command.

```
# /usr/proc/bin/pmap 25888

1197:   /bin/ksh
00010000    192K read/exec         /usr/bin/ksh
0004E000      8K read/write/exec   /usr/bin/ksh
00050000     40K read/write/exec    [ heap ]
FF180000    656K read/exec         /usr/lib/libc.so.1
FF232000     32K read/write/exec   /usr/lib/libc.so.1
FF280000    512K read/exec         /usr/lib/libnsl.so.1
FF30E000     40K read/write/exec   /usr/lib/libnsl.so.1
FF318000     32K read/write/exec    [ anon ]
FF330000     16K read/exec         /usr/platform/sun4u/lib/libc_psr.so.1
FF340000     16K read/exec         /usr/lib/libmp.so.2
FF352000      8K read/write/exec   /usr/lib/libmp.so.2
FF370000     32K read/exec         /usr/lib/libsocket.so.1
FF386000     16K read/write/exec   /usr/lib/libsocket.so.1
FF390000      8K read/exec         /usr/lib/libdl.so.1
FF3A0000      8K read/write/exec    [ anon ]
FF3B0000    120K read/exec         /usr/lib/ld.so.1
FF3DC000      8K read/write/exec   /usr/lib/ld.so.1
FFBEC000     16K read/write/exec    [ stack ]
 total     1760K
```

The pmap command shows us the size and protections for each segment and, where possible, the name of the file mapped into the process. In this example, we can see the binary (/usr/bin/ksh) and the libraries mapped into the Korn shell.

11.5.1 Mapping Options

Certain flags allow different options to be passed to mmap to control the way a file is mapped into the process's address space (see Table 11-7). These are passed in through the flags argument.

Table 11-7 Solaris 7 mmap Flags from <sys/mman.h>

Type	Description
MAP_FIXED	Maps at the address supplied.
MAP_NORESERVE	Does not reserve swap space for this mapping.
MAP_SHARED	Changes are reflected across all mappings.
MAP_PRIVATE	Changes are not reflected; a copy of the page is made so that the changes are local only.

The MAP_FIXED option requests that the file range be mapped exactly at the address supplied by *addr*. If MAP_FIXED is not set, the system uses *addr* to derive an address used to map the file. The address chosen will be an area of the address space that the system deems suitable for a mapping of len bytes to the file. If MAP_FIXED is not set and *addr* is 0, then the system chooses the address to map the file range into.

If the MAP_NORESERVE option is specified, no swap space is reserved for a mapping. Without this flag, the creation of a writable MAP_PRIVATE mapping reserves swap space equal to the size of the mapping. When writing into a MAP_NORESERVE segment, if space is available, the write succeeds and a private copy of the written page is created; if space is not available, the write fails and a SIGBUS or SIGSEGV signal is delivered to the writing process.

11.5.1.1 Mapping Files into Two or More Processes

A file can be mapped into more than one process when another process calls mmap on the same file with an overlapping range. The system does this by mapping the same pages of memory into each address space. When this mapping occurs, the memory is shared between the processes, and by default, each process sees all modifications made by another process. This behavior can be used as an alternative method of sharing memory to System V shared memory. In fact, the POSIX interprocess communication facility for shared memory is built on shared memory mapped files. The options MAP_SHARED and MAP_PRIVATE can be passed to mmap to allow different sharing semantics, rather than the default of sharing everything.

If MAP_SHARED is specified, write references will change the memory that is being shared by all processes with mappings to the file range. If MAP_PRIVATE is specified, the initial write reference creates a private copy of the memory page, and from this point on, the process will have a private copy of that page of the mapping.

11.5.1.2 Permission Options

The memory address range is created in the process's address space with the permissions provided with the prot argument. The permissions control whether a process can read, write, or execute memory within the memory range of the mapping. The protection/permission options are shown in Table 11-8.

Table 11-8 Solaris 7 mmap Protection Options from <sys/mman.h>

Type	Description
PROT_READ	Data can be read.
PROT_WRITE	Data can be written.
PROT_EXEC	Data can be executed.
PROT_NONE	Data cannot be accessed.

If we examine the mappings for ksh from our previous pmap example, we can see that the first portion of ksh is mapped read-only/execute, and the second half is mapped read/write/execute.

```
00010000    192K read/exec        /usr/bin/ksh
0004E000      8K read/write/exec   /usr/bin/ksh
```

If a process were to attempt to write to the memory range between 0x010000 and 0x04e000, a SIGSEGV signal would be sent to the process to notify it that a segmentation violation had occurred. Incidentally, the first segment is the text portion of the process, which is always read-only, and the second mapping is the data section for uninitialized variables, both of which are shared among processes. The second segment is mapped read/write with MAP_PRIVATE; so, if a process updates an initialized variable (say, i = 1), that variable does not change across all ksh processes. Rather, a copy-on-write operation creates a local page, which is then used to hold a page-length mapping for the file at that location, private to the process.

11.5.2 Providing Advice to the Memory System

We can provide advice to the memory system about the pages of memory within the range of the mapping by using the madvise system call. The madvise system call allows us to tell the memory system if we need or don't need a range of memory or if we are going to access the memory in a sequential or random order. This information allows the memory system and file systems to proactively read in portions of the file with the range of memory.

```
int madvise(caddr_t addr, size_t len, int advice);
```

Header File <sys/mman.h>

The advice is given for a memory range and is specified with the advice argument. The arguments may be one of MADV_DONTNEED, MADV_WILLNEED, MADV_SEQUENTIAL, or MADV_RANDOM.

11.5.2.1 The MADV_DONTNEED Flag

When we map a file into a process's address space and read the file by touching memory locations, we allocate physical memory for that range and fill the memory with the respective range of the file. Once we are done with that range of the file, we may never want it again, in which case we can let the operating system know that this memory range is no longer needed. This notification is especially important since the memory is not freed, even when we unmap the memory segment. The MADV_DONTNEED flag allows us to give back memory for a given range. The following example shows how this can be done.

```c
#include <stdio.h>
#include <unistd.h>
#include <stdlib.h>
#include <sys/sysmacros.h>
#include <sys/types.h>
#include <fcntl.h>
#include <sys/mman.h>

void
main(int argc, char ** argv)
{
        int fd;
        caddr_t addr;
        off_t size;
        off_t length;
        off_t offset;
        off_t chunk = 1<<30;

        if (argc != 2) {
                (void) fprintf(stderr, "Usage: mmap_dontneed filename\n");
                exit(1);
        }

        if ((fd = open(argv[1], O_RDONLY)) < 0) {
                perror("Open failed");
                exit(1);
        }

        size = lseek64(fd, (off_t)0, SEEK_END);

        /*
         * mmap a chunksize segment and issue madvise(DONTNEED)
         * against it.
         */
        for (offset = 0; offset < size; offset += chunk) {

                length = MIN(size - offset, chunk);

                if ((addr = mmap64((caddr_t)0, length, PROT_READ,
                    MAP_SHARED, fd, offset)) == NULL) {
                        perror("mmap failed");
                        exit(1);
                }

                (void) madvise(addr, length, MADV_DONTNEED);
                (void) munmap(addr, length);
        }

}
```

We can execute the preceding program to free the range of a file back to the memory system. We can observe what happens when we run the program by looking at the amount of free memory on the system with the `vmstat` command. An example is shown below.

```
# vmstat 3
procs     memory              page            disk          faults      cpu
 r b w   swap  free  re  mf pi po fr de sr f0 s2 s3 s5   in   sy   cs us sy id
 0 0 0 155868  2992   0  92  0  0 12  0  2  0  0  0  1   23  172   96  0  2 98
 0 0 0 155868  3020   0  33  1  0  0  0  0  0  1  0  0   20  187   95  1  2 98
 0 0 0 155868  3012   0  50  2  0  0  0  0  0  1  0  0   22  181   97  0  1 99
 0 0 0 155868  3012   0  50  0  0  0  0  0  0  0  0  0   18  123   92  0  1 99
 0 0 0 155868  3012   0  50  0  0  0  0  0  0  0  0  0   21  126   95  0  1 99
 0 0 0 155804 17244 186 112 78  0 98  0 27  0 13  0  0   86  223  131  0 12 88
 0 0 0 155868 45840   0  50  0  0  0  0  0  0  0  0  0    7  119   50  0  1 99
 0 0 0 155868 45840   0  50  0  0  0  0  0  0  0  0  0   15  130   55  0  1 99
 0 0 0 155868 45840   0  50  0  0  0  0  0  0  0  0  0   14  122   52  0  1 99
```

11.5.2.2 The MADV_WILLNEED Flag

The pages of a file are read, one at a time, the first time we access the location of a file that is not already in memory. This approach may be suboptimal if we know we will be reading most or all of a given file range, and we can use the `MADV_WILLNEED` flag to read ahead all of a given range, as shown below.

```
if ((addr = mmap64((caddr_t)0, length, PROT_READ,
    MAP_SHARED, fd, offset)) == NULL) {
        perror("mmap failed");
        exit(1);
}

(void) madvise(addr, length, MADV_WILLNEED);
(void) munmap(addr, length);
```

The range requested by `MADV_WILLNEED` is read in synchronously, so the `madvise` system call will wait until the entire range is read in before returning. A simple test program demonstrates how free memory falls as a file is read in after a `MADV_WILLNEED`. The output of the test program is shown below.

```
# ./mmmap_willneed testfile&
# vmstat 3
procs     memory              page            disk          faults      cpu
 r b w   swap  free  re  mf pi po fr de sr f0 s2 s3 s5   in   sy   cs us sy id
 0 0 0 155908 45760   0  50  0  0  0  0  0  0  0  0  0    7  121   53  0  1 99
 0 0 0 155864  3100   1  53  0 336 342 0 27 0  0  0 41  205  131   57  0  1 99
 0 0 0 155864  3964   2  54  0  0  0  0  0  0  0  0  0   15  122   53  0  1 99
 0 0 0 155864  3944   1  53  0  0  0  0  0  0  0  0  0    9  131   54  0  1 99
```

11.5.2.3 The MADV_SEQUENTIAL Flag

By default, the memory system reads in a file as it is allocated and then leaves it in memory. The `MADV_SEQUENTIAL` flag can tell the memory system that a range is being accessed sequentially and can free memory behind that which is being read. An example of how `MADV_SEQUENTIAL` can be used on a range is shown below.

```
if ((addr = mmap64((caddr_t)0, length, PROT_READ,
    MAP_SHARED, fd, offset)) == NULL) {
        perror("mmap failed");
        exit(1);
}

(void) madvise(addr, length, MADV_SEQUENTIAL);
(void) munmap(addr, length);
```

If we run a simple process that reads sequentially through a process, we can see by looking at the output of the `vmstat` command that memory is freed as it is read.

```
# ./mmmap_seqread testfile&
# vmstat 3
procs     memory            page              disk          faults      cpu
 r b w   swap  free  re  mf pi po fr de sr f0 s2 s3 s5   in   sy   cs us sy id
 0 0 0 155864 3100   1  53 336 0 336 0 0  0  0  0 41  205  131   57  0  1 99
 0 0 0 155864 3100   1  53 339 0 339 0 0  0  0  0 41  205  131   57  0  1 99
 0 0 0 155864 3100   1  53 332 0 332 0 0  0  0  0 41  205  131   57  0  1 99
 0 0 0 155864 3100   1  53 338 0 338 0 0  0  0  0 41  205  131   57  0  1 99
```

Another benefit of `MADV_SEQUENTIAL` is that files are read in advance, in groups of 64 kilobytes. You can see this by looking at the I/O sizes with the `iostat` command. Our `iostat` example, below, shows that 98 I/Os per second are being read, and a total of 6272 kilobytes per second is being read, with an average I/O size of 64 kilobytes.

```
# iostat -x 5

device    r/s  w/s    kr/s   kw/s wait actv  svc_t  %w  %b
fd0       0.0  0.0     0.0    0.0  0.0  0.0    0.0   0   0
sd6       0.0  0.0     0.0    0.0  0.0  0.0    0.0   0   0
ssd11     0.0  0.0     0.0    0.0  0.0  0.0    0.0   0   0
ssd12     0.0  0.0     0.0    0.0  0.0  0.0    0.0   0   0
ssd13    98.0  0.0  6272.0    0.0  0.0  3.7   73.7   0  93
ssd15     0.0  0.0     0.0    0.0  0.0  0.0    0.0   0   0
ssd16     0.0  0.0     0.0    0.0  0.0  0.0    0.0   0   0
ssd17     0.0  0.0     0.0    0.0  0.0  0.0    0.0   0   0
```

11.5.2.4 The MADV_RANDOM Flag

By default, read-ahead is implemented on file reads (as described for the `MADV_SEQUENTIAL` flag). In some cases, we may know that our access pattern will be completely random. In such cases, read-ahead offers no benefit and may, in fact, add additional overhead, since I/Os will be done in 64-kilobyte chunks rather than page-sized chunks (usually 8 kilobytes). We can disable read-ahead by specifying the `MADV_RANDOM` flag, as shown in the following example.

```
if ((addr = mmap64((caddr_t)0, length, PROT_READ,
    MAP_SHARED, fd, offset)) == NULL) {
        perror("mmap failed");
        exit(1);
}

(void) madvise(addr, length, MADV_RANDOM);
(void) munmap(addr, length);
```

A simple test program shows that we are now reading 151 I/Os per second, with an I/O rate of 1,198 kilobytes per second, an average I/O size of 8 kilobytes, as shown below.

```
# iostat -x 5

device    r/s   w/s    kr/s    kw/s wait actv   svc_t  %w   %b
fd0       0.0   0.0     0.0     0.0  0.0  0.0     0.0    0    0
sd6       0.0   0.0     0.0     0.0  0.0  0.0     0.0    0    0
ssd11     0.0   0.0     0.0     0.0  0.0  0.0     0.0    0    0
ssd12     0.0   0.0     0.0     0.0  0.0  0.0     0.0    0    0
ssd13   151.0   0.0  1198.0     0.0  0.0 10.2   150.2    0  100
ssd15     0.0   0.0     0.0     0.0  0.0  0.0     0.0    0    0
ssd16     0.0   0.0     0.0     0.0  0.0  0.0     0.0    0    0
ssd17     0.0   0.0     0.0     0.0  0.0  0.0     0.0    0    0
```

11.6 64-bit Files in Solaris

For many years Sun shipped systems with a maximum file system and file size of 2 gigabytes. This size was a constraint imposed by the number of bits in the offset data types in the kernel. The size limitation occurred in three main places: the disk address type, daddr_t; the file system interface, off_t data type; and the uio structure used for device drivers and some file system interfaces. The pre-Solaris 2.0 types are both 32 bits, as shown below.

```
typedef long    daddr_t;
typedef long    off_t;

struct  uio {
        struct  iovec *uio_iov;
        int     uio_iovcnt;
        off_t   uio_offset;
        short   uio_segflg;
        short   uio_fmode;
        int     uio_resid;
};
```

The daddr_t and uio_t structures are used by device drivers and by some of the file system interfaces in the kernel, and the off_t data type is used extensively throughout the kernel and user-land application programming interfaces.

11.6.1 64-bit Device Support in Solaris 2.0

Solaris 2.0 was implemented with partial 64-bit device support, with the aid of the 64-bit data type, `longlong_t`. Solaris 2.0 shipped with an additional disk address type (`lldaddr_t`), an additional offset type (`lloff_t`), and a 64-bit-capable `uio` structure. The expanded disk addresses and `uio` structure allow device support beyond 2 Gbytes and allow file systems to span past the 2-Gbyte limit, to a theoretical maximum of $2^{63}-1$. The UFS file system in Solaris 2.x is expandable to 1 terabyte, which is a UFS-specific limitation.

```
typedef long            daddr_t;        /* <disk address> type */
typedef long            off_t;          /* ?<offset> type */

typedef longlong_t      offset_t;
typedef longlong_t      diskaddr_t;

/*
 * Partial support for 64-bit file offset enclosed herein,
 * specifically used to access devices greater than 2 GB.
 * However, support for devices greater than 2 GB requires compiler
 * support for long long.
 * XXX These assume big-endian machines XXX
 */
typedef union lloff {
        offset_t        _f;     /* Full 64-bit offset value */
        struct {
                long _u;        /* upper 32 bits of offset value */
                off_t _l;       /* lower 32 bits of offset value */
        } _p;
} lloff_t;

typedef union lldaddr {
        diskaddr_t      _f;     /* Full 64-bit disk address value */
        struct {
                long _u;        /* upper 32 bits of disk address value */
                daddr_t _l;     /* lower 32 bits of disk address value */
        } _p;
} lldaddr_t;
```

Header File <sys/types.h>

No user interfaces in Solaris 2.0 accessed large devices, which limited device access and file sizes to 2 gigabytes.

11.6.2 64-bit File Application Programming Interfaces in Solaris 2.5.1

With databases growing to over 1 terabyte in size and single disk devices growing past 2 gigabytes, application vendors required a mechanism to access data sizes beyond 2 gigabytes. Full, large-file support was destined to appear in Solaris 2.6, but in Solaris 2.5., two interfaces were added to provide large-device support for raw devices. While this may not have seemed like a significant addition, many database vendors use raw devices for storage for database tables. The large-device interfaces enable database vendors to address more than 2 gigabytes of space on raw devices.

Since the read and write system calls do not contain disk offset addresses, large-device interfacing was possible by the mere addition of an interface to seek to a 64-bit address. The new interface added was `llseek`, appropriately named as a long `lseek`. Note the use of the new offset type, `offset_t`, rather than the old `off_t`.

```
typedef longlong_t      offset_t;

offset_t llseek(int fdes, offset_t off, int sbase)
```

Header File   <sys/unistd.h>

The new `llseek` interface allowed a process to seek across a 64-bit file offset in any device that supports large access. Only raw disk devices permit large access. Since the `llseek` interface was added primarily for database vendors, and since many database vendors take advantage of asynchronous I/O, two new interfaces were created for asynchronous I/O on large (greater than 2 Gbyte) files.

```
typedef longlong_t      offset_t;

int aioread64(int fd, caddr_t *buf, int bufsz, offset_t offset,
              int whence, aio_result_t *resultp)

int aiowrite64(int fd, caddr_t *buf, int bufsz, offset_t offset,
               int whence, aio_result_t *resultp)
```

Header File   <sys/asynch.h>

Note that all of the Solaris 2.5.1 large-device interfaces require application changes.

11.6.3 Solaris 2.6: The Large-File OS

Solaris 2.6 was the first Solaris release to provide support for files greater than 2 gigabytes. The file systems were enhanced to deal with files crossing the 2-gigabyte boundary, and a 64-bit file API was introduced to allow applications to access large files.

Since the existing API had been using 32-bit offsets in all of the file seek interfaces, the existing APIs could not change without breaking Unix 95, POSIX, and binary compatibility. For this reason, a transitional large-file interface was provided in Solaris 2.6.

11.6.3.1 The Large-File Summit

Sun was not the only vendor to have to address the large-file compatibility issues, and an industry summit was called to specify a common set of large-file application interfaces for 32-bit environments (see the large-file summit documentation at `http://www.sas.com/standard/large.file/`). The large-file summit specified a new set of interfaces, similar to the Unix 95/POSIX interfaces, but with an extension of 64 added to the name of the interface. For example, the 32-bit `lseek()` has an equivalent 64-bit interface, `lseek64()`. In addition to the new interfaces, all of the existing interfaces are made large-file safe, so that appropriate error conditions are returned if a large file is accessed (or a file grows beyond the 2-Gbyte limit). Within the context of large-file support, a program is considered to be in one of two possible states:

- **Large-file safe.** The program will detect an operation being performed on a large file and handle the errors without causing data loss or corruption.
- **Large-file aware.** The program can properly process large files.

The following changes in Solaris 2.6 provide large-file support:

- Appropriate error handling and checking in the 32-bit interfaces for large files. The `open` system call will fail to open a large file in a non-large-file application, and all 32-bit file APIs return `E_OVERFLOW` when they encounter a regular file whose size is greater than or equal to 2 Gbytes.

- A new set of large-file summit APIs to access large files.

- File systems capable of large files, limited initially to UFS.

- Solaris commands enhanced to be large-file aware and large-file safe.

- An NFS implementation that is large-file compatible and safe.

11.6.3.2 Large-File Compilation Environments

Two compilation environments implement large-file support in Solaris 2.6 and 32-bit Solaris 7:

- **The transitional compilation environment.** The transitional compilation environment simply adds the new 64-bit interfaces by using the `64()` extension. You enable it by setting `_LARGEFILE64_SOURCE` to 1 before including any system headers.

- **The large-file compilation environment.** The large-file compilation environment uses the same interface names, with large offset types (`off_t` becomes a `longlong_t`). You enable it by setting `_FILE_OFFSET_BITS` to 64 before including any system headers.

Converting an application to use large files requires cleaning up code that contains undetected type clashes. Frequently, a fundamental type of similar size has been used instead of the variable's defined type. Also, much code has never been updated to reflect standards such as POSIX.

Data types that have been extended to include the 64-bit version are listed in Table 11-9.

Table 11-9 Large File Extended 64-bit Data Types

Type	Description
ino_t	File serial number
off_t	Relative file pointer offsets and file sizes
fpos_t	Unique file positions
rlim_t	Resource limit values
blkcnt_t	Number of disk blocks
fsblkcnt_t	File system block counts
fsfilecnt_t	File system inode counts

You should also inspect code for incorrect casts and assignments and for correct return types. lint is our friend here. Consider the example in the code segment below.

```
long curpos;
curpos = lseek(fd, 0L, SEEK_CUR);
```

In a large-file environment, this code would truncate the returned 64-bit offset to 32 bits, which might lead to data corruption later on. The code should be changed to:

```
off_t curpos;
curpos = lseek(fd, (off_t)0, SEEK_CUR);
```

Any output or in-memory formatting strings used in reference to the large-file sizing entities must be converted. In the current environment, a formatting string for an offset can look like %ld. In the new environment, it must be converted to %lld to accommodate values of type long long. Additionally, if any byte count information accompanies the format, it, too, must be modified to accommodate larger potential values.

For example,

```
off_t offset;
printf(" %7ld", offset);
```

should be modified to:

```
off_t offset;
printf(" %7lld", offset);
```

If the compilation environment can be set for either small files or large files, it is safest to place #ifdef around the format string, such as:

```
off_t offset;
#if _FILE_OFFSET_BITS - 0 == 64
printf(" %7lld", offset);
#else
printf(" %7ld", offset);
#endif
```

You can find more information on the transitional and large-file interfaces in the system manual pages, under interface64(5), lf64(5), and lfcompile(64).

Note that the transitional interfaces exist for 32-bit Solaris. Beginning with 64-bit Solaris 7, the file interfaces use the 64-bit data types for file offsets.

11.6.4 File System Support for Large Files

Starting with Solaris 2.6, large-file support was added to the UFS, CACHEFS, and NFSV3 file systems. Each of these file systems can contain files larger than 2 gigabytes and can provide support to seek within the large offsets.

The UFS provides a mount option to control how it handles large files. By default, it supports large files. Support for large files was also added to swapfs, which allows us to add swap devices and swap files of sizes up to 1 terabyte. Note that the tmpfs in Solaris 2.6 has a maximum file size of 2 gigabytes. The maximum file size is unlimited with Solaris 7 in 64-bit mode.

12

FILE SYSTEM OVERVIEW

In the last chapter, we explored how an application accesses files and we examined the different interfaces that are available to access the data stored within a file. In this chapter, we discuss how the file system provides the facilities that allow us to do file I/O and how the file system manages files. Different types of file systems are available within Solaris, and in this chapter we look at those different types and explain some of the important file system features.

12.1 Why Have a File System?

The file system is an essential component of all Unix environments; it provides the mechanism for the storage and retrieval of files and a hierarchical directory structure for naming of multiple files. A single Unix file system can hold thousands of files, and the task of organizing the storage structures required to store files and directories is insulated from the application.

A basic Unix file system enables the operating system to do the following:

- Create and delete files
- Open files for reading and writing
- Seek within a file
- Close files
- Create directories to hold groups of files

- List the contents of a directory
- Remove files from a directory

These functions have grown into what we have become accustomed to today as the complex file manipulation facilities offered in the modern Unix environment. The capabilities of the file systems have grown immensely, and the data management interfaces they provide are much more extensive.

An application uses the file as an abstraction to address a linear range of bytes, which are to be stored on some form of input/output medium, typically a storage device such as a SCSI disk. To access a file, the operating system provides file manipulation interfaces to open, close, read, and write the data within each file. In addition to read and write, the operating system provides facilities to seek within each file to allow random access to the data.

The storage devices also provide access to a linear series of data bytes, organized into groups of bytes known as blocks, for example, a 1-Gbyte disk stores 2^{30} (1,073,741,824) bytes of data that can be accessed in 512-byte blocks. Each block of data is individually addressable and can be accessed in a random order. By using the basic file interfaces, an application can access all of the data in a storage device by seeking to individual locations and retrieving the data. However, without any organized storage of multiple files, each storage device appears to the application as a single file. The job of the file system is to provide a layer between the application's notion of files and the storage device, so that multiple files can reside on a single storage device, with the file system managing the storage of each file. The file system presents each storage device as a series of directories, each of which holds several files.

12.2 Support for Multiple File System Types

Solaris provides a flexible framework that allows multiple and different file system types within the environment. The most common file system is the Unix file system (UFS), which is used by default to hold all of the files in the root directory hierarchy of the Unix file system. UFS is known as an "on disk" or "regular" file system, which means that it uses a storage device to hold real file data.

In contrast, there are also file systems that look like regular file systems but represent virtual devices. These are known as pseudo file systems. For example, in Solaris the list of processes can be mounted as a file system and each process appears as a file. The Solaris pseudo file systems represent processes, network sockets, character device drivers, and some other virtual file abstractions. Table 12-1 summarizes the different file systems available in the Solaris environment.

Table 12-1 File Systems Available in the Solaris File System Framework

File System	Type	Device	Description
ufs	Regular	Disk	Unix Fast File system, default in Solaris
pcfs	Regular	Disk	MS-DOS file system
hsfs	Regular	Disk	High Sierra file system (CD-ROM)
tmpfs	Regular	Memory	Uses memory and swap
nfs	Pseudo	Network	Network file system
cachefs	Pseudo	File system	Uses a local disk as cache for another NFS file system
autofs	Pseudo	File system	Uses a dynamic layout to mount other file systems
specfs	Pseudo	Device drivers	File system for the /dev devices
procfs	Pseudo	Kernel	/proc file system representing processes
sockfs	Pseudo	Network	File system of socket connections
fifofs	Pseudo	Files	FIFO file system

In addition to the file systems provided with Solaris, a number of third-party file systems provide an additional set of features to the regular UFS file system, as listed in Table 12-2.

Table 12-2 Third-Party File Systems Available for Solaris

File System	Type	Device	Description
vxfs	Regular	Disk	Veritas file system
qfs	Regular	Disk	QFS file system from LSC Inc.
samfs	Regular	Disk	Veritas file system

12.3 Regular (On-Disk) File Systems

Regular file systems are those that allow storage of files and data on some form of storage media and are the most commonly known type of file system. Regular file systems implement the basic operating system facilities, which include the following:

- Facilities to read and write file data
- Facilities for creating and deleting files themselves
- Facilities for creating and deleting directories to manage files

- Implementation of a hierarchical directory structure
- File access control and authentication
- File locking

File systems that are implemented on local storage are known as "on disk" file systems and use a rigid file system structure on the storage media. In this chapter, we explore three disk-based file systems for Solaris:

- Solaris UFS — Blocked, allocated, logging file system with extentlike performance
- VxFS — Extent-based logging file system from Veritas Corp.
- QFS — Extent-based file system from LSC Corp.

12.3.1 Allocation and Storage Strategy

A file system stores data on the storage device by managing the allocation of each file's blocks within the file system. The file system maintains the location of each block for each file in an on-disk structure. Each file system uses a different method for allocation and retrieval of file blocks.

There are two common types of file system space allocation strategies: block allocation and extent allocation. Block-based allocation creates incremental disk space for a file each time it is extended, whereas extent-based allocation creates a large series of contiguous blocks each time the file exhausts the space available in its last extent.

12.3.1.1 Block-Based Allocation

The block-based allocation mechanism is used by the traditional Unix file system, such as UFS, and provides a flexible and efficient block allocation policy. Disk blocks are allocated as they are used, which means that a minimal number of file system blocks are allocated to a file in an attempt to conserve storage space.

When a file is extended, blocks are allocated from a free block map, so that blocks are sometimes allocated in a random order. This random allocation can cause excessive disk seeking, and subsequent reads from the file system will result in the disk mechanism seeking to all of the random block locations that were allocated during the extension of the file. Random block allocation can be avoided by optimization of the block allocation policy so that it attempts to allocate a sequential series of blocks.

A smarter block allocation achieves large sequential allocations, resulting in greatly reduced disk seeking. Continuous file system block allocation will, however, eventually end up with file blocks fragmented across the file system, and file system access will eventually revert to a random nature.

The block allocation scheme also stores information about where each new block is allocated every time the file is extended and whether the file is being extended a block at a time. Extra disk I/O is required to read and write the file system block structure information. File system block structure information is known as metadata. File system metadata is always written synchronously to the storage device, which means operations that change the size of a file need to wait for each metadata operation to complete. As a result, metadata operations can significantly slow overall file system performance.

12.3.1.2 Extent-Based Allocation

Extent-based file systems allocate disk blocks in large groups at a time, thus forcing sequential allocation. As a file is written, a large number of blocks are allocated when the file is first created; then, writes can occur in large groups or clusters of sequential blocks. File system metadata is written when the file is first created; subsequent writes within the first allocation extent of blocks do not require additional metadata writes until the next extent is allocated.

This approach optimizes the disk seek pattern, and the grouping of block writes into clusters allows the file system to issue larger physical disk writes to the storage device, saving the overhead of many small SCSI transfers. Figure 12.1 compares block-based and extent-based allocation. We can see that the block address number is required for every logical block in a file on a block-allocated file, resulting in a lot of metadata for each file. In the extent-based allocation method, only the start block number and length are required for each contiguous extent of data blocks. A file with only a few very large extents requires only a small amount of metadata.

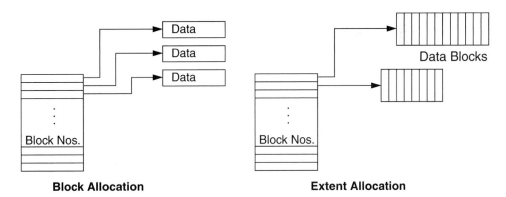

Figure 12.1 Block- and Extent-Based Allocation

Extent-based file systems provide good performance for sequential file access thanks to the sequential allocation policy and block clustering into larger writes. However, many of the benefits of extent-based file systems may not be realized when the file system is being used for random I/O.

For example, if we want to read sequentially through an extent-based file, we only need to read the start block number and the length; then, we can continue to read all of the data blocks in that extent, which means there is very little metadata read overhead in reading sequentially. In contrast, if we were to read a file in a random manner, we would need to look up the block address for the block we want for every data block read, which is similar to what we would have to do with a block-based file system.

Table 12-3 summarizes the allocation format for third-party file systems.

Table 12-3 File System Structure and Allocation

File System	Allocation Format
UFS	Block
VxFS	Extent
QFS	Extent

12.3.1.3 Extentlike Performance from Block Clustering

The sequential access performance of the block-allocated file systems quickly became a major limiting factor for overall system performance. That was the motivation for several enhancements to block allocation of file systems. In 1991, Kleiman and McVoy at Sun showed that when UFS was modified to allocate large sequential series of disk blocks, and reads and writes were grouped into larger clusters, UFS performed at rates similar to those of an extent-based file system. The UFS file system allocator was enhanced so that UFS can allocate up to 16-Mbyte extents at a time when a file is sequentially written. This rate lays the foundation to perform reads and writes larger than the block size when a file is accessed sequentially, since the file system blocks are now in adjacent order on the storage device.

Other enhancements to the UFS write code delay writes long enough so that one large write can be performed instead of several smaller writes.

Similarly, the UFS read paths were changed so that if sequential access is being made to a file, a whole group of blocks is read in at a time, effectively reading ahead into the file being accessed. The read enhancements also enabled UFS to generate large read requests of the storage device in place of smaller requests, which eliminated the need to wait for many small individual disk I/Os for each read.

The size of the groups or "block clusters" read and written is controlled by the file system `maxcontig` parameter; it defaults to either 128 Kbytes or 1 Mbyte. We talk more about cluster sizes in the following chapter.

The initial tests showed an increase in throughput of 100 percent, with a reduction of CPU overhead of 25 percent. Today, block clustering allows sequential reads of single files at over 100 MB/s with some configurations. To make best use of the block clustering and sequential allocation, you should preallocate a file when possible. Doing so provides proper sequential allocation of the disk blocks, so that future disk I/O can take advantage of the block clustering capability for extended performance.

12.3.2 File System Capacity

File system capacity has become more important as a limiting factor in recent years because of the rapid growth of storage capacity. This growth is the result of two important factors: disk capacity has grown from average sizes of 50 Mbytes to over 36 Gbytes per spindle, and the introduction of logical storage (RAID) has meant that storage device article size is now a function of the number of drives in the storage device. Storage devices provide virtual disk representation of multiple disks, and often 10 or more disks will be combined into a single virtual disk, with sizes now exceeding the 1-Tbyte mark.

Many Unix file systems were designed in the early 1980s to use disk sizes on the order of 50 megabytes, and at the time, sizes of 1 terabyte sounded unrealistic; by contrast, today's storage devices are often configured with several terabytes of capacity.

The mechanism by which devices are addressed in many Unix implementations is a function of 32-bit addressing, which limits file and file system addresses to 2 gigabytes. As a result, early file systems were limited to a maximum file system size of 2 gigabytes. When Solaris implemented 64-bit file offset pointers in the disk device drivers, it enabled a file system to grow beyond the 2-gigabyte limit. The file system could provide support beyond that limit because Solaris divides the file system addresses into 512-byte sectors, which translates into a maximum file and file system size of $2^{31} * 512 = 1$ Tbyte.

Solaris 2.6 added support to the operating system to allow logical file sizes up to 2^{63} bytes, which means that a file on UFS may be as large as the file system, 1 terabyte.

The Veritas VxFS and LSC QFS file systems provide support beyond 1 terabyte; in fact, file system sizes up to 2^{63} bytes are supported.

Table 12-4 summarizes file system capacities.

Table 12-4 File System Capacities

File System	Max Capacity	Max File Size
SunOS 4.x UFS	2 GB	2 GB
Solaris UFS	1 TB	1 TB
VxFS	2^{63} bytes	2^{63} bytes
QFS	2^{63} bytes	2^{63} bytes

12.3.3 Variable Block Size Support

The block size used by each file system often differs with the type of file system, and in many cases each file system can support a range of different block sizes. The block size of a file system is typically configured by a tunable parameter at the time the file system is created.

The block size of a file system affects the performance and efficiency of the file system in different ways. When a file is allocated, the last block in the file is partly wasted. If the file is small, then the amount of overhead in the file system can be large in proportion to the amount of disk space used by the files. A small block size provides efficient space utilization since the space wasted in the last block of each file is minimal; however, small block sizes increase the amount of information required to describe the location and allocation of each disk block, which means that sequential performance of large files can be adversely affected. A large block size provides greater file system performance at the penalty of efficiency, since more space is wasted at the end of each file.

Table 12-5 shows the amount of space wasted for 1,000 files of two different sizes on file systems with various block sizes. The efficiency trade-off is clearly only applicable for file systems containing many small files. File systems with file sizes an order of magnitude higher than the block size have no significant space overhead from the different block sizes, and since disk space is so cheap, the efficiency overhead is rarely an issue.

Table 12-5 Space Efficiency for 1,000 Files with Different File/Block Sizes

Space Used	% Waste	File Size and File System Block Size
2 MB	0	2-KB files on 512-byte blocks
2 MB	0	2-KB files on 1024-byte blocks
4 MB	50	2-KB files on 4096-byte blocks
8 MB	75	2-KB files on 8192-byte blocks
1 GB	0	1-MB files on 512-byte blocks
1 GB	0	1-MB files on 1024-byte blocks
1 GB	0	1-MB files on 4096-byte blocks
1 GB	0	1-MB files on 8192-byte blocks
1 GB	6	1-MB files on 64-Kbyte blocks

Another important factor for block sizes is the data access size. Although the average file system size has mushroomed over the years, the average size of data that is accessed is often still very small. For example, an OLTP database with tables containing customer information such as name, address, and ZIP code occupies only a few hundred bytes, and the read/write operations to the file systems will be very small. Databases typically access the file systems in 2-, 4-, 8-, or 16-Kbyte sizes. Here, the smaller block size may well be better suited to the size of the database access size. A larger block size may provide better sequential performance, but the small and random access from a database will not benefit from having to retrieve a larger block, since they are only using a small portion of the block.

A block size of 4 or 8 Kbytes is often optimal for databases, where the largest possible block size is optimal for large sequential file access. At this time, the Solaris UFS only supports a 4- or 8-Kbyte block size. Table 12-6 shows the different block sizes supported on different file systems.

Table 12-6 File System Block Size Support

File System	Block Size Support	Sub-Block Support
Solaris UFS	4 or 8 Kbytes	512-byte – 8-Kbyte fragments
VxFS	512 bytes to 8 Kbytes	N/A
QFS	1 Kbyte to 32 Mbytes	N/A

The UFS file system provides an additional allocation unit known as a fragment, which is smaller than the file system block size. A fragment can be allocated in the last block of a file to provide more space efficiency when many small files are being stored. The UFS fragment can be configured between 512 bytes and the block size of the file system; it defaults to 1 Kbyte.

12.3.4 Access Control Lists

The traditional Unix file system provides a simple file access scheme based on users, groups, and world, where each file is assigned an owner and a Unix group, and then a bit map of permissions for user, group, and world is assigned, as illustrated in Figure 12.2.

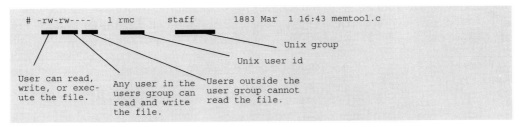

Figure 12.2 Traditional File Access Scheme

This scheme is flexible when file access permissions align with users and groups of users, but it does not provide any mechanism to assign access to lists of users that do not coincide with a Unix group. For example, if we want to give read access to file1 to Mark and Chuck, and then read access to file2 to Chuck and Barb, then we would need to create two Unix groups, and Chuck would need to switch groups with the chgrp command to gain access to either file.

To overcome this drawback, some operating systems use an access control list (ACL), where lists of users with different permissions can be assigned to a file. Solaris introduced the notion of access control lists in the B1 secure version, known as Trusted Solaris, in 1993. Trusted Solaris ACLs were later integrated with the commercial Solaris version in 1995 with Solaris 2.5.

Solaris ACLs allow the administrator to assign a list of Unix user IDs and groups to a file by using the `setfacl` command and to review the ACLs by using the `getfacl` command, as shown below.

```
# setfacl -m user:jon:rw- memtool.c
# getfacl memtool.c

# file: memtool.c
# owner: rmc
# group: staff
user::r--
user:jon:rw-              #effective:r--
group::r--                #effective:r--
mask:r--
other:r--

# ls -l memtool.c
-r--r--r--+  1 rmc        staff           638 Mar 30 11:32 memtool.c
```

For example, we can assign access to a file for a specific user by using the `setfacl` command. Note that the Unix permissions on the file now contain a +, signifying that an access control list is assigned to this file.

Multiple users and groups can be assigned to a file, offering a flexible mechanism for assigning access rights. ACLs can be assigned to directories as well. Note that unlike the case with some other operating systems, access control lists are not inherited from a parent, so a new directory created under a directory with an ACL will not have an ACL assigned by default. Table 12-7 lists file system support for ACLs.

Table 12-7 File System ACL Support

File System	ACL Support?
Solaris 2.0-2.4 UFS	No
Solaris 2.5 UFS	Yes
VxFS	Yes
QFS	No

12.3.5 File Systems Logging (Journaling)

Important criteria for commercial systems are reliability and availability, both of which may be compromised if the file system does not provide the required level of robustness. We have become familiar with the term *journaling* to mean just one thing, but, in fact, file system logging can be implemented in several ways. The three most common forms of journaling are:

- Metadata logging — Logs only file system structure changes
- File and metadata logging — Logs all changes to the file system
- Log-structured file system — The entire file system is implemented as a log

A file system must be able to deliver reliable storage to the hosted applications, and in the event of a failure, it must also be able to provide rapid recovery to a known state.

The original implementations of Unix file systems did not meet these criteria. They left the file system in an unknown state in the event of a system crash or power outage, and often took a very long time (30+ hours for a 50-Gbyte file system) for consistency checking at boot time.

We can dramatically increase the robustness of a file system by using logging to prevent the file system structure from becoming corrupted during a power outage or a system failure. The term journaling describes a file system that logs changes to on-disk data in a separate, sequential, rolling log. The primary reason for using this procedure is that it maintains an accurate picture of file system state, so that in the event of a power outage or system crash, the state of the file system is known. Then, rather than scanning the entire file system with fsck, we can check the file system log and correct the last few updates as necessary. A logging file system can mean the difference between mounting a heavily populated file system in 20 seconds versus 30+ hours without a log.

Logging does not come for free and incurs a significant performance overhead. Logging does require more slow synchronous writes, and the most popular implementation of logging (metadata logging) requires at least three writes per file update, which is significantly more than would be required without logging.

Because of those costs, we should evaluate our requirements. Do we want the file system to go fast, or do we need maximum reliability? For example, if we are using a file system for a high-performance HPC task that creates a lot of output files, we want absolute performance but may not care about file system robustness if a power outage occurred, and in this case we should choose not to use logging. On the other hand, if we are building a clustered database system, we absolutely require file system reliability, and logging is mandatory, even considering the performance overhead.

Table 12-8 shows the types of logging used in different file systems.

Table 12-8 File System Logging Characteristics

File System	Logging Characteristics	Comments
UFS (2.6 & earlier)	No logging without SDS	

Table 12-8 File System Logging Characteristics (Continued)

File System	Logging Characteristics	Comments
Solaris 2.4-2.5.1 UFS with SDS 3.0-4.x	Metadata logging with logging of small sync data	Can have separate LOG device
Solaris 2.6 with SDS 3.0-4.x	Metadata logging only	Can have separate LOG device
Solaris 7 UFS	Metadata logging	Log is embedded in file system
VxFS	Data and metadata logging	Default is metadata logging only
VxFS with NFS Acc.	Data and metadata logging	Log is placed on a separate device
QFS	Logging not necessary	Can do quick mount on reboot without `fsck` after crash

12.3.5.1 Metadata Logging

The most common form of file system logging is metadata logging. When a file system makes changes to its on-disk structure, it uses several disconnected synchronous writes to make the changes. If an outage occurs halfway through an operation, the state of the file system is unknown, and the whole file system must be consistency checked.

For example, if one block is appended to the end of a file, the on-disk map that tells the file system the location of each block for the file needs to be read, modified, and rewritten to the disk before the data block is written. When a failure occurs, the file system must be checked before it is mounted at boot, and the file system doesn't know if the block map is correct and also doesn't know which file was being modified during the crash. This situation means a full file system scan, often taking minutes or hours.

A metadata logging file system has a cyclic, append-only log area on the disk that it can use to record the state of each disk transaction. Before any on-disk structures are changed, an intent-to-change record is written to the log. The directory structure is then updated, and when complete, the log entry is marked complete. Since every change to the file system structure is in the log, we can check the consistency of the file system by looking in the log, and we need not do a full file system scan. At mount time, if an intent-to-change entry is found but not marked complete, then the file structure for that block is checked and adjusted where necessary. Figure 12.3 illustrates how metadata logging works.

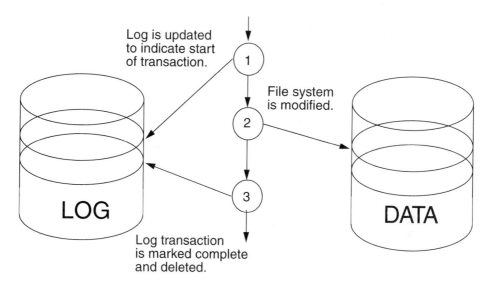

Figure 12.3 File System Metadata Logging

This method of logging has been implemented successfully on several file systems and is the basis for the logging UFS file system used in Solaris. It retains the on-disk file system structure for UFS and can be enabled or disabled at any time without the need to change on-disk data. The Veritas VxFS file system also uses metadata logging.

Some file systems have the log embedded in the same partition as the file system data, whereas others allow separation of the log from the file system. The unbundled UFS logging in Solstice DiskSuite allows a separate log and data; the bundled logging UFS in Solaris 7 does not. Veritas allows the log to be separated only when the Veritas NFS Accelerator option is purchased to enable this feature.

12.3.5.2 Data and Metadata Logging

Some file systems provide an option to put file data into the log in conjunction with the metadata. This approach can be particularly useful for small synchronous writes, which would require two or more writes to different parts of the disk for every application write (one for the data and one for the log write). By putting the data into the log, we can avoid the second seek and write. The data is first written to the log and then replayed into the file system. This technique does two things: it ensures data integrity up to but not including the last block written, and it can help performance for small synchronous writes. The Veritas VxFS file system has an option to log both data and metadata.

12.3.5.3 Log-Structured File Systems

Traditional file systems are block allocated, and device blocks are allocated from a map of free blocks. An alternative file system format is a log-structured file system that implements the entire file system as a log. The log-structured file system appends data blocks to the end of the log each time blocks are written to a file, invalidating earlier-written blocks as it goes. This approach allows every file to be written to sequentially, regardless of the block order of the writes and thus provides very fast write performance.

The log-structured file system provides extremely high write performance at the cost of read performance and increased complexity. Read performance is often much slower since blocks are allocated in the order they are written, which may mean that files are fragmented across the disk in an arbitrary order. Complexity increases because a separate garbage collector or cleaner process is needed to scan the file system and remove invalidated blocks. Moreover, a complex caching/lookup mechanism is required to enable efficient lookup because blocks are allocated in a random order, and the location of the blocks for each file must be maintained.

Log-structured file systems prove to be efficient in metadata-intensive environments but have yet to be proven more efficient for data-intensive workloads. It is important to note the difference between log-structured and logging file systems. Log-structured file systems are also known as "write anywhere file system layout" (WAFL).

No log-structured file systems are currently available for Solaris.

12.3.6 Expanding and Shrinking File Systems

A common requirement for on-line storage management is the ability to grow and shrink file systems. Early file systems did not support this requirement, since a disk was fixed in size. Now that we have virtual disks by means of volume managers, we can change the size of the underlying device. Without the ability to grow a file system, we would need to back up the file system, make the file system again with mkfs/newfs, and then restore all the file system data. A file system that can grow in size online removes the need for this disruptive process. A Solaris UFS file system can be extended by the mkfs command with the -M option for a mounted file system and the -G option for an unmounted file system.

In addition to growing a file system, we sometimes need to do the reverse. For example, if we want to reclaim some space from one device to assign to another, we would need to shrink the file system first, so that any allocated file blocks are moved away from the end of the file system that is being shrunk.

Table 12-9 lists the support for expanding and shrinking in different file systems.

Table 12-9 File System Grow/Shrink Support

File System	Grow	Shrink
Basic UFS	Yes, with `mkfs -M`	No
VxFS	Yes, with `fsadm`	Yes, with `fsadm`
QFS	Yes, with `growqfs`	No

12.3.7 Direct I/O

To provide near-device performance, many file systems offer the option to bypass the file system cache through a mechanism known as direct I/O. This option reduces the overhead of managing cache allocation and completely removes all interaction between the file system and the memory system. In many cases, the resulting performance can be many times worse, since there is no cache to buffer reads and writes, but when caching is done in the application, direct I/O can be a benefit. Another important use of direct I/O is backups, where we don't want to read a file into the cache during a backup.

Applications such as databases do their own caching, and direct I/O offers a mechanism to avoid the double caching that would occur if applications were to use a regular file system. Without direct I/O, an application reads a file block into the Solaris file system cache, and then reads it into the database shared buffer (e.g., Oracle's block cache), so the block exists in two places. However, with direct I/O, the block is read directly into the database cache without passing through the regular file system cache.

Because direct I/O bypasses the file system cache, it also disables file system read-ahead. This means that small reads and writes result in many I/O requests to the storage device that would have otherwise been clustered into larger requests by the file system; hence, direct I/O should only be used for random I/O or large-block sequential I/O.

Another side effect of direct I/O is that it does not put a load on the Solaris memory system and removes the typical paging that can be seen when a regular file system is used. This effect is a frequent motivator for the use of direct I/O, but note that the new Priority Paging feature of Solaris provides similar separation between the file systems and applications. Refer to "Is All That Paging Bad for My System?" on page 595 for details on how Priority Paging improves file system behavior.

Direct I/O was initially implemented in the UFS, and VxFS has subsequently been enhanced to provide a wide range of direct I/O facilities. The UFS direct I/O facility provides a mechanism to enable direct I/O per file or per file system. The VxFS file system implements direct I/O automatically for I/O sizes larger than 256 Kbytes by default (this size can be tuned) and also provides a mechanism to create a raw device that represents direct access to the file. QFS has options similar to those for UFS to allow direct I/O on a per-file basis.

12.3.7.1 Sparse Files

Some file systems allow the creation of files without allocation of disk blocks. For example, you can create a 1-Gbyte file by opening a file, seeking to 1 Gbyte, and then writing a few bytes of data. The file is essentially created with a hole in the middle, and although the file size is reported as 1 Gbyte, only one disk block would be used to hold such a file.

Files with allocation holes are known as sparse files. Accesses to locations with a sparse file that has no blocks allocated simply return a series of zeros, and blocks are not allocated until that location within the file is written to. Sparse files are particularly useful when memory mapped files or files for databases are used, since they remove the need for complex file allocation algorithms within an application. For example, a simple database application can store records in a file by seeking to the required offset and storing the record; then the file will only use as much space as there are records in the file and will leave holes where there are empty records.

12.3.7.2 Integrated Volume Management

Volume management allows multiple physical disks to be used as a single volume to provide larger aggregate volume sizes, better performance, and simpler management. Volume managers are typically implemented as a separate layer between the physical disks and present themselves as a virtual disk device. Databases and file systems can be mounted on these larger virtual disk devices, and the same management techniques can be used to manage data within each virtual volume.

Some file systems provide volume management capabilities within the file system. The QFS file system from LSC provides integrated volume management and allows striping and concatenation of files within the file system. The file system is configured on multiple devices, rather than on the traditional single device. Each file within the file system can be concatenated or striped with different interlace sizes, on a file-by-file basis.

12.3.7.3 Summary of File System Features

In this section, we have explored the most common file system features and drawn some comparisons between some different file systems. Table 12-10 summarizes the file system features we have covered so far.

Table 12-10 Summary of File System Features

Feature	UFS	VxFS	QFS	Notes
Max file size	1TB	2^{63}	2^{63}	Maximum file size.
Max file system size	1TB	2^{63}	2^{63}	Maximum size of file system.
Logging	Yes	Yes	No	Greater data integrity, faster reboot, faster `fsck`.

Table 12-10 Summary of File System Features (Continued)

Feature	UFS	VxFS	QFS	Notes
Separate log	Yes, with SDS	Yes, with NFS Acc.	No	A separate log device can be attached to the file system to avoid seeking backward and forward from the log to the data.
Extent based	No	Yes	Yes	Fewer disk seeks due to simpler block allocation schemes.
Direct I/O	Yes, 2.6	Yes	Yes	Direct I/O options allow bypassing of the page cache based on mount options and runtime directives.
Expandable	Yes	Yes	No	The file system size can be expanded online.
Shrinkable	No	Yes	No	The file system size can be shrunk online.
Snapshot, by locking file system	Yes	Yes	No	The file system can be locked and frozen for a backup snapshot. Locking suspends all file system activity during the backup.
Online snapshot	No	Yes	No	A frozen version of the file system can be mounted while the main file system is online. This version can be used for online backup.
Quotas	Yes	Yes	No	Disk space quotas can be enforced.
ACLs	Yes	Yes	No	Enhanced file permissions via Access Control Lists.
HSM capable	No	Yes	Yes	Automatic hierarchical storage management options available.
Page cache friendly	Yes	No	Yes	UFS will not cause memory shortage when used in sequential mode. VxFS must be used in direct or sequential advise mode to avoid causing a memory shortage.
Stripe alignment	No	Yes	Yes	Ability to align clustered writes with storage stripe to allow whole stripe writes. Provides superior RAID-5 performance.
Integrated Volume Manager	No	No	Yes	Striping and concatenation across multiple storage devices possible from file system.

13

FILE SYSTEM FRAMEWORK

$\mathbf{I}$n this chapter, we introduce the kernel file system framework and discuss the implementation of the kernel file system architecture.

13.1 Solaris File System Framework

Solaris includes a framework, the *virtual file system framework*, under which multiple file system types are implemented. Earlier implementations of Unix used a single file system type for all of the mounted file systems, typically, the UFS file system from BSD Unix. The virtual file system framework was developed to allow Sun's distributed computing file system (NFS) to coexist with the UFS file system in SunOS 2.0; it became a standard part of System V in SVR4 and Solaris.

Each file system provides file abstractions, arranged in a hierarchical directory structure. We can categorize Solaris file systems into the following types:

- **Storage based** — Regular file systems that provide facilities for persistent storage and management of data. The Solaris UFS and PC/DOS file systems are examples.
- **Network file systems** — File systems that provide files which appear as if they are in a local directory structure, but are stored on a remote network server; for example, NFS.

- **Pseudo file systems** — File systems that present various abstractions as files in a file system. The /proc pseudo file system represents the address space of a process as a series of files.

13.1.1 Unified File System Interface

The framework provides a single set of well-defined interfaces that are file system independent; the implementation details of each file system are hidden behind these interfaces. Two key objects represent these interfaces: the virtual file, or *vnode,* and the virtual file system, or *vfs* objects. The vnode interfaces implement file-related functions, and the vfs interfaces implement file system management functions. The vnode and vfs interfaces direct functions to specific file systems, depending on the type of file system being operated on. Figure 13.1 shows the file system layers. File-related functions are initiated through a system call or from another kernel subsystem and are directed to the appropriate file system by the vnode/vfs layer.

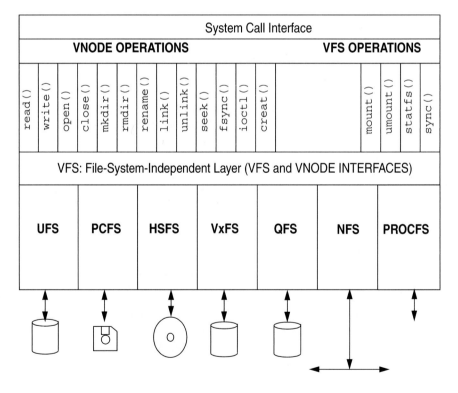

Figure 13.1 Solaris File System Framework

13.1.2 File System Framework Facilities

The vnode/vfs interfaces—the "top end" of the file system module—implement vnode and vfs objects. The "bottom end" of the file system uses other kernel interfaces to access, store, and cache the data they represent. Disk-based file systems interface to device drivers to provide persistent storage of their data, and they interface to network file systems access the networking subsystem to transmit and receive data to remote systems. Pseudo file systems typically access local kernel functions and structures to gather the information they represent.

- **Loadable file system modules** — A dynamically loadable module type is provided for Solaris file systems. File system modules are dynamically loaded at the time each file system type is first mounted (except for the root file system, which is mounted explicitly at boot).

- **The** vnode/vfs **framework** — As discussed, a unified interface framework that uses the vnode and vfs interfaces allows file functions and file system management functions to be implemented.

- **File system caching** — File systems that implement caching interface with the HAT layer of the virtual memory system to map, unmap, and manage the memory used for caching. File systems use physical memory pages and the HAT layer of the virtual memory system to cache files. The kernel's seg_map driver maps file system cache into the kernel's address space when accessing the file system through the read() and write() system calls.

- **Path-name management** — Files are accessed by means of path names, which are assembled as a series of directory names and file names. The file system framework provides routines that resolve and manipulate path names by calling into the file system's lookup() function to convert paths into vnode pointers.

- **Directory name caching** — A central directory name lookup cache (DNLC) provides a mechanism to cache pathname-to-vnode mappings, so that the directory components need not be read from disk each time they are needed.

13.2 The vnode

A vnode is a representation of a file in the Solaris kernel. The vnode is said to be objectlike because it is an encapsulation of a file's state and the methods that can be used to perform operations on that file. A vnode represents a file within a file system; the vnode hides the implementation of the file system it resides in and exposes file-system-independent data and methods for that file to the rest of the kernel.

A vnode object contains three important items (see Figure 13.2):

- **File-system-independent data** — Information about the vnode, such as the type of vnode (file, directory, character device, etc.), flags that represent state, pointers to the file system that contains the vnode, and a reference count that keeps track of how many subsystems have references to the vnode.
- **Functions to implement file methods** — A structure of pointers to file-system-dependent functions to implement file functions such as open(), close(), read(), and write().
- **File-system-specific data** — Data that is used internally by each file system implementation; typically the in-memory inode that represents the vnode on the underlying file system. UFS uses an inode, NFS uses an rnode, and tmpfs uses a tmpnode.

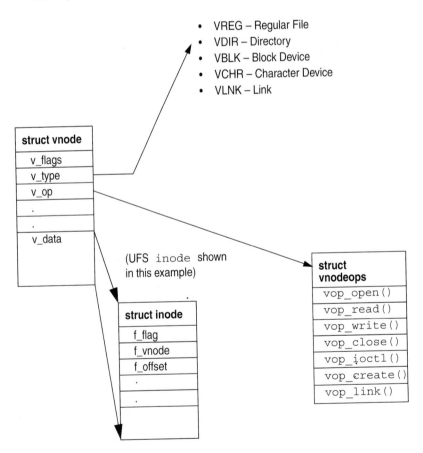

Figure 13.2 The vnode Object

The kernel uses macros to call vnode functions. In that way, it can perform vnode operations (e.g., read(), write(), open(), close()) without knowing what the

underlying file system containing the vnode is. For example, to read from a file
without knowing that it resides on a UFS file system, the kernel would simply call
the file-system-independent macro for read(), VOP_READ(), which would call the
vop_read() method of the vnode, which in turn calls the UFS function,
ufs_read(). A sample of a vnode macro from sys/vnode.h is shown below.

```
#define VOP_READ(vpp, mode, cr) \
        (*(*(vpp))->v_op->vop_read)(vpp, mode, cr)
```

Header File   <sys/vnode.h>

The structure of a vnode in Solaris can be found in sys/vnode.h and is shown
below. It defines the basic interface elements and provides other information contained in the vnode.

```
typedef struct vnode {
        kmutex_t          v_lock;                   /* protects vnode fields */
        ushort_t          v_flag;                   /* vnode flags (see below) */
        uint_t            v_count;                  /* reference count */
        struct vfs        *v_vfsmountedhere;        /* ptr to vfs mounted here */
        struct vnodeops   *v_op;                    /* vnode operations */
        struct vfs        *v_vfsp;                  /* ptr to containing VFS */
        struct stdata     *v_stream;               /* associated stream */
        struct page       *v_pages;                 /* vnode pages list */
        enum vtype        v_type;                   /* vnode type */
        dev_t             v_rdev;                   /* device (VCHR, VBLK) */
        caddr_t           v_data;                   /* private data for fs */
        struct filock     *v_filocks;               /* ptr to filock list */
        struct shrlocklist *v_shrlocks;             /* ptr to shrlock list */
        kcondvar_t        v_cv;                     /* synchronize locking */
} vnode_t;
```

Header File   <sys/vnode.h>

13.2.1 vnode Types

Solaris has specific vnode types for files. The v_type field in the vnode structure
indicates the type of vnode, as described in Table 13-1.

Table 13-1 Solaris 7 vnode Types from sys/vnode.h

Type	Description
VNON	No type
VREG	Regular file
VDIR	Directory
VBLK	Block device
VCHR	Character device
VLNK	Hard link
VFIFO	Named pipe
VDOOR	Doors interface
VPROC	procfs node

Table 13-1 Solaris 7 vnode Types from `sys/vnode.h`   (Continued)

Type	Description
VSOCK	`sockfs` node (socket)
VBAD	Bad vnode

13.2.2 Vnode Methods

The vnode interface provides the set of file system object methods, some of which we saw in Figure 13.1 on page 532. The file systems implement these methods to perform all file-system-specific file operations. Table 13-2 shows the vnode interface methods in Solaris.

Table 13-2 Solaris 7 Vnode Interface Methods from `sys/vnode.h`

Method	Description
vop_access()	Checks access to the supplied vnode.
vop_addmap()	Increments the map count.
vop_close()	Closes the file given by the supplied vnode. When this is the last close, some file systems use vop_close() to initiate a writeback of outstanding dirty pages by checking the reference count in the vnode.
vop_cmp()	Compares two vnodes.
vop_create()	Creates the supplied path name.
vop_delmap()	Decrements the map count.
vop_dispose()	Frees the given page from the vnode.
vop_dump()	Dumps data when the kernel is in a frozen state.
vop_dumpctl()	Prepares the file system before and after a dump.
vop_frlock()	Does file and record locking for the supplied vnode.
vop_fsync()	Flushes out any dirty pages for the supplied vnode.
vop_getattr()	Gets the attributes for the supplied vnode.
vop_getpage()	Gets pages in the range offset and length for the vnode from the backing store of the file system. Does the real work of reading a vnode. This method is often called as a result of read(), which causes a page fault in seg_map, which calls vop_getpage.
vop_getsecattr()	Gets security access control list attributes.
vop_inactive()	Frees resources and releases the supplied vnode. The file system can choose to destroy the vnode or put it onto an inactive list, which is managed by the file system implementation.
vop_ioctl()	Performs an I/O control on the supplied vnode.
vop_fid()	Gets a unique file ID for the supplied vnode. Used for NFS client consistency.

Table 13-2 Solaris 7 vnode Interface Methods from `sys/vnode.h` (Continued)

Method	Description
`vop_link()`	Creates a hard link to the supplied vnode.
`vop_lookup()`	Looks up the path name for the supplied vnode. The `vop_lookup()` does file-name translation for the open, stat system calls.
`vop_map()`	Maps a range of pages into an address space by doing the appropriate checks and calling `as_map()`.
`vop_mkdir()`	Makes a directory of the given name.
`vop_open()`	Opens a file referenced by the supplied vnode. The `open()` system call has already done a `vop_lookup()` on the path name, which returned a vnode pointer and then calls to `vop_open()`. This function typically does very little, since most of the real work was performed by `vop_lookup()`.
`vop_pageio()`	Paged I/O support for file system swap files.
`vop_pathconf()`	Establishes file system parameters with the `pathconf` system call.
`vop_poll()`	File system support for the `poll()` system call.
`vop_putpage()`	Writes pages in the range offset and length for the vnode to the backing store of the file system. Does the real work of reading a vnode.
`vop_read()`	Reads the range supplied for the given vnode. `vop_read()` typically maps the requested range of a file into kernel memory and then uses `vop_getpage()` to do the real work.
`vop_readdir()`	Reads the contents of a directory.
`vop_readlink()`	Follows the symlink in the supplied vnode.
`vop_realvp()`	Gets the real vnode from the supplied vnode.
`vop_remove()`	Removes the file for the supplied vnode.
`vop_rename()`	Renames the file to the new name.
`vop_rmdir()`	Removes a directory pointed to by the supplied vnode.
`vop_rwlock()`	Holds the reader/writer lock for the supplied vnode. This method is called for each vnode, with the `rwflag` set to 0 inside a `read()` system call and the `rwflag` set to 1 inside a `write()` system call. POSIX semantics require only one writer inside `write()` at a time. Some file system implementations have options to ignore the writer lock inside `vop_rwlock()`.
`vop_rwunlock()`	Releases the reader/writer lock for the supplied vnode.
`vop_seek()`	Seeks within the supplied vnode.
`vop_setattr()`	Sets the attributes for the supplied vnode.

Table 13-2 Solaris 7 Vnode Interface Methods from `sys/vnode.h` (Continued)

Method	Description
`vop_setfl()`	Sets file locks on the supplied vnode.
`vop_setsecattr()`	Sets security access control list attributes.
`vop_shrlock()`	ONC shared lock support.
`vop_space()`	Frees space for the supplied vnode.
`vop_symlink()`	Creates a symbolic link between the two path names.
`vop_write()`	Writes the range supplied for the given vnode. The `write` system call typically maps the requested range of a file into kernel memory and then uses `vop_putpage()` to do the real work.

13.2.3 vnode Reference Count

A vnode is created by the file system at the time a file is first opened or created and stays active until the file system decides the vnode is no longer needed. The vnode framework provides an infrastructure that keeps track of the number of references to a vnode. The kernel maintains the reference count by means of the VN_HOLD() and VN_RELE() macros, which increment and decrement the v_count field of the vnode. A vnode stays valid while its reference count is greater than zero, so a subsystem can rely on a vnode's contents staying valid by calling VN_HOLD() before it references a vnode's contents. It is important to distinquish a vnode reference from a lock; a lock ensures exclusive access to the data, and the reference count ensures persistence of the object.

When a vnode's reference count drops to zero, VN_RELE() invokes the VOP_INACTIVE() method for that file system. Every subsystem that references a vnode is required to call VN_HOLD() at the start of the reference and to call VN_RELE() at the end of each reference. Some file systems deconstruct a vnode when its reference count falls to zero; others hold on to the vnode for a while so that if it is required again, it is available in its constructed state. The UFS file system, for example, holds on to the vnode for a while after the last release so that the virtual memory system can keep the inode and cache for a file, whereas the PCFS file system frees the vnode and all of the cache associated with the vnode at the time VOP_INACTIVE() is called.

13.2.4 Interfaces for Paging vnode Cache

Solaris unifies file and memory management by using a vnode to represent the backing store for virtual memory. A page of memory represents a particular vnode and offset. The file system uses the memory relationship to implement caching for vnodes within a file system. To cache a vnode, the file system has the memory system create a page of physical memory that represents the vnode and offset.

The virtual memory system provides a set of functions for cache management and I/O for vnodes. These functions allow the file systems to cluster pages for I/O and handle the setup and checking required for syncing dirty pages with their backing store. The functions, described in Table 13-3, set up pages so that they can be passed to device driver block I/O handlers.

Table 13-3 Solaris 7 vnode Paging Functions from `vm/pvn.h`

Function	Description
`pvn_getdirty()`	Queries whether a page is dirty. Returns 1 if the page should be written back (the iolock is held in this case), or 0 if the page has been dealt with or has been unlocked.
`pvn_plist_init()`	Releases the iolock on each page and downgrades the page lock to shared after new pages have been created or read.
`pvn_read_done()`	Unlocks the pages after read is complete. The function is normally called automatically by `pageio_done()` but may need to be called if an error was encountered during a read.
`pvn_read_kluster()`	Finds the range of contiguous pages within the supplied address / length that fit within the provided vnode offset / length that do not already exist. Returns a list of newly created, exclusively locked pages ready for I/O. Checks that clustering is enabled by calling the `segop_kluster()` method for the given segment. On return from `pvn_read_kluster`, the caller typically zeroes any parts of the last page that are not going to be read from disk, sets up the read with `pageio_setup` for the returned offset and length, and then initiates the read with `bdev_strategy()`. Once the read is complete, `pvn_plist_init()` can release the I/O lock on each page that was created.
`pvn_write_done()`	Unlocks the pages after write is complete. For asynchronous writes, the function is normally called automatically by `pageio_done()` when an asynchronous write completes. For synchronous writes, `pvn_write_done()` is called after `pageio_done` to unlock written pages. It may also need to be called if an error was encountered during a write.

Table 13-3 Solaris 7 `vnode` Paging Functions from `vm/pvn.h` (Continued)

Function	Description
`pvn_write_kluster()`	Finds the contiguous range of dirty pages within the supplied offset and length. Returns a list of dirty locked pages ready to be written back. On return from `pvn_write_kluster()`, the caller typically sets up the write with `pageio_setup` for the returned offset and length, then initiates the write with `bdev_strategy()`. If the write is synchronous, then the caller should call `pvn_write_done()` to unlock the pages. If the write is asynchronous, then the `io_done` routine calls `pvn_write_done` when the write is complete.
`pvn_vplist_dirty()`	Finds all dirty pages in the page cache that have an offset greater than the supplied offset and calls the supplied `putapage()` routine. `pvn_vplist_dirty()` is often used to synchronize all dirty pages for a `vnode` when `vop_putpage` is called with a zero length.

13.2.5 Block I/O on vnode Pages

The block I/O subsystem provides support for initiating I/O to and from `vnode` pages. Three functions, shown in Table 13-4, initiate I/O between a physical page and a device.

Table 13-4 Solaris7 Paged I/O Functions from `sys/bio.h`

Function	Description
`bdev_strategy()`	Initiates an I/O on a page, using the block I/O device.
`pageio_done()`	Waits for the block device I/O to complete.
`pageio_setup()`	Sets up a block buffer for I/O on a page of memory so that it bypasses the block buffer cache by setting the `B_PAGEIO` flag and putting the page list on the `b_pages` field.

13.3 The vfs Object

The `vfs` layer provides an administrative interface into the file system to support commands like `mount` and `umount` in a file-system-independent manner. The interface achieves independence by means of a virtual file system (vfs) object. The vfs object represents an encapsulation of a file system's state and a set of methods for each of the file system administrative interfaces. Each file system type provides its own implementation of the object. Figure 13.3 illustrates the vfs object.

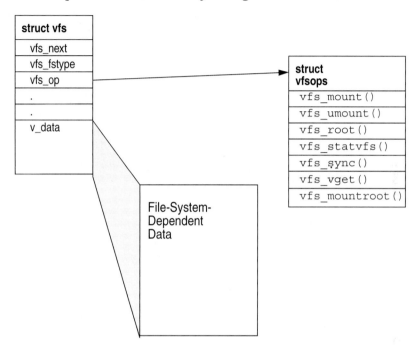

Figure 13.3 The vfs Object

Table 13-5 lists all the vfs interface methods.

Table 13-5 Solaris 7 vfs Interface Methods from sys/vfs.h

Method	Description
vfs_mount()	Mounts a file system on the supplied vnode.
vfs_unmount()	Unmounts the file system.
vfs_root()	Finds the root vnode for a file system.
vfs_statvfs()	Queries statistics on a file system.
vfs_sync()	Flushes the file system cache.
vfs_vget()	Finds a vnode that matches a unique file ID.
vfs_mountroot()	Mounts the file system on the root directory.
vfs_swapvp()	Not used.

The vfs interface, with the relevant data structures from sys/vfs.h, is shown below.

```
/
 * Structure per mounted file system. Each mounted file system has
 * an array of operations and an instance record.
 *
 * The file systems are kept on a singly linked list headed by "rootvfs" and
 * terminated by NULL. File system implementations should not access this
 * list; it's intended for use only in the kernel's vfs layer.
 */
typedef struct vfs {
        struct vfs       *vfs_next;              /* next VFS in VFS list */
        struct vfsops    *vfs_op;                /* operations on VFS */
        struct vnode     *vfs_vnodecovered;      /* vnode mounted on */
        uint_t           vfs_flag;               /* flags */
        uint_t           vfs_bsize;              /* native block size */
        int              vfs_fstype;             /* file system type index */
        fsid_t           vfs_fsid;               /* file system id */
        caddr_t          vfs_data;               /* private data */
        dev_t            vfs_dev;                /* device of mounted VFS */
        ulong_t          vfs_bcount;             /* I/O count (accounting) */
        ushort_t         vfs_nsubmounts;         /* immediate sub-mount count */
        struct vfs       *vfs_list;              /* sync list pointer */
        struct vfs       *vfs_hash;              /* hash list pointer */
        ksema_t          vfs_reflock;            /* mount/unmount/sync lock */
}

/*
 * Operations supported on virtual file system.
 */

typedef struct vfsops {
        int      (*vfs_mount)(struct vfs *, struct vnode *, struct mounta *,
                        struct cred *);
        int      (*vfs_unmount)(struct vfs *, struct cred *);
        int      (*vfs_root)(struct vfs *, struct vnode **);
        int      (*vfs_statvfs)(struct vfs *, struct statvfs64 *);
        int      (*vfs_sync)(struct vfs *, short, struct cred *);
        int      (*vfs_vget)(struct vfs *, struct vnode **, struct fid *);
        int      (*vfs_mountroot)(struct vfs *, enum whymountroot);
        int      (*vfs_swapvp)(struct vfs *, struct vnode **, char *);
}
```

Header File　<sys/vfs.h>

13.3.1 The File System Switch Table

The file system switch table, shown below, is a systemwide table of file system types. Each file system type that is loaded on the system can be found in the virtual file system switch table. The file system switch table provides an ASCII list of file system names (e.g., ufs, nfs), the initialization routines, and vfs object methods for that file system. The vfs_fstype field of the vfs object is an index into the file system switch table.

```
/*
 * File system type switch table.
 */
typedef struct vfssw {
        char             *vsw_name;        /* type name string */
        int              (*vsw_init)(struct vfssw *, int);
                                           /* init routine */
        struct vfsops    *vsw_vfsops;      /* file system operations vector */
        int              vsw_flag;         /* flags */
} vfssw_t;
```

Header File　<sys/vfs.h>

File systems install entries into the file system switch table when they are first loaded, usually during their initialization function. There is only one entry for each type of file system, regardless of how many mounts exist for that type of file system. An example of the virtual file system switch table is shown below. Each slot lists the name of the file system and tells where to find the relative functions for that file system.

```
struct vfssw vfssw[] = {
        "BADVFS",       NULL,           &vfs_strayops,  0,      /* invalid */
        "specfs",       specinit,       NULL,           0,      /* SPECFS */
        "ufs",          ufsinit,        &ufs_vfsops,    0,      /* UFS */
        "fifofs",       fifoinit,       &fifo_vfsops,   0,      /* FIFOFS */
        "namefs",       namefsinit,     &name_vfsops,   0,      /* NAMEFS */
        "proc",         proc,           &proc_vfsops,   0,      /* PROCFS */
        "s5fs",         s5fsinit,       &s5_vfsops,     0,      /* S5FS */
        "nfs",          nfsinit,        &nfs_vfsops,    0,      /* NFS Ver 2 */
        "hsfs",         hsfsinit,       &hs_vfsops,     0,      /* HSFS */
        "lofs",         lofsinit,       &lo_vfsops,     0,      /* LOFS */
        "tmpfs",        tmpfsinit,      &tmp_vfsops,    0,      /* TMPFS */
        "fd",           fdinit,         &fd_vfsops,     0,      /* FDFS */
        "pcfs",         pcfsinit,       &pc_vfsops,     0,      /* PCFS */
        "swapfs",       swapinit,       &swap_vfsops,   0,      /* SWAPFS */
};
```

To dump the vfs switch table, issue the crash command, as shown below.

```
# crash
dumpfile = /dev/mem, namelist = /dev/ksyms, outfile = stdout
> vfssw
FILE SYSTEM SWITCH TABLE SIZE = 29
SLOT    NAME        FLAGS
   1    specfs        0
   2    ufs           0
   3    fifofs        0
   4    namefs        0
   5    proc          0
   6    s5fs          0
```

The file system framework provides functions for accessing file systems in the file system switch table. These functions, described in Table 13-6, find file system entries, locate and load the file system modules for given types, and allocate new entries in the file system switch table.

Table 13-6 Solaris 7 vfs Support Functions from <sys/vfs.h>

Method	Description
getvfs()	Gets a pointer to the vfs that matches the supplied fsid. Used by the nfs server.
vfs_getvfssw()	Finds a vfssw entry by file system type name. Tries to autoload the file system if entry is not found.
allocate_vfssw()	Allocates an entry in the file system switch table for a given file type.

13.3.2 The Mounted vfs List

The system starts with only one `vfs` object, the root file system, which is identi-fied by the `rootvfs` kernel pointer. You can subsequently mount file systems by looking up the `vfsops` structure in the switch table and calling the `mount` opera-tion for that file system. The `mount` operation initializes a new `vfs` object and links it to the `rootvfs` object by using the `vfs_next` structure in the object. Each time a new file system is mounted, its `vfs` structure is linked onto the chain. You can obtain a list of mounted file systems by starting at `rootvfs` and following the `vfs -> vfs_next` chain, as shown in Figure 13.4.

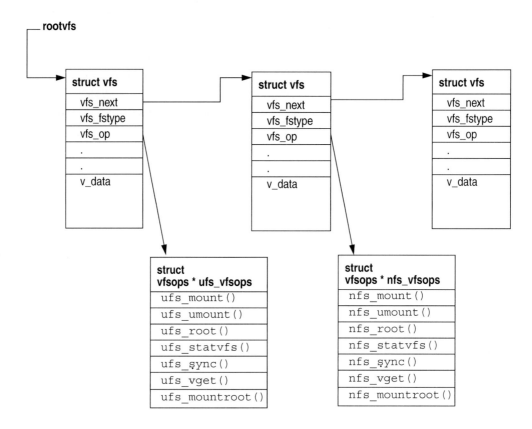

Figure 13.4 The Mounted `vfs` List

The file system framework provides functions, described in Table 13-7, for searching, adding, and removing file systems from the mounted file system list.

Table 13-7 Solaris 7 `vfs` Support Functions

Method	Description
`vfs_add()`	Called by a file system `mount` function to mount over an existing mount point. For example, the `vfs_mountroot()` method uses this call to mount and unmount root.
`vfs_remove()`	Removes a `vfs` object from the chain. Usually called only when unmounting a root overlay.
`vfs_lock()`	Locks the entire file system.
`vfs_unlock()`	Unlocks the entire file system.
`vfs_make_fsid()`	Called by a file system to generate the file system ID from the device.
`getvfs()`	Gets a pointer to the `vfs` that matches the supplied `fsid`. Used only by the nfs server.
`vf_to_stf()`	Maps `vfs` flags to `statfs` flags.

To display the list of file system `vfs` objects, issue the `crash` or `adb` command, as shown below.

```
# crash
dumpfile = /dev/mem, namelist = /dev/ksyms, outfile = stdout
> vfs
 FSTYP  BSZ  MAJ/MIN       FSID    VNCOVERED         PDATA BCOUNT  FLAGS
   ufs 8192  118,104    1d80068            0  30000067888      0  notr
  lofs 8192    65,5     1040005  300032b99f8  300029265e0      0
namefs 1024   179,0     2cc0000  300011ff5a0  300011ff440      0  nolnk
  lofs 8192    65,7     1040007  30002b0fb70  30002932978      0
  lofs 8192    65,5     1040005  30000070958  30002932918      0
   nfs 3276   175,2     2bc0002  30002b0e670  30002ecfe00      0  nosu
  hsfs 2048    91,1    31ba36b3  300013780a0  30001335e20      0  rd
   nfs 8192   175,1     2bc0001  30001378af0  300012e2200      0
namefs 1024   179,0     2cc0000  30001139710  30000dde670      0  nolnk
  lofs 8192  65,57000   104dea8  30000070dd8  300001a8720      0
   ufs 8192  65,57000   104dea8  30000d5fcd8  30000067348      0  notr
 tmpfs 8192     0,1           1  30000960ec0  300001260b0      0  notr
    fd 1024   172,0     2b00000  300009715d0            0      0
  proc  512   168,0     2a00000  30000adb290  300009550c0      0
> q
# adb -k

$<vfslist


                  vfs 10458730
root:
root:             next              op                vnodecovered
                  300031b2e90       ufs_vfsops        0
root+0x18:        flag              bsize             fstype
                  20                8192              2
root+0x24:        fsid              data              dev
                  1d8006800000002   30000067888       7600000068
root+0x40:        bcount            nsubmounts        list
                  0                 19                0
root+0x58:        hash
                  0
root+0x60:        reflock

root+0x60:        sleepq            count
                  0                 1




                  vfs 300031b2e90
300031b2e90:      next              op                vnodecovered
                  30001260cc8       lo_vfsops         300032b99f8
300031b2ea8:      flag              bsize             fstype
                  0                 8192              10
300031b2eb4:      fsid              data              dev
                  104000500000002   300029265e0       4100000005
300031b2ed0:      bcount            nsubmounts        list
                  0                 0                 138b13500000000
300031b2ee8:      hash
                  0
300031b2ef0:      reflock

300031b2ef0:      sleepq            count
                  0                 1
```

13.4 File System I/O

Two distinct methods perform file system I/O:

- read(), write(), and related system calls
- Memory-mapping of a file into the process's address space

Both methods are implemented the same way: a file is mapped into an address space and then paged I/O is performed on the pages within the mapped address space. Although it may be obvious that memory mapping is done when we memory-map a file into a process's address space, it is less obvious that the read() and write() system calls also map a file before reading or writing it. The major differences between these two methods are where the file is mapped and who does the mapping; a process calls mmap() to map the file into its address space for memory mapped I/O, and the kernel maps the file into the kernel's address space for read and write. The two methods are contrasted in Figure 13.5.

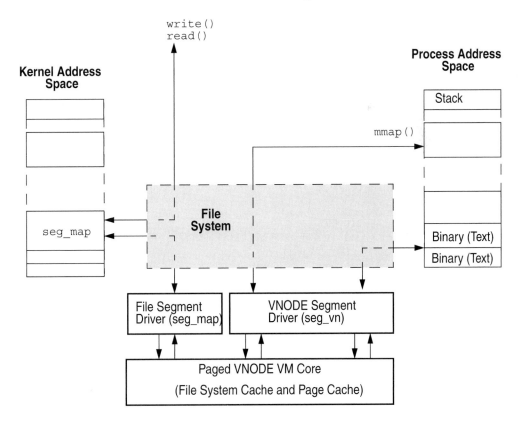

Figure 13.5 The read()/write() vs. mmap() Methods for File I/O

13.4.1 Memory Mapped I/O

A request to memory-map a file into an address space is handled by the file system vnode method vop_map() and the seg_vn memory segment driver (see "The seg_map Segment" on page 549). A process requests that a file be mapped into its address space. Once the mapping is established, the address space represented by the file appears as regular memory and the file system can perform I/O by simply accessing that memory.

Memory mapping of files hides the real work of reading and writing the file because the seg_vn memory segment driver quietly works with the file system to perform the I/Os without the need for process-initiated system calls. I/O is performed, in units of pages, upon reference to the pages mapped into the address space; reads are initiated by a memory access; writes are initiated as the VM system finds dirty pages in the mapped address space.

The system call mmap() calls the file system for the requested file with the vop_map() vnode method. In turn, the file system calls the address space map function for the current address space, and the mapping is created. The protection flags passed into the mmap() system call are reduced to the subset allowed by the file permissions. If mandatory locking is set for the file, then mmap() returns an error.

Once the file mapping is created in the process's address space, file pages are read when a fault occurs in the address space. A fault occurs the first time a memory address within the mapped segment is accessed because at this point, no physical page of memory is at that location. The memory management unit causes a hardware trap for that memory segment; the memory segment calls its fault function to handle the I/O for that address. The segvn_fault() routine handles a fault for a file mapping in a process address space and then calls the file system to read in the page for the faulted address, as shown below.

```
segvn_fault (hat, seg, addr, len, type, rw) {

        for ( page = all pages in region ) {

                advise = lookup_advise (page);  /* Look up madvise settings for page */
                if (advise == MADV_SEQUENTIAL)
                        free_all_pages_up_to (page);

                /* Segvn will read at most 64k ahead */
                if ( len > PVN_GETPAGE_SZ)
                        len = PVN_GETPAGE_SZ;

                vp = segvp (seg);
                vpoff = segoff (seg);

                /* Read 64k at a time if the next page is not in memory,
                 * else just a page
                 */
                if (hat_probe (addr+PAGESIZE)==TRUE)
                        len=PAGESIZE;

                /* Ask the file system for the next 64k of pages if the next*/
                VOP_GETPAGE(vp, vp_off, len,
                        &vpprot, plp, plsz, seg, addr + (vp_off - off), arw, cred)
        }
}
```

For each page fault, seg_vn reads in an 8-Kbyte page at the fault location. In addition, seg_vn initiates a read-ahead of the next eight pages at each 64-Kbyte boundary. Memory mapped read-ahead uses the file system cluster size (used by the read() and write() system calls) unless the segment is mapped MA_SHARED or memory advice MADV_RANDOM is set.

Recall that you can provide paging advice to the pages within a memory mapped segment by using the madvise system call. The madvise system call and (as in the example) the advise information are used to decide when to free behind as the file is read.

Modified pages remain unwritten to disk until the fsflush daemon passes over the page, at which point they will be written out to disk. You can also use the mem-cntl() system call to initiate a synchronous or asynchronous write of pages.

13.4.2 read() and write() System Calls

The vop_read() and vop_write() vnode methods implement reading and writing with the read() and write() system calls. As shown in Figure 13.5 on page 547, the seg_map segment driver maps a file into the kernel's address space during the read() and write() system calls. The seg_vn segment could be used to map the file into the kernel's address space; however, the seg_vn driver is a complex segment driver that deals with all of the process address space requirements (such as mapping protections, copy-on-write fault handling, shared memory, etc.), so a lighter-weight driver (seg_map) performs the mapping. The read and write file system calls require only a few basic mapping functions since they do not map files into a process's address space. Instead, they copy data to or from the process during a system call to a portion of the file that is mapped into the kernel's address space by seg_map. The lighter-weight seg_map driver enhances performance by virtue of a shorter code path and reduced locking complexities.

13.4.3 The seg_map Segment

The seg_map segment maintains mappings of pieces of files into the kernel address space and is used only by the file systems. Every time a read or write system call occurs, the seg_map segment driver locates or creates a virtual address space where the page of the file can be mapped. Then, the system call can copy the data to or from the user address space.

The seg_map segment provides a full set of segment driver interfaces (see "Memory Segments" on page 143); however, the file system directly uses a small subset of these interfaces without going through the generic segment interface. The subset handles the bulk of the work that is done by the seg_map segment for file read and write operations. The functions used by the file systems are shown in Table 13-8.

Table 13-8 seg_map Functions Used by the File Systems

Function Name	Description
segmap_getmap() segmap_getmapfault()	Retrieves or creates a mapping for a range of the file at the given offset and length.
segmap_release()	Releases the mapping for a given file at a given address.
segmap_pagecreate()	Creates new page(s) of memory and slots in the seg_map segment for a given file. Used for extending files or writing to holes during a write.
segmap_pageunlock()	Unlocks pages in the segment that was locked during segmap_pagecreate().

At any time, the seg_map segment has some portion of the total file system cache mapped into the kernel address space. The maximum size of the seg_map segment differs among hardware architectures, is often only a fraction of the total physical memory size, and contains only a small proportion of the total file system cache. Note that even though the size of the seg_map segment is fixed, the pages which it references can be stolen by the page scanner, and as a result, only a portion of the seg_map segment may be resident (especially on machines where the seg_map segment is close to the size of physical memory).

A single seg_map segment is created at boot time. The segment is sized according to a table of machine types (see Table 13-9) and is capped at the amount of free memory just after the kernel has booted. For example, if the machine is an Ultra-1 or sun4u architecture, the maximum size of the seg_map is 256 Mbytes. A 64-Mbyte machine booting the Solaris kernel will most likely end up with a seg_map segment about 50 Mbytes in size, as 50 Mbytes was the free memory when the system was being booted. A 512-Mbyte sun4u system will have a seg_map size of 256 Mbytes, since free memory will be much larger than 256 Mbytes while it is booting.

Table 13-9 Architecture-Specific Sizes of Solaris 7 seg_map Segment

Architecture	Systems	Maximum Size of seg_map
sun4c	SPARC 1, 2	4 Mbytes
sun4m	SPARC 5, 10, 20	16 Mbytes
sun4d	SPARC 1000,2000	32 Mbytes
sun4u	UltraSPARC	256 Mbytes

We can take a look at the seg_map segment on a running system by using adb
with the $seg macro, as shown below.

```
# adb -k /dev/ksyms /dev/mem
physmem 3b73

segkmap/J
segkmap:
segkmap:        3000022df50

3000022df50$<seg

3000022df50:    base            size            as
                2a750000000     7432000         104236e0
3000022df68:    next            prev            ops
                104234a0        3000022df88     segmap_ops
3000022df80:    data
                300001b1d68
```

We can see that on this system, the segkmap segment has been created at boot
as 0x7432000 bytes, or 121,839,616 bytes. This system was a 128-Mbyte Ultra-1,
and we can see that free memory was smaller than the 256-Mbyte maximum segment size for the sun4u architecture. Hence, the segment was created at whatever the size of free memory was at that point. Once segkmap is created, the
segment interfaces are called directly from the file system code during the read
and write operations.

The seg_map segment driver divides the segment into block-sized slots that
represent blocks in the files it maps. The seg_map block size for the Solaris kernel
is 8,192 bytes. A 128-Mbyte segkmap segment would, for example, be divided into
128-MB/8-KB slots, or 16,384 slots. The seg_map segment driver maintains a hash
list of its page mappings so that it can easily locate existing blocks. The list is
based on file and offsets. One list entry exists for each slot in the segkmap segment. The structure for each slot in a seg_map segment is defined in the
<vm/segmap.h> header file, shown below.

```
/*
 * Each smap struct represents a MAXBSIZE-sized mapping to the
 * <sm_vp, sm_off> given in the structure. The location of
 * the structure in the array gives the virtual address of the
 * mapping. Structure rearranged for 64-bit sm_off.
 */
struct  smap {
        struct  vnode   *sm_vp;             /* vnode pointer (if mapped) */

        /*
         * These next 3 entries can be coded as
         * ushort_t's if we are tight on memory.
         */
        struct  smap    *sm_hash;           /* hash pointer */
        struct  smap    *sm_next;           /* next pointer */
        struct  smap    *sm_prev;           /* previous pointer */
        u_offset_t      sm_off;             /* file offset for mapping */

        ushort_t        sm_bitmap;          /* bitmap for locked translations */
        ushort_t        sm_refcnt;          /* reference count for uses */
};

struct  smfree {
        struct  smap    *sm_free;           /* free list array pointer */
                kmutex_t        sm_mtx;         /* protects smap data of this color */
        kcondvar_t      sm_free_cv;
        ushort_t        sm_want;            /* someone wants a slot of this color */
};
```

Header File   <vm/seg_map.h>

The smap structures are:

- **sm_vp** — The file (vnode) this slot represents (if slot not empty)
- **sm_hash, sm_next, sm_prev** — Hash list reference pointers
- **sm_off** — The file (vnode) offset for a block-sized chunk in this slot in the file
- **sm_bitmap** — Bitmap to maintain translation locking
- **sm_refcnt** — The number of references to this mapping caused by concurrent reads

The important fields in the smap structure are the file and offset fields, sm_vp and sm_off. These fields identify which page of a file is represented by each slot in the segment.

We can observe the seg_map slot activity with the kstat statistics that are collected for the seg_map segment driver. These statistics are visible with the netstat command, as shown below.

```
# netstat -k segmap
segmap:
fault 8366623 faulta 0 getmap 16109564 get_use 11723 get_reclaim 15257790 get_reuse
825178
get_unused 0 get_nofree 0 rel_async 710244 rel_write 749677 rel_free 16370
rel_abort 0 rel_dontneed 709733 release 15343517 pagecreate 1009281
```

Table 13-10 describes the `segmap` statistics.

Table 13-10 Statistics from the `seg_map` Segment Driver

Field Name	Description
fault	The number of times `segmap_fault` was called, usually as a result of a read or write system call.
faulta	The number of times the `segmap_faulta` function was called. It is called to initiate asynchronous paged I/O on a file.
getmap	The number of times the `segmap_getmap` function was called. It is called by the read and write system calls each time a read or write call is started. It sets up a slot in the `seg_map` segment for the requested range on the file.
get_use	The number of times `getmap` found an empty slot in the segment and used it.
get_reclaim	The number of times `getmap` found a valid mapping for the file and offset already in the `seg_map` segment.
get_reuse	The number of times `getmap` deleted the mapping in a nonempty slot and created a new mapping for the file and offset requested.
get_unused	Not used—always zero.
get_nofree	The number of times a request for a slot was made and none was available on the internal free list of slots. This number is usually zero because each slot is put on the free list when `release` is called at the end of each I/O. Hence, ample free slots are usually available.
rel_async	The slot was released with a delayed I/O on it.
rel_write	The slot was released as a result of a write system call.
rel_free	The slot was released, and the VM system was told that the page may be needed again but to free it and retain its file/offset information. These pages are placed on the cache list tail so that they are not the first to be reused.
rel_abort	The slot was released and asked to be removed from the `seg_map` segment as a result of a failed aborted write.
rel_dontneed	The slot was released, and the VM system was told to free the page because it won't be needed again. These pages are placed on the cache list head so they will be reused first.
released	The slot was released and the release was not affected by `rel_abort`, `rel_async`, or `rel_write`.
pagecreate	Pages created in the `segmap_pagecreate` function.

Our example segmap statistics show us that 15,257,790 times a slot was reclaimed out of a total 16,109,564 getmap calls, a 95% slot reuse with the correct file and offset, or a 95% cache hit ratio for the file system pages in segmap. Note that the actual page-to-cache hit ratio may be higher because even if we miss in segmap, we could still have the pages in the page cache and only need to reload the address translations for the page. A lower segmap hit ratio and high page-to-cache hit ratio is typical of large memory machines, in which segmap is limited to only 256 megabytes of potential gigabytes of physical memory.

Writing is a similar process. Again, segmap_getmap is called to retrieve or create a mapping for the file and offset, the I/O is done, and the segmap slot is released. An additional step is involved if the file is being extended or a new page is being created within a hole of a file. This additional step calls the segmap_pagecreate function to create and lock the new pages, then calls segmap_pageunlock() to unlock the pages that were locked during the page_create.

The segmap cache can grow and shrink as pages are paged in and out and as pages are stolen by the page scanner, but the maximum size of the segmap cache is capped at an architecture-specific limit.

13.5 Path-Name Management

All but a few of the vnode methods operate on vnode pointers, rather than on path names or file descriptors. Before calling file system vnode methods, the vnode framework first converts path names and file descriptors into vnode references. File descriptors may be directly translated into vnodes for the files they referenced, whereas path names must be converted into vnodes by a lookup of the path-name components and a reference to the underlying file. The file-system-independent lookuppn() function converts path names to vnodes. An additional wrapper, lookupname(), converts path names from user-mode system calls.

13.5.1 The lookupname() and lookupppn() Methods

Given a path name, the lookupppn() method attempts to return a pointer to the vnode the path represents. If the file is already opened, then a new reference to the file is established, and if not, the file is first opened. The lookuppn() function decomposes the components of the path name, separating them by "/" and ".", and calls the file-system-specific vop_lookup() method for each component of the path name.

If the path name begins with a "/", path-name traversal starts at the user's root directory. Otherwise, it starts at the vnode pointed to by the user's current directory. lookuppn() traverses the path one component at a time, using the vop_lookup() vnode method. vop_lookup() takes a directory vnode and a component as arguments and returns a vnode representing that component.

If a directory vnode has v_vfsmountedhere set, then it is a mount point. If lookuppn() encounters a mount point while going down the file system tree, then it follows the vnode's v_vfsmountedhere pointer to the mounted file system and calls the vfs_root() method to obtain the root vnode for the file system. Path-name traversal then continues from this point.

If lookuppn() encounters a root vnode (VROOT flag in v_flag set) when following "..", then lookuppn() follows the vfs_vnodecovered pointer in the vnode's associated vfs to obtain the covered vnode.

If lookuppn() encounters a symbolic link, then it calls the vn_readlink() vnode method to obtain the symbolic link. If the symbolic link begins with a "/", the path name traversal is restarted from the root directory; otherwise, the traversal continues from the last directory. The caller of lookuppn() specifies whether the last component of the path name is to be followed if it is a symbolic link.

This procedure continues until the path name is exhausted or an error occurs. When lookuppn() completes, it returns a vnode representing the desired file.

13.5.2 The vop_lookup() Method

The vop_lookup() method searches a directory for a path-name component matching the supplied path name. The vop_lookup() method accepts a directory vnode and a string path-name component as an argument and returns a vnode pointer to the vnode representing the file. If the file cannot be located, then ENOENT is returned. Many regular file systems will first check the directory name lookup cache, and if an entry is found there, the entry is returned. If the entry is not found in the directory name cache, then a real lookup of the file is performed.

13.5.3 The vop_readdir() Method

The vop_readdir() method reads chunks of the directory into a uio structure. Each chunk can contain as many entries as will fit within the size supplied by the uio structure. The uio_resid structure member shows the size of the getdents request in bytes, which is divided by the size of the directory entry made by the vop_readdir() method to calculate how many directory entries to return.

Directories are read from disk with the buffered kernel file functions fbread and fbwrite. These functions, described in Table 13-11, are provided as part of the generic file system infrastructure.

Table 13-11 Functions for Cached Access to Files from Within the Kernel

Function Name	Description
fbread()	Returns a pointer to locked kernel virtual address for the given <vp, off> for len bytes. The read may not cross a boundary of MAXBSIZE (8192) bytes.
fbzero()	Similar to fbread(), but calls segmap_pagecreate(), not segmap_fault(), so that SOFTLOCK can create the pages without using VOP_GETPAGE(). Then, fbzero() zeroes up to the length rounded to a page boundary.
fbwrite()	Direct write.
fbwritei()	Writes directly and invalidates pages.
fbdwrite()	Delayed write.
fbrelse()	Releases fbp.
fbrelsei()	Releases fbp and invalidates pages.

13.5.4 Path-Name Traversal Functions

Several path-name manipulation functions assist with decomposition of path names. The path-name functions use a path-name structure, shown below, to pass around path-name components.

```
/*
 * Path-name structure.
 * System calls that operate on path names gather the path name
 * from the system call into this structure and reduce it by
 * peeling off translated components. If a symbolic link is
 * encountered, the new path name to be translated is also
 * assembled in this structure.
 *
 * By convention pn_buf is not changed once it's been set to point
 * to the underlying storage; routines which manipulate the path name
 * do so by changing pn_path and pn_pathlen. pn_pathlen is redundant
 * since the path name is null-terminated but is provided to make
 * some computations faster.
 */
typedef struct pathname {
        char    *pn_buf;                /* underlying storage */
        char    *pn_path;               /* remaining pathname */
        size_t  pn_pathlen;             /* remaining length */
        size_t  pn_bufsize;             /* total size of pn_buf */
} pathname_t;
```

Header File   <sys/pathname.h>

The path-name functions are shown in Table 13-12.

Table 13-12 Path-Name Traversal Functions from `<sys/pathname.h>`

Method	Description
`pn_alloc()`	Allocates a new path-name buffer.
`pn_get()`	Copies path-name string from user and mounts arguments into a struct path name.
`pn_set()`	Sets a path name to the supplied string.
`pn_insert()`	Combines two path names.
`pn_getsymlink()`	Follows a symbolic link for a path name.
`pn_getcomponent()`	Extracts the next delimited path-name component.
`pn_setlast()`	Appends a component to a path name.
`pn_skipslash()`	Skips over consecutive slashes in the path name.
`pn_fixslash()`	Eliminates any trailing slashes in the path name.
`pn_free()`	Frees a `struct` path name.

13.5.5 The Directory Name Lookup Cache (DNLC)

The directory name lookup cache is based on BSD 4.2 code. It was ported to Solaris 2.0 and threaded and has undergone some significant revisions. Most of the enhancements to the DNLC have been performance and threading, but a few visible changes are noteworthy. Table 13-13 summarizes the important changes to the DNLC.

Table 13-13 Solaris DNLC Changes

Year	OS Rev	Comment
1984	BSD 4.2	14-character name maximum
1990	SunOS 2.0	31-character name maximum
1994	SunOS 5.4	Performance (new locking/search algorithm)
1998	SunOS 5.7	Variable name length

13.5.5.1 DNLC Operation

Each time we open a file, we call the `open()` system call with a path name. That path name must be translated to a `vnode` by the process of reading the directory and finding the corresponding name that matches the requested name. No place in the `vnode` stores the name of the file; so, to prevent us from having to reread the directory every time we translate the path name, we cache pathname-to-`vnode` mappings in the directory name lookup cache. The cache is managed as an LRU cache, so that most frequently used directory entries are kept in the cache. The early-style DNLC in Solaris uses a fixed name length in the cache entries. Hence, if a file name is opened with a name larger than can fit, it will not be entered into the DNLC. The old-style (pre-SunOS 5.4) DNLC is shown in Figure 13.6.

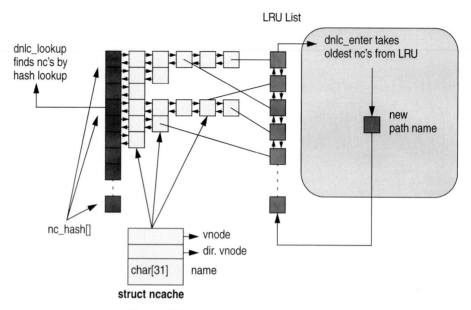

Figure 13.6 Solaris 2.3 Name Cache

The number of entries in the DNLC is controlled by the ncsize parameter, which is initialized to 4 * (max_nprocs + maxusers) + 320 at system boot.

Most of the DNLC work is done with two functions: dnlc_enter() and dnlc_lookup(). When a file system wants to look up the name of a file, it first checks the DNLC with the dnlc_lookup() function, which queries the DNLC for an entry that matches the specified file name and directory vnode. If no entry is found, dnlc_lookup fails and the file system reads the directory from disk. When the file name is found, it is entered into the DNLC with the dnlc_enter() function. The DNLC stores entries on a hashed list (nc_hash[]) by file name and directory vnode pointer. Once the correct nc_hash chain is identified, the chain is searched linearly until the correct entry is found.

The original BSD DNLC had 8 nc_hash entries, which was increased to 64 in SunOS 4.x. Solaris 2.0 sized the nc_hash list at boot, attempting to make the average length of each chain no more than 4 entries. It used the total DNLC size, ncsize, divided by the average length to establish the number of nc_hash entries. Solaris 2.3 had the average length of the chain dropped to 2 in an attempt to increase DNLC performance; however, other problems, related to the LRU list locking and described below, adversely affected performance.

Each entry in the DNLC is also linked to an LRU list, in order of last use. When a new entry is added into the DNLC, the algorithm replaces the oldest entry from the LRU list with the new file name and directory vnode. Each time a lookup is done, the DNLC also takes the entry from the LRU and places it at the end of the

list so that it won't be reused immediately. The DNLC uses the LRU list to attempt
to keep most-used references in the cache. Although the DNLC list had been made
short, the LRU list still caused contention because it required that a single lock be
held around the entire chain.

The old DNLC structure is shown below. Note that the name field is statically
sized at 31 characters.

```
#define NC_NAMLEN       31        /* maximum name segment length we bother with */

struct ncache {
        struct ncache *hash_next;        /* hash chain, MUST BE FIRST */
        struct ncache *hash_prev;
        struct ncache *lru_next;         /* LRU chain */
        struct ncache *lru_prev;
        struct vnode *vp;                /* vnode the name refers to */
        struct vnode *dp;                /* vnode of parent of name */
        char namlen;                     /* length of name */
        char name[NC_NAMLEN];            /* segment name */
        struct cred *cred;               /* credentials */
        int hash;                        /* hash signature */
};
```

Header File   <sys/dnlc.h>

13.5.5.2 The New Solaris DLNC Algorithm

In Solaris 2.4, replacement of the SVR4 DNLC algorithm yielded a significant
improvement in scalability. The Solaris 2.4 DNLC algorithm removed LRU list
lock contention by eliminating the LRU list completely. In addition, the list now
takes into account the number of references to a vnode and whether the vnode
has any pages in the page cache. This design allows the DNLC to cache the most
relevant vnodes, rather than just the most frequently looked-up vnodes.

```
struct ncache {
        struct ncache *hash_next;        /* hash chain, MUST BE FIRST */
        struct ncache *hash_prev;
        struct ncache *next_free;        /* freelist chain */
        struct vnode *vp;                /* vnode the name refers to */
        struct vnode *dp;                /* vnode of parent of name */
        struct cred *cred;               /* credentials */
        char *name;                      /* segment name */
        int namlen;                      /* length of name */
        int hash;                        /* hash signature */
};
```

Header File   <sys/dnlc.h>

The lookup algorithm uses a rotor pointing to a hash chain, which switches
chains for each invocation of dnlc_enter() that needs a new entry. The algorithm starts at the end of the chain and takes the first entry that has a vnode reference count of 1 or no pages in the page cache. In addition, during lookup, entries
are moved to the front of the chain so that each chain is sorted in LRU order. Figure 13.7 illustrates the Solaris 2.4 DNLC.

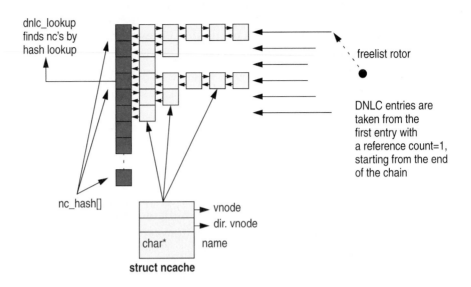

dnlc_lookup
finds nc's by
hash lookup

freelist rotor

DNLC entries are
taken from the
first entry with
a reference count=1,
starting from the end
of the chain

nc_hash[]

vnode
dir. vnode

char*   name

struct ncache

Figure 13.7 Solaris 2.4 DNLC

The Solaris 7 DNLC was enhanced to use the kernel memory allocator to allocate a
variable length string for the name; this change removed the 31-character limit. In
the Solaris 7 DNLC structure, shown below, note that the name field has changed
from a static structure to a pointer.

13.5.5.3 DNLC Support Functions

Table 13-14 lists the DNLC support functions.

Table 13-14 Solaris 7 DNLC Functions from `sys/dnlc.h`

Function	Description
`dnlc_lookup()`	Locates an ncache entry that matches the supplied name and directory vnode pointer. Returns a pointer to the vnode for that entry or returns NULL.
`dnlc_update()`	Enters a new ncache entry into the DNLC for the given name and directory vnode pointer. If an entry already exists for the name and directory pointer but the vnode is different, then the entry is overwritten. Otherwise, the function returns with no action.
`dnlc_enter()`	Enters a new ncache entry into the DNLC for the given name and directory vnode pointer. If an entry already exists for the name and directory pointer, the function returns with no action.

Table 13-14 Solaris 7 DNLC Functions from `sys/dnlc.h` (Continued)

Function	Description
`dnlc_remove()`	Removes the entry matching the supplied name and directory `vnode` pointer.
`dnlc_purge()`	Called by the `vfs` framework when an `umountall()` is called.
`dnlc_purge_vp()`	Purges all entries matching the `vnode` supplied.

13.5.6 File System Modules

A file system is implemented as an instance of the `vfs` and `vnode` objects in a self-contained, loadable kernel module. The operating system provides the infrastructure for mounting and interfacing with the file system, and each file system implementation can abstract the file system object methods in different ways. The modules are loaded from the file system directory in `/kernel/fs` during the first mount operation. File systems provide module initialization functions; a typical file system initialization section declares a module constructor and destructor, as described in "Kernel Module Loading and Linking" on page 116.

13.5.7 Mounting and Unmounting

When a file system is first mounted, the file system framework attempts to autoload the file system from the `/kernel/fs` directory. The autoload procedure calls the initialization routines in the file system; at that point, the file system can register itself in the file system switch table. The file system is required to fill in the `vfssw` structure during the initialization function. Once this phase is completed, the file system is available for mount requests and the mount method of the file system is called.

When the mount method is called for the file system, a `vfs` object for the instance of the mounted file system is created; then, the mount method must fill in the `vfs` structures. Typically, the root `vnode` of the file system is either created or opened at this time. The following example shows a simple file system and its initialization functions.

```
extern struct mod_ops mod_fsops;
static struct modlfs modlfs = {
        &mod_fsops,
        "vnode file pseudo file system",
        &vfw
};

static struct modlinkage modlinkage = {
        MODREV_1,
        &modlfs,
        NULL
};

int
_init(void)
{
        int     error;

        mutex_init(&vnfslock, NULL, MUTEX_DEFAULT, NULL);
        rw_init(&vnfsnodes_lock, NULL, RW_DEFAULT, NULL);
        error = mod_install(&modlinkage);
        if (error) {
                mutex_destroy(&vnfslock);
                rw_destroy(&vnfsnodes_lock);
        }
        myfs_init_otherstuff();
        return (error);
}

int
_fini(void)
{
        int     error;

        vnfs_vnlist_destroy();
        error = mod_remove(&modlinkage);
        if (error)
                return (error);
        mutex_destroy(&vnfslock);
        rw_destroy(&vnfsnodes_lock);
        return (0);
}

int
_info(struct modinfo *modinfop)
{
        return (mod_info(&modlinkage, modinfop));
}

static struct vfssw vfw = {
        "myfs",
        myfsinit,
        &myfs_vfsops,
        0
};

static int
myfsinit(struct vfssw *vswp, int fstype)
{
        vswp->vsw_vfsops = &myfs_vfsops;
        myfstype = fstype;
        (void) myfs_init();
        return (0);
}
```

13.6 The File System Flush Daemon

The `fsflush` process writes modified pages to disk at regular intervals. The `fsflush` process scans through physical memory looking for dirty pages. When it finds one, it initiates a `write` (or `putpage`) operation on that page.

The `fsflush` process is launched by default every 5 seconds and looks for pages that have been modified (the modified bit is set in the `page` structure) more than 30 seconds ago. If a page has been modified, then a page-out is scheduled for that page, but without the free flag so the page remains in memory. The `fsflush` daemon flushes both data pages and inodes by default. Table 13-15 describes the parameters that affect the behavior of `fsflush`.

Table 13-15 Parameters That Affect `fsflush`

Parameter	Description	Min	Solaris 2.7 Default
`tune_t_fsflushr`	The number of seconds between `fsflush` scans.	1	5
`autoup`	Pages older than `autoup` in seconds are written to disk.	1	30
`doiflush`	By default, `fsflush` flushes both inode and data pages. Set to `0` to suppress inode updates.	0	1
`dopageflush`	Set to `0` to suppress page flushes.	0	1

14

THE UNIX FILE SYSTEM

T he Unix File System (UFS) is the general-purpose, disk-based file system that is shipped with Solaris. It has been the standard disk-based file system since early versions of SunOS 4.x. Over the life of Solaris, UFS has undergone extensive changes to keep pace with the required application performance, security, and reliability constraints.

14.1 UFS Development History

The original version of UFS is derived from the Berkeley Fast File System (FFS) work from BSD Unix, architected by Kirk McKusick and Bill Joy in the late 1980s. The Berkeley FFS was the second major file system available for Unix and was a leap forward from the original System V file system. The System V file system was lightweight and simple but had significant shortcomings: poor performance, unreliability, and lack of functionality.

During the development of SunOS 2.0, a file-system-independent interface was introduced to provide support for concurrent, different file systems within an operating system instance. This interface, known today as the vnode/vfs interface, is the mechanism all file systems use to interface with the file-related system calls. (The vnode/vfs architecture is discussed further in "The vnode" on page 533.) At that time, UFS was modified so that it could be used within the vnode/vfs framework. Since then, UFS has been the focus of much of the file system development effort in Solaris.

A second major overhaul for UFS was at the time of SunOS 4.0, when the virtual memory system was redeveloped to use the vnode as the core of virtual memory operations. The new VM system implemented the concept of virtual file caching—a departure from the traditional physical file cache (known as the "buffer cache" in previous versions of UNIX). The old buffer cache was layered under the file systems and cached the physical blocks from the file system to the storage device. The new model is layered above the file systems and allows the VM system to act as a cache for files rather than blocks. The VM system caches page-sized pieces of files, where the file and a particular offset are cached as pages of memory. From this point forward, the buffer cache was used only for file system metadata, and the VM system implements file system caching. The new VM system affected the file systems in many ways and required significant changes to the vnode interface. At that point, UFS was substantially modified to provide support for the new vnode and VM interfaces.

The third major change to UFS was in Solaris 2.4 in 1994, which saw the introduction of file system metadata logging to provide better reliability and faster reboot times after a system crash or outage. The first versions of logging were introduced in the unbundled Online: Disk Suite 3.0, the precursor to Solstice Disk Suite (SDS). Solaris 7 saw the integration of logging into the base Solaris UFS.

Table 14-1 summarizes the major UFS development milestones.

Table 14-1 Unix File System Evolution

Year	SunOS Version	Annotations
1984	SunOS 1.0	FFS from 4.2 BSD.
1985	SunOS 2.0	UFS rearchitected to support vnodes/vfs.
1988	SunOS 4.0	UFS integrated with new VM virtual file cache.
1991	SunOS 4.1	I/O clustering added to allow extentlike performance.
1992	SunOS 4.1	1TB file system and ability to grow UFS file systems with Online: Disk Suite 1.0.
1992	Solaris 2.0	1TB file system support included in base Solaris.
1994	Solaris 2.4	Metadata logging option with Online: DiskSuite 3.0.
1995	Solaris 2.6	Large file support allows 1TB files. Direct I/O uncached access added.
1998	Solaris 7	Metadata logging integrated into base Solaris UFS.

14.2 UFS On-Disk Format

The on-disk format of the UFS file system has largely remained unchanged with the introduction of new features, maintaining forward compatibility across all releases. This allows Solaris to be upgraded without the need to back up and restore file systems.

14.2.1 UFS Inodes

Information about which data blocks relate to each file are stored in a special file index node: the inode. The inode contains all of the information about the file, except for the file name, which is stored in the directory. Inode information includes:

- File type (regular, special, fifo, link, etc.)
- Owner of file (`uid`)
- Group of file (`gid`)
- File size
- Attributes (read, execute, modify)
- Timestamps (last modified, etc.)
- Number of references to the file (links)
- Arrays of disk block addresses that contain the file's data

14.2.2 UFS Directories

The file-name information and hierarchy information that constitute the directory structure of UFS are stored in *directories*. Each directory stores a list of file names and the inode number for each file; this information allows the directory structure to relate file names to real disk files.

The directory itself is stored in a file as a series of chunks, which are groups of the directory entries. Each directory entry in the chunk contains the following information (see Figure 14.1):

- Inode number
- Size of the file-name entry
- Length of the directory entry
- File-name string (null terminated)

Earlier file systems like the System V file system had a fixed directory record length, which meant that a lot of space would be wasted if provision was made for long file names. In the UFS, each directory entry can be of variable length, thus

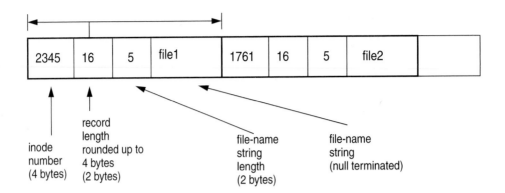

Figure 14.1 UFS Directory Entry Format

providing a mechanism for long file names without wasting a lot of space. UFS file names can be up to 255 characters long.

The group of directory chunks that constitute a directory is stored as a special type of file. The notion of a directory as a type of file allows UFS to implement a hierarchical directory structure: directories can contain files which are directories. For example, the root directory / has a name "/" and an inode number, 2, which holds a chunk of directory entries holding a number of files and directories. One of these directory entries, named etc, is another directory containing more files and directories. For traversal up and down the file system, the chdir system call opens the directory file in question and then sets the current working directory to point to the new directory file. Figure 14.2 illustrates the directory hierarchy.

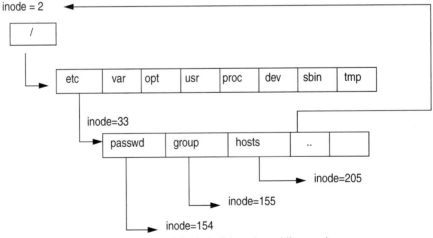

Figure 14.2 Unix Directory Hierarchy

Each directory contains two special files. The file named "." is a link to the directory itself; the file named ".." is a link to the parent directory. Thus, a change of directory to .. leads to the parent directory.

14.2.3 UFS Hard Links

There is one inode for each file on disk; however, with hard links, each file can have multiple file names. With hard links, file names in multiple directories point to the same on-disk inode. The inode reference count field reflects the number of hard links to the inode. Figure 14.3 illustrates inode 1423 describing a file; two separate directory entries with different names both point to the same inode number. Note that the reference count, refcnt, has been incremented to 2.

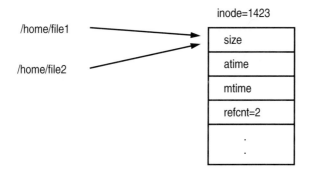

Figure 14.3 UFS Links

14.2.4 UFS Layout

To avoid excessive seeking between data and inode information, UFS tries to place inodes in close proximity to the data blocks for each file. The inodes are grouped at evenly spaced points across the file system in areas known as cylinder groups. Information about the location of each cylinder group is stored in the superblock, which is at the start of the file system. The on-disk layout of the UFS file system is shown in Figure 14.4.

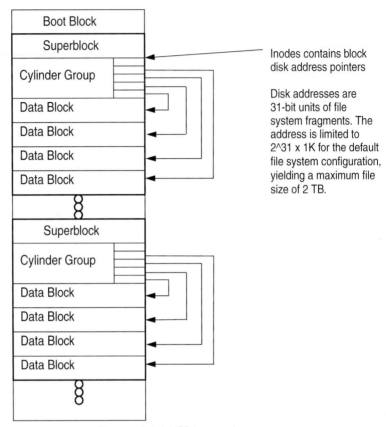

Figure 14.4 UFS Layout

14.2.4.1 The Boot Block

At the start of the file system is the boot block. This is a spare sector reserved for the boot program when UFS is used as a root file system. At boot time, the boot firmware loads the first sector from the boot device and then starts executing code residing in that block. The firmware boot is file system independent, which means the boot firmware has no knowledge about the file system. We rely on code in the file system boot block to do the mount of the root file system. When the system starts, the UFS boot block is loaded and executed, which, in turn, mounts the UFS root file system. The boot program then passes control to a larger kernel loader, in `/platform/sun4[mud]/ufsboot`, to load the Unix kernel.

The boot program is loaded onto the first sector of the file system at install time with the `installboot(1M)` command. The 512-byte install boot image resides in `/usr/platform/sun4[mud]/lib/fs/ufs/bootblk` in the platform-dependent directories.

14.2.4.2 The Superblock

Immediately after the boot block is the superblock. The superblock contains the information about the geometry and layout of the file system and is critical to the file system state. As a safety precaution, the superblock is replicated across the file system with each cylinder group so that the file system is not crippled if the superblock becomes corrupted. The superblock contains a variety of information, including the location of each cylinder group and a summary list of available free blocks. The major information in the superblock that identifies the file system geometry is shown below.

- `fs_sblkno` — Address of superblock in file system; defaults to block number 16
- `fs_cblkno` — Offset of the first cylinder block in the file system
- `fs_iblkno` — Offset of the first inode blocks in the file system
- `fs_dblkno` — Offset of the first data blocks after the first cylinder group
- `fs_cgoffset` — Cylinder group offset in the cylinder
- `fs_time` — Last time written
- `fs_size` — Number of blocks in the file system
- `fs_dsize` — Number of data blocks the in file system
- `fs_ncg` — Number of cylinder groups
- `fs_bsize` —Size of basic blocks in the file system
- `fs_fsize` — Size of fragmented blocks in the file system
- `fs_frag` — Number of fragments in a block in the file system
- `fs_magic` — A magic number to validate the superblock; the number is Bill Joy's birthday.

The file system configuration parameters also reside in the super block. The file system parameters include some of the following, which are configured at the time the file system is constructed. You can tune the parameters later with the `tunefs` command.

- `fs_minfree` — Minimum percentage of free blocks
- `fs_rotdelay` — Number of milliseconds of rotational delay between sequential blocks. The rotational delay was used to implement block interleaving when the operating system could not keep up with reading contiguous blocks. Since this is no longer an issue, `fs_rotdelay` defaults to zero.
- `fs_rps` — Disk revolutions per second
- `fs_maxcontig` — Maximum number of contiguous blocks, used to control the number of read-ahead blocks
- `fs_maxbpg` — Maximum number of data blocks per cylinder group
- `fs_optim` —Optimization preference, space, or time

14.2.5 Disk Block Location

The disk blocks for a file are represented by disk address pointers in the inode for the file. Each inode has space for 12 disk block addresses, which, when used on their own, limit the maximum size of a file to 12 * 8K = 96K. To allow for larger files, indirect blocks provide more space for disk address blocks. With one level of indirection, one of the disk addresses points to a file system block containing further disk addresses, greatly increasing the number of data blocks per file. A second level of indirection can also be used, allowing even more data blocks. The inode contains a slot for triple indirect pointers, although triple indirection is currently not implemented within UFS. Figure 14.5 illustrates the inode format.

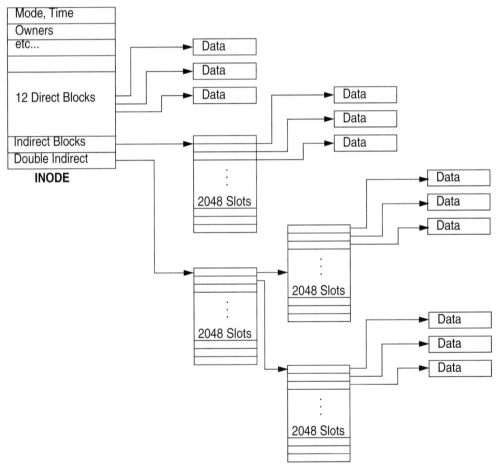

Figure 14.5 The UFS inode Format

UFS allocates space, known as fragments, in file system blocks and subblocks. Assuming 8-Kbyte file system blocks:

- The first 12 direct blocks allow 12 blocks, or 98,304 bytes
- The first level of indirection allows a full file system block of disk addresses, which means that an 8-Kbyte block can hold 2,048 32-bit disk addresses; 12 + 2048 blocks, or $(12 + 2048) \times 8 = 1{,}687{,}520$ bytes.
- The second level of indirection (double indirect) allows $12 + 2048 + (2048 \times 2048) \times 8\text{KB} = 34{,}376{,}613{,}888$ bytes.

There is, however, a limit to the maximum offset in each disk address, which is expressed as a number of file system fragments; using the default fragments size of 1 Kbyte, the maximum offset for each block is $2^{31} \times 1\text{KB} = 2$ terabytes.

14.2.6 UFS Block Allocation

UFS uses block sizes of 4 and 8 Kbytes, which provides significantly higher performance than the 512-byte blocks used in the System V file system. The downside of larger blocks was that when partially allocated blocks occurred, several kilobytes of disk space for each partly filled file system block were wasted. To overcome this disadvantage, UFS uses the notion of file system fragments. Fragments allow a single block to be broken up into 2, 4, or 8 fragments when necessary.

UFS block allocation tries to prevent excessive disk seeking by attempting to co-locate inodes within a directory and by attempting to co-locate a file's inode and its data blocks. Where possible, all of the inodes in a directory are allocated in the same cylinder group. This scheme helps reduce disk seeking when directories are traversed; for example, executing a simple `ls -l` of a directory will access all of the inodes in that directory. If all the inodes reside in the same cylinder group, most of the data will be cached after the first few files are accessed. A directory will be placed in a cylinder group different from that of its parent.

Blocks are allocated to a file sequentially, starting with the first 96 Kbytes (the first 12 direct blocks), skipping to the next cylinder group and allocating blocks up to the limit set by the file system parameter `maxbpg`, maximum-blocks-per-cylinder-group. After that, blocks are allocated from the next available cylinder group.

By default, on a file system greater than 1 Gbyte, the algorithm allocates 96 Kbytes in the first cylinder group, 16 Mbytes in the next available cylinder group, 16 Mbytes from the next, and so on. The maximum cylinder group size is 54 Mbytes, and the allocation algorithm only allows one-third of that space to be allocated to each section of a single file when it is extended. The `maxbpg` parameter is set to 2,048 8-Kbyte blocks by default at the time the file system is created; it is also tunable but can only be tuned downward, since the maximum cylinder group size is 16-Mybte allocation per cylinder group.

Selection of a new cylinder group for the next segment of a file is governed by a rotor and free-space algorithm. A per-file-system allocation rotor points to one of the cylinder groups; each time new disk space is allocated, it starts with the cylinder group pointed to by the rotor. If the cylinder group has less than average free space, then it is skipped and the next cylinder group is tried. This algorithm makes the file system attempt to balance the allocation across the cylinder groups.

14.2.7 UFS Allocation and Parameters

Figure 14.6 shows the default allocation that is used if a file is created on a large UFS. The first 96 Kbytes of file 1 are allocated from the first cylinder group. Then, allocation skips to the second cylinder group and another 16 Mbytes of file 1 are allocated, and so on. When another file is created, we can see that it consumes the holes in the allocated blocks alongside file 1. There is room for a third file to do the same.

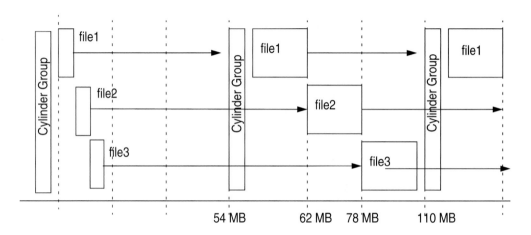

Figure 14.6 Default File Allocation in 16-Mbyte Groups

The actual on-disk layout will not be quite as simple as the example shown but does reflect the allocation policies discussed. We can use an add-on tool, `filestat`, to view the on-disk layout of a file, as shown below.

```
# /usr/local/bin/filestat testfile
Inodes per cyl group:   128
Inodes per block:       64
Cylinder Group no:      0
Cylinder Group blk:     64
File System Block Size: 8192
Block Size:             512
Number of 512b Blocks:  262288

Start Block     End Block    Length (512 byte Blocks)
-----------     -----------  ------------------------
       144 -> 335            192
       400 -> 33167          32768
    110800 -> 143567         32768
    221264 -> 221343         80
    221216 -> 221263         48
    221456 -> 254095         32640
    331856 -> 331999         144
    331808 -> 331855         48
    332112 -> 364687         32576
    442448 -> 442655         208
    442400 -> 442447         48
    442768 -> 475279         32512
```

The `filestat` output shows that the first segment of the file occupies 192 (512-byte) blocks, followed by the next 16 Mbytes, which start in a different cylinder group. This particular file system was not empty when the file was created, which is why the next cylinder group chosen is a long way from the first.

We can observe the file system parameters of an existing file system with the `fstyp` command. The `fstyp` command simply dumps the superblock information for the file, revealing all of the cylinder group and allocation information. The following example shows the output for a 4-Gbyte file system with default parameters. We can see that the file system has 8,247,421 blocks and has 167 cylinder groups spaced evenly at 6,272 (51-Mbyte) intervals. The maximum blocks to allocate for each group is set to the default of 2,048 8-Kbyte, 16 Mbytes.

```
# fstyp -v /dev/vx/dsk/homevol |more
ufs
magic    11954     format  dynamic  time     Sat Mar  6 18:19:59 1999
sblkno   16        cblkno  24       iblkno   32       dblkno   800
sbsize   2048      cgsize  8192     cgoffset 32       cgmask   0xffffffe0
ncg      167       size    8378368  blocks   8247421
bsize    8192      shift   13       mask     0xffffe000
fsize    1024      shift   10       mask     0xfffffc00
frag     8         shift   3        fsbtodb  1
minfree  1%        maxbpg  2048     optim    time
maxcontig 32       rotdelay 0ms     rps      120
csaddr   800       cssize  3072     shift    9        mask     0xfffffe00
ntrak    32        nsect   64       spc      2048     ncyl     8182
cpg      49        bpg     6272     fpg      50176    ipg      6144
nindir   2048      inopb   64       nspf     2
nbfree   176719    ndir    10241    nifree   956753   nffree   21495
cgrotor  152       fmod    0        ronly    0        logbno   0
```

The UFS-specific version of the fstyp command dumps the superblock of a UFS file system, as shown below.

```
# fstyp -v /dev/vx/dsk/homevol |more
ufs
magic     11954    format  dynamic  time      Sat Mar  6 18:19:59 1999
sblkno    16       cblkno  24       iblkno  32      dblkno  800
sbsize    2048     cgsize  8192     cgoffset 32     cgmask  0xffffffe0
ncg       167      size    8378368  blocks  8247421
bsize     8192     shift   13       mask    0xffffe000
fsize     1024     shift   10       mask    0xffffc00
frag      8        shift   3        fsbtodb 1
minfree   1%       maxbpg  2048     optim   time
maxcontig 32       rotdelay 0ms     rps     120
csaddr    800      cssize  3072     shift   9        mask    0xffffffe00
ntrak     32       nsect   64       spc     2048     ncyl    8182
cpg       49       bpg     6272     fpg     50176    ipg     6144
nindir    2048     inopb   64       nspf    2
nbfree    176719   ndir    10241    nifree  956753   nffree  21495
cgrotor   152      fmod    0        ronly   0        logbno  0
fs_reclaim is not set
file system state is valid, fsclean is 0
blocks available in each rotational position
cylinder number 0:
   position 0:       0      4      8     12     16     20     24     28     32     36     40     44
                    48     52     56     60     64     68     72     76     80     84     88     92
                    96    100    104    108    112    116    120    124
   position 2:        1      5      9     13     17     21     25     29     33     37     41     45
                    49     53     57     61     65     69     73     77     81     85     89     93
                    97    101    105    109    113    117    121    125
   position 4:        2      6     10     14     18     22     26     30     34     38     42     46
                    50     54     58     62     66     70     74     78     82     86     90     94
                    98    102    106    110    114    118    122    126
   position 6:        3      7     11     15     19     23     27     31     35     39     43     47
                    51     55     59     63     67     71     75     79     83     87     91     95
                    99    103    107    111    115    119    123    127
cs[].cs_(nbfree,ndir,nifree,nffree):
      (23,26,5708,102) (142,26,5724,244) (87,20,5725,132) (390,69,5737,80)
      (72,87,5815,148) (3,87,5761,110) (267,87,5784,4) (0,66,5434,4)
      (217,46,5606,94) (537,87,5789,70) (0,87,5901,68) (0,87,5752,20)
                      .
                      .
cylinders in last group 48
blocks in last group 6144


cg 0:
magic     90255    tell    6000     time      Sat Feb 27 22:53:11 1999
cgx       0        ncyl    49       niblk   6144     ndblk   50176
nbfree    23       ndir    26       nifree  5708     nffree  102
rotor     1224     irotor  144      frotor  1224
frsum     7        7        3        1        1        0        9
sum of frsum: 102
iused:  0-143, 145-436
free:   1224-1295, 1304-1311, 1328-1343, 4054-4055, 4126-4127, 4446-4447, 4455,
4637-4638,
```

14.3 UFS Implementation

UFS is implemented as a loadable file system module containing instances of the vfs and vnode objects. The UFS vnode interfaces implement file operations, and the UFS vfs interfaces implement file system administration.

The UFS file system implementation can be divided into five major components:

- An instance of the vfs object and methods for mounting and unmounting a file system and gathering file system statistics
- An implementation of the vnode methods for file operations
- A directory implementation that uses the standard directory name lookup cache
- A block map algorithm to map files to disk blocks on the storage device
- An inode cache to keep vnodes in memory after they are no longer referenced

Figure 14.7 shows the relationship between the components of the UFS file system. UFS implements the vnode interface for file access and the vfs interface for file system management. UFS interfaces with device drivers for persistent storage, the block buffer cache to store and retrieve metadata, the directory name lookup cache for caching path names, and the virtual memory system for caching of file data.

In the following paragraphs, we discuss the implementation of each of the blocks within the UFS file system.

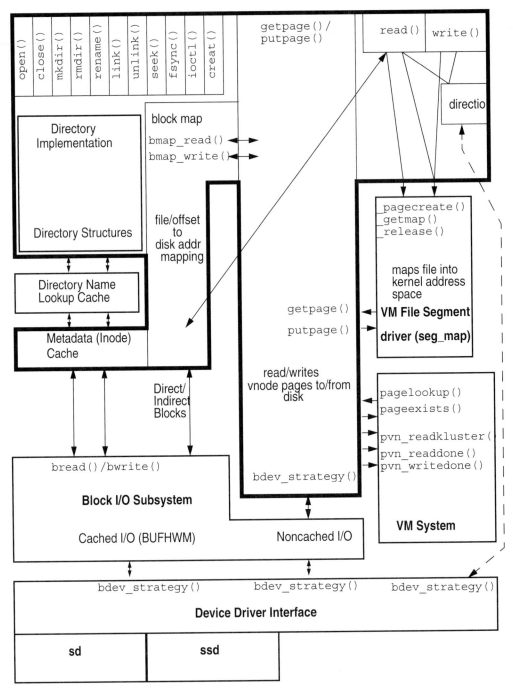

Figure 14.7 The UFS File System

14.3.1 Mapping of Files to Disk Blocks

At the heart of a disk-based file system are the block map algorithms, which implement the on-disk file system format. These algorithms map UFS file and offsets pairs into disk addresses on the underlying storage. For UFS, two main functions—bmap_read() and bmap_write()—implement the on-disk format. These functions are called to do the following:

- bmap_read() queries the file system as to which physical disk sector a file block resides on; that is, requests a lookup of the direct/indirect blocks that contain the disk address(es) of the required blocks.

- bmap_write() allocates new disk blocks when extending or allocating blocks for a file.

The bmap_read() function is used for both reading and writing to locate disk blocks; it accepts an inode and offset as input arguments, and a pointer to a disk address and length as output arguments.

```
int
bmap_read(struct inode *ip, u_offset_t off, daddr_t *dap, int *lenp)
```

Header File   <fs/ufs_inode.h>

The bmap_read() function is used for both file reads and writes. In both cases, the file system uses the bmap_read() algorithm to locate the physical blocks for the file being read or written. The bmap_read() function searches though the direct, indirect, and double indirect blocks of the inode to locate the disk address of the disk blocks that map to the supplied offset. The function also searches forward from the offset, looking for disk blocks that continue to map contiguous portions of the inode, and returns the length of the contiguous segment in the length pointer argument. The length and the file system block clustering parameters are used within the file system as bounds for clustering contiguous blocks to provide better performance by reading larger parts of a file from disk at a time.

```
int
bmap_write(struct inode *ip, u_offset_t off, int size,
           int alloc_only, struct cred *cr);
```

Header File   <fs/ufs_inode.h>

The bmap_write() function allocates file space in the file system when a file is extended or a file with holes has blocks written for the first time. bmap_write() searches though the block free lists, using the rotor algorithm (discussed in "UFS Block Allocation" on page 573), and updates the local, direct, and indirect blocks in the inode for the file being extended.

14.3.1.1 Reading and Writing UFS Blocks

A file system read calls bmap_read() to find the location of the underlying physical blocks for the file being read. UFS then calls the device driver's strategy routine for the device containing the file system to initiate the read operation by calling `bdev_strategy()`.

A file system write operation that extends a file first calls `bmap_write()` to allocate the new blocks and then calls `bmap_read()` to obtain the block location for the write. UFS then calls the device driver's strategy routine, by means of `bdev_strategy()`, to initiate the file write.

14.3.1.2 Buffering Block Metadata

The block map functions access metadata (local/direct and double indirect blocks) on the device media through the buffer cache, using the `bread()` and `bwrite()` buffered block I/O kernel functions. The block I/O functions read and write device blocks in 512-byte chunks, and they cache physical disk blocks in the block buffer cache (note: this cache is different from the page cache, used for file data). The UFS file system requires 1 Mbyte of metadata for every 2 Gbytes of file space. This relationship can be used as a rule to calculate the size of the block buffer cache, set by the `bufhwm` kernel parameter.

14.3.2 Methods to Read and Write UFS Files

Files can be read or written in two ways: by the `read()` or `write()` system calls, or by mapped file I/O. The `read()` and `write()` system calls call the file system's `vop_read()` and `vop_write()` method. These methods map files into the kernel's address space and then use the file system's `vop_getpage()` and `vop_putpage()` methods to transfer data to and from the physical media.

14.3.2.1 ufs_read()

An example of the steps taken by a UFS read system call is shown in Figure 14.8. A read system call invokes the file-system-dependent read function, which turns the read request into a series of `vop_getpage()` calls by mapping the file into the kernel's address space with the `segmap` driver, as described in "File System I/O" on page 547.

The `vop_read` method calls into the `seg_map` segment to create a virtual address in the kernel address space for the file and offset requested with the `segmap_getmap()` function. The `seg_map` driver determines whether it already has a slot for the page of the file at the given offset by looking into its hashed list of mapping slots. Once a slot is located or created, an address for the page is created, and a page fault for the page that is mapping the file is initiated to read in page at the virtual address of the `seg_map` slot. The page fault is initiated while we are still in the `segmap_getmap()` routine, by a call to `segmap_fault()`, which in turn calls back into the file system with `vop_getpage()`, which calls `ufs_getpage()`.

The `ufs_getpage()` routine handles the task of bringing the requested range of the file (vnode, offset, and length) from disk into the virtual address and length passed into the `ufs_getpage()` function. The `ufs_getpage()` function locates

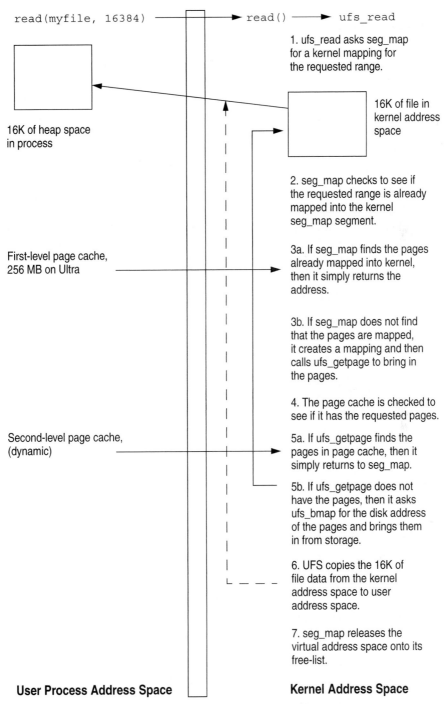

Figure 14.8 ufs_read()

the file's blocks (through the block map functions discussed in "Mapping of Files to Disk Blocks" on page 579) and reads them by calling the underlying device's strategy routine.

Once the page is read by the file system, the requested range is copied back to the user by the uio_move() function. Then, the file system releases the slot associated with that block of the file with the segmap_release() function. At this point, the slot is not removed from the segment because we may need the same file and offset later (effectively caching the virtual address mapping); instead, it is added onto a seg_map free list so it can be reclaimed or reused later.

14.3.2.2 ufs_write()

Writing to the file system is performed in a similar manner, although it is more complex because of some of the file system write performance enhancements, such as delayed writes and write clustering. Writing to the file system follows the steps shown in Figure 14.9.

The write system call calls the file-system-independent write, which in our example calls ufs_write(). UFS breaks the write into 8-Kbyte chunks and then processes each chunk. For each 8-Kbyte chunk, the following steps are performed.

- UFS asks the segmap driver for an 8-Kbyte mapping of the file in the kernel's virtual address space. The page for the file and offset is mapped here so that the data can be copied in and then written out with paged I/O.

- The segmap segment looks in its cache of mappings. If a mapping exists, it is returned. If there is no mapping for this file and offset, then a new one is created by replacement of one of the existing mappings.

- If the write is to a whole file system block, then a new zeroed page is created with segmap_pagecreate(). In the case of a partial block write, the block must first be read in so the partial block contents can be replaced.

- The new page is returned, locked, to UFS. The buffer that is passed into the write system call is copied from user address space into kernel address space.

- The ufs_write throttle first checks to see if too many bytes are outstanding for this file as a result of previous delayed writes. If more than the kernel parameter ufs_HW bytes are outstanding, the write is put to sleep until the amount of outstanding bytes drops below the kernel parameter ufs_LW.

- The file system calls the seg_map driver to map in the portion of the file we are going to write. The data is copied from the process's user address space into the kernel address space allocated by seg_map, then seg_map is called to release the address space containing the dirty pages to be written. This is when the real work of write starts, because seg_map calls ufs_putpage() when it realizes there are dirty pages in the address space it is releasing.

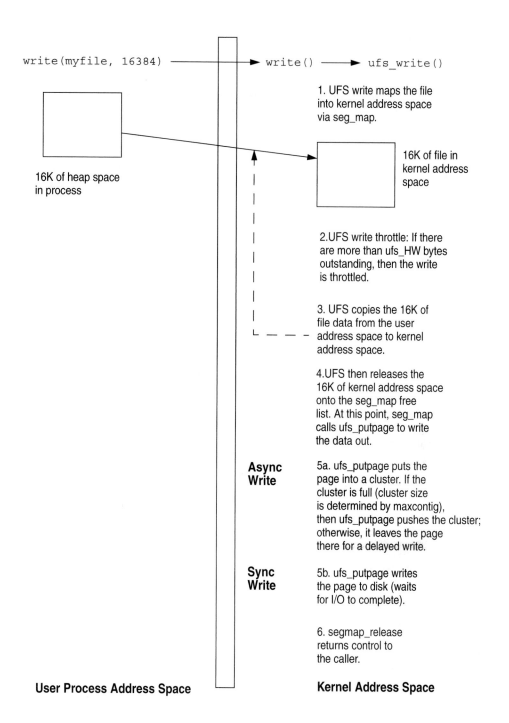

Figure 14.9 ufs_write()

14.3.3 In-Core UFS Inodes

Each file system has two forms of an inode: the in-core (in-memory) inode and the on-disk inode. The on-disk inode resides on the physical medium and represents the on-disk format and layout of the file; the in-core inode resides in memory and contains the file-system-dependent information, kernel locks, and state.

The vnode is typically contained in an in-core inode, so that when an inode is created, a vnode is automatically created. In that way, simple macros can convert from a file-system-dependent inode to a file-system-independent vnode. The in-core UFS inode contains an embedded vnode, as shown in Figure 14.10.

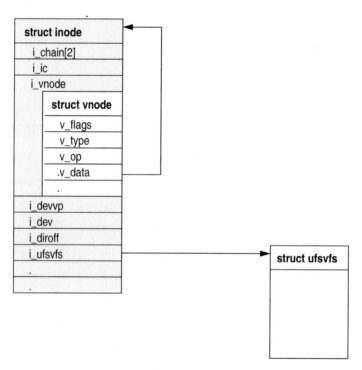

Figure 14.10 The UFS inode

Embedding the vnode in the inode also allows file systems to easily convert between inode and vnode references. File systems use macros to convert a vnode reference to an inode reference, and vice versa. UFS uses the macro VTOI to convert a vnode pointer to an inode pointer, and the macro ITOV to convert an inode pointer to a vnode pointer.

```
/*
 * Convert between inode pointers and vnode pointers
 */
#define        VTOI(VP)           ((struct inode *)(VP)->v_data)
#define        ITOV(IP)           ((struct vnode *)&(IP)->i_vnode)
```

Header File   <fs/ufs_inode.h>

14.3.3.1 Freeing inodes—the Inode Idle List

When the last reference to a vnode is released, the vop_inactive() routine for the file system is called. (See vnode reference counts in "vnode Reference Count" on page 538.) UFS uses vop_inactive() to free the inode when it is no longer required. UFS implements an idle list because if we were to destroy each vnode when the last reference to a vnode is relinquished, we would throw away all the data relating to that vnode, including all of the file pages cached in the page cache. This practice could mean that if a file is closed and then reopened, none of the file data that was cached would be available after the second open and would need to be reread from disk.

14.3.3.2 Caching Inodes—the Inode Idle List

Each time the last reference to a file is made, the vop_inactive() method for the file system is called to handle the last reference to the vnode. UFS implements an idle queue to cache recently closed inodes in their constructed state, to keep their in-kernel state and file system cache pages intact.

For idling inodes, UFS implements a thread that maintains a list of idle inodes on a queue. The ufs_inactive() routine puts UFS inodes into the idle queue. The ufs_inactive() routine is passed a vnode, and the UFS uses the VTOI macro to convert an inode reference, which is then placed onto the idle queue. The inodes on the idle queue retain all of their state, keeping any pages in the page cache in memory. The inodes stay on the idle queue until the idle queue reaches a high watermark, at which point the UFS idle thread is awakened to free half of the inode idle queue. Figure 14.11 illustrates the process.

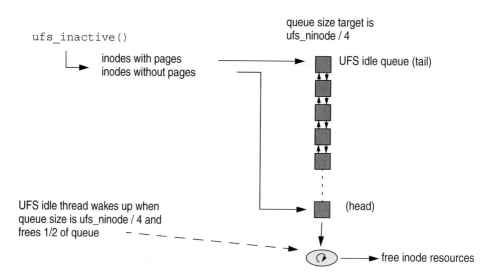

Figure 14.11 UFS Idle Queue

The ufs_inactive() routine attempts to free inodes with no pages in the page cache in preference to inodes that still have pages in the page cache. The goal—to keep as many file pages in the page cache as possible—is realized by the following procedure: inodes that have pages associated with them are placed at the tail of the idle queue, and inodes with no pages are placed at the head of the inode queue. When inodes are removed from the idle queue, they are removed from the tail of the queue, that is, the inodes without pages are taken first.

```
# sar -g 3 3333

SunOS devhome 5.7 Generic sun4u      08/01/99

09:42:52  pgout/s ppgout/s pgfree/s pgscan/s %ufs_ipf
09:42:55    0.00     0.00    30.90     0.00     0.00
09:42:58    0.00     0.00    34.55     0.00     0.00
09:43:01    0.00     0.00    45.15     0.00     0.00
09:43:04    0.00     0.00    64.00     0.00     0.00
09:43:07    0.00     0.00    69.44     0.00     0.00
09:43:10    0.00     0.00    84.95     0.00     1.21
09:43:13    0.00     0.00    86.67     0.00     0.00
09:43:16    0.00     0.00    35.88     0.00     0.00
09:43:19    0.00     0.00    71.33     0.00     0.00
```

The UFS idle thread is awakened when the size of the idle queue exceeds one-fourth of the system-tunable parameter ufs_ninode. When the thread wakes up, it attempts to remove half the inodes from the idle queue, to discard all of the pages associated with the inode, and to free the kernel memory used to store the in-memory inode. Inodes that are removed from the idle queue update kernel statistics in the virtual memory system; you can obtain the statistics with sar. The statistics show how many inodes that have pages associated with them in the page cache were freed. Note that the %ufs_ipf column in the sar output for this example shows that almost no inodes that are freed had associated pages.

14.3.4 UFS Directories and Path Names

The file system directory and path-name code are responsible for managing the on-disk directory format and translating file-name lookups into vnode references. Four vnode methods implement directory and path-name services: vop_lookup(), vop_readdir(), vop_mkdir(), and vop_rmdir().

Path names are converted to vnode references by the file-system-independent lookuppn() function. The lookuppn() function calls into the file system's vop_lookup() method. Directories are traversed by means of the vop_readdir() method; they are created and deleted with the vop_mkdir() and vop_rmdir() methods.

14.3.4.1 ufs_lookup()

The ufs_lookup() function traverses the directory to find a file matching the supplied path name and returns a reference to a vnode for the file. For example, the open system call for a UFS file translates the path name of the file into a vnode by calling lookuppn(), which calls ufs_lookup() for each component of the path name. Opening /etc/passwd causes vop_lookup() to be called for the root directory /, the etc subdirectory, and the password file passwd.

The ufs_lookup() implementation first searches the directory name lookup cache (DNLC), using dnlc_lookup(), to check if an entry exists in the DNLC. If not, the directory is read in and searched for the path name. Once located, the path name is entered into the DNLC with dnlc_enter(), and an open vnode is returned to the caller.

14.3.4.2 ufs_readdir()

The ufs_readdir() method reads chunks of UFS directories from disk and returns them to the caller. The ufs_readdir() method is typically called as a result of the readdir() system call. The raw UFS directory data is cached in the file system cache (compared with the DNLC, which caches the inode and path name information for individual files).

15

SOLARIS FILE SYSTEM CACHE

O ne of the most important features of a file system is its ability to cache file data, but, ironically, the file system cache is not implemented in the file system. In Solaris, the file system cache is implemented in the virtual memory system. In this section, we explain how Solaris file caching works, and we explore the interactions between the file system cache and the virtual memory system.

15.1 Introduction to File Caching

Traditional Unix implements file system caching in the I/O subsystem by keeping copies of recently read or written blocks in a block cache. This block cache sits just above the disks, and it caches data corresponding to physical disk sectors.

Figure 15.1 shows an example in which a process reads a piece of a file. The process reads a segment of a file by issuing a `read` system call into the operating system. The file system must then look up the corresponding disk block for the file by looking up the block number in the direct/indirect blocks for that file, after which the files system requests that block from the I/O system. The I/O system retrieves the block from disk the first time; then, the file systems satisfies subsequent reads by reading the disk block from the block buffer cache. Note that even though the disk block is cached in memory—because this is a physical block cache—we have to invoke the file system and look up the physical block number for every cached read.

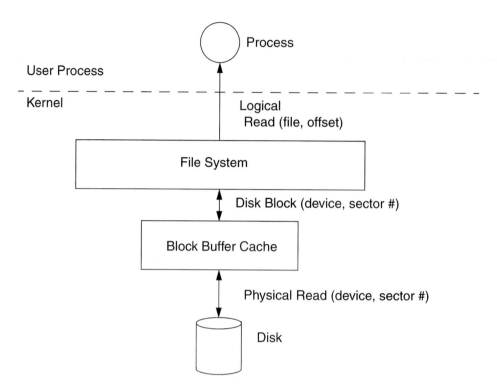

Figure 15.1 The Old-Style Buffer Cache

Typically, the old buffer cache is sized statically by a kernel configuration parameter. Changing the size of the buffer cache requires a kernel rebuild and a reboot.

15.1.1 Solaris Page Cache

Solaris has a new method, the page cache, of caching file system data. The page cache was developed at Sun as part of the virtual memory rewrite in SunOS 4 in 1985 and is used by System V Release 4 Unix. Page cache derivatives are now also used in Linux and Windows NT. The page cache has two major differences from the old caching method. First, it's dynamically sized and can use all memory that is not being used by applications. Second, it caches file blocks rather than disk blocks. The key difference is that the page cache is a virtual file cache rather than a physical block cache. A virtual file cache allows the operating system to retrieve file data by simply looking up the file reference and seek offset. The old way, the operating system invoked the file system, which looked up the physical disk block number corresponding to the file and retrieved that block from the physical block cache. The virtual file cache is far more efficient.

Figure 15.2 shows the new page cache. When a Solaris process reads a file the first time, file data is read from disk through the file system into memory in page-sized chunks and returned to the user. The next time the same segment of file data is read, it can be retrieved directly from the page cache without a logical-to-physical lookup through the file system. The old buffer cache is still used in Solaris, but only for internal file system data (which is just the metadata items) that is only known by physical block numbers—direct/indirect blocks and inodes. All file data is cached through the page cache.

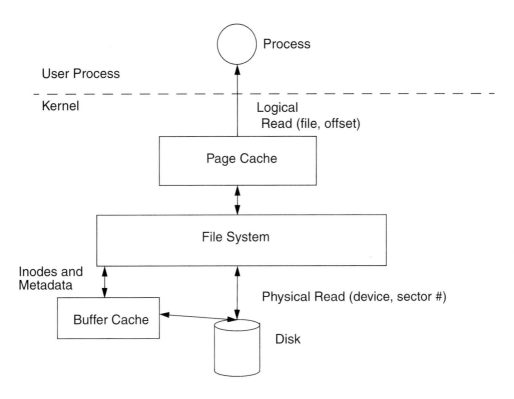

Figure 15.2 The Solaris Page Cache

The diagram in Figure 15.2 is somewhat simplified because the file system is still involved in the page cache lookup, but the amount of work that the file system needs to do is dramatically reduced. The page cache is implemented in the virtual memory system; in fact, the virtual memory system is architected around the page cache principle. Each page of the physical memory is identified the same way: by file and offset. Pages associated with files point to regular files, whereas pages of memory associated with process private-memory space point to the swap device. We don't go into too much detail about the Solaris virtual memory system in this section; you can find a more detailed description of the Solaris memory system in Chapter 5. The important thing to remember is that file cache is just like process memory, and as we will see, file caching shares the same paging dynamics as the rest of the memory system.

15.1.2 Block Buffer Cache

The old buffer cache is used in Solaris for caching of inodes and file metadata and is now also dynamically sized. In old versions of Unix, the buffer cache was fixed in size by the `nbuf` kernel parameter, which specified the number of 512-byte buffers. We now allow the buffer cache to grow by `nbuf`, as needed, until it reaches a ceiling specified by the `bufhwm` kernel parameter. By default, the buffer cache is allowed to grow until it uses 2 percent of physical memory. We can look at the upper limit for the buffer cache by using the `sysdef` command.

```
# sysdef
*
* Tunable Parameters
*
 7757824        maximum memory allowed in buffer cache (bufhwm)
    5930        maximum number of processes (v.v_proc)
      99        maximum global priority in sys class (MAXCLSYSPRI)
    5925        maximum processes per user id (v.v_maxup)
      30        auto update time limit in seconds (NAUTOUP)
      25        page stealing low water mark (GPGSLO)
       5        fsflush run rate (FSFLUSHR)
      25        minimum resident memory for avoiding deadlock (MINARMEM)
      25        minimum swapable memory for avoiding deadlock (MINASMEM)
```

Now that we only keep inode and metadata in the buffer cache, we don't need a very large buffer. In fact, we only need 300 bytes per inode and about 1 megabyte per 2 gigabytes of files that we expect to be accessed concurrently (note that this rule of thumb is for UFS file systems).

For example, if we have a database system with 100 files totaling 100 gigabytes of storage space and we estimate that we will access only 50 gigabytes of those files at the same time, then at most we would need 100×300 bytes = 30 kilobytes for the inodes, and about 50 / 2 * 1 megabyte = 25 megabytes for the metadata (direct and indirect blocks). On a system with 5 gigabytes of physical memory, the defaults for `bufhwm` would provide us with a `bufhwm` of 102 megabytes, which is more than sufficient for the buffer cache. If we are really memory misers, we could limit `bufhwm` to 30 megabytes (specified in kilobytes) by setting the `bufhwm` parameter in the `/etc/system` file. To set `bufhwm` smaller for this example, we would put the following line into the /etc/system file.

```
*
* Limit size of bufhwm
*
set bufhwm=30000
```

You can monitor the buffer cache hit statistics by using `sar -b`. The statistics for the buffer cache show the number of logical reads and writes into the buffer cache, the number of physical reads and writes out of the buffer cache, and the read/write hit ratios.

```
# sar -b 3 333
SunOS zangief 5.7 Generic sun4u     06/27/99

22:01:51 bread/s lread/s %rcache bwrit/s lwrit/s %wcache pread/s pwrit/s
22:01:54       0    7118     100       0       0     100       0       0
22:01:57       0    7863     100       0       0     100       0       0
22:02:00       0    7931     100       0       0     100       0       0
22:02:03       0    7736     100       0       0     100       0       0
22:02:06       0    7643     100       0       0     100       0       0
22:02:09       0    7165     100       0       0     100       0       0
22:02:12       0    6306     100       8      25      68       0       0
22:02:15       0    8152     100       0       0     100       0       0
22:02:18       0    7893     100       0       0     100       0       0
```

On this system we can see that the buffer cache is caching 100 percent of the reads and that the number of writes is small. This measurement was taken on a machine with 100 gigabytes of files that are being read in a random pattern. You should aim for a read cache hit ratio of 100 percent on systems with only a few, but very large, files (e.g., database systems) and a hit ratio of 90 percent or better for systems with many files.

15.2 Page Cache and Virtual Memory System

The virtual memory system is implemented around the page cache, and the file system makes use of this facility to cache files. This means that to understand file system caching behavior, we need to look at how the virtual memory system implements the page cache.

The virtual memory system divides physical memory into chunks known as pages; on UltraSPARC systems, a page is 8 kilobytes. To read data from a file into memory, the virtual memory system reads in one page at a time, or "pages in" a file. The page-in operation is initiated in the virtual memory system, which requests that file's file system to page in a page from storage to memory. Every time we read in data from disk to memory, we cause paging to occur. We see the tally when we look at the virtual memory statistics. For example, reading a file will be reflected in vmstat as page-ins.

```
# ./rreadtest testfile&

# vmstat
   procs        memory              page                  disk            faults            cpu
 r b w  swap    free  re  mf  pi   po fr de sr s0 -- -- --   in   sy    cs us sy id
 0 0 0 50436   2064    5   0  81    0  0  0  0 15  0  0  0  168  361    69  1 25 74
 0 0 0 50508   1336   14   0 222    0  0  0  0 35  0  0  0  210  902   130  2 51 47
 0 0 0 50508    648   10   0 177    0  0  0  0 27  0  0  0  168  850   121  1 60 39
 0 0 0 50508    584   29  57  88  109  0  0  6 14  0  0  0  108 5284   120  7 72 20
 0 0 0 50508    484    0  50 249   96  0  0 18 33  0  0  0  199  542   124  0 50 50
 0 0 0 50508    492    0  41 260   70  0  0 56 34  0  0  0  209  649   128  1 49 50
 0 0 0 50508    472    0  58 253  116  0  0 45 33  0  0  0  198  566   122  1 46 53
```

In our example, we can see that by starting a program that does random reads of a file, we cause a number of page-ins to occur, as indicated by the numbers in the pi column of vmstat. Note that the free memory column in vmstat has dropped to a low value; in fact, the amount of free memory is almost zero. This situation occurs because the file system consumes a page of physical memory every time it pages in a page-sized chunk of a file. Have you ever noticed that when you boot your machine there is a lot of free memory, and as the machine is used, memory continues to fall to zero, then just hangs there? Here is why: the file system is using all available memory to cache the reads and writes to each file—and it's completely normal.

Memory is put back on the free list by the page scanner, which looks for memory pages that have not been used recently. The page scanner runs when memory falls to a system parameter known as lotsfree. In this example, we can see from the scan rate (sr) column that the page scanner is scanning about 50 pages per second to replace the memory used by the file system.

There is no parameter equivalent to bufhwm for the page cache. The page cache simply grows to consume all available memory, which includes all process memory that has not been used recently by applications. The rate at which the system pages and the rate at which the page scanner runs are proportional to the rate at which the file system is reading or writing pages to disk. On large systems, you should expect to see large paging values—it's completely normal.

Consider a system that is reading 10 megabytes per second through the file system; this translates to 1,280 page-ins per second and means that the page scanner must scan enough memory to be able to free 1,280 pages per second. The page scanner must actually scan faster than 1,280 pages per second, since not all memory the page scanner comes across will be eligible for freeing (the page scanner only frees memory that hasn't been used recently). If the page scanner finds only one out of three pages eligible for freeing, then it would need to run at 3,840 pages per second. Don't worry about high scan rates; if you are using the file system heavily, then they are normal. There are many myths about high scan rates meaning you have a shortage of memory; perhaps this explanation reassures you that high scan rates can be normal in many circumstances.

Having all of the free memory used for a cache makes it harder to observe how much memory is really free and also makes it hard to see how much memory is being used as a file system cache. The MemTool package (see "File System Caching Memory" on page 234) can display the amount of memory that is being used as a file system cache.

```
# prtmem

Total memory:            242 Megabytes
Kernel Memory:            35 Megabytes
Application memory:      139 Megabytes
Executable  memory:       50 Megabytes
Buffercache memory:        7 Megabytes
Free memory:
```

15.2.1 File System Paging Optimizations

Some file systems try to reduce the amount of memory pressure by doing two things: invoking free-behind with sequential access and freeing pages when free memory falls to `lotsfree`. Free-behind is invoked on UFS when a file is accessed sequentially so that the cache is not polluted when we do a sequential scan through a large file. This means that when we create or sequentially read a file, we don't see high scan rates.

Also, some checks in some file systems limit the file system's use of the page cache when memory falls to `lotsfree`. An additional parameter, `pages_before_pager`, used by the UFS, reflects the amount of memory above the point where the page scanner starts; by default `pages_before_pager` is 200 pages. This means that when memory falls to 1.6 megabytes (on UltraSPARC) above `lotsfree`, the file system throttles back the use of the page cache. To be specific, when memory falls to `lotsfree + pages_before_pager`, the following happens:

- Solaris file systems free all pages after they are written
- UFS and NFS enable free-behind on sequential access
- NFS disables read-ahead
- NFS writes synchronously, rather than asynchronously
- VxFS enables free-behind (some versions only)

15.3 Is All That Paging Bad for My System?

Although we stated earlier that it may be normal to have high paging and scan rates, it is likely that the page scanner will be putting too much pressure on your application's private process memory. If we scan at a rate of several hundred pages or more per second, then the amount of time that the page scanner takes to check whether a page has been accessed falls to a few seconds. This means that any pages that have not been used in the last few seconds will be taken by the page scanner when you are using the file system. This behavior can negatively affect application performance and is the reason why *priority paging* was introduced.

If your system seems slow while file system I/O is going on, it's because your applications are being paged in and out as a direct result of the file system activity.

For example, consider an OLTP application that makes heavy use of the file system. The database is generating file system I/O, making the page scanner actively steal pages from the system. The user of the OLTP application has paused for 15 seconds to read the contents of a screen from the last transaction. During this time, the page scanner has found that those pages associated with the user application have not been referenced and makes them available for stealing. The pages are stolen, and when the user types the next keystroke, the user is forced to wait until the application is paged back in—usually several seconds. Our user is forced to wait for an application to page in from the swap device, even though the application is running on a system with sufficient memory to keep all of the application in physical memory!

The priority paging algorithm effectively places a boundary around the file cache so that file system I/O does not cause unnecessary paging of applications. The algorithm prioritizes the different types of pages in the page cache, in order of importance:

- Highest — Pages associated with executables and shared libraries, including application process memory (anonymous memory)
- Lowest — Regular file cache pages

When the dynamic page cache grows to the point where free memory falls to almost zero, the page scanner wakes up and begins scanning, but as long as the system has sufficient memory, the scanner only steals pages associated with regular files. The file system effectively pages against itself rather than against everything else on the system.

Should there be a real memory shortage where there is insufficient memory for the applications and kernel, the scanner is again allowed to steal pages from the applications. By default, priority paging is disabled. It is likely to be enabled by default in a Solaris release subsequent to Solaris 7. To use priority paging, you will need either Solaris 7, Solaris 2.6 with kernel patch 105181-13, or Solaris 2.5.1 with 103640-25 or higher. To enable priority paging, set the following in /etc/system:

```
*
* Enable Priority Paging
*
set priority_paging=1
```

To enable priority paging on a live 32-bit system, set the following with `adb`:

```
# adb -kw /dev/ksyms /dev/mem

lotsfree/D
lotsfree: 730 <- value of lotsfree is printed

cachefree/W 0t1460 <- insert 2 x value of lotsfree preceded with 0t (decimal)
dyncachefree/W 0t1460 <- insert 2 x value of lotsfree preceded with 0t (decimal)


cachefree/D
cachefree: 1460
dyncachfree/D
dyncachefree: 1460
```

To enable priority paging on a live 64-bit system, set the following with adb:

```
# adb -kw /dev/ksyms /dev/mem

lotsfree/E
lotsfree: 730 <- value of lotsfree is printed

cachefree/Z 0t1460 <- insert 2 x value of lotsfree preceded with 0t (decimal)
dyncachefree/Z 0t1460 <- insert 2x value of lotsfree preceded with 0t (decimal)
cachfree/E
cachefree: 1460
dyncachfree/E
dyncachefree: 1460
```

Setting `priority_paging=1` in /etc/system causes a new memory tunable, `cachefree`, to be set to twice the old paging high watermark, `lotsfree`, as the system boots. `cachefree` scales with `minfree`, `desfree`, and `lotsfree`.

Priority paging distinguishes between executable files and regular files by recording whether they are being mapped into an address space with execute permissions. That is, if regular files have the execute bit set when the memory map system call maps them into an address space, then those files are treated as executables. Be careful to ensure that data files that are being memory mapped do not have the execute bit set.

Under Solaris 7, an extended set of paging counters allows us to see what type of paging is occurring. We can now see the difference between paging caused by an application memory shortage and paging through the file system. The paging counters are visible under Solaris 7 with the `memstat` command. The output from the `memstat` command is similar to that of `vmstat`, but with extra fields to differentiate paging types. In addition to the regular paging counters (sr, po, pi, fr), the `memstat` command shows the three types of paging: executable, application, and file. The `memstat` fields are shown in Table 15-1.

Table 15-1 Paging Counters from the `memstat` Command

Column	Description
pi	Total page-ins per second
po	Total page-outs per second
fr	Total page-frees per second
sr	Page scan rate in pages per second
epi	Executable page-ins per second
epf	Executable pages freed per second
api	Application (anonymous) page-ins per second from the swap device
apo	Application (anonymous) page-outs per second to the swap device
apf	Application pages freed per second
fpi	File page-ins per second
fpo	File page-outs per second
fpf	File page-frees per second

If we use the `memstat` command, we can now see that as we randomly read our test file, the scanner is scanning several hundred pages per second through memory and causing executable pages to be freed and application (anonymous) pages to be paged out to the swap device as they are stolen. On a system with plenty of memory, this is not the desired mode of operation! Enabling priority paging will stop this excessive swapping when there is sufficient memory.

```
# ./readtest testfile&

# memstat 3
memory ---------- paging ------ -executable- - anonymous - -- filesys - --- cpu ---
free re mf   pi   po   fr de   sr epi epo  epf api  apo  apf  fpi fpo  fpf us sy wt id
2080 1   0  749  512  821  0  264   0   0  269   0  512  549  749   0    2  1  7 92  0
1912 0   0  762  384  709  0  237   0   0  290   0  384  418  762   0    0  1  4 94  0
1768 0   0  738  426  610  0 1235   0   0  133   0  426  434  738   0   42  4 14 82  0
1920 0   2  781  469  821  0  479   0   0  218   0  469  525  781   0   77 24 54 22  0
2048 0   0  754  514  786  0  195   0   0  152   0  512  597  754   2   37  1  8 91  0
2024 0   0  741  600  850  0  228   0   0  101   0  597  693  741   2   56  1  8 91  0
2064 0   1  757  426  589  0  143   0   0   72   8  426  498  749   0   18  1  7 92  0
```

With priority paging enabled, we can see the different behavior of the virtual memory system.

```
# ./readtest testfile&

# memstat 3
memory  ---------- paging ----------- - executable -  - anonymous -  -- filesys -- --- cpu ---
  free  re  mf  pi   po   fr  de  sr  epi epo epf  api apo apf  fpi  fpo  fpf us sy wt id
  3616   6   0 760    0  752   0  673    0   0   0    0   0   0  760    0  752  2  3 95  0
  3328   2 198 816    0  925   0 1265    0   0   0    0   0   0  816    0  925  2 10 88  0
  3656   4 195 765    0  792   0  263    0   0   0    2   0   0  762    0  792  7 11 83  0
  3712   4   0 757    0  792   0  186    0   0   0    0   0   0  757    0  792  1  9 91  0
  3704   3   0 770    0  789   0  203    0   0   0    0   0   0  770    0  789  0  5 95  0
  3704   4   0 757    0  805   0  205    0   0   0    0   0   0  757    0  805  2  6 92  0
  3704   4   0 778    0  805   0  266    0   0   0    0   0   0  778    0  805  1  6 93  0
```

With the same test program, random reads on the file system again cause the system to page, and the scanner is actively involved in managing the pages, but now the scanner is freeing only file pages. The zeros in the executable and anonymous memory columns clearly show that the scanner is choosing file pages first. The activity shown in the fpi and fpf columns means that file pages are being read in and an equal number are freed by the page scanner to make room for more reads.

15.4 Paging Parameters That Affect File System Performance

When priority paging is enabled, you will notice that the file system scan rate is higher. Because the page scanner must skip over process private memory and executables, it needs to scan more pages before it finds file pages that it can steal. High scan rates are always found on systems that make heavy use of the file system and so should not be used as a factor for determining memory shortage. If you have Solaris 7, then the memstat command will reveal if you are paging to the swap device; such paging suggests that you are short of memory.

If you have high file system activity, then you will find that the scanner parameters are insufficient and will limit file system performance. To compensate, you must set the scanner parameters fastscan and maxpgio to allow the scanner to scan at a high enough rate to keep up with the file system.

By default, the scanner is limited by the fastscan parameter, which reflects the number of pages per second that the scanner can scan. It defaults to scan one-fourth of memory every second and is limited to 64 megabytes per second. The scanner runs at half of fastscan when memory is at lotsfree, which limits it to 32 megabytes per second. If only one in three physical memory pages is a file page, then the scanner will only be able to put $32 / 3 = 11$ megabytes per second of memory on the free list, limiting file system throughput. So, to allow the page scanner to scan fast enough, increase fastscan to, say, one-fourth of memory, with an upper limit of 1 gigabyte per second. That upper limit translates to 131072 for the fastscan parameter.

The `maxpgio` parameter is the maximum number of pages the page scanner can push. `maxpgio` can also limit the number of file system pages that are pushed, thus limiting the write performance of the file system. If your system has sufficient memory, then we recommend setting `maxpgio` to something large, say, 1024. On the E10000 systems, this is the default for `maxpgio`. For example, on a 4-gigabyte machine, one-fourth of memory is 1 gigabyte, so we would set `fastscan` to 131072. Our parameters, set in `/etc/system`, for this machine are shown below.

```
*
* Parameters to allow better file system throughput
*
set fastscan=131072
set handspreadpages=131072
set maxpgio=1024
```

In summary, we have seen the a strong relationship between the VM system and file system behavior. The parameters that control the paging system have the most influence on file system performance, since they govern the way pages are made available to the file system. Figure 15.3 depicts the paging parameters that affect file systems and the memory parameters that control paging as the amount of free memory falls to the point where it hits these parameters.

15.5 Bypassing the Page Cache with Direct I/O

In some cases we may want to do completely unbuffered I/O to a file. A *direct I/O* facility in most file systems allows a direct file read or write to completely bypass the file system page cache.

15.5.1 UFS Direct I/O

Support for direct I/O was added to UFS starting with Solaris 2.6. Direct I/O allows reads and writes to files in a regular file system to bypass the page cache and access the file at near raw disk performance. Direct I/O can be advantageous when you are accessing a file in a manner where caching is of no benefit. For example, if you are copying a very large file from one disk to another, then it is likely that the file will not fit in memory and you will just cause the system to page heavily. By using direct I/O, you can copy the file through the file system without reading through the page cache and eliminate the memory pressure caused by the file system and the additional CPU cost of the layers of cache.

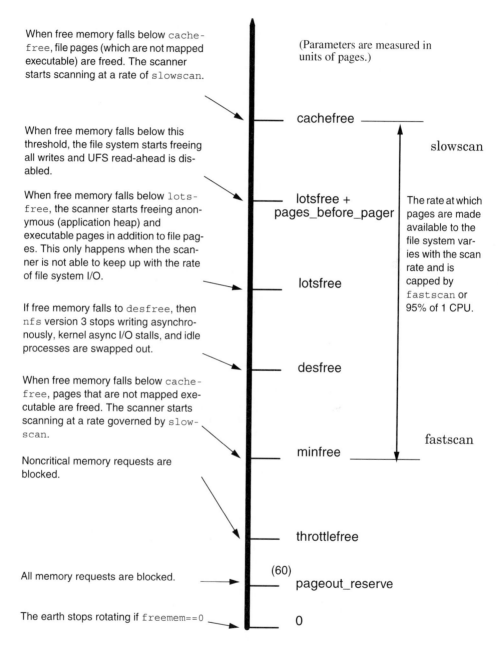

When free memory falls below `cache-free`, file pages (which are not mapped executable) are freed. The scanner starts scanning at a rate of `slowscan`.

(Parameters are measured in units of pages.)

cachefree

slowscan

When free memory falls below this threshold, the file system starts freeing all writes and UFS read-ahead is disabled.

When free memory falls below `lots-free`, the scanner starts freeing anonymous (application heap) and executable pages in addition to file pages. This only happens when the scanner is not able to keep up with the rate of file system I/O.

lotsfree + pages_before_pager

The rate at which pages are made available to the file system varies with the scan rate and is capped by `fastscan` or 95% of 1 CPU.

lotsfree

If free memory falls to `desfree`, then `nfs` version 3 stops writing asynchronously, kernel async I/O stalls, and idle processes are swapped out.

desfree

When free memory falls below `cache-free`, pages that are not mapped executable are freed. The scanner starts scanning at a rate governed by `slow-scan`.

Noncritical memory requests are blocked.

fastscan

minfree

throttlefree

All memory requests are blocked.

(60)

pageout_reserve

The earth stops rotating if `freemem==0`

0

Figure 15.3 VM Parameters That Affect File Systems

Direct I/O also eliminates the double copy that is performed when the read and write system calls are used. When we read a file through normal buffered I/O, the file system (1) uses a DMA transfer from the disk controller into the kernel's address space and (2) copies the data into the buffer supplied by the user in the read system call. Direct I/O eliminates the second step by arranging for the DMA transfer to occur directly into the user's address space.

Direct I/O will only bypass the buffer cache if all of the following are true:

- The file is not memory mapped.
- The file is not on a logging file system.
- The file does not have holes.
- The read/write is sector aligned (512 byte).

You enable direct I/O by mounting an entire file system with the force-directio mount option, as shown below.

```
# mount -o forcedirectio /dev/dsk/c0t0d0s6 /u1
```

You can also enable direct I/O with the directio system call, on a per-file basis. Note that the change is file based, and every reader and writer of the file will be forced to use directio once it's enabled.

```
int directio(int fildes, DIRECTIO_ON | DIRECTIO_OFF);
```

Header File   <sys/fcntl.h>

Direct I/O can provide extremely fast transfers when moving data with big block sizes (>64 kilobytes), but it can be a significant performance limitation for smaller sizes. If an application reads and writes in small sizes, then its performance may suffer since there is no read-ahead or write clustering and no caching.

Databases are a good candidate for direct I/O since they cache their own blocks in a shared global buffer and can arrange to do their own clustering of reads and writes into larger operations.

A set of direct I/O statistics is provided with the ufs implementation by means of the kstat interface. The structure exported by ufs_directio_kstats is shown below. Note that this structure may change, and performance tools should not rely on the format of the direct I/O statistics.

```
struct ufs_directio_kstats {
        uint_t  logical_reads;  /* Number of fs read operations */
        uint_t  phys_reads;     /* Number of physical reads */
        uint_t  hole_reads;     /* Number of reads from holes */
        uint_t  nread;          /* Physical bytes read */
        uint_t  logical_writes; /* Number of fs write operations */
        uint_t  phys_writes;    /* Number of physical writes */
        uint_t  nwritten;       /* Physical bytes written */
        uint_t  nflushes;       /* Number of times cache was cleared */
} ufs_directio_kstats;
```

You can inspect the direct I/O statistics with an engineering utility from our website at http://www.solarisinternals.com.

```
# directiostat 3
  lreads lwrites  preads pwrites     Krd      Kwr holdrds  nflush
       0       0       0       0       0        0       0       0
       0       0       0       0       0        0       0       0
       0       0       0       0       0        0       0       0
```

15.5.2 Direct I/O with Veritas VxFS

VxFS also provides a direct I/O implementation, which by default switches on whenever the read or write size is 256 kilobytes or greater. This VxFS feature is known as *discovered direct I/O*.

15.6 Directory Name Cache

The directory name cache caches path names for vnodes, so that when we open a file that has been opened recently, we don't need to rescan the directory to find the file name again. Each time we find the path name for a vnode, we store it in the directory name cache. (See "The Directory Name Lookup Cache (DNLC)" on page 557 for further information on the DNLC operation.) The number of entries in the DNLC is set by the system-tunable parameter, ncsize, which is set at boot time by the calculations shown in Table 15-2. The ncsize parameter is calculated in proportion to the maxusers parameter, which is equal to the number of megabytes of memory installed in the system, capped by a maximum of 1024. The maxusers parameter can also be overridden in /etc/system to a maximum of 2048.

Table 15-2 DNLC Default Sizes

Solaris Version	Default ncsize Calculation
Solaris 2.4, 2.5, 2.5.1	ncsize = (17 * maxusers) + 90
Solaris 2.6, 2.7	ncsize = (68 * maxusers) + 360

The size of the DNLC rarely needs to be adjusted because the size scales with the amount of memory installed in the system. Earlier Solaris versions had a default maximum of 17498 (34906 with maxusers set to 2048), and later Solaris versions have a maximum of 69992 (139624 with maxusers set to 2048).

Use adb to determine the size of the DNLC.

```
# adb -k
physmem b919
ncsize/D
ncsize:
ncsize:             25520
```

The hit rate of the directory name cache shows the number of times a name was looked up and found in the name cache. A high hit rate (>90%) shows that the DNLC is working well. A low hit rate does not necessarily mean that the DNLC is undersized; it simply means that we are not always finding the names we want in the name cache. This situation can occur if we are creating a large number of files. The reason is that a create operation checks to see if a file exists before it creates the file, causing a large number of cache misses.

```
# vmstat -s
        0 swap ins
        0 swap outs
        0 pages swapped in
        0 pages swapped out
   405332 total address trans. faults taken
  1015894 page ins
      353 page outs
  4156331 pages paged in
     1579 pages paged out
  3600535 total reclaims
  3600510 reclaims from free list
        0 micro (hat) faults
   405332 minor (as) faults
   645073 major faults
    85298 copy-on-write faults
   117161 zero fill page faults
        0 pages examined by the clock daemon
        0 revolutions of the clock hand
  4492478 pages freed by the clock daemon
     3205 forks
       88 vforks
     3203 execs
 33830316 cpu context switches
 58808541 device interrupts
   928719 traps
214191600 system calls
 14408382 total name lookups (cache hits 90%)
   263756 user    cpu
   462843 system  cpu
 14728521 idle    cpu
  2335699 wait    cpu
```

15.7 Inode Caches

Disk-based file systems attempt to keep a number of inodes in memory, even if the file for that inode is not open or referenced. This is done for two reasons: to minimize disk inode reads by caching the inode in memory and to keep the inode's vnode in memory so that file pages remain in the page cache. The number of inodes that the system will attempt to keep in memory is indirectly controlled by a system parameter: `ufs_ninode`.

15.7.1 UFS Inode Cache Size

The UFS uses the `ufs_ninode` parameter to size the file system tables for the expected number of inodes. To understand how the `ufs_ninode` parameter affects the number of inodes in memory, we need to look at how the UFS maintains inodes. Inodes are created when a file is first referenced. They remain in memory much longer than when the file is last referenced because inodes can be in one of two states: either the inode is referenced, or the inode is no longer referenced but is on an idle queue. Inodes are eventually destroyed when they are pushed off the end of the inode idle queue. Refer to "Freeing inodes—the Inode Idle List" on page 585 for a description of how `ufs` inodes are maintained on the idle queue.

The number of inodes in memory is dynamic. Inodes will continue to be allocated as new files are referenced. There is no upper bound to the number of inodes open at a time; if one million inodes are opened concurrently, then a little over one million inodes will be in memory at that point. A file is referenced when its reference count is nonzero, which means either the file is open for a process or another subsystem such as the directory name lookup cache is referring to the file.

When inodes are no longer referenced (the file is closed and no other subsystem is referring to the file), the inode is placed on the idle queue and eventually freed. The size of the idle queue is controlled by the `ufs_ninode` parameter and is limited to one-fourth of `ufs_ninode`. The maximum number of inodes in memory at a given point is the number of active referenced inodes plus the size of the idle queue (typically, one-fourth of `ufs_ninode`). Figure 15.4 illustrates the inode cache.

We can use the `sar` command and inode kernel memory statistics to determine the number of inodes currently in memory. `sar` shows us the number of inodes currently in memory and the maximum reached. We can find similar information by

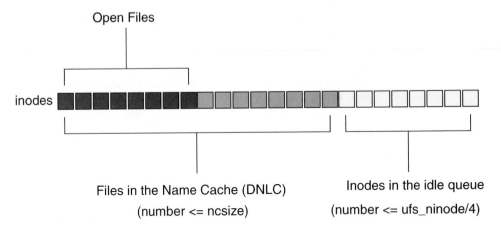

Figure 15.4 In-Memory Inodes (Referred to as the "Inode Cache")

looking at the `buf_inuse` and `buf_total` parameters in the inode kernel memory statistics.

```
# sar -v 3 3

SunOS devhome 5.7 Generic sun4u     08/01/99

11:38:09  proc-sz    ov  inod-sz      ov  file-sz    ov   lock-sz
11:38:12  100/5930    0  37181/37181   0  603/603     0    0/0
11:38:15  100/5930    0  37181/37181   0  603/603     0    0/0
11:38:18  101/5930    0  37181/37181   0  607/607     0    0/0

# netstat -k ufs_inode_cache
ufs_inode_cache:
buf_size 440 align 8 chunk_size 440 slab_size 8192 alloc 1221573 alloc_fail 0
free 1188468 depot_alloc 19957 depot_free 21230 depot_contention 18 global_alloc 48330
global_free 7823 buf_constructed 3325 buf_avail 3678 buf_inuse 37182
buf_total 40860 buf_max 40860 slab_create 2270 slab_destroy 0 memory_class 0
hash_size 0 hash_lookup_depth 0 hash_rescale 0 full_magazines 219
empty_magazines 332 magazine_size 15 alloc_from_cpu0 579706 free_to_cpu0 588106
buf_avail_cpu0 15 alloc_from_cpu1 573580 free_to_cpu1 571309 buf_avail_cpu1 25
```

The inode memory statistics show us how many inodes are allocated by the `buf_inuse` field. We can also see from the ufs inode memory statistics that the size of each inode is 440 bytes. We can use this value to calculate the amount of kernel memory required for desired number of inodes when setting `ufs_ninode` and the directory name cache size.

The `ufs_ninode` parameter controls the size of the hash table that is used to look up inodes and indirectly sizes the inode idle queue (`ufs_ninode` / 4). The inode hash table is ideally sized to match the total number of inodes expected to be in memory—a number that is influenced by the size of the directory name cache. By default, `ufs_ninode` is set to the size of the directory name cache, which provides approximately the correct size for the inode hash table. In an ideal world, we could set ufs_ninode to four-thirds the size of the DNLC, to take into account the size of the idle queue, but practice has shown this unnecessary.

We typically set ufs_ninode indirectly by setting the directory name cache size (ncsize) to the expected number of files accessed concurrently, but it is possible to set ufs_ninode separately in /etc/system.

```
* Set number of inodes stored in UFS inode cache
*
set ufs_ninode = new_value
```

15.7.2 VxFS Inode Cache

The Veritas file system uses a similar parameter, vxfs_ninode, to control the size of the inode cache. It also attempts to keep one-fourth of the vxfs_ninode parameter number of inodes on the inode idle queue.

```
* Set number of inodes stored in VxFS inode cache
*
set vxfs:vxfs_ninode = new_value
```

A

KERNEL TUNABLES,
SWITCHES, AND LIMITS

In this appendix, we provide several tables showing the various kernel settable parameters. The variables listed here do not represent every kernel variable that can be altered. Almost any kernel variable that is visible to the kernel linker can be altered with an entry in the /etc/system file or with a debugger like adb(1). Certainly, it was never intended that each and every kernel variable, along with its meaning and possible values, be documented as user settable. Most have never been intended for public use, but rather exist for debugging or experimentation. Here we list what we consider the mainstream variables—those that have always been intended to be user settable—and several that are not as well known but that have proved to be useful for some installations.

A.1 Setting Kernel Parameters

You establish settable kernel tunable parameters by adding an entry to the /etc/system file, in the form of:

set *parameter* = *value*

or

set *kernel_module:parameter* = *value*

The second example applies to those kernel variables that are part of a loadable kernel module, where the module name is separated by a colon from the variable name in the entry. The values in the `/etc/system` file are read at boot time, so any changes made to this file require a reboot to take effect.

These settable kernel variables are traditionally referred to as *kernel tunable parameters*. The settable kernel variables can be more accurately categorized into one of three groups:

- `Switches` — Refers to a kernel parameter that simply turns on or off a particular behavior or functional component, which, of course, affects system behavior and performance. An example of a switch is the `priority_paging` parameter, which is either on (value of 1) or off (value of 0).

- `Limits` — Refers to kernel variables that impose hard limits on a particular resource. The System V IPC tunables fall into the limit category. Several others do as well.

- `Tunables` — Refers to kernel variables that will alter performance or behavior. Think of these as a tuning knob that has a range of values (0 to N, where N represents that maximum allowable value).

Kernel parameters can be further divided into those parameters that are set on typical installations and impose minimal risk, and those that are less well known and not well understood. Changing the value of any kernel parameter imposes some level of risk. However, many of the kernel limit parameters, such as those set for System V IPC resources, are set on many installations and are generally well understood. Others can alter system behavior and performance, and sometimes it is not easy (or even possible) to predict which direction performance will move in (better or worse) as a result of changing a particular value.

In the tables that follow, we list the various kernel settable parameters, indicating their category (switch, limit, tunable) and whether or not we believe that the parameter is something that may impact system behavior in an unpredictable way, where such a warning is applicable. We also provide a reference to the page number in the book where more information about the kernel variable can be found.

As a practice, you should never change a kernel settable parameter in a production system without first trying the value in a lab environment and then testing extensively.

A.2 System V IPC - Shared Memory Parameters

Table A-1 describes shared memory parameters. For more information, refer to "System V Shared Memory" on page 425.

Table A-1 System V IPC - Shared Memory

Parameter	Default	Category	Description / Notes
shmmax	1048576	Limit	System V IPC shared memory. Maximum shared memory segment size, in bytes.
shmmin	1	Limit	System V IPC shared memory. Minimum shared memory segment size, in bytes.
shmmni	100	Limit	System V IPC shared memory. Maximum number of shared memory segments, systemwide.
shmseg	6	Limit	System V IPC shared memory. Maximum number of shared segments, per process.
segspt_minfree	5% of available memory	Limit	Number of pages of physical memory not available for allocation as ISM shared segments. Default value translates to allowing up to 95% of available memory get allocated to ISM shared segments.

Table A-2 lists System V IPC semaphores. For more information, refer to "System V Semaphores" on page 436.

Table A-2 System V IPC - Semaphores

Parameter	Default	Category	Description / Notes
semmap	10	Limit	Size of the semaphore map.
semmni	10	Limit	Maximum number of semaphore identifiers, systemwide.
semmns	60	Limit	Maximum number of semaphores, systemwide. Should be the product of semmni and semmsl.
semmnu	30	Limit	Maximum number of semaphore undo structures, systemwide.
semmsl	25	Limit	Maximum number of semaphores per semaphore ID.
semopm	10	Limit	Maximum number of semaphore operations per semop() call.
semume	10	Limit	Maximum per-process undo structures.
semvmx	32767	Limit	Maximum value of a semaphore.
semaem	16384	Limit	Maximum adjust-on-exit value.

Table A-3 describes message queues. For more information, refer to "System V Message Queues" on page 442.

Table A-3 System V IPC - Message Queues

Parameter	Default	Category	Description/Notes
msgmap	100	Limit	Maximum size of resource map for messages.
msgmax	2048	Limit	Maximum size, in bytes, of a message.
msgmnb	4096	Limit	Maximum number of bytes on a message queue.
msgmni	50	Limit	Maximum number message queue identifiers, systemwide.
msgssz	8	Limit	Message segment size.
msgtql	40	Limit	Maximum number of message headers, systemwide.
msgseg	1024	Limit	Maximum number of message segments.

A.3 Virtual Memory Parameters

Table A-4 lists parameters that relate to the virtual memory system and paging activity. Such activity is closely tied to file system I/O because of the buffer caching done by file systems such as UFS and VxFS.

You can read more about the memory paging parameters in "Summary of Page Scanner Parameters" on page 186, "Solaris File System Cache" on page 589, "Page Cache and Virtual Memory System" on page 593, and "In summary, we have seen the a strong relationship between the VM system and file system behavior. The parameters that control the paging system have the most influence on file system performance, since they govern the way pages are made available to the file system. Figure 15.3 depicts the paging parameters that affect file systems and the memory parameters that control paging as the amount of free memory falls to the point where it hits these parameters." on page 600.

Table A-4 Virtual Memory

Parameter	Default	Category	Description/Notes
fastscan	1/4th of physical memory, or 64 MB, whichever is larger.	Tunable	The maximum number of pages per second the page scanner will scan.
slowscan	100	Tunable	Initial page scan rate, in pages per second.
lotsfree	1/64th of physical memory, or 512 KB, whichever is larger.	Tunable	Desired size of the memory free list (number of free pages). When the free list drops below lotsfree, the page scanner runs.

Table A-4 Virtual Memory (Continued)

Parameter	Default	Category	Description/Notes
desfree	lotsfree / 2.	Tunable	Free memory desperation threshold. When freemem drops below desfree, the page scan rate increases and the system will alter its default behavior for specific events. desfree must be less than lotsfree.
minfree	desfree / 2.	Tunable	Minimum acceptable amount of free memory. minfree must be less than desfree.
throttlefree	minfree	Tunable	Memory threshold at which the kernel will block memory allocation requests. Must be less than minfree.
pageout_reserve	throttle-free / 2	Tunable	Memory pages reserved for pageout and memory scheduler threads. When freemem drops below pageout_reserve, memory allocations are denied for anything other than pageout and sched.
priority_paging	0	Switch	Enables priority paging when set to 1. Priority paging relieves memory pressure on executable pages due to cached file system activity. Priority paging is available for Solaris 2.6 with kernel jumbo patch 105181-10 or greater. It is in Solaris 7.
cachefree	*	Tunable	The memory page threshold that triggers the priority paging behavior, where file system cache pages are marked for pageout only as long as freemem is below cachefree but above lotsfree. cachefree must be greater than lotsfree. * If priority_paging is 0, then cachefree = lotsfree. If priority_paging is 1 (enabled), then cachefree = (lotsfree * 2)
pages_pp_maximum	*	Limit	Number of pages the system requires remain unlocked. * 200, or tune_t_minarmem, or 10% of available memory, whichever is greater.
tune_t_minarmem	25	Limit	Minimum number of memory pages reserved for the kernel. A safeguard to ensure that a minimum amount of nonswappable memory is available to the kernel.
min_percent_cpu	4	Tunable	Minimum percentage of CPU time pageout can consume.

Table A-4 Virtual Memory (Continued)

Parameter	Default	Category	Description/Notes
handspreadpages	fastscan	Tunable	Number of pages between the first and second hand of the page scanner.
pages_before_pager	200	Tunable	Used in conjunction with lotsfree to establish the point at which the kernel will free file system pages after an I/O. If available memory is less than lotsfree + pages_before_pager, then the kernel will free pages after an I/O (rather than keep them in the page cache for reuse).
maxpgio	40	Tunable	Maximum number of pageout operations per second the kernel will schedule. Set to 100 times the number of disks with swap files or swap partitions.

A.4 File System Parameters

The file system and page flushing parameters in Table A-5 provide for tuning file system performance and manage the flushing of dirty pages from memory to disk.

You can read more about the fsflush and associated parameters in "Bypassing the Page Cache with Direct I/O" on page 600. "Directory Name Cache" on page 603 and "Inode Caches" on page 605 have more information on the file system parameters directory and inode caches.

Table A-5 File System and Page Flushing Parameters

Parameter	Default	Category	Description/Notes
tune_t_flushr	5	Tunable	fsflush interval; the fsflush daemon runs every tune_t_flushr seconds.
autoup	30	Tunable	Age in seconds of dirty pages. Used in conjunction with tune_t_fsflushr; modified pages that are older than autoup are written to disk.
dopageflush	1	Switch	When set, enables dirty page flushing by fsflush. Can be set to zero to disable page flushing.
doiflush	1	Switch	Flag to control flushing of inode cache during fsflush syncs. Set to 0 to disable inode cache flushing.

Table A-5 File System and Page Flushing Parameters (Continued)

Parameter	Default	Category	Description/Notes
ncsize	*	Limit	Size of the directory name lookup cache (DNLC); a kernel cache that caches path names for vnodes for UFS and NFS files. * ncsize defaults to (17 * maxusers) + 90 on 2.5.1, and (68 * maxusers) + 360 on Solaris 2.6 and 7.
bufhwm	2% of physical memory	Limit	Maximum amount of memory (in Kbytes) allocated to the I/O buffer cache, which caches file system inodes, superblocks, indirect blocks, and directories.
ndquot	((maxusers * 40) / 4) + max_nprocs	Limit	Number of UFS quota structures to allocate. Applies only if quotas are enabled for UFS.
maxphys	126976 (sun4m and sun4d), 131072 (sun4u), 57344 (x86)	Limit	Maximum physical I/O size, in bytes. For some devices, the maximum physical I/O size is set dynamically when the driver loads.
ufs_ninode	ncsize	Limit	Number of inodes to cache in memory.
ufs:ufs_WRITES	1	Switch	Enables UFS per-file write throttle. See below.
ufs:ufs_LW	256 Kbytes	Tunable	UFS write throttle low watermark. See below.
ufs:ufs_HW	384 Kbytes	Tunable	UFS write throttle high watermark. If the number of outstanding bytes to be written to a file exceeds ufs_HW, then writes are deferred until ufs_LW or less is pending.
nrnode	ncsize	Limit	Maximum number of rnodes allocated. rnodes apply to NFS files, and are the NFS equivalent of a UFS inode.
tmpfs_maxkmem	Set dynamically when tmpfs is first used.	Limit	Maximum amount of kernel memory for tmpfs data structures. The value is set the first time tmpfs is used, to a range somewhere between the memory page size of the platform, to 25% of the amount of available kernel memory.
tmpfs_minfree	256 pages	Limit	Minimum amount of swap space tmpfs will leave for non-tmpfs use (i.e., the rest of the system).

Table A-6 lists parameters related to `swapfs`—the pseudofile that is a key component in the management of kernel anonymous memory pages. These parameters are generally not changed from their defaults.

Table A-6 Swapfs Parameters

Parameter	Default	Category	Description/Notes
swapfs_reserve	4 MB or 1/16th of memory, whichever is smaller	Limit	The amount of swap reserved for system processes. Those processes owned by root (UID 0).
swapfs_minfree	2 MB or 1/8 of physical memory, whichever is larger.	Limit	Amount of memory the kernel keeps available for the rest of the systems (all processes).

A.5 Miscelaneous Parameters

Table A-7 lists miscellaneous kernel parameters. You can read more about many of the tunable parameters in "Kernel Bootstrap and Initialization" on page 107.

Table A-7 Miscellaneous Parameters

Parameter	Default	Category	Description/Notes
maxusers	MB of RAM	Limit	Generic tunable for sizing various kernel resources.
ngroups_max	16	Limit	Maximum number of supplementary groups a user can belong to.
npty	48	Limit	Number of pseudodevices, /dev/pts slave devices, and /dev/pty controller devices.
pt_cnt	48	Limit	Number of pseudodevices, /dev/pts slave devices, and /dev/ptm master devices.
rstchown	1	Switch	Enables POSIX_CHOWN_RESTRICTED behavior. Only a root process can change file ownership. A process must be a current member of the group to which it wishes to change a files group, unless it is root.
rlim_fd_cur	64	Limit	Maximum per-process open files.
rlim_fd_max	1024	Limit	Per process open files hard limit. rlim_fd_cur can never be larger than rlim_fd_max.

Table A-7 Miscellaneous Parameters (Continued)

Parameter	Default	Category	Description/Notes
physmem	number of pages of RAM	Limit	Can be set to reduce the effective amount of usable physical memory. Values are in pages.
kobj_map_space_len	1 MB	Limit	Amount of kernel memory allocated to store symbol table information. In Solaris 2.6, it defines to total space for the kernel symbol table. In Solaris 7, space is dynamically allocated as needed, in units of kobj_map_space_len.
kmem_flags	0	Switch	Solaris 2.6 and later. Enable some level of debug of kernel memory allocation. Values: 0x1 – AUDIT: maintain an activity audit log. 0x2 – TEST: Allocator tests memory prior to allocation. 0x3 – REDZONE: Allocator adds extra memory to the end of an allocated buffer, and tests to determine if the extra memory was written into when the buffer is freed. 0x4 – CONTENTS: Logs up to 256 bytes of buffer contents when buffer is freed. Requires AUDIT also be set.
kmem_debug_enable	0	Switch	Kernel memory allocator debug flag. Allows kma debug information for any or all kmem caches. Value of –1 in all caches. Solaris 2.6 and 7 only. Removed in Solaris 7, 3/99.
moddebug	0	Switch	Turn on kernel module debugging messages. The many possible values for moddebug can be found in /usr/include/sys/modctl.h. Some useful values are: 0x80000000 – print loading/unloading messages. 0x40000000 – print detailed error messages.
timer_max	32	Limit	Number of POSIX timers (timer_create(2) system call) available.
consistent_coloring	0	Switch	sun4u (UltraSPARC) only. Establishes the page placement policy for physical pages and L2 cache blocks. Possible values are: 0 – page coloring 1 – virtual address = physical address 2 – bin-hopping

A.6 Process and Dispatcher (Scheduler) Parameters

The parameters listed in Table A-8 relate to the process and scheduler subsystem in Solaris. For more information, refer to "The Kernel Process Table" on page 286.

Table A-8 Process and Dispatcher (Scheduler) Parameters

Parameter	Default	Category	Description/Notes
reserved_procs	5	Limit	The number of process table slots reserved for system processes.
maxpid	30,000	Limit	Maximum value for a PID, and the maximum number of processes that can exist on the system at any one time.
max_nprocs	(10 + 16 * max-users)	Limit	Maximum number of process that can exist on the system. Will be set to maxpid if it is set to a value greater than maxpid.
maxuprc	max_nprocs - reserved_procs	Limit	Maximum number of processes a non-root user can create.
noexec_user_stack	0	Switch	If set to 1, stack pages are mapped noexec, providing protection against buffer overflow attacks. 64-bit Solaris 7 maps stack pages no-exec by default.
rechoose_interval	3	Tunable	Clock tick count for thread-to-processor affinity scheduling. The dispatcher attempts to place a thread on the same processor it last ran on, for optimal hardware cache hits. After rechoose_interval ticks, the next available processor is chosen.
hires_tick	0	Tunable	Default of 0 has the system generate 100 clock interrupts per second (10 ms interval). Setting this value to 1 results in a 1 ms interval (1000 clock interrupts per second).

A.7 STREAMS Parameters

Table A-9 lists tunable parameters available for the kernel STREAMS subsystem. STREAMS are not covered in this version of the book.

Table A-9 STREAMS Parameters

Parameter	Default	Category	Description/Notes
nstrpush	9	Limit	Number of modules that can be pushed onto a STREAM.
strmsgsz	65536	Limit	Maximum size (in bytes) of a STREAMS data message.
strctlsz	1024	Limit	Maximum size (in bytes) of a STREAMS control message.
sadcnt	16	Limit	Number of STREAMS administrative driver (sad) devices.
nautopush	32	Limit	Number of sad autopush structures.

B

KERNEL VIRTUAL ADDRESS MAPS

In this appendix, we illustrate the allocation- and location-specific information for the segments that constitute the Solaris 7 kernel address space.

The kernel address space is represented by the address space pointed to by the system object, kas. The segment drivers manage the manipulation of the segments within the kernel address space. Figure B.1 illustrates the architecture.

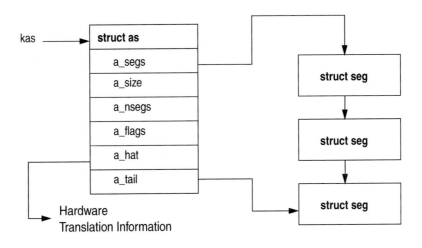

Figure B.1 Kernel Address Space and Segments

You can look at the kernel address space with the as adb macro, using the kernel address space pointer. The as macro will show the kernel address space and the pointer to the list of kernel segments.

```
# adb -k
physmem b91a
kas$<as

10423320:      contents (mutex)
10423320:      owner/waiters
               0
10423328:      flags    vbits    cv
               0        0        0
10423330:      hat               hrm            seglast
               300000ebf88       0              300002a9f88
10423350:      lock (rwlock)
10423350:      wwwh
               0
10423368:      segs              size           tail
               10434678          2052c0000      104230e0
10423380:      nsegs             lrep  hilevel
               6                 0     0
10423386:      unused   updatedir        objectdir
               0        01               0
10423390:      sizedir           wpage          nwpage
               0                 0              0
10423340:      userlimit
               0
```

You can then use the seglist adb macro to print a list of the kernel's memory segments.

```
10434678$<seglist

ktextseg:
ktextseg:           base             size           as
                    10000000         4a0000         10423320
ktextseg+0x18:      next             prev           ops
                    1041fd60         0              segkmem_ops
ktextseg+0x30:      data
                    0

kvalloc:
kvalloc:            base             size           as
                    104a0000         e20000         10423320
kvalloc+0x18:       next             prev           ops
                    104233a0         10434678       segkmem_ops
kvalloc+0x30:       data
                    0

kvseg32:
kvseg32:            base             size           as
                    78000000         4000000        10423320
kvseg32+0x18:       next             prev           ops
                    300002a9f88      1041fd60       segkmem_ops
kvseg32+0x30:       data
                    0
```

The next figures illustrate Solaris 7 address space, as follows:

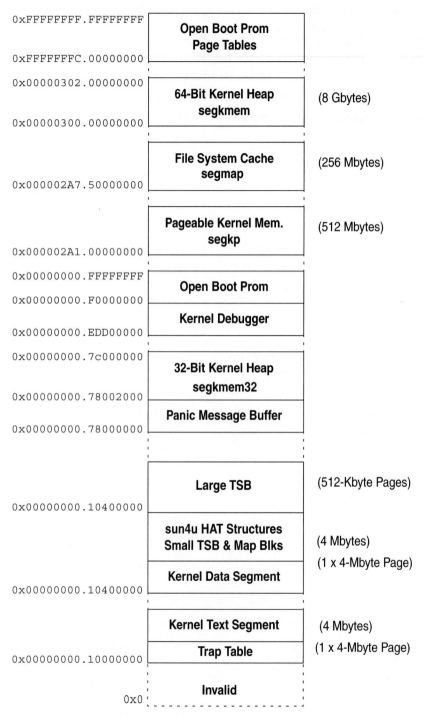

Figure B.2   Solaris 7 sun4u 64-Bit Kernel Address Space

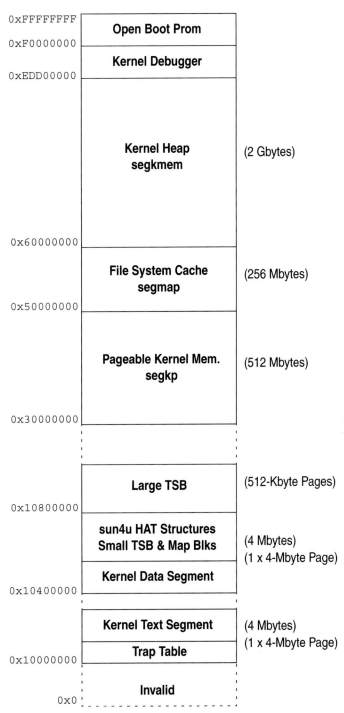

Figure B.3 Solaris 7 sun4u 32-Bit Kernel Address Space

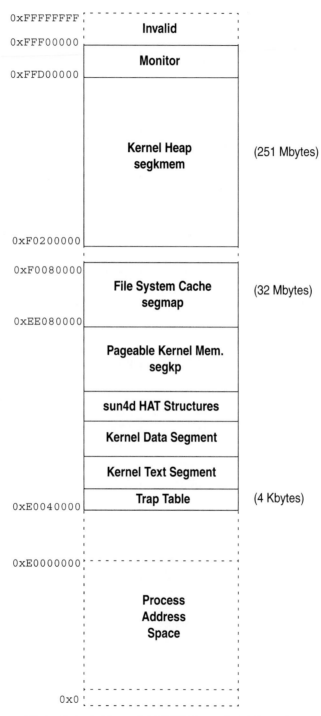

Figure B.4   Solaris 7 sun4d 32-Bit Kernel Address Space

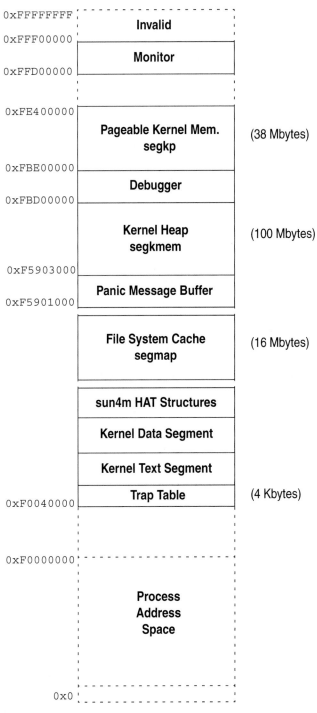

Figure B.5 Solaris 7 sun4m 32-Bit Kernel Address Space

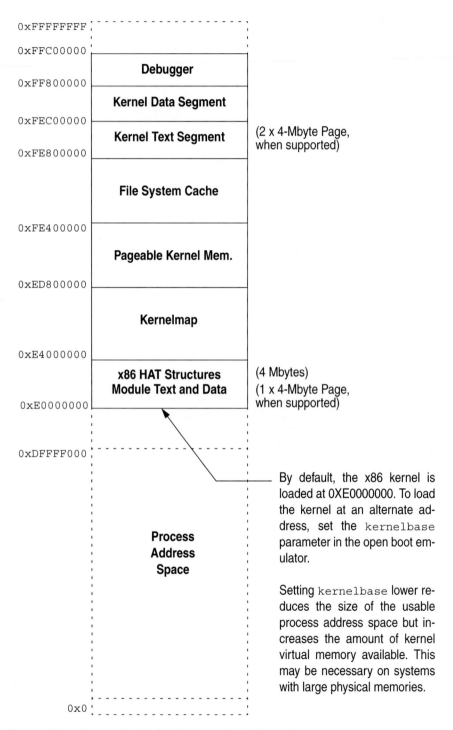

Figure B.6 Solaris 7 x86 32-Bit Kernel Address Space

A SAMPLE PROCFS UTILITY

```
$ msacct ls -lR
.:
total 3012
drwxrwxrwx   9 jmauro    tech        2560 Oct 22 13:02 2.X
[a LOT of output snipped]
....
-rwxrwxrwx   1 jmauro    staff       5166 Feb 12 18:11 msacct.c
-r--r--r--   1 jmauro    staff       4401 Feb  6 22:02 ptime.c

*** Usage Counters ***
        Minor Faults:.................0
        Major Faults:.................0
        Swaps:........................0
        Input Blocks:.................0
        Output Blocks:................0
        STREAMS Messages Sent:........0
        STREAMS Messages Received:....0
        Signals:......................0
        Voluntary Context Switches:...1684
        Involuntary Context Switches:.25
        System Calls:.................3693
        Read/Write Characters:........53305
*** State Times ***
        Total Elapsed Time:..........11.065
        Total User Time:.............0.403
        Total System Time:...........0.429
        Other System Trap Time:......0.000
        Text Page Fault Sleep Time...0.000
        Data Page Fault Sleep Time...0.000
        Kernel Page Fault Sleep Time..0.000
        User Lock Wait Sleep Time.....0.000
        All Other Sleep Time.........10.201
        Time Waiting for a CPU........0.038
        Stopped Time.................0.000
```

```c
/*
 * Turn on microstate accounting, and print all field resource
 * usage and microstat accounting fields when process terminates.
 *
 * Borrowed largely from ptime.c
 * (Thanks Roger Faulkner and Mike Shapiro)
 *
 * Usage: msacct command
 *
 */

#include <sys/types.h>
#include <sys/time.h>
#include <procfs.h>
#include <stdio.h>
#include <stdlib.h>
#include <unistd.h>
#include <fcntl.h>
#include <string.h>
#include <errno.h>
#include <math.h>
#include <wait.h>
#include <signal.h>

static          int         look(pid_t);
static          void        hr_min_sec(char *, long);
static          void        prtime(char *, timestruc_t *);
static          int         perr(const char *);

static          void        tsadd(timestruc_t *result, timestruc_t *a, timestruc_t *b);
static          void        tssub(timestruc_t *result, timestruc_t *a, timestruc_t *b);

static          char        *command;
static          char        procname[64];

main(int argc, char **argv)
{
        int ctlfd;
        long ctl[2];
        pid_t pid;
        struct siginfo info;
        int status;

        if ((command = strrchr(argv[0], '/')) != NULL)
                command++;
        else
                command = argv[0];

        if (argc <= 1) {
                (void) fprintf(stderr,
                        "usage:%s command [ args ... ]\n", command);
                (void) fprintf(stderr,
                        " (time a command using microstate accounting)\n");
                return (1);
        }

        switch (pid = fork()) {
        case -1:
                (void) fprintf(stderr, "%s: cannot fork\n", command);
                return (2);
        case 0:
                /* newly created child process */
                /* open the /proc ctl file and turn on microstate accounting */
                (void) sprintf(procname, "/proc/%d/ctl", (int)getpid());
                ctlfd = open(procname, O_WRONLY);
```

```
                ctl[0] = PCSET;
                ctl[1] = PR_MSACCT;
                (void) write(ctlfd, ctl, 2*sizeof (long));
                (void) close(ctlfd);
                (void) execvp(argv[1], &argv[1]);
                (void) fprintf(stderr, "%s: exec failed\n", command);
                if (errno == ENOENT)
                        _exit(127);
                else
                        _exit(126);
        }

        (void) sprintf("%d", procname, (int)pid);        /* for perr() */
        (void) signal(SIGINT, SIG_IGN);
        (void) signal(SIGQUIT, SIG_IGN);
        (void) waitid(P_PID, pid, &info, WEXITED | WNOWAIT);

        (void) look(pid);

        (void) waitpid(pid, &status, 0);

        if (WIFEXITED(status))
                return (WEXITSTATUS(status));
        else
                return ((status & ~WCOREFLG) | 0200);
}

static int
look(pid_t pid)
{
        char pathname[100];
        int rval = 0;
        int fd;
        prusage_t prusage;
        timestruc_t real, user, sys;
        prusage_t *pup = &prusage;

        (void) sprintf(pathname, "/proc/%d/usage", (int)pid);
        if ((fd = open(pathname, O_RDONLY)) < 0)
                return (perr("open usage"));

        if (read(fd, &prusage, sizeof (prusage)) != sizeof (prusage))
                rval = perr("read usage");
        else {
                real = pup->pr_term;
                tssub(&real, &real, &pup->pr_create);
                user = pup->pr_utime;
                sys = pup->pr_stime;
                tsadd(&sys, &sys, &pup->pr_ttime);
                (void) fprintf(stderr, "\n");
                printf("*** Usage Counters *** \n");
                printf("Minor Faults:................%ld\n", pup->pr_minf);
                printf("Major Faults:................%ld\n", pup->pr_majf);
                printf("Swaps:.......................%ld\n", pup->pr_nswap);
                printf("Input Blocks:................%ld\n", pup->pr_inblk);
                printf("Output Blocks:...............%ld\n", pup->pr_oublk);
                printf("STREAMS Messages Sent:.......%ld\n", pup->pr_msnd);
                printf("STREAMS Messages Received:...%ld\n", pup->pr_mrcv);
                printf("Signals:.....................%ld\n", pup->pr_sigs);
                printf("Voluntary Context Switches:..%ld\n", pup->pr_vctx);
                printf("Involuntary Context Switches:.%ld\n", pup->pr_ictx);
                printf("System Calls:................%ld\n", pup->pr_sysc);
                printf("Read/Write Characters:.......%ld\n", pup->pr_ioch);
                printf("*** State Times *** \n");
                prtime("Total Elapsed Time:..........", &real);
```

```
                        prtime("Total User Time:..............", &user);
                        prtime("Total System Time:............", &sys);
                        prtime("Other System Trap Time:.......", &pup->pr_ttime);
                        prtime("Text Page Fault Sleep Time....", &pup->pr_tftime);
                        prtime("Data Page Fault Sleep Time....", &pup->pr_dftime);
                        prtime("Kernel Page Fault Sleep Time..", &pup->pr_kftime);
                        prtime("User Lock Wait Sleep Time.....", &pup->pr_ltime);
                        prtime("All Other Sleep Time..........", &pup->pr_slptime);
                        prtime("Time Waiting for a CPU........", &pup->pr_wtime);
                        prtime("Stopped Time..................", &pup->pr_stoptime);
                }

                (void) close(fd);
                return (rval);
        }

        static void
        hr_min_sec(char *buf, long sec)
        {
                if (sec >= 3600)
                        (void) sprintf(buf, "%ld:%.2ld:%.2ld",
                                sec / 3600, (sec % 3600) / 60, sec % 60);
                else if (sec >= 60)
                        (void) sprintf(buf, "%ld:%.2ld",
                                sec / 60, sec % 60);
                else {
                        (void) sprintf(buf, "%ld", sec);
                }
        }

        static void
        prtime(char *name, timestruc_t *ts)
        {
                char buf[32];

                hr_min_sec(buf, ts->tv_sec);
                (void) fprintf(stderr, "%s%s.%.3u\n",
                        name, buf, (u_int)ts->tv_nsec/1000000);
        }

        static int
        perr(const char *s)
        {
                if (s)
                        (void) fprintf(stderr, "%s: ", procname);
                else
                        s = procname;
                perror(s);
                return (1);
        }

        static void
        tsadd(timestruc_t *result, timestruc_t *a, timestruc_t *b)
        {
                result->tv_sec = a->tv_sec + b->tv_sec;
                if ((result->tv_nsec = a->tv_nsec + b->tv_nsec) >= 1000000000) {
                        result->tv_nsec -= 1000000000;
                        result->tv_sec += 1;
                }
        }

        static void
        tssub(timestruc_t *result, timestruc_t *a, timestruc_t *b)
        {
                result->tv_sec = a->tv_sec - b->tv_sec;
```

```
        if ((result->tv_nsec = a->tv_nsec - b->tv_nsec) < 0) {
                result->tv_nsec += 1000000000;
                result->tv_sec -= 1;
        }
}
```

BIBLIOGRAPHY

1. Bach, M. J., *The Design of the UNIX Operating System*, Prentice Hall, 1986.
2. Bonwick, J., *The Slab Allocator: An Object-Caching Kernel Memory Allocator*. Sun Microsystems, Inc. White paper.
3. Bourne, S. R., *The UNIX System*, Addison-Wesley, 1983.
4. Catanzaro, B., *Multiprocessor System Architectures*, Prentice Hall, 1994.
5. Cockcroft, A., *Sun Performance and Tuning — Java and the Internet*, 2nd Edition, Sun Microsystems Press/Prentice Hall, 1998.
6. Cockcroft, A., *CPU Time Measurement Errors*, Computer Measurement Group Paper 2038, 1998.
7. Cypress Semiconductor, *The CY7C601 SPARC RISC Users Guide*, Ross Technology, 1990.
8. Eykholt, J. R., et al., *Beyond Multiprocessing — Multithreading the SunOS Kernel*, Summer '92 USENIX Conference Proceedings.
9. Gingell, R. A., Moran, J. P., Shannon, W. A., *Virtual Memory Architecture in SunOS*, Proceedings of the Summer 1987 USENIX Conference.
10. Goodheart, B., Cox, J., *The Magic Garden Explained — The Internals of UNIX System V Release 4*, Prentice Hall, 1994.
11. Hwang, K., Xu, Z., *Scalable Parallel Computing*, McGraw-Hill, 1998.
12. Intel Corp, *The Intel Architecture Software Programmers Manual, Volume 1, 2 and 3*, Intel Part Numbers 243190, 24319102, and 24319202, 1993.
13. Kleiman, S. R., *Vnodes: An Architecture for Multiple File System Types in Sun UNIX*, Proceedings of Summer 1986 Usenix Conference.

14. Kleiman, S., Shah, D., Smaalders, B., *Programming with Threads*, Prentice Hall, SunSoft Press, 1996.

15. Leffler, S. J., McKusick, M. K., Karels, M. J., Quarterman, J. S., *The Design and Implementation of the 4.3BSD UNIX Operating System*, Addison-Wesley, 1989.

16. Lewis, B., Berg, D. J., *Threads Primer. A Guide to Multithreaded Programming*, SunSoft Press/Prentice Hall, 1996.

17. Lewis, B., Berg, D. J., *Multithreaded Programming with Pthreads*. Sun Microsystems Press/Prentice Hall. 1998

18. McKusick, M. K., Bostic, K., Karels, M. J., Quarterman, J. S., *The Design and Implementation of the 4.4 BSD Operating System*, Addison-Wesley, 1996.

19. McKusick, M. K., Joy, W., Leffler, S., Fabry, R., *A Fast File System for UNIX*, ACM Transactions on Computer Systems, 2(3):181–197, August 1984.

20. Moran, J. P., *SunOS Virtual Memory Implementation*, Proceedings of 1988 EUUG Conference.

21. Pfister, G., *In Search of Clusters*, Prentice Hall, 1998.

22. Rosenthal, David S., *Evolving the Vnode Interface*, Proceedings of Summer 1990 USENIX Conference.

23. Schimmel, C., *UNIX Systems for Modern Architectures*, Addison-Wesley, 1994.

24. Seltzer, M., Bostic, K., McKusick, M., Staelin, C. *An Implementation of a Log-Structured File System for UNIX*, Proceedings of the Usenix Winter Conference, January 1993.

25. Shah, D. K., Zolnowsky, J., *Evolving the UNIX Signal Model for Lightweight Threads*, Sun Proprietary/Confidential Internal Use Only, White paper, SunSoft TechConf '96.

26. Snyder, P., *tmpfs: A Virtual Memory File System*, Sun Microsystems White paper.

27. SPARC International, *System V Application Binary Interface — SPARC Version 9 Processor Supplement*, 1997.

28. Sun Microsystems, *Writing Device Drivers - Part Number 805-3024-10*, Sun Microsystems, 1998

29. Sun Microsystems, *STREAMS Programming Guide - Part Number 805-4038-10*, Sun Microsystems, 1998

30. Sun Microsystems, *UltraSPARC Microprocessor Users Manual - Part Number 802-7220*, Sun Microsystems, 1995.

31. Stevens, W. R., *Advanced Programming in the UNIX Environment*, Addison-Wesley, 1992.

32. Stevens, W. R., *UNIX Network Programming, Volume 2. Interprocess Communication. 2nd Edition.* Addison-Wesley, 1998.

33. Talluri, M., *Use of Superpages and subblocking in the address translation hierarchy,* Thesis for the doctorate of Computer Science, 1995

34. Tanenbaum, A. *Operating Systems: Design and Implementation.* Prentice Hall, 1987.

35. Tucker, A., *Scheduler Activations,* PSARC 1996/021, Sun Internal Proprietary Document. March, 1996.

36. Tucker, A., *Scheduler Activations in Solaris,* SunSoft TechConf '96. Sun Proprietary/Confidential – Internal Use Only Document.

37. Tucker, A., Private Communication.

38. UNIX Software Operation, *System V Application Binary Interface – UNIX System V.* Prentice Hall/UNIX Press. 1990.

39. Vahalia, U., *UNIX Internals — The New Frontiers,* Prentice Hall, 1996.

40. Van der Linden, P., *Expert C Programming — Deep C Secrets,* SunSoft Press/Prentice Hall, 1994.

41. Weaver, D., Germond, T., (editors), *The SPARC Architecture Manual, Version 9,* Prentice Hall, 1994.

42. Wong, B., *Configuration and Capacity Planning on Sun Solaris Servers,* Sun Microsystems Press/Prentice Hall, 1996.

43. Zaks, R., *Programming the Z80,* Sybex Computer Books, 1982.

INDEX

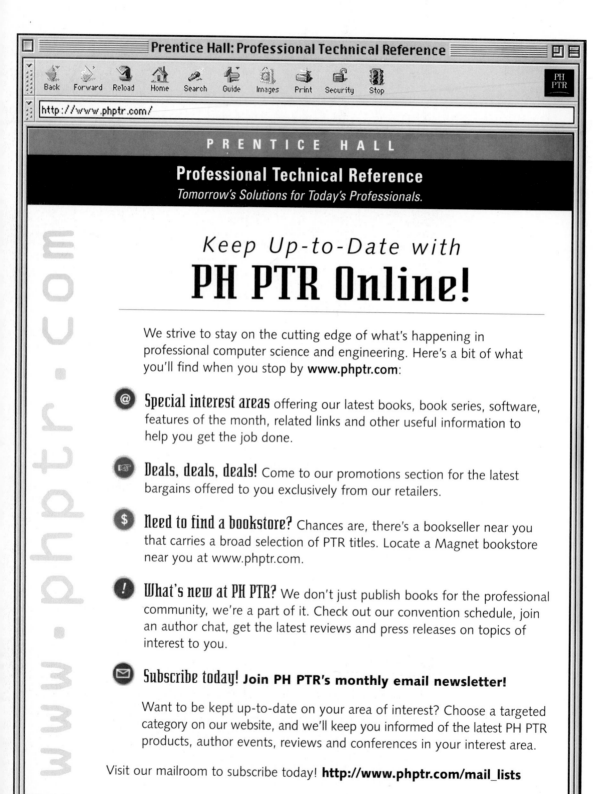